WORKS

OF

JOHN KNOX.

THE WORKS

OF

JOHN KNOX

COLLECTED AND EDITED BY

DAVID LAING, LL.D.

VOLUME THIRD.

Wipf & Stock
PUBLISHERS
Eugene, Oregon

AD SCOTOS TRANSEUNTIBUS PRIMUS OCCURRIT MAGNUS ILLE JOANNES CNOXUS; QUEM SI SCOTORUM IN VERO DEI CULTU INSTAURANDO, VELUT APOSTOLUM QUENDAM DIXERO, DIXISSE ME QUOD RES EST EXISTIMABO.

THEOD. BEZA.

Wipf and Stock Publishers
199 West 8th Avenue, Suite 3
Eugene, Oregon 97401

The Works of John Knox, Volume 3: Earliest Writings 1548-1554
Edited by Laing, David
ISBN: 1-59244-527-6
Publication date 1/30/2004
Previously published by James Thin, 1895

TABLE OF CONTENTS.

	PAGE
ADVERTISEMENT,	vii
AN EPISTLE TO THE CONGREGATION OF THE CASTLE OF ST ANDREWS; WITH A BRIEF SUMMARY OF BALNAVES ON JUSTIFICATION BY FAITH, 1548,	1
A VINDICATION OF THE DOCTRINE THAT THE SACRIFICE OF THE MASS IS IDOLATRY, 1550,	29
A SUMMARY, ACCORDING TO THE HOLY SCRIPTURES, OF THE SACRAMENT OF THE LORD'S SUPPER, 1550,	71
A DECLARATION OF THE TRUE NATURE AND OBJECT OF PRAYER, 1553,	
A Confession or Prayer on the Death of Edward VI.,	77
AN EXPOSITION UPON THE SIXTH PSALM OF DAVID, ADDRESSED TO MRS BOWES, 1554,	111
A GODLY LETTER OF WARNING, OR ADMONITION TO THE FAITHFUL IN LONDON, NEWCASTLE, AND BERWICK, 1554,	157
CERTAIN QUESTIONS CONCERNING OBEDIENCE TO LAWFUL MAGISTRATES, WITH ANSWERS BY HENRY BULLINGER, 1554,	217

TABLE OF CONTENTS.

	PAGE
TWO COMFORTABLE EPISTLES TO HIS AFFLICTED BRETHREN IN ENGLAND, 1554,	227
A FAITHFUL ADMONITION TO THE PROFESSORS OF GOD'S TRUTH IN ENGLAND, 1554,	251
EPISTLES TO MRS ELIZABETH BOWES, AND HER DAUGHTER MARJORY, 1553–1554,	
LETTERS I. TO XXVI.,	331

APPENDIX.

BIOGRAPHICAL NOTICES AND LETTERS OF HENRY BALNAVES OF HALHILL,	405
A TREATISE BY BALNAVES ON JUSTIFICATION BY FAITH, REVISED BY KNOX IN 1548,	431

ADVERTISEMENT.

The first two Volumes of Knox's Works, containing his History of the Reformation in Scotland, were published for the Members of the Wodrow Society, and also for the Bannatyne Club. According to the plan which was then proposed, of arranging his Miscellaneous Writings in nearly chronological order, the present Volume forms the commencement of the series; as it contains the earliest of his Works which are known to be preserved, extending from the year 1548 to 1554. The next, or fourth Volume, will embrace the period of his settlement as Minister of the English Congregation at Frankfurt, and afterwards at Geneva.

In the prefatory notice to each separate tract or division, the several printed editions or early manuscripts employed are carefully indicated; and to enable the Reader more clearly to understand the position which the Reformer occupied at the time, occasional incidents connected with his personal history are introduced.

Should the number of Subscribers be sufficient to encourage the Publishers to complete this series of the

Reformer's Works, the Editor indulges the hope that he may be enabled to accomplish his task in three additional Volumes, to be published successively, and as speedily as the nature of such an undertaking admits. He can scarcely anticipate that such encouragement will not be afforded to the extent required, in order to erect this Literary Monument to the Reformer's memory; and some progress has already been made in printing the fourth Volume.

AN EPISTLE

TO THE CONGREGATION

OF THE CASTLE OF ST ANDREWS,

PREFIXED TO THE TREATISE

BY HENRY BALNAVES

ON JUSTIFICATION BY FAITH;

WITH A BRIEF SUMMARY

OF THE WORK.

M.D.XLVIII.

In April 1547, being upwards of ten months subsequent to the murder of Cardinal Beaton, KNOX, with his three pupils, entered the Castle of St Andrews, as a temporary place of refuge. His mode of catechising, and his private lectures on the Gospel of St John, having attracted the attention of Henry Balnaves of Halhill, Sir David Lyndsay of the Mount, and John Rough, he was urged to undertake the office of a preacher; but this, he says, he utterly refused, alleging, "He would not run where God had not called him."

The manner of his public vocation to the ministry in the Great Church of St Andrews, he has recorded in his "History of the Reformation."[1] At this time he was in the forty-second year of his age; and his previous scholastic studies may have served to qualify him for thus unexpectedly being called upon to assume the ministerial office. But whatever reluctance he may have felt in complying with this public desire of the Congregation at St Andrews, he seems on no subsequent occasion to have faltered in his resolution, under the greatest difficulties or discouragements. The notices of his first Sermon, and of his Disputation with Friar Arbuckle in St Leonard's College, contained in his History,[2] were probably extracted from the account which he transmitted from France to his brethren who remained at St Andrews, and these may be referred to as the earliest specimens of his literary composition that have been preserved.

In the winter of 1548, Balnaves, who remained a prisoner in the old palace of Rouen, had sent to Knox, while still detained on

[1] Vol. i. pp. 186–189.   [2] Ib. pp. 193–200.

board the French galley on the Loire, a Treatise which he had written on the doctrine of Justification by Faith.[1] With this work Knox was so much pleased, that having revised it carefully, divided it into chapters, and added a brief Summary of the book, it was conveyed with the Author's permission to Scotland, probably for publication, with an Epistle by Knox addressed "to his best beloved Brethren of the Congregation of the Castle of St Andrews." As the old copy bears the title of "The Confession of Faith," and in the following Epistle, he refers to it by that title, this work may have been "The Confession" to which he elsewhere alludes as having been sent to his friends in Scotland, and which is usually supposed to be lost.[2] Of Balnaves's Treatise, in 1566, he remarks, "how it is suppressed, we know nott;"[3] but the manuscript was accidently recovered, some years after his death,[4] and was first published at Edinburgh in 1584.

Knox's Epistle, and Brief Summary of the book, are here inserted; and as the Work itself embodies his views on an important point of Christian doctrine, it will be reprinted as a suitable Appendix to the present volume, and will be accompanied with some account of the Author.

[1] Vol. i. p. 226.   [2] Ib. p. 200, note 4.   [3] Ib. p. 227.
[4] See "the Epistle Dedicatorie," prefixed by the Printer of the work, in 1584.

JOHN KNOX, THE BOUND SERVANT OF JESUS CHRIST, UNTO HIS BEST BELOVED BRETHREN OF THE CONGREGATION OF THE CASTLE OF ST ANDREWES, AND TO ALL PROFESSOURS OF CHRISTS TRUE EVANGELL, DESIRETH GRACE, MERCY, AND PEACE FROM GOD THE FATHER, WITH PERPETUALL CONSOLATION OF THE HOLY SPIRITE.

BLESSED bee God, the Father of our Lord Jesus Christ, whose infinite goodness and incomprehensible wisdome, in every age, so frustrats the purpose, and maketh of none effect the slight of Sathan, that the same things, which appeare to be extreme destruction to the just, and damnage to the small flocke of Jesus Christ, by[1] all men's expectation (yea, and Sathan himselfe) by the mercy of our good God, are turned to the laude, praise, and glorie of his own name, utilitie and singuler profite of his Congregation, and to the pleasure, confort, and advancement of them that suffer. How the name of the onely living God hath beene magnified in all ages by them which were sore troubled, by persecution of tyrants, exiled from their owne countrey, long were to rehearse. Yet one or two principall will wee touche, for probation of our words foresaid.

Sathan moved the hatred of the rest of his Brethren against GEN 37. young Joseph, to whom God promised honours, and authoritie, above his brethren and parentes. To the impediment whereof Sathan procured, he should be sould as a boundman or slave, caried in a strange countrie, where many yeares injustly hee suf-

[1] "By," *prep.* beyond.

fered imprisonment. And Sathan wrought this, to the intent that he which reproved the wickedness of his brethren, should perish altogether. For nothing is to Sathan more noysome, as these men in whom godlines, and in whome puritie of life, and hatred of iniquitie, appeareth, that they should floorish in dominion, or authoritie. But all his counsels were frustrate, when by the singular mercy and prouidence of God, Joseph was exalted in most high honours, made principall governour of Egypt by Pharao, the potent king therof, who gave in charge, that all princes of his kingdom should obey his wil, and that his senatours should learne wisedome at the mouth of Joseph: who, no doubt, with all studie set foorth the true knowledge, worshipping, and religion of the onely living God, which in that countrey was unknowen before. And after certaine yeares, hee receaved his Father and Brethren in this same countrey, whome hee with all godlinesse and wisedome, in the yeares of hunger, susteined and nourished. And so was Sathan frustrate, and all his deceate turned to nought.

<sub_marginalia>GEN. 41.</sub_marginalia>
<sub_marginalia>PSAL. 104.</sub_marginalia>
<sub_marginalia>GENE. 15.</sub_marginalia>

When, after this, God of his great mercy, according to his owne promise, sometyme made to Abraham, had placed the people of Israel in the land of Canaan, Sathan, to corrupt the true religion, which they had receaved from God by his faithfull servant Moyses, invented abominations of idolatrie, under the pretext of the true worshipping of God. And albeit frequently they were reproved by true prophetes, yet ever superstition preuailed; while God, of his righteous judgement, was compelled to punish, first Israel, and thereafter Juda, giving them in the power of their enemies, which translated them from their owne countreyes; Salmanaser, Israel unto Assyria, and Nebucadnetzar, Juda unto Babylon. Then Sathan beleeved the true knowledge and worshipping of God to have decayed for ever. But he was farre deceaved; when first Nebucadnetzar, king of Babylon, and the mightiest prince in the earth, and after him Darius, the potent king of Media, receaveth the true knowledge of the Lord God by

<sub_marginalia>JOSUE 11.</sub_marginalia>
<sub_marginalia>3. REG. 12.
3. REG. 13.
& 16.</sub_marginalia>
<sub_marginalia>ESA. 1.
JER. 3.
4. REG. 17.
ET VLTIMO.</sub_marginalia>

Daniel the prophet, one of the same nomber, whiche were transported from their owne countrey; and not only receaved the kings (then having the whole empyre in earth) the true religion of God, but also commanded the same to be observed by their subjectes. For after this manner it was written, "Then Darius wrote unto all people, nations, and toungs in the universal earth, saying, Peace bee multiplied with you. A decreite is ordeined by mee, that in my universal empyre and kingdom, all men shall feare, dread, and honour the God of Daniel; for he is the living and eternall God for ever. He is a deliverer, and Saviour, working signes and wonderfull thinges in heaven and earth; which hath delivered Daniel from the denne of lions." Secondly, after Darius, the most prosperous, valiant, and mighty Cyrus, the first monarche of the Persians and Medians, not onely of the true living God (by the same Prophete) obteined knowledge, but also for singuler affection which he bare to the true religion, restored unto libertie the people of Israell, permitting unto them to build a new temple of Solomon, and to repare the walles of Jerusalem, which by the Babylonians sometyme were brought to ruine. And albeit that by the perpetuall hatred of Sathan, working by his members, some years they were impedite, yet at the last (to the great consolation of all the people) was the work finished, where, many years after, God's true religion was observed.

Sathan never beleeved his purpose rather to take effect, then when, after the death of Jesus Christ, hee moved the princes of the priests (who then were estemed the true church of God) to persecute the Apostles, and other professours of Christ's Evangel. For, who beleeved not great damnage to followe the congregation, when, after the death of Steven (who was stoned to death) the professours were dispersed, banished, and exiled from Jerusalem. But what entres therby tooke the church of God, the 11. chap. of the Acts of the Apostles, showeth in these wordes: "And they whiche were scattered abroad, because of the affliction that arose about Steven, went through till they

Act. 7.

came unto Phenice, and Cyprus, and Antiochia, preaching plainly the Evangell of Jesus Christ."

Of these, and other testimonies of the Scripture, we may consider (dearely beloved Brethren) that the infinite goodnesse of our Father, turned the same thinges, whereby Sathan and his members intende to destroy and oppresse the true religion of God, to the advancement and forthsetting thereof: And that no lesse in these latter, wicked, and dangerous dayes, than he did in any age before us. Which thing shall openly declare this godly Worke subsequent. The counsell of Sathan in the persecution[1] of us, first, was to stoppe the wholesome winde of Christ's Evangell to blow upon the parts where we converse and dwell; and secondlie, so to oppresse our selves by corporall affliction, and worldly calamities, that no place should wee finde to godly studie.[2] But by the great mercy and infinite goodnesse of God our Father, shall these his counsels be frustrate and vaine. For in despite of him, and all his wicked members, shall yet that same word (O Lord! this I speake, confiding in thy holy promisse) openly be proclaimed in that same countrey.

And how that our mercifull Father, amongst these tempestuous stormes, by all men's expectation, he hath provided some rest for us, as this present Worke shall testifie; which was sent to mee in Roane, lying in irons, and sore troubled by corporall infirmitie, in a galley named *Nostre Dame*, by an honourable man and faithfull Christian brother, M. HENRY BALNAVES, of Halhill, for the present holden as prisoner (though unjustly) in the old Pallaice of Roane. Which worke, after I had once again read, to the great confort and consolation of my spirite, by counsell and advise of the foresaid noble and faithfull man, authour of the same Worke, I thought expedient it should be digested in chapters; and to the better memory of the Reader,

---

[1] In the edit. 1584, "perfection."

[2] This may be explained by a reference to Knox's previous intention to have visited some of the learned seminaries in Germany. Vol. i. p. 185.

the contents of every chapter proponed[1] briefly unto them, with certaine annotations, to the more instruction of the simple, in the margent. And also that an Epitome of the same work should be shortly collected, wee have likewise digested the same in chapters, which follow the worke in place of a Table: Which thing I have done, as imbecillitie of ingine[2] and incommoditie of place would permit; not so much to illustrate the Worke, (which in the self is godly and perfite) as, together with the foresaid noble man and faithfull Brother, to give my Confession of the article of Justification therein conteined. And I beseech you, beloved Brethren, earnestly to consider if we deny any thing presently, or yet conceale or hide, which any time before we professed in that Article.

And now we have not the Castle of St Andrewes to bee our defence, as some of our enemies falsely accused us, saying, "If we wanted our walls we would not speak so boldly." But we pray the Eternal God, that the same affection, which now and then remained in us, remaine with them eternally. The Lorde shall judge if all which we spak was not of pure heart, having no respect either to love or hatred of any person, but onely to the Word of God, and veritie of his Scriptures, as we must answere in the great day of the Lorde, where no man shall have place to dissemble. But blessed be that Lord, whose infinite goodnes and wisdome hath tane from us the occasion of that slaunder, and hath showen unto us that the Serpent hath power only to stang the heele; that is, to molest and trouble the fleshe, but not to move the spirite from constant adhearing to Jesus Christ, nor publick professing of his true Word. O, blessed bee thou, Eternall Father! which by thy only mercy hast preserved us to this day, and provided that the Confession of our Faith, (which ever wee desired all men to have knowen), should by this Treatise come plainely to light. Continue, O Lord! and graunt unto us, that as now with pen and ink, so shortly wee may confesse with voice and toung, the same be-

---

[1] In the edit. 1584, "preponed."   [2] *i. e.*, genius, or knowledge.

fore thy Congregation; upon whome looke, O Lord God, with the eyes of thy mercy, and suffer no more darknes to prevaile. I pray you pardon me, beloved Brethren, that on this maner I digresse: vehemency of spirite (the Lord knoweth I lye not) compelleth me thereto. The head of Sathan shall be troaden down, when he beleeveth surely to triumphe. Therefore, most deare Brethren (so call I all professing Christes Evangell), continue in that purpose which yee have begunne godly; though the battell appeare strong, your Captaine is unexpugnable: To him is given all power in heaven and earth. Abide, stand, and call for his support; and so the ennemies, which now affraye you, shortly shal be confounded, and never againe shall appeare to molest you.

Consider, Brethren, it is no speculative Theolog which desireth to give you courage, but even your Brother in affliction, which partly hath experience what Sathan's wrath may doe against the chosen of God. Rejoyse (yet I say) spiritually, and bee glad; the time of the battell is short, but the reward is eternall. Victorie is sure, without yee list to fly (which God forbid) from Christ. But that ye may plainly know wherby are Sathan and the world overcome, and which are the weapons against whome they may not stand, yee shall reade diligently this Work following; which, I am sure, no man having the Spirite of God shal thinke tedious, nor long, because it conteineth nothing except the very Scriptures of God, and meditations of his Law; wherein is the whole study of the godly man, both day and night, knowing that therein are found onely wisedome, prudence, libertie, and life. And therefore, in reading, talking, or meditation thereof, he is never satiate. But, as for the ungodly, because their works are wicked, they may not abide the light. And therefore they abhore all godly writings, thinking them tedious, though they conteine not the length of the Lord's Prayer. But according to the threatning of Esay the prophet, saying, "Because they contemne the law of the Lord God, hee shall contemne them. Their harts shall be indured, in the daye of anguish and trouble they shall dispaire, and curse the Lord God into their harts. They shal be nombred to the sword, and in the slaughter shall they fall. Then shal they know that their workes were vaine, and that they placed their refuge in lies. Their vestiments of spiders webbes (which ar their vaine workes) shall not abide the force of the Lord's winde; but they shall stand naked, and the workes of iniquitie in their handes, to their extreame confusion. And this ᴇꜱᴀ. 59. shall apprehend and overtake them, because they call light darknes, and darknes light; that which was sweete they called bitter, and by the contrarie, that which was bitter they called sweet; seeking salvation where none was to be found." But yee, most Christian Brethren, humbly I beseeche, and in the bloud of Jesus Christ I exhort, that ye reade diligently this present Treatise; not onely with earnest prayer, that yee may understand the same aright, but also with humble and due thankesgiving unto our most mercifull Father, who of his infinite power so hath strengthned the hartes of his Prisoners, that in despite of Sathan, they desist not yet to worke, but in the most vehemency of tribulation seeke the utilitie and salvation of others.

It is not my purpose to commend, or advance this Worke with wordes (as commonly writers of prophane or humane science do), seeing the verity by the selfe is onely to be commended. But one thing bouldly I dare affirme, that no man which commeth with a godly hart hereto, shall passe from the same without satisfaction. The firme and weake shall find strength and confort; the rude and simple, true knowledge and erudition; the learned and godly humbly rejoycing, by the omnipotent spirite of Jesus Christ, to whome bee glorie before his congregation. Amen.

TO THE READER.

IF it please thee, good Reader, of these plesant floures, amongst the which thou hast walked at large, again to take a taste[1] or smelling; thou shalt read these short Abbreviations subsequent. Exhorting thee, that where any obscuritie appeareth, that thou make recourse unto the preceeding places, where every thing is manifestly expressed. Thou shalt doe well, if earnestlie thou shalt pray that Lord onely, to whom the harvest perteineth, that it would please him send true workemen thereto; to the manifestation of his owne glorie before his congregation, by Jesus Christ; whose omnipotent Spirite satiate the harts of them which thirst [after] ryghteousnesse. Amen.

[1] It may be necessary to mention that this Address, and the following Summary are subjoined, not prefixed, to the original edition of Balnaves's Treatise.

A BRIEFE SOMMARIE OF THE WORK BY BALNAVES ON JUSTIFICATION.

The Sommarie of the First Chapter.

Our whole study should be to adhear unto God; running to him in the time of tribulation, (as doeth the wild hart in the birning heate to the could river,) with sure hope of deliverance by him allone; not inquiring his name, that is, the maner how hee shall deliver vs.

The Sommarie of the Second Chapter.

By Faith have we knowledge of God, whom we should seeke in his Scriptures, and receave him as he is offered to us thereinto; that is, a Defender, Protector, Refuge, and Father, inquiring no further speculation of him. For, Philip desiring to see the Father, answeared Christ, "Who hath seene me, hath seene the Father." Meaning that the love, goodnes, and mercy, which God the Father beareth unto mankinde, hee had expressed in doctrine and workes; and also should show a most singular token of love, giving his owne life for his ennemies. And therefore would all men come to him, to whome the Father hath given all power.

The Sommarie of the Third Chapter.

Tribulations are profitable to the faithfull; for thereby the strength of the flesh somewhat is dantoned, and ceaseth to rebell against the spirite: and beginneth to seeke God, who is a peculiar Father to the faithfull, delivering them from all tribulations, not for their worthynesse, but for his own mercie. Worldly tribulations are the signe and token of God's love;

albeit, the wicked and unfaithfull judge otherwise, which in tyme of tribulation runne from God, seeking help at man (which is but vaine), whereof they being frustrate and deceaved, fall in desperation.

The Sommarie of the Fourth Chapter.

The faithfull thanke God in tribulation; and albeit our wicked nature teacheth us to flye from God, as did our first parent Adam, after his transgression; yet Faith in Jesus Christ leadeth us to the throne of our Father's grace, where we finde goodnes, mercy, and justice, given to us freely by Jesus Christ, as they were given to Adam; who, albeit fled from God; yet He, moved of love toward his own handywork, followed him: and albeit Adam, at the voice of God, repented not, but obstinately excused his sinne; yet God made to him the promisse of salvation, before hee pronounced his wrath contrary sinne (which of his righteous judgement hee must punish.) And so Adam wrought nothing which might move God to make this promisse, more then hee wrought that of dust and clay, hee should be made a living creature, to the image and similitude of God. And to Abraham, being an idolater, was made the promisse, hee should be the father of many nations (which hee merited not), to whiche promisse Abraham giving credite, was reckoned just. By the which it is plaine, that the mercy of God, and not our workes, is the cause that hee calleth us by his Worde, whereto wee giving credite are reckoned just, all our deservinges or merites being excluded.

The Sommarie of the Fifth Chapter.

Adam, expelled forth of Paradise, had no consolation, except in the blessed Seede promised; by whom hee beleeved him to stande in God's favour; for all bodily consolation, which hee had of his two sonnes, was turned in dolour when Cain killed Abell. In the which dolour Adam many yeares remained, whill God having compassion upon him, gave him another sonne named

Seth, of whome descended the blessed Seede. For this sonne Adam gave thankes unto God, taking all afflictions in patience, knowing himself worthie of greater punishment; by whose example we should patiently (with thanksgiving unto God) suffer all tribulation. For none descending of Adam by naturall propagation, are juster then hee was after his fall, which all his life suffered trouble, having no confort, but that he should overcome all worldly calamitie (yea, and also the slightes of Sathan, which had deceaved him) by the blessed Seede promissed. And this same should be our confort in all tribulations.

The Sommarie of the Sixth Chapter.

By bodily afflictions our faith is tryed, as gold by the fire. They are also a communion with the passions of Jesus Christ. And therefore in them have we matter and cause to rejoyce, considering we suffer without cause, committed contrarie man. Notwithstanding, the wicked persecute the faithfull in all ages as if they had beene mischievous or evill doers; as may be seene in the persecution of the Prophets, Apostles, and of Jesus Christ himself. The cause hereof is the neglecting of God's Word, and taking from Faith her due office, whereof riseth all dishonouring of God; for none may or can honour God except the justified man. And albeit, in diverse men there be diverse opinions of Justification; yet they alone, in whome the Holy Spirit worketh true Faith (which never wanteth good workes) are just before God. The substance of Justification is, to cleave fast unto God, by Jesus Christ, and not by our selfe, nor yet by our workes. And this article of Justification should be holden in recent memorie, because without the knowledge thereof, no workes are pleasant before God

The Sommarie of the Sevinth Chapter.

As by perswasion of Sathan, Adam and Eve seeking wisdome contrarie God's commandement, were deceaved, and fell in extreame miserie; so they, seeking Justification otherwise then teach the Scriptures, remaine under the wrath of God, for Faith alone reconcileth[1] man to God, which the Lawe, whose office is onely to utter sinne, and trouble the conscience, (as it did to Adam after his transgression,) may not doe. Therefore, who list to resist Sathan, let him cleave to Faith, for it is the onely shield which his dartes may not pearse.

The Sommarie of the Eight Chapter.

Cain, a wicked hipocrit, killed his brother Abell, for no other cause, but that his brother's sacrifice pleased God because it was offered into faith. And the posteritie of Cain pursued perpetually them which depended upon the blessed Seede; while God was compelled to drown the whole world, eight persons being reserved, amongst whom yet was keept the seed of Sathan, in the third sonne of Noe, Cham. From the dayes of Noe to Abraham, this article of Justification altogether was obscured, idolatry spreading over all. The cause thereof was, they followed the external works of the holy Fathers in sacrifice, but had no respect to Faith, without the which all sacrifices ar idolatrie.

The Sommarie of the Ninth Chapter.

God, of his mercy, providing that his Church should not perish altogether, renewed to Abraham the promisse of the blessed Seede, made to Adam; whereto Abraham giving credit, is, without his workes, reckoned just. But shortly after, began Sathan newly to pursue the just by his members, stirring up Ismaell against Isaac, Esau against Jacob; but the just, at the end, shall prevaile, as hath done Jesus Christ, whose brethren we ar, by reason he is very man of the seed of Adam; and also because in him wee are adopted, and made the sonnes of God. The fleshly man is ever deceaved, judging the wicked to bee the chosen, as Abraham beleeved Ismaell, and Isaac beleeved Esau, to have beene their heires. But Faith judged righteously,

---

[1] In the edit. 1584, "reconciliateth."

which caused Rebecca to labour with diligence that Jacob, the youngest sonne, should be blessed by his father.

The Sommarie of the Tenth Chapter.

THE Jewes, having a carnall opinion of the Seede promissed, (that their Messias should rule temporally, as did David,) refused Jesus Christ, appearing simple and poore. But the cause which moved Sathan to stirre up his members against Christ was, that hee plainly taught, that by Faith, without all Workes, man is reckoned just. For the wicked, thinking to make their foolishe workes a part of their Justification, may never suffer them to bee damned. And the true preacher can never but exclude them from the Justification of man; as did the Prophetes, Jesus Christ him selfe, and his Apostles, for which they suffered death; leaving to us a sure testimonie for confirmation of this Article, which after Christ's death was plainly preached.

The Sommarie of the Elevinth Chapter.

SATHAN, perceaving his crafts, wherewith hee deceaved Mankinde, discovered, and his head troden downe by the death of Christ, cled him in a new arrayement; and finding them whiche should have truely preached, idle, perswaded man to invent new works, by the which they should seeke Justification, neglecting true Faith. Whiche pestilent workes so hath abolished the effect of perfite Faith, that they which are called Bishops understand nothing thereof, but pursue all them which truely preache or defende the same; by the which they showe them selves the Church Malignant: For the chosen never pursue, but ever is pursued.

The Sommarie of the Twelfth Chapter.

JUSTICE, in generall, is an outward obedience or honestie, which a man may performe of his owne power: And is devided in the justice of man, that is, which commeth of the law which man maketh; and in the justice of the law of God. The justice of man is devided in politick and ceremoniall. Politicke justice is, an obedience which the inferiour estate giveth to their superiour; which should be keept, because it is the command of God that Princes be obeyed. Ceremoniall justice is, the observing of statutes and traditions commanded by the Bishope of Rome, Counsels, or Schoolemaisters; which ar to be keept, so that they repugn not to the law of God, nor yet that by them men seeke remission of sinns. The Justice of the law of God is, to fulfill the same as it requireth; that is, to love, feare, serve, and honour God, with all thy harte, and strength thereof. Which because no creature in earth doeth, there is no man justified by the workes of the Law; for in all man (Jesus Christ excepted) is found sinne: as prove the examples of Abraham, Moyses, Noe, and others most holie Fathers, in whom all sinne was found. For, by the transgression of Adam, all his posteritie became rebels to the Lawe, and are compelled to pray with David: "Enter not in judgement with thy servaunt, O Lord; for in thy sight no living creature shal be found just."

THE SOMMARIE OF THE THIRTEINTH CHAPTER.

SEING then our Forefathers were not just by the Law, nor workes thereof, of necessitie must we seeke the Justice of another (that is, of Jesus Christ), which the Law may not accuse. In whom if we beleeve, we ar receaved in the favour of God, accepted as just without our merits or deservinges. But here objecte the wicked (as their use is, when any thing transcendeth their capacitie in understanding) these questiones: First, Wherefore gave God the Law, if man may not fulfill the same? Secondly, Wherefore shuld we work good works, seing by them we are not made just? Thirdly, Whereby were the Fathers made just?

THE SOMMARIE OF THE FOURTEINTH CHAPTER.

FOR understanding of the first question, Man should learne to know God as hee is declared in the Scripture; That is, to know him Creator and Maker of all; which also made all his creatures, in their first creation, good and perfite; who not onely gave a law to man, but also to the rest of his creatures; as to beasts, sunne, moone, sea, and elements; that thereby he might be glorified, and knowen Lord. And so to man hee gave a lawe, to the effect he should know his Maker, and obey him. Which law when Adam transgressed, he lost his perfection and righteousnesse. And so the cause why man may not fulfill the Law is, that the Law remaineth in the owne perfection, in the which it was first created by God. But man, by his disobedience and foolishnesse, fell from his perfection; and therefore should he accuse him selfe and not God, that he may not fulfill the Law which is perfite.

The Sommarie of the Fifteinth Chapter.

In Adam, after his transgression, remained a litle of that knowledge and power, with the which he was indewed by God; and from him it descended in his posteritie; whereby man may worke the outward workes of the Law; but the whole obedience thereto giveth no man. For these wordes prove all men (Jesus Christ excepted) to be sinners by the Law: "Of the deeds of the law shall no fleshe be justified before God." Which wordes Sophistes would abolish, saying, " Paull speaketh of the ceremoniall Law, and not of the morall or law of nature." But the plaine wordes of Paull prove them to be lyers; he sayeth, "The Law speaketh to all which are under the Law." And all men is under the Law morall; and therefore Paull speaketh of the Lawe morall, which condemneth al men, Jesus Christ excepted.

The Sommarie of the Sixteinth Chapter.

The Justice which is acceptable before God hath diverse names. First, it is called the Justice of God, becaus it proceedeth onely of the mercy of God. Secondly, it is called the Justice of Faith, because Faith is the instrument whereby we apprehend the mercy of God. And last, it is called Justice, because by Faith in Christ, it is given us freely without our deservinges. But even as the dry earth receaveth the raine but all deservinges of the self; so receave we the justice, which is of value before God, without all our workes: but yet we must suffer God to worke in us. And this Justice is plainly revealed in the Evangel, from faith to faith, that is, wee should continue in this faith all our life. For the just live by faith, ever trusting to obteine that which is promised, whiche is eternall life, promissed to us by Jesus Christ.

The Sommarie of the Sevinteinth Chapter.

The Faith of the Fathers, before Christ's comming in the flesh, and ours in the New Testament, was and is one thing. For they beleeved them to stande in the favour of God, by reason of that promissed Seede which was to come; whome wee beleeve is come already, and hath fulfilled all which was spoken of him in the Law and Prophets. By this faith were the Fathers made safe, without all their works, as testifieth Peter. And where our adversaries aske them, What availed workes? wee answere, That workes are an outward testimony to Faith, by which only man is first made just, and therafter his workes pleas God, because the persone is acceptable. And so no godly man forbiddeth good workes, but of necessitie must they bee excluded from the justification of man. For Paull saith, "If justice bee of the lawe, Christ's death is in vain." For albeit justice sometime be ascribeth to man, that is, not because it proceedeth of man, but because it is given to man freely by God. Like as our Faith is called the faith of Jesus Christ, because by him we are repute just; for he is made to us from God, wisedome, justice, holynes, and redemption. And so al the Scripture testifieth us to bee made just, freely, by the mercy of God, that all glory may be given to him. And therefore, who maked[1] workes a part of their owne Justification, spoile God of his glorie.

[1] "Who maked," or, whoever make.

The Sommarie of the Eighteinth Chapter.

God loveth us because wee are his own handywork, created unto good workes in Christ Jesus; in whom we remaine as branches in the vine roote, bringing forth good fruites, not of our owne strength, but of the power of the spirite of Jesus Christ, remaining in us by true faith; which works the Law may not condemne, becaus they are the works of Jesus Christ, and not ours. And so the glorie of works is excluded by the law of faith. For in our Justification, wee onely receave, as did our father Abraham (whose sonnes wee are by Faith), which was reakoned just before he wrought any good works. The veritie of the Scripture proveth, that the heritage commeth not by the Law; for by the Law, Ismaell and Esau, the eldest sonnes, should have succeeded to the heritage, and not Isaac and Jacob, which were yonger. And so, by the promise commeth the heritage, and not by the Law; for the Law ever accuseth, and craveth more of us then we ar able to pay; and therfore, damnation abydeth us, without we apprehend Jesus Christ, which payeth for us that which the Law requireth. For hee alone taketh away the sinnes of the world. Hee called all to him self, and sendeth none to the Law to seek Justification. And therfore, who seeketh any parte thereof by their Workes, spoile Christ of his office.

The Sommarie of the Nineteinth Chapter.

As the good tree beareth good fruites, so the just man worketh good workes; but neither maketh the fruite the tree good, nor yet the workes the man just; for as the tree is before the fruit, so the man is just before the worke be good. We should worke good workes, becaus, wee, being sometime the sonnes of God's wrath, and subjects to Sathan, are bought by the blood of Jesus Christ to serve in his kingdome; in the which ruled faith, hope, and charitie, ever working righteousnes unto life. By the contrarie, in the kingdom of the Devill rule incredulitie, dispaire, and envy, ever working unrighteousnes. And so we owe obedience to him, whose servants we ar. There be divers princes, realmes, subjects, and rewardes; no man can serve both, nor of both the rewardes no man shall be participant: but who serveth sinne, receaveth eternall death for his reward; and who serveth righteousnes, receaveth life everlasting by Jesus Christ.

The Sommarie of the Twentieth Chapter.

Workes are commended in the Scripture; not that they justifie before God, but that they are the fruites of a justified man, wrought to testifie his true Faith; which onely justifieth, without workes, either preceeding or following the same. And that proveth Paull, saying, "Without faith, it is impossible to please God:" and also, "All which is not of faith is sin." Whereof it is plaine, that Sophistes alledging that workes preceeding faith deserve the grace of God *de congruo*,[1] say as much as, Sin deserveth the grace of God: for all workes preceeding faith, is sinne. And that workes following faith justifieth not, testifieth the same Apostle, saying, "Not of the works of righteousnes which we have wrought, shall we be safe, but acording to his mercy God hath made us safe." And so neither Works preceeding nor following Faith justifie.

The Sommarie of the Twentie-First Chapter.

The wicked, by works of their own invention,[2] would be a part of their owne salvation, because thay seek their own glorie (as did the Scribes and Pharisies) and not the glory of God. But, seing the works commanded by God, done without faith, to deserve remission of sinnes, are abomination before God, as testifieth Esay; "What shal be of the vaine workes of man, set up without the command of God, by which hypocrites would be made just?" And if we should confesse, as commandeth Jesus Christ, "When we have done all, yet wee are but unprofitable servauntes." Where is the merite of the workes of supereroga-

---

[1] "*De congruo*," from congruity.   [2] In the edit. 1584, "intention."

tion, which hypocrites would sell to others? And if Paull, which had right excellent workes, esteemed them al to be but filthinesse, "that he might winne Christ, and be found in him, not having his owne justice, which is of the lawe, but the justice which is of the faith of Jesus Christ;" if Paull (I say) sought no justice in his own workes, how shal we (whose workes are on no maner equall to the workes of Paull) be justified thereby? And therefore, with the Scriptures and Apostles we conclude, That by Faith onely in Christ we ar made just, without all law or workes. And after man be made just by Faith, and possesseth Jesus Christ in his hart, then can he not bee idle. For with true Faith is also given the Holie Spirite, which suffereth not man to bee idle, but moveth him to al godly exercise of good workes.

The Sommarie of the Twentie-Second Chapter.

AFTER the article of Justification, Christians should bee instructed to doe good Workes; not these which are invented by man, but which are commanded by God; amongst which the principall is, to rejoyce in tribulation, giving thankes to God in all things, with sure hope and patience, abyding his deliverance; knowing that the life of man is a perpetuall battell upon earth; the law of the members ever rebelling against the law of the mind. The law of the members wee call the tyrannie of the Devill, ever drawing us to the lustes of the flesh, not onely in externall works, but also in the inwarde affections of the minde: as, to doubt of the goodnesse and mercy of God, to be sloughtful, and not to love and feare him with our whole hart. The law of the minde, or of the spirite, is, the motion of the Holie Ghost, stirring us up to all justice and righteousnes; which we know to bee good, and yet finde no power in our selfe to performe the same. And this battell is most vehement in the most holy, as witnesseth Paull. And therefore, to kill this outwarde man, which is our wit, reason, and will, we should offer our bodies unto God in a quicke, lively, and holy sacrifice. But before this sacrifice bee pleasant to God, must the minde (which is the fountaine of all good workes) bee renewed with the Spirite of God, and made cleane; which is, when we cast from us our wisedome, righteousnes, holynes, and redemption, and receave the same from Jesus Christ. Some there is which put their whole trust in their own works, thinking thereby to obteine the eternall glorie. And these men go before Christ, and are called Antichristes. Others there is, which thinke Faith not sufficient, but will have their workes joyned to helpe Christ; and these goe astray from him. For none of these two kindnes suffereth Jesus Christ death; but for them onely which follow him, laying all their sinnes upon his backe.

THE SOMMARIE OF THE TWENTIE-THIRD CHAPTER.

THE foolish reason of man perswadeth us to leave the workes commanded by God; and to set up workes of our own invention, thinking God to bee pleased therewith, becaus they are done of good zeale and intention. The Scriptures of God showeth all the thoughtes and cogitations of man to be evill at all time. And if so bee, what is our good intention? But whether the intent of man bee good or not, the fruites proceeding therefrom shall testifie. For, as sometime in Israell abounded all idolatrie (they having gods according to the multitude of their cieties), so nowe, amongst them which are called Christians, are set up carved images, defended, adorned, and worshipped, contrarie the expresse commandement of God. The blessed sacrament of Christ's body and bloud abused and prophaned before them. And all this, and much more abomination, proceedeth from that zeale, which wee call good. But how good that ever it appeare in our sight, the adhearers thereto shall receave the malediction of God.

THE SOMMARIE OF THE TWENTIE-FOURTH CHAPTER.

No better Workes can be, then John the Baptist taught to the people; which are the workes of mercy, and to desist from fraude, injurie, and oppression. And these workes (and not the vaine inventions of man) pastours should teach their flocks, instructing them first in perfite Faith. For Jesus Christ (being asked by the Jewes, what they shuld do that they might worke the workes of God, that is, that they might please God) answered, "This is the worke of God, that yee beleeve in Him whome he hath sent." By the which words our Maister understandeth, that without Faith, whiche is the worke of God, and not of man, no worke pleaseth God.

The yoke of Christ is easie, and his burden is light to the faithfull, because they lay all their sinns upon Christ's backe, and follow him, every man in his owne vocation. There is two maner of vocations: one immediate by God, as the Prophetes and Apostles were called to be preachers without authoritie of man. Another is, mediate, as when one man called another; as Paull called Timothie and Titus to be bishops. There is a generall vocation, by which all the chosen are called to a Christian religion, having one Lorde, one Faith, one Baptisme. In this vocation there is no difference of persons, but all are equally loved by God; becaus we ar all the sonns of one Father, and al bought with one price; all servaunts to one Lord, all guided with one Spirite, all tending to one end, and shall all be participant of one heritage; that is, the life eternall by Jesus Christ, by whom we are all made priests and kings. But let no man herefore usurpe the authoritie of a King in dignitie, nor the office of a Priest in administration of God's word and sacraments; for that perteineth to a speciall vocation.

The Sommarie of the Twentie-Fifth Chapter.

ALL Estate of man is conteined within one of these four special vocations: either is he Prince or subject, Pastor or one of the flocke, Father or sonne, Lord or servaunt. In the Prince is conteined all magistrats having jurisdiction in a commounweall; whose duety is, First, To know God, and his lawe, which hath placed them in that authoritie. Secondly, To guide, feed, and defend their subjects; knowing them selves to be no better of their nature then is the poorest in their realme. Thirdly, To defend the just, and punish the wicked, but respect of persons. having their harts and eyes cleane and pure from all avarice. They are called the sonnes of God, and should be obeyed in all things not repugning to the command of God; because they ar ordeined and placed by God to punish vice and mainteine vertue: And therefore their owne life should be pure and cleane; first, because otherwise they can not punish sinne; and secondly, because the wickednesse of princes provoketh their subjects to the imitation thereof; and therefore the life of princes shuld be pure and cleane, as a mirrour to their subjects; and should admitte into their kingdomes no worshipping of God, except that which is commanded in the Scriptures. For God, being commoved by idolatry and strange worshipping, hath destroyed many kingdomes, as all prophecyings witnesse.

The Sommarie of the Twenty-Sixt Chapter.

The principall office of a Bishop is, to preach the true Evangell of Jesus Christ; knowing that if the flocke perish, the bloud shal be required at his handes; and that he, neglecting the preaching of the Evangell, is no bishop, nor can doe no worke plesant before God. And therefore, no bishope should mixt him selfe with temporall or seculer busines, for that is contrarie his vocation; but continually should preache, reade, and exhort his flocke to seeke their spirituall foode in the Scriptures. And so the tyrantes in these dayes, forbidding men to reade the Scriptures, declare them selves wolves and no pastors; whom God shall shortly punish (because they have contemned his command, attending altogether upon their owne vaine superstitions), as he did Hely and his two sonnes under the law; and the whole priesthood after Jesus Christ.

The Sommarie of the Twenty-Sevinth Chapter.

The office of the Father (under whom is comprehended al householders) is to rule and guide his children, family, and servaunts, in all godlinesse and honestie, instructing them in the lawe and Worde of God. For honest householders, who lived in chast matrimonie, ruled and guided their householdes well, nurished their children in the feare and reverence of God, were chosen to be bishoppes in the Primitive Church. And therefore they are blasphemous to the Holy Spirite, which inhibit the Laickes (so style they the chosen of God) learning, reading, and teaching of the Holy Scriptures, wherein is conteined the foode of the soule; whereof Antichrists willing to deprive them, would also kill the soule: For the soule, without God's Word, hath nor may have no life. The office of the Husband is, to love and defend his wife, giving to her onely his body. The office of the Wife is likewise, to love and obey her husbande, usurping no dominion over him. And the office of them both is, to instructe their children in God's law; giving ever to them example of good life, and holding them at godly occupations; labouring also them selves faithfully for sustentation of their families.

The Sommarie of the Twentie-Eight Chapter.

The office and duetie of the Lord is, to pay unto his servaunts the reward promised. And the office of the Servaunt is, to worke faithfully and labour, to the profite and utility of his lord, but fraude or simulation, as hee would serve Jesus Christ. The office of the Subject is, to obey his prince and rulers placed by him; giving unto them honour, custome, and tribute, not requiring the cause why they receave the same; for that perteineth not to the vocation of a subject. The office of the Sonne is, to love, feare, and honour his parents; which honour standeth not in words only, but in ministring of all thinges necessary unto them; which if the Sonne doe not to the father and mother, hee can doe no good worke before God. And therefore, devilish doctors are they, which teach men to found Soule Masses of their substance, suffering father and mother to labour in indigence and povertie.

FINIS.

The Workes before written, are they in the which every Christian should be exercised, to the glory of God, and utilitie of his neighbour.

A VINDICATION

OF THE DOCTRINE

THAT THE SACRIFICE OF THE MASS

IS IDOLATRY.

M.D.L.

THE exact time when Knox was liberated from his confinement on board the French galley, is somewhat doubtful. In a letter, dated in December 1559, he refers to his bodily sufferings during the space of nineteen months, in which, with the other prisoners in the galleys, he was "miserably entreated." As the Castle of St Andrews surrendered on the 30th of July 1547, and the French vessels sailed, "after certane days," laden with the spoils,[1] this would fix the period of his release to February or March 1548-9. On the other hand, he mentions his having received a letter from William Kirkaldy of Grange, asking his counsel respecting some plan for effecting his escape from the fortress of Mount St Michel.[2] This might obviously have been several months before it was accomplished; but Knox expressly states that he obtained his own release the winter before he met Kirkaldy in England. Now it seems to be an ascertained fact, that Kirkaldy, and three of his companions, succeeded in their bold attempt on the 5th of January 1549-50,[3] and having separated for the better chance of escaping discovery, he and Peter Carmichael wandered about as poor mariners for upwards of twelve weeks before they found a vessel to take them to England.[4] It is therefore most probable that Knox, in consequence of the entreaty of some of his friends, and the certainty of his having had no concern in Cardinal Beaton's murder, was set at liberty in the earlier part of the year 1549. This supposition is confirmed by a letter from Sir John Mason, English ambassador at the Court of France, in June 1550, in which he details his negotiations for the release of "the

[1] Vol. i. p. 206.   [2] Ib. p. 229.   [3] Ib. p. 230, note 1.   [4] Ib. p. 231.

Scots of St Andrews," at the special instance of Edward the Sixth; and he alludes to Kirkaldy having escaped from prison, and to the previous liberation of two others[1] (probably Knox himself and Alexander Clerk); the rest of the prisoners, who had been detained in violation of the treaty with the garrison in 1547, being released in the course of that year, 1550.

The state of parties in Scotland prevented Knox from returning to his native country, and he proceeded to London. The zeal which he had already displayed in proclaiming the Protestant doctrines, having recommended him as a fit person to be employed in the northern parts of England, where the Romish services were still continued, he was speedily nominated by the Privy Council, at the suggestion of Cranmer, as preacher at Berwick. Dr Cuthbert Tonstall, one of the most learned of the Romish prelates, still held the See of Durham; and wishing to curb Knox's zeal in denouncing the Idolatry of the Mass, he summoned him before the Council of the North for Public Affairs, in April 1550. He accordingly presented himself at Newcastle, and on the 4th of that month delivered the following Confession or Vindication of his Doctrine regarding the Sacrifice of the Mass.

The text is here given from the manuscript volume in the possession of the Rev. Dr M'Crie, compared, and in some places corrected by the old printed copy, without date, which is annexed to the first edition of Knox's Letter to the Queen Regent in 1556. On the title-page (of which an exact copy will afterwards be given) it bears: "Here is also a notable Sermon, made by the sayde John Knox, wherin is euydentlye proued that the Masse is and alwayes hath ben abhominable before God, and Idolatrye." It has supplied the marginal notes, which are mostly omitted in the MS., and also some lines at the top of the pages too closely cut by the binder.

[1] Tytler's Edward VI., &c., vol. i. p. 295.

THE FOURT OF APRYLE, IN THE YEIR 1550, WAS APPOYNTIT TO JOHNE KNOX, PREACHER OF THE HALIE EUANGELL OF JESUS CHRYST,[1] TO GIF HIS CONFESSSIOUN WHY HE AFFIRMED THE MASSE IDOLATRIE: WHILK DAY, IN PRESENCE OF THE CONSALE AND CONGREGATIOUN, AMANGIS WHOME WAS ALSO PRESENT THE BISCHOPE OF DUREHAM[2] AND HIS DOCTOURIS, ON THIS MANNER HE BEGYNNETH:—

THIS day I do appeir in your presence, Honorable Audience, to gif a reasone why so constantlie I do affirme the Masse to be, and at all tymes to haif bene, Idolatrie, and abominatioun befoir God. And becaus men of great eruditioun in your audience affirmed the contrarie, most gladlie wold I that heir thai wer present, ether in proper persone, or ellis by thair learnit men, to ponder and wey the causis movyng me thairto; for unles I evidentlie prufe myne intente be Godis halie[3] Scriptures, I will recant it as wickit doctrine, and confes my self maist worthie of grevous punishment.

How difficill it is to pull furth of the hartes of the pepill the thing whairin opinion of holynes standeth, declareth the great tumult and uprore moveit aganis Paule by Demetrius and his fellowis, who, by Idolatrie, gat great vantage,[4] as oure preistis have done be the Masse in tyme past. The people, I say, heiring that the honour of thair great goddes Diana stude in jeopardie,

[1] In the old black letter edition, the words "Preacher, &c.," are omitted.
[2] In the MS. "Duram."
[3] In the old edit. "halie," omitted.
[4] In the old edit. "advantage."

with furious voyces cryed, "Great is Diana of the Epheseianis;" As thai wold say, We will not haif the magnificence of our great goddes Diana, whome not onlie Asia but the haill warld wirschippeth, called in doubt, cum in questioun, or contraversie: Away with all men intending that impietie. And heirunto wer thai movit be lang custome and false opinioun.

I knaw that in the Masse hath not onlie bene estemit great holines and honoring of God, but also the ground and foundatioun of oure religioun. So that, in opinioun of many, the Masse takin away, thair resteth no trew wirschipping nor honouring of God in the erth. The deiper hath it persit the hartis of men, that it occupyeth the place of the last and misticall Supper of our Lord Jesus. But yf I sall, be plane and evident Scriptures, prove the Masse, in hir maist honest garment, to haif bene Idolatrie befoir God, and blasphemous to the Death and Passioun of Chryst, and contrarie to the Supper of Jesus Chryst; than gude hope have I, Honourable Audience and belovit Brethrene, that the feir, love, and obedience of God, who, in his Scripturis, hath spokin all veritie, necessarie for oure salvatioun, will have you to gif place to the same.

O Lord Eternall! move and governe my toung to speak the veritie, and the hartis of thy pepill to understand and obey the same.

That ye may the better perceave and understand the manner of my doctrine in this my Confessioun; first, will I collect and gather the summe thairof in a breif and schort *Syllogismus;* and heirefter explane the same more largelie.

THE MASSE IS IDOLATRIE. All wirschipping, honoring, or service inventit by the braine of man in the religioun of God, without his own express commandment, is Idolatrie: The Masse is inventit be the braine of man, without any commandement of God: Thairfoir it is Idolatrie.

For probation of the First part, I will adduce none of the Gentillis sacrifices, in whilk, notwithstanding, was les abominatioun than hath bene in our Masse:[1] but furth of Godis Scriptures will I bring the witnessis of my wordis. And, first, let [1. REG. 13.] us heir Samuell speiking unto Saule, efter that he had sacrificeit[2] unto the Lord upon Mont Gilgall, what tyme his enemyis aprochit aganis him: "Thou art becum foolische, (sayith Samuell,) thou hast not observit the preceptes of the Lord, whilk he commandit[3] thee· Trewlie the Lord had preparit to have stablissit this kingdome above Israel for ever; but now thy kingdome sall not be sure."

Let us considder what was the offence committit be Saule. His enemyis aprocheing, and he considdering that the pepill declynit fra him, and that he had not consulted with the Lord, nor offerit sacrifice for pacificatioun of the Lordis wrath, by reason that Samuell, the principall Prophet and hye preist, was not present, offereth him self brunt and peace offeringis.

Heir is the ground of all his iniquitie; and of this proceideth the caus of his dejection[4] from the kingdome, that he wald honour God utherwayes than wes commandit by his express word. For he, being none of the tryb of Levi, apoyntit be Godis commandment to mak sacrifice, usurpeth that office not dew to him, whilk was maist high abominatioun befoir God, as by the punisment apeireth.

Considder weill that no excusationis ar admittit by [God; as that his][5] enemyes approchit, and his awn pepill departit from him: he culd not haif a lawfull minister, and gladlie wold he have bene reconcilit to God, and consultit with him of the end and chance of that jurney: and thairfoir he, the King, anoyntit be Godis commandement, makith sacrifice. Bot none of all theis wer admittit be God; but Saule was pronunced fulische and vane. For no honoring knaweth God, nor will accept, without it have the express commandement of his awn Word to be done in all poyntis. And no commandement

---

[1] In the MS. "the Mase."
[2] In the old edit. "made sacrifice."
[3] In the old edit. "hath commandit."
[4] In the old edit. "eiection."
[5] These words are not found in the old copies.

was gevin unto the King to mak or offer unto God any maner of sacrifice; whilk becaus he tuke upon him to do, he and his posteritie was depryvit frome all honouris in Israell.

Nether availled his pre-eminence; the necessitie whairin he stude; nor yit his gude intent. But lat us heir mair: When commandement was gevin unto Saule by Samuell, in Godis name, to distroy Amaleck, because that sumtyme thai trubillit the pepill of Israell passing up from Egypt, (advert, ye that presentlie persecut the pepill of God, albeit your painis be deferrit, yit ar thai alreddie prepareit of God;) this pepill of Amaleck wer not immediatlie efter the violence done aganis Israell punissit; but lang efter, thai wer commandit to be distroyit by Saule, man, woman, infant, suckling, oxin, cattell, camellis, and assis; and finallie, all that liveit[1] in that land.

^{1 REGUM. 15.}

Terribill suld the rememberance heirof be to all sic as trubill or molest sic as wold follow the commandement and vocatioun of God, leaving[2] spirituall Egypt, the kingdome of the Antichrist, and the abominatioun thairof. But Saule saved the King, named Agag, and permittit the pepill to saif the best and fattest of the bestiall, to the intent sacrifice suld be made thairof unto God. But lat us heir how this is acceptit. Samuell befoir admonished of his innobedience, cuming unto Saule askit, "What voyce was it whilk he heard?" The King answereth, "The pepill hath saved the fattest and best beastis, thairof to mak sacrifice unto thair God." Heir may be marked, that Saule had no sure confidence in God: for he speikes as thought God apertenit[3] nothing unto him. Samuell answereth, "Suffer and I sall declair unto thee what the Lord hath spokin unto me this nycht." And schortlie he rebukit him maist scharplie that he had not obeyit the voyce of the Lord.

But Saule standing in opinioun that he had not offendit, becaus he did all of gud intent, sayeth, "I haif obeyit the Lordis voce: I have destroyit the synnaris of Amaleck, and onlie I have

---

[1] In the old edit. "lyved."
[2] In the MS. "living."
[3] In the old edit. "He speaketh as thoughe God apperteyned."

saved the King; and the pepill have reserved certane bestiall to be offerit unto God:" and so defendit he his awn work to be just and rychteous. But thairto answereth Samuell, "Delyteth God in brunt offering, and not rather that his voyce be obeyit?" The sin of Witchcraft is not to obey his voyce, and to be stuburne is the sin of Idolatrie. As Samuell wald say, Thair is nothing that God mair requyreth of man than obedience to his commandement; yea, he preferreth obedience to the self same sacrifice ordanit be him self, and no sin is more odius in Godis presence than to disobey his voyce; for that esteameth God so odius, that he doith compare it to the two synnis most abominabill, Incantation and Idolatrie: so that disobedience to his voyce is verie Idolatrie.

Disobedience to Godis voyce is not onlie when man doith wickitlie contrarie to the preceptis of God, but also when of gud zeall, or gud intent, as we commonlie speak, man doith any thing to the honour or service of God not commandit by the express Word of God, as in this matter plainlie may be espyit. For Saule transgressit not wickitlie in murther, adulterie, or lyke externall synnis, but saveit ane aigeit and impotent King (whilk thing who wold not call a gude deid of mercie?); and permitted the pepill, as said is, to save certaine bestiall to be offerit unto the Lord; thinking that God suld thairwith stand content and appleasit,[1] becaus he and the pepill did it of gud intent. But boith theis callit Samuell Idolatrie: first, becaus thai wer done without any commandement of God; and, secondlie, becaus in doing thairof he thocht him self not to haif offendit. And that is principall Idolatrie when our awn inventionis we defend to be rychteous in the sycht of God, becaus we think thame gude, laudable, and pleasant. We may not think us so frie nor wyse, that we may do unto God, and unto his honour, what we think expedient. No! the contrarie is commandit by God, saying, "Unto my Word sall ye add nothing; nothing sall ye deminische thairfrom,

NOTA

DEUT 4.

---

[1] In the MS. "appeasit."

that ye mycht observe the preceptes of your Lord God:" Whilk wordis ar not to be understand of the Decalogue and Law Morall onlie, but of statutis, rytis, and ceremonyis; for equall obedience of all his Lawis requyreth God.

<small>LEVI. 10.</small>   3. And in witnes thairof, Nadab and Abihu offirring strange fyre, whairof God had gevin unto thame na charge, war instantlie as thai offerit punissit to death by fyre. Strange fyre whilk thai offerit unto God was a common fyre, and not of that fyre whilk God had commandit to burne day and nycht upon the alter of brunt sacrifice, whilk onlie aught to haif bene offirit unto God.

O Bischops! ye suld have keipit this fyre: at morne and at evin aucht ye to haif laid fagottis thairupon; your selves aught to haif cleansit and careit away the assis;[1] but God sall behald.

In the puniment of theis tuo afoirsaid is to be observit, that Nadab and Abihu wer the principall preistis nixt to Aaron, thair father; and that thai wer comprehendit neyther in adulterie,[2] covetousnes, nor desyre of warldlie honour, but of a gud zeall and simpill intent wer making sacrifice; desyreing no profit of the pepill thairby, but to honour God and to mitigat his wraith. And yit in the doing of this self same act and sacrifice wer thai consumed away with fyre. Whairof it is plane, that nether the pre-eminence of the persone or man that maketh or setteth up any religioun, without the express commandement of God, nor yit the intent whairof he doith the same, is acceptit befoir God. For nothing in his religioun will he admit without his awn Word; but all that is addit thairto doith he abhoir, and punisseth the inventouris and doeris thairof, as ye haif hard in Nadab and Abihu, by Gedion and dyvers uthiris Israellites setting up sumthing to honour God, whairof thai had no express commandement.

4. A storie, whilk is recytit in the Popes Cronicles, will I recyt, whilk differeth nothing fra the punissment of Nadab, &c. Gregorius Magnus, in the tyme of the maist contagious pestilence

---

[1] In the old edit. "asches."   [2] In the old edit. "aduoutry."

whairwith God punissit the iniquitie of Rome, (for now was the
wickit houre that Antichryst sprung up and set in authoritie);
in this tyme, I say, Gregorie the Pope divysit a new honoring of
God, the Invocation of Sanctis callit the Letanie,[1] whairof in the
Scripturis nether is thair autoritie nor commandement. Upon
whilk sacriledge and idolatrie God declareit his wraith, evin as
he did upon Nadab and Abihu; for in the instant hour when
first the Letanie[2] was recytit in opin processioun (as thai call it),
four scoir of the principall men that recytit the same, horribillie
wer strikin by the plaige of God to death, all in ane hour. The
Papistis attributit this to the contagious aire and vehemencie
of the plague;[3] but it was no other thing but a manifest de-

[1] Knox here refers to "the Greater Litany" of the Church of Rome, containing invocation to saints, and ascribed by that Church to Pope Gregory the First. Basnage, a divine of the Reformed Church, in his Ecclesiastical History, has noticed very fully the subject of the ancient Litanies; and states, that the earliest Litanies now extant, which contain addresses to saints, were not written before the conclusion of the eighth or the beginning of the ninth century. The Litanies, when regularly celebrated, were recited in Ascension week; persons walked in the processions barefooted and fasting. Such invocations were added to the earlier Litanies in more corrupt times; and the names of saints to whom prayers for intercession were offered, were frequently changed at different periods. The variety of formularies used in the Church of Rome was a subject which came under the notice of the Council of Trent. The revisal of the Service-book was committed to Pope Pius V.; and the Roman Litany now contains direct invocations only to forty-three saints.—(*Note abridged from the British Reformers, Knox*, p. 187.)

[2] "Gregorie, in the tyme of a common pestilence, ordeyned this service, called LETANY, whiche is a Greeke worde, and as moch in Englyshe to say, as Supplication or Prayer." (The Prymer in Englyshe, M.D.XXXVIII., sign I ij.) In this edition, the Litany contains eighty-three distinct Invocations.

[3] The historical event referred to by Knox, is thus related by the earliest biographers of Pope Gregory I. In 590, Rome suffered very severely from an infectious distemper, when Gregory, not then installed in the Popedom, preached a sermon, earnestly calling upon the people to repent. The conclusion is preserved in his works, and contains an exhortation to the people to unite publicly in supplication to God, appointing that they should meet at day-break in seven different companies, according to their several ages, sex, and stations, and walk in seven processions, reciting Litanies or Supplications, till they all met at one place. They did so, and proceeded singing and uttering the words, "Kyrie eleison," or "Lord, have mercy upon us." In the space of one hour, while thus engaged, eighty

claration of Godis wraith for inventing and bringing in into the Kirk a false and diabolicall religion. For while we desyre Sanctis to mak intercessioun and to pray for us, what othir thing do we then estemo the advocatioun of Jesus Chryst not to be sufficient for us? And what can be more devillische?

Of theis presidentis, it is plane that na man in earth hath power nor autoritie to statute any thing to the honour of God not commandit be his awn Word.

OBJECTIOUN. 5. It profiteth nothing to say the Kirk hath power to set up, devyse, or invent honoring of God, as it thinketh maist expedient for the glorie of God. This is the continewall crying of the Papistis, The Kirk, the Kirk hath all power; it can not err, for Chryst sayeth, "I wil be with you to the end of the warld." "Whairsoevir is two or three gatherit in my name, thair am I in the middis of thame." Off this falslie conclude thai, the Kirk may do all that semeth gude for the glorie of God; [and whatsoever the Church[1] doeth, that accepteth and approveth God.][2]

6. I culd evidentlie prufe that whilk thai call the Kirk, not to be the Kirk and immaculat spouse of Jesus Chryst, whilk doith not err; but presentlie I ask, yf the Kirk of God be bound to this perpetuall precept? "Not that thing whilk apeireth ryghteous in thyne awn eis that sall thow do, but what God hath commandit, that observe and keip." And yf thai will deny, I desyre to be certifeit wha hath abrogatit and maid the same of none effect? In my judgement Jesus Chryst confirmeth the same, saying, "My scheip heir my voyce, and a stranger

persons fell to the ground, and breathed their last. (Vit. Gregor. a Jo. Diacon. xlii. et seq. See also Fleury, liv. 35, § 1. Baron. Annal. 590, p. 6.) Baronius relates, that Gregory caused an Image of the Virgin to be carried on this occasion. With regard to the persons who died while thus engaged, we may remember, that the plague then raged fiercely, and doubtless many had assembled who were already infected by it. Such deaths occurred in the congregation assembled in London during the plague of 1666."—(*Part of a Note by the Editor of the British Reformers*, p. 187.)

[1] In the old black letter edit. "the Churche," is uniformly employed in place of "the Kirk."

[2] The words inclosed within brackets, supplied from the old edit., are omitted in the MS.

thai will not heir, but flie frome him." To heir his voce (whilk is also the voce of God the Father), is to understand and obey the same; and to flie from a stranger, is to admit none uthir doctrine, worschipping, nor honoring of God than hath proceidit furth of his awne mouth; as he him self testifieth, saying, "All that is of the veritie, heir my voyce." And Paule sayith, " The Kirk is foundit upon the fundatioun of the Prophettis and Apostillis;" whilk fundatioun, no doubt, is the Law and the Evangile. So that it may command nothing that is not contanit in ane of the two; for yf so it doith, it is removit from the onlie fundatioun, and so ceasseth to be the trew Kirk of Chryst.

7. Secondlie, I wold aske, yf that Jesus Chryst be not King and Heid of his Kirk? This will no man deny. Yf he be King, then must he do the office of a King; whilk is not onlie to gyd, reule, and defend his subjectis, but also to mak and statute lawis, whilk lawis onlie, ar his subjectis bound to obey, and not the lawis of any Forrane Princes. Then it becumeth the Kirk of Jesus Chryst to advert what he speiketh, to receave and imbrace his lawis, and whair he maketh end of speiking or law giving [here to rest;][1] so that all the power of the Kirk is subject to Godis Word. And that is maist evident by the commandement gevin of God unto Josua, his chosin captane and leidder of his pepill, in theis wordis, " Be strong and valiant that thai may do according to the holie law, whilk my servand, Moses commandit unto thee. Declyne not frome it, nether to the ryght hand nor to the left, &c." " Let not the buke of the Law depart from thi mouth, but meditate in it boith day and nyght that you may keip and do, in all thingis, according to that whilk is writtin thairin," &c. Heir was it not permittit to Josua to alter one jote, ceremonie, or statute in all the Law of God, nor yet for to add thairunto, but diligentlie for to observe that whilk was commandit. No les obedience requyreth God of us than he did of Josua, his servand. For He will haif

---

[1] These words omitted in the MS. are supplied in an old hand on the margin of a copy of the black letter edition.

the religion ordeanit be His onlie son, Jesus Chryst, most straitlie observit, and not to be violatit in any part.

<small>ʀᴏᴄᴀ. 2.</small> 8. For that I find gevin in charge to the Congregatioun of Thiatira in theis wordes: "I say unto you, and unto the rest that ar in Thiatira, who that hath not the doctrine (meanyng of the diabolicall doctrine befoir rehersit), and who that knaweth not the deipnes of Sathan; I will put upon you none uther burdene but that whilk ye have, Hold till I cum." Mark weill, the Spreit of God calleth all whilk is addit to Chrystis religioun, the doctrine of the Devill, and deip inventioun of the adversarie Sathan. As also did Paule wrytting to Timothie. And Jesus Chryst sayeth, "I will lay upon you none uther burdene than I haif alredie; and that whilk ye haif, observe diligentlie."

O God Eternall! hast thou laid none uther burdene upon our backis than Jesus Chryst laid be his Word? Then who hath burdenit us with all theis Ceremonyis, prescrybed Fasting, compellit Chistitie, unlawfull Vowis, Invocatioun of Sanctis, and with the Idolatrie of the Masse? The Divill, the Divill, Brethrene, inventit all theis burdenis to depress imprudent men to perditioun.

9. Paule wryting of the Lordis Supper, sayith, *Ego accepi a Domino quod et tradidi vobis,* "I have ressavit and learnit of the Lord that whilk I have taught you." And consider yf one ceremony he addeth or permitteth to be usit other than Chryst did use him self; but commandeth thame to use with reverence the Lordis institutioun untill his returnyng to judgement.

10. Albeit Moses wes replenissit with the Spreit of wisdom, and was more familiar with God than ever was any mortall man; yit was thair not of all the ceremonies referrit to his wisdome one jote. But all was commandit to him, to be maid according to the similitude schawin unto him, and according as the word expresseth. Of the whilk presidentis I think it is plane, that all whilk is addit to the religioun of God, without his awn express Word, is Idolatrie.

11. Yit must I answer to ane objectioun, objectit be the Pa- OBJECTIOUN pistis; for never may thai abyd to be subject unto Godis Word. The Apostillis (say they), in the Consall haldin at Jerusalem, set up a religioun, and maid lawis whairof na jote was conteanit in Godis Word: Thairfoir the Kirk may do the same.

That thair was any religion (that is honoring of God, whairby thai myght merit, as ye call it, any thing befoir God) inventit in that Consall, ye never ar abill to prove. Preceptis wer gevin, but nether suche, nor to that intent that ye alledge: All preceptis gevin in that Consall had the commandement of PRECEPTIS WER GEVIN. God, as efter sal be heard.

First, lat us heir the cause of the Consall. Paule and Bar- THE CAUSE OF THE CONSALL AT nabas had taught amangis the Gentillis that onlie Faith in JERUSALEM. Chrystis blude justifieth; and a great multitude of Gentillis by thair doctrine embraceit Jesus Chryst, and by him trewlie wirschippit God. Unto Antiochia from Judea came certane fals teacheris, affirming, That unless thai wer circumcisit according to Moses law, thai culd not be saveit: As our Papistis say this day, that trew fayth in Chrystis blude is not sufficient purgatioun for oure synnis, onless also we bye thair mumbled Masses.[1] This contraversie trubillit the hartis and consciences of the brethrene, in so muche that Paule and Barnabas wer compellit to go unto Jerusalem unto Petir and James, and otheris, I think, of the Apostillis; whair a Conventioun had,[2] the question was proponit, Whether the Gentillis suld be subject to the observatioun of Moses law or not? That is, whether onlie Faith in Jesus Chryst did justifie, or necessarie was also to justificatioun the Law observit.[3] Efter great contentioun, Petir expoundit, How that the house of Cornelius, being all CORNELIUS. Gentillis, had, by his preaching, receaved Jesus Chryst, and wer declarit in his presence just and ryghteous befoir God. For thai did receave the Halie Gaist visibillie, not onlie without observatioun of Moses law, but also befoir thai had ressavit any

---

[1] Meaning, private masses.
[2] "Had," or, being held.
[3] "The Law observit;" that is, the observance of the Ceremonial Law.

sacramentall signe of Chrystis religion. Petir concludeth, that to put a yok upon the brethrenis neckis, whilk yok myght none of the Jewis beir thame selfis, was nothing but to tempt God; that is, to prove yf God wold be pleasit with such lawis and ordinances as thai wold lay upon the neckis of men, without his awn Word, whilk wer maist extreame impietie: And sa concludeth he, that the Gentillis aught not to be burdenit with the Law. Heirefter declared Paule and Barnabas what wonderous workis God had schewed by thame amangis the Gentillis, who nevir observit Moses law. And last, James, who appeareth unto me Principall in that Consall, (for he collecteth the Scriptures and pronunceth the finall sentence, as ye sall heir planelie,) declareth that the vocatioun of the Gentillis was prophesied befoir, and that thai suld be acceptit and accomptit to be the pepill of God without observatioun of Moses law; adding, that no man aught to inquyre a cause of Godis work. And so pronunceth he the sentence, that thair libertie suld not be diminissit.

<small>CONCLUSION OF THE CONSALL.</small>

Advert now the cause, the process, and determinatioun of this Consall. The cause was, to inquyre the veritie of certane doctrine; that is, Whether the Gentillis suld be chargeit with the observatioun of Moses law, as was affirmed and taught by sum. In this mattir thai procedit be exampill of Godis workes; finding that his gracious Majestie had[1] acceptit the Gentillis, without any thraldome or ceremony observit. Last ar produceit Scriptures, declareing so to be foirspokin; and according to all this it is concludit and defynit, that the Gentillis sall not be burdenit with the Law. What congruence, I pray you, hath the Antichrystis Consallis with this Consall of the Apostillis? The Apostillis gatherit to consult upon the veritie. The Papisticall Consallis ar gatherit for privat commoditie, upsetting of idolatrie, and all abominatioun, as thair determinationis manifestlie prove. The Apostillis proceidit in thair Consallis, be consideratioun of Godis workes, and applying of thame to the

<small>QUESTIOUN.</small>

---

[1] In the old edit. "finding that he had," &c.

present cause, whairupon deliberatioun was to be tackin and determined as Godis Scriptures commandit. But the Padistis in thair Consallis proceid according as thair wisdome and folische braine thinkis gude and expedient, and concluding not onlie without authoritie of Godis Scriptures, but also manifestlie contrarie to the same. And that I offir me most cleirlie for to prufe, yf any wold deny or alledge that so it is not.

But yit, say thai, the Apostillis commandit the Gentillis to absteane from certane thingis, whairof thai had no commandement of God. Let us heir the thingis inhibitit: "Ye sall absteane (sayeth the Apostill sent to Antiochia) frome fornicatioun." This is the commandement of God. So, althocht the Gentillis estemit it to be no sin, yit is it expreslie forbiddin in Godis Law. But it followeth, "Frome thingis offerit unto idollis, from strangillit, and frome blude, sall ye absteane." Yf the caussis moving the Apostillis to forbid theis thingis be weill considderit, it sal be found that thai had the express commandement of Jesus Chryst so to do. The Spreit of treuth and knowledge working in the Apostillis with all abundance, schewit unto thame, that nothing was mair profitabill, and mair myght avance the glorie of God, and incresse the Kirk of Chryst, than that the Jewis and Gentillis suld use together in familiaritie and daylie conversatioun, that by mutuall company, love mycht increase. One thing was easie to be espyit, that the Jewis culd not haistelie be persuadit that the eatting of meattis forbiddin in Moses Law was no sin befoir God. For difficill it is to pull furth of the hairt that whilk is plantit by Godis awn Word; so that the Jewis wold have abhorrit the company of the Gentillis yf thai had eattin in thair presence such meattis, as was forbiddin in the Law. The Apostillis considderit that the absteanyng frome suche thingis was nothing prejudiciall to the libertie of Christianis; for with the tyme, and as the Jewis grew more strang, and wer better instructit, thai wold be nothing offendit for suche matteris; and thairfoir commandit thai

OBJECTIOUN

the Gentillis to absteane for a time. For that it wer not a perpetuall precept declareth this day, when no man holdeth the eatting of suche thingis sin.

But what precept had thai so to do? The last and new precept gevin by Jesus Chryst to his Discipillis, "That everie ane love another, as he hath loved us." May not Christian love command, that none of us do in the sycht of uther that whilk may offend or trubill the conscience of the infirme and weake? So witnesseth Paule, affirmyng, "that yf a man eat with offence he synneth." And by vertew of this same precept, the Apostillis forbid that the Gentillis sall eat thingis offerit unto idollis, &c., that beiring sum part with the infirmitie of the Jewis, thai mycht grow togethir in mutuall amitie and Christian love. And theis ar the traditionis of the Seniouris[1] whilk Paule commandit to be observit. I pray you, what similitude hath oure Papisticall lawis with this precept of the Apostillis?

NOTA. But greatlie it is to be mervalit that men do not advert that the buke of Godis Law, that is, of all his Ordinances, Testament, Promeis, and exhibitioun thairof, was seallit and confermit in the dayis of the Apostillis; the effect and contentis thairof promulgat and publischit; so that maist extreame impietie it is to mak any alteratioun thairin; yea, and the wraith and feirfull maledictioun of God is denuncit to fall upon all thame that dar attempt to add or diminische any thing in his religioun, confirmit and proclamit by his own voyce. O Papistis! whair sall ye hyd yow frome the presence of the Lord? Ye haif pervertit his Law, ye haif takin away his Ordinances, ye haif placeit up[2] your awn Statutis insteid of his: Wo and dampnatioun abydeth you! Albeit that the Apostillis had made lawis other than the express word commandit, what aperteneth that to you? Have ye the Spreit of treuth and knowledge in aboundance as thai had? Was the Kirk of Chryst left imperfyt efter the Apostillis dayis? Bring your selves to mynd, and

---

[1] The Seniors, or Elders of the Church.
[2] That is, set up, or, substituted.

be aschamit of your vanitie. For all men, whais eis Sathan hath not blindit, may espy, that nether wisdome nor autoritie of man may change or set up any thing in the religioun of God, without his awn express commandement and word.

And thus, I think, the First part of my Argument sufficientlie proved; whilk is, That all wirschipping, honoring, or service of God inventit be the braine of man, in the religion of God, without his awn express commandement, is Idolatrie.

But in vane, will sum think, that all this labour I have takin; for na man of haill judgement any part of this wold haif denyit; nor yit doith it prove any thing of myne intent: for the Masse is not the inventioun of man, but the verie ordinance of God. Then discend I to prove the Masse to be the meir inventioun of man, set up without all commandement of God.

And first, of this name MISSA, whilk we call THE MASSE, wold I ask at suche as wold defend that Papisticall abominatioun, Of what spreit is it inventit that *Missa*[1] sall signifie a Sacrifice for the synnis of the quick and the deid? Of the Spreit of God? or of the spreit of man? Or of what originall is it discendit? Sum will answer, from the Hebrew dictioun, *Missah*, whilk, eftir sum, doith signifie ane oblatioun or a gift; lyke as tribut whilk the Inferiour offereth or payeth to the Superiour. In the Hebrew toung I confes my self ignorant, but have (as God knaweth) fervent thrist to have sum entrance thairin: and sa of the Hebrew dictioun can not contend. But men of great judgement in the same toung say, That na whair in Scriptures *Missah* betokeneth ane oblatioun. But admitting that so it did, What sall thai be abill to prove thairby? My question is, Yf the Spreit of God hath inventit and pronunceit this dictioun *Missa* to signifie a sacrifice for the synnis of the quick and the deid? Whilk yf thai be not abill to prove, then must thai neidis confes that it is of manis inventioun, and not of Godis impositioun. I culd gif unto thame a moir apperand cause and

[1] The Latin name for the Mass.

derivatioun of that dictioun *Missa*; but of the name I am not greatlie sollist.

Secundly, I desyre to be certifeit what thai call thair Masse? Whether the haill actioun, with all ceremonies, useit now of olde, or a part thairof? It will not satisfie the hairtis of all godlie to say. St James and St Petir celebrated the first Masse in Jerusalem or Antiochia. Yf it so wer, one of the two celebratit first, and the other eftir; but nether of the two can be proved be Scripture. Great mervale it is that sa manifestlie men schame not to lie! Petir and James (say the Papistis) celebratit the first Masse. But I sall prove that Pope Sixtus was the first that did institut the aulteris. Felix, the first of that name, did consecrat thame and the tempillis boith. Bonifacius commandit the aulteris to be coverit with cleane clothis. Gregorius Magnus commandit the candellis to be lychtit at the Evangile; and did institute certane clothis. Pontianus commandit *Confiteor*[1] to be said. And wharfoir suld I trubill you and my self boith, in recyting what everie Pope addit. Ye may for two-pence[2] have the knawledge what everie Pope addit, untill at last wes compact and set up the haill bodie of the blasphemous Ydoll. And yit eschame thai not to say, St Petir said the first Masse, althocht that many hundreth yeiris eftir him na sic abominable ceremonyis wer inventit.

PAPÆ QUI MISSAM INSTITUERUNT.

EVASION.

But thai say, All theis ceremonies ar not of the substance of the Masse, but ar addit for gude caussis. What commandement haif thai ressavit to add any thing to the ordinance of God, for any cause apeiring to thame? But lat thame certifie me what is the Masse. The Canon,[3] will thai answer, with the wordes of

---

[1] That is, the general Confession in the Ordinary of the Mass, beginning, "Confiteor Deo omnipotenti, beatæ Mariæ semper Virgini, beato Michaeli archangelo," &c.

[2] The price of many of the smaller tracts published at this time. In an account given by Foxe the Martyrologist of the troubles of Gertrude Crokey, we find that Dr Mallet, the Romish master of St Katherine's, London, told her, she was deceived by "little new-fangled two-penny books."

[3] The ritual or service of the Romish Sacrament of the Altar is called *Canon Missæ*, the Canon of the Mass.

consecration. Who is author of the Canon, can thai precislie tell? Be weill avysit befoir ye answer, lest by neglecting your self ye be proved lyaris. Will ye say that the Apostillis usit your Canon? So ye haif affirmit in tymes past. Yf the Canon discendit frome the Apostillis to the Popes, bold and maleperte impietie it had bene to haif addit any thing thairto; for a Canon is a full and sufficient reule, whilk in all partes and poyntis is perfyte. But I will prove dyverse Popes to haif addit thair portionis to this halie Canon. Yf thai will deny, advyse what addit Sergius; and what addit Leo;[1] and what addit the two Alexanderis, for I may not abyd presentlie to recyte all; but yf thai doubt, thair awn law sall certifie thame.

IMPROBATION OF THE CANON.

Secundlie, the rememberance of the names of suche men, wha wer not borne many hundred yeiris eftir the dayes of the Apostillis, declaireth the Canon not to have bene inventit many yeiris eftir the Apostillis. For who useit to mak mentioun of a man in his prayeris befoir he be borne? And masteris memorie[2] is maid in the Canon of suche men and women of whois halines and godlie lyfe credibill histories mak litill mentioun, whilk is ane evident testimony that your halie Canon is vane and of none effect. And yf any will tak upon him to defend the same, I will prove that thairin is indigest, barbarous, fulische congestioun[3] of wordis, imperfectioun of sentences, ungodlie invocationis, and diabolicall conjurationis. And this is that halie Canon whois authoritie precelleth all Scripture. O! it was so holie, it mycht not be spokin planelie as the rest, but secretlie it behoved to be whisperit![4] That was not evill devysit, for yf all men had hard it, men wold have espyit the vanitie thairof.

[1] In both the MS. and the old edition, the words, "what Leo," are uselessly repeated.

[2] So in the old edition as well as the MS. The phrase "masteris memorie," referring to the commemoration of holy men in the Ritual of the Romish Church, is unusual, and is perhaps incorrectly given.

[3] Heaping together.

[4] That is, some parts of the Mass are repeated by the priest in a tone inaudible to the people.

A VINDICATION OF THE DOCTRINE

But to the wordis of Consecration: By whome haif thai that name, I desyre to know? By Jesus Chryst, will thai say? But no whair ar thai abill to prove that the wordis whilk he pronuncit in his last Supper, callit he, or any of his Apostillis efter him, "wordis of Consecration." And so have thai ressaveit the name by authoritie of man. Whilk ar the wordis? Lat us heir. *Accipite et manducate ex hoc omnes. Hoc est enim corpus meum. Similiter et calicem post quam coenavit, dicens,* &c.[1] Let us inquyre yf any thing be heir addit to Chrystis wordis, or yf any thing be changeit or alterit thairin. First, in whilk of the Evangelistis ar theis wordis, *ex hoc omnes*,[2] spoken of the breid? Jesus Chryst did speik thame of the cuppe, but not of the breid. O Papistis! ye have maid alteration, not so mekill in wordis as in deid; and of the self same action commandit to be usit be him: ye permittit all to eat of the bread; but of the cuppe ye reservit to yow, clippit in the crounis and annoyntit upon the fingeris;[3] and in pane of your great Anathematization, of your great Cursing, ye forbad that any layit[4] presumit to drink thairof. But tell me, Papistis, wer the Apostillis clippit and smeirit[5] as yow be? or will ye than say, that the Congregation of the Corinthianis wer Papist preistis? I think ye will not. And yit thai all drank of the cuppe, lyke as thai eate of the bread. Mark, Brethren, that of Chrystis own wordis thai mak alteration.

NOTA.

But let us proceid. Thay say, *Hoc est enim corpus meum*. I pray thame, schew whair find thay *enim*.[6] Is not this thair awn inventioun, and addit of thair awn braine? O! heir mak thai a great matter, and heir lyeth a secreit misterie and hid operatioun; for in fyve wordis conceaved the Virgin Marie, say thay when sche conceavit the Sone of God. What yf sche had spokin seven, ten, or tuentie wordis? or what yf sche had not spokin thrie? Suld thairby the determinat consalle bene

---

[1] "Take and eat ye all of this, for this is my body. In like manner he took the cup after supper, saying," &c.
[2] "All of this."
[3] The Romish Priests.
[4] In the old edit. "layed," any layman.
[5] Clipped, or shorn, and besmeared.
[6] "For this is my body."

impedit? But, O Papistis! is God a juglar? Useth he certane nomber of wordis in performing his intent? But whairto ar ye ascendit, to be exaltit in knawledge and wisdome above Jesus Chryst. He sayeth onlie, *Hoc est corpus meum.* But ye, as thocht thair lackit sumthing necessarie requysite, have addit *enim*,[1] saying, *Hoc est enim corpus meum.* So that your affirmatioun makith all perfyte.

Considder, I exhort you, belovit Brethrene, yf thai haif not addit heir of thair awn inventioun to Chrystis wordis. And as thai add, so steall thai frome thame. Chryst sayith, *Hoc est corpus meum, quod pro vobis datur,* or *frangitur.* "This is my body whilk is gevin for yow, or whilk is brokin for yow." Theis last wordis, whairin standis our haill comfort, omit thai, and mak no mentioun of thame. And what can be judgeit more bold or wickit than to alter Chrystis wordis, to add unto thame, and to diminische frome thame? Had it not bene convenient, that eftir thai had introduceit Jesus Chryst speiking, that his awn wordis had bene recytit, nothing interchangeit, addit, or diminischit; whilk seing thai haif not done, but haif done the express contrarie, as befoir is proved.

In vain I think it is further to labour to prove the rest of this abominabill action to be inventit and devysit by the folische braine of man, and sa can it not be denyit to be Idolatrie. It sall not profit thame to say, The Epistill and Evangile is in the Masse, heirunto is no thing addit. What sall they prove thairby? For the Epistill and Evangile, as thame selves do confess, are not of the substance of the Masse. And althocht thai wer, it did no thing excuse the rest of that Idolatrie. For the Devill may speik the wordis of God, and his false Prophetis also, and yit thairby ar thai nether better nor mair halie. The Epistill and Evangile ar Godis wordis, I confess, but thair ar thai spokin for no edification of the peple, but for to be a clok unto the bodie of that mischevous Idolatrie. All the ac-

---

[1] "For:" the Editor of the British Reformers remarks, "The distinction which Knox makes here, is, however, hardly to be considered of moment."

tion is abominable, becaus it is the inventioun of man; and so a few or certane gud wordis can not sanctifie that haill Mass and bodie of abominatioun. But what yf I sall admit to the Papistis, that the haill action of the Masse wer the institutioun and verie ordinance of God, and never one jote of manis inventioun thairin : [if] I admit it be the ordinance of God (as it is not), yet will I prufe it abominatioun befoir God.

The Second Syllogisme.

All honoring or service of God, whairunto is addit a wickit opinioun, is abominatioun. Unto the Masse is addit a wickit opinioun. Thairfoir it is abominatioun.

The first part, I think, no godlie man will deny; and yf any wold, I ask, What maid the self same sacrifice, institute and ordeanit to be useit be Godis express commandement, odious and abominabill in his sycht? As it is writtin, "Bring unto me no more your vane sacrifices, your brunt offeringis is abominatioun, your new moones, Sabbothis, and conventionis I may not abyd; your solemne feastis, I hate thame from the hart." And also, "Who slayith ane oxe in sacrifice, killeth a man;" that is, doth me no les dishonour than yf he killed a man: "Who slayith a scheip (sayeth he) choketh a dog: Who brocht meat offeringis unto me, doith offer swynis blude." Theis two beastis, the dog and swyne, wer abominabill to be offerit in sacrifice, the ane for the crueltie, the other for filthines. But, O Preistis! your sacrifices ar mixt with the blude of dogis and swyne; whill that on the ane part, most cruellie ye do persecut the professouris of Chrystis word · upon the other part, your selves live most filthilie. The Prophet proceideth; "Who makith a memoriall of incense, praiseth the thing that is vane." Amos says, "I hait and detest your solemne feastis. I will not accept your incense, your brunt offeringis and meat offeringis ar not thankfull befoir me." And why all this? Becaus, sayith the Prophet Esay, "They have chosin theis in thair awin wayis, and thair own hartis haif delytit in thair abominations." And plane it is, that

ESAY I.

AMOS THE 5.

ESAY 66.

thair foirsaid sacrifices wer commandit to be done be God, and wer not inventit, no, not one jote thairof, by manis wisdome. Read the bukis of Moses, Exodus, and Leviticus, and thow sall perceave thame to be verie[1] commandements of God. And yit sayith the Prophet, "Thai haif chosin thame in thair awn wayis." Whairby the Prophet meant and understude, that thai had addit unto thame ane opinioun, whilk maid thame to be abominable befoir God.

This opinioun was, as in the same Prophet and diverse uthiris may be spyit, That be working of the externall work, thai mycht purchese the favour of God, and mak satisfactioun for thair synnis by the same sacrifices. And that I collect of Jeremie saying, "Ye beleif fals wordis whilk sall not profit you: JEREM. 7. For when ye haif stollin, murtherit, committit adulterie, and perjurie, &c., then ye cum and stand befoir me in this house, whilk hath my name gevin unto it; and ye say, We ar delyvered or absolved, albeit we haif done all theis abominations." Thay thocht and verelie belevit thair synnis to have bene remittit by vertew of thair sacrifice offerit. But Esay asketh of thame, ESAY 55. "Why spend ye silver for that whilk is not sure, and consume labour for that whilk dois not saciate?" "Ye do hyd your selves with lies[2] (but thai estemit thame to have bene verities) and ye mak a band or covenant with death, but it sall not stand, for when distructioun cumeth it sall overwhelme you." Thair fals prophetis had taught thame to cry, Peace, peace, when yit thair was no peace in thair consciences. For thai whilk did eat the sin of the pepill, (as our Preistis have lang done,) for the mair wickit men wer, the mair desyre thai had of the Masse, thinking be vertew thairof all was purgeit. The pestilent preistis of Moses law, as witnesseth the Prophetis, OSE. 7. JERE. 2. causit the pepill to beleive, that by oblatioun of the sacrifice thai wer just and innocent; and durst desyre, for sic offeringis, plage, and the wraith of God[3] to be removit. But it is answerit

[1] "Verie," or, the true.
[2] In the old edit. "leasinges."
[3] In the old edit. "plague and the furor of God."

unto thame be the Prophet Michas, "Sall I cum in his presence with brunt offeringis, and yeirlie lambis? Or doith a thousand rammes please him, or ten thousand boit[1] of oyle? Sall I gif my first-borne sone for expiation of myne iniquitie; or the frute of my wombe a sin offering for my saule?" Heir the Prophet planlie witnesseth that no externall work, how excellent that ever it be, doith purge or mak satisfaction for sin; and sa, of the presidentis,[2] it is playn, that a wickit opinioun addit to the verie work, sacrifice, or ceremony commandit to be done and usit by God, makith it abomination and ydolatrie. For Idolatrie is not onely to wirschip the thing whilk is not God, but also to trust or leane unto that thing whilk is not God, and hath not in it self all sufficiencie. And thairfoir Paule calleth covetous men idolatouris, becaus thair confidence and trust is in thair ryches; much more wald he call him ane ydolater whois hart beleveth remissioun of synnis by a vane work, done by him self or by any uthir in his name.

NOTA.

But now let us heir yf unto the Masse be joynit a wickit opinioun. It hath bene haldin in commoun opinioun. It planelie hath bene taught, by law it is decreit, and in the wordis of the Masse it is expressit, That the Masse is a Sacrifice and oblatioun for the synnis of the quick and the deid: so that remissioun of synnis undoubtedlie was belevit by that same actioun and work presentlie done by the Preist. Sufficient it wer for me, by the plane wordis of the foirsaid Prophetis, heirfor to conclude it abominatioun; seing thai planelie schaw that remissioun of synnis cumeth onlie of the meir mercie of God, without all deserving of us, or of our work proceiding of oure selves; as Esay wrytteth saying, "I am he whilk removeth thyne iniquitie, and that for my awn sake."

OPINIOUN HALDIN OF THE MASS.

But yf I sall prove this foirsaid opinion which hath bene haldin of the Masse to be fals, deceavable, and vane, and that it is no sacrifice for sin, sall than either consuetude, lang process of tyme, or multitude of Papisticall patronis, defend that

---

[1] In the old edit. "boyt," casks or butts.   [2] Ib. "precedentes."

it is not abomination and Idolatrie? And first I ask, Who offerith this sacrifice, and what is offerit? The Preist (sayeth the Papistis) offerith Jesus Chryst unto the Father. Then demand I, Yf a man can offer unto God a more pretious thing than him self? And it appeireth that not, for Paule commandith that "We offer unto God a holie, lyvelie, and reasonable Sacrifice," whilk he calleth oure awn bodies. And Jesus Chryst, having nothing more pretious than him self, did offer up him self. Yf Paule had knawin any other sacrifice, efter the death of Jesus Chryst, (that is in all the tymes of the New Testament) more acceptabill unto God than the mortificatioun of our awn bodies, wold he not have advertisit us thairof? Yf thair was any other sacrifice, and he did not knaw thairof, then led not the Spreit him in to all veritie, whilk to say wer blasphemie. If he knew it, and yit did not advertise us thairof, than did he not the deutie and office of a trew preacher, and that to affirme wer lyk impietie. If any man mycht have offerit Jesus Chryst but him self onlie, in vaine had it bene to him to haif sufferit so cruell torment in his awn persone by oblatioun of him self. And so to affirme that mortall man may offer him who is immortall God, in my opinioun is malapert[1] proudnes. NOTA.

But let us heir more. Paule sayeth, "By one Oblatioun hath he made perfyt for evir thame whilk ar sanctifeit;" and also, "Remissioun of synnis anis gotten, thair resteth na mair Sacrifice." Thay will not avoyd Paullis wordis, althocht thai say Paule speiketh of the Leviticall sacrifice. No, Papistis! he excludeth all maner of sacrifice, saying, *Nulla amplius restat Oblatio*, "No more Sacrifice resteth." And thairto testifieth Jesus Chryst him self upon the cross, saying, *Consummatum est*;[2] that is, what ever is requyrit for pacifeing my Fatheris wraith justlie moveit aganis sin; what ever is necessarie for reconciliatioun of mankynd to the favour of my Eternall Father; and what ever the purgation of the synnis of the haill warld requyrit, is now compleit and endit, so that no further sacrifice resteth for sin. HEBRE. 10.

---

[1] Impudent.   [2] "It is finished."

Heir, ye Papistis! tuo Witness speik agains yow. How can ye deny the opinion of your Masse to be false and vaine? Ye say it is a sacrifice for sin, but Jesus Chryst and Paule say, The onlie death of Chryst was sufficient for sin, and efter it resteth none uther sacrifice: Speak! or els ye ar lyke to be condempnit. I knaw ye will say, it is none uther sacrifice, but the self same, save that it is iteratit[1] and renewit. But the wordis of Paule bind you more straitly than that so ye may eschaip: for in his haill disputation, contendeth he not onlie that thair is no uther sacrifice for sin, but also that the self same sacrifice, anis offerit, is sufficient, and nevir may be offerit againe. For uthirwayis of no greatter pryce, value, nor extenuation, suld the death of Chryst be, then the death of thois beastis whilk wer offerit under the Law: whilk ar proved to be of none effect, nor strenth, becaus it behoveth thame often tymes to be iterit.[2]

The Apostle, be comparing Jesus Chryst to the Leviticall preistis, and his sacrifice unto thairis, maketh the matter plane that Chryst mycht be offerit but anis. First, the Leviticall preistis wer mortall, and thairfoir it behoved thame to haif successouris: But Chryst is ane eternall Preist, and thairfoir is allone, and neideth no successour. The Leviticall preistis offerit the blude of beistis: But Jesus Chryst offerit his awn bodie and blude. The Leviticall preistis, for impotence of thair sacrifice, did iterat the same: But the sacrifice of Jesus Chryst, having in it self all perfectioun, neideth not to be iterat; yea, to affirme that it ought (or may be) iterat, is extreme blasphemie; for that wer to impute imperfection thairupon, contrarie to the haill religioun, and the plaine wordis of Paule, saying, "Suche is our High Preist, holie, just, unpolute, seperate from synneris, and higher than the heavinis; to whome it is not necessarie everie day to offer, as did thois preistis first offer for thair awn synnis, and than for the synnis of the pepill: For that he hath done anis, when he offerit him self." What wordis

[1] In the old edit. "iterated," repeated.   [2] Ib. "iterate."

THAT THE MASS IS IDOLATRY. 57

can be more plaine? Heir Paule scheweth all caussis, whairfore it neideth not Chryst to be offerit agane; and wold conclude, that he may not be offerit agane.

Yit say thay, it repugneth nothing that we offer Chryst, so *PAPISTIS ANSWER.* that he offer not him self. The text sayeth planelie, as befoir is schewit, that Chryst onlie mycht offer him self; whilk sacrifice is sufficient, and never may be offerit agane: "For yf it had behovit him to have bene oftener offerit than anis, he suld have sufferit often tymes from the begynning of the warld. But *HEBR. 9.* anis hath he appeired for the away taking of sin, offering him self;" that is of his awn bodie, anis slane, now lyving, and may suffer death no more: "For by his onlie ane sacrifice hath he *HEBR. 10.* maid us perfyte, and sanctifeit for evir."

Heir is answerit to that objectioun, that sum object; Men *NOTA.* everie day sin: thairfoir it is necessarie that everie day be sacrifice maid for sin. Paule sayeth, "Be ane sacrifice hath he consummat us for ever;" for uthirwayis his death wer not the onlie and sufficient sacrifice for oure synnis; whilk to affirme wer blasphemie. And so thair resteth of oure haill redemption nothing but his secund cuming, whilk salbe to judgement; whair we, depending upon him, sall ressave glorie and honour; but his enemyis salbe maid a futstule to his feit. Not that I meane that his death ought not to be preachit, and the remembrance thairof extollit and praisit in the rycht ministration of his Supper; but none of theis tuo be sacrifice for sin. What will ye *QUESTION.* answer to this, whilk Paule produceth aganis your Masse? He planelie sayeth, Thair is no sacrifice for sin, but Chrystis death onlie, &c.; and that neither may ye offer him, nor yit that he may offer him self any more.

Ye will say, It is a memoriall sacrifice, under the whilk Jesus *PAPISTIS ADVERT* Chryst is offerit unto the presence of God the Father by the Kirk,[1] under the apeirance of bread and wyne, for remissioun of synnis. I answer with Paule, *Apparet nunc in conspectu Dei* *EVASION.* *pro nobis*, "He apeireth now in the presence of God for us."

[1] In the old edit. "the Church."

So that it is not requisit that any man offer or represent him to the Father; for that he doith him self, making continewall intercession for us.

But let us consider this Doctrine mair deiplie. The Kirk,[1] say they, offered Jesus Chryst unto God the Father for a memoriall sacrifice, or in a memoriall sacrifice. Is thair any oblivion or forgetfulnes fallin on God the Father? Hath he forgottin the Death and Passion of Jesus Chryst, sa that he neideth to be brocht in memorie thairof be any mortall man? Behold, Brethren, how that impietie discloseth and declareth it self! Can thair be any greatter blasphemie than for to say, God the Father hath forgotten the benefittis whilk he gave to mankynd in his onlie Son Jesus! And who that ever will say, that thai offer any memoriall sacrifice or rememberance thairof unto God, doith plainlie say that God hath forgottin thame. For uthirwayis, what neideth a representation or rememberance?

<small>PAPISTIS</small>

Advert, Papistis, and consider how Sathan hath blinded you; ye do manifestlie lie, and do not espy the same. Ye do blaspheme God at everie word, and can ye not repent? Thay say it is *Sacrificium* speaking here; for a memoriall sacrifice it can not be. Thay say it is *Sacrificium applicatorium*,[2] a sacrifice whairby thai do and may[3] apply the merittis of Chrystis passion unto synneris. Thay will be layaris to of plaisteris! but I feir the wound be not weill rypit, and thairfoir that the plaisteris be unprofitable. Ye say ye may apply the merittis of Chrystis Passioun to whome ye list. This is proudlie spokin. Then may ye mak peace with God at your pleasure. But the

<small>ESAY 27.</small>

contrarie speikith he in theis wordis, "Who may make." Heir God sayeth, that as none may move his wraith aganis his chosin, (and heirof aught ye to rejoise, Brethren: the Pope, nor his Preistis, nor Bischopis whatsomever may not cause God to be angrie aganis yow, albeit thai Curse yow with cross, bell, and candill,[4]) so may no man compell him to love or receave in fa-

---

[1] In the old edit. "the Church."
[2] An applicatory Sacrifice.
[3] In the old edit. "may and do."
[4] The Romish form of Cursing.

vour but whome it pleaseth his infinit gudnes. Moses, I confess, prayit for the pepill when God was displeasit with thame. But he speiketh not so proudlie as yow do, but either desyreth God to remit the offence of the pepill, or els to distroy him altogether with thame. I feir that your love be not so fervent. He obteyned his petition of God.

But will ye say, So it was[1] determinat befoir in the counsall of God? Avyse yow weill. The nature of God is to be frie, and thrall unto nothing. For althocht he is bond and oblissit to fulfill all that his Word promissis to the faithfull beleiveris, yit is that neither subjection nor thraldom; for frielie he maid his promeis, and frielie he doth fulfill the same. I desyre to be certifeit whair God maid his promeis unto yow Papist preistis, that ye suld have power to apply (as ye speik) the merittis of Chrystis passion to all and sindrie who told or numbered money to yow for that purpois? Taketh God any part of the profit that ye ressave? Allace, I have compassion upon your vanitie, but moir upon the simpill pepill that haif bene disceavit be yow and your fals doctrine. Ar ye better heard with God than Samuell was? He prayit for King Saule, and that maist ferventlie, and yit obteanit not his petition, nor mycht not apply any merittis or holines unto him. And it is said to Jeremie, "Pray thow not for this pepill, JERE 14 for my hart is not towardis it; no, thocht Moses and Helias suld pray for thame, yit wold I not heir thame, for thai love to go wrong, and do not absteane frome iniquitie. Albeit thei fast and cry, yit will I not heir thame; and althocht thai offer brunt sacrifice, I tak no pleasure in it. And thairfoir pray not for this pepill, nor yit mak any intercessioun for thame, for I will not heir thee."

What say yow to theis wordis, Papistis? The Prophet is forbiddin to pray, for God sayeth, he neither will heir him nor yit the pepill: He will accept none of thair sacrifices; and that

[1] In the margin of a copy of the old edit., corrected, in an old hand, "So it was not."

becaus the pepill manifestlie rebellit aganis God, rejoiseit in iniquitie, committit idolatrie and abomination. And he manifestlie schewith, that nothing may appease him but trew repentance and conversioun agane unto God. O Preistis! hath thair not as great iniquitie aboundit in your dayis as ever did from the beginning? Have ye not bene intyseris and leidaris of the pepill to all idolatrie? Yea, hath not the mischeivous exampill of your abominabill lyves provokit thousandis unto iniquitie? And yit do ye say, that ye may apply the merittis of Chrystis Passion to whome ye list! Heir ye not that God never will accept prayeris nor sacrifice whillis trew repentance wer found? Of that ye wer dum, and alwayis keipit silence. Your clamour and crying was, "Cum, cum to the Mass; buy with money, substance, and possessionis, remissioun of your synnis: We have the merittis of Chrystis Passioun: We may offer Jesus Chryst unto the Father, whome he must neidis receave for an acceptabill sacrifice and satisfactioun of all your synnis." Think not, Brethrene, that I alledge any thing upon thame whilk thai thame selves do not speik, as thair awn Law and Masse sall testifie.

In the beginning of the Canon,[1] the proude Preist, lifting up his eis, as that he had God evin always bound to his commandement, sayeth, "We beseche thee, maist mercifull Father, by Jesus Chryst our Lord, that you ressave and bliss this untaistit Sacrifice (unsavourie Sacrifice, trewlie he mycht have said) whilk we offer to thee for thyne Universall Kirk."

O proude and pervers Prelatis[2] and Preistis! who gave you that authoritie? Is it not expreslie forbidden by the Apostill Paule that any man suld usurpe the honour to mak sacrifice, except he be callit by God, as was Aaron? Have ye the same commandement whilk was gevin to Aaron? His sacrifices ar abrogatit by Chryst. Let us heir whair ye ar commandit to mak sacrifices. Searche the Scriptures, but searche thame with

---

[1] The Service of the Mass.   [2] In the old edit. "Papist Prelates."

judgement. It will not be, *Hoc facite*,¹ for that is spokin of eatting, drinking, and thankisgeving, and not of sacrifice making. Nor yit with the ordour of Melchizedeck, nor the text of Malachie prove yow Preistis to mak sacrifice. Advyse with others that have more appearance to prove your intent; for yf theis be weill ponderit, the wecht of thame will depress the proudnes of your Papisticall Preisthoode.

Now will I collect schortlie, all that is said for probatioun, that the Masse is no sacrifice for synne. Advert: The New Testament is eternall, that is, anis maid, can never be dissolved, and ESAY 9. JEREM. 31. thairfoir the blude whairwith this Testament is confirmed is eternall: For it is the blude of the Eternall Sone of God. Onlie the blude of Jesus Chryst takith away oure synnis; for it is he allone that takith away the synnis of the warld; and who by his awn blude hath reconcilit all. For yf uthirwayis sin mycht have bene takin away, than Chryst had died in vane. COLLOS. 1. And yf full admission stude not in him alone, than thai that NOTA eat him yet hungerit, and thay that drank him yet thrystit; and that wer contrarie to his own wordis: "The blude of Chryst JOHNE 6. is anis offerit," and is sufficient, for it is the eternall blude of the eternall Son of God; and "by his awn blude hath he anis enterit into the halie place." Thairfoir the blude of Chryst anis offerit remaneth for ever, for purgatioun of all synis; and sa resteth thai na sacrifice in the Masse. Advert theis reasonis president² and gif place to the veritie: For whill the Scriptures of God salbe haldin of autoritie, never ar ye abill to resolve theis argumentis.

Considder now, Brethrene, yf the opinioun of the Masse be not vane, fals, and deceavabill? Causit thai not you to beleive it was a Sacrifice, wheirby remissioun of synnis was obteynit? And ye may planelie perceave that na sacrifice thair is, nor at any time was, for synnis, but the death of Jesus Chryst onlie. For the sacrifice of the Ald Law were onlie figures of that verie and trew sacrifice anis offerit by Jesus Chryst. And in thame was com-

¹ " Do this." ² In the old edit. " precedent."

memoration of synnis maid, but nether was remission of synnis obteanit, nor purgation maid by any suche sacrifice. What will ye do, Papist Preistis? Thair resteth no sacrifice to be offerit for sin by yow, nor by any mortall man. Theis ar dolorous tydingis unto your hartis, and no marvale; for by that vane oppinioun that the Masse was a sacrifice for sin, have ye so quyetlie restit into that flude of Euphrates,[1] that is, in all warldlie felicitie, whilk flowit unto yow as a continuall flude. But the Masse knawin not onlie to be no sacrifice, but also to be idolatrie, the watteris appeir to dry up; and it is lyke that ye lack sum licour to refresche your tungis, being cruciat with drought and heat intollerabill.

Wold ye then hear glad tydingis? What, yf that I suld permit unto you (as one willing to play the gude fellow, and not to be stifneckit) that the Masse wer a sacrifice for sin, and that ye did offer Jesus Chryst for sin, wold ye be content that this wer permittit unto yow? I think ye wold, for thairfoir have ye lang contendit. Than let us consider, what suld subsequentlie follow thairupon.

A sacrifice for sin was never perfyt untill that the beast offerit was slane. If in your Masse ye offer Jesus Chryst for sin, than necessarilie in your Masse must ye neidis kill Jesus Chryst. Do not esteme, Belovit Brethrene, these wordis schortlie spokin, to be vane or of small effect. Thay ar collectit of the verie ground of Scriptures, for thay planelie testifie that Chryst to be offerit, Chryst to suffer, and Chryst to sched his blude or die, ar all one thing. Paule, in the Epistill to the Hebrews, sayith, "He appeirith now in the presence of God for us, not to offer him self often tymes for us, for uthirwayis it behoved him to have sufferit often tymes, from the begynning of the warld." Mark weill, that Paule maketh to offer and suffer both one thing, and thairfoir proveth he that Chryst maid but one Sacrifice, becaus he anis did suffer the death. Jesus Chryst sayith, as it is writtin in Mathew, "This is my blude of the New

---

[1] The waters of Babylon.

THAT THE MASS IS IDOLATRY. 63

Testament, whilk salbe sched for yow and for many, in remissioun of synnis." Mark, that remissioun of synnis is attributit to the schedding of Chrystis blude. And Paule sayeth, " Chryst is deid for our synnis;" and in another place, "By one oblatioun or sacrifice hath he made us perfyt for ever." Considder diligentlie that remissioun of synnis is attributit sumtyme to the schedding of Chrystis blude, sumtyme to his death, and sumtyme to the haill sacrifice whilk he maid in suffering all pane. And why is this? Whether yf thair be dyvers maneris to obtene remissioun of synnis? No, but becaus everie ane of theis thrie necessarilie followeth other. Remissioun of synnis is commonlie ascrybit to any of thame, for whair so that ever Chryst is offerit, thair is his blude sched, and his death subsequentlie followeth.

And so Papistis, yf ye offer Chryst in sacrifice for sin, ye sched his blude, and thus newlie slay him. Advert to what fyne[1] your awn desire sall bring yow, evin to be slayeris[2] of Jesus Chryst. Ye will say, ye never pretendit sic abominatioun. I disput not what ye intendit; but I onlie schaw what absurditie doith follow upon your awne doctrine. For necessarilie yf ye do offer Chryst for sin, as ye confess, and your Law doith teache, ye cruellie sched his blude, and finallie do slay him.

But now will I releif yow of this anguische: dolorous it wer daily to commit manslaughter, and oftentymes to crucifie the King of glorie. Be not affrayit; ye do it not: For Jesus Chryst may suffer no more, sched his blude no more, nor dye no more. For that he hath dyed, he sa dyed for sin, and that anis; and now he liveth, and death may not prevaile aganis him. And sa do ye not slay Chryst, for no power ye have to do the same. Onlie ye haif deceavit the pepill, causing thame beleive that ye offerit Jesus Chryst in sacrifice for sin in your Masse; whilk is frivole and false; for Jesus Chryst may not be offerit because he may not die.

I maist gentillie exhort all desyreing to object aganis theis

[1] " What fyne," what end.   [2] In the old edit. " kyllers."

precedentis, ryplie to considder the ground thairof, whilk standeth not upon the opinion of man, but upon the infallibill Word of God; and to resume everie part of their argumentis and lay thame to the haill bodie of Godis Scriptures; and then, I dout not, but all men whois sensis the Prince of Darknes and of this Warlde hath not execatit,[1] sall confesse with me, that in the Masse can be no Sacrifice for sin. And yit, to the great blasphemy of Chrystis death, and opin denyall of his Passion, hath it bene affirmit, taught, and beleivit, that the Masse was a Sacrifice for the synnis of the quick and the dead: whilk opinioun is maist false, vane, and wickit. And so, I think, the Masse to be abominabill and Idolatrie no man of indifferent judgement will deny.

Let no man intend to excuse the Masse with the pretext of the Lordis Supper. For now will I prove that thairwith it hath no congruence,[2] but is express contrarie to it; and hath tackin the rememberance of the same out of mynd. And farther, it is blasphemous to the death of Jesus Chryst. First, Thai ar contrarie in institutioun; for the Lordis Supper was institutit to be a perpetuall memorie of theis benefittis whilk we haif ressavit be Jesus Chryst, and be his death. And first we suld call to mynd in what estait we stude in the loynis of Adam, when that we all blasphemit the majestie of God in his face. Secundlie, that his awne incomprehensibill gudnes moveit him to love us, maist wreachit and miserabill, yea maist wickit and blasphemous; and love most perfyte compellit him to schaw mercie. And mercie pronuncit the sentence, whilk was, that his onlie Sone suld pay the pryce of oure redemptioun. Whilk thing being rychtlie callit to memorie in the present actioun of the Supper, culd not but move us to unfeaned thanksgeving unto God the Father, and to his onlie Sone Jesus, who hath restorit us agane to libertie and lyfe, and this is it whilk Paule commandeth, saying, " As oft as ye sall eat of this bread, and drink of this cup, ye sall declair the

---

[1] In the old edit. "execated," blinded.   [2] Agreement.

THAT THE MASS IS IDOLATRY.

Lordis death till he cum." That is, ye sall laude, magnifie, and extoll the liberall kyndnes of God the Father, and the infinit benefittis whilk ye haif ressaveit by Chrystis death.

But the Masse is institutet,[1] as the plane wordis thairof, and thair awn lawis do witness, to be a Sacrifice for the synnis of the quick and the dead: for doing of the whilk Sacrifice, God is bound not onlie to remit our synnis, but also to gif unto us what ever we will ask. And that sall testifie dyvers Massis celebratit for dyvers caussis: sum for peace in tyme of war; sum for raine; sum for fair weather; yea, and (allace, my hart abhorreth sic abominatioun!) sum for sicknes of bestiall.[2] Thay will say, thay severallie take prayeris for obteanyng sic thingis; and that is all whilk I desyre thay say; for the obteanyng sic vane triffillis, destinat thay thair haill purpoise, and so prophane the Sacrament of Chrystis bodie and blude, (yf that wer any Sacrament whilk thai abusit so,) whilk suld never be usit but in memorie of Chrystis death. Then suld it not be useit to pray that the tuthe-acke be takin away from us; that oure oxen suld not tak the lowing ill, oure horse the spavin or fersie,[3] and so of all maner discassis for oure cattell. Yea, what was it whairfoir ye wald not say Masse, perversit Preistis? But lat us heir more.

The Supper of the Lord is the gift of Jesus Chryst, in whilk we suld laude the infinite mercie of God. The Masse is a Sacrifice whilk we offer unto God, for doing whairof we alledge God suld love and commend us.

In the Supper of the Lord, confes we our selves redeamit from sin by the death and blud of Jesus Chryst onlie. In the Masse, crave we remissioun of sinnes, yea, and whatsoever thing we list, by working of that same work, whilk we presentlie do our self. And heirin is the Masse blasphemous unto Chryst and his Passioun. For in so far as it offereth or permitteth remissioun of synnis, it imputeth imperfectioun upon Chryst and his sacrifice; affirmyng that all synnis wer not remittit by his death, but that

---

[1] In the MS. "institute."
[2] Cattle.
[3] In the old edit. "spaven or farsye."
— Distempers incident to cattle.

a great part ar reservit to be purgeit by vertew and the value of the Masse. And also it is injurious unto Chryst Jesus, and not onlie speiking most falslie of him, but also usurping to it self that whilk is propir to him allone. For he affirmeth that he allone hath, by his awn death, purged the synnis of the warld; and that no part resteth to be changed by any other meanis. But the Masse singeth ane other song, whilk is, that everie day, by that oblatioun offerit by the Preistis, is sin purgeit and remission obteanit. Considder, Papistis, what honour your Masse giveth unto Chryst Jesus!

Last, in the Supper of the Lord, we grant[1] our selves eternall dettouris to God, and unabill any way to mak satisfactioun for his infinit benefittis whilk we haif ressaveit. But in the Masse, alledge we God to be a dettour unto us for oblatioun of that Sacrifice, whilk we thair presentlie offer, and dar affirme that we thair mak satisfactioun by doing thairof, for the synnis of oure self and of othiris.

Yf theis precedentis be not contrarie, lat men judge with indifferencie.[2] Thay differ in use; for in the Lordis Supper, the Minister and the Congregatioun sat boith at ane tabill; no difference betuix thame in pre-eminence nor habit, as witnesseth Jesus Chryst with his Discipillis, and the practise of the Apostillis efter his death. But in the Papisticall Masse, the Preistis (so will thai be styllit) ar placeit by thame selves at ane altar.

QUESTIOUN. And I wold ask of the autoritie thairof, and what Scripture commandeth so to be done. Thay must be cled in a severall habit,[3] whairof no mentioun is maid in the New Testament. It will not excuse thame to say, Paule commandit all to be done with ordour and decentlie. Dar thai be so bold as to affirme, that the Supper of Jesus Chryst was done without ordour and undecentlie, whairin wer sene no suche disagysit vestamentis?

[1] Confess.
[2] Impartiality.
[3] Knox here refers to the dresses worn by the Romish priests while saying Mass, as they are described in some of their works of devotion. The colours of the priestly ornaments used in the Romish church service vary at different seasons; and to each colour a mystical meaning is attached.

Or will thai set up to us agane the Leviticall Preistheid? Suld not all be taught by the plane Word?

Prelattis or Preistis, I aske one questioun: Ye wald be lyke to the vestamentis of Aaron in all thingis. Aaron had affixed unto his garmentis certane bellis, whilk wer commandit to ring, and to mak sound, as oft as he was cled thairwith. But, Preistis, your bellis want[1] toungis, thai ring not, thai sound of nothing but of the Earth. Nothing understandeth the pepill of all your ceremonyis. Feir ye not the wraith of God? It was commandit Aaron, that the sound of the bellis suld be heard, that he died not.

Advyse with this, for the matter[2] apperteaneth unto yow.

In the Supper of the Lord all wer equallie participant: The bread being broken, and the cup being distributit amangis all, according to his holie commandement. In the Papisticall Masse, the congregation getteth nothing except the beholding of your jukingis,[3] noddingis, crossingis, turnyng, uplifting, whilk all ar nothing but a diabolicall prophanation of Chrystis Supper. Now, juke,[4] cross, and nod as ye list, thai ar but your awn inventionis. And finallie, Brethrene, ye gat nothing, but gaseit[5] and beheld whill that one did eat and drink all.

It sall not excuse you to say, the Congregatioun is participant spirituallie. O, wickit Antichrystis! sayeth not Jesus Chryst, "Eat of this, and drink of this, all do this in rememberance of me?" Chryst commandeth not that one suld gase upon it, bow, juke,[6] and beck thairto, but that we suld eat and drink thairof our selves; and not that we suld behold utheris do the same; unles we wold confes the death of Jesus Chryst to aperteane nothing to us. For when I eat and drink at that tabill, I opinlie confes the frute and vertew of Chrystis bodie, of his blude and passion, to aperteane to my self; and that I am a member of his misticall bodie; and that God the Father

---

[1] In the old edit. "lacke."
[2] Ib. "Advyse herewith, for thys matter."
[3] Ib. "duckings."
[4] Ib. "ducke."
[5] Ib. "gased," gazed.
[6] Ib. "ducke."—The phrase, "to juke," or "to douk," signifies to make obeisance.

is appeasit with me, notwithstanding my first corruptioun and present infirmities.

Judge, Brethrene, what comfort hath this takin frome us, whilk will that the sycht thairof salbe sufficient. I wald ask, first, yf the sycht of corporall meat or drink doith feid or nurische the bodie? I think thai will say, Nay. And I affirme, that na mair profit receaveth the saule in beholding ane other eat and drink the Lordis verie Supper, (as for their Idolatrie, it is alwayis dampnable) than the bodie doith in behalding ane other eate and drink, and thow receaving no part thairof.

But now brieflie, lat this contraritie be collectit.[1] In the Lordis Supper ar offerit thankis for the benefittis whilk we haif receaved of God. In the Masse, will the Papist compell God to grant all that he asketh of him, be vertew of that Sacrifice; and sa alledgeth, that God suld refer thankis unto him that doith Masse.

In the Supper of the Lord, the actouris humillie doith confes thame selfes redemit onlie by Chrystis blude, whilk anis was sched. In the Masse, the Preist vanteth him self to mak a Sacrifice for the synnis of the quick and the deid.

In the Lordis Supper, all the partakeris at that tabill granteth and confesseth thameselves dettouris unto God; unabill to refer thankis for the benefittis whilk we haif receavit of his liberalitie. In the Papisticall Masse, alledgeth the Preist that God is a dettour to him, and unto all thame for whome he maketh that Sacrifice. For he doith affirme remissioun of synnis to be obteanit thairby: And in that the Masse is blasphemous to Chrystis death.

In the Lordis Supper, all sit at ane tabill; na difference in habit nor vestament betuene the Minister and the Congregatioun. In the Papisticall Masse, the Preistis ar placeit by thameselves at ane Alter (as thai call it); and ar cled in disagysit garmentis.

In the Lordis Supper, finallie, all dois eat of ane bread and

---

[1] That is, Let these contradictions be examined.

drink of ane cupe. But in the mischevous Masse, ane man did eat and drink all.

Considder now, belovit Brethrene, what hath the frutis of the Masse bene, evin in hir greatest puritie. The Masse is nothing; but the inventioun of man, set up without all autoritie of Godis Word, for honoring of God; and thairfoir it is Idolatrie. Unto it is addit a vane, fals, deceavable, and maist wickit opinioun; that is, that by it is obteanit remissioun of synnis: And thairfoir it is abominatioun befoir God. It is contrarious unto the Supper of Jesus Chryst, and hath takin away boith the rycht use and rememberance thairof, and thairfoir it is blasphemous to Chrystis death. Manteane or defend the Papisticall Masse who so list, this honour and service did all whilk useit the same. And heir I speik not of the maist abominabill abussis, as of bying and selling, useit now of lait by the mischevous Preistis; but of the Masse in hir maist hie degree, and maist honest garment; yea, even of the great *Gaudeamus*[1] song or said by Gregorie the Great, as Papistis do call him.

Let no man think, that because I am in the Realme of Ingland, that thairfoir so boldlie I speak aganis this abominatioun. Naye, God hath takin that suspicioun frome me, for this bodie lying in maist panefull bandis, amangis the middis of cruell tyrantis,[2] his mercie and gudnes provydit that the hand suld wryt, and beir witness to the confessioun of the heart more aboundantlie than ever yet the toung spoke.

And heir I call my God to recorde, that neither profit to my self, hatred of any persone or personis, nor affectioun or favour that I beir towardis any privat man, causeth me this day to speak as ye haif heard; but onlie the obedience whilk I aucht[3] unto God in ministratioun, schawing of his Word, and the common love whilk I beir to the salvatioun of all men.[4] For so odious and abominable I knaw the Masse to be in Godis pre-

---

[1] "*Gaudeamus omnes in Domino*," &c., sung in the Mass on the festival of the Assumption of the Virgin.—(*Missale Romanum.*)

[2] During his imprisonment on board the French gallies. See *supra*, page 9.
[3] In the old edit. "I owe."
[4] Ib. "I bear to your salvation."

sence, that unles ye declyne from the same, to lyfe can ye never atteane. And thairfoir, Brethrene, flie from that Idolatrie, rather than from the present death.

Heir wold I haif spokin of the diversitie of Sacrifice, but neither doeth tyme nor the wickednesse[1] of myne owne flesh permit that so I do. I will ye observe,[2] that whair I say thair resteth no sacrifice, nor yit is thair any preistis; that I meane, thair resteth no sacrifice to be offerit for sin, nor yit is thair any preistis haveing power to offer sic oblationis. Otherwyse, I do knaw that all trew Christianis ar kingis and preistis, and do daylie offer unto God a sacrifice most acceptabill; the mortificatioun of thair affectionis, as Paule commandit the Romanis. But heirof may not I remayne to speak presentlie.

Such Doctrine as was taught in your audience, upon Sunday befoir none, I will prove, as opportunitie sall permit, by Godis Scriptures, not onlie unprofitabill, but also erronious and dissavabill. But first, according to my promeis, I will send unto the Teacher, the extract thairof, to add or diminische, as by his wisdome salbe thocht maist expedient. For God knowith my mynd is not captiouslie to trappe[3] men in wordis; but, my onlie desyre being, that ye, my Audience, be instructit in the veritie; whairfrom dissenteth sum doctrine taught yow, (yf trewlie I haif collectit), moveth me to speik aganis all that may have appeirance of lies and superstitioun.

And pray with me, Brethrene, that the Spreit may be ministerit unto me in aboundance, to speik at all tymes as it becumeth a trew messinger. And I will lykewyse pray, that ye may heir, understand, and obey with all reverence, the gud will of God, declaired unto the Warld by Jesus Chryst, whois omnipotent Spreit remayne with yow for ever. Amen.[4]

Gif the glorie to God alone.

JOHNE KNOX.

[1] The feebleness or frailty.
[2] I will you should observe.
[3] In the old edit. "to tryppe."
[4] The words that follow, are omitted in the old edition.

A SUMMARY,

ACCORDING TO THE HOLY SCRIPTURES,

OF THE SACRAMENT OF

THE LORD'S SUPPER.

M.D.L.

THIS brief statement respecting the Sacrament of the Lord's Supper has no date, but it may be assigned to the year 1550, as it is annexed to the previous Vindication, both in the old printed copy, and in Dr M'Crie's manuscript volume.

It may here be noticed, that in the several articles printed from that Manuscript, a few peculiarities of orthography, which are calculated to mislead the reader, have been corrected, such as *Masse, Aaron, Egypt, he, heard, voyce, voyces,* written sometimes *Mess* and *Mase, Aron* and *Aharon, Igept* and *Igipt, hie, hard, voce, voces,* &c.

HEIR IS BREIFLIE DECLARIT IN A SUMME, ACCORDING TO THE HOLIE SCRIPTURES, WHAT OPINIOUN WE CHRISTIANS HAIF OF THE LORDIS SUPPER, CALLIT THE SACRAMENT OF THE BODIE AND BLUDE OF OUR SAVIOURE JESUS CHRYST.

FIRST, We confess that it is ane holie actioun, ordaynit of God, in the whilk the Lord Jesus, by earthlie and visibill thingis sette befoir us, lifteth us up unto hevinlie and invisibill thingis. And that when he had prepareit his spirituall banket, he witnessit that he him self was the lyvelie bread, whairwith our saullis be fed unto everlasting lyfe.

And thairfoir, in setting furth bread and wyne to eat and drink, he confirmeth and sealleth up to us his promeis and communioun, (that is, that we salbe partakeris with him in his kingdome); and representeth unto us, and maketh plane to our sensis, his hevinlie giftis; and also giveth unto us him self, to be receaveit with faith, and not with mouth, nor yit by transfusioun of substance. But so through the vertew[1] of the Halie Gaist, that we, being fed with his flesche, and refrescheit with his blude, may be renewit both unto trew godlines and to immortalitie.

And also that heirwith the Lord Jesus gathereth us unto ane visibill bodie, so that we be memberis ane of another, and mak altogether one bodie, whairof Jesus Chryst is onlie heid. And finallie that by the same Sacrament, the Lord calleth us to rememberance of his Death and Passioun, to steir[2] up our hartis to prais his maist holie name.

[1] The power.   [2] In the old edit. "to styrre."

Farther more, we acknowledge that this Sacrament aught to be cum unto reverentlie, considering thair is exhibited and gevin a testimony of the wonderfull societie and knytting togidder of the Lord Jesus and of the receaveris; and also, that thair is included and conteanit in this Sacrament, that he will preserve his Kirk. For heirin we be commandit to schaw the Lordis death untill he cum.

Also, we beleive that it is a Confessioun, whairin we schaw what kynd of doctrine we profess; and what Congregatioun we joyne our selves unto; and lykwyse, that it is a band of mutuall love amangis us. And finallie, we beleive that all the cummeris unto this holie Supper must bring with thame thair conversioun unto the Lord, by unfeaned repentance in Faith; and in this Sacrament receave the seallis and confirmatioun of thair faith; and yit must in no wyse think, that for this workis sake thair synnis be forgevin.

And as concerning theis wordis, *Hoc est corpus meum*, "This is my bodie," on whilk the Papistis dependis so much, saying, That we must neidis beleive that the breid and wyne be transubstantiated into Chrystis bodie and blude; We acknawledge that it is no artikill of our faith whilk can saif us, nor whilk we ar bound to beleive upon pane of eternall dampnatioun. For yf we suld beleive that his verie naturall bodie, both flesche and blude, wer naturallie in the bread and wyne, that suld not save us, seing many beleif that, and yit receave it to thair dampnatioun. For it is not his presence in the bread that can save us, but his presence in our hartis through faith in his blude, whilk hath waschit out our synnis, and pacifeit his Fatheris wraith towardis us. And again, yf we do not beleive his bodilie presence in the bread and wyne, that sall not dampn us, but the absence out of our hart throw unbeleif.

OBJECTION.   Now, yf thai wald heir object, that though it be trewth, that the absence out of the breid culd not dampn us, yit ar we bound to beleive it because of Godis Word, saying, "This is my bodie," whilk who beleiveth not as muche as in him lyith, maketh God a lier: and thairfoir, of ane obstinat mynd not to beleive his Word, may be oure dampnatioun. To this we answer, That we beleive Godis Word, and confess that it is trew, but not so to be understand as the Papistis grosslie affirme. For in the Sacrament we receave Jesus Chryst spirituallie, as did the Fatheris of the Old Testament, according to St Paulis saying. And yf men wald weill wey, how that Chryst, ordeyning this Halie Sacrament of his bodie and blude, spak theis wordis Sacramentallie, doutless thai wold never so grosslie and foolischlie understand thame, contrary to all the Scriptures, and to the expositioun of St Augustine, St Hierome, Fulgentius, Vigilius, Origines, and many other godlie wrytteris.

margin: ANSWER. 1 COR. II.

A DECLARATION

OF THE TRUE NATURE
AND OBJECT OF PRAYER.

M.D.LIII.

IN a previous sheet, reference is made to the conflicting statements regarding the precise time when Knox obtained his release from the French galleys. The following extract from the Records of the Privy Council of England,[1] confirms the inference to be drawn from his own statement of the duration of his captivity,[2] that he was liberated in February or March 1549, according to the present mode of reckoning:—

"*Sunday, the 7th of Aprill* 1549.

"Warrant to the Receivour of the Duchy for 5 lib. to JOHN KNOCK, preacher, by way of reward."

His first employment, as already noticed, was at Berwick; and towards the close of the year 1550, he was removed to Newcastle, as a wider sphere of usefulness. Twelve months later, in order to mark the estimation in which he was held, Knox was appointed by the Privy Council one of six Chaplains in Ordinary at the Court of Edward the Sixth; of whom two in succession should always be resident, the others, in their turn, to serve as itinerary preachers in destitute parts of the country. This was in December 1551; and the annual salary of £40 was allotted to each of the persons thus nominated.

While holding this appointment, Knox was consulted in the preparation of the Formularies of the Church of England. Having always evinced a strong aversion to the English Service-Book, and as he refers with some satisfaction, in his "Admonition to the Professors of God's Truth in England"

[1] Obligingly communicated, along with two subsequent extracts, by Mr Lemon, junior, through his father, Robert Lemon, Esq. F.S.A., of the State Paper Office.

[2] In this volume, *supra*, p. 31.

to his having obtained an important change to be made in the communion service, this circumstance is worthy of notice.

The First Liturgy of Edward the Sixth was published in March 1548-9; in this the Popish doctrine of the real and corporal presence in the elements of communion remained unaltered. The Second, or revised Book of Common Prayer, was completed at press in August 1552, but the printer was directed not to publish it until some corrections or additions concerning the posture of kneeling at the communion should be inserted.[1] Towards the end of October, the Council had ordered this addition; and, on the 1st of November, the Prayer Book came into general use. This addition appears in the form of a rubric, inserted in some copies of the earliest edition as an extra single leaf, explaining, that by the act of kneeling no adoration of the sacramental bread or wine was meant, "for that were idolatry, to be abhorred of all faithfull Christians."[2] There can be no doubt, therefore, that in the Disputation with Latimer at Oxford, in April 1554, it was Knox to whom Dr Weston the Prolocutor alluded, when he said, "A runnagate Scot dyd take awaye the adoration or worshipping of Christe in the Sacrament; by whose procurement that heresie was put into the last Communion Booke: *so much prevailed that one man's authoritie at that tyme.* You never agreed with the Tygurines, or Germanes, or with the Churche, or with yourselfe."[3] This rubric is in substance still retained in the Book of Common Prayer.

During the same year, the King and Privy Council had directed Archbishop Cranmer to form a Book of Articles of Religion, to be subscribed by all such as should be admitted to

---

[1] Strype's Ecclesiastical Memorials, vol. ii. p. 366. Todd's Life of Cranmer, vol. ii. p. 272.

[2] See the Parker Society edition of the Liturgies of King Edward the Sixth, edited by the Rev. Joseph Ketley, p. 285, Cambridge, 1844, 8vo. In Dr Cardwell's edition of the Two Books of Common Prayer, &c., p. 317, Oxford, 1838, 8vo, no mention is made of this addition; but he refers to it in his second edition, 1844, as quoted in the Parker Society's volume.

[3] Foxe's Acts and Monuments, vol. ii. p. 1388, edit. 1576.

be preachers or ministers, with the view of preserving and maintaining peace and unity of doctrine in the church. These Articles, partly founded upon the Augsburg Confession, after being revised " by the Bishops and other godly men," were presented to the King, on the 2d of October, and they were delivered to the six Royal Chaplains, Harley, Bill, Horn, Grindall, Perne, and Knox, who were enjoined "to make report of their opinion touching the same."[1] The Articles were sent to the Archbishop for "the last corrections of his judgment and pen," in November, but they were not published, with the King's mandate, till after an interval of six months, or within a few days of his death.[2] These Articles, in the 5th of Queen Elizabeth, were reduced to thirty-nine, their present number.

Knox's individual share in this matter was probably of no great importance, but such occupation recommended him for higher preferment in the Church. The following letter from the Duke of Northumberland to Secretary Cecil, first published by Mr Tytler,[3] shows that he was recommended to fill the See of Rochester. He had at this time (27th of October) been sent to the North; and a warrant was addressed to four gentlemen, to pay to him, "as preacher in the North," the sum of £40.

"I WOULD to God it might please the King's Majesty to appoint MR KNOCKS to the office of Rochester Bishoprick; which, for three purposes, should do very well. The first, he would not only be a whetstone, to quicken and sharp the Bishop of Canterbury, whereof he hath need; but also he would be a great confounder of the Anabaptists lately sprung up in Kent. Secondly, he should not continue the ministration in the North contrary to this[4] set forth here. Thirdly, the family of the Scots, now inhabiting in Newcastle chiefly for his fellow-

---

[1] In Todd's Life of Cranmer, vol. ii. p. 288, it is mentioned that a copy of the Articles, in Latin, as it was subscribed by the six chaplains, is preserved in the State Paper Office.

[2] Todd's Cranmer, vol. ii. p. 290.
[3] Tytler's Edward VI., &c., vol. ii. p. 142.
[4] That is, not conforming to the usual form prescribed at this time.

ship, would not continue there, wherein many resorts unto them out of Scotland, which is not requisite.

"Herein I pray you desire my Lord Chamberlain and Mr Vice-Chamberlain to help towards this good act, both for God's service and the King's.

"And then for the North, if his Majesty make the Dean of Durham[1] Bishop of that See, and appoint him one thousand marks more to that which he hath in his deanery, and the same houses which he now hath, as well in the city as in the country, will serve him right honourably, so may his Majesty receive both the castle, which hath a princely site, and the other stately houses which the Bishop had in the country, to his Highness; and the Chancellor's living to be converted to the deanery, and an honest man to be placed in it; the Vice-Chancellor to be turned into the Chancellor; and the Suffragan, who is placed without the King's Majesty's authority, and also hath a great living, not worthy of it, may be removed, being neither preacher, learned, nor honest man; and the same living, with a little more to the value of it, a hundred marks, will serve to the erection of a Bishop within Newcastle. The said Suffragan is so pernicious a man, and of so evil qualities, that the country abhors him. He is most meet to be removed from that office and from those parts.

"Thus may his Majesty place godly ministers in these offices as is aforesaid, and receive to his crown 2000 lib. a year of the best lands within the North parts of his realm. Yea, I doubt not it will be iiii^m marks a year of as good revenue as any is within the realm; and all places better and more godly furnished than ever it was from the beginning to this day.

"Scribbled in my bed, as ill at ease as I have been much in all my life.—Your assured friend,

"NORTHUMBERLAND."

---

[1] The Dean of Durham, here referred to, was Robert Horne, one of the King's chaplains, and afterwards promoted by Queen Elizabeth to the Bishopric of Winchester.

In a letter to the King's two principal Secretaries, on the 23d of November, the Duke writes: "And forder, I have thought good to putt you, and so my Lordes, in memory, that some order be taken for KNOKKS, otherwys you shall not avoyd the Scottes from out of Newcastell, which, all things consyderyd, my thinke, should not be forgotten."[1] It appears, however, from a subsequent letter, dated on the 7th of December, and brought to light by Mr Tytler's researches, that Knox had neither eagerly grasped at such promotion, nor expressed himself sufficiently grateful for the Duke's solicitations in his behalf.

"MASTER KNOX'S being here to speak with me, saying that he was so willed by you, I do return him again, because I love not to have to do with men which be neither grateful nor pleasable. I assure you I mind to have no more to do with him but to wish him well; neither also with the Dean of Durham, because, under the colour of a false conscience, he can prettily malign and judge of others against good charity upon a froward judgment. And this manner you might see in his letter, that he cannot tell whether I be a dissembler in religion or not: but I have for twenty years stand [stood] to one kind of religion, in the same which I do now profess; and have, I thank the Lord, past no small dangers for it." Two days later (on the 9th of December) a letter in Knox's favour was addressed to Lord Wharton, Lord Warden in the Northern Borders.[2]

Another letter, first published by Mr Tytler, may also be quoted, as illustrating this period of Knox's life. On his return to Newcastle, his custom of alluding in the pulpit to affairs of state raised up many enemies, among whom was Lord Wharton, the most powerful man in that quarter, and also Sir Robert Brandling, Mayor of Newcastle, who preferred new accusations, which, as Mr Tytler remarks, "embittered Knox's life, and drew from him a letter to this nobleman (the Duke

---

[1] Haynes's Burghley State Papers, p. 127, Lond. 1740, folio.

[2] Council Register, as quoted by Strype. Life of Cranmer, p. 292.

of Northumberland), which, from the manner in which he alludes to its contents, must have been desponding and melancholy, a tone very different from that in which he generally expressed himself: it is much to be regretted that this letter of Knox, which was sent enclosed by Northumberland to Cecil, is not to be found."[1] It is somewhat unexpected, so soon after the date of his former letter, to find the Duke expressing so much commiseration in behalf of " poor Knoxe," when annoyed by malicious accusers.

"AFTER my right hearty commendations—Herewith I do return unto you as well Mr Morison's letters as also the Lord Wharton's, and do also send with the same such letters as I have received from the said Lord Wharton of the 2d and 3d of this instant, with also one letter from poor KNOXE, by the which you may perceive what perplexity the poor soul remaineth in at this present; the which, in my poor opinion, should not do amiss to be remembered to the rest of my Lords, that some order might be taken by their wisdoms for his recomfort. And as I would not wish his abode should be of great continuance in those parts, but to come and to go as shall please the King's Majesty and my Lords to appoint him, so do I think it very expedient that his Highness pleasure should be known, as well to the Lord Wharton as to those of Newcastle, that his Highness hath the poor man and his doings in gracious favour; otherwise some hindrance in the matters of religion may rise and grow amongst the people, being inclined of nature to great inconstancy and mutations. And the rather do I think this meet to be done, for that it seemeth to me that the Lord Wharton himself is not altogether without suspicion how the said Knox's doings hath been here taken: wherefore I pray you that something may be done whereby the King's Majesty's pleasure to my Lords may be indelayedly certified to the said

---

[1] Tytler's England under the Reigns of Edward and Mary, vol. ii. p. 158. Lond. 1839, 2 vols. 8vo.—The letter is addressed, "To my very loving friend, Sir William Cecil, Knight."

Lord Wharton, of the King's Majesty's good contentation towards the poor man and his proceedings, with commandment that no man shall be so hardy to vex him or trouble him for setting forth the King's Majesty's most godly proceedings, or [what he] hereafter by his Majesty's commandment shall do; for that his Majesty mindeth to employ the man and his talent from time to time in those parts, and elsewhere, as shall seem good to his Highness for the edifying of his people in the fear of God. And that something might be written to the Mayor for his greedy accusation of the poor man, wherein he hath, in my poor opinion, uttered his malicious stomach towards the King's proceedings if he might see a time to serve his purpose; as knoweth God, to whose infinite goodness let us pray that all things may prosper, to his glory, and to the honour and surety of the King's Majesty.

"From Chelsey, this 9th of January 1552.

"Your assured loving friend,

"NORTHUMBERLAND."

Another preferment was placed at this time within Knox's reach, but was also declined. On the 2d of February 1552-3, a letter was addressed to Archbishop Cranmer, to collate him to the Church of Allhallows, London, which had become vacant by the advancement of Thomas Sampson to the Deanery of Chichester.

"*At Westminstre, the seconde of February* 1552.

"A lettre to the Archebusshop of Caunterbury in favour of MR KNOKES, to be presented to the Vicaredge or Personage of Allhallowes, in Bredstrete, in his Lordship's disposition, by the preferment of Thomas Sampson to the Deanry of Chichester."[1]

Knox's refusal of this living was one of the grounds upon which he was summoned to appear before the Privy Council, as we learn from a letter written by him in April 1553. The letter itself has not been discovered; but Calderwood has pre-

[1] Counc. Register, Edward VI., vol. iii.

served what seems to be a full abstract of it, in his larger Manuscript History,[1] in connection with some extracts from his "Admonition," which was written and published in the following year. "These passages of the Admonition, printed anno 1554, (he says) lett us see how painfullie and powerfully Mr Knox taught in England the three yeeres preceding, the libertie and boldnes of his spirit, and fidelitie in delivering the word, in what account he was before publick reformation in Scotland." Strype also mentions Knox's examination before the Privy Council, and quotes nearly the same words, simply stating that such "were collected from a letter of Knox's own writing."[2]

"In a letter, dated the 14th of April 1553, and written with his own hand, I find (says Calderwood) that he was called before the Council of England for kneeling, who demanded of him three questions. First, Why he refused the benefice provided for him? Secondly, Whether he thought that no Christian might serve in the ecclesiastical ministration according to the rites and lawes of the realme of England? Thirdly, If kneeling at the Lord's Table was not indifferent?

"To the first he answered, That his conscience did witness that he might profit more in some other place than in London; and therefore had no pleasure to accept any office in the same. Howbeit he might have answered otherwise, that he refused that parsonage because of my Lord of Northumberland's command. To the second, That many things were worthy of reformation in the ministry of England; without the reformation whereof, no minister did discharge or could discharge his conscience before God; for no minister in England had authority to divide and separate the lepers from the heal,[3] which was a chief point of his office; yet did he not refuse such office as might appear to promote God's glory in utterance of Christ's

---

[1] Addit. MSS. in the British Museum, No. 4734, p. 196, collated with the MS. of Calderwood's History, 1636, in the Advocates Library.

[2] Strype's Ecclesiastical Memorials, vol. ii. p. 400.

[3] The whole, or sound.

gospel in a mean degree, where more he might edify by preaching of the true Word than hinder by sufferance of manifest iniquity, seeing that reformation of manners did not appertain to all ministers. To the third he answered, That Christ's action in itself was most perfect, and Christ's action was done without kneeling; that kneeling was man's addition or imagination; that it was most sure to follow the example of Christ, whose action was done sitting and not kneeling."

In this last question there was great contention betwixt the whole table of the Lords and him.[1] There were present there the Bishops of Canterbury, and Ely, my Lord Treasurer, the Marquis of Northampton, the Earl of Bedford, the Earl of Shrewsbury, Master Comptroller, my Lord Chamberlain, both the Secretaries, and other inferior Lords. After long reasoning, it was said unto him, that he was not called of any evil mind; they were sorry to know him of a contrary mind to the common Order. He answered, that he was more sorry that a common Order should be contrary to Christ's institution. With some gentle speeches he was dismissed, and willed to advise with himself if he would communicate after that Order."

In the ensuing month of June, Knox was sent as one of the itinerary preachers into Buckinghamshire.

"*At Grenewich, the 2d of June* 1553.

"A Letter to the Lord Russell, Lord Windesour, the Justices of Peace, and the rest of the Gentlemen within the countie of Buckingham, in favour of MR KNOCKES the preacher, according to the minute."[2]

Edward the Sixth died on the 6th of July 1553, in the sixteenth year of his age. For a few months his successor, Queen Mary, tolerated the Protestant ministers, and Knox availed himself of this interval to resume his labours in Buckinghamshire and Kent. "Wherever he went, he earnestly exhorted the peo-

---

[1] In MS. 1636, "betwixt the Lords of the English Council and him."

[2] Council Register, Edward VI., vol. iii.

ple to repentance under the tokens of Divine displeasure, and to a steady adherence to the faith which they had embraced." He was attended by large congregations, and he continued preaching until the end of October. It seems to have been at this time, as Dr M'Crie remarks, "that he composed the Confession and Prayer, commonly used by him in the congregations to which he preached, in which he prayed for Queen Mary by name, and for the suppression of such as meditated rebellion."[1]

The following Treatise on Prayer is contained in Dr M'Crie's MS. volume, and was published after Knox had left England, under the fictitious imprint, "At Rome, before the Castle of St Aungel, at the signe of Sainct Peter,"[2] in July 1554. It has been conjectured, that the alterations which appear on collation with the manuscript, were made by the author while it was passing through the press. His "Godly Letter to the Faithfull," was published at the same time; and from the small woodcut device, in the last page of both tracts, we may conclude that the printer was Hugh Singleton.[3] An exact copy of the title-page is given on the following leaf. It will be observed, that this title chiefly bears a reference to the concluding Prayer,[4] in which Knox so pathetically laments the death of the young and pious Monarch, as being a judgment upon the sins of the nation, as well as of himself as an individual. This Prayer is not contained in Dr M'Crie's Manuscript, which also omits most of the titles to the several paragraphs, and the Table at the end of the Treatise.

[1] Life of Knox, vol. i. p. 113.
[2] It contains signatures A to C 3, in eights, (or 19 leaves,) in small 8vo, not paged.
[3] In Ames's Typographical Antiquities, by Herbert (vol. ii. p. 740), and Dibdin (vol. iv. p. 289), there is given a list of the works printed by Singleton between 1553 and 1588; also of those without date, some of them distinguished by his device, others with his name, as dwelling "at the signe of the gylden tunne."
[4] *Infra*, p. 106.

A confession

& declaratiō of praiers added thervnto / by Jhon Knox / minister of Christes moste
sacred Euangely / vpon the death of that moste
verteous and moste famous king / Edward the
VI. kynge of Englande / Fraunce and Ireland /
in whiche confession / the sayde Jhon doth accuse no lesse his owne offences / then the
offences of others / to be the cause
of the awaye takinge / of that
moste godly prince / nowe
raininge with Christ
whyle we abyde
plagues for
our vnthā
fulnesse.

¶ & ❦

¶ Imprinted in Rome, before the
Castel of S. Aungel / at the signe of saint
Peter. In the moneth of July / in
the yeare of our Lorde.
1 5 5 4. (⁂)

In small 8vo, black letter, A to C iii, in eights, (or 19 leaves), not paged. It was printed in connection with his "Godly Letter to the Faithfull in London," &c. (See page 163.)

A DECLARATIOUN WHAT TREW PRAYER IS, HOW WE SULD PRAY, AND FOR WHAT WE SULD PRAY. SET FURTH BE JOHNE KNOX, PREACHER OF GODIS HOLIE WORD:

VNTO THE SMALL AND DISPERSIT FLOCK OF JESUS CHRYST.

How necessarie is the rycht Invocatioun of Godis name (otherwyse called perfyt Prayer) becumeth no Christian to misknaw;[1] seing it is the verie branche whilk springeth furth of trew Faith, whairof yf any man be destitute, notwithstanding he be indewit with whatsoever other vertewis, yit in the presence of God is he reputit for no Christiane at all. Thairfoir a manifest signe it is, that sic as in prayer alwayis ar negligent, do understand nothing of perfyt Faith: For yf the fyre be without heit, or the burnyng lamp without lycht, then trew Faith may be without fervent Prayer. But because, in tymis past was (and yit allace! with no small number is) that raconit[2] to be Prayer whilk in the sycht of God was and is nothing less, I intend schortlie to touche the circumstances thairof. _{PRAYER SPRINGETH OUT OF TREW FAITH. ROM. 10.} _{MEN NEGLIGENT IN PRAYER ARE NOT PERFYYTE IN FAYTH.}

WHAT PRAYER IS.— Who will pray, must knowe and understand that Prayer is ane earnest and familiar talking with God, to whome we declair oure misereis, whois support and help we implore and desyre in our adversiteis, and whome we laude and prais for oure benefittis receaved. So that Prayer conteaneth the expositioun of our dolouris,[3] the desyre of Godis defence, and the praising of his magnificent name, as the Psalmis of David cleirlie do teache.

[1] To be ignorant or mistaken.   [2] Reckoned.   [3] Troubles, sorrows.

WHAT IS TO BE OBSERVIT IN PRAYER.—That this be maist reverentlie done, suld provock us the consideratioun in whois presence we stand, to whome we speik, and what we desyre; standing in the presence of the Omnipotent Creatour of heavin and earth, and of all the contentis thairof; to whome assist and serve a thousand thousand of angellis, giving obedience to his eternall Majestie; and speiking unto Him who knawith the secreittis of oure hartis, befoir whome dissimulatioun and lies ar alwayis odius and haitfull, and asking that thing whilk may be maist to his glorie, and to the confort of our conscience. But diligentlie suld we attend, that sic thingis as may offend his godlie presence, to the uttermaist of our power, may be removeit. And first, that warldlie caris and fleschlie cogitationis (sic as draw us frome contemplatioun of our God), be expellit frome us, that we may frelie, without interruptioun, call upon God. But, how difficill and harde is this one thing in Prayer to performe, knawith nane better than sic as in thair prayeris ar not content to remane within the bandis of thair awn vanitie, but, as it wer ravischit, do intend¹ to a puritie, allowit of God; asking not sic thingis as the fulische reasone of man desyreth, but whilk may be pleasand and acceptabill in Godis presence. Oure adversarie, Sathan, at all tymis compassing us about, is never more busie than when we adress and bend our selves to Prayer. O! how secreitlie and subtelie creipeth he into our breistis, and calling us back frome God, causeth us to forget what we have to do; so that frequentlie when we (with all reverence) suld speik to God, we find our hartis talking with the vaniteis of the warld, or with the fulische imaginationis of our awn conceat.

HOW THE SPREIT MAKETH INTERCESSIOUN FOR US.—Sa that without the Spreit of God supporting our infirmiteis (mychtelie making intercessioun for us with incessibill² groanis, whilk can not be expressit with toung), thair is no hoip that any thing we can desyre according to Godis will. I meane not that the

¹ Do strive to attain. ² Unceasing.

Halie Gaist doith murne or pray, but that he steireth up our myndis, giving unto us a desyre or boldnes for to pray, and causeth us to murne when we ar extractit or pullit thairfra. Whilk thingis to conceave, no strenth of man suffiseth, nether is abill of it self; but heirof it is plane, that suche as understand not what thai pray, or expound not, or declar not the desyre of thair hartis cleirlie in Godis presence, and in tyme of prayer (to thair possibilitie) do not expell vane cogitationis frome thair myndis, profit nothing in prayer. who prayeth not.

WHY WE SULD PRAY, AND ALSO UNDERSTAND WHAT WE DO PRAY.—But men will object and say, Albeit we understand not what we pray, yit God understandeth, who knawith the secreitis of oure hartis; he knawith also what we neid, althocht we expone not, or declair not, our necessiteis unto him. Sic men verelie declair thame selves never to have understanding what perfyt Prayer meant, nor to what end Jesus Chryst commandeth us to pray; whilk is, First, That our hartis may be inflamit with continewall feir, honour, and love of God, to whome we run for support and help whensoever danger or necessitie requyreth; that we, so learnyng to notifie oure desyres in his presence, he may teache us what is to be desyrit, and what not. Secundlie, That we, knawing our petitionis to be grantit by God allone, to him onlie we must rendir and gif laud and prais, and that we ever having his infinit gudnes fixit in our myndis, may constantlie abyd to receave that whilk with fervent prayer we desyre. objection. answer.

WHY GOD DEFERRETH TO GRANT OUR PRAYER.—For sum tyme God deferreth or prolongeth to grant our petitionis, for the exercise and tryell of our faith, and not that he sleipeth or is absent frome us at any tyme, but that with more gladnes we mycht receave that whilk with lang expectatioun we haif abiddin; that thairby we assureit of his eternall providence (sa fer as the infirmitie of our corrupt and maist weak nature will permit), dout not but his mercifull hand sall releif us, in maist urgent necessitie, and extreame tribulatioun. Thairfoir, sic men as teache us that necessarilie it is not requyrit that we understand what we pray, becaus God knawith what we neid, wold also teache us that nether we honour God, nor yit refer or gif unto him thankis for benefittis receavit; for how sall we honour and prais him, whois gudnes and liberalitie we knaw not? And how sall we knaw, unles we receave and sum tyme haif experience? And how sall we knaw that we haif receavit, unless we knaw verelie what we haif askit?

The Secund thing to be observit in perfyt Prayer is, That standing in the presence of God, we be found sic as do beir to his halie law reverence; ernistlie repenting oure iniquitie passit, and intending to leid a new lyfe; for uthirwayis in vane ar all oure Prayeris, as it is written, "Who so withdraweth his eare that he may not heir the law, his Prayer salbe abominabill." Lykwyse Esay and Jeremie say thus, "Yow sall multiplie your Prayeris, and I sall not heir, because your handis ar full of blud," that is, of all crueltie and mischevous workis. Also the Spreit of God appeirith by the mouth of the blind (whome Jesus Chryst did illuminat) by theis wordis, "We knaw that God heireth not synneris," (that is, sic as glorie and do continew in iniquitie); sa that of necessitie, trew repentance must neidis be had, and go befoir perfyt Prayer, or sinceir Invocatioun of Godis name.

WHEN SYNNERIS AR NOT HEARD OF GOD.—And unto theis tuo precedentis must be annexit the Thrid, whilk is, The dejectioun of our selves in Godis presence, utterlie refusing and casting of our awn justice, with all cogitationis and opinioun thairof. And lat us not think that we suld be hard for any thing proceiding of our selves, for all suche as avance, boast, or depend any thing upon thair awn justice, from the presence of his mercie, repelleth and holdeth with the high proud Pharisie: and thairfoir, the maist halie men we find in prayeris maist dejectit and humillit. David sayeth, "O Lord, oure Saviour, help us, be mercifull unto our synis for thy awn sake. Remember not our ald iniquiteis. But haist thou, O Lord, and lat thy mercie prevent us." Jeremie sayith, "Yf our iniquiteis

beir testimony aganis us, do thow according to thy awn name:"
and behold Esay, "Thou art angrie,[1] O Lord, becaus we haif ESAY 64.
synnit, and ar replenissit with all wickitnes; and oure justice is
lyke a defyllit cloth. But now, O Lord, thou art oure Father;
we ar clay, thow art the workman, and we ar the workmanship
of thy handis: Be not angrie,[2] O Lord, remember not our iniquiteis for ever." And Daniell, greatlie commendit of God, DANIEL 9.
makith in his prayer maist humill confessioun, in theis wordis,
" We be synneris, and have offendit; we have done ungodlie, and
fallin from thy commandement, thairfoir, not in oure awn righteousnes mak we oure prayeris before thee, but thy maist rycht
and great mercies bring we furth for us. O Lord, heir! O
Lord, be mercifull and spair us! O Lord, attend, help, and ceas
not; my God, evin for thy awn name's sake do it; for thy citie
and thy people ar callit efter thy awn name." Behold that in
theis prayeris is no mentioun of thair awn justice, thair awn
satisfactioun, or thair awn merittis. But maist humill confessioun, proceiding frome a sorowfull and penitent hart; haveing
nothing whairupon it mycht depend, but the frie mercie of God
allone, who had promissit to be thair God, (that is, thair help,
comfort, defender, and delyverer), as he hath also done to us
by Jesus Chryst in tyme of tribulatioun; and that thai dispair
not, but efter the acknawledgeing of thair synnis, callit for mercie and obteanit the same. Whairfoir it is plane, that suche men
as, in thair prayeris, have respect to any vertew proceiding of
thame selves, thinking thairby thair prayeris to be acceptit,
never prayit arycht.

WHAT FASTING AND ALMIS DEIDIS AR WITH[3] PRAYER.—
And albeit to fervent prayer be joynit fasting, watcheing, and
almis-deidis, yit ar none of them the cause that God doith accept
oure prayeris; but thai ar spurris whilk suffer us not to varie,
but mak us mair abill to continew in prayer, whilk the mercie
of God doith accept. But heir it may be objectit, that David

[1] In the edit. 1554, "Thou art crabbid."   [2] Ib. "Be not crabbid."
[3] Ib. "Without."

prayeth, "Keip my lyfe, O Lord, for I am holie; O Lord, save my saule, for I am innocent; and suffer me not to be consumeit." Also Ezechiah,[1] "Remembir, Lord, I beseche thee, that I have walkit rychteouslie befoir thee, and that I have wrocht that whilk is gud in thi sycht." Theis wordis ar not spokin of men glorious, neither yit trusting in thair awn workis. But heirin thai testifie thame selves to be the sonis of God, by regeneratioun; to whome he promisseth alwayis to be mercifull, and at all tymes to heir thair prayeris.

THE CAUSE OF THAIR BOLDNES WAS JESUS CHRYST.—And sa thair wordis sprung frome a wontit, constant, and fervent faith, surelie beleiving that as God of his infinit mercie had callit thame to his knawledge, not suffering thame to walk efter thair awn naturall wickitnes, but partlie had taught thame to conforme thame to his halie law; and that for the promissit Seidis sake; sa mycht he not leif thame destitut of confort, consolatioun, and defence in so great and extreme necessitie. And sa thair justice alledge thai not to glorie thairof, or to put trust thairin, but to strenthin and confirme thame in Godis promissis. And this consolatioun I wolde wische all Christianis in thair prayeris; a testimony of a gud conscience to assure thame of Godis promissis; but to obtene what thai ask must onlie depend upon him, all opinioun and thocht of our awn justice laid asyd. And, moreover, David, in the wordis above, compaireth him self with King Saule, and with the rest of his enemyis, who wrangfullie did persecut him; desyreing of God that thai prevaile not aganis him, as he wold say, Unjustlie do thai persecut me, and thairfoir, according to my innocence defend me. For uthirwayis he confesseth him self maist grevouslie to haif offendit God, as in the precedent places he clearlie testifieth.

IPOCRISIE IS NOT ALLOWED WITH GOD.—Thridlie, in Prayer is to be observit, that what we ask of God, that we must ernistlie desyre the same, knawledgeing us to be indigent and voyd thairof; and that God allone may grant the petitioun of our

---

[1] In the edit. 1554, "Ezechius."

hartis, when his gud will and pleasure is. For nathing is mair odius befoir God then ipocrisie and dissimulatioun, that is, when men do ask of God thingis whairof thai haif no neid, or that thai beleive to obtene by otheris than God allone. As yf a man ask of God remissioun of his synnis, thinking never the less to obtene the same by his awn workis, or by uthir mennis merittis, doith mok with God and disceave him self. And in sic cassis do a great number offend, principallie the mychtie and ryche of the earth, who, for a common custome will pray this part of the Lordis Prayer, "Gif us this day our daylie breid," that is, a moderat and reasonable sustentatioun; and yit thair awn hartis will testifie that thai neid not so to pray, seing thai abound in all warldlie solace and felicitie. I meane not that ryche men suld not pray this part of prayer, but I wold thai understude what thai aught to pray in it, (whairof I intend efter to speik,) and that thai ask nothing whairof thai felt not thame selves mervellous indigent and neidfull. For unles we call in veritie, we sall not grant; and except we speik with oure haill hart, we sall not find him. <small>MERK WEILL IPOCRISIE IS ABOMINABLE TO GOD.</small> <small>DAYLIE BREID.</small>

The Fourth Rule necessarie to be followit in Prayer is, A sure hoip to obtene what we ask. For nothing more offendeth God, than when we ask doubting whether he will grant oure petitionis; for in so doing we dout yf God be trew, yf he be mychtie and gude; sic (sayeth James) obtene nothing of God: And thairfoir Jesus Chryst commandeth that we firmlie beleive to obtene whatsoever we aske; for all thingis is possibill unto him that beleiveth. And thairfoir, in our prayeris alwayis is to be expellit disperatioun. I meane not that any man in extreamitie of trubill can be without a present dolour, and without a greater feir of trubill to follow. <small>JAMES I.</small> <small>NOTE.</small> <small>NOTE WELL.</small>

TRUBILLIS AR THE SPURRIS TO STIR US TO PRAY.—Trubill and feir are verie spurris to prayer; for when man compassit about with vehement calamiteis, and vexit with continewall solicitude, having, by help of man, no hope of deliverance, with soir oppressit and punissit hart, feiring also greater punisment to follow, from the deip pit of tribulatioun doith call to God for confort and support; suche prayer ascendeth into Godis presence and returneth not in vane.

GOD DELYVERETH HIS AWN FROM THAIR TRUBILL AND ENEMYIS.—As David, in the vehement persecutioun of Saule, huntit and chasit frome everie hold, fearing that ane day or uther he suld fall into the handis of his persecutouris, efter he had compleanit that no place of rest was left to him, vehementlie prayit, saying, "O Lord, whilk art my God, in whome I onlie trust, save me frome thame that persecut me, and delyver me frome my enemyis. Lat not this man (meanyng Saule) devoure my lyfe, as a lyoun doith his prey: for of none seik I confort but of thee alone."

In the midst of theis anguischis the gudnes of God susteanit him, that the present tribulatioun was tollerabill, and the infallibill promissis of God so assured him of delyverance, that feir was partlie mitigat and gone, as planelie appeireth to suche as diligentlie marketh the process of his prayeris. For efter lang menassing and threatnyng maid to him of his enemie, he concludeth with theis wordis, "The dolour whilk he intendit for me sall fall upon his own pate; and the violence whairwith he wold haif oppressit me sall cast doun his awn heid. But I will magnifie the Lord according to his justice, and sall prais the name of the Most Hiest." This is not written for David onlie, but for all suche as sall suffer tribulatioun to the end of the warld. For I, the wrytter heirof, (lat this be said to the laude and prais of God allone,) in anguische of mynd and vehement tribulatioun and afflictioun, called to the Lord when not onlie the Ungodlie, but evin my faithfull Brether, yea, and my awn self, that is all naturall understanding, judgeit my cause[1] to be irremeadable: And yit in my greatest calamitie, and when my pains wer most cruell, wold His eternall wisdome that my handis suld wryt far contrarie to the judgement of carnall

A COMFORT TO THE WRYTTER, BEING IN GREAT ADVERSITIE.

---

[1] Knox here refers to his bodily and mental sufferings during the time of his confinement on board the French galley.

reason, whilk His mercie hath proved trew. Blissit be His halie name! And thairfoir dar I be bold, in the veritie of Godis Word, to promeis[1] that notwithstanding the vehemencie of trubill, the lang continewance thairof, the disperatioun of all men, the feirfulnes, danger, dolour, and anguische of oure awn hartis, yit yf we call constantlie to God, that beyond expectatioun of all men he sall delyver.

WHAIR CONSTANT PRAYER IS, THAIR THE PETITIOUN IS GRANTIT. NOTE WELL. —Let no man think him self unworthie to call and pray to God, becaus he hath grevouslie offendit his Majestie in tymis past; but lat him bring to God a sorowfull and repenting hart, saying with David, "Heall my saule, O Lord, for I have offendit against thee. Befoir I was afflictit, I transgressit, but now let me observe thy commandementis." To mitigate or ease the sorowis of our woundit conscience, two plaisteris hath oure maist prudent Phisitioun provydit to gif us incouragement to pray (notwithstanding the knawledge of offences committit), that is, a precept and a promeis. The precept or commandement to pray is universall, frequentlie inculcat and repeatit in Godis Scriptures: "Aske, and it salbe gevin unto yow." MAT. 7. "Call upon me in the day of trubill." PSA. 40. "Watche and pray that ye fall not into temptatioun." "I command that ye pray ever without ceassing." MAT. 26. "Mak deprecationis incessabill, and gif thankis in all thingis." TIMO. 2. Whilk commandementis, I. THESSA. 5. who so contempneth or dispyseth, doith equallie sin with him that doith steill; for in this commandement thow sall not steill NOTE. is a precept *negative;* sa thou sall pray is a commandement *affirmative.* And God requyreth equall obedience of and to all his commandementis. Yit more boldlie will I say, He who, when necessitie constraincth, desyreth not support and help of God, doith provoke his wraith no less than suche as mak fals Godis, or opinlie deny God.

[1] In the edit. 1554, "And therefore dare I be in the veryte of Godes worde *to permit.*" But several such typographical mistakes, rendering the sense obscure, occur in that old edition.

HE THAT PRAYETH NOT IN TRUBILL, DENYITH GOD.—For lyke as it is to knaw no phisitioun or medicine, or in knawing thame refuse to use and ressave the same; so not to call upon God in thy tribulatioun, is lyke as yf thow didest not knaw God, or ellis utterlie deny him.

NOT TO PRAY, IS A SIN MAIST ODIUS.—O! why ceass we then to call instantlie to his mercie, haveing his commandement so to do. Above all oure iniquiteis, we work manifest contempt and dispysing of him, when, by negligence, we delay to call for his gracious support. Who doith call upon God obeyith his will, and findeth thairin no small consolatioun, knawing nothing is mair acceptable to his Majestie than humill obedience.

To this commandement he addeth his maist undoutit promeis in many places, "Aske, and ye sall receave; seik, and ye sall find." And by the Prophet Jeremie, God sayeth, "Ye sall call upon me, and I sall heir yow." "Ye sall seik and sall find me." And by Esay, he sayeth, "May the Father forget his naturall son, or the Mother the chyld of hir wombe? and althocht thai do, yit sall I not forget suche as call upon me." And heirto correspond and agrie the wordis of Jesus Chryst, saying, "Yf ye being wickit can gif gud giftis to your children, muche more my heavinlie Father sall gif the Halie Gaist to thame that aske him." And that we suld not think God to be absent, or not to heir us, accuseth Moses, saying, "Thair is no natioun that have thair Godis so adherent, or neir unto thame as oure God, whilk is present at all oure prayeris." Also the Psalmist, "Neir is the Lord unto all that call upon him in veritie." And Chryst sayeth, "Whairsoever tuo or thrie ar gatherit together in my name, thair am I in the middis of thame."

READINESS OF GOD TO HEIR SINNERS.—That we sall not think that God will not heir us, Esay sayith, "Befoir ye cry I sall heir, and whill thai speak I sall answer;" and also, "Yf at evin cum sorrow or calamitie, befoir the mornyng spring I sall reduce[1] and bring gladnes." And theis most comfortabill wordis,

---

[1] To bring back, (Lat. *reducere*.)

doith the Lord speik not to carnall Israell onlie, but to all men soir oppressit, abyding Godis delyverance, "For a moment and a litill seasone haif I turnit my face from thee, but in everlasting mercie sall I confort thee."

THE HOPE TO OBTEYN OURE PETITIONS SHOULD DEPEND UPON THE PROMISES OF GOD.—O! hard ar the hartis whome so many-fold, most sueit, and sure promissis doith not molefie; whairupon suld depend the hoip to obtene our petitionis. The indignitie or unworthines of our selvis is not to be regardeit; for albeit, to the chosin whilk ar departit in holines and puritie of lyfe, we be far inferiouris, yit in that part we ar equall, in that we have the same commandement to pray, and the same promeis to be hard. For nis Gracious Majestie estemeth not the prayer, nether granteth the petitioun for any dignitie of the persone that prayith, but for his promeis sake onlie; and thairfoir sayith David, "Thou hes promeisit unto thy servand, O Lord, that thow wilt build a house for him, whairfoir thy servand hath found in his hart to pray in thy sycht, now evin so, O Lord, thou art God, and thy wordis ar trew: Thow hes spokin theis thingis unto thy servand, begyn thairfoir to do according to thy promeis; multiplie, O Lord, the houshald of thy servand." Behold, David altogether dependeth upon Godis promeis. As also did Jacob, who efter he had confessit him self unworthie of all the benefittis ressavit, yit durst he ask greatter benefittis in tyme to cum, and that becaus God had promissit. In the lyke maner, lat us be incorageit to aske what so ever the gudnes of God hath frelie promissit. What we suld ask principallie, we sall heirefter declair. [I. KING. 7. GEN. 32.]

OBSERVATIOUN IN GODLY PRAYER.—The Fyft Observatioun whilk godlie Prayer requyreth, is perfyt knawledge of the Advocat, Intercessour, and Mediatour.

OF NECESSITIE WE MUST HAVE A MEDIATOUR.—For, seing no man is of him self worthie to compeir or appeir in Godis presence, be reasone that in all men continewallie resteth sin, whilk by the self doith offend the Majestie of God; raising all debait, stryfe, hatred, and divisioun betuix his inviolabill justice and us: For the whilk, unles satisfactioun be maid be another than by our selves, so litill hoipe resteth that any thing frome him we can atteane, that na suretie with him may we have at all. To exeme us fra this horribill confusion, oure maist mercifull Father hes gevin unto us his onlie belovit Sone to be unto us justice, wisdome, sanctificatioun, and halines. Yf in him we faithfullie beleive, we ar so cled that we may with boldnes compeir and appeir befoir the throne of Godis mercie; doubting nothing but whatsoever we ask, be oure Mediatour, that sam we sall obtene most assuredlie.

<small>1 JOH. 2.</small>
<small>HEBR. 8.</small>
<small>HEBR. 4.</small>

NOTE DILIGENTLY, BY WHOM WE MUST PRAY.—Heir is maist diligentlie to be observit, that without our Mediatour, Foirspeaker, and Peace-maker, we enter not into prayer; for the incalling of suche as pray without Jesus Chryst, ar not onlie vane, but also thai ar odius and abominable befoir God. Whilk thing to us, in the Leviticall Preisthood, most evidentlie was prefigurat and declarit: for as within the *Sanctum Sanctorum* (that is the most Holie Place), enterrit no man but the Hie Preist allone; and as all sacrifices offerit by any other than by preistis onlie, provokit the wrath of God upon the sacrifice maker; so who doith intend to enter into Godis presence, or to mak prayeris without Jesus Chryst, sall find nothing but feirfull judgement and horribill dampnatioun.

<small>PAR. 26.</small>

TURKES AND JEWES.—Whairfoir it is plane, that Turkis and Jewis, notwithstanding that thai do, appeirantlie, most ferventlie pray unto God, who creatit heavin and erth, who gydeth and reuleth the same, who defendeth the gude and punisseth the evill, yit never ar thair prayeris plesand unto God; nether honour thai his halie Majestie in any thing, becaus thai acknawledge not Jesus Chryst, for who honoureth not the Sone honoureth not the Father.

WHEN WE BE NOT HEARD.—For as the Law is a statute that we sall call upon God, and as the promeis is maid that he sall heir us, so ar we commandit onlie to call by Jesus Chryst.

by whome allone our petitionis we obtene; for in him allone ar all the promissis of God confirmit and compleit; whairof, without all contraversie, it is plane, that suche as haif callit, or calleth presentlie unto God by any uther name then by Jesus Chryst allone, doith nothing regarde Godis will, but obstenatlie prevaricateth, and doith aganis his commandementis. And thairfoir, obtene not thai thair petitionis, nether yit haif entress to his mercie. For na man cumeth to the Father (sayith Jesus Chryst) but by me. He is the rycht way; who declyneth frome him erreth, and goith wrang; he is oure Leider, whome without we follow we sall walk in darknes; and he allone is oure Captaine, without whome neither prais nor victorie ever sall we obtene. 2 COR. 1.

INTERCESSIOUN TO SAINTS.—Against suche as depend upon the Intercession of Sanctis na uthirwayis will I contend, but schortlie tuiche the properties of a perfyte Mediatour. First, ar the wordis most sure of Paule, "A mediatour is not the mediatour of one," that is, whairsoever is requyreit a mediatour, thair ar also tuo parteis; to wit, ane partie offendant, and the other partie whilk is offendit; whilk parties be thame selves may in no wyse be reconcilit. Secundlie, the mediatour whilk taketh upon him the reconciling of theis tuo parties must be suche a one as having trust and favour of both parteis, yit in sum thingis must differ frome both, and must be cleare and innocent also of the cryme committit aganis the partie offendit. Let this be more plane by this subsequent declaratioun: The Eternall God standing upon the one part, and all naturall men descending of Adame upon the other part. The infinit Justice of God is so offendit with the transgressioun of all men, that in na wyse can amitie be maid, except suche one be found as fullie may mak satisfactioun for manis offences. Among the sonnis of men none was found abill: for all thai wer found cryminall in the fall of one. And God, infinit in justice, must abhorre the societie and sacrifice of synneris.

ANGELLIS CAN NOT BE MEDIATOURIS.—And unto the Angellis

OURE HEVIE AND GREAT SYNNIS EX-CEIDIS THE STRENGTH OF ANY OF US. WHAIR-FOR IT IS NECESSAR THAT THOU, O CHRYST, THI SELF MAK SATIS-FACTIOUN FOR US. what prevallit the prevaricatioun of man, who (albeit thai wold haif interponit thame selves mediatouris), yit thai had not the justice infinit. Who then sall heir be found the Peace-maker? Surelie the infinit gudnes and mercie of God mycht not suffer the perpetuall loss and repudiatioun of his creaturis; and thairfoir his eternall wisdome provydit sic a Mediatour, having whairwith to satisfie the justice of God; differing also frome the Godheid; his onlie Sone, clad in the nature of manheid, who interponit himself a Mediatour, not as man onlie.

JESUS CHRYST, GOD AND MAN, OUR MEDIATOUR.—For the pure humanitie of Chryst (of it self) mycht nether mak intercessioun nor satisfactioun for us, but God and Man: In that he is God, he mycht compleit the will of the Father, and in that he is Man, pure and cleane without spot or sin, he mycht offer sacrifice for the purgatioun of our synnis and satisfactioun of Godis Justice. So, without Sanctis haif theis tuo, Godheid equall with the Father, and Humanitie without sin, the office of mediatouris Sanctis may not usurpe.

OBJECTIOUN. But heir wilbe objectit, Who knaweth not Jesus Chryst to be the onlie Mediatour of oure redemptioun; but that impedeth or letteth nothing Sanctis and Holie Men to be Media-
AUNSWER. touris and to mak intercessioun for us. As thocht that Jesus Chryst had bene but one hour our Mediatour, and efter had resignit the office unto his servandis!

WHO MAKETH OTHIR MEDIATOURIS NOR JESUS CHRYST TAKETH HONOUR FRA HIM.—Do not suche men gentillie[1] intreat Jesus Chryst, detracting from him suche portioun of his honour? Otherwayis speakith the Scriptures of God, testifieing him to haif bene maid man, and to haif proved oure infirmiteis; to have sufferit death willinglie; to haif overcum the same; and all to this end, that he mycht be oure perpetuall High Soveraine Preist, in whois place or dignitie none uthir mycht entir. As *HEBRE. 6, 7, 9, 10.* Johne sayith, "Yf any man sin, we have an Advocat with the Father, evin Jesus Chryst the just."

[1] Gentilly, that is, respectfully, (spoken ironically.)

Mark weill theis wordis: Johne sayith, We haif presentlie a sufficient Advocat, whome Paule affirmeth to sit at the rycht hand of God the Father, and to be the onlie Mediatour betuene God and Man. "For he allone, (sayith Ambrose,) is oure mouth, by whome we speik to God; he is oure eis, by whome we see God, and also oure rycht hand, by whome we offer any thing unto the Father;" who, unless he mak intercessioun, neither we, neither any of the Sanctis, may have any societie or fellowschip with God. What creature may say to God the Father, Lat mankynd be ressavit into thy favour, for the paine of his transgressioun that have I susteanit in my awn bodie? For his cause was I compassit with all infirmiteis, and so became the most contempnit and dispysit of all men; and yit in my mouth was found no gyle nor disceat, but alwayis obedient to thy will, suffering maist grevous death for mankynd: And, thairfoir, behold not the synner but me, who, be my infinit Justice,[1] hath perfytlie satisfeit for his offences. May any other (Jesus Chryst exceptit[2]) in theis wordis mak intercessioun for synneris? Yf thai may not, than ar thai neither mediatouris nor yit intercessouris. "For albeit (sayith Augustine) Christianis do commend ane another unto God in thair prayeris, yit mak thai not intercessioun, neither dar thai usurpe the office of a Mediatour; no not Paule, albeit under the Heid he was a principall member, becaus he commendith him self to the prayeris of faithfull men." But yf any do object, Suche is not the conditioun of the Sanctis departit, who now hath put off mortallitie, and beireth no langer the fragilitie of the flesche: Whilk albeit I grant to be maist trew, yit ar thai all compellit to cast thair crownis befoir Him that doith sit in [on] the throne, acknawledgeing thame selves to have bene delyverit frome great afflictioun, to have bene purgeit by the blude of the Lamb; and thairfoir none of thame do attempt to be a Mediatour, seeing thai neither have being, nor justice, of thame selves.

JOHN 3.
ROM. 8.

LIBRO DE ISAAC ET ANIMA.

TRUE MEMBERS.

NOTE DILIGENTLY.

OBEDIENCE OF OURE SAVIOUR.

LIBRO CONTRA [EPIST.] PARMEN.

OBJECTIOUN.

AUNSWER.

---

[1] Justice, or righteousness.   [2] In the MS. "except"; in the edit. 1554, "except I."

But in so great lycht of the Gospell whilk now is begynning, (praise be to the Omnipotent!) it is not necessarie upon suche matter lang to remane. Sum say, We will use but one Mediatour, Jesus Chryst, to God the Father; but we must haif Sanctis, and cheiflie the Virgin Mary, the mother of Jesus Chryst, to pray for us unto him.

Note this weill.

AGAINST SUCHE AS WOULD HAVE MEDIATOURS TO JESUS CHRYST.—Allace! whosoever is so myndit, scheweth planelie thame selves to knaw nothing of Jesus Chryst rychtlie. Is he who discendit from heaven, and vouchsaffit to be conversant with synneris, commanding all soir vexit and seik to cum unto him, (who, hanging upon the Cross, prayit first for his enemyis) becum now so untractable, that he will not heir us without a persone to be a meane? O Lord! oppin the eis of suche, that thai may cleirlie persave thy infinit kyndnes, gentilnes, and love toward mankynd.

Math. 2.

Above all precidentis[1] is to be observit, that what we ask of God aught to be profitabill to oure selves and to others, and hurtfull or dangerous to no man. Secundlie, we must considder whether oure petitionis extendeth to Spirituall or Corporall thingis. Spirituall thingis, sic as ar delyverance frome impietie, remissioun of synnis, the gyft of the Halie Gaist, and of Lyfe everlasting, suld we desyre absolutlie, without any conditioun, by Jesus Chryst, in whome allone all theis ar promissit. And in asking heirof, we suld not pray thus: O Father! forgive our synnis gif thow will. For his will he hath expressit, saying, "As I live, I desyre not the death of a synner, but rather that he convert, and live;" whilk immutabill and solempnit othe who calleth in doubt maketh God a liar, and so far as in him lyeth, wolde spoyle God of his Godheid: For he can not be God except he be eternall and infallibill veritie. And Johne sayith, "This is the testimonie whilk God hath testifeit of his Sone, that who [so] beleiveth in the Sone hath eternall lyfe;" to the veritie whairof, we suld stedfastlie cleave; althocht warldlie dolour apprehend us.

Spirituall things shuld be axed without condition.

Merk weill.
1 Joh. 5.

---

[1] That is, Above all these things.

As David, exyllit from his kingdome, and depryvit of all his glorie, secludit not frome God, but stedfastlie beleivit reconciliatioun by the promeis maid, nochtwithstanding that all creatures in earth had refusit, abjectit, and rebellit aganis him: "Happie is the man whome thow sall inspyre, O Lord." <small>3 REG. 15</small>

In asking Corporall thingis, first lat us inquyre yf we be at peace with God in oure conscience be Jesus Chryst, firmelie beleiving oure synnis to be remittit in his blude? Secundlie, lat us inquyre of oure awin hartis, yf we knaw temporall ryches or substance not to cum to man be accident, fortune, or chance, neither yit be the industrie and diligence of mannis labour; but to be the liberall gift of God onlie, whairof we aught to laude and prais his gudnes, wisdome, and providence allone? <small>CORPORALL THINGIS.</small>

WHAT SULD BE PRAYIT FOR.—And yf this we do trewlie acknawledge and confes, lat us boldlie aske of him whatsoever is necessarie for us, as sustentatioun of this bodie; health thairof; defence frome miserie; delyverance frome trubill; tranquillitie and peace to oure Commoun weill; prosperous success in oure vocatiounis, labouris, and effairis, whatsoever thai be, whilk God will, we aske all of him, to certifie us that all thingis stand in his regement and dispositioun. And also by asking and ressaving theis corporall commoditeis, we have taist of his sueitnes, and be inflamed with his love, that thairby oure faith of reconciliatioun and remissioun of oure synnis may be exercisit and tak incress.

WHY GOD DIFFERRETH OR PROLONGETH TO GRANT US OUR PETITIOUNIS.—But in asking for temporall thingis, we must observe, first, That yf God differreth or prolongeth to grant oure petitiounis, evin sa lang that he semeth appeirandlie to reject us, yit lat us not cease to call, prescrybing him neither tyme, neither maner of delyverance; as it is writtin, "Yf he prolong tyme, abyde patientlie upon him," and also, "Lat not the faithfull be too haistie, for God sumtyme differeth, and will not haistelie grant to the probatioun of oure continewance," as the wordis of Jesus Chryst testifie; and also, that we may ressave with <small>NOTE WEILL.</small>

greatter glaidnes that whilk, with ardent desyre, we lang haif luikit for: as Anna, Sara, and Elizabeth, efter great ignominie of thair barrennes and sterilitie, receaved frute of thair bosomes with joy. Secundlie, because we knaw the Kirk at all tymes to be under the Cross, in asking temporall commoditeis, and speciallie delyverance from trubill, lat us offer unto God obedience, yf it sall please his gudnes we langer be exercisit that we may pacientlie abyd it; as David, desyreing to be restoirit to his kingdome (what tyme he was exyllit be his awn sone) offereth to God obedience, saying, "Yf I have found favour in the presence of the Lord, he sall bring me home agane; but yf he sall say, Thow pleases me not langer to beir autoritie, I am obedient: let him do what seemeth gude unto him."

<small>2 REG. 15.</small>

BETTER IT IS TO OBEY GOD THAN MAN.—And the Three Childrene unto Nebuchadnezzar did say, "We knaw that oure God whome we wirschip may delyver us; but yf it sall not pleas him so to do, let it be knawin to thee, O King, that thy Godis we will not wirschip." Heir gave thai a trew confessioun of thair perfyt faith, knawing nothing to be impossibill to the Omnipotence of God; affirmyng also thame selves to stand in his mercie; for uthirwayis the nature of man culd not willinglie give the self[1] to so horribill a torment; but thai offer unto God most humill obedience, to be delyverit at his gud pleasure and will. As we suld do in all afflictionis, for we knaw not what to ask or desyre as we aught; that is, the fraill flesche, oppressit with feir and pane, desyreth delyverance, ever abhoring and drawing back frome obedience giving.

<small>DANI. 3.</small>

O Christiane Brethrene, I wryt be experience: but the Spreit of God calleth back the mynd to obedience, that albeit it doith desyre and abyd for delyverance, yit suld it not repyne aganis the gudwill of God, but incessantlie ask that it may abyde with pacience: How hard this battell is, no man knawith but he whilk in himself hath sufferrit tryell.

THE PETITIOUN OF THE SPREIT.—It is to be noted, that God

---

[1] "The self," or "itself," as in edit. 1554.

sumtyme doith grant the petitioun of the Spreit, whill he yit <small>NOTE WEILL.</small> differreth the desyre of the flesche. As who doubteth but God did mitigat the heaviness of Joseph, althocht he sent not haistie delyverance in his lang imprisonment; and that as he gave him favour in the sycht of his jaylour, sa inwardlie also gave he <small>GEN. 39.</small> unto him consolatioun in spreit. And moreover God sumtymes granteth the petitioun of the spreit, whair alluterlie he repelleth the desyre of the flesche; for the petitioun alwayis of the spreit is, that we may atteine to the trew felicitie, whairunto we must neidis enter by tribulatioun, and the finall death, whilk both the nature of man doith ever abhorre, and thairfoir the flesche, under the cross, and at the sycht of death, calleth <small>FLESCHE STRYVETH AGANIS THE SPREIT.</small> and thristis for haistie delyverance. But God, who allone knawith what is expedient for us, sumtyme prolongeth the delyverance of his chosin, and sumtyme permitteth thame to drink before the maturitie of age, the bitter cupe of corporall death, that thairby thai may receave medicine and cure frome <small>PERSECUTIOUN OF THE FAITHFULL.</small> all infirmitie. For who doubteth that Johne the Baptist desyrit to have seene more the dayis of Jesus Chryst, and to have bene langer with him in conversatioun? Or that Stevin wald not have labourit mo dayis in preaching Chrystis gospell, whome, nevertheles, he sufferit haistilie to taist of this generall <small>ACT. 7.</small> sentence? And, albeit we sie thairfoir no appeirand help to oure selves, nor yit to othiris afflictit, lat us not ceiss to call, thinking our prayeris to be vane. For, whatsoever cum of <small>COMFORT TO THE AFFLICTIT.</small> our bodies, God sall gif unspeakabill confort to the spreit, and sall turne all to oure commodities beyond oure awn expectatioun.

IMPEDIMENTS CUMMETH OF THE WEAKENESSE OF THE FLESCHE. —The cause that I am so lang and tedious in this matter is, for that I knaw how hard the battell is betuix the Spreit and the Flesche, under the heavie cross of afflictioun, whair no warldlie defence, but present death dois appeir. I knaw the grudgeing and murmuring complayntes of the flesche; I knaw the angir, wraith, and indignatioun whilk it consavith aganis God, calling all his promissis in doubt, and being reddie everie hour utterlie to fall frome God. Aganis whilk restis onlie faith,[1] provoking us to call ernistlie and pray for assistance of Godis Spreit; whairin yf we continew, oure maist desperat calamiteis sall he turne to gladnes, and to a prosperous end. To thee, O Lord, allone be prais, for with experience I wryte this and speak.

WHAIR, FOR WHOME, AND AT WHAT TYME WE AUGHT TO PRAY, is not to be passit over with silence.

PRIVAT PRAYER.—Privat prayer, suche as men secreitlie offer unto God by thame selves, requyres no speciall place; althocht that Jesus Chryst commandeth when we pray to enter into our chamber, and to clois the dur, and sa to pray secretlie unto our Father. Whairby he wald that we suld chuse to oure prayeris sic places as mycht offer leist occasioun to call us back from prayer; and also, that we suld expell furth of oure myndis in tyme of our prayer, all vane cogitatiounis. For utherwayis Jesus Chryst himself doith observe no speciall place of prayer; for we find him sumtyme pray in Mont Olivet, sumtyme in the Desert, sumtyme in the Tempill, and in the Garden. And Peter covetteth to pray upon the top of the house. Paule prayed in prisone, and was hard of God. Who also commandeth men to pray in all places, lifting up unto God pure and cleane handis; as we find that the Propheitis and maist Holie men did, whensoever danger or necessitie requyrit.

APPOYNTIT PLACES to PRAY IN, MAY NOT BE NEGLECTIT.— But publict and commoun prayeris suld be useit in place appoyntit for the Assemblie, from whence whosoever negligentlie extracteth thame selves is in no wyse excusabill. I meane not, that to absent from that place is syn, because that place is more holie than another; for the haill earth creatit be God is equallie holie. But the promeis maid, that "Whairsoever tuo or thrie be gatherit togither in my name, thair sall I be in the middis of thame," condempneth all sic as contempneth the con-

[1] In the edit. 1554, " Against which all resteth in faith."

MARGIN: MATH 6.
MARGIN: ACT. 10
MARGIN: PRIVATE PLACES TO PRAY IN.

gregatioun gatherit in his name. But mark weill the word "gatherit;" I mene not to heir pyping, singing, or playing; nor to patter upon beidis, or bukis whairof thai haif no understanding; nor to commit idolatrie, honoring that for God whilk is no God in deid. For with suche will I neither joyne my self in commoun prayer, nor in ressaveing externall sacramentis; for in so doing I suld affirme thair superstitioun and abominabill idolatrie, whilk I, be Godis grace, never will do, neither counsall uthir to do, to the end.

WHAT IT IS TO BE GATHERED IN THE NAME OF CHRIST.—This congregatioun whilk I meane, suld be gatherit in the name of Jesus Chryst, that is, to laude and magnifie God the Father, for the infinit benefittis thai had ressavit be his onlie Sone oure Lord. In this congregatioun suld be distributed the mysticall and last Supper of Jesus Chryst without superstitioun, or any mo ceremonyis than he him self useit, and his Apostillis eftir him. And in distributioun thairof, in this congregatioun suld inquisitioun be maid of the poore amang thame, and support provydit, whill the tyme of thair nixt conventioun, and it suld be distributit amangis thame. Also, in this congregatioun suld be maid commoun prayeris, suche as all men heiring mycht understand; that the hartis of all, subscryving[1] to the voyce of one, mycht, with unfeaned and fervent mynd, say, Amen. Whosoever doith withdraw him self frome suche a congregatioun, (but allace, whair sall it found?) do declair thame selves to be no memberis of Chrystis bodie.

FOR WHOM, AND AT WHAT TYME WE SHOULD PRAY.—Now thair remaneth, For whome, and at what tyme, we suld Pray. For all men, and at all tymes, doith Paule command that we suld pray. And principallie for sic of the houshald of faith as suffer persecutioun; and for commounwealthis tirannouslie oppressit, incessantlie suld we call, that God, of his mercie and power, will withstand the violence of suche tyrantis.

1 TIM. 2.

GOD'S SENTENCE MAY BE CHANGED.—And when we sie the

[1] Subscribing, agreeing.

plagues of God, as hunger, pestilence, or weir[1] cuming or appeiring to ring,[2] then suld we, with lamentabill voyces and repenting hartis, call unto God, that it wold pleas his infinit mercie to withdraw his hand; whilk thing, yf we do unfeanedlie, he will without doubt revoke his wraith, and in the middis of his furie think upon mercie; as we ar taught in the Scripture be his infallible and eternall verities. As in Exodus, God sayeth, "I sall distroy this Natioun frome the face of the Erth;" and when Moses addressit him self to pray for thame, the Lord proceideth, saying, "Suffer me that I may utterlie distroy thame." And then Moses falleth doun upon his face, and fourtie dayis continewit in prayer for the saiftie of the pepill; for whome at the last he obteanit forgivenes. David, in the vehement plague, lamentabillie callit unto God. And the King of Ninivie sayeth, "Who can tell? God may turne and repent, and cease frome his fierce wraith, that we perische not." Whilk exempillis and scriptures ar not writtin in vane, but to certifie us, that God of his awn native gudnes will mitigate his plagues, (by oure prayeris offerit by Jesus Chryst,) althocht he hath threatenit to puniss, or presentlie doith punische: Whilk he doith testifie by his awn wordis, saying, "Yf I have prophesied aganis any natioun or pepill, that thai salbe distroyit, yf thai repent of thair iniquitie, it sall repent me of the evill whilk I haif spokin aganis thame." This I wryte, lamenting the great caldnes of men, whilk under so lang scurgeis of God, is nothing kendillit to pray by repentance, but cairlesslie sleipeth in a wickit lyfe; evin as thocht the continewall warris, urgent famine, and quotidiane plagues of pestilence, and uther contagious, insolent,[3] and strange maladies, wer not the present signis of Godis wraith, provokit be oure iniquiteis.

2 KINGS, LAST CH.

JONAS

JEREM. 18.

WEAKNESS IN PRAYER.

A PLAGUE THREATNED TO ENGLAND.—O England! lat thy intestin battell, and domesticall murther provok thee to puritie

[1] War.   [2] To reign, or prevail.   [3] Insolent, unaccustomed.

of lyfe, according to the word whilk oppinlie hath bene proclamed in thee, otherwise the cuppe of the Lordis wraith thow salt drink!¹ The multitude sall not eschape, but sall drink the dregis, and have the cupe brokin upon thair heidis. For judgement begynneth in the house of the Lord, and commounlie the leist offender is first punissit, to provoke the mair wickit to repentance. But, O Lord! infinit in mercie, yf thow salt puniss, mak not consummatioun, but cut away the proude and luxuriant branches whilk beir no frute: and preserve the Commounweillis² of sic as gif succour and harbour³ to thy contempnit messingeris, whilk lang have sufferit exyle in desert. And⁴ lat thy Kingdome schortlie cum that sin may be endit, death devorit, thy enemyis confoundit; that we thy pepill, be thy Majestie delyverit, may obtene everlasting joy and felicitie, throw Jesus Chryst oure Savioure, to whom be all honour and prais, for ever. Amen.

JOHNE KNOX.

THE GODLY PUNISHED.

Haisten, Lord, and tarie not.

¹ In the edit. 1554, "thou shalt shortly drinke of."
² Ib. "the Commonwealth."
³ Ib. "herber."

⁴ In the edit. 1554, this concluding sentence is omitted, and after the words "in desert," there is merely added, "So be it. Amen."

HERE AFTER FOLLOWETH A CONFESSION,
[OR PRAYER.]

OMNIPOTENT and everlasting God, Father of our Lord Jesus Chryst, who by thy eternall providence disposes kyngdomes, as best seameth to thy wysdome: we acknowledge and confesse thy judgmentes to be righteous, in that thow hast taken from us, for our ingratitude, and for abusinge of thy most holy worde, our Native Kyng and earthlye comforter.

Justly maye thow poure forth upon us the uttermoste of thy plagues; for that we have not knowen the dayes and tymes of oure mercifull visitation. We have contempned thy worde and despised thy mercies; we have transgressed thy lawes; for deceytfully have we wroughte, every man with oure neyghbours; oppression and violence we have not abhorred; charitie hath not appeared amonge us, as our profession requireth. We have little regarded the voyces of thy prophetes: thy threatnings we have estemed vanytie and wynd. So that in us, as of our selfs, restes nothing worthy of thy mercies; for all are founde fruitless; even the princes with the prophetes, as wythered trees apt and mete to be burnt in the fyre of thy eternall displeasure.

But, O Lord, behold thy own mercy and goodness, that thou may purge and remove the most fylthye burden of oure moste horrible offences. Let thy love overcome the severitie of thy judgments, even as it did in geving to the world thy onely Sonne, Jesus, when all mankynde was lost, and no obedience was left in Adam nor in his seede. Regenerate our hartes, O Lorde, by the strength of thy Holy Ghoste. Convert thou us, and we shall be converted: Worke thou in us unfayned repentance, and move thou oure hartes to obey thy holy lawes.

Behold our troubles and apparent destruction, and staye the sworde of thy vengeance before it devoure us. Place above us, O Lorde, for thy great mercies sake, such a head, with such rulers and magistrates as feareth thy name, and willeth the glory of Christ Jesus to spred. Take not from us the light of thy Evangely,[1] and suffer thou no Papistrie to prevaile in this realme. Illuminate the harte off our Soveraigne Lady Quene Marie with pregnant[2] giftes of thy Holy Ghoste. And inflame the hartes of her Counsayl with thy trew feare and love. Represse thou the pryde of those that wold rebelle; and remove from all hartes the contempte of the Worde. Let not our enemyes rejoyce at our destructioun, but looke thou to the honour of thy own name, O Lord; and let thy Gospell be preached with boldnes in this Realme. If thy justice must punish, then punish our bodies with the rodde of thy mercy. But, O Lorde, let us never revolte, nor turne backe to Idolatrie agayne. Mytigate the hartes of those that persecute us; and let us not faynt under the Crosse of our Saviour, but assist us with the Holy Ghoste, even to the ende.

[1] Gospel.   [2] Fruitful.

HERE AFTER FOLLOWETH THE TABLE OF THIS BOKE.[1]

A

	Page
A Confession of Christes most sacred Evangely upon the Death of that moste verteous and moste famous King, Edward the VI.,	106
A Plague threatened to England,	104
Appoynted places to Praye in may not be neglected,	102
Aungels maye not be Mediators,	95
Agaynste suche as wolde have Mediators to Jesus Christ,	98

B

Better it is to obey God than Man,	100
By whome we must Praye,	94

[1] The references to the pages in the present volume are substituted in place of the folios in the edition of 1554, to which this Table is subjoined.

THE TABLE.

                        Page

C

Corporall thinges,	99
Comforte to the Afflicted,	101

D

Dayly Bread,	89

F

Flesche stryveth agaynste the Spreit,	101
For Whom, and at what Tyme we should Pray,	103

G

God's sentence may be chaunged,	103
God delyvereth his Chosen from their Trubill and Enemyis,	90

H

How the Sprite maketh Intercession for us,	84

J

Jesus Christ, God and Man, is Mediator,	96
Impedimentes cummeth of the weakenesse of the flesche,	101
Intercession to Sainctes,	95
Ipocrisie is not allowed with God,	88

L

Let every man judge hys owne hart,	84

N

Not to pray is synne most odious,	92

O

Obedience of Christ,	97
Observation in godly Prayer,	93
Of Necessitie we must have a Mediator,	93

R

Reddines of God to heare synners,	92

S

Spurris stirre us to Prayer,	89

T

Turkes and Jewes,	94

THE TABLE.

	Page
The hope to obtayn our Peticion should depend upon the Promises of God,	93
The Cause of their boldness was Jesus Chryst,	88
The Peticion of the Sprete,	100

W

What Prayer is,	83
Who Prayeth not in Tribulation	92
When Synners are not harde of God,	86
Why we shoulde Praye, and also understande what we do Praye,	85
What Fasting and Almis Deidis ar with Prayer,	87
When we be not Harde,	94
What is to be Gathered in the Name of Christ,	103
Who maketh other Mediators than Jesus Christ taketh honor from him,	96
What shoulde be Prayed for,	99
When, and for Whom, we should Praye,	102
Why God differeth or prolongeth to grant us our Peticion,	85
Whair constant Prayer is, there is grantit the Peticion,	91
Who Prayeth not,	85
What is to be observed in Prayer,	84

HERE ENDETH THE TABLE.

AN EXPOSITION

UPON THE SIXTH PSALM OF DAVID,

ADDRESSED TO MRS BOWES.

M.D.LIV.

DIEPPE, a well known sea-port in Upper Normandy, was formerly a place of importance both for navigation and manufactures. It then afforded the most direct communication with the French capital; and is now, like Brighton on the opposite coast, a place of resort for the advantage of sea-bathing, and as a fashionable summer residence. On visiting it, a few years ago, although the town or its neighbourhood contains no memorials of our Scottish Reformer, I could not fail to recall the time when Knox arrived here an afflicted and solitary exile, to escape the persecution which had driven so many of his Protestant brethren from their native land. We find him likewise, on more than one occasion, returning hither to obtain certain tidings of the state of affairs both in Scotland and England.

After his first arrival at Dieppe, in January 1554, he employed himself in writing two treatises, one of which, at least, he had commenced in England. The English Parliament assembled on the 5th of October 1553; and while Queen Mary's title as Supreme Head of the Church was retained, bills were introduced which repealed all the laws made in favour of the Reformation, and restored the Roman Catholic religion, but liberty to observe the forms of Protestant worship was extended to the 20th of December. Three days after that period had elapsed, Knox was still continuing his labours, and, in a letter to Mrs Bowes, he says, "I may not answer your places of Scripture, nor yet write the Exposition of the Sixth Psalm, for every day of the week must I preach, if this wicked carcase will permit."

Of this Exposition, which was completed while he remained at Dieppe, there are two early editions. In its printed form, the work exhibits no appearance of having been composed at different periods; but the autograph original of the first portion, defective at the beginning, is still preserved, and the concluding paragraph, omitted in the later copies, shows that this portion had been sent to his mother-in-law, most probably from London, on the sixth of January. This very interesting fragment, although unsigned, is beyond doubt in Knox's own hand: it is contained in a miscellaneous volume of letters and papers which belonged to Foxe the Martyrologist, and now deposited in the British Museum, (Harleian MSS., No. 416, fol. 40-45.)

Another copy, corresponding with the printed editions, occurs in Dr M'Crie's manuscript volume, and furnishes the date, the last day of February, when it was completed. Knox was then on the eve of leaving Dieppe on his first journey to Switzerland. This manuscript, which was transcribed in the year 1603, and will afterwards be more particularly noticed, came into the possession of Wodrow the historian,[1] who also had acquired another manuscript volume in folio, containing some of Knox's treatises. As this volume cannot now be traced, it may not be out of place to present a description of its contents, as furnished by Wodrow and Crawfurd.

"The one Manuscript," says Wodrow, "is a folio, in an old hand, though very fairly written, nicely ruled with red ink, and the capital letters, running titles, and other embellishments in red; and most correctly finished, as far as I can guess, before Mr Knox's death. At the end of it is 'J. G.,' and then follows, 'John Gray, scribe.' And before it is 'MARGARET STEWART, *with my hand.*' By the Registers to the Assembly 1579 [1570], I find one John Gray, Scribe to the Assembly, and it is not improbable that this book might be written by him for Mrs Knox's use, who, I suppose, is meant here by Margaret Stewart."

---

[1] (See page 335.)—Wodrow, in his MS. Life of Knox states, that this quarto manuscript "once belonged to the Rev. Mr Thomas Wilkie, minister, since the Revolution, in the Canongate of Edinburgh." He died 19th of March 1711.

The Rev. Matthew Crawfurd, in a Life of the author, prefixed to his edition of Knox's History, makes a similar statement: "There is a volume in folio (in Mr Wodrow's hands) in an old hand, fairly written; it seems to have been copied by John Gray, who was Scribe to the General Assembly, for the use of Margaret Stewart, Mr Knox's widow, for both their names are written upon the book." It contained,

1. The Preparatioun to Prayer, and necessare Observatione thereof, drawin be ane faythfull Minister of the Evangell of Jesus Christ, John Knox, at the request of ane faythfull brother. It is signed J. K., and consists of four sheets and a half of paper.

2. The Sext Psalme of David godlie expoundit, and sent to ane ancient faithfull Mother, for consolatioun of ane troubled conscience. It consists of ten sheets; it was written in the year 1553, when he was leaving England; at the end of it is written, "At the very point of my journey, last January [February] 1553, your Son, with sorrowful heart, J. K."

3. The Epistle sent to several Congregations in England, shawand the Plaigs which sall schortlie cum upon that Realme for refusing God's Worde, and imbrassing Idolatrie, by John Knox.

4. To the Faithfull in London, Newcastle, and Berwick; it has at the end, "Upon my departure from Deipe 1553, whidder God knawis," &c., signed John Knox.

It will be observed that each of these treatises has been preserved, both in a printed and manuscript form; it would, however, have been satisfactory to have collated these copies, which were no doubt transcribed under the author's own inspection during the later period of his life. It may be added, that "Mr John Gray, Scribe to the General Assemblie," died in April 1574.[1]

Of the two early editions referred to, accurate copies of the

---

[1] Register of Confirmed Testaments, 21st March 1575-6; and Booke of the Universall Kirk, vol. i. pp. 299, 311.

title-pages are here annexed. The first is a diminutive volume, without any indication of the printer's name, place, or date, but apparently printed in the year 1556. The other, printed at London in 1580, has the accompanying prefatory address by Abraham Fleming, a person of considerable literary reputation, and afterwards Rector of a church in London.[1] Although this is merely a republication, no notice is taken of the former edition. To both these editions are added Knox's "Comfortable Epistle," written from Dieppe on the last day of May 1554, and the "Letter of Wholesome Counsell," written in 1556.

In the following text, the autograph portion has been carefully adhered to, except so far as regards the omission of the contractions which occur in the MS.; and the commencement, as well as the later portion, is supplied from Dr M'Crie's manuscript volume, collated with the old printed copies.

This Exposition, says the Biographer of Knox, "is an excellent practical discourse upon that portion of Scripture, and will be read with peculiar satisfaction by those who have been trained to religion in the school of adversity."[2]

[1] See note 2, page 118.   [2] M'Crie's Life of Knox, vol. i. p. 127.

TO THE RELIGIOUS READER.

[*Prefixed to the Edition printed at London*, 1580.]

WHO art thou (O Christian) that beeing sicke in soule, and desirest to be sound? sorowfull in spirit, and cravest comfort? unquiet in minde, and seekest to be at rest? wounded in conscience, and wouldest be in safetie? tormented in thought, and longest for reliefe? Who art thou (I say) that having offended thy God, and art therefore punished? tried with tribulation, and criest out to be refreshed? visited with affliction, and faine wouldest be delivered? Get thee to God's Woorde, and there learne thy lesson: heare his holy Gospell preached, and thereby receave instruction: peruse and ponder, examine and consider, meditate and exercise thy selfe in the good bookes of God's faithfull Servants, and they shall teach thee wisdome.

And among all bookes tending to this purpose, I commende to thy memory (O Christian) to bee embraced and followed, this notable Exposition of that zealous man of God, Maister JOHN KNOXE, uppon the Sixt Psalme, contayning sundry comfortable and excellent doctrines, in number many, in matter weightie, under the person of that Princely Prophet David, and after his example and patterne too bee applied unto all suche as are touched eyther in minde or bodie with any kind of crosse or calamitie, to direct them to the path of patience, and to shew them by a president, unto whom they must run for refuge in the time of their visitation, if they desire eyther partly too have their miseries mitigated, or themselves wholly from troubles to be delivered.

The benefite of this Booke belongeth to every particular member of Christes Mysticall Bodie, and they onlie have the grace to use this and the like at convenient seasons. Moreover, the manifolde comfortes of this woorthy Author's most fruitefull Epistle,[1] written for the consolation of Christes afflicted flocke, are of no lesse force and vertue, in cases of calamitie, than his other Treatise; the one commodious, the other necessary, both beneficiall.

Thine to doe thee good,

ABRAHAM FLEMMING.[2]

---

[1] His Epistle, written from Dieppe, on the last day of May 1554, and annexed to both the old editions of the Exposition on the Sixth Psalm.

[2] Fleming, who was a native of London, was born in 1551, and educated for the ministry, probably at Cambridge. Among his various publications are several translations from classical authors. In his Bucolics of Virgil, printed in 1575, he styles himself "Student." In 1589, he added the Georgics, with a new version of the Bucolics, and dedicated them to Archbishop Whitgift. He had previously assisted in revising and enlarging the second edition of Holinshed's Chronicles. (Warton's *Hist. of English Poetry*, vol. iii. p. 326, edit. 1840). Fleming was preferred to the Rectorship of St Pancras, Soperlane, London, in October 1593; and died 29th of February 1607. (Newcourt's *Repertorium Ecclesiasticum Parochiale Londinense*, vol. i. p. 519.)

An Expositioun upon the Sext Psalme of David; whairin is declairit his Cross, Complayntis, and Prayeris; necessarie[1] to be read of all thame, for thair singular confort, that under the Banner of Chryst are by Sathan assaltit, and feill the heavie burdene of Sin with whilk thai ar oppressit.

The pacient abyding of the soir afflictit was never yet confoundit.

To his belovit Mother, Johne Knox[2] sendeth greiting, in the Lord.

The desyre that I have to heir of your continewance with Chryst Jesus, in the day of this his battell, whilk schortlie sall end to the confusion of his proude enemyis, neither by toung nor[3] by pen can I express, beloved Mother. Assuredlie it is suche that it vanquisseth and overcumeth all rememberance and solicitude, whilk the flesche useth to take for feiding and defence of hir self. For in everie realme and natioun, God will steir[4] up sum ane or other to minister theis thingis that appertene to this wreachit lyfe. And yf men will ceiss to do thair office, yet will He send his ravenis; so that, in everie place, perchance I may find sum featheris[5] to my bodie. But allace! whair I sall find children to be begottin unto God by the Word of lyfe, that can I not presentlie considder. And thairfore the spirituall lyfe of suche as sum tymes boldlie professit Chryst (God knaweth), is, to my hart, more deir than all the glorie,

---

[1] In the first edit., "moste necessarie."
[2] In the old editions, "J. K."
[3] Ib. "neither yet."
[4] Ib. "styr," or "stirre."
[5] Ib. "fethers," raiment, clothing.

ryches, and honour in earth. And the falling back of suche men, as I heir daylie do turne back to that Ydoll[1] agane, is to me more dolorous then, I trust, the corporall deith salbe, whenever it sall cum at Godis apoyntment. Some will ask then, Why did I flie? Assuredlie I can not tell; but of one thing I am sure, the feir of death was not the chief cause of my flieing. I trust the one cause hath bene, to lat me sie with my corporall eyis that all had not a trew hart to Chryst Jesus that in the day of rest and peace bare a fair face. But my flieing is no matter; by Godis grace, I may cum to battell befoir that all the conflict be endit. And haist the tyme, O Lord, at thy gud pleasure, that anis agane my toung may yit prais thy Holie Name, befoir the Congregatioun, yf it wer but in the verie hour of death.

I have writtin a large Treatise tuiching the plagues that assuredlie sall apprehend obstinat ydolateris,[2] and thois also that, dissembling with thame, deny Chryst in obeying[3] ydolatrie, whilk I wold ye suld reid diligentlie. Yf it cum not to yow frome the South, I sall provyde that it sall cum to yow be sum other meanes.

Tuiching[4] your continewall trubill, gevin unto yow by God for better purpois than we can presentlie espy, I have begun unto yow the Expositioun of the Sext Psalme; and as God sall grant unto me opportunitie and helth of bodie, (whilk now is verie weak,) I purpose to absolve the same.

THE ARGUMENT.[5]

IT appeireth that David, efter his offences,[6] fell into sum great and dangerous seaknes, in the whilk he was soir tormentit, not so muche by corporall infirmiteis, as by susteanyng and drink-

---

[1] The Romish Mass.
[2] The Treatise to which Knox refers, is his "Letter to the Faithful in London," &c., which immediately follows this Exposition.
[3] In the old edit. "obeying to."
[4] "Touching."
[5] In the first edit., "The Argument of the Syxte Psalme."
[6] Ib. "offence."

ing sum large portioun of the cupe of Godis wraith. And albeit that he was delyverit (as then) frome the corporall death, yit it apeireth, that long efter (yea and I verelie beleive that all his lyfe) he had sum sense and rememberance of the horribill feir whilk befoir he suffirit in the tyme of his seaknes. And thairfoir the Holie Ghost, speiking in him, scheweth unto us what be the complayntis of Godis elect under suche crosse; how diverslie thai ar tormentit; how that thai appear to have no sure hold of God, but to be abject[1] frome him. And yit what ar the signis that thai ar Godis elect? And so doith the Holie Ghost to teache us to seik help of God, even when he is punissing, and appeireth to be angrie with us.

THE SIXTH PSALME.

O Lord, rebuke me not in thine anger, nor chasten me in thy hote displeasure. <small>THE BEGINNING OF THE 6. PSALME.</small>

DAVID, sore trubillit in bodie and spreit, lamentabillie prayeth unto God, whilk, that ye may mair surelie understand, I will attempt to express in mo wordis. David speiketh unto God, as he wold speik unto a man, in this maner: "O Lord, I feill what is the wecht and strenth of thi displeasure. I have experience how intollerabill is the hevines of thy hand, whilk I, maist wrechit man, have provokit aganis my self by my horribill synis. Thow whippis me and scourgeis[2] me bitterlie; yea, sa thow vexeis me, that, unless thow withdraw thy hand, and remit thy displeasure, thair resteth nothing unto me but utterlie to be confoundit. I beseche thee, O Lord, rage not, neither be commoveit aganis me above measure. Remitte[3] and take awaie thy hevie displeasure, which, by my iniquitie I have provoked against my selfe." This appeareth to have bene the meanyng <small>THE DOLOROUS COMPLAYNT OF DAVID IN HIS TROUBLE.</small> <small>HIS PRAIER.</small> <small>HIS CONFESSIOUN.</small>

---

[1] "Abject," cast out.
[2] In the old editions, "thou whippest me and scourgest."
[3] The original MS. commences at the top of the page with this word.

of David in his first wordes, wherbie he declareth himselfe to have felt the grevous wraith of God before that he bursted forth in these words.

In which, First, is to be noted, that the Prophet doth acknowlege all trouble that he sustayned, as well in bodie as in mind, to be sent of God, and not to happen unto him by chaunce. For herein peculiarlie differ the sonnes of God from the reprobate; that the sonnes of God knowe both prosperitie and adversitie to be the giftes of God onelie, as Job doth witnes. And therfore in prosperitie commonlie thei are not insolent nor proude; but even in the daie of joye and rest thei loke for trouble and sorowe. Nether yet in the time of adversitie are thei altogether left without comforte; but by one meane or other God sheweth to them that trouble shal have an end. Where contrarywise, the reprobate, either taking all thing of chaunce, or els makyng an idoll of their owne wisdome, in prosperitie are so puft up, that thei forget God, without any care that trouble shulde folowe, and in adversitie thei are so dejecte, that thei loke for nothing but hell.

<small>ALL TROUBLE COMMETH OF GOD.</small>

Here must I put you in mynde, Dearlie Beloved, how oft have you and I talked of these present daies, till nether of us both coulde refrayne teares, whan no such appearaunce there was sene by man. How oft have I saide unto you, that I loked dailie for trouble, and that I wondred at it, that so long I dyd escape it? What moved me to refuse, and that with displeasure, of all men, (even of those that best loved me), those high promotions that were offred, by him[1] whom God hath taken from us for our offences? Assuredlie, the foresight of trouble to come. How oft have I saide unto you, that the tyme wold not be long, that England wold geve me bred? Advyce with[2] the last letter that I wrote unto your Brother-in-law, and consider what is therein conteyned.

<small>KING EDWARD.</small>

[1] This evidently refers to the offers made to Knox of being promoted to the See of Rochester, in October 1552, and to a vacant living in London, in April following. See vol. i. pp. xv, xvi.

[2] In MS. M. "Advyse with," refer to, compare.

THE SIXTH PSALM OF DAVID. 123

While I had this trouble, you had the greater, sent, I doubte not, to us both of God; that, in that greate rest, and, as we maie call it, whan the Gospell tryumphed, we shulde not be so careles and so insolent as others were. Who, albeit thei professed Christ in mouth, yet sought thei nothing but the world, with hand, with foote, with counsaill, and wisdome. And albeit at this present our comforte appeareth not; yet, before that all the plages be poured forth, it shalbe knowne that there is a God who taketh care of his owne.

Secondarely, is to be observed, that the nature and ingyne of the very sonnes of God, in the tyme of their trouble, is to impute unto God some other affection then ther is, or can be in him, towards his children; and somtyme to complayne upon God, as that he dyd those thinges, that, in very dede, he can not do to his electe. David and Job often complayne that God had lefte them, was become their enemie, regarded not their praiers, and toke no hede to delyver them: And yet impossible it is, that God either shal leave his chosen, or that he shal despise the humble peticions of such as do yncalle[2] his supporte. But such complayntes are the voyces of the fleshe, wherewith God is not offended to the rejection of his electe, but pardoneth them among their innumerable infirmities and synnes. And therfore, Dearlie Beloved, despaire you not, albeit the flesh somtyme bursteth out in hevy complaynts, as it were against God. You are not more perfect then was David and Job, and you cannot be so perfecte as Christ himselfe was, who upon the cross cried, "My God, my God, why hast thou forsaken me?" Considre, Dear Mother, how lamentable and horrible were these wordes to the onelie Sonne of God. And David, in the 88 Psalme, (which, for better understanding, I desyre you read,) complayneth upon God, that night and daie he had cryed, and yet he was not delyvered. "But (saith he)

GOD'S VERY ELECT SOME TIMES ACCUSE GOD.[1]

GOD SHEW-ETH MERCIE WHER NONE YS DESERVED.

---

[1] The marginal notes are not in the original manuscript, but appear to have been subsequently added.

[2] "Yncall," implore, pray for.

my soule was replenished with dolour: I am as a man without strength: I am lyke unto those that are gone downe into the pitt, of whom thou hast no more mynde; lyke unto those that are cut of by thy hande: Thou hast put me in a depe dongeon: All thy wraith lyeth upon me. Why leavest thou me, O Lorde? Why hydest thou thy face so fare fro me? Thou hast removed all my frendes fro me; thou hast made me odyous unto them." And thus he endeth his Psalme and complaynt, without mencion of eny comforte receaved. And Job, in dyverse places of his boke, maketh even the like complaynts; Somtyme sayeng, that God was his enemie, and had set him, as it were, a marck to shute at. And therfore that his soule desyred the very destruction.

Thes things I recyte unto you, Dearlie Beloved, understanding what hath bene your troubles heretofore, and knowing that Satan wyll not ceasse now to persuade to your tender conscience, that none of God's electe hath bene in lyke case as you are. But by these presedents, and of many other places (which now to collecte I have no oportunyte), it planelye doth appeare, God's chosen vessels[1] hath suffred the lyke tentations. I remembre, that oft ye have complayned upon the grudging and murmuryng that you founde within your selfe, fearing that it provoked God to more displeasure. Beholde and consider, Deare Mother, what God hath borne with his saynts before; will he not beare the same with you, beyng most sorie for your imperfection? He can none otherwise do; but as his wisdome hath made us all of one masse and nature, erth and erthie; and as he hath redemed us with one pryce, the bloude of his onlie Sonne, so must He, acording to his promes, loke mercifullie upon the offences of all those that yncalle[2] the name of the Lorde Jesus· Of these I meane, that refuse all other justice[3] but his alone.

ROMA. 10.

But to our matter: Of thes presidentes, playne it is, that God is

---

[1] In MS. M. "chosin children."   [3] "Justice," righteousness.
[2] Ib. "incall," call on, pray in.

electe, before you, suffred the lyke crosse, as presentlie you suffre; that thei have complayned, as you complayne; that thei have thought themselves abjecte, as you have thought, and yet maie thinke yourselfe; and yet, nevertheles, thei were sure in Godis favor. Hope, Deare Mother, and loke you for the same; hope (I saie) against hope. How horrible the payne is to suffre that crosse, can none expresse, excepte such as have proved it. Fearfull it is, for the very payne it selfe; but most fearful it is, for that the godlie so tormented, judgeth God to be angrie, in furour, and in rage against them, as is before expressed. Seynge we have found this crosse to apperteyne to Godis children, profitable it shalbe to serche out the causes of the same.

Playne it is, that not onelie God worketh all to the profit of his electe, but also that he worketh it of such love towardes them, and with such wisdome, that otherwise thinges coulde not be. And this to understande is very profitable, partlie to satisfie the grudging complayntes of the flesh, which, in trouble, commonlie doth question, Why doth God this or that? And albeit the flesh in this erth can never be fullie satisfied; but even as hunger and thirst from tyme to tyme assaulteth it, so do others more grosse imperfections. Yet the inwarde man, with sobbes unto God, knowing the causes why the very just[1] are sore troubled and tormented in bodie and sprete in this life, receave sure comforte, and get sume staye of Godis mercie, by knowing the causes of the trouble. All causes maie I not here recite, but two or three of the pryncipall will I touche.

The first is, to provoke in Godis electe a hatred of synne, and unfeyned repentaunce of the same; which cause, yf it were rightuouslie considred, were sufficient to make all spirituall and corporall troubles tollerable unto us. For seyng it is, that without repentaunce no man doth attayne to Godis mercie; (for it is now appoynted by Him, whose wisdome is infinite, I meane of those that are coverted to the felyng of synne,) and

[1] "The very just," the truly righteous.

that without mercie no man can come to joye: Is not that which letteth us understand[1] what repentaunce is, gladlie to be receaved and embraced?

Repentaunce conteyneth in it,[2] a knowlege of synne, a dolour for it, and a hatred of it, together with hope of mercie. It is very evident that Godis owne children have not at all tymes the right knowlege of synne, that is to saie, how odyous it is before God; much lesse have thei the dolour for it, and hatred of it. Which yf thei had, as thei coulde not synne, so coulde thei never be able (havyng allwaies that very sence[3] of Godis wraith against synne) to delight in any thing that apperteyneth to the flesh, more then the woman whom God hath appoynted by the helpe of man to produce mankynde, coulde ever delight in man, yf at all tymes she felt the same panges of dolour and payne, that she doth in hir childe birthe. And therfore doth God, for such purposes as is knowne to himselfe, somtyme suspende from his owne children this foresaide sense and felinge of his wraith against synne: as no doubte he here dyd with David, not onelie before his synne, but also somtyme after. But lest that the sonnes of God shulde become alltogether insolent, like the children of the world, he sendeth unto them some portion of this foresaide cup; in drynking wherof, thei come to such knowlege as thei never had before. For, first, thei fele the wraith of God working against synne; wherbie thei lerne the justice of God to be even such as he himself pronounceth; that he maie suffre no synne unpunished. And thus begynne thei, as well to mourne for their offences, as also to hate the same, which otherwise thei coulde never do. For nothing is so pleasing to the corrupte nature of man, as is synne; and thinges pleasing to nature, cannot nature by the selfe[4] hate.

But in this conflicte, as Godis children fele tormentes, and that most grevous; as thei mourne, and by Godis Holie Sprete

---

[1] In MS. M., and the old editions, "whilk causeth us to understand."
[2] Ib. "within it."
[3] Ib. "having that same verie sense."
[4] Ib. "Of it self."

begynne to hate synne, so come thei also to a more high knowlege; that is, that a man can not be saviour to himselfe. For how shale he save himselfe from hell, that can not save himselfe from anguishe and trouble here in the flesh, while that he hath strength, witte, reason, and understanding? And therefore must he be compelled in his hert to acknowlege, that another Mediatour must ther be betwixte Godis justice and mankynde, then eny that ever descended of the corrupted sede of Adam; yea, than eny creature that onelie is creature. And by the knowlege of this Mediatour, at last the afflicted commeth by[1] some sense and lyvelie fealing of Godis great mercies declared unto mankynde, albeit thei be not so sensible as is the payne. And albeit that torment, by this knowlege, is not haistelie removed, yet hath the pacient some hope that all dolour shal have end. And that is the cause why he sobbeth and groneth for an end of payne; why also he blasphemeth not God, but crieth for his helpe, even in the myddes of his anguishe.

How profitable this is to the children of God, and what it worketh in to them, as the playne Scripture teacheth, so experience letteth us[2] understand. And verelie even so profitable as it is to mourne for synne, to hate the same; to knowe the Mediatour betwixte God and man; and, finallie, to knowe his love and mercie towardes them, so necessary is it to drynke this foresaide cuppe. What it worketh in them, none knoweth but such as taisteth it.

In David, it is playne that it wrought humilite and abjection of himself: it toke from him the great trust that he had in himself; it made him dailie to feare, and ernestlie to praie, that after he shulde not offende in lyke maner, nor yet be left to his owne handes. It made him lowelie,[3] although he was a kyng; it made him mercifull, whan he might have bene rygorous; yea, it caused him to mourne for Absalom his wicked sonne. But to the rest of the causes.

[1] "Commeth by," attaineth.
[2] "Letteth us," causeth us.
[3] In the MS. "lowe"; in the old editions "lowly."

The second cause why God permitteth his Electe to taist of this bitter cuppe, is to reise up our herts from thes transitorie vanities. For so foolishe and so forgetfull of nature, and so addicted are we to the thinges that are present, that onlesse we have another scoolmaster then manlie reason,[1] and some other spurre and perpetuall remembraunce then anye that we can chose, or devyce ourselves, we nether can desyre, nether yet ryghtuouslie remembre, the departure from this vayne and wicked worlde, to the kyngdome that is prepared.

We are commaunded dailie to praie, THY KYNGDOME COME. Which peticion asketh that synne maie ceasse; that death maie be devoured; that transitory troubles maie have an end; that Sathan maie be troden under our fete; that the hole body of Christ maie be restored to life, libertie, and joye; that the powers and kingdomes of this erth maie be dissolved and destroyed; and that God the Father maie be all in all thinges, after that his Sonne Christ Jesus, our Saviour, hath rendred up the kingdome for ever.

Thes thinges are we all commaunded to praie. But which of us, at the tyme whan all aboundes with us, whan nether bodie ner spirite hath trouble, from our hert, and without symulation, can wishe thes thinges? Verely none. With our mouthes we maie speake the wordes, but the hert can not thirst the effecte to come, excepte we be in such estate that wordlie thinges be unsaverie unto us: And so can thei never be, but under the crosse; nether yet under all kynde of crosses are wordlie thinges unpleasaunt. For in povertie, riches do greatlie delight many; for allthough thei lack them, yet desyre thei to have them, and so are thei nether unsavery ner unpleasaunt; for thinges that we ernestlie covet are not unpleasaunt unto us. But whan thinges apperteyning to the flesh are sufficientlie mynistred unto us, and yet none of them can mollifye our anguishe nor payne, then sobbes the hert unto God, and unfeynedly wisheth an ende of miserie. And therfore our heavenlie

---

[1] "Manlie reason," human reason.

An Exposition vppon the syxt Psalme of Dauid, wherein is declared hys crosse, complayntes and prayers, moste necessarie too be red of them, for their singular comforte, that vnder the banner of Christe are by Satan assaulted, and feele the heauye burthen of synne, with whiche they are oppressed.

☞ The patiente abydinge of the sore afflicted was neuer yet confounded.

☞ **9∶6** ☜

In 16to, black-letter, without date, place, or the name of the printer. This little volume contains signatures A to I, in eights. The Exposition of the Sixth Psalm ends with signature F. Then follows on G i, with a separate title, "A Comfortable Epistle," &c. "Written at Depe, the last of May, An. M.D.Liiij." This ends on H (6). The next leaf is blank, and the volume concludes with the Letter "of Wholesome Counsell," dated the 7th of July 1556. It was probably printed in that year, after Knox had reached Dieppe, on his way to Geneva.

A
¶ *Fort for the affli-*
cted.

Wherin are miniſtred many notable & excellent remedies against the stormes of tribulation.

Written chiefly for the comforte of *Christes little flocke,* which is the smal number of the Faithfull, by Iohn Knoxe.

Iohn. 16. 33.
In the vvorlde yee shall haue affliction, but be of good comfort: I haue ouercome the vvorld.

Imprinted at London at the three Cranes in *the Vintree, by Thomas Dawſon,* 1580.

In 12mo, signatures ❦ in four, and A to F 4, in eights, Roman letter. The "Comfortable Epistle" begins on the reverse of D 6; the "Letter of Wholesome Counsel," on E 7. On the last page is this colophon:

Imprinted at London by Thomas Dawſon, dwelling at the three *Cranes in the Vintree.*
1580.

Father, of his infinite wisdome, to holde us in contynuall remembraunce that in this wretched world ther is no rest, permitteth and suffreth us to be tempted and tried with this crosse, that with an unfeyned hert we maie desyre not onelie an end of our owne troubles, (for that shal come to us by death), but also of all the troubles of the Church of God; which shal not be before the agayn commyng of the Lorde Jesus.

The thirde cause, I collecte of Moses wordes to the Israelites, saienge: "The Lord thy God shal cast out thes nacions by litle and litle before thee. He wil not cast them out all at ones, lest, perchaunce, the wylde beastes be multiplied against thee." And also, "Whan thou shalt entre in that good land, and shalt dwell in the howses that thei never buyldet, and that thou shalt eate and be filled, geve thankes unto the Lord thy God, and beware that thou forget him not; and that thou saie not in thy hert, The strength of myne owne hand hath brought thes greate riches unto me." <small>DEUT. 7.</small> <small>DEUT. 8.</small>

In thes wordes are two thinges apperteyning to our matter, most worthelie to be noted. First, that Moses saieth, that the Lorde will not at ones, but by litle and litle destroie thes nacions; adding the cause, lest, perchaunce, (saieth he) the wilde beastes be multiplied, and make uproare against thee. The second, that whan thei had abundaunce, that then thei shulde declare them selves myndfull of Godis benefits; and that thei shulde not thinke that their owne power, wisdome, nor provision was eny cause that thei had the fruition of those commodities.

By these presidents, the Holie Goost teacheth unto them, that like as thei dyd not possesse nor opteyne the first interest of that land by their owne strength, but that the Lord God dyd frelie geve it unto them; so likewise were thei not able to broke nor enjoye the same by eny power of their selfe: for albeit that God shulde have in one moment destroied all their enemies, yet, yf he shulde not have bene their perpetuall savegard, the wilde beastes shulde have troubled them. And yf thei had demaunded the question, Why wilt thou not destroie the wilde beastes also? He answereth: Lest thou forget the Lord thy God, and saie unto they hert, My strength hath opteyned this quietnes to my selfe.

Considre, Dearlie Beloved, that such thinges as the Spirite of God foresawe daungerous and damnable unto them, the same thinges are to be feared in us; for all thinges happened to them in figures.[1] Thei were, in Egipte, corporally punished by a cruell tyrant: We were in spiritual bondage of the Devell by synne and incredulitie. God gave to them a land that flowed with mylke and hony, for which thei never laboured: God hath opened to us the knowlege of Christ Jesus, which we never deserved, nor yet hoped for the same. Thei were not able to defende the land, after thei were possessed in it: We are not able to reteyne our selves in the true knowlege of Christ, but by his grace onelie. Some enemies were left to exercise them: Synne is left in us, to lerne us to fight: Yf enemies had not bene, wilde beestes shulde have multiplied amonges them. Yf such thinges[2] as we thinke most doth trouble us were not permitted so to do, worse beests shulde have domynion over us: To wete,[3] trust in our selfe, arrogancy, oblyvion, and forgetfulnes of that estate from which God had delyvered us, together with a light estimation of all Christis merits; which synnes are the beests that, alas! devoure no small nombre of men. Nether yet let eny man thinke, that yf all kynde of crosses were taken from us, during the tyme that we beare the erthlie ymage of Adam, that we shulde be more perfecte in usyng the spirituall giftes of God, to wete,[4] free remission of synnes, his free graces, and Christis justice[5]; for which we never laboured, nor that people shulde have bene in usyng of those corporall giftes.

And Moses saieth unto them: Beware that thou forget not the Lorde thy God. He who knoweth the secrets of herts,

---

[1] "Happened unto them for ensamples."—1 Cor. x. 11.

[2] In the old edit. "such beastes"

[3] Ib. "that is, to wit."

[4] Ib. "to wit."

[5] Or righteousness.

geveth not his preceptes in vayne; but knowing what thinges be most able to blynd and disceave man, the wisdome of God, by his contrarie precepts, geveth him warnyng of the same. Experience hath taught us, how such beasts have troubled the Church of God, to speak nothing of the tyme of the Prophets, of the Apostels, or of the Primityve Church.

What trouble made Pelagius[1] by his heresie! Affirmyng that man, by naturall power and fre will, might fulfill the lawe of God, and deserve for himself remission and grace. And to come a litle nearer to our owne age, hath it not been openlie preached, affirmed in scooles, and set out by wrytinges, that onelie faith doth justifie, but that works doth also justifie? Hath it not bene taught, that good workes maie go before faith, and maie provoke God to geve his graces? What hath bene taught of menis merites, and of the workes of supereroga- tioun? Some openlie affirmyng, that some men have wrought more good workes than were necessary to their owne salva- tioun. I praie you consider, yf thes men saide not, Our hand and our strength hath geven thes thinges unto us? What were these develishe heresies aforesaid, and others that have justi- fied[2] the whole Papistrie? Assuredly thei were cruell and raven- yng beasts, able to devoure the soules of all those upon whom thei get the upper hand. But the mercifull providence of our God, willing our salvatioun, wil not suffre us to come to that unthankfullnes and oblyvion: And therfore he[3] permitteth us to our enemies, with his Apostle Paul, to be buffeted to the end, and that we maie mourne for synne, and hate the same; that we maie knowe the onelie Mediator and the dignitie of his office; that we maie unfeynedlie thirst the commyng of the Lorde Jesus; and that we nether be presumptuous, lightlie estemyng Christis death, nether yet unmyndefull of our former estate

---

[1] Pelagius, who flourished about the beginning of the fifth century, was probably a native of Ireland. His heresy, which occasioned great dis- sension in the British Church, con- sisted in denying the doctrine of Ori- ginal Sin, and in teaching that men might be saved by their own works.

[2] In the old edit. "have infected."

[3] Ib. "heere he."

and miseries. And so this cupp is, as it were, a medicyne prepared by the wisdome of our eternall Phisician, who onelie knoweth the remedies for our corrupt nature.

Adverte and marke, Deare Mother, that all commeth to us for oure most singular profite: It is a medicyne, and therfore presently it can not be pleasinge. But how gladlie wold we use and receave, when the bodies were sick, (how unpleasant and bitter that ever it were to drink,) that medicyne which wold remove sickness and restore helth. But O how much more ought we, with pacience and thankesgevyng, receave this medicyne of our Fatheris handes, that from our soules removeth so many mortall diseases, (his Holie Ghost so working by the same;) such as pryde, presumptioun, contempt of grace, and unthankfullnes; which be the very mortall diseases, that by unbelefe killeth the soule, and doth restore unto us lowlynes, feare, invocation of Godis name, remembring of our owne weaknes, and of Godis infinite benefites, by Christ receaved; which be the very evident signes that Jesus Christ liveth in us. What signes and tokens of thes presidents hath appeared in you (and others that be in your company) since your first profession of Christ, it nedeth me not to rehearce. God grant that the eyes of men be not blynded to their owne perdicion.[1] Amen.

Presently I maie wryte no more unto you in this matter, Beloved Mother; but as God shal grant unto me more oportunitie, by his grace who geveth all, you shal receave from my handes the rest of Davides mynde in this Psalme. Most ernestlie beseching you in the bowelles of Christ Jesus, paciently to beare your present cross and dolores, which shortlie shal vanish, and after shal never appeare. I can not expresse

---

[1] The two following paragraphs are not contained in either the old printed editions, or in Dr M'Crie's manuscript volume; but in each of these copies after the above words— "blynded to their owne perdicion," the Exposition of the Psalm is continued without break or division, as at the top of page 134, "But to our purpois," &c.

the payne which I thinke I might suffre to have the presence of you, and of others that be lyke troubled, but a few daies. But God shal gather us at his good pleasure: Yf not in this wretched and miserable life, yet in that estate where death maie not dissever us. My dailie praier is, for the sore afflicted in those quarters. Somtyme I have thought that impossible it had bene, so to have removed my affection from the Realme of Scotland, that eny Realme or Nation coulde have bene equall deare unto me. But God I take to recorde in my conscience, that the troubles present (and appearing to be) in the Realme of England, are double more dolorous unto my hert, then ever were the troubles of Scotland. But herof to speake, I now supersede; beseching God of his infinite mercie so to strengthen you, that in the weakest vessels Christes power maie appeare.

My hartie commendacion to all whom effeires: I meane unto such as now boldlie abydeth with Christ. I byd you so hartelie Farewell as can eny wicked and corrupte man do to the most especiall frendes. In great haist and troubled hert, this 6th of Januarij, [1553-4.]

[THE SECOND PART.]

But to our purpois: Deirlie Belovit, accept this cuppe from the handis of our Heavinlie Father, and albeit your panis be almost intollerabill, yit cast your self, becaus yow haif no uthir refuge, befoir the trone[1] of Godis mercie, and with the Prophet David, being in lyke trubill, say unto him:—

Have mercy upon me, O Lord, for I am weak: O Lord, heall me, for all my bonis ar vexit.

Now proceideth David in his Prayer, adding certane caussis why he suld be heard, and obtene his petitionis. But first, we will speak of his prayeris, as thai be in ordour throucht[2] this haill Psalme.

David, in soume[3] desyreth four thingis in this his vehement troubill. In the first verse, he asketh, that God punische him not in his heavie displeasure and wraith. In the secund verse, he asketh, that God suld haif mercie upon him. And in the third verse, he desyreth, that he suld heall him. And in the fourth verse, he asketh, that God suld returne unto him, and that he suld saif his saule. Everie ane of theis thingis wer so necessarie unto David, that lacking any ane of thame, he judgeth him self maist miserabill. He felt the wraith of God, and thairfoir desyreth the same to be removeit. He had offendit, and thairfoir desyreit mercie. He was fallin in most dangerous sicknes, and thairfoir he cryit for corporall health. God appeired to be departit from him, and thairfoir desyreit he that the confort of the Halie Gaist suld returne unto him. And thus was David, not as commonlie ar the maist part of

---

[1] In the old edit. "the throne."
[2] Ib. "through."
[3] Ib. "in summa"; or "in summe."

men in thair prayeris, who, of a consuetude and custome, oftentymes do ask with thair mouthis suche thingis as the hart do not greatlie desyr to obtene.

But lat us mark principallie what thingis ar to be notit in theis his prayeris, whilk he, with ernist mynd, powrit furth befoir God. Evident it is that David in theis his prayeris, susteanit and felt the verie sense of Godis wraith; and also that he understude cleirlie that it was God onlie that trubillit him, and that had laid that soir scourge upon him. And yit no whair else but at God allone (who appeireth to be angrie with him) seeketh he support or ayde. This is easie to be spokin, and the maist part of men will judge it but a lycht matter to flie to God in thair trubillis. I confes, in deid, that yf our trubillis cum be mannis tyranny, that then the maist sure and maist easie way is to rin[1] to God for defence and ayde. But lat God appeir to be oure enemye, to be angrie with us, and to haif left us, how hard and difficill it is then to call for his grace and for his assistance none knaweth, except suche as have learnit it in experience; neither yit can any man so do, except the elect children of God. For so strong ar the enemyis that, with great violence, invade the trubillit conscience in that trubilsum battell, that unles the hid[2] seid of God suld mak thame hoip aganis hoip, thai culd never luke for any delyverance or confort. The flesche lacketh not reassonis and persuasionis to bring us frome God. The Devill, by himself and by his messingeris, dar boldlie say and affirme that we haif nothing to do with God; and a weak faith is oft compellit to confes boith the accusationis and reasonis to be moist trew.

LET THIS BE WEILL NOTIT.

ENEMIES DRIVE US FROM GOD UNDER THIS CROSSE.

In tyme of trubill, the flesche doith reasone, "O wrechit man, perceaveit thow not that God is angrie with thee? He plagueth thee in his hait displeasure, thairfoir it is in vane for thee to call upon him." The Devill, by his suggestioun or by his ministeris, doith amplifie and aggravate theis presidentis,[3] affirmyng

---

[1] "Rin," run.
[2] "Hid," hidden.
[3] "Theis presidentis," that is, these things already mentioned.

and beatting into the conscience of the soir afflictit in this maner. "God plagueth thee for thy iniquitie; thow has offendit his halie law, thairfoir it is labour lost to cry for mercie or relief; for his justice must neidis tak vengeance upon all inobedient offenderis." In this mene seassone, a weak faith is compellit to confess and acknawledge the accusationis to be moist trew; for who can deny that he hath not deservit Godis punishmentis? The flesche feilleth the tormentis, and our awin weaknes cryeth, All is trew, and no poynt can be denyit.

The vehemencie of this battell in the seiknes of Ezechias, and in the historie of Job, playnlie may be espyit. Ezechias, after that, with lamentabill teiris, he had complaynit that his lyfe was takin away, and cut of befoir his tyme; that violence was done unto him, and that God had bruisit all his bonis lyke a lyoun, at last he sayith, "Be thow suretie for me, O Lord;" but immediately upon theis wordis, as it were correcting him selff, he sayith, "What sall I say, it is He that hath done it;" as who suld say, to what purpois compleane I to him? Yf he had any pleasure in me, he wold not haif intreatit me on this maner: It is he him selff whome I thocht suld have bene my suretie and defender, that hath wrappit me in all this wreachit miserie. He cannot be angrie and mercifull at anis (so judgeth the flesche), for in Him thair is no contrarietie. I feill him to be angrie with me, and thairfoir it is in vane that I compleane or call upon him. This, also, may be espyit in Job, who, efter that he was accusit by his freindis, as ane that had deserveit the plague of God; and after that his wyfe had willit him to refuse all justice, and to curse God and so to die; efter his most grevous complayntes, he sayith, Whan I callit upon him, and he hath answerit, yit beleive I not that he hath heard my voce. As Job wold say, So terribill ar my tormentis, so vehement is my pane and anguische, that albeit verilie God hath heard my petitionis, yit feill I not that he will grant me my requeist. Heir is a strong battell, whan perfytlie thow understand that remedie is in none, but in God onlie, and yit from

Godis hand thai luke for no support, as mycht appeir to manis judgement: for he that sayith that God punisseth him, and thairfoir can not be mercifull, and he that doubteth whether God heireth him or not, appeirith to haif cast away all hoip of Godis delyverance.

Theis thingis put I yow in mynd of, Belovit Mother, that albeit your panis sumtymes be so horrible, that no release nor confort ye find, neither in spreit nor bodie, yit yf the hart can onlie sob unto God, dispair not, yow sall obtene your hartis desyre; and destitute ye ar not of Faith. For at suche tyme as the flesche, naturall reasone, the law of God, the present torment, and the Devill, at anis doith cry, God is angrie, and thairfoir is thair nether help nor remedie to be hoipit for at his handis: At suche tyme, I say, to sob unto God is the demonstratioun of the secreit seid of God, whilk is hid in Godis elect childrene; and that onlie sob, is unto God a moir acceptabill sacrifice, than, without this cross, to give our bodies to be brunt, evin for the truthis sake. For yf God be present by assistance of his Halie Spreit, or that no dout is in our conscience, but that assuredlie we stand in Godis favour, what can corporall trubill hurt the saule or mynd? Seing the bitter frostie wind can not hurt the bodie it self, whilk is maist warmlie coverit and cled from violence of the cold.

But when the Spreit of God appeireth to be absent, yea, whan God him selff appeireth to be our enemy, then to say, or to think, with Job in his trubill, "Albeit he suld destroy or sla me, yit will I trust in him." O, what is the strenth and vehemence of that faith, whilk so luketh for mercie, when the haill man feilleth nothing but dolouris on everie syd? Assuredlie that hoip sall never be confoundit; for so it is promissit by Him who can not repent of his mercie and gudnes. Rejoice, Mother, and fight to the end, for sure I am that ye ar not utterlie destitute of that Spreit who taught David and Job. What obedience I have heard yow gif unto God, in your most strong torment, it neideth now not to wryt; onlie I desyre, whilk is a portioun of my daylie prayer, God oure Father, for Chryst Jesus his Sonis sake, that in all your trubill ye may continew as I haif left yow, and that with David, ye may sob, albeit the mouth may not speik, yit lat the hart grone and say, "*Have mercie upon me, O Lord, and heall me.*" And then I nothing doubt your grevous tormentis sall not molest yow for ever, but schortlie sall haif ane end, to your everlasting consolation and confort.

<small>OBJECTION OF THE FLESH.</small> Ye think, peradventure, that ye would gladlie call and pray for mercie, but the knawledge of your synis do hinder yow.

<small>ANSWERE BY A SIMI-LITUDE.</small> Considder, Deirlie Belovit, that all phisick or medecine serveth onlie for the pacient. So doith mercie serve onlie for the synner, yea, for the wreatchit and maist miserabill synner. Did not David understand him selff to be a synner, and adulterer, and a schedder of innocent blude? Yea, knew he not also that he was punissit for his synnis? Yes, verelie he did, and thairfoir he callit for mercie; whilk he that knaweth not the heaviness and multitude of synnis can in no wyse do, but most commonlie dois dispyse mercie when it is offerit; or, at least the man or woman that feilleth not the burdene of syn, lichtlie regardeth mercie, becaus he feilleth not how necessarie it is unto him; as betuix Chryst and the proude Phariseis, in many places of the New Testament it is to be seene. And thairfoir, Dear Mother, yf your adversarie trubill yow either with your synnis past or present, objecting that mercie apperteneth not unto yow by reasone of your synnis, answer unto him as ye ar taught be oure Saviour Chryst Jesus, That the haill neideth no physicioun, neither yit the just mercie, nor pardone; but that our Chryst is cum to gif sycht to the blynd, and to call synneris to repentance, of whome ye acknawledge your selff to be the greattest, and yit that ye doubt nothing to obtene mercie, because it was never denyit to none that askit the same in faith, and thus no doubt ye sall obtene victorie by Chryst Jesus, to whome be prais for ever. Amen.

THE SIXTH PSALM OF DAVID.

In the rest of Davidis prayeris now will we be schorter, that we may cum to the ground of the same.

After the desyring of mercie, now desyreth David a corporall benefit, saying, "*Heall me, O Lord.*" Heirof is to be notit, that bodilie health being the gift of God, may be askit of him without syn, albeit that we understand oure selves to be punissit for our offences. Neither yit in so praying, ar we contrarie to Godis will; for his providence hath plantit in the nature of man a desyre of helth, and a desyre that it may be conserveit. And thairfoir is he not offendit that we ask helth of bodie, when we lack it, neither yit that we seik preservatioun of our helth by suche ordinarie meanis as his Majestie hath apoyntit; provydit alwayis that God him selff be first socht, and that we desyre neither lyfe nor helth to the hinderance of Godis glorie, nor to the hurt or distructioun of utheris oure brethrene; but rather that by us Godis glorie may be promotit, and that utheris, oure brethrene, by our strenth, helth, and lyfe, may be confortit and defendit. Theis presidentis now rychtlie observit, it is no sin ernistlie to aske at God helth of bodie, albeit we knaw oure seiknes to be the verie hand of God punissing or correcting oure former evill lyfe.

This I wryt, becaus sum men ar so seveir, that thai wold not that we suld aske bodilie helth of God, because the seiknes is sent to us by him. But suche men do not rychtlie understand, neither yit considder, that seiknes is a trubill to the bodie, and that God commandeth us to call for his help in all oure trubillis. Surelie, oure submissioun and prayers in suche extremitie, is the greattest glorie that we can gif unto oure God. For so doing, we think that his mercie aboundeth above his judgement, and so we ar bold to pray for the withdrawing of his scourge. Whilk petitioun, no doubt, he must grant; for so he promisseth by Jeremie his propheit, saying, "If I have spokin aganis any natioun or citie, saying, that I will destroy it, and yf it turne from iniquitie, and repent, it sall repent me also of the plagues that I have spokin aganis it." God promisseth to _{JEREM. 18.} _{MARK WELL.}

schew mercie to a whole citie or natioun yf it repent; and will he not do the same to a particular persone, yf, in his seiknes, he call for grace? He hath schewit unto us, that he will, by dyvers exampillis, and speciallie to the leprosie of Miriam,[1] the sister of Moses and Aaron, whilk she ressaveit of the Lordis hand, punissing hir high and haughtie mynd. And agane, upon hir submissioun, and at the prayer of Moses, sche schortlie was restoreit to helth.

But to proceid. David, moirover, prayeth, "*Turne agane, O Lord.*" It appeireth into David, being in the extremitie of his pane, that God was altogether departit frome him; for so alway judgeth this flesche (yea, the haill man) when trubill worketh by any continewance of tyme. David had susteanit trubill many dayis; he had prayit, and yit was not delyverit. And thairfoir judgeth he that God, being offendit for his synis, had left him. And yit plane it is that God was with him, working in his hart, by his Holie Spreit, repentance. Expressing furth thois sobbis and gronis, as also the desyre he had to be restorit to that confort and consolatioun whilk sumtymes he had felt, by the familiaritie whilk he had with God. All theis motionis, I say, wer the operatiounis of Godis Holie Spreit; and yit culd David perceave no confort nor presence of God in his trubill, but lamentabillie complayneth, as befoir ye haif heard. Heirof it is plane, that the verie elect sumtymes ar without all feilling of consolatioun; and that thai think thame selves altogether destitute, as may be sene in David.

But it is cheiflie to be notit, that David in this his anguische remembreth that God sumtymes had bene familiar[2] with him, for he sayeth, "*Turne agane, O Lord,*" signifeing heirby, that befoir he had felt the sueitnes of Godis presence; but now he was left to him self, without feilling of confort or consolatioun. For thus appeireth David to complane: Hast thow not bene familiar with me, O Lord, thy unprofitabill servand? Didest

---

[1] In the old edit. as well as MS. M. it is "Marie."

[2] "Bene familiar," been present.

thow not call me frome keiping scheip, to be anoyntit King over thy people Israel? Didest not thow so incorage my mynd, that I feirit not the fresche strength of the cruell lyoun, nether yit the devouring teith of the hungrie beare; frome whois jawis I delyverit my scheip? Didest not thow anis inflame my hart with the zeale of thy halie name, that when all Israell wer so effrayit that none durst encounter with that monster Goliath, yit thy Majesties spreit maid me so bold and so valiaunt, that without harnes or weaponis (except my sling, staf, and stonis) I durst interpryes singular battell aganis him? Was it not thy awin strenth that gave me victorie, not onlie at that tyme, but also of all uther enemyis that have socht my lyfe since? Hast thou not maid me so glaid by the multitude of thy mercies and thy most gracious favour, whilk thow fra tyme to tyme most aboundantlie hast pourit upon me, that boith saule and bodie hath rejoseit throucht the glaidnes of thy countenance? Hast thow not bene sa effectuallie with me present in trubillis and dangeris, that my verie enemyis have knawin and confessit that thy power was alwayis with me, and that thow didest tak my defence upon thy awin self? And wilt thow now so leif the habitation that thow has chosin? Sall it be left desolat for ever? Can thy mercies have an end, and sall thy fatherlie pitie never appeir moir unto me? Salt thow leif me for ever thus to be tormentit, whome thy gudnes afoir so abundantlie confortit? O Lord, I am sure thy free mercies will not so intreat me; and thairfoir turne agane, O Lord my God; and mak me glad with thy countenance, whome of long tyme thow has left voyd of consolatioun and joy.
<small>IN TRUBILL DAVID REMEMBERET GODIS FORMER WORKIS TO HIM.[1]</small>
<small>WILT THOW FORSAKE THE PURE CREATURE? THAT THOW HES DONE SO MUCHE FOR?</small>

Advert and consider, Deirlie Belovit, in what estait was David when that he had no uthir confort, except the onlie rememberance of Godis former benefittis schewit unto him. And thairfoir mervale ye not, nor yit dispair, yea, albeit that ye find

---

[1] In the first edit., the marginal note reads, "In truble David remembreth what God somtymes had wrought by him."

[2] In the first edit., "Wilt thou forsake thy servaunte that thou haste done so muche for?"

your self in the same case that David was. Sure I am, that your awin hart must confes that ye haif ressaveit evin lyke benefittis of the handis of God as David did. He hath callit yow frome a moir vyle office than from the keiping of scheip, to as great a dignitie (tuiching the everlasting inheritance) as he did David. For, frome the service of the Devill and Sin, he hath anoyntit us preistis and kingis by the blude of his onlie Sone Jesus. He hath gevin yow corage and boldnes to fight[1] aganis enemyis, that be moir neir unto yow than either was the lyoun, the beare, or Goliath to David. Against the Devill, I mene, and his assaltis; against your awin flesche, and most inward affectionis; against the multitude of thame that wer (and yit remane) enemyis to Chrystis religioun; yea, and against sum of your maist naturall freindis, whilk appeir to profes Chryst with yow, and in that part the battell is mair vehement. What boldnes I haif sene with you in all suche conflictis, it neideth not me to reherse. I wryt this to the prais of God, I haif wonderit at that bold constancie whilk I haif found in yow at suche tyme as my awin hart was faynt. Sure I am, that flesche and blud culd never haif persuadit yow to haif contempnit and set at nocht thois thingis that the warld maist estemeth. Ye haif taistit and felt of Godis gudnes and mercies in suche measure, that not onlie ye ar abill to reasone and speak, but also, by the Spreit of God working in yow, to gif confort and consolatioun to suche as wer in trubill. And thairfoir, Deir Mother, think not that God will leif his awin mansion for ever. No, impossible it is that the Devill sall occupie Godis inheritance, or yit that he sall so leif and forsaik his holie tempill, that God will not sanctifie the same. Agane, God sumtyme suspendeth his awin presence frome his elect, as heir by David may be espyit, and verie often suffereth he his elect to taist of bitternes and greif for suche caussis as ar befoir expressit. But to suffer thame to be reft out of his handis,

---

[1] In the old edit., "to fight againste more cruel, more subtle, more dangerous, and against enemyis that be more nye unto you, than either," &c.

THE SIXTH PSALM OF DAVID. 143

that he neither will nor may permit; for so wer he a mutabill God, and gaif his glorie to another, yf he permittit him self to be overcum of his adversarie, whilk is as lyke impossibill, as it is that God sall ceas to be God.

Now last, David prayeth, "*Delyver my saule, and saif me.*" In this prayer, no doubt David desyreit to be delyverit frome the verie corporall death at that tyme, and his saule to be saved frome the present plagues and grevous torments that he susteanit. In whilk it mycht appeir to sum that he was mair addictit to this present lyfe, and that he loved mair the quyetnes of the flesche than it became spirituall man to do. But, as befoir is said, God hath naturallie ingraftit and plantit in man this love of lyfe, tranquillitie, and rest, and the maist spirituall man oftymes desyreth thame. Becaus thai ar seallis and witnessis of that leag¹ and felowschip that is betuene God and his elect. And albeit that trubill maist commonlie doith follow the freindis of God, yit is he nothing offendit that ernistlie we ask our quyetnes; neither is that our desyre any declaratioun of carnalitie or of inordinat love that we haif to the warld, considdering that the finall caus whairfoir we desyre to leif is not for enjoying of worldlie pleasures, for many tymes in the middis of theis, we grant and confess, that better it is to be absent frome the bodie. But the chief caus why Godis elect do desyre lyfe, or to haif rest in earth, is for the maintenance of Godis glorie, and that utheris may sie that God taketh a cair over his elect.

<small>THE MOST SPIRITUALL MAN DESYRETH RESTE.</small>

But now to the groundis and foundationis of Davidis prayeris, and whairupon his prayeris do stand.

1. The First is takin frome the vehement trubill whilk he susteanit, and from the long continewance of the same.

2. The Secund is takin frome the goodness of God.

3. And the Third, frome Godis glorie, and frome the insolent rage of his enemyis.

---

¹ "Leag," and in other places, "leig," league, covenant.

Heir is to be observit and notit, that neither is trubill, neither long continewance of the same, neither yit the proude and hawtie myndis of wickit men, the cheif moving cause why God heireth oure prayeris, and declareth him self mercifull unto us; and thairfoir thai may not be the sure and sound foundationis of our prayeris. But onlie Godis infinit gudnes is the frie fontane of all mercie and grace, whilk springeth and cumeth unto us be Chryst Jesus his Sone. But thai ar caussis, by operatioun of the Holie Spreit, helping oure weaknes to beleive, and to trust that God, who is Father of mercies, will not be angrie for ever at the soir afflictit; neither yit that he will punische without mercie suche as call for his help and confort. As also that God, who hath alwayis declareit him self enemy to pryde, will not suffer the proude and obstinat contempneris of his pure sanctis long to blaspheme his lenitie and gentilnes, but that he will poure furth his plagues upon thame according to his threatnyngis. And sa ar oure trubillis, and the tiranny of oure enemyis in that behalf, fundamentis whairupon our prayeris may stand: As heir appeireth.

David declareth[1] his dolour, and the continewance thairof, in theis wordis:—

I am consumed away with seiknes, all my bones ar vexit, and my saule is in horribill feir. But, Lord, how long wilt thou thus intreat me? I am wearied for sobbing; I watter my bed with my teiris.

Let us think[2] that David thus speiketh: O Lord, mayest thow, who ever hast takin cair for me frome my motheris wombe, now forget me, the workmanship of thy awn handis? Mayest thow, that has declareit thy self so mercifull unto me in all my tribulationis, now in the end tak thy mercies cleane frome me? Hast thow no pitie, O Lord! Dost thou not behold that I am pynit and consumed be this grevous torment, whairin not onlie is my tendir flesche, but also my very bonis (the strongest part of the bodie) so vexit, that neither is thair bew-

---

[1] In the first edit., " describeth." [2] Ib. " Let us ymagyn."

tie nor strenth left unto me? Yf theis anguischeis occupyit the bodie onlie, yit wer the pane almost insufferabill: But, O Lord, how horribillie is my saule tormentit, that, albeit it be immortal, yit it so quaketh and trembilleth as verie death suld devoure it. And thus do I sustene most grevous tormentis, both in bodie and saule, of suche long continewance, that it appeireth unto me thow hast forgotten to be mercifull. O Lord, how long wilt thou intreat me in this manner? Hast thow forgotten thy loving mercies? or hast thow lost thy fatherlie pitie? I have no longer strenth to cry; yea, and for sobbis and groanis I am so werie, that my breth failleth me; the teiris of my eyis, whairwith nychtlie I have wet my bed, hath borne witness of my unfeaned dolour; but now my eyis ar waxin dim, and my haill strenth is dryit up.

In all theis lamentabill complayntes, David speiketh unto God as he wold speik unto a man that wer ignorant what ane uthir man sufferit; whairof it may be understand how the maist prudent and the maist spirituall man judgeth of God in the tyme of trubill. Assuredlie he thocht that God taketh na cair for him, and thairfoir doith he, as it wer, accuse God of unmyndfulnes, and that he lukeit not upon him with the eyis of his accustomit mercie, as cleirlie be theis wordis may be espyit. And yit ar Davidis trubillis the first ground and cause why he maketh his prayeris, and claimeth to be heard. Not that trubillis (as befoir is notit) ar sufficient by thameselves for Godis delyverance, bot, in recompting his dolour, David hath a secreit access to Godis mercie, whilk he challengeit and claimeth of dewtie to apertene to all his, who, in the tyme of trubill call for his support, help, and ayd. And it is the same ground that Job taketh, whair he sayeth, "Is it profitable unto thee that thow violentlie oppress me? Wilt thow dispyse the work of thy awin handis? Thow hast formit and maid me altogether, and wilt thow now devour me? Remember, I beseiche thee, that thow hes fasshionit me as a mould, and that thow shalt bring me to dust. Thow hast coverit me with skin and flesche; with

<small>MERCIE APPERTENETH TO ALL THE CREATURIS OF GOD THAT CALL FOR THE SAME UNFEANEDLY FOR CHRYSTIS SAKE.

JOB 9.</small>

sinewis and bonis hast thow joynit me; with lyfe and comliness hast thow beautifeit me; and thy prudence hath keipit my spreit." Heir may be espyit upon what ground theis tuo stude in thair most grevous paynis. Their trubill moveit thame to compleane, and to appele to the great mercie of God, whilk, as thai alledgeit, evin so it is most sure, he may deny to none that aske it. For as the trubillis of his creatures is none advantage unto God, so to deny mercie when it is asked, wer to deny him self.

And heirin, Deirlie Belovit, I hartelie wische yow to rejoyce, for I can be witness how constantlie ye haif callit for grace in your anguischeis; and your awin conscience must testifie, that oftentymes ye haif found release[1] and confort in sic measure, that ye haif bene bold to triumph against your adversareis, in Chryst Jesus your Saviour. Be not effrayit, albeit presentlie ye feill not your accustomed consolatioun; that sall hurt yow na mair than the trubillis of David and Job did hurt thame, who, in the tyme that thai spak theis former wordis, found na mair consolatioun than ye do now in the maist extremetie of your trubill. Neither yit did thai haistelie obtene confort, for David sayeth, "O Lord, how long wilt thow so cruellie punische me?" And yit we knaw most assuredlie that thai wer heard, and that thai obtenit thair hartis desyre; as, no doubt, everie man sall, that in tyme of trubill, be it spirituall or corporall, appealeth onlie to Godis mercie.

The Second ground and fundatioun whairupoun the prayeris of David do stand, is, the infinit gudnes[2] of God: for thus he sayeth, "*Save me, O Lord, for thy gudnes.*" David befoir had askit mercie, and declared his complayntis; but now serching and reasonyng with himself secreitlie in his conscience efter this maner: Why suld God schaw mercie unto him that so haynouslie had offendit, and that justlie was tormentit by Godis hand for his transgressioun and syn? No other ground, that is

NOTE.

---

[1] In the MS. "releis." [2] Goodness.

THE SIXTH PSALM OF DAVID. 147

alwayis sure and permanent, findeth he except Godis infinit gudnes, whilk he espyeth to be the onlie stay; whilk neither tempest of windis, neither fludis of watter, ar abill to overthraw nor undermynd. And O! how persing ar the eyis of faith, that, in so deip a doungeon of desperatioun, can yit espy, in the middis of theis trubilsum darknessis, plentifull gudnes to remane in our God; yea, and suche gudness as is sufficient and abill to overcum, devour, and swallow up all the iniquiteis of his elect, so that none of thame ar abill to ganestand or hinder Godis infinit gudnes to schew his mercie to his trubillit childrene. <small>THE EYE OF FAITH.</small>

Heirby ar we taught, Belovit,[1] in the extremitie of our trubill, to runne to Godis onlie gudnes; thair to seik confort by Chryst Jesus, and no whair els. I feir nothing the blasphemous voyces of such, nor thair rageing[2] aganis God, and aganis his onlie eternall veritie, that ar not eschamit to affirme that this kynd of doctrine maketh men negligent to do gude workis; aganis whome no uthirwayis will I contend than doith the Apostill, saying, "Thair dampnatioun is just." For my purpois and mynd is to edifie yow whome God hath callit from darknes to lycht, whois eyis it hath pleasit his mercie so to open, that evidentlie thai feill the flesche to rebell aganis the spreit, evin in the hour of thair greattest perfectioun; in suche maner, that all power, all justice, and all vertew proceiding from us is so contaminat and defyllit, that the verie gude workis whilk we do must be purgeit be ane other, and that, thairfore, can none of thame be an infallible ground of oure prayer, neither yit a sufficient cause why we suld be heard. <small>THE CLEANEST WORKIS THAT WE CAN DO AR IN GODIS SYGHT UNCLEANE.[3]</small>

But the gudnes of God, as it is infinit, so can it not be defyllit by our iniquitie; but it perseth throuch the same, and will schaw it self to oure consolatioun, even as the beames of the brycht sone perseth throuch the mistie and thick cloudis,

---

[1] In the old edit. "Beloved Mother."
[2] In the first edit. "raygynges."
[3] In the first edit. this marginal note reads, "The moste purest workes that man can do, are in the sight of God unclene." In the edit. 1580, "The most pure"

and bringeth doun his naturall heit, to confort and quicken suche hearbis and creatures as, throuch violence of cold, wer almost fallin into deadlie decay; and thus the onlie gudness of God remaneth in all stormes, the sure fundatioun to the afflictit, aganis whilk the Devill is never abill to prevaile. The knawledge of this is so necessarie to the afflictit conscience, that without the same it is verie hard to withstand the assaltis of the adversarie. For as he is a spreit most subtill, and vigilant to trubill the Children of God, so it is easie to him to deface and undermynd all the groundis and caussis that be within man; and especiallie, when we ar in trubill; yea, he can persuade that we want thois thingis quhilk, most assuredlie, we haif by Godis free gift and grace.

As, for exampill, yf we desyre to be delyverit frome trubill and anguische of conscience, with David and Job, suddenlie can the Devill object, What apperteneth thair exempill unto thee? They had many notabill and singular vertewis whilk thow lackest. Yf we desyre remission of synnis, with Magdalene, with Petir, or with any uthir offenders, he hath these dartis readie to schute: They had Faith, but thow hast none! They had trew repentance, thow art but ane hypocrite! They haited syn and continewit in gud workis, but thow rejoysest in syn, and doest no gude at all! By these meanis can he who is the accuser of us and of our brethrene, ever find out sum craftie accusatioun to trubill the weak conscience of the afflicted, so long as ever it resteth upon any thing that is within it self; and till, by operatioun of the Halie Gaist, we ar ravischeit and reft up to the contemplatioun of our God, so that our myndis ar fixit onlie upon Godis infinit gudnes, claimyng by the same to ressave mercie; as Job doith in his former wordis, the sense and meanyng whairof is this: O Lord, thow maidest me when yit I was not; Thow gavest me saule and bodie when I neither knew nor understude what thy power was; Thow feddest and nurissit[1] me when I culd do nothing but weip and murne; and

[1] In the old edition, "norishedest," "nourishedst."

thy Majesteis providence unto this day hath preserveit my lyfe; and yit neither I nor my workis culd profit Thee! For Thow (whois habitatioun is in heavin) neidis not the help of man. And as for my workis, suche as the fountaine is, suche must the watter be. My heart is corruptit, how then can any thing that is cleane proceid frome the same? And so, whatever I have ressavit, that either was, is, or heirefter salbe, within my corrupt nature, all proceideth frome thy infinit gudnes, whilk began to schaw thy mercie befoir that I knew thee. Canst thow, O Lord, leave me thus, then, in my extremitie? I grant and confess that I have offendit. But is thair any creature cleane and perfyte in such perfectioun, that without mercie he may abyde the tryell of thy justice? Or is thair any iniquitie now in me whilk thy wisdome did not knaw befoir? And thus appeale I to thy onlie mercie, whilk springeth frome thy infinit gudnes.

O Belovit! when thy afflictit saule[1] can thus forsaik and refuse what ever is in man, and can stay it self (how litill so ever it be) upon Godis infinit gudnes, then ar all the fyrie dartis of the Devill quenchit, and he is repulschit as a confundit Spreit.[2] It sall hurt nothing, albeit the stormie tempest cease not suddanelie; that is sufficient that this anker be cast out, whilk assuredlie sall preserve your schip, that sche violentlie runne not upon the foirland of desperatioun.

This I wryt, Belovit in the Lord, knawing what hath bene your complayntis heirtofoir; in that ye found your faith faynt, that ye culd not repent your former evill lyfe, that ye found no dispositioun nor readines to gude workes, but wer rather careit away of sin and wickitnes. If all this had bene trew, yit had ye bene in no worse case than was the Apostill Paule, when he cryit, "O wretcheit and unhappie man that I am! who sall delyver me frome this bodie of sin?"

But I assuredlie knaw, that the cheif part of your trubill

---

[1] In the first edit. "O deir Mother, when the afflicted soul."

[2] Ib. "Quenched, and he is repulsed as a confounded Spirit."

proceideth frome malice and envy of the Devill, who wold persuade to your hurt, that ye delytit in thois thingis whilk, to yow, wer most displeasing. For how oft have ye complainit upon the weaknes of your faith! How oft have ye lamentit the imperfectioun of your flesche! the teiris of your eyis have witnessit before God that ye delytit not in suche thingis as your adversarie falslie layeth to your charge. For who useth continewallie to murne for thois thingis that are pleasing to his hart, yf thai be present with him at all tymes? Or who will desyre thingis pleasing to be removeit frome him? Ye haif murnit for your weaknes, and haif desyreit your imperfectionis to be removeit; and ye haif detestit all sortis of idolatrie. How then can ye think that ye tak any pleasure in the same! Despair not, althocht all rememberance of Godis gudnes or worthines be removeit frome your mynd. Ye haif David, Job, Daniell, and all uther the Sanctis of God in equall sort with yow. Of David and Job ye haif heard. And Esay, making his heavie complaynt for the plague of the pepill of Israell, opinlie confesseth that all hath synnit, that thair rychteousnes was nothing but filthines; that none socht God; that none callit upon his name. And Daniell, in his prayer, lykewyse confesseth that all had wrocht wicketlie, that all had declynit frome God, yea, that none had submittit thame selves to God, nor yit had maid supplicatioun unto him, albeit he had punissit thair former inobedience; and thairfoir sayeth he, that thai did not alledge thair awin justice in thair prayeris.

Considder, Deir Mother, that no mentioun is maid of any rychteousnes that was within thame selves; neither yit do thai glorie of any workis or vertewis that thai had wrocht befoir; for thai understude that God was authour of all gudnes, and thairfoir to him onlie appertened the prais. But as for thair synnis, thai understude thame to be the infirmiteis of thair awin flesche, and thairfoir boldlie callit thai for mercie, and that onlie be Godis infinit gudnes, whilk is no les frie unto yow than unto thame, according to the ryches of his liberall graces, whilk plentifullie he poureth forth upon all thame that incall the name of the Lord Jesus.

The Thrid and last ground of Davidis prayeris was, The glorie and prais of Godis name to be schawit and utterit in his lyfe, as in theis wordis he declareth, "*For thair is no rememberance of thee in death: Who laudeth thee in the pitt?*" As David wold say, O Lord, how sall I pray and declair thy gudnes when I am deid, and gone doun into the grave? It is not the ordinarie course to have thy miracles and wonderous workis preacheid unto men by thois that ar buried and gone doun into the pit. Thois that ar deid mak no mentioun of thee in the earth: And thairfoir, O Lord, spair thy servand, that yit for a tyme I may schaw and witnes thy wonderous workis unto mankynd. Theis most godlie affectionis in David did engender in him a vehement horrour and fear of death, besydes that whilk is naturall and common to all men, becaus he perfytlie understude that, by death, he salbe lettit any further to advance the glorie of God. Of the same he compleaneth most vehementlie in the 88th Psalme, whair, appeiringlie, he taketh frome thame that ar deid, sense, rememberance, feilling, and understanding; alledgeing that God wirketh no miracles by the deid; that the gudnes of God cannot be preacheit in the grave, nor his faith in perditioun; and that his mervelous workis ar not knawin in darknes. By whilk speacheis we may not understand that David taketh all sense and feilling from the deid, neither yit that thai whilk ar deid in Chryst ar in suche estait, that by God thai haif not consolatioun and lyfe; no, Chryst him self doith witnes the contrarie. But David so vehementlie depressis thair estait and conditioun, because that efter death thai ar depryveit from all ordinarie ministratioun in the Kirk of God. None of thois that ar departit ar appointit to be preacheris of Godis glorie unto mankynd. But efter death, thai ceas any moir to advance Godis halie name heir amangis the liveing on earth; and so sall evin thai, in that behalf, be unprofitabill to the

Congregatioun, as tuiching any thing that thay can do either in bodie or saule efter death. And thairfoir most ernistlie desyred David to live in Israell for the further manifestatioun of Godis glorie.

Heir is to be observeit a schort, but yit a most necessarie note, whilk is this: What ar the thingis that we ought principallie to seik in this transitorie lyfe? Not thois for whilk the blind warld contendeth and stryveth; but God, and his loving kyndnes towardes mankynd, his amiabill promisses, and trew religioun, to be advanced and preached unto otheris, our brethrene, that be ignorant; yf so we do not, we may rather be countit beastis then men, dead stockis nor lyveing creatures; yea, rather thingis that be not at all, then substance haveing either being or lyfe. Seing that the heavenis declair the glorie of God, the earth, with the haill contentes thairof, what ever thai be, do gif prais to his holie name; the sea, fludis, and fontainis, with the wonderis contenit in the same, do not cease to mak manifest the wisdom, the power, and the providence of thair Creatour. What then salbe said of Man, that neither seiketh, neither regardeth Godis glorie? Yea, what salbe judgeit of thois that not onlie hinder Godis glorie, but also declair thame selves enemyis to suche as wold promote it?[1] I must speik my conscience with a sorrowfull hart; they ar not onlie deid, but they ar also of the nature of him by whois malice and envy Death enterit into the warld, that is of the Devill. But thame I omit at this present, because thair accusatioun doith not much appertene to this our matter, whairof now I must mak ane end, sumwhat contrarie to my mynd; for so I am compellit be sum present trubillis as weill of bodie as of spreit.

The Fourt Part of this Psalme I omit to mair opportunitie; for it doith not much appertene to the Spirituall cross, but it is,

[1] The following marginal note, in Dr M'Crie's manuscript volume, is evidently by the amanuensis in 1603, and of course does not occur in the old editions:—" Lord, be mercifull to us in this unthankfull Land, and to Magestratis that stopis the mouthis of his Servandis."

as it wer, a Prophesie, spokin aganis all suche as rejoyce at the trubillis of Godis elect, who assuredlie salbe confoundit, and suddanlie brocht to schame, when the Lord sall heir the voices of his soir afflictit. Now, Deirlie Belovit in our Saviour Chryst Jesus, seing that the Spirituall cross is proper to the children of God, seing that it is gevin to us as a most effectuall medicine, as weill to remove disseasses as to plant in our saullis most notabill vertewis, suche as is humilitie, mercie, contempt of our selves, and continewall rememberance of our awin weaknes and imperfectioun; and seing that ye have had most evident signis that this same medicine hath wrocht in yow a part of all the premisses,[1] ressave it thankfullie of your Fatheris hand, what trubill so ever it bring with it. And albeit that the flesche grudge, yit lat the spreit rejoyce, stedfastlie luking for deliverance; and assuredlie ye sall obtene, according to the gudwill and promeis of Him who can not deceave: To whome be glorie for ever and ever, befoir his Congregatioun. Amen.

Now seing it is uncertane, Belovit Mother, yf ever we sall meit in this corporall lyfe; whilk wordis I will ye tak not in any displeasure, for yf God continew you in lyfe, and me in corporall helth, I sall attempt and assay to speik with you, face to face, within less tyme then is passit since the one of us last saw the uther. And be ye assured, Belovit Mother, that neither sall it be the feir of death, nor the rage of the Devill, that sall impeid or hinder me; and thairfoir I beseik yow, tak not my wordis in that part, as althocht I wer not myndit to visit yow agane: No, I assure yow, that onlie Godis hand sall withhold me. But because oure lyfe doith vanische as the smoke befoir the blast of wind, my conscience moveth me to wryte unto yow, as thocht I suld tak frome yow my last Gud nycht in earth. The summe whairof is this, to exhort and admonische yow, evin as that ye

[1] "All the premisses,"—All that I have spoken of.

will haif part with Chryst Jesus, to continew in the doctrine to the end, whilk befoir the warld ye haif professit.

For, befoir God, befoir Chryst Jesus his Sone, and befoir his Halie Angellis, neither aschame I to confess, nor doubt I to affirme, that the doctrine quhilk ye and others haif heard, not onlie of my mouth, but also faithfullie taught by the mouthis of many utheris, (of whome sum ar exyllit, sum cruellie cast in prisone, and the rest commandit to sylence,) is the onlie word of lyfe, and that all doctrine repugnyng to the same is diabolicall and erronious, whilk assuredlie sall bring death and perpetuall condempnatioun, to all thois whilk thairto sall condiscend and agrie. And thairfoir, Mother, be not moveit with any wind, but stick to Chryst Jesus in the day of this his battell. And also, admonische yow to avoyd that abominatioun, whilk oft ye haif heard by me affirmit to be dampnabill ydolatrie. And God I tak to record in my conscience, that neither then nor now I spak, neither do speake, for pleasure or hatred of any liveing creature in earth, whatsoever that it be; but as my conscience was certifeit by the infallibill and plaine word of God, frome whilk, I prais my maist mercifull Father, I am not this day one jote removeit. Neither repent I of that my blissit and maist happie societie with the treuth of Chrystis Gospell, unto whilk it hath pleasit God to call me the maist wreacheit of otheris. Neither forthink I[1] that God hath maid me ane open and manifest enemye to Papistrie, to Superstitioun, and to all that filthie Ydolatrie, whilk newlie is erectit in Godis hoit displeasure. Neither yit wold I recant (as thay terme it) one sentence of my former doctrine, for all the glorie, ryches, and reste that is in earth.

And, in conclusioun, I wold not bow my knee befoir that most abominabill ydoll[2] for all the tormentis that earthlie tyrantis can devyse, God so assisting me, as his Holie Spreit presentlie moveth me to wryt unfeanedlie. And albeit that I haif in the begynnyng of this battell, appeired to play the faynt-heartit and febill souldeour (the cause I remit to God), yit my prayer is,

---

[1] That is, Neither do I regret. [2] The Romish Mass.

that I may be restoirit to the battell agane. And blessit be God the Father of oure Lord Jesus Chryst, I am not left so baire without confort, but my hoip is to obtene such mercie, that yf a schort end be not maid of all my misercis by finall death, (whilk to me wer no small advantage,) that yit, by him who never despyseth the sobbis of the soir afflictit, I salbe so encourageit to fight, that England and Scotland sall baith knawe that I am readie to suffer more than either povertie or exyle, for the professioun of that doctrine, and that heavinlie religioun, whairof it hes pleasit his mercifull providence to make me, amangis utheris, a simpill souldiour and witness beirer unto men. And thairfoir, Mother, let no feir entir into your hart, as that I, eschaping the furious rage of thois ravening wolves, (that for oure unthankfulnes ar laitlie lousit frome thair bandis), do repent any thing of my former fervencie. No, Mother, for a few Sermonis by me to be maid within England, my heart at this hour culd be content to suffer more that nature wer abill to sustene; as by the grace of the most mychtie and most mercifull God, who onlie is God of confort and consolatioun throuch Chryst Jesus, one day salbe knawin.

In the meane seassone, yit anis agane, and as it wer my finall Gud nycht and last Testament in this earth, in the bowellis of Chryst Jesus, I exhort and admonische yow constantlie to continew with the veritie whilk yit sall triumphe and obtayne victorie, in dispyte of Sathane and his malice. And avoyd idolatrie, the manteneris and obeyeris whairof sall not eschape the suddane vengeance of God, whilk salbe pourit furth upon thame, according to the rypnes of thair iniquitie; and when thai sall cry quyetnes and peace, (whilk never remainit of any continewance with the ungodlie,) then sall thair suddane distructioun cum upon thame without provisioun.

The God of peace and consolatioun, who, of his power infinit and invincibill, hath callit from death the onlie trew and great Bischope of our saullis, and in him hath placeit oure flesche above principalliteis and poweris of what pre-eminence that ever thai be, in heavin or in earth, assist you with his Halie Spreit, in such constancie and strenth, that Sathan and his assaltis be confoundit, now and ever, in yow, and in the Congregatioun, by Chryst Jesus our Lord: To quhome, with the Father and with the Halie Gaist, be all praise and honour eternallie. Amen.

Upon the verie poynt of my journey, the last of Februar, 1553.[1]

Yours with sorowfull hart,

JOHNE KNOX.

Watche and pray.

---

[1] That is, the 28th of February 1553-4, as the year was then reckoned to begin on the 25th of March. This sentence containing the date, is omitted in the old editions.

A GODLY LETTER

OF WARNING OR ADMONITION

TO THE FAITHFULL IN LONDON,

NEWCASTLE, AND BERWICK.

M.D.LIV.

This "Godly Letter," is the first of a series of Admonitions and Consolatory Epistles, which Knox, during his residence on the Continent, addressed to his friends in England. One of the copies has this Postscript: "The peace of God rest with you all, frome ane sore trubillit heart, *upon my departure frome Deip*, 1553, whither, God knaweth." This seems to fix the period to the last of February 1553-4; but the Treatise had been commenced in England. In his Exposition of the Sixth Psalm,[1] he thus mentions it: "I have written a large Treatise touching the plagues that assuredly shall apprehend (or overtake) obstinate Idolaters." It was suggested, no doubt, in accordance with that feeling so strongly expressed, of his willingness to undergo any bodily sufferings, provided he could enjoy a renewed opportunity of preaching the gospel in England.[2] As, however, he could no longer instruct his people by preaching or conversation, he adopted this mode of conveying to them suitable advices, and warnings against defection from the religion which they had professed, or giving countenance to the idolatrous worship now practised by public authority.

For the purpose of giving this "Godly Letter" a wider circulation, it was committed to the press, and the first edition bears the imprint, "From Wittonburge, by Nicholas Dorcaster, Anno 1554, the 8 of May." Two months later, what appears to have been a revised edition, was published along with his Treatise on Prayer (see page 77), under the fictitious imprint, "in Rome, before the Castel of S. Aungel," and it bears the device of Hugh Singleton. Both editions are now of great rarity, more especially the first; but whether either of them

[1] See *supra*, p. 120.   [2] See ib. p. 155.

was printed with the Author's knowledge, or under his immediate superintendence, can only be conjectured. Accurate copies of the title-pages are annexed. The earliest edition is the most correct,[1] and the occasional variations in the second edition may safely be assigned to the printer or editor. A contemporary transcript, preserved among Foxe's Collections, in the British Museum,[2] corresponds very closely with the first printed edition, and was evidently a copy intended for private circulation. The same Tract is also contained in Dr M'Crie's manuscript, from which the present text was at first taken, before I was fully aware of the numerous discrepancies in these copies; and it proved no very easy task to adjust the text, and to avoid overloading the foot notes with various readings. It is however hoped that nothing of any importance has been overlooked.

This Letter of Knox's is written in a very impressive and eloquent manner, highly characteristic of the Author. While pointing out the plagues threatened to such as were idolaters, he encourages those whom he addressed to adhere to their former profession, and escape from the apostasy which generally prevailed. The reader of this Letter, or Admonition, as his learned Biographer remarks, "cannot fail to be struck with its animated strain, when he reflects that it proceeded from a forlorn exile, in a strange country, without a single acquaintance, and ignorant where he would find a place of abode, or the means of subsistance."[3]

---

[1] It may be noticed, that the lines (somewhat varied) on the opposite title-page, form part "of the wordes that Maister John Houper wrote on the wall with a cole, in the New Inne in Gloucester, the night before he suffered."—(*Hooper's Later Writings, Parker Society*, p.xxx.) Bishop Hooper suffered martyrdom on the 9th of February 1555, but this edition of the Admonition in which the lines occur was printed at least nine months earlier, or in May 1554.

[2] MSS. Harl. 416, fol. 47–92.

[3] M'Crie's Life of Knox, vol. i. p. 127.

AN ADMONITION
or vvarning that the faithful
Chriſtiās in London, Newcaſtel, Barwycke, & others, may auoide Gods vengeaūce, both in thys life and in the life to come. Com= pyled by the Seruaunt of God
John Knokes.

The Perſecuted ſpeaketh.

I fear not for death, nor passe not for bands:
  Only in God put I my whole trust,
For God wil requyre my blod at your hands,
  And this I know, that once dye I must:
Only for Christ, my lyfe if I gyue;
  Death is no death, but a meane for to lyue.

VOL. III.   L

In small 8vo, black letter, sign. A to E in 8ˢ. The running title is, "An Admonition to the Faithfull;" and the colophon on the last page:

¶ From Wittonburge by Nicholas Dorcastor. Anno. M.D.Liiii. the . viii . of May.

Cum priuilegio ad imprimendum solum.

A godly let=

ter sent too the fayethfull in London / Newcastell / Barwyke / and to all
other within the realme off Eng=
lande / that loue the cōminge
of oure LORDE Jesus
by Jhon Knox.

Math. 10.
☞ He that continueth unto the ende /
shall be saued.

¶ Imprinted in Rome, before the
Castel of s. Aungel / at the signe of sainct
Peter. In the moneth of July / in
the yeare of our Lord.
1554. (⁂)

In small 8vo, black letter, A to D iiij in 8°. In the opposite title, after the words, in the fourth line, "in godliness to the end," there is added, "With a Declaracion of Prayer, annexeth to the same." This clearly indicates that both tracts had appeared at one and the same time. The Printer's device (as follows) occurs on the last page of each tract.

John Knox, to the faithfull in Londoun, Newcastell, and Barwick, and to all uthiris within the realme of England, that luffeth[1] the cumming of oure Lorde Jesus, wissheth continewance in godliness to the end.

When I remember the feirfull threatnyngis of God, pronunced aganis realmes and nationis, to whome the lycht of Godis Word hath bene offerit, and contemptouslie be thame refusit; as my heart unfeanedlie mourneth for your present estait, Deirlie Belovit in oure Saviour Jesus Chryst, so doith the haill poweris of bodie and saull,[2] trembill and schaik for the plagues that ar to cum. But that Godis trew Word hes bene offerit to the realme of England, can none deny, except suche as be the Devill ar haldin in bondage, (God justlie sa punisching thair proude inobedience,) have neither eyis to sie, nor understanding to discerne gude from bad, nor darkness frome lycht: Aganis whome, at this present, no uthirwyse will I contend, nor did[3] the Prophet Jeremie aganis the stif-nekit and stuburne pepill of Judea, saying, "The wraith of the Lord sall not be turnit away, till he have fulfillit the thochtis of his heart." And thus leif I thame (as of whois repentance thair is small hoip) to the handis of Him that sall not forget thair horribill blasphemeis spokin in dispyte of Chrystis treuth, and of his trew messengeris.[4] And with yow that unfeanedlie mournis for the great shipwrack of Godis trew religion, purpois I to communicat suche counsell and admonitioun, now be my rude pen,[5] as sumtymes it pleasit

LEVIT. 26.
MATTH. 10

1 TIMO. 2.

JEREM. 23

---

[1] In MS. F. and the first edit. "love."
[2] Ib. "the whole powers of my body." [3] Ib. "then did."
[4] Ib. "true minysters."
[5] In MS. F. and the first edit. "now by myne owne pen"; in the second edit. "suche counsailes and admonicions, now by my writinge."

God I suld[1] proclaim in your earis. The end of whilk my Admonitioun is, That evin as ye purpois and intend to avoyd Godis vengeance, baith in this lyfe and in the lyfe to cum; that sa ye avoyd and flie, as well in bodie as in spreit, all felowschip and societie with Idolateris in thair idolatrie.

THE SOWM OF THE ADMONITIOUN.

Ye schrink, I knaw, evin at the first, but gif ane Oratour had the matter in handelling, he wald prove it honest, profitabill, easie, and necessarie to be done: And in everie ane poynt wer stoir yneugh for ane lang orisone.[2] But as I never labourit to persuade any man in matteris of religioun, (God I tak to recorde in my conscience,) except by the verie simplicitie and playne infallible trewthe[3] of Godis Word, no more intend I to do in this behalf. But this I affirme, that to flie from idolatrie is sa profitabill and sa necessarie for a Christiane, that onles he sa do, all warldlie profit turneth to his disprofit and perpetuall condemnatioun. Profit either pertenis[4] to the bodeis or to the saullis of oure selves, or of oure posteritie. Corporall commoditeis consistis in suche thingis as man cheiflie covetis for the bodie; as ryches, estimatioun, lang lyfe, helth, and quyetnes in earth. The onlie confort and joy of the saule, is God by his Word expelling ignoraunce, syn, and death, and in the place of theis planting trew knawledge of him self, and with the same, justice,[5] and lyfe be Chryst Jesus his Sone. Gif either profit of bodie or of saule move us,[6] than of necessitie it is that we avoyd idolatrie. For plane it is, that the saule hes neither lyfe nor confort, but by God allone, with whome idolateris hes no uther fellowschip nor[7] participatioun than hes the devillis. And albeit that abhominable idolateris triumphe for a moment, yit approcheis the hour when Godis vengeance sall stryke not onlie thair saullis, but evin thair vyle

TO FLIE IDOLATRIE IS PROFITABILL AND NECESSARIE.

DIVISION OF PROFIT.

CORPORALL COMMODITIE.

THE JOY OF THE SOULE.

1 CORI. 6.

---

[1] In the second edit. "I did."

[2] Supplication or discourse: In MS. F. and the old editions, "a lang oration."

[3] In MS. M., "except be verie simplicitie."

[4] In the first edit. "aperteyneth eyther;" in the second edit. "aperteyning either."

[5] Righteousness.

[6] In MS. F. and the old editions, "Yff any of these aforsaid move us."

[7] In MS. F. and the first edition, "fellowschip nor," omitted.

carcassis salbe plaguit, as befoir he hes threatnit.¹ Thair cities LEVI. 26.
salbe brunt, thair land salbe laid waist, thair enemyis sall dwell
in thair strangholdis, thair wyffis and thair dochteris salbe de- JEREM. 4.
fyllit, thair children sall fall in the edge of the sworde; mercie
sall thai find none, becaus thai haif refusit the God of all mer- LEVIT. 26.
cie, when lovinglie and lang he called upon thame. Ye wald
knaw the tyme, and what certaintie I haif thairof. To God
will I appoynt no tyme, but thir and ma plagues sall fall upon
the Realme of England, (and that or it be lang, except repentance prevent,) I am sa sure as that I am that my God liveth.

This, my affirmatioun, sall displease many, and sall content
few. God, wha knaweth the secreitis of all hartis, knaweth
that it also displeaseth my self, and yit lyke as of befoir, I haif
bene compellit to speik in your audience, and in audience of
uthiris, sic thingis as was not plausibill to the earis of men,
whairof, allace! ane great part is this day cum to pass; so I
am compellit to wryt, with the teiris of my eyis, I knaw to your
displeasure. But, Deir Brethrene, be subject unto God, and
gif place to his wraith, that ye may eschape his everlasting
vengeance. My pen, I trust, sall now be na mair vehement,
nor my toung hes bene oftner than anis, not onlie befoir yow,
but also befoir the cheif of the Realme. What was said in
Newcastell and Berwick befoir the Sweitting seiknes,² I trust
sum in thai partis³ yit beiris in mynd. And upon the day of
All Sanctis (as thai call it), in the yeir that the Duck of Somerset was last apprehendit,⁴ let Newcastell witness!⁵ What befoir

---

¹ In MS. F. and the old editions, "as God before hath threatned."

² Ib. "the Sweate." This fatal and infectious disease was prevalent in England during the reign of Edward the Sixth. A letter from the Duke of Northumberland, printed by Mr Tytler, describes its symptoms as exhibited when his daughter died, 2d June 1552:—"The night before she died, she was as merry as any child could be."—(*England under the reigns of Edward VI. and Mary*, vol. ii. p. 115.)

³ Ib. "in those places."

⁴ Edward Seymour, Duke of Somerset, and Lord Protector of England, was finally apprehended 16th October 1551. He was tried and executed on Tower Hill, 22d January 1552.

⁵ In the second edition, these words are placed in the margin.

him that then was Duck of Northumberland, in mo places nor one.[1] What befoir the Kingis Majestie, whom God hes callit from warldlie miserie for our offences, at Wyndsoir, Hamptoun Court, and Westminster.[2] And finallie, what was spokin in Londone in mo places nor ane, when fyreis of joy and ryottous banketting wer at the proclamatioun of Marie, your Quene.[3] Gif men will not speik, yit sall the stanis and tymber of thai places crye in fyre, and sall beir record that the treuth was spokin, and sall absolve me in that behalfe in the day of the Lord.

Suspect not, Brethrene, that I delyte in your calamiteis, or in the plagues that sall fall upon that unthankfull Natioun. No, God I tak to recorde that my heart mourneth within me, and that I am cruciate[4] with rememberance of your trubillis: But gif I suld ceas, then suld I do aganis my conscience, as also aganis my knawledge, and so suld I be guiltie of the blude of thame that perischeth for lack of admonitioun, and the plague not a moment the langer be delayit. For the Lord hes appoyntit the day of his vengeance, befoir the whilk he sendis his trompettis and messingeris, that his elect, watcheing, and praying, with all sobrietie, may, be his mercie, eschaipe the vengeance that sall cum.

But ye wald knaw the groundis of my certitude; God grant that hearing thame ye may understand and stedfastlie beleive the same. My assurances are not the Mervallis of Merlin,[5] nor yit the dark sentences of prophane Prophesies; But (1.) the plane treuth of Godis Word; (2.) the invincibill justice of the everlasting God; and (3.) the ordinarie course of his punishmentis and

---

[1] In the old editions, "in the towne of Newcastell, and in other places mo."

[2] That is, when Knox was officiating in his turn at these places, as one of the preachers to Edward the Sixth.

[3] On the 20th of July 1553, when Lady Jane Gray, who had previously been proclaimed Queen, was deposed.

[4] "I am cruciate," suffering excruciating sorrow.

[5] Referring to the vague but popular predictions, under the names of Merlin the magician, Beid, Berlington, and others, which long continued in both countries to be accommodated by the minstrel-poets to passing events.

plagues from the begynning, ar my assurance and groundis. Godis Word threatneth distructioun to all inobedient; his immutabill justice must¹ requyre the same. The ordinary punishmentis and plagues schawis exempillis. What man then can ceis to prophesie? The Word of God planelie speikis, that gif a man sall heir the curses of Godis Law, and yet, into his heart, sall promeis to him self felicitie and gude luck, thinking that he sall haif peace, albeit he walk efter the imaginatiounis of his awn will and heart; to sic a man the Lord will not be mercifull, but his wrath salbe kendillit aganis him, and he sall distroy his name from under Heaven. How the Lord threatneth plague efter plague, and ever the last to be soirest, whili, finallie, He will consume realmis and nations gif they repent not, reid the twenty-sixth chaptour of Leviticus; whilk chaptour oft haif I willit you to mark, and yit I do unfeanedlie. And think not it apperteaneth to the Jewis onlie. No, Brethrene, the Prophetis ar the interpretouris of the Law, and thai mak the plagues of God commoun to all offenderis. The punishment ever begynneth at the houshald of God. DEUT. 28. JERM. 5. AMOS 3. DEUT. 29. LEVI. 26.

And heir must¹ I touche a poynt of that devilische Confessioun maid, (alas!) by the miserabill man, whois name, for sorrow, I can not recyte.³ This argument usit he to preve the doctrine of lait yeiris, preicheit in the realme of England, to be wickit:⁴ "Trubillis and plagues (said he) hes followit the samyn, not onlie heir in England, but also in Germanie," as he willit yow to mark. This fragill and vaine argument at this tyme na uthirwayis will I labour to confute, then be plane and NORTHUMBERLAND. 2

---

¹ In MS. M. "man," and "maun."

² In MS. F. and the first edit. "The Duke of Northumberland's Confession." In the second edit. "The wicked protestation of the late Duke of Northumberland, at the hour of his death, agaynste hys owne conscience in hope off lyfe."

³ It is to be noticed, that John Dudley, Earl of Warwick and Duke of Northumberland, deceived by hopes of pardon, professed to be a Papist at the time of his death, 22d August 1553. The Duke's Confession is printed by Mr Tytler in his *Edward VI. and Mary*, vol. ii. p. 230.

⁴ In the second edit. "This argument he useth to prove the doctrine of late years done, taught amongst yow to be wicked."

evident Scriptures; declareing that the vengeance and plagues of God do appertene to all inobedient,[1] howbeit he begyn to punische whair his graces hes bene offerit and obstinatelie refuseit. And that is the cause why Germanie and England hes bene plaguit thir yeiris bypast; whilk may be an ansueir to the blind rage of ignorantis, who never will knaw the verie cause of Godis plagues.

ESAY 13, 15, 17, 18, 19.
JEREM. 50, 51.
EZEC. 25, 26, 27.

The Scriptures declaring God to punische all nations, efter he hes correctit his awn pepill, ar writtin be the Prophetis Esay, Jeremie, and Ezekiell, as also be uthiris; who, efter thai had proclamed and denunced plagues to fall upon the pepill of Israel, and upon the house of Juda, for the contempt of God and of his Law, prophesies also aganis certane Nationis and Citeis, not onlie adjacent to Jerusalem, but also aganis suche as wer fer distant; as aganis Moab, Ammoun, Egypt, Palestina, Tirus, Damascus, and aganis Babilone. And, in conclusioun, generall Prophesies wer spokin aganis all inobedient, as in the twenty-fourth chapter of Esay planlie appeiris.

JEREM. 25.

As also, the Lord commandeth Jeremie to gif the cuppe of his wraith to all nationis round about, who suld drink of the same althocht thai refuseit it of his hand; that is, albeit thai wald not beleive the threatnyngis and voyce of the Prophet, yit suld

JEREM. 6.

thai not eschaip the plagues that he spak; "For everie Natioun lyke unto this will I punische, sayeth the Lord of Hoistis."

AMOS 9.

As also, Amos agreeth with him, saying, "The eyis of the Lord ar upon everie synfull Natioun, to rute it oute of the earth."

Theis, and many mo places, evidentlie preveis[2] that the plagues spokin in the law of God, do appertene to everie rebellious pepill, be thai Jew or be thai Gentill; Christianis in titill,

---

[1] In MS. F. and the old editions, the rest of this sentence reads, "beginning fyrste where Godis mercies hath bene offered, and obstinatlye refused; and that may aunswere the blynde rage of ignorauntes;" or, "of ignoraunce." And the next sentence, omitting the first part of it as above, begins, "The Prophetes Esai, Jeremi, and Ezechiell, after they had proclamed plagues to fall upon the people of Israel, and upon the house of Juda, prophecied particularly against certain Nations," &c.

[2] Ib. "evidently prove."

or Turkis in professioun. And the ground and assurance of the Prophetis wes the samyn, whilk I haif rehersit to be my assurance, that England salbe plagued; that is, Godis immu-tabill and inviolabill Justice, whilk can not spair in a realme and natioun the offences that he maist seveirlie punissis in another; for so wer he inequale, and maid difference as tuiching executioun of his just judgmentis betuix realme and realme, and betuix persone and persone, whilk is maist contrarious to the integritie of his Justice. For as the ryghteous Judge of the haill Earth can not distroy the just with the wickit, so can he not spair a sort of obstinat malefactouris and punische another;[2] as Himself witnesseth be the Prophet Jeremie, saying, "I haif begun to punische in the house whair my name is incallit, and sall I spair the rest?" As the Lord God wald say, How can my Justice suffer and permit their crymes and offenssis unpunissit in proude contempnaris, wha neither regardis me nor my law, seing I haif not spareit my awn pepill and children, who externallie beiris sum reverence to my name? The Justice of God.[1] Jerem. 25.

That God hath punissit other nationis and realmes neidith no probatioun, for experience doth teache it.[3] But whether lyke crymes hes bene, and yit ar committit within the realme of Ingland, as wer committit in those Nationis befoir thair last destructioun, that is to be inquyreit. In this case, nothing can better instruct us than Godis plane word, rebuking the vyces that rang in thai dayis.[4] And omitting to recyt all,[5] it sall suffice to rehers for this present sum places of the Prophet Jeremie, the tyme of whois prophesie, weill considderit, sall mak the matter mair sensibill, and better to be understude. He begynnis his prophesie in the 13 yeir of King Josias his England synfull.

---

[1] In MS. M., on the margin, "God can not spair in a Realme thai crimes that he hes punissit in another."

[2] The previous words of this sentence are not found in MS. F. or the old editions, which read: "Thus he speaketh by Jeremy his prophet, 'Behold, I haif,' &c."

[3] In the first edit. "That God hath punyshed other Realmes and Nations, men of small understanding will easily confesse."

[4] Ib. "which raigned in those daies."

[5] In the old editions, "And omitting all such as prophesied before."

reign, and continewith till efter the destructioun of Jerusalem, whilk came in the eleventh yeir of the ring of King Zedikias.

[Long[1] preached this godly man, to wite, thirty and nyne yeares and sixe monethes,[2] before the uttermost of the plagues apprehended this stubborne nation, and that he did with much troble and injurie susteined, as in his Prophesyes[3] is to be sene. Be all lykelyhood then, there were some Cob Carles, that wer not pleased with the Prophet,[4] neither yit with hys preachinges. And yit plane it is, that no Kyng so truly turned unto God with all hys heart, with all hys soule, and with all hys strength, according to all the law of Moyses, as did Josias; and yit (as said is) the Prophet of God was troubled, and that not by a mene number, for I fynd hym complaining universally and generally upon the peoples iniquitie, for thus induceth he[5]] God speakinge: "My people hes committit dowbill iniquitie, thay haif forsakin me the fountane of liveing watter, and hes diggit unto thame selves cisternis that can conteine no watter. Why will you justifie thy awn way? sayeth the Lord. Under thy wingis ar found the blude of the saullis of the pure innocentis, whome thow found not in corneris; and yit thow sayis, I am innocent. Thow hes gottin ane horische foirheid:[6] thow can not think schame: my pepill is fulische, thai knaw not me; thai ar fulische childrene, and hes no wisdome: wyse thai ar to commit mischeif, but to do gude thai ar altogether ignorant. Everie man may be war of his nychtbour, and no man assured-

JEREM. 2.
NOTE WEILL.

JEREM. 3.
JEREM. 4.

JEREM. 9.

---

[1] In Dr M'Crie's manuscript volume, in place of the sentences inclosed within brackets, the passage reads as follows: "Sa that the haill tyme of his preaching befoir the plages come, was xxxix yeiris and sex monethis; sa lang preached and prophesied that godlie man amang that stubborne Natioun, with mekill trubill and mokyng sustenit, as by his complayntis evidentlie appeiris. For this induceis he, God speaking: 'My pepill,' &c."

[2] In the first edit. "two monethes."

[3] Jeremiah began to prophesy, B. C. 629. Jerusalem was taken, B. C. 588. An interval of nearly forty-one years. —(*Townshend's Chronology of the Old Testament.*)

[4] In the second edit. "proffit."

[5] Ib. "not by no small number, for, &c., thus judgeth he God speakinge."

[6] Ib. "a whoores forehead."

lie may trust in his brother, for everie man is becumin deceat- <small>THE OF-FENCES OF JUDA BE-FORE THE CAPTYVI-TIE.</small>
full; thay haif practisit thair toungis to leis and guyle. Thay
haif left my law, sayeth the Lord, and hes followit the wickit
imaginatiounis of thair awn hairtis. They haif followit efter
Balaam whome thair fatheris teachit thame."

Of these, and of many mo places lyke, the generall offences of
that pepill appeiris to haif bene, defectioun frome God, embrassing of fals religioun, schedding of innocent blude, justificatioun of thame selves, and defence of thair iniquitie; while yit
thay aboundit in reif, murther, oppressioun, leis, crafty practeis,
deceat, and manifest idolatrie, following the tred[1] of thair fa- <small>JEREM. 5.</small>
theris; who, under Manasses and Ammon Kingis, (of whome the
ane in the begynning, the other all his lyfe, maintainit ydolatrie,)
had bene the ring leaderis to all abominatioun, suche as in
Englande ar Winchester[2] and mo.

The Prophet of God, wondering at suche manifest iniquitie,
judgeit that sic ignorance and inobedience was onlie among the
rascall sort of men, and thairfoir he sayis, " Theis be but pure <small>JEREM. 4.</small>
anis; for lack of wisdome thai ar fulische, thai knaw not the way
of the Lord, nor the judgement of thair God. I will go to the
Nobillis, and I will talk with thame; for thai knaw the way of
the Lord, and the judgmentis of thair God." But what he
findeth amang that sort, he declaris in theis wordis: "Thay haif
all brokin the yoke, and thay haif heipit sinne upon sinne, and
mischeif upon mischeif;[3] from the least unto the maist thai ar <small>EZEC. 8.</small>
all bent upon avarice, and thay gape for lucre; from the preist
to the propheit, everie man dealleth disceitfullie. Behold, thair
earis ar uncircumcisit thay can not advert; the Word of God
is a rebuke unto thame, thay delyte not in it. Thay haif
committit abominabill mischeif; thay can not repent, neither
think schame."

---

[1] In the old edit. "trade," or footsteps.

[2] Stephen Gardiner, Bishop of Winchester, and Lord Chancellor of England. He died in November 1555.

The latter words of this sentence occur only in MS. M.

[3] In the old edit. "one mischeif upon another."

[What this abhominatioun was, God sheweth to Ezechiell: all had forsaken God in thair heartes, insomuch, that a great nomber openlie had turned thair backes unto God, and made sacrifice to the Sunne, every man in his owne secret closet; yea, women mourned, for that they were not permitted to commit open abhominatioun. Is it not to be wondered that all Estates were so corrupte under so godlye a Prince? But our Prophet Jeremie proceadeth in his complaintis, saying,][1]

JEREM. 5. "Thay haif denyit the Lord, and said it is not he, (that is, thay haif denyit and oppugnit Godis Word,) that it is not the treuth, for thay haif said, We sall neither see sword nor honger." This was the obedience that this Prophet found amang the Princes of Juda, as also amang the commoun pepill.[2] And is it not to be wonderit at, that the vyneyaird that wes sa weill

HERKEN ENGLAND. manurit brocht furth na better grapes? Thay had a King maist godlie myndit,[3] for so witnesseth the Halie Gaist of him, "That thair was no king that so trewlie turnit to God with all his heart, with all his saule, and all his strength, according to all the law of Moses, as did Josias." Thay had Prophetis (for Jeremie was not allone) most faithfull and fervent. Thay wer admonissit be dyvers plagues; and ever the Prophetis callit for repentance. And yet nothing followit but opin contempt of

OSEI. 6. God and of his messingeris. "Thair repentance," sayis Hosie, "is lyke the mornyng dew, it abydis not. Albeit thay can say,

JEREM. 5. 'The Lord leivis,' yit ar[4] thair oathes nothing but leis. Find me ane man that doith equitie and justice, and to him will I be mercifull, sayeth the Lord." Heir was narrow inquisitioun amang so great a multitude. Great scarcitie of gude counsalouris with so godlie a King; for belyke thair hes not bene many, when that He who knawis the secreitis of hartis so earnistlie

---

[1] The words enclosed within brackets are not in MS. M., but are found in MS. F. and the early printed copies.

[2] In MS. M. is this note: "Whidder the lyk was, or is, in England, lat sic as ar not blind judge, and allace! this day, for our selves."

[3] The rest of this sentence is omitted in the second edit.

[4] In the old edit. "The Lord lyveth, yet were."

seiketh for one man.¹ But before we proceid further in this matter, it salbe necessarie² to sie how theis presidentis dois agrie with oure estait and tyme.

And First, that we had not Godis Word trewlie preachit amangis us, will none, except ane errent and dispytfull Papist,³ deny. We had ane King of sa godlie dispositioun towardis vertew and the treuth of God, that none⁴ from the begynning passit him; (and to my knawledge, none of his yeiris did ever matche him in that behalf, gif he mycht haif bene lord of his awn will). In this meane tyme, yf synnis did abound, lat everie man accuse his awn conscience. For heir I am not myndit to specifie all that I knaw; neither yit is it necessarie, seing sum crymes wer so manifest and haynous that the Earth culd not hyde the innocent blude; neither yit culd the Heavens behold, without schame, the craft, the deceit, the violence, and oppressioun that universallie wer wrocht;⁵ and in the meane seasoun, the hand of God was busie over us, and his trew messingeris keipit not silence.

COMPARISON BETWIXTE ENGLAND AND JUDA BEFORE THE DESTRUCTION.

KYNG EDWARD THE SIXTH.

Ye knaw that the realme of England wes visited with dyvers and strange plagues, and whether that it was not ever propheseit (unless that with more obedience we embrace Godis Word) that the worse plagues was to follow, I appele to the testimony of your awn conscience. But what ensewit heirupon? Allace! I eschame to reherse it. Universall contempt of all Godis admonitiounis; haitred of thame that rebukeit vyce, authorising of thame that could invent most villany aganis the preacheris of Godis Word. In this matter, I may be admittit for a sufficient witness; for I heard and saw, I understude and knew, with the sorrow of my heart, the manifest contempt and craftie devyces of the Devill aganis those most godlie and learnit Preacheris that this last Lent, Anno M.D.LIII., wer appoyntit to preache befoir the Kingis Majestie; as also, aganis all utheris whose toungis

WITNESS CERTEYNE BALLATES.

1553.

---

¹ In MS. F. and the old editions, "searcheth so diligently."
² Ib. "salbe profitable."
³ Ib. "excepte ane arrant Papist."
⁴ In the old edit. "towards vertue, and chiefly towards God's truth."
⁵ Ib. "and wrong, that openly was wrought."

wer not temperat with the halie watter of the Court; planelie to speak, wha culd not flatter aganis thair conscience, and say[1] all wes weill, and na thing neidit Reformatioun. What reverence and audience, I say, wes gevin to the Preacheris this last Lent by suche as than wes in autoritie,[2] thair awn consciences[3] declairit; assuredlie, evin suche as be the wickit Princes of Juda wes gevin to Jeremie. Thay haitit such as rebukeit vyce, and stubburnlie thay said, we will nocht amend. And yit how boldlie thair synnis were rebukeit, evin in thair faces, suche as wer present can witness with me.

Almost thair wes none that occupyit the place, but he did prophesie and planelie speake the plagues that ar begun and assuredlie sall end. MAISTER GRINDALL[4] planelie spak the death of the Kingis Majestie; complaynyng on his houshald servandis and officeris, who neither eschameit nor feirit to raill aganis Godis trew Word, and aganis the Preacheris of the same. The godlie and fervent man, MAISTER LEVER,[5] planelie spak the desolatioun of the commoun weill, and the plagues whilk suld follow schortlie. MAISTER BRADFURDE (whome God for Chrystis his Sonis sake comfort to the end!)[6] spared not the proudest, but boldlie declareit that Godis vengeance suld schortlie stryke thame that then wer in autoritie, becaus thay abhorrit and loathed the trew Word of the everlasting God. And, amangis many uthir, willit thame to tak exempill be the lait Duck of Somerset,[7] who became so cold in hearing Godis Word, that the

MAISTER GRINDALL.

MAISTER LEVER.

MAISTER BRADFURD.

---

[1] In MS. F. and the old editions, "were not tempered by the holy water of the Court, to speake it plainlye, who, flatteringe agaynste their own consciences, culd not saye."

[2] In the margin of MS. M., "Our case, this day, 1603."

[3] In the old edit. "their owne countenances."

[4] Dr Edmund Grindall. In the reign of Queen Elizabeth, he was successively Bishop of London, Archbishop of York, and afterwards of Canterbury.

[5] Thomas Lever, a learned, zealous Protestant minister, and one of the King's Chaplains in Ordinary. He afterwards obtained preferment at Durham, but was ejected for non-conformity.

[6] At this time John Bradford was imprisoned. He suffered martyrdom at Smithfield, on the 1st of July 1555.

[7] Edward Seymour, Earl of Hertford and Duke of Somerset, uncle of Edward the Sixth, was executed on the 22d of January 1552.

year befoir his last apprehensioun, he wald ga visit his masonis, and wald not dainyie himself to ga frome his gallerie to his hall for heiring of a sermone.¹ "God punissit him (said the godlie Preacher) and that suddanelie, and sall He spair yow that be dowbill mair wickit? No, He sall not! Will ye, or will ye not, ye sall drink the cuppe of the Lordis wrath. *Judicium Domini, Judicium Domini,* The judgement of the Lord, The judgement of the Lord;" lamentabillie cryit he, with weipping teiris.² MAISTER HADDON³ most learnedlie oppinit the causes of the bypast plagues, affirmyng⁴ that the worse wer to follow, unless repentance suld schortlie be found. This then, and mekill mair, I herd planelie spokin, efter that the haill Counsaile had said, Thay wald heir no mo of thair sermonis: thay wer but indifferent fellowis; (yea, and sum of thame eschameit not to call thame pratting knaves).⁵ But now will I not speik all that I knaw; for yf God continew my lyfe in this trubill, I intend to prepair ane dische for such as than led the ring in the Gospell; but now thay haif bene at the scule of Placebo,⁶ and amangis ladyis hes lernit to dance, as the Devill list to pype. Agaynst those whom God hath stryken, seeing now

MAISTER HADDON.

---

¹ This sentence in the second edition is thus abridged :—" And willed them to take exemple by a noble man, who became so colde in hearing Godis worde that the yeare before his death, he would not disease hymself to heare a sermon."

² In MS. F. and the printed copies, " cryed he with a lamentable voyce, and weaping teares."

³ Dr Walter Haddon, celebrated for his eloquence and learning, was, for a short period, President of Magdalene College, Oxford. He was Master of Requests to Queen Elizabeth. His Latin Orations and Epistles were collected in a posthumous volume, 1567. The Queen being asked whether she preferred Haddon or Buchanan as men of learning, answered, " Buchananum omnibus antepono, Haddonum nemini postpono."

⁴ In MS. F. and the first edit. " and assured them that the worse wer after to come."

⁵ This sentence in MS. F. and the two old editions, runs thus : " Muche more I harde of these foure, and of others, which now I may not rehearce; and that (which is to be noted) after that the whole Counsail had sayd, Thay wolde heare no mo of their sermons, (thay were undiscreate felowes, yea, and prating knaves)."

⁶ Of pleasing men. From the Lat. "I will please," applied to designate a Parasite.—(*Jamieson's Dictionary.*)

resteth to them no place of repentance, nothing mynd I to speake. But such as lyve to this day would be admonished, that He who hes punished the one will not spair the rest, gif thay be found lyke wicked and treasonabill.¹ But to our purpois.

Thir presidentis I judge sufficient to prove the haill multitude, and all estaitis in this oure age, to haif bene, and yit to remaine, lyke wickit, yf thay be not worse, with thame against whome Jeremie did prophesie. Now let us sie what followit in Juda; mischeif upon mischeif, while, finallie, in the Lordis anger, he tuke away King Josias, becaus he was determinat to distroy Juda, as befoir he had distroyit Israell. Efter the death of this godlie King great was the trubill, dyverse and suddane wer the alterationis of that Commounwealth: The Kingis wer takin prisoneris ane after another in schort space; And what uther wer the misereis of that stubburne natioun, O God, for thy great mercies sake, lat never thy small and soir trubillit flock within the realme of England preve nor learne in experience! But in all their trubillis no repentance appeirit, [as by the Prophet ye may learne, for thus he cryith, "Thou hast stryken them, O Lorde, but they have not mourned; thou hast destroyed them, but they have not receaved discipline. Thay have hardened thair faces harder than stanes, thay will not convert. The whole land is wasted, but no man will wey, ponder, and consider the cause. This people will not heare my worde. Thay walk in the wicked invention of thair awn hartes. Thay go after other goddes to worship and serve them. And of the prophetis naturall frendes of the men of Anathotes, some plainlie said, 'Speake no more to us in the name of the Lorde, least thou dye in our handes.'" Belyke these men had smal fantasye of Godis prophet.]² But mair and mair

---

¹ This sentence differs in the various copies by the omission, or slight variation of some of the words.

² The words within brackets are supplied from MS. F. and the old copies; but it will be observed, that the same passage, with some slight variations, is introduced again at page 179. See note 3, page 181.

the pepill wer bent upon idolatrie, as be ane sermone (and that whilk conseivit upon the same), maid in the beginning of the ring of Jehoikim, sone to Josias, is evident. For be God the Propheit was commandit to stand in the entress of the Lordis house, and to speik to all the cieties of Juda that come to wirschip in the house of the Lord; and was commandit to keip no word aback, gif peradventure, sayeth the Lord, thay will herkin and turne everie man frome his wickit way. Heir is to be notit, that immediatlie efter the death of the gude King, thay wer entirit into iniquitie, frome whilk God, be his Prophetis, labourit to call thame aback, befoir he began to plague thame moir extremelie.[1]

The tennour of the Sermone was this: "Thus sayeth the Lord, Gif ye will not obey, to walk in my lawis whilk I have gevin yow, and to heir the wordis of my servandis the Prophetis, whome I send to yow, ryseing up betymes, and still sending; gif ye will not heir thame, (I say) then will I do unto this house as I did unto Silo, and will mak this citie to be abhorrit of all pepill in the Earth. Hear not the wordis of the Prophetis that say unto yow, Ye sall not serve the King of Babylone. I haif not sent thame, sayeth the Lord, howbeit thay ar bold to prophesie lyes in my name. Gif ye gif eare unto thame, baith ye and your fals prophetis sall perische." JEREM. 26. JEREM. 27.

Heir is first to be notit,[2] as befoir we haif tuichit, that immediatlie efter the death of thair King, whais studie and ernest diligence wes to rute out all monumentis of superstitioun and idolatrie, the pepill efter his death, I say, with haill consent, revoltit back to ydolatrie; for such is the ingyne of this oure corrupt nature, that no religioun can content nor please us, except

---

[1] This sentence is not contained in the old printed copies.

[2] In MS. F. and the two old edition, in place of the following paragraph, there is this sentence: "Here is first to be noted, that the people was alreddy entered into iniquitie, and especially (straighte after the death of thair King,) into idolatry; from which the Lorde by his Prophet labored to call them backe, threatning unto them desolation yf they proceded to rebel."

that whilk we oure selves haif devysit.¹ For lyke as the wisdome of the maist wyse erthlie man in Godis presence is nothing but fulischnes, so ar the ordinances of God in manis presence so wickit and so bair, that man alwayis thinkis he can devyse ane mair perfyt honoring of God than that whilk him self hath commandit: Witness the Ysraellittis in the Desert; the Ten Trybis under Jeroboam; the Phariseis and the rest of the sectis in Chrystis tyme; and the Papistis befoir and in oure own tyme. For lat any of thame be demandit, How knaw ye that theis your workis, rytis, and ceremoneis pleasis God, seing ye haif not his commandement to do the same? Straight thay sall ansuer, Thay ar laudabill, thay ar honest and decent, thay haif gude significationis, thay pleasit oure Fatheris, and the maist part of the warld useit the same. And thus into ydolatrie, the corrupt childrene follow the futesteppis of thair foirfatheris.

Secundlie, It is to be notit and observeit, that amangis thame wer false prophetis;² not that thay wer so knawn and esteamit of the pepill: No, thay wer haldin the trew Kirk of God, (for sa thay boistit thame selves to be,) that culd not err. Thir false propheitis wer manteaneris of ydolatrie, (as Winchester, Duresme, Londone,³ I meane thay memberis of the Devill stylit Bischopis of suche places, ar now in England,) and yit boldlie promissit thay to the pepill prosperitie and gude luck. Whairwith, and be whome, the pepill were so abuseit and blindit, that the wordis of Jeremie wer nothing regardit as the consequent declared. For his Sermone endit, the preistis, prophetes, and

---

¹ In the margin of the second edit. "Denie will I nothing except Idolatrie. But the like was done in England."

² In the margin of the second edit. "Suche false Prophetes at this presente are muche estemed in Englande."

³ Gardiner, Bishop of Winchester, Tonstall, Bishop of Durham, and Bonner, Bishop of London.—The words of this parenthesis are only found in MS. M. The other copies read, "So known and holden of the people: No, they were holden and estemed (for so they bosted themselves to be) the trew Churche of God, that culde not erre. For how shulde the Lawe peryshe from the mouthe of the preist? These false prophets were mayntenaris of idolatrye, and bauldlie they promissed to the people," &c.

the haill pepill apprehendit Jeremie, and with one voyce cryit, "He sall die, he is worthie of the death." Great was the uprore aganis the poore[1] Prophet, in whilk appeirandlie he culd not haif eschaipit, gif the Princes of Juda had not haistelie cumit frome the Kingis house into the Tempill, and taken upon thame the heiring of the cause; in whilk, efter mekill debait, whill sum defendit, and uther sum maist vehementlie accuseit the Prophet, the text sayith, that the hand of Ahakin, the sone of Sapham, was with Jeremie, that he suld not be gevin in the handis of the pepill to be killed.[2] *JEREM. 26.*

Albeit the Prophet verie narowlie eschaipit death, yet ceassit he not frome his office; but sumtymes he compleanis unto God, and sumtymis he admonissis the pepill. To God he complainis, saying, "Thow hes strikin thame, O Lord, but thay haif not murnit: Thow hes destroyit thame, but thay haif not ressaveit discipline. Thay haif hardened thair faces harder than stanis: Thay will not convert. The haill land is waistit, but na man will wey, ponder, nor considder the cause. This pepill will not heir my wordis: Thay walk in the wickit inventiounis of thair awin hartis: Thay go after thair Godis to wirschip thame." Be thir complayntis, we may understand the fervencie of the Prophet, that he had to call the pepill back from thair abominabill ydolatrie. But what he profittit, may be understand be the wordis of his awn freindis, the men of Anothoth; for thay planelie said unto him, "Speik na mair unto us in the name of the Lord, leist thow die in our handis." Belyke thir men had small delyte in the doctrine of the prophetis, or thair exhortationis. In conclusioun, he was prohibited to enter into the Tempill,[3] and so mycht he not preache; and than was he *JEREM. 5. JEREM. 12. JEREM. 13.*

---

[1] In the MS. "pure."

[2] In the margin of the second edit. "In England, the true preachers are caste into prison, and no cause knawen whi."

[3] In place of the preceding sentences of this paragraph, as introduced *supra* page 178, in MS. F. and the old editions we read, "Heirof you may easlye consider (Beloved Brethren) what were the maneris of that wicked generacion immediately after the death of thair good King, and how they were encoraged to idolatrye by

commandit be God to wryt his sermonis, whilk he obeyis, and caussis the samyn be read opinlie in the Tempill, (allace! I feir Baruch sall not be found,[1]) and efter the samyn sermonis cumis to the earis of the Consall, and last to the King; and albeit that in dispyt thay wer anis brunt, yit is Jeremie commandit to wryt agane, and boldlie to say, "Jehoiakim sall haif no seid that ever sall sit upon the seat of David. Thair carionis sall be cassin to the heit of the day, and to the frost of the nycht: and I sall visit, sayeth the Lord, the iniquitie of him, of his seid, and of his servandis; and I sall bring upon thame, upon the induellaris of Jerusalem, and upon all the men of Juda, all the calamiteis I have spokin aganis thame." And albeit that when thir wordis wer spokin and writtin, so thai contempnit that banketting and feisting wer proclamit in dispyt, yit no word[2] of all his threatnyngis wer spokin in vane: For efter many plagues sustenit be the mischevous father, the wickit and miserabill sone, in the third moneth of his raigne, was led prisoner to Babilone. But now when the tyme of thair desolatioun approcheit, God steiris up abone this wickit generatioun sic a king, sic preastis, and sic prophetis, as thair awn hartis wissit;[3] evin sic as suld leid filthie dogis to thair vomit agane. Zedikias was king, and such as lang had resistit; poore Jeremie had gottin be thair handis the feirfull whip of correctioun; Paschur and his companionis led the King as thay list; up gat Topheth, the hill alteris smokit with incense; Baall and his bellie goddis (befoir the vengeance of God was pourit furth upon thame) gettis the day thay lang lukit for. And, in conclusion, so horribill wer the abominationis of thay dayis, that

JEREM. 36.

4 REGUM. 24.

ADVERTE ENGLAND, THYS DID JUDA.

JEREM. 33.

WINCHESTER.

false prophetes; but in all this tyme, the Prophet ceaseth not most faythfully to execute his office, for albeit after this he might not enter into the Temple," &c.

[1] Ib. "Alace! I feare we lacke Baruck."

[2] In the second edition, "Albeit, when these wordes were spoken and written, so they were contempned that they durst crye, 'Let the consaill of the Holy One of Israell cese, we will follow the devyses of oure owne hartes,' (Jerem. xviii.) yet no word," &c.

[3] In the margin of the second edit. "There are too many off suche preachers now in Englande."

the Lord cryis to his contempnit noumber,[1] (sum thair wes that yit feirit God), "What has my beloveit to do in my house, (meanyng the Tempill of Jerusalem,) seeing that the multitude committis in it abominabill idolatrie. Thay have provokit me to angir, burnyng incense unto Baall." Whilk great abominationis, when God had schawin, not onlie to Jeremie, but also to Ezechiel, then being at Babylon amangis the prisoneris thair, God moved thai Prophetis to agrie in ane voyce, that haill Israell suld be distroyit.[2] For thus wryttis Ezechiell: "Ah! upon all the abominationis of the house of Israell, thay sall fall be the sword, be pestilence, and famyne; he that is far off sall die of the plague; he that is neir, sall die be the sword; he that is left, and beseigit sall die of hunger: and I sall compleit my wraith upon thame." And Jeremie sayis, "Behold I will gif this citie into the hand of the Caldeis, in the handis of Nebuchadnezar, King of Babilon, wha sall tak it. The Caldeis verelie sall entir into it, and they sall burne it with fyre; thay sall burne it, and the houssis in the whilk thay burnt incense unto Baall." He proceidis, and giveis the reasone and cause of Godis plaguis, saying, "The children of Israell, and the children of Juda, hes done nathing from thair youthheid but wickitnes, evin befoir my eyis, to provoke me to anger: Thay haif turnit to me thair backis and not thair faces; thay, thair Kingis, thair Princes, thair Prophetis, thair Preistis, haill Juda, and all the citie of Jerusalem; thay wald not heir nor be reformit. Thay haif placeit thair doung (sa termit he thair abominabill ydollis) in the place that is consecrat unto my name, to defyle it."[3]

And when the King of Babylon wes lying about the citie,

[1] In the old editions, "cryith to hys sore trobled flocke;" and in the margin of the second edition, "As Pashur ruled the King than at his pleasur, so doth the B. of Winchester rule the Quene now, and doth what him lusteth in England. O wickednes intollerable."

[2] In M.S. F. and the old edit. "But also to Ezechiel being prisoner in Babylon. Their bodies being seperated, in prophecie they did bothe agre, that whole Israel and Juda shuld be destroyed."

[3] In the margin of the second edit. "All the glystering ceremonies off the Papistes are very donge, and abomination before God."

he sayis to the messingeris of Zedekias, who than had send to ask what suld becum of the citie, " The Caldeans sall tak the citie, (sayis the Prophet,) and sall burne it with fyre: yea, yf ye had slane all the hoist of the Caldeans that besege you, and yf the slane men be left, everie man suld ryse in his tent, and suld burne this citie with fyre: He that abydis within the citie sall die either be sword, be honger, or be pestilence; But he that sall go forth and fall to the Caldeans, sall leif and sall win his saule for a pray." Lat a thing be heir notit, that the Prophetis of God sumtymes may teache[1] treasone aganis kingis, and yit neither he, nor sic as obeyis the word spokin in the Lordis name be him, offendis God.[2] And the mair planelie speiketh the Prophet unto the King in secreit, asking his counsale. For thus he sayis, " Gif suddenelie thow sall go furth and subdew thy self to the Princes and chief captanis of the Babilonianis, thy saule sall leif, and this citie sall not be set in fyre; but gif thow go not furth to the cheif captanis of the King of Babylon, this citie salbe gevin over into the handis of the Caldeans, who sall burne it with fyre, neither yit sall thow eschaip thair handis."

Thir wer plane advertismentis, and thus, without flatterie or feir, did thir true[3] Prophetis planelie and opinlie proclame the desolatioun of that place, for suche offensis as befoir hes bene rehersit. But how plesit[4] sic message the Citie of Jerusalem, and principallie thois delicate dames, that maid sacrifice to the Queen of Heaven? Or how lykit the Preistis, Prophetis, and

WHO WOULD NOT HAVE CALLED THE PROPHET A TRAITOUR.

JEREM. 37.

JEREMIES COUNSALE TO THE PEPILL APPEIRIT TREASONE AGANIS THE KING.

THE CRYMES LAID AGAINST JEREMIE.

JEREM. 9, 23. EZEC. 29.

---

[1] " May teach," what some may call.

[2] This sentence is not in the old editions.

[3] In the first edit. "these ij prophetis."

[4] In MS. F. and the old edit. " But how pleaseth suche message the citie of Jerusalem, the priestis, princes, and people of Juda? and what reward receaveth Jeremie for his longe travayle and painfull preachinge? Verely, even such as Pashur and his coun- sall judgeth meete. ' He spake against the Temple, he prophecied mischief against the citie, he fainted the hartes of the souldiours and of the people, but principally, he was unfriendly to the faythe that Pashur taught the people,' to wete, the fayth of their forefathers, who alwayes rebelled against God. And therefore he was reputed a heretycke, accused of sedicion, and dampned of treasone."

Princes of Juda, this ambassadour? That sall we knaw be his intreatment and reward. I find schortlie efter this, Jeremie apprehendit and cassin in prisone as a traitour. He was accusit of seditioun, and dampnit of treasone.

Plane preacheingis wer maid aganis all that he had spokin befoir, and suche felicitie and gud luck wes promissit to the pepill, that within tuo yeiris suld Nebuchadnezaris yok be brokin frome the nekis of all pepill.[1] And the veschellis of the Lordis house, togidder with all the prisonneris, suld be brocht agane to Jerusalem. JEREM. 28.

Had[2] not thir presidentis sum apperances? Yes, verelie thay had. The King of Babylon had many enemyis, and he was not abill to resist thame all; the pepill aboundit in wyne and oyle, who than culd say but God was appeasit with thame? Thair prophetis mainteanit and autorisit all that the pepill did. How culd thay than do wrang? JEREM. 14.

Now lat us consider the Prophetis part. Jeremie had spokin aganis the Tempill, saying, it suld be destroyit, and maid lyk to Silo, (whilk place the Lord had distroyit,) removeing frome thame the Ark of his Covenant, principallie for the iniquitie of the Preistis. And was not this judgeit heresie, think ye? No less I warrand yow, nor now it is in England to say, that all the doctrine that Winchester and his schavellingis now maintene, is the doctrine of his father the Devill; and thairfoir that it schortlie sall provock Godis vengeance to stryke all that adheiris thairto. Jeremie said, that Jerusalem suld be set on fyre, and laid waist, unless that Zedekias suld render him self in the handis of Nebuchadnezzar. And was not this as great treasone, as to say that the Citie of London suld be maid a

---

[1] In the margin of the second edit. "Suche wealthe do the Papistes promise the people for receiving the Idolatrous Masse againe into England."

[2] In MS. F. and the old edit. after these words, is added, " Now, dyd they abound with wyne and with oyle? O pleasing and blessed amongst the people were suche prophetes;" with this marginal note, "Habundance cam before the destruction."—But the greater portion of this and the following paragraph is not contained in MS. F. or the old printed copies.

desert, gif Jesabell be mainteanit in hir autoritie? Jeremie commandit opinlie all such as wold avoid Godis vengeance to leif the citie of Jerusalem, and to seik the favouris of thair enemyis. And was not this as great seditioun as now to say that England salbe gevin over in the handis of strange nationis? Jeremie did opinlie preache that the religioun whilk than thai usit was devillische, albeit thair foirfatheris had followit the same. And what is this else, than to affirme that Generall Consallis, and that whilk is callit the Universall Kirk, is the Malignant Kirk and the Congregatioun of the Antichryst. To be schort, gif menis judgementis may haif place, Jeremie was ane heretick, he was ane seditious fellow, ane seducer of the pepill. He was ane that discouregeit the hartis of the strang men of war; and he was unfreind to that faith whilk Paschur and his companionis teichit the pepill. And thairfoir he is dampnit to prisone, and judgeit worthie of the death. For the King can deny nothing to his Princes. Amangis whom, I think, Paschur hes bene, as it wer, Cheif Chancellour, (ane ald enemie he was to Jeremie,) by whome was not onlie the King, but also the haill multitude of the pepill so blindit, that boldlie thay durst cry, "No mischance sall cum to us: We sall neither sie pestilence, nor honger; the King of Babylon sall never cum aganis this citie nor land."

Considder now, Deir Brethren, the estait of Godis trew Prophet; what anguische wes this in his hart, whan not onlie wer his admonitionis contempnit, but almost everic creature wes conjurit aganis him to his distructioun. In the middis of these stormie trubillis, no uther comfort had the Prophet than to complane to his God, at whois commandement he had spokin: And in his complaynt he is sa kendillit aganis ydolatrie and great unthankfulness, that he cryis as in a rage, "O thow Lord of Hostis, the tryer of the just, thow that seis the reynis and the heart, lat me sie thy vengeance takin on thame, for unto thee have I referrit my cause." As this prayer was maist feirfull to his enemyis, gif thay had sene the efficacie thairof, sa

JEREM. 27.

JEREM. 20.

wes the Prophet assureit be the same that Godis wraith was kendillit aganis that sinfull and unthankfull natioun; and that it suld not turne back till he had performit the cogitationis of his awn hart; whilk wes either to call thame back from ydolatrie, or ellis to bring upon thame the plagues that he had threatnit.

Hitherto haif I recytit the estate of Juda befoir the distructioun of Jerusalem and subversioun of that commonwelth. Now, I appele to the conscience of any indifferent[1] man, in what ane poynt differis the maneris, estait, and regiment[2] of England this day from the abuse and estait rehersit of Juda in theis dayis, except that thay had a King, a man of his awin nature (as appeirit), mair facill nor cruell, who sumtymes was intreatit in the Prophetis favouris, and also in sum caisis heard his consall. And ye haif a Quene, a woman of a stout stomak,[4] more styffe in opinioun nor flexibill to the veritie, who no wyse may abyde the presence of Godis prophets.[5] In this one thing you disagrie, in all uthir thingis sa lyke as ane beane or nut is lyke to another. (1.) Thair King was led by pestilent preistis.[6] Who guydis your Quene; it is not unknawin. (2.) Under[7] Zedikias and his consaill, the ydolatrie whilk be Josias was suppressit came to the light agane. But more abominabill idolatrie was never in the earth, than is that whilk of lait is now set up agane be your pestilent Papistis amang yow. (3.) In Jerusalem, was Jeremie persecutit and cast in prisone, for speiking the treuth and rebuking thair ydolatrie. What prisone within London tormenteth not sum trew Prophet of God for the same caussis? And O thow dongeoun of darknes, whair that abominabill ydoll of lait dayis wes first erectit, (thow Tower

DIFFERENCE BETUIX JUDA AND ENGLAND.[3]

[1] Impartial.
[2] Government.
[3] In the second edit. "A comparison betweene England and Juda."
[4] (Queen Mary)—of a haughty spirit.
[5] In the margin of the second edit. "The Queene stubburne against the truthe of Godis Worde, and hateful to the preachers of the same."
[6] In MS. M. "be preistis and fals prophets."
[7] In the old edit. "Under suche came Idolatrie to the lighte agane. O would to God that the worse wer not among you!"

of London¹ I meane,) in thee ar tormentit ma Jeremyis nor ane,² whom God sall comfort according to his promeis, and sall reward thair persecutoris evin as thay haif deservit; in whilk day also sall thow trembill for feir, and suche as pretend to defend thee sall perische with thee, because thow was first defyllit with that abominabill ydoll.

<small>ENGLAND WORSE THAN JUDA.</small>

Considder, Deir Bretherne, gif all thingis be alyke betuene England and Juda befoir the destructioun thairof: Yea, gif England be worse than Juda was, sall we think that the Lordis vengeance sall sleip, mannis iniquitie being so rype? No, Deir

<small>JEREM. 9.</small>

Brethrene, "He that hes understanding must knaw the contrarie, and he to whom the Lordis mouth hes spokin, must

<small>WHEREIN JUDA WAS BETTER THAN ENGLAND IS NOWE.</small>

schaw the caussis why the land salbe waistit." It may offend yow that I call England worse than unthankfull Judea. But gif gude reassonis adduceit and declarit may tak place, than I

<small>CAUSSIS.</small>

feir not judgement. (1.) From Jerusalem many passit at the admonitioun of the Prophet, leaving all that they had rather than thay wald abyde the danger of Godis plagues that wer threatned. Godis Prophetis hes threatnit and cryit many plagues to fall upon England, but I hear not of many that preparis to flitt: God grant that thay repent not! (2.) In Jerusalem wer princes and nobles wha defendit Jeremie, and also that did absolve him when he was accuseit and unjustlie condempnit be the pestilent preistis. But how many of the nobilitie within England boldlie speikis now in the defence of Godis messingeris, is easie to be tald! (3.) In Jerusalem, had the Prophet of God libertie to speik in mantenance of his doctrine. How suche as seik to haif the tryell of thair doctrine be Godis Word, hes bene, and yit ar entreatit amangis yow, is heard in strange contreyis. (4.) In Jerusalem was Abdemelech, who boldlie said to the King that Jeremie was injureit be the fals priestis, and thairfoir ob-

---

¹ In the margin of the second edit. "The Idolatrous Masse of late first erected in the Tower of London. The B. of Canterb., D. Ridleye, M. Latimer, Bradford, Sandes, Bacon, Veron, &c., preachers and prisoners in the Tower of London."

² In the second edit. "In thee doth mo Jeremies than one suffer injurye and trouble."

tenit his libertie, when he was dampnit to death. But in England, I heir of none (God steir sum!) that dar put thair hands betuix the blude-thristic lyonis and thair pray: that is, betuix those cruell tirantis that now ar lowsit from thair dennis, and the pure sanctis of God. (5.) In Jerusalem, Jeremie, being in prisone, was daylie fed upon the Kingis chargeis, and that when great skairstie of bread was in the haill Citie. In London, whair all plentie aboundis, ar Godis messingeris permittit to honger; yea, and ancient Fatheris sa cruellie entreattit, that seldome hes it bene that theif or murtherer hes bene so cruellie handellit.

In theis caisis, do I not blame yow, Belovit Brethrene, for I assuredlie knaw your hartis to murne for the trubillis of your Brethrene, the faithfull Preacheris; and that ye seik all meanis possibill how thay may be comfortit and releiffit. But thir thingis do I reherse to the end that ye may sie, that thair abominatioun and less feir of God, mair unjust dealling and less schame, mair cruell persecutioun and less mercie and gentilnes is now amang the cheif Reularis in the realme of England, than in those dayis wer in Judea. And yit did not Jerusalem eschaip the puneisment of God. Sall we than belief that England sall avoyd the vengeance that is threatnit? No, Deir Brethrene, gif ydolatrie continew as it is begun, na mair may England eschape Godis vengeance, nor God himself may lose his Justice.[1] And thairfoir, Deirly Belovit in oure Savioure Jesus Christ, gif profit to yourselves or your posteritie may move you any thing, than must ye avoyd ydolatrie: For gif the messingeris of the Lord that salbe sent to execute his wraith and vengeance sall find you amang ydolateris, your bodeis committing lyke abominationis with thame, ye haif na warrand that ye sall eschape the plagues prepareit for the wickit. The haill trybe of Benjamin perischit with the adulteraris, and yit

JUDIC. 20.
1 REG. 15.

---

[1] In the margin of the second edit. "Be ware yie dissembling Gopellers, which for the safegard of youre warldly pelfe, defile yourselves with all Popishe abominations.

thay wer not all adulteraris in fact. Haill Ameleck wes commandit to be destroyit, and yit was not ane of thame leving that trubillit the Israellites in thair passing from Egypt. Pharo was not drounit allane, (as in ane uther Treatise[1] I have planelie writtin,) neither yit eschapit Jonathan when God punissit Saule his father. And why? The Apostle gives the answer: "Because (sayes he) men knaweth the Justice of God, and doing the contrarie, ar worthie of death, not onlie thay that committis iniquitie, but also suche as consentis to the same." And who can deny but suche men as daylie dois accompany wickit men, and yit never declairis thame selves offendit nor displeasit with thair wickitnes, dois consent to thair iniquitie. But of this salbe spokin mair planelie heirefter. And so yit anis agane, I say, that gif profit may move us, most profitabill it salbe, yea, evin for the bodie in this present lyfe, to avoyd ydolatrie; for gif sa we do, than is God oblisit to be oure Father, oure portioun, oure inheritance, and defence. He promissis, and will not dissave us, to carrie us upon his owne wingis from all dangeris, to feid us in the tyme of honger, to plant us and our posteritie in everlasting memoriall, and finallie to fecht for us, and save us from all miseries and craftis of Sathan.

But now to the subsequent: As it is maist profitabill for bodie and saull to avoyd ydolatrie, so is it necessarie, that onless so we do, we refuse to be in league with God, we schaw our selves to haif no faith, and we deny to be witnessis unto God, and to his treuth; and so must he, of his Justice, expressit in his Word, deny us to pertene to him or his kingdome. And then, allace! what ellis is the haill lyfe of man but ane heip of misereis, leiding suche as ar not in league with God to dampnation perpetuall. This is the league betuixt God and us, that He alone sall be oure God, and we salbe his pepill: He sall communicat with us of his graces and gudness; We sall serve him in bodie and spreit: He salbe oure saifgard frome death and dampnatioun; We sall seik to him, and sall flie frome all

---

[1] In MS. F., and the old edit., "in another Letter."

strange Godis. In making whilk league, solemnedlie we sweir never to haif fellowschip with ony religioun, except with that whilk God hath confirmit be his manifest Word. Gif thir presidentis by Godis Scriptures be so plane that no man of reasone can deny any one poynt of the same, than haif I gude hoip that ye will admit it to be necessarie that ydolatrie be avoydit, yf the league betuix God and us stand inviolatit.

First, it is to be observit, that Godis Justice being infinit and immutabill, requireth lyke obedience in matteris of religioun of all thame that be within his league, in all ageis, that He requyris of any one natioun, or of any particular man in any age befoir us. For all that be in this league¹ ar one bodie, as Moses doth witness, recompting men, wemen, childrene, servandis, princes, preastis, reularis, officeris, and strangeris within the Covenant of the Lord: Then plaine it is, that of one bodie thair must be one law; sa that whatever God requyreth of one, in that behalf, he requyreis the same of all. For his Justice is immutabill, and what he dampneth in any one, the same can he neither absolve nor excuse in others; for He is rychteous without partialitie. Then lat us searche, understand, and considder, what God requyrit of that pepill that sumtyme wes in league with him, and what he commandit to be punissit amangis thame. Moses, the mouth of God to the Israellitis, speiketh as followeth: "Gif thy brother, the sone of thy mother, or thy sone, or thy dochter, or the wyfe of thy awn bosome, or thy nychtbour whome thow luffis as thy awn lyfe, sall privilie solist thee, saying, 'Let us go serve uther Godis whilk thow hes not knawin, &c.,' Obey him not, heir him not, neither yit let thy eye spair him, be not mercifull unto him, nor hyde him not; but alluterlie slay him. Let thy hand be first upon him, that suche ane may be slane. And then the handis of the haill pepill stane him with stanis that he may die, &c." And lykewyse commandeth he to be done with ane haill citie, gif the induellaris

NOTE WEILL.

DEUT. 29.

DEUT. 13.

MARK WHAT GOD COMMANDETH SHOULD BE DONE TO ALL IDOLATOURS.

¹ In MS. M. *league* is variously written "leig," "leag," "lieg;" also *ane* for *one*, and *man* for *must*.

thairof turne back to idolatrie; adding also that the haill citie and the spoyle of the same sall be brunt, and that na portioun thairof suld be saved; neither yit that the citie suld be re-edifeit or buildit agane for ever, becaus it wes accursit of God.

Here is a playne declaration, what God requyreth of them that will continue in league with him; and what he hath damned by his expresse Word.[1] And do we esteme, Belovit Brethrene, that the immutable God will wink at oure idolatrie as that he saw it not? seing that he commandit judgement to be execut sa seveirlie aganis ydolateris, and aganis sic as onlie provokit or solistit to ydolatrie, that neither suld blude nor affinitie, multitude nor ryches, save suche as offendit; neither yit that the husband suld conceill the offence of his awn wyfe; neither the father the iniquitie of his sone or of his dochter, but that the father, husband, or brother, suld be the first to accuse sone, dochter, brother, or wyfe. And why? "Because he intendit (sayeth Moses) to bring thee from the Lord thy God, who led thee furth of the Land of Egypt. And thairfoir let him die, that all Israell heiring may feir, and that efter thay commit not sic abominatioun in the middis of thee. Let nothing appertenyng to suche a man or citie cleif unto thy hand, that the Lord may turne from thee the furie of his wraith, and be moveit to have compassioun over thee, and multiplie thee as he hes sworne unto thy fatheris."

In these wordis most evidently is expressed unto us, why God will that we avoyd all fellowship with idolatry, and with the maintainers of the same; in which ar thrie thingis appertenyng to our purpois cheiflie to be notit.[2] First, That the Halie Gaist pronounces and gives warnyng unto us, that mainteaneris of idolatrie, and provokeris to the same, intendis to draw us frome God; and thairfoir will he, that neither we obey thame, be thay Kingis or be thay Quenis, neither yit that

---

[1] This sentence is omitted in MS. M.
[2] The first part of this sentence is omitted in MS. M.—In the margin of the second edit. is this note, "Why idolatrie is to be eschewed, and the mainteners thereof."

we conceill thair impietie, wer thay sone, dochter, or wyfe, gif we will haif the league to stand betuix God and us. And heir is the firmament[1] of my first cause, Why it is necessarie that we avoyd ydolatrie, because that otherwise we declair oure selves little to regard the league and covenant of God; for that league requyreis that we declair oure selves enemyis to all sortis of ydolatrie.

Secundlie, it is to be noted, that ydolatrie so incenssis and kendillis the wraith of God, that it is never quenchit till the offenderis, and all that they possess, be destroyit frome the earth; for He commandis thameselves to be stonit to the death, thair substance to be brunt, and, gif ane citie offend, that it salbe altogidder destroyit without mercie. This may appeir a severe and rigorous judgement. But yf ye sall considder the caus, Godis great mercie towardis us salbe espyit; for thairinto declareis He himself enemie unto oure enemyis. For all those that wold draw us from God (be they Kings or Quenes), being of the Devil's nature, are enemyis unto God, and therefore will God that in such cases we declare our selves enemyis unto them.[2] Because He wald that we suld understand how odius is ydolatrie in his presence, and how that we cannot keip the league betuix him and us inviolatit gif we favour, follow, or spair idolateris: Lord! open oure eyis that we may understand the great necessitie of this thy precept. Amen. Drawers of men from God are of the Devil's nature.

Thirdlie, it is to be noted,[3] that obedience gevin to Godis preceptis in this case, is the cause why God schawis his mercie upon us, why he multiplyis us, and dois embrace us with fatherlie lufe and affectioun. Whair be the contrair, by consenting to ydolatrie, by haunting or favouring of the samyn, ar the mercies of God schut up frome us, and we cutt off from the body of Chryst, left to wither and rotte as treis without sap or moysture; and then, allace! in what estait stand we? In the same assuredlie that Chryst declairis the unfruitfull branches to be,

---

[1] Or, the confirming.
[2] This sentence occurs only in MS. M.
[3] In the old edit. "And last, it is to be noted."

whilk is cutted frome the stock, witheris, and ar gadered in fagottis to the fyre.

O, deirly Belovit, gif we will stand in league with God, and be recomptit[1] the children of fayth, we must follow the futestepis of Abraham, who, at Godis commandement, left his native contrie, becaus it was defylit with ydolatrie. God gave to him but a commandement, saying, "Pass out of thy Fatheris house," and he, without further reasonyng, did obey. And, allace! sall not sa mony preceptis as be gevin to us to flee and avoyd ydolatrie, move us, seing that God schawis him self sa offendit with ydolateris, that he commandis all suche to be slane without mercie?[2]

QUESTION. But now, sall sum demand, What then? Sall we go and
ANSWERE. slay all ydolateris? That wer the office, deir Brethrene, of everie Civill Magistrate within his realme. But of yow is requyreit onlie to avoyd participatioun and company of thair abominationis, as well in bodie as in saule; as David and Paule planelie teachis unto yow. David in his exyle, in the
PSALM 16. middis of ydolateris, sayeth, "I will not offer thair drink offeringis of blude, neither yit will I tak thair name in my mouth."
1 COR. 10. And Paule sayis, "Ye may not be partakeris of the Lordis tabill and of the tabill of the Devillis, ye may not drink the Lordis cuppe and the cuppe of the Devillis." As thir tuo places of Godis maist Sacred Scripture planelie resolves the former questioun, sa do thay confirme that whilk is befoir said, that the league betuixt God and us requyreth avoyding of all ydolatrie.
1 REGUM. 27. First, plane it is, that in Gathe, amangis the Philistines, whair David was in exyle, and in Corinthus, when S. Paule wrote his Epistles, wer no small number of ydolateris; yet neither sayeth David that he will slay any man in that place, neither yit gives Paule any sic commandement; whairfoir it is plane, that the slaying of ydolateris appertenis not to everie particular man. But in ane thing thay do baith agrie, that is to say, that sic as

[1] Accounted.
[2] Several of the preceding sentences are not contained in MS. F. and the old printed copies.

hes societie and fellowschip with God, must so abhorre idolatrie, that na part of the bodie be defylit thairwith. For David sayis, " I will not tak thair names in my mouth;" as he wald say, Sa odius ar the names of fals and vane goddis, that the mentioun of thame to the godlie is lyke to stinking carioun, whilk neither can be eittin nor yit smellit without displeasure of sic as hes not thair senses corrupt: And thairfoir I will neither gif my presence befoir thame, neither yit will I defyle my mouth with thame. That is, I will never speake one favourable worde of them. I think much lesse woulde he have crouched and kneeled before them for any manis pleasure.

Advert, Brethren, that David, inspired with the Halie Gaist, knew not sic schyftis as warldlie wyse men ymagine now-a-dayis, that thai may keip thair hartis pure and cleane unto God, howbeit thair bodies dance with the Devill.[1] Not so, deir Brethren, not so, the Tempill of God hes nothing to do with ydollis. The cause expressis David in these wordes: " For the Lord himself is my portioun, and myne inheritance." Great is the cause yf it be deiplie considderit. David, illuminated be the Halie Gaist, seis evin the samyn self thing that befoir we haif alledgeit of the Apostillis wordis, to wit, That God will not part spoyle with the Devill, permitting him to haif the service of the bodie, and God to stand content with the saule or mynd. No, Brethren, David makis this the fundament and reason why he will neither offer sacrifice to ydollis, nor yit defyle his mouth with thair names. " Because (sayeth he) the Lord is my portioun:" As he wald say,[2] Such is the condition of the league betwene me and my God, that as he is my tower of defence against my enemyis, preserving and nourishing both the bodie and soule, so must I be wholie his in bodie and soule, for my God is of

<small>SHYFTE MAKERS ARE DOUBLE DISSEMBLERS.</small>

<small>WHAT THE LEAGUE BETWENE US AND GOD REQUYRETH.</small>

---

[1] "An opinion held by many who had been gospellers in the days of King Edward, and who afterwards outwardly professed Popery to avoid persecution. Several letters of Bradfurd, Hooper, Latimer, and other Reformers, condemn this practice."— (*Note, Editor of the British Reformers.*)

[2] In MS. M. "Sic is the conditioun of the league betuix the Lord and me, that as he is myne in the necessitie, sa man I be his, bodie and saule."

that nature, that he will suffer no portioun of his glorie to be gevin to another.

In confirmatioun of this, sayeth Esay the Prophet, efter he had rebukit the Jewis of thair idollis and inventionis, "These ar thy portioun." And Jeremie lykewyse in mokage of thame, sayis, "Lat thy loveris[1] delyver thee; call upon thame, and lat thame heir thee! Thow hast committed fornicatioun with thame, and hes committit huredome with stoke and stone." The Prophetis meanyng thairby, that ydolateris can haif no league, nor Covenant with God, in sa far as thair hartis be alienated frome him, whilk the service of thair bodeis testifeis. And thairfoir renunceis God such league and band as befoir was offerit; for Esay would say, Even such as thou hast chosen, such shall be thy portion; and Jeremy would say, Thou hast put thy trust in them (which he meaneth by lying with them in bedde), and therefore let thame shew their power in thy deliverance: and thus he sendeth thame, as it were, to suck watter of hoit burnyng coillis.

It shall nothing excuse us to saye, We trust not in Idols, for so will every Idolatour alledge; but if either yow or they in Godis honour do any thing contrary to Godis Worde, yow shew your selfe to put your trust in somewhat els besydis God, and so are yow idolatours. Marke, Brethren, that many maketh an idoll of thair awne wisdome or fantasye: more trusting to that which thay thinke good, nor unto God, who plainly sayeth, not that things which seameth good in thy eyes, do unto thy God, but what thy Lord God hath commanded them. But of this some other tyme, God willing, more shall be spoken.

Heirof I suppose it to be plane, that lyke as God is immutabill, who by his Law hes not onlie forbidden all fellowschip with ydolateris, but straitlie hes commandit also, that vengeance and punisment be taken on them; and as the sanctis of God wer inspyrit with the Holie Ghost, wha sa refusit all ydolatrie, that thai wald not do sa mekill honour unto ydollis, as anis

---

[1] In the first edit. "thy belfellowes."

favorabillie to speik of thame. And last, as the Scriptures of MARKE. God be infallibill, whilk pronounceth that God may not abyd that our bodeis serve the Devill in joyning our selves with ydolatrie; sa is it of meir necessitie that baith in bodie and saule we absteyne from the samyn, gif we will haif the league to stand sure betuix God and us.

I will not answer at this tyme[1] to any sic objectionis as men that seikis to live as thai list dois now-a-dayis invent, seing that partlie in another Letter I haif answerit the same: And gif God sall grant me ony rest in this wickit lyfe, be ane occasioun or uthir,[2] I purpois, be Godis grace, fullie to answer what can be said for thair defence, whilk in verie deid, when all is said that thai can, thai haif said nothing that God will admit; unless[3] that thai can persuade His Majestie to send doun some new messingeris to repell, retreat, and call back all that is spokin in his Law and Evangell.

But we proceid: Now resteth it to schaw, that trew faith and the confessioun of the samyn, necessarilie requyreis that bodie and saule be cleane frome ydolatrie. It is not neidfull that I labour in the first, seeing that almost no man denyeth it: But ane perfyt faith, as it purgeth[4] the hart, so dois it remove, and cast out frome the samyn superstitioun and abominabill ydolatrie. But whither ane inward faith requyreth ane exter- BY FRE-QUENTING nall confessioun, and that the bodie avoyd ydolatrie, sum per- OF IDOLA-TRIE MEN chance may doubt. To the ane part the Apostill answeris, SHEWS THAME SELF TO saying, "The heart beleivis unto Justice, but be the mouth is HAVE NO FAITH. confessioun to Salvatioun." And David lykewise, "I have be- ROM. 10. leivit and thairfoir haif I spokin; but I was soir trubillit." As David would say, I could not conceale the confession of my PSAL. 116. faith, howbeit trouble did ensue the same. In this place, the voice of the Holie Spirit joyneth togidder faith, as thinges that be inseperable the one from the other; and thairfoir dare I not

---

[1] In the first edit. "I will not truble this tyme with answering."
[2] Ib. "as occasion shall be offered."
[3] The rest of this sentence is not in the old printed copies.
[4] In the old edit. "perseth."

tak upon me to dissever thame; But must say, that whair trew faith is, that thair is also confessioun of the samyn when time and necessitie requyreth; and that whair confessioun is absent, that thair faith is asleip, or ellis (whilk moir is to be feirit) far frome home. For lyke as eiting, drinking, speiking, moving, and utheris operationis of ane lyveing bodie, declairis the bodie to be alyve, and not to be deid; so dois confessioun, in tyme convenient, declair the faith to be lyveing. And as impotence to do any of the foir-named offices of the bodie, declairis the samyn either to be deid, or ellis schortlie and assuredlie to die; so lyk confessioun not gevin in dew tyme makis manifest that the saule hes no lyfe be trew faith.

<small>WHETHER THIS TYME REQUYRETH CONFESSIOUN OF OUR FAITH.</small> But now it is to be considderit, gif this tyme requyreth that we gif confessioun of oure faith, and that we absteane frome manifest ydolatrie. Chryst and his gospell are oppugned, his holy sacramentes are prophaned: Chrystis messengers are some exiled, some cruelly tormented in prison: Oure adversareis, that lang hes fouchtin aganis Chryst, hes now, as thay think, gottin the upper hand. Thay opposing the doctrine that befoir we confessit to be Chrystis treuth; and for ane seill of all abominationis thai haif erectit and set up that ydoll. What <small>THE MASSE.</small> sall we do now, in this the battell for our Soverane Lord? We are persuadit that all whilk oure adversareis dois is diabolicall. Sall we now cum in oppin presence of the pepill, and do evin as the rest doith? God forbid! For so doing we declair our selves to be of mynd and opinion with thame; for neither dois feit, hand, nor mouth declair the contrarie. The feit careis the bodie to serve ane ydoll. The eye beholdis it with ane certane reverence. The toung speikis nothing in the contrarie; yea the handis ar extendit in significatioun of humill obedience.[1] What

---

[1] In the old printed copies, this paragraph reads:—"Now it is to be considered, if this tyme requyreth the confessioun of our faith. Christ and his Evangile are oppugned, his holye Sacramentis are prophaned. Christis messengers are some exiled, some cruelly tormented in pryson; our adversaries have gotten the upper hande, and an execrable Idol erected up in confirmatioun of all iniquitie. What now shall I do, that am as-

greater signis can we gif, that we haif refusit the fellowschip of God, and hes schakin handis with the Devill? That we ar emptie and voyd of faith, and that we ar replenissit with the bitter gall of incredulitie? Assuredlie, I can persave none greatter, nor more evident.

But lat me haif no credit in this behalf, unless the same be provin be manifest plane demonstratioun of Godis Word. The Lord our God, be his Prophet Esay, sayeth to the pepill of Israell, (and this is answer also to the Seconde question, If I may not do as the worlde doth, and yet have faithe?) "Ye are my witnessis, whether thair be any God but I allone. Is thair any creature that I suld not knaw him?" These wordis wer spokin, as it wer, to mak ane witness to rebuke ydolatrie and the vaine inventaris of the samyn. As the Lord wald say, Thow house of Jacob, and ye the naturall children descending of Abraham; ye ar my pepill, whom peculiarlie I haif chosin, be yow to schaw to the warld the greatness¹ of my name. And to that end have I spokin unto yow hid thingis frome the begynnyng, that ye may understand and knaw that thair is na knawledge but in me allone: And thairfoir I will, that ye, persuadit of my power and wisdome, testifie and beare witness of the same to suche as hath not the lyke understanding with yow. Hereof it is playne, that of suche as to whome God granteth knawledge, He requyreis ane confessioun to provoke the ignorant to embrace God and his Word, or at the leist to schaw thame thair vanitie and blind fulischenes.² For so zealous is God over his giftis, that gif we labour

<small>ESAY 44.</small>

<small>NOTE.</small>

sured that all this is abhominatioun? Here Christ is in battaile: Shall I do as the multitude, or as Christis enemies doth? What confessioun give I then? Assuredly even such as the rest doth, for neither doth foot, hande, eye, nor mouth wytnes the contrary. The feete carieth the bodye to serve an Idoll. The eye beholdeth it with a certayn reverence. The mouth dare not whisper what the hart thinketh: yea, the handes are extended and gives signifatioun of humble obedience. Have I not nowe justified the Devill, and damned Christ? It can not be denyed."

¹ In MS. M. "magnificence."

² In the old edit. "or at least that by the understanding man, the vanitie of the foolische shuld be rebuked."

not to employ thame to the glorie of God, and to the profit of utheris his creatures, He will, according unto the threatnyng of Jesus Chryst, tak the talent from us, and will gif it to him that will labour thairupon. Some perchance would gladly labour, but thay see not what fruit shall succeed, and therefoir judge thay better to cease: even as though God could bryng forthe no fruit except he made us fyrst of counsaile. Neither yit sall it excuse us till alledge that we can sie no suche frute that oure confessioun sall bring furth. Considder, deir Brethren, that God is to be obeyit in his commandements, and the frute and success is to be committit to Him whois wisdome is unsearchabill. He commandis us to refraine from ydolatrie: This precept aught we to obey, albeit the present death suld follow; for we ar callit as witnessis betuixt God and the blind Warld, as it is befoir said, "Israell, thou art my witness."

The question and debait standis yit undecydit nor resolvit,[1] Whether is the Masse Godis trew service, or, Is it ydolatrie? In this questioun or contraversie are we, to whome God hes reveallit his treuth, callit for witnesses. When we crouch and kneill, when we beck, and when we bow, and finallie, when we gif and it wer but oure presence befoir that ydoll, What witness beir we? Assuredlie fals witness aganis God and aganis our nychtbour: Aganis God, in so far as we honour ane ydoll with oure bodelie presence, whilk is no small derogatioun to his glorie in this tyme of his battell. Aganis our nychtbour, for that we confirme ignorantis in errour to boith oure condempnationis. But when we abstaine from all fellowship of idolatrie, whatever ensue therupon, we bear trew witnessing, and dois oure dewtie to Godis glorie. And thairfoir of necessitie sall frute ensew, how unapeirand that ever it be to us. Lat no man judge that I am more rigorous and severe in requyring that we abstene frome all ydolatrie nor necessitie re-

---

[1] In the old edit. "The Worlde asketh, Is the Masse Godis service? or, Is it Idolatry? God hath opened to us that it is abbominable idolatry; but when that we, for feare of our vyle carcases, do as the blind World doth, What witness beare we? Assuredly," &c.

quyreth. No, Brethrene, I haif learnit alwayis to contene and keip my affirmatioun within the boundis of Godis Scriptures. And that sall Jeremie the Prophet witness, who, wrytting to thame that either then wer prisoneris in Babylone, or ellis that schortlie suld be prisoneris for thair offences, to whome the Prophet giffis his consall and exhortatioun, efter that he had forbiddin thame in any wise to follow the vane religioun of that pepill, by many reasonis preving that thair idollis wer no Goddis. At the last he says, "Ye sall say to thame, The Goddis that maid neither heaven nor earth sall perische frome the earth and frome under the heavin." *JEREM. 10.*

Heir is to be observit, as that singular instrument of God, Johne Calvin, maist diligentlie noteth, that the rest of the Prophetis warkis wes writtin in the Hebrew toung, whilk than wes peculiar to the Jewis.¹ But the verses and wordis above rehersit wer writtin in the Chaldee toung, in the toung of that pepill amangis whome thai wer to suffer trubill.² As that the Prophet wald constraine thame to change thair naturall toung, and in plane wordis, declair the hatred and alienatioun whilk thai had aganis all ydollis and wirschipping of false goddis. Considder, deare Brethren, what God requyris by his Prophet of his pepill whan thai wer in the middis of thair enemyis wha wer ydolateris. Will He not requyre the same of us, being in oure awn countrie, and amangis suche as suld be Christianis? Gif He be immutabill, He must requyre the samyn. *THE PROPHET CONSTRAINETH THE JEWES TO DECLARE THAIR CONFESSION AGAINST IDOLS, AND THAT CHAUNGING THAIR NATURAL TOUNG.*

---

¹ That is, verse 11 of chapter x. of Jeremiah is written in a different dialect from the rest of his prophetical writings. In the passage referred to, Calvin says, "This is the only verse in the whole book written in Chaldee; and the Chaldee differs much from the Hebrew. We have seen before that Daniel wrote in Chaldee, when he spoke of things pertaining to the Chaldeans; but when he addressed his own people and announced prophecies, belonging especially to the Church of God, he wrote in Hebrew. Hence the book of Daniel is written in Hebrew, except in those parts which he wished to be understood by the Chaldeans; and so does the Prophet in this place."—(*Jeremiah*, vol. ii. p. 29. Edit. *Calvin Translation Society*, Edinb. 1851, 8vo.)

² In the old edit. (in which the last part of this paragraph is omitted) "in the tongue of that people where the Jewes were then in thraldome."

I beseech you, Brethren, mark weill the wordis of the Prophet: He sayis not, Ye may think in your heart that thai ar vane, and that thai sall perische; but, Ye sall say it, and that sall ye do, not privilie, but opinlie to thame that put thair trust in such vanitie; as did the Three Childrene, denying baldlie in the presence of a King (when feirfull death was prepareit[1]) to gif the reverence of thair bodies befoir ane ydoll. And also Daniell wald not keip secreit the confessioun of his faith onlie threttie[2] dayis, (as in my uther Letter 1 haif mair planelie spokin,[3]) but opinlie prayit, his windowis oppin, and his face turnit toward Jerusalem, declaring thairby that the Kingis laws and commandement, devysit be his nobillis, wes wickit, and thairfoir it was not to be obeyit, but baldlie to be contempnit of all suche as had faith towardis God. And this he did not without great appeirance of domage and trobill to follow. As gif any of us suld oppinlie tak that ydoll, maist abominabill of all uthiris, that now, allace, is wirschippit of the blind warld,[4] and tred it under our feit in presence of wickit Winchester and his fellow messingeris and servandis of the Devill.

DAN. 7, 8, 9.

Heirof it is plane, that requyring yow not to prophane your bodeis with ydolatrie, I requyre no more nor Godis most sacred Scriptures be plane preceptis and ensampillis teachis unto us. And of everie man, and at all tymes, I requyre not so mekill, for I constrane no man to go to ydolateris in the tyme of thair ydolatrie, and to say, Your Godis maid neither Heavin nor Earth, and thairfoir sall thai perische, and ye with them, for all your wirschipping is abominabill ydolatrie. But I requyre onlie that we absent oure bodeis (callit of the Apostill the Tempill of the Halie Gaist) frome all suche diabolicall conventionis, whilk gif we do, is baith profitabill and necessarie, no

1 COR. 5.

---

[1] The words of this parenthesis are not in the old printed copies.
[2] In the first edit. "thre dayis."
[3] In the old edit. "as in my former Letter more planelye is expressed."

The rest of this paragraph to the wordis "servandis of the Devill," is not contained in the old printed copies.
[4] The consecrated wafer used in the Romish sacrament.

less to our selves than to our posteritie, of whom now at the end must we speik sumwhat.

Everie man that is not degenerated to the nature of brute beastis,[1] will appeir to beir suche lufe to his childrene, that to leif thame ryches, in felicitie and in gude estait, he will pacientlie suffer trubillis, and will do many thingis for the weill of his children, that utherwise wer contrarious to his pleasure. And I wische to God[2] that the perfectioun of this lufe wer mair deiplie groundit in mannis heart: I mene trew lufe; and not fond fulischenes, whilk under the name of lufe procureth the destructioun of bodie and saule; whair be the contrarie, trew lufe and perfyte, maist cairfullie laboureth for salvatioun of baith. Gif this lufe, I say, towardis our children and posteritie to cum, whilk everie man pretendeth to haif, be in us, then of necessitie it is that, for thair caussis, he avoyd all societie and fellowschip of those filthie abominationis. This my affectioun may appeir strange, but gif it be with indifferencie perceavit, it salbe verie easie to be understand. The onlie way to leive our children blissit and happie, is to leif thame rychtlie instructit in Godis trew religioun. For what availeth all that is in the erth gif perpetuall condempnatioun follow death, yea, and Godis vengeaunce also go befoir the same, as of necessitie thai must, whair the trew knawledge of God is absent; and thairfoir God straitlie commandis the fatheris to teache thair sonis the lawis, ceremonies, and ryttis. And unto Abraham he opennit the secreit of his counsall tuicheing the destructioun of Sodom and Gomortha: "Because, sayeth the Lord, I knaw that Abraham will teache his childrene that thai feir my name." Then God wald that the lyfe and conversatioun of the fatheris suld be ane sculemaister to the children. Plane it is, that the true knowledge of God is not borne with man, neither yet cometh it unto him by natural power, but he must have Scolemasteris

<small>1 CCR. 13.

NOTE YE FATHERS.

NOTE.

THE TREW KNOW-LEDGE OF GOD IS NOT BORNE WITH MAN.</small>

---

[1] In the old edit. "of a brute beast."
[2] In the old edit. "And with my hart I wish to God."
[3] The old printed copies vary slightly from the text, as here printed, in the arrangement of the sentences.

to traine him up in that which he lacketh. The chiefe Scolemaster (the Holy Ghost excepted) of the age following, is the workes, practises, and the life of the forefathers. And experience dois so teache us, that so bound and adict ar the childrene to the workis and practises of thair fatheris, (and speciallie yf it be in ydolatrie,) that skarslie can the power of God, speikand be his awn Word, (as the Prophetis oft complayne,) ryfe or pluck any aback frome thair fatheris futestepis.[1] Now, yf that ye altogether refusing God, stoup under ydolatrie, what scolemasteris ar ye to your posteritie? Assuredlie evin suche as thai evill and fulische fathers, that, consenting to Jeroboam and to his idolatrie, left to thair children a paterne of perditioun. What ymage schaw ye to your childerne, yea, in what estait leif ye thame, baith tuiching bodie and saule? blindit[2] in ydolatrie (allace, I feir and trembill to pronunce it) and bound slaves to the Devill, without hoip of redemptioun, or lycht to be ressavit, befoir that God take vengeance upon thair unobedience. Tusche (will sum object) the Lord knaweth his awne. Trew it is, but his ordinarie meanis apoyntit be his eternall wisdome, to reteine in memorie his benefittis and graces ressavit, ar no wyse to be contempnit. God commandis yow to teache your children his lawis, statutis, and ceremonies, that thai lykwyse may teache the samyn to the generations following. This his precept is to be obeyit, not only for the love of the children, (whilk greatlie aught to move yow,) but also for the reverence ye awe to Godis high Majestie; whais preceptis giff ye contempne, ye and your posteritie, to the thrid and fourth generatioun, sal be plagued, and sal lack the lycht of lyfe everlasting. But yet will some object, What taught our fatheris to us? O dear Brethren, be not so ingrate and unthankfull to God, neither yet I would that you shuld flatter yourselves,[3] think-

---

[1] In the first edit. "that God crying by the mouthis of his messingeris hath muche to do to reave or plucke any man back from their forefatheris futesteppis."

[2] In the old edit. "To speake it plainly, you leave them blinded."

[3] In place of this sentence, MS. M. has "Be not dissaveit, flattering yourselves, belovit Brethrene."

ing that sic a trumpet sal be blawin to your posteritie as hes bene blawin unto yow. Giff all cum to close siknes, as the messingeris of the Lord fand the beginning of this oure age,[1] when the haill realme of Ingland was drounit in sa deidlie a sleip, that the sound of the Lordis trumpet wes not understand; whill first the maist pairt of the blaweris gave thair blude in a testimony that thair doctrine was the same, whilk be blude was plantit, be blude was keipit in mynd, and be blude did increase and fructifie.

But will the Lord, think ye, have his messengeris to ficht alone; or will he bestow sic aboundance of blude upon your children to incourage thame, as he did upon you for your instructioun and incoragement, gif ye all sa traiterouslie flie from him in this day of his battell? The contraire is to be feirit.

NOTE.

Oft revolving how God hes usit my toung (my toung, I say, the maist wicked as of my self[2]) planelie to speik the trubillis that are cum,[3] oft occurris to my mynd a certane Admonitioun that God wald I commonlie suld use in all congregations: The Admonitioun wes this, That the last Trumpet wes then in blawing within the Realme of England, and thairfoir aucht everie man to prepair himself for battell. For gif the trumpet suld altogether cease, and be put to silence, then suld it never blaw agane with the lyke force within the said realme till the cuming of the Lord Jesus. O, deare Brethren! how soir these threatnings persis my awin heart this day, onlie God knaweth; and in what anguische of heart I write the same unto you, God sall declair when the secreitis of all hartis sal be disclosit. I wische my self to be accursit of God, as tuiching all earthlie pleasures or comfort, for ane yeir of that tyme, whilk is, allace! neither ye nor I, (God be mercifull to us!) did rychteouslie esteme quhen all aboundit with us. I sob and grone, I call and pray, that

---

[1] In the second edition is this marginal note, "Let the Reader understand."

[2] In the old edit. "hath used my toung (my tounge, I say, being most wretched of others)."

[3] In the first edit. "that are present;" in the second edit. "that are perfet."

in that poynt I may be disceaveit. But I am commandit to stand content, for it is God himself that performis the word of his awn trew messengeris. His justice and ordour cannot be pervertit.

The Sunne keipeth his ordinare course, and starteth not back frome the West to the South; but when it goeth doune, we lack lycht of the same till it ryse the nixt day towards the Eist agane. And sa is it with the lycht of the Gospell, whilk hes his day appointed whairin it schynis to realms and nations; gif it be contempnit, darknes suddenlie followeth, as Chryst himself in his exhortation dois witness, saying, " Whill ye haif the lycht, beleif in the lycht, that darknes apprehend yow not, lest whill ye haif the lycht." And Paule sayis, " The night is passed, and the day is come (meaning of the Gospel);" And also, " This day yf ye heir his voyce harden not your hartis;" and in dyvers uthir places, the tyme of ye gospell offerit is callit the day. And albeit this day be all tyme frome Chrystis Incarnatioun or Ascensioun to the heavinis in his humane nature till his last gaincoming ; yit evident it is, that all nationis at anis, neither hes had, neither perfectlie hes the lycht of Godis Word offerit and trewlie preichit unto thame. But sum wer and yit remane in darknes, when other sum had the lycht planelie schynyng, as God be his eternall wisdome hes appoyntit the tymes. But, be the contrare, maist evident it is, that whair the lycht of Godis Word for the unthankfulnes of men hes bene tane away, that thair it is not to this day restored agane. Witness haill Israell, and all the countries of the Gentillis, whair the Apostillis first preacheit. What is in Asia? Ignorance of God. What in Africa? Abnegatioun of the verie Saviour,[1] of our Lord Jesus. What in those maist notabill churches of the Grecianis, whair Chryst Jesus was plantit be Paule, and lang eftir watterit be utheris? Mahomet and his false sect. Yea, and what is in Rome? The greatest ydoll of all utheris,

---

[1] Or, rejecting.—In the second edit. is this marginal note, " Examples of God's vengeaunce against unthankfulness."

that adversarie, that man of syn, extollit above all that is callit God, wha, under the name of Chryst, maist cruellie persecutis trew memberis.

Mark, Brethren: Hathe God punishit the nationis foirnamit befoir us? Not onlie the first offenderis, but evin thair posteritie to this day; and sall he spair us, gif we be lyke unthankfull as thai wer; yea, gif we be worse nor thai wer? For of thame na small number sufferit persecutioun, banishment, sclander, povertie, and, finallie, the death for professioun of Chryst (who, haveing onlie the knawledge that ydollis wer odius befoir God, culd neither for loss of temporall gudis, for honouris offerit gif thai wald obey, nor yit for maist cruell tormentis sufferit in resisting, be persuadit to bow befoir ydollis.) And allace! sall we, eftir so many graces that God hes offerit in our dayis, for pleasure or for vaine threatnyng of thame whome our heartis knaweth and oure mouthis have confessit to be odius ydolateris, altogidder without resistance turne back to our vomitt and dampnabill ydolatrie, to the perditioun of ourselves and of our posteritie to come? O horribill to be heard! Sall Godis halie preceptis work no godlier obedience in us? Sall nature no othirwayis mollify oure hartis? Sall not fatherlie pitie overturn this cruelnes? I speik to yow, O naturall Fatheris: Behold your children with the eye of mercie, and considder the end of thair creatioun. Crueltie it wer to saif your selves and dampne thame. But O, more than crueltie and madnes that can not be expressit, gif, for the pleasure of a moment, ye depryve yourselves and your posteritie of that eternall joy that is ordanit for thame that continew in confessioun of Chrystis name to the end, which assuredlye ye do, yf without resistance altogether, ye returne to idolatrie again. Gif naturall lufe, fatherlie affectioun, reverence of God, feir of torment, or yit hoip of lyfe, move yow, then will ye gane stand that abominabill ydoll; quhilk gif ye do not, then, allace! the sunne is gone doun, and the lycht is quyte lost; the trompet is ceissit, and ydolatrie is placeit in quyetnes and rest. But gif God sall strenthen

Feirful is the expectatioun.

Note.

yow, (as unfeanedlie I pray that his Majestie may,) then is thair but ane darke mistye cloude overspred the sunne for ane moment, whilk schortlie sall vanische, so that the beames efter sal be sevinfold mair brycht and amiabill nor thai wer befoir. Your patience and constancie sal be a louder trompet to your posteritie, than wer all the voyces of the prophetis that instructit yow: and so is not the trompet ceissit sa lang as any baldlie resisteth ydolatrie.

<small>GOD GRANT YOU MAY UNDERSTAND.</small>

And thairfoir, for the tender mercies of God, arme yourselves to stand with Chryst in this his schort battell. Fly from that abhominable idoll, the maintainers whereof shall not escape the vengeaunce of God. Lat it be knawin to your posteritie, that ye wer Chrystianis and not ydolateris; that ye learnit Chryst in tyme of rest, and baldlie professit him in tyme of trubill. The preceptis, think ye, are scharpe, and hard to be observit! And yit agane I affirme, that compared with the plagues that assuredlie sall fall upon obstinat ydolateris, thai sall be found easie and lycht. For avoyding of ydolatrie ye may perchance be compellit to leave your native countrie and realme;[1] but obeyeris of ydolatrie, without end, sall be compellit, body and soule, to burne in hell.[2] For avoyding ydolatrie, your substance sal be spoillit; but for obeying ydolatrie, heavenlie ryches sal be lost. For avoyding of ydolatrie ye may fall in the handis of earthlie tyrantis; but obeyeris, maintaineris, and consentaris to ydolatrie sall not eschaip the handis of the liveing God. For avoyding ydolatrie, your childrene sal be depryvit of father, of freindis, ryches, and of earthly rest; but by obeying ydolatrie, thai sal be left without the knawledge of his Word, and without hoip of his kingdome.

<small>THE OBJECTION OF THE FLESH. ANSWER.</small>

Considder, deare Brethrene, that how mekill mair dolorous and fearfull it is to be tormentit in hell, than to suffer trubill in erth; to be depryvit of heavinlie joy, than to be robbit of transitorie ryches; to fall in the handis of the liveing God, than

---

[1] In the old edit. "it may chance that you be contempned in the worlde, and compelled to leave the Realme."

[2] In the second edit. is the marginal note, "Note this Antithesis and consider it well."

to obey mannis vane and uncertane displeasure; to leif oure childrene destitute of God, than to leif thame unprovydit befoir the warld: Sa mekill mair feirfull it is to obey ydolatrie, or by dissembling to consent to the same, than be avoyding and flying from the abominatioun, to suffer what inconveniences may follow thairupon by mannis tyrrany. For the extremitie of the ane is but transitorie pane, and the maist easie of the other is, to suffer in the fyre that never sall haiff end.

I am not prejudiciall[1] to Godis mercies, as that suche as sall repent sall not find grace. No, Brethrene, this I must assuredlie knaw, in[2] whatsoever hour ane synner sall repent, God sall not remember ane of his iniquities; but albeit that his offences wer as reid as skarlet, yit sall thai be maid as whyt as snow; and albeit in multitude thai wer passit number, yit so sall thai be blottit out, that nane of thame sall appeir to condempnatioun of the trewlie penitent. For sic is his promise, that nane trewlie beleiving in Chryst Jesus sall entir into judgement; for the blude of Chryst Jesus, his Sone, purgeth thame frome all syn; so that how far the heavin is distant from the earth, so far does he remove the synnis frome the penitent. EZECH. 18, 23.
ESAI. 1.
JOHN 3, 5.
1 JOHN 1.
PSAL. 103.

But considder, deare Brethrene, that these and the lyk promissis (that be infallibill) ar maid to penitent synneris,[3] and dois nothing apperteine to prophane personis, idolateris, nor to fearfull shrinkeris from the truth for feare of worldly troubles, or to suche as alwayis contempnis Godis admonitionis. And gif any alledge that God may call thame to repentance, how prophane and wicked that ever men be: I ansuere, that I acknawledge and do confess Godis omnipotencie to be so frie, that he may do what pleaseth his wysdome, but yet is not bounde to do all that our fantasie requyreth; and in lykwyse, I acknawledge that God is so luffing and so kynd to such as feare him, that he will performe thair wills and pleasure, although NOTE.

---

[1] Opposed.
[2] In the first edit. "God forbydde, for heirin am I most assuredlye persuaded, that in."
[3] In the second edit. is this marginal note: "The comfortable promises of God are made to penitent sinners onely."

Kyngis and Princes had sworn to the contrary: and so thair is no doubt but God may call to repentance.

But this is greatlie to be doubted,[1] Whither, gif suche as for pleasure of men, or for avoyding temporall punishment, defile themselves with idolatry, feare God? And whether thay which all thair lyfe deny Christ, by consenting to idolatry, shall, at the last hour,[2] be callit to repentance. No suche promeis haif we within the scriptures of God, but rather the express contrarie. And thairfore God is not to be tempted, but is to be heard, feared, and obeyed: When he callis us ernestlie, and threateneth not without cause: "Flie frome ydolatrie, pass frome the middes of thame, O my pepill, that ye be not partakeris of thair plagues." And that is meant of that abhominable whore and of her abhomination. "How long will ye halt on both partis." "Ye may not both be partakeris of the Lordis cuppe and of the cuppe of devillis." "He that denyis me befoir men, I will deny him befoir my Father. He that refuseth not himself, and takis not up his croce and followis me, is not worthie of me. No man putting his hand to the plewch, and luiking bakward, is worthie of the kingdome of God." And Paule to the Hebrewes onlie meaneth of this syn, when he sayis, That suche as willinglie synneth efter the knawledge of the treuth, can not be renewit agane to repentance.

O, deare Brethrene, remember the dignitie of oure vocatioun:[3] you haif followit Christ: you haif proclamit warre against ydolatrie: you haif laid hand upon the treuth, and hes communicate with the Lordis tabill: Will ye now suddanelie slyde back? Will ye refuse Christ and his truth, and mak pactioun with the Devill and his discevable doctrine? Will ye tread the maist precious blude of Chrystis Testament under your feit, and sett up an idoll befoir the people? Whilk thingis assuredlie ye do as oft as ever ye present your bodies amangis ydolateris befoir that blasphemous ydoll. God, the Father of all mercies, for

---

APOC. 18.

3 REG. 18.
1 COR. 10.
MATH. 10.

HEBR. 6, 10.

---

[1] In the old edit. "But here stands the doubt."
[2] In MS. M. "at their pleasure."
[3] Ib. "oure confession."

Chryst his Sonnes sake, preserve yow frome that soir temptatioun, whose dolouris and dangeris verie sorowe will not suffer me to express. Alas, Brethren, it is to be feared, that if ye fall once aslepe, you lye too long before you be awakened.

But yit will sum object, Peter the denyer obtenit mercie. To whome I answer, Particular ensamplis makis no commoun law, neithir yit is thair any resemblance or likelihude betuix the fall of Peter and our daily idolatry. Peter upon a suddane, without any former purpois, within ane schorte space,[1] thryse denyit Christ. We, upon determinat purpose and advysit mynd, denyit Chryst daylie. Peter had Chrystis assurance and promeis, that efter his denyall he suld be converted: We haif Chrystis threatnyngis, that gif we deny we sal be denyit. Peter, in the middis of men of weir, following Chryst to the Bischopis house,[2] committit his offence for feir of death present:[3] We, in our awn houshaldis and citeis, seiking the warld, dois no less, onlie for feir to lose wickit mammoun. Peter, at the warnyng of the cock, and at Chrystis looke, left the company that provokit his syn: We, efter Chrystis admonitiouns, yea, efter gentill exhortationis and fearefull threatnyngis, obstinatlie will continew in the myddis of ydolatrie; and for thair pleasure, denying Chryst Jesus, we will haunt and frequent abominabill ydolatrie.[4]

What resemblance or likelihude can now be found betuix the fall of Peter and oure daylie ydolatrie, lat everie man judge. But mekill I wonder that men can espy sa narowlie schiftis as to see with thair father, auld Adam, the schadow of a busche to hyd thame frome Godis presence; that also thai can not espy that Judas was ane Apostell, in presence of men, sumtymes of no less autoritie and estimatioun than Peter was; that

---

[1] In the old edit. "within the space of a hour or two:" and the second edit. has this marginal note: "A comparison between Peter and our disembling Gospellers."

[2] To the High Preist's house.

[3] In the old edit. "Peter in the Bishopes hall, and amonges wicked men of warre, committed his offence for feare of life."

[4] Ib. "We will crouche and kneel as the Devill commandeth."

<small>1 REG. 10.</small> Cayn wes the first borne in the warld; that Saule was the first
<small>1 REG. 16.</small> anoyntit King over Godis pepill, be the hand of the Prophet,
at Godis commandement; and that Achitophell wes a man of
so singular wisdome, that his counsall was haldin as the oracle
<small>1 REG. 1.</small> of God: And yit none of these found place of repentance. And
have we any other assurances and particular warrantes within
the scriptures of God than they had, that all oure lyfe we
<small>NOTE.</small> may be in league with the Devill, and than at oure pleasure
that we may lay hand upon Chryst Jesus, and when we list
clothe us with his justice?[1] Be not disceavit, beloved Breth-
<small>JOEL 2.
ROM. 10.
2 TIMO. 2.</small> rene, for albeit maist trew it is, that who so ever incalleth the
name of the Lord sal be saved, yit lyk trew it is, that who so
ever incalleth the name of the Sone, sall avoyd and eschew all
manifest iniquitie; and that who so ever contineweth obstinat-
<small>JOB 9.</small> lie in iniquitie, the same man incalleth not the name of the
<small>JOB 35.</small> Lord, neither yit hes God any respect to his prayer. And
<small>THE MASSE
THE DE-
VILLS SA-
CRAMENT
AND SEALE.</small> greatter iniquitie was never frome the beginning, than is con-
tainit in worshipping of an abominabill ydoll; for it is the seill of
the league whilk the Devill hes maid with the pestilent sons of
the Antichryst, and is the verie cheif cause why the blude of
Godis Sanctis hes bene sched neir the space of ane thousand
yeirs; for so long hes it bene almost in devysing and in decking
with that whorische garment,[2] whairin now it triumphis aganis
Christ, aganis the halie institutioun of his last Supper, aganis
that onlie one sacrifice acceptabill for the synis of all faithfull
beleiveris;[3] quhilk haill mass of iniquitie ye confirme, and in a
manner subscryve with your hand, schawing your selves also
consenting to the blude-schedding of all thame that have sufferit for speiking aganis that abominatioun, als oft as ever ye
<small>NOTE.</small> decoir[4] that idoll with your presence. And thairfoir avoyd it,
as that ye will be partakeris[5] with Chryst, with whome ye have

---

[1] It will be observed, that Knox uniformly uses the word *Justice*, as signifying *Righteousness*.

[2] Marg. note in second edit.: "The longe patching of the Papiste Masse."

[3] In the old edit. "against the onely one sacrifice of his death and merites of his passion."

[4] In the first edit. "garnishe."

[5] In MS. M. "will haif part."

sworne to die and to live in baptisme and in his holy supper. Schame it wer to break promeis to men; but is it not mair schame to break it unto God? Fulischeness it wer to leave that King whose victorie ye saw present, and to tak part with him, whome you understude and perceived to be sa vanquished, that neither mycht he ganestand, neither yit abyde the cuming of his adversarie.

O, Brethrene, is not the Devill, the prince of this warld, vanquished and casten out? Hath not Chryst Jesus, for whome we suffer, maid conquest of him? Hath he not, in despite of Sathanis malice, carried oure flesche up to glory? And sall not our Champion returne? We knaw that he sall, and that with expeditioun, when Sathan and his adherentis, idolateris, and worschipperis of that blasphemous beast, filthie personis, and feirfull schrinkeris frome the treuth of God, sal be casten in the stank[1] burning with fire, whilk never sal be quencheit. But in the meanetyme, you feir corporall death: gif nature admittit any man to live ever, then had your feir some apperance of reasone. But gif corporall death be commoun to all, why will ye jeoparde to loise eternall life, to decline and eschaip that quhilk neither ryche nor pure, neither wyse nor ignorant, proude of stomoke nor febill of courage, and, finallie, no earthlie creature, be no craft or ingyne of man, did ever avoyd? Gif any eschaipit the uglie face and horribill feir of death, it wes thai that baldlie confessit Chryst befoir men.[2]

But yit grudgeth the flesche (say you,) for feir of pane and torment. Lat it do the awin nature and office; for sa must it do, whill it be burdenit with Chrystis cross, and than no doubte sall God send comfort, that now we neither can feill nor understand. But why aucht the way of lyfe be so feirfull be reasone of any pane, considdering that a great number of oure brethrene hes past befoir us be lyke dangeris as we feir?[3] A stout and

JOB 12. 16.
ACTS. 1.
CUM, LORD JESUS!
APO. 20.
FOLISHE FEARE.
THE FLESHE CAN DOE NOTHING BUT GRUDGE.

---

[1] The lake: so in the first edit. "the stanke or lake."
[2] In the old edit. "it was suche as boldlye did gainstand mennes iniquitie in the earthe."
[3] In the old editions, "Let us not

prudent marinell[1] in tyme of tempest, seing but one or tuo schippis, or lyke weschellis to his, pass throuch any danger, and to win a sure harbour, will have gud esperance be the lyke wind to do the same. Allace! sall ye be mair feirfull to win lyfe eternall, than the naturall man is to have the corporall lyfe? Hath not the maist part of the sanctis of God, from the begynning, enterit into thair rest be torment and trubillis? Of whome, as witnesseth Paule, sum wer rackit, sum hewin asunder, sum slane with swordis, sum walkit up and down in scheip skynnis; in neid, in tribulatioun, and vexatioun; in mountainis, dennes, and in caves of the earth! And in all their extremities, what complaintes hear we of thair mouthes, except it be that thay lament the blindness of the world, and the perditioun of thair persecutoris? Did God comfort thame, and sall his Majestie dispyse us, gif in fichting aganis iniquitie we[2] will follow thair futstepis? He will not, for he hes promissit the contrarie, and thairfoir be of gud corage, the way is not so dangerous as it appeareth; prepair in tyme, and determyne with your selves to abyde in Chryst Jesus, and his croce sall never oppress you as presentlie ye feir. And thairfoir, deirlie Belovit in oure Savioure Jesus Chryst, as ye purpose to avoyd the grevous vengeance to cum, that schortlie and assuredlie sall stryk all obstinat ydolateris; as ye would haif the league betuix God and yow to stand sure and inviolated, and as you will declare yourselves to have trew faith, without which no man ever shall enter into life; and finally, as ye will leif the trew knawledge of God in possessioun to your childrene; avoyde all idolatry and all participation thereof, for it is so odious before Godis presence, that not only doth he punish the inventors and fyrst offenders, but often times thair posterity are striken with

OTHERS BEFORE US HATH PAST TO LYF BY TORMENT.
HEBR. II.

DEUT. 23.

turne back from Christ, albeit the flesche complaine, and feareth the tormentis. Wonder it is that the waye to life is so fearfull unto us, considering that so great a number of our brethren hath passed before us, in at the same gate that we so much abhorre." The next two sentences are not contained in these copies.

[1] Mariner.
[2] In the old edit. "dispyse us if in obedience to him, we."

blindness and deadness[1] of mind. The battail shall appeare strang, which ye are to suffer, but the Lord hym selfe shall be your comfort. Flie from ydolatrie, and stand with Chryst Jesus in this day of his battell, whilk sal be schort and the victorie everlasting! For the Lord himself sall cum in our defence with his michtie power; He sall gif us the victorie when the battell is maist strang; and He sall turn our teares into everlasting joy. He sall consume[2] oure enemyis with the breath of his mouth, and he sall lat us see the destructioun of thame that now ar maist proude, and that maist pretendeth to molest us. Frome God allone we abyde redemptioun. ZACHA. 2.
PSALM 46, 57, 61.
APOC. 7, 23.
PSALM 51.

The God of all comfort and consolatioun, for Chryst Jesus his Sonnes sake, grant that this my simple and plaine Admonitioun (yea, rather the warning of the Holie Ghost) may be ressaved and accepted of yow, with no less feare and obedience than I haif writtin it unto yow with unfained lufe and sorowfull heart. And then I dout not but baith you and I sal be comforted, when all suche as now molestis us sall trembill and schaik, by the comming of our Lord Jesus, whois omnipotent Spirit preserve and keip yow undefylit, bodie and saule, to the end. Amen.[3]

The peace of God rest with yow all. Frome ane sore trubillit heart, upon my departure frome Deipe, (1553,[4]) whither God knaweth. In God is my trust, through Jesus Christ his Sone, and thairfoire I feir not the tirannye of man, neither yit what the Devill can invent againis me. Rejois, ye faithfull, for in joy sall we meit whair death may not dissever us.

Your Brother in the Lord,

JOHNE KNOX.

[1] In the first edit. "dasednes."
[2] Ib. "confound."
[3] The old printed copies end here, omitting the following paragraph, or postscript. The words, "Lord, increase our Faith," occur in the first edition, immediately before the imprint, as given at page 162. In the second edition, there is added the Godly Prayer, which is annexed on the following page.
[4] See *supra*, page 159.

A GODLY PRAYER.[1]

AH, LORDE! most strong and mightye God, which destroyest the counsayles of the ungodly, and ryddest away the tyrauntes of thys worlde out of the earth at thy pleasure, so that no counsaill or force can resiste thyne eternal counsaill and everlasting determination. We, thyne poore creatures and humble servauntes, do moste instantly desyre thee, for the love that thou hast to thyne welbeloved and onely begotten Sonne oure Lorde and Saviour Jesus Chryst, that thou will loke upon thyne cause, for it is tyme, O Lorde, and bringe to naught all those thinges that ar or shalbe apoynted, determined, and fully agreed agaynste Thee and thy Holy Worde. Let not the enemyes of thy truth too miserablye oppresse thy Word and thy servauntes which seke thy glorie, tender the advancement of thy pure religion, and, above all thinges, wishe in their hartes that thy holy name may onely be glorified amonge all nations. Geve unto thy Servauntes the mouth of thy truthe and wysedom, whiche no man maye resiste: And althoughe we have moste justlye deserved thys plague and famyne of thyne worde, yet upon our trew repentance, grante, we beseke Thee, we may be thereof released; and here we promise before thy Devyne Majestie, better to use thy gyftes than we have done, and more strayghtlye to order oure lyves, according to thy holye will and pleasure, and we will synge perpetuall prayses to thy moste blessed name, worldes without ende, throughe Jesus Christe oure Lorde. Amen.

FINIS.

[1] See note 3, page 215.

CERTAIN QUESTIONS

CONCERNING OBEDIENCE TO

LAWFUL MAGISTRATES,

WITH ANSWERS BY BULLINGER.

M.D.LIV.

IN a letter from Henry Bullinger, the eminent divine of Zürich, addressed to Calvin on the 26th of March 1554, he says, "I have enclosed in this letter the Answer I made to the Scotsman whom you commended to me. You will return it to me when you have an opportunity:" (*Quid Scoto isti a te nobis commendato responderimus, hisce inclusi. Remittes, cum per opportunitatem licuerit.*)[1]

The following translation of these Questions and Answers is that given in the publication by the Parker Society, of the very interesting and valuable series of Original Letters relative to the English Reformation, chiefly from the Archives of Zürich, translated and edited by the Rev. Hastings Robinson, D.D., in 1847. The learned Editor, in a foot-note, says that "Simler conjectures either Knox or Goodman to be the Scotsman here referred to." He adds, "It was probably the latter," judging from the mention made by Goodman, in a subsequent letter, of his having submitted certain Propositions to Calvin and Peter Martyr. There can, however, be no doubt that Knox was the individual alluded to; for it is ascertained that he visited Geneva in that month of March, and obtained from Calvin a letter of introduction to Bullinger. Christopher Goodman, who afterwards became Knox's colleague at Geneva, was an Englishman, and his letter, to which Dr Robinson alludes, was not written till August 1558, or four years subsequent to Bullinger's communication.

This paper is the more interesting, as it exhibits the Questions respecting which Knox was desirous of obtaining the sentiments of the more eminent Swiss Divines. "I have travellit

[1] Epistolæ Tigurinæ, &c., p. 482. Cantabr. 1848, 8vo.

(he writes, on the 10th of May,[1]) through all the congregations of Helvetia, and hes reasonit with all the Pastouris, and many other excellentlie learnit men, upon sic matteris as now I canot commit to wrytting: gladlie I wold be toung or be pen utter the same to Godis glorie."

[1] *Infra,* page 235.

AN ANSWER GIVEN TO A CERTAIN SCOTSMAN, IN REPLY TO SOME QUESTIONS CONCERNING THE KINGDOM OF SCOTLAND AND ENGLAND.

1. *Whether the Son of a King, upon his father's death, though unable by reason of his tender age to conduct the government of the kingdom, is nevertheless by right of inheritance to be regarded as a lawful magistrate, and as such to be obeyed as of divine right?*

That person is, in my opinion, to be esteemed as a lawful King, who is ordained according to the just laws of the country. And thus it is clear that Edward VI. of happy memory was ordained. For his Father on his death-bed appointed him King, and so claimed for him the right of sovereignty, which they say is hereditary. The States of the kingdom acknowledged him, as they testified by his coronation. They provided him with

---

RESPONSUM SCOTO CUIDAM DATUM, AD QUÆSTIONES ALIQUOT DE REGNO SCOTIÆ ET ANGLIÆ.

1. *Utrum Filius Regis, patre rege mortuo, jure nativitatis, utcunque propter pueritiam regnum administrare non possit, habendus sit pro legitimo magistratu, cui jure divino oporteat parere?*

Pro legitimo rege is mihi habendus videtur, qui secundum leges patrias non iniquas ordinatus est. Ita vero constat ordinatum esse beatæ memoriæ Edvardum VI. Hunc enim Pater moriens designavit Regem, ac ita deposcebat jus regni, quod aiunt esse hæreditarium: receperunt illum regni ordines: id quod coronatione testati sunt. Instruxerunt illum consiliariis,

councillors, endued as he was with great gifts of God; nor was any thing wanting to that kingdom, which is wont to be looked for in the most prosperous kingdom elsewhere. He was therefore a lawful Sovereign, and his laws and ordinances demanded obedience; and he ruled the kingdom after a more godly manner than the three most wise and prosperous kings of that country who immediately preceded him.

2. *Whether a Female can preside over, and rule a kingdom by divine right, and so transfer the right of sovereignty to her Husband?*

The law of God ordains the woman to be in subjection, and not to rule; which is clear from the writings of both the Old and the New Testament. But if a woman in compliance with, or in obedience to the laws and customs of the realm, is acknowledged as Queen, and, in maintenance of the hereditary right of government, is married to a Husband, or in the meantime holds the reins of government by means of her councillors, it is a hazardous thing for godly persons to set themselves in

---

alioqui magnis Dei dotibus præditum. Nec defuit ei regno quicquam, quod in felicissimo alioqui regno requiri solet: legitimus ergo rex fuit, et parendum est illius legibus et constitutis. Sanctius ille regnum instituit, quam tres prudentissimi et felicissimi hujus regni reges, qui ante ipsum regnarunt.

2. *Utrum Fœmina jure divino regno præsidere et hoc gubernare possit, adeoque Marito suo jus regni tradere?*

Lex Dei fœminam subesse, et non dominari jubet: id quod clarum est in utriusque Testamenti libris. Si vero, legibus et ritibus regni permittentibus vel jubentibus, recipitur fœmina Regina, jure hæreditario regni ita exigente, quæ Marito nubat, interim per consiliarios moderetur imperii habenas; periculosum erit piis se objicere legibus politicis, maxime cum evangelium

opposition to political regulations; especially as the gospel does not seem to unsettle or abrogate hereditary rights, and the political laws of kingdoms; nor do we read that Philip the eunuch, by right of the gospel, drove out Candace from the kingdom of Ethiopia. And if the reigning Sovereign be not a Deborah, but an ungodly and tyrannous ruler of the kingdom, godly persons have an example and consolation in the case of Athaliah. The Lord will in his own time destroy unjust governments by his own people, to whom he will supply proper qualifications for this purpose, as he formerly did to Jerubbaal, and the Maccabees, and Jehoiada. With respect, however, to her right of transferring the power of government to her Husband, those persons who are acquainted with the laws and customs of the realm can furnish the proper answer.

3. *Whether obedience is to be rendered to a Magistrate who enforces idolatry and condemns true religion; and whether those authorities, who are still in military occupation of towns and fortresses, are permitted to repel this ungodly violence from themselves and their friends.*

---

non videatur hæreditarium jus et regnorum leges politicas convellere aut abrogare: neque legimus Philippum jure evangelii deturbasse Candacem a regno Ethiopiæ. Si Debora non sit, sed impia magis quæ præest, et tyrannide consequuta imperium, habent pii exemplum et consolationem in Athalia. Injustas Dominus dominationes per suos, quos ad hoc instruit facultatibus, ut olim Jerubbaal et Machabæos et Joiadas, suo tempore deturbat. An vero hæc tradere possit jus regni Marito suo, commode respondebunt, qui leges et ritus regni noverunt.

3. *Utrum Magistratui, imperanti idololatriam et damnanti veram religionem, obtemperandum sit; et an proceres, tenentes adhuc oppida et arces manu armata, vim istam impiam a se et suis propulsare possint?*

The history of Daniel, and the express command of God, Matt. x., and the examples of the apostles in Acts iv. and v., as also that of many of the martyrs in ecclesiastical history, teach us that we must not obey the king or magistrate when their commands are opposed to God and his lawful worship; but rather that we should expose our persons, and lives, and fortunes to danger. This power is the power of darkness, as the Lord saith in the gospel. And Eusebius records, in the ninth book and eighth chapter of his Ecclesiastical history, that the Armenians took arms against their lawful sovereigns, the Roman emperors, who desired to force them to idolatry. And this conduct of theirs is not reproved. Those very Armenians, many years after, by reason of the ungodliness of the kings of Persia, slew their ungodly commanders, and revolted to the Emperor Justin, as is recorded by Evagrius. (Eccl. Hist. v. 8.) For the Holy Scripture not only permits, but even enjoins upon the magistrate a just and necessary defence.

But as other objects are often aimed at under the pretext of

Non obtemperandum esse regi aut magistratui impia contra Deum et cultum ejus legitimum mandanti, sed potius et corpus et vitam et fortunas in periculum objiciendas esse, docet historia Danielis, et disertum Dei mandatum, Matth. x. et exemplum apostolorum, Act iv. et v. et multa martyrum in ecclesiastica historia. Hæc potestas est potestas tenebrarum, ut dicit in evangelio Dominus. Ac Eusebius, (Hist. Eccles. lib. ix. cap. viii.) commemorat, Armenios arma sumpsisse contra legitimum suum magistratum, contra imperatores Romanos cogere volentes ad idololatriam. Nec improbatur illorum factum. Illi ipsi Armenii, multos post annos, propter impietatem regum Persicorum, defecerunt ad Justinum imperatorem, cæsis præsidibus impiis: quod commemorat Evagrius, (Eccles. Hist. lib. v. cap. viii.) Nom et Scriptura sancta justam necessariamque defensionem non modo concedit, sed etiam mandat magistratui.

Ceterum cum sub assertionis vel defensionis justæ et neces-

a just and necessary assertion or maintenance of right, and the worst characters mix themselves with the good, and the times too are full of danger; it is very difficult to pronounce upon every particular case. For an accurate knowledge of the circumstances is here of great importance; and as I do not possess such knowledge, it would be very foolish in me to recommend or determine any thing specific upon the subject. For even Paul, we read, made use of the Roman soldiery against those who plotted against him, and was right in doing so: yet at another time, though under almost the same or similar circumstances, he is recorded to have used only the arms of patience, and none else. There is need, therefore, in cases of this kind, of much prayer, and much wisdom, lest by precipitancy and corrupt affections we should so act as to occasion mischief to many worthy persons. Meanwhile, however, death itself is far preferable to the admission of idolatry.

4. *To which party must Godly persons attach themselves, in the case of a religious Nobility resisting an idolatrous Sovereign?*

---

sariæ prætextu sæpe quærantur alia, et bonis se misceant pessimi, temporaque sint periculosissima, difficile est pronunciare de causis singularibus. Circumstantiæ enim bene cognitæ hic plurimum conferunt, quæ cum nobis perspectæ non sint, stultum esset jubere aut definire hic aliquid certi. Nam et Paulus Romanorum armis contra conjuratos legitur esse usus, et recte quidem usus, qui tamen alibi in eadem fere aut simili causa, patientia tantum pugnans, nullius armis usus legitur. Multis ergo hic precibus, multa sapientia opus est, ne quid præcipitantes et affectibus pravis tentemus, quod in multorum bonorum detrimentum vergat. Interim vero mori præstat quam idololatriam recipere.

4. *Utri parti adhærendum sit Piis, si religiosi Proceres bello resistant Regi idololatræ?*

I leave this to be decided by the judgment of godly persons, who are well acquainted with all the circumstances, who look up in all things to the Word of God, who attempt nothing contrary to the laws of God, who obey the impulses of the Holy Ghost, and who are guided by circumstances of place, time, opportunity, persons, and things, without making any rash attempt, and who can therefore be directed more safely by their own sense of duty than by the consciences of others. But I would advise them, above all things, that those causes may be removed, on account of which hypocrites are predominant; iniquities, I mean, that we may become reconciled to God by a true repentance, and implore his counsel and assistance. He is the only and the true deliverer; and, as we read in the books of Judges and Kings, and the Ecclesiastical histories, has never been wanting to his Church. Let us lift up our eyes to Him, waiting for his deliverance, abstaining in the meantime from all superstition and idolatry, and doing what he reveals to us in his Word.

Hoc relinquimus piorum judicio æstimandum, qui et totum negotium perspectum habent, et in omnibus verbum Dei respiciunt, nihil tentant adversum legibus Dei, Spiritus Sancti suggestionibus obtemperant, et ex loco, tempore, occasione, personis, rebusque capiunt consilium, neque quicquam temere tentant, ideoque ex suis ipsorum quam alienis conscientiis certius judicium petunt. Suademus tamen ante omnia, ut tollantur causæ, propter quas regnant hypocritæ, scelera; ut, inquam, per veram pœnitentiam redeamus cum Deo in gratiam, et hujus auxilium et consilium imploremus. Hic est liberator unicus et verus; qui in libris Judicum et Regum, et in Ecclesiasticis historiis, nunquam defuit suæ Ecclesiæ. Ad hunc attolamus oculos, exspectantes illius redemptionem. Abstineamus interim ab omni superstitione et idololatria, facientes illud quod Verbo suo nobis revelat.

TWO
COMFORTABLE EPISTLES
TO HIS AFFLICTED BRETHREN

IN ENGLAND.

MAY M.D.LIV.

THE two following Epistles were written by Knox after his return to Dieppe, and are dated the 10th and 31st of May 1554. As a portion of the earliest letter is repeated nearly verbatim, they were no doubt addressed by him to his friends, who resided in different parts of the country. In the previous months of March and April, he had travelled through France and Switzerland, visiting particular congregations, and conferring with the Swiss divines, and other learned men. "On making himself known," says his biographer, "Knox was cordially received by them, and treated with the most affectionate hospitality... The kind reception which he had met with, and the agreeable company which he enjoyed, during his short residence in Switzerland, had helped to dissipate the cloud which hung upon his spirits when he landed in France, and to open his mind to more pleasing prospects as to the issue of the present afflicting events. This appears from a letter written by him at this time, and addressed 'To his afflicted Brethren.'"[1]

Of these two Epistles, the first is preserved in the series of Knox's early Letters, contained in Dr M'Crie's manuscript volume. The other is annexed (with the separate title, as given at page 237) to the original publication of his Exposition of the Sixth Psalm, which has already been described. It is also included in the republication, at London 1580, of that little volume, by Abraham Fleming.[2]

[1] M'Crie's Life of Knox, vol. i. p. 132.   [2] See pages 116, 118.

An Epistle to his Afflicted Brethren in England.

The great Bishop of our Saulis sall shortlie appear, to the comfort of us that now mourne.

When I ponder within myself, rycht dearlie belovit Brethrene, what was the estait of Chrystis trew Kirk immediatelie efter the death and passioun of our Saviour Jesus, and what were the changeis and greit mutationis in the commounweill of Judea, befoir the finall desolatioun of the same: As I can not but feir lyke plagues to stryke the realme of Ingland; and in feiring, God knaweth, I lament and mourne; sa can I not but rejoise, knawing that Godis maist mercifull providence is na less cairfull this day over his weak and feabill servandis, than he was that day over his dispersit and sair oppressit flock.

What was the estait of Chrystis Kirk betuene his death and resurrectioun, betuene his resurrectioun and ascensioun, betuene his ascensioun and the sending of the Halie Gaist upon his discipillis, and fra that tyme to the finall destructioun of Jerusaleme? The plane Scriptures do witness it was maist afflictit, without all comfort and warldlie consolatiounis, and that sumtymes it wes sa oppressit with cair, dolour, and desperatioun, that neither culd the witnessing of the women, the appeiring of the Angellis, nor the verie voce and presence of Chryst Jesus him self, remove all doubtis of a lang continewance fra the hartis of his Apostillis. What wer the mutationis and trubillis in Judea and Jerusalem befoir the destructioun thairof, sic as be exercisit in reiding Histories, and principallie in Josephus and Ægisippus,[1] can not be ignorant. What wer the

[1] See Note 1, page 240.

plagues that rang¹ over that unthankfull pepill? to wit, cruell, tiranfull, and ungodlie magestratis, by whome the pepill war oppressit and spoilzeit of their liberties; of whilk occasioun was steirit up seditioun, and thair upon followit sa cruell persecutioun, under the name of justice, that na small noumber wer burnit quick. After whilk crueltie, followit sic murther universallie in the citie and in the feildis, that the fatheris feirit their sonis, and the brether thair brethrene. Whilk unquyetnes ceassit not, till Godis sever vengence was at anis pourit furth upon sic as obstinatlie refusit, and cruellie persecutit Chryst Jesus and his doctrine.

And yit amangis the extreamitie of theis calamiteis sa wounderouslie was Chrystis Kirk preservit, that the remembrance thairof is unto my hart greit matter of consolatioun. For yit my gud hoip is, that ane day or uther Chryst Jesus, that now in Ingland is crucifeit, sall ryse agane in dispyt of his enemyis, and sall appeir to his weak and sair trublit discipillis, (for yit sum he hath in that wreachit and miserable Realme), to whome he sall say, Peace be unto yow. It is I, feir not: And this sall he do for his awn mercies sake, to lat us knaw, and in practise understand, that his promissis ar infallibill, and that he will not intreat us according to the offences of oure corrupt and fraill nature, whilk alwayes is reddie to fall frome oure God, to distrust his promisses, and to forget that ever we had ressavit benefit or comfort at his hand, when trubill or danger appeireth.

This I wryt, belovit in the Lord, that albeit ye find your hartis sumtymes assaltit with dolour, grudgeing, or with desperatioun, that yit ye be not trubillit above measure, as that Chryst Jesus suld never visit yow agane; thair fallis na thing to yow, nor yit to the flock of Chryst Jesus this day within the miserabill realme of Ingland, whilk did not fall on Chrystis trew and beloved discipillis befoir and efter his death.

Befoir his death, thay wer advertisit and planelie admonishit

¹ Reigned.

that truble suld apprehend thame; that he suld suffer a cruell and ignominious death, that thay suld everie ane be aschamit and fle fra him. This culd thay not beleive, but baldlie durst promeis the contraire, and yit as Chryst Jesus foirspak all came to pas. He oftentymes promisit and did assure thame that he suld ryse agane, that he suld visit thame and suld give thame consolatioun, and suld remove thair dolour.

But trust ye, that in the tyme of thair anguische any remembrance of Chrystis resurrectioun, comfort, or returnyng, was in thair hartis. It is easie to be espyit, that thair was nane, but that dolour and disperatioun had sa persit thair tender hartes, that efter many apparitionis thair wavering myndis fullie culd not be establishit.

In the same case, considder I now the trew professoris of Chrystis halie and sacred Evangell to be within the realme of Ingland. The dayis of this oure dolour hes bene blawin in oure earis, oure weaknes and oure infirmities hath bene payntit out befoir oure eyis, but allace, then culd we not beleive that the tyme approcheit sa neir, nether yit that sa schort a tempest suld have overthrawin sa great a multitude, (O Lord, incres oure faith, be mercifull unto us, and lat us not droun in the deip for ever!); but, deirlie belovit, the same voice that foirspak oure dolours, foirspak also oure everlasting comfort with Chryst Jesus, whilk promeis, peradventure, doith not greatlie now rejose oure hartis, be reasone that the bodie standis in feir, and our saullis ar in anguische be tormentis that ar threatnit be sic as sall schortlie perische. Sic imperfectionis wer in Chrystis apostillis, and yit thay did not impeid his gane cuming unto thame, na mair sall thay do unto us, provyding that Judas obstinacie, his impenitent and tratourous hart be absent fra us; and thairfoir, beloved in the Lord, hoip now against all warldlie appeirance, the power of oure God salbe knawin unto his awn glorie in dispyt of theis conjured enemys, whais judgement sall not sleip, but suddanlie sall fall upon thame to thair perpetuall confusioun. Haist Lord, and tarie not, for thay have violatit thy law and prophanit thy halie testament!

Ye wald knaw perchance my judgement, be what meanis sall the tirantis of Ingland, and maist obstinat and abominabill idolateris, be punissit. To determinate unto thame a certane kynd of warldlie punishment it aperteaneth not to me, but heirof am I sa sure, as that I am that my God liveth, that besyd thair perpetuall condempnatioun and torment in hell, thay sall also be plaguit in this present lyfe, except thay repent; that lykwys as men hes heard thair abominationis and enormities schawin to thair faces, in so muche, that thay have bitten thair toungis for verie dispytfull anger, and yit did never repent fra thair iniquiteis; sa sall also men that this day seis thair tiranny, behold the plagues of Godis vengeance pourit furth upon thame evin in this present lyfe, and yit sall thay not ceas to rebell aganis his Halie Majestie, for the deidlie venoume of that malicious serpent, thair fathir the Devill, can never be purgeit fra thair cankirrit hartis; and thairfoir efter warldlie punishment (whilk thay sall not eschape), is the fyre that never salbe quencheit prepareit for thair portioun, and sa theis tirantis is mair to be piteit and lamentit than either feirit or haitit, except it be with a perfyt hatred, whilk the Spreit of God moveth in the hartis of Godis elect aganis the rebellious contempnaris of his halie statutis, whairwith Jeremie the prophet was inflamit when that he prayeth, "Lat me see thy vengeance takin upon thy enemyis, O Lord." Whilk also he obteanit and beheld with his corporall eis, as I am assureit sum that at this day sobbis under thair cruell tiranny sall see of the pestilent Papistis within the realme of Ingland; but what salbe the kynd of thair plagues, and whome God sall use to execute his wraith, I can not say; but lat it be sufficient that they sall not eschape the punishment that is prepareit, na mair than Haman did the gallous that hie maid for Mordiche the Jew.

Now, belovit in the Lord, seeing that neither can the crueltie of tiranns, nor yit the infirmitie that resteth in this oure corrupt nature, withhald fra us the mercifull presence of oure Saviour Chryst Jesus, but that he will visit us agane be the bryghtnes of his word to oure comfort and consolatioun, when all oure enemyis sall trembill, feir, and be confoundit. Lat us pacientlie abyd, with gronyng and with sobbis, the tyme that is apoyntit to oure correctioun, and to the full rypnes of thair malicious myndis, avoyding with all studie sic offences as separatis man fra the societie and fellowschip of God. And theis ar synnes knawin, manteanit obstinatlie, useit and defendit as that thay wer na syn nor offensive befoir God; thais sortis of synis, becaus thay ar without repentance, devydis man fra Godis favour. God the Father, for Chryst Jesus his Sonis sake, preserve and keip your hartis fra that temptatioun, and be his Halie Gaist sa quickin your senssis and purge your understanding, that what ye have professit in the dayis of rest, now in the dayis of trubill in your hartis ye may acknawledge, and with your mouthis confes (when the glorie of His halie name sall requyre the same) to be the infallibill and undoutit veritie of God. As also, to abhorre, detest, and avoyd, be all meanis possibill, that whilk ye knaw, and opinlie befoir the warld hes professit to be abominable idolatrie, the manteneris whairof sall not eschaip Godis vengeance.

My awne estait is this: since the 28th of Januar, I have travellit through all the congregationis of Helvetia,[1] and hes reasonit with all the Pastouris and many other excellentlie learnit men upon sic matters as now I can not commit to wrytting: gladlie I wold be toung or be pen utter the same to Godis glorie. Gif I thocht that I myght have your presence, and the presence of sum other assured men, I wald jeopard my awn lyfe to let men see what may be done with a saif conscience in theis dolorous and dangerous dayis; but seing that it can not be done instantlie without danger to utheris than to me, I will abyd the tyme that God sall appoynt.

[1] The classical name of Switzerland.

But heirof be assureit, that all is not lawfull nor just that is statute be Civill lawis, nether yet is everie thing syn befoir God, whilk ungodlie personis alledgeis to be treasone; but this I superceid to mair oportunitie, gif be any meanis I may, I intend to speak with yow or it be lang. God of his infinit mercie, for Chryst Jesus his Sonis sake, grant that I may find yow sic as my heart thristis. Amen. The peace of God rest with yow: in great haist, fra Deip the 10th of Maij 1554.

    Youris whome ye knaw

JOHNE KNOX.

A comfor=
table Epistell sente

to the afflicted church of Chryst,
exhortyng thē to beare hys crosse
wyth paciēce, lokyng euery houre
for hys commynge agaynne to the
greate comfort and consolacion of
hys chosen, with a prophecy of the
destruction of the wycked. Wher-
vnto is ioyned a moste wholsome
counsell, how to behaue oure
selues in the myddes of thys
wycked generacion tou-
ching the daily exer-
cise of Gods most
holy & sacred
worde.

¶ Wrytten by the man
of God.
J.   K.

Contains 14 leaves on signatures G and H, in the little volume of his Exposition upon tne Sixth Psalm. (See page 111.) The running title of these leaves is, " A Comfort to Christes Afflicted Churche." In the republication at London, 1580, it begins on the reverse of sign. D 6. The "Wholesome Counsell," mentioned in the preceding title, having been addressed by Knox to his friends in Scotland, on the 7th of July 1556, will be inserted under the proper date.

A COMFORTABLE EPISTELL SENTE TO THE AFFLICTED CHURCH OF CHRYST, EXHORTYNG THEM TO BEARE HYS CROSSE WYTH PACIENCE.¹

"Passe throughe the Citie, and put a sygne on the foreheades of those that mourne for the abominations that are commytted."—EZE. ix. 4.

WHEN I ponder wyth my selfe, beloved in the Lord, what was the state of Christes true churche immediatlie after his death and passion, and what were the chaunges and greate mutacions in the commonwealth of Judea before the finall desolation of the same: As I cannot but feare that like plagues, for lyke offences shall strike the Realme of Englande; and in fearing, God knoweth, I lament and mourne; so can I not but rejoice, *THE CARE OF GOD IS ALWAY ONE OVER HYS CHOSEN.* knowing that Godis most mercifull providence is no lesse carefull this day, over his weake and feeble servantes in the Realme of Englande, than it was that day, over his weake and sore oppressed flocke in Jurye.

What was the state of Chrystes Church betwene his death and resurrection, and from hys resurrection to the sendyng of the Holy Ghost upon hys Disciples, and from that time also to the finall destruction of Hierusalem? The playne Scripture doth witnes that it was most afflicted, without all comfort and worldly consolation, and that it was so persecuted, that havok was made over the Churche of God. And what were the mu-

¹ In the edit. 1580, the title, as given on page 237, is preceded with the words, "The Argument of the Epistle."

tations and troubles in Judea and Hierusalem before the destruction of the same, such as bee exercised in Histories, and principally in Josephus and Egesippus,[1] cannot be ignorant. For thei witnes, that over that unthankful people wer permitted to reigne cruel, tiranful,[2] and most ungodly magistrates, by whom the people wer oppressed and spoyled of their liberties; by which occasion was styrred up sedicion; and thereupon followed so cruell tyranny, that under the name of justice no smal nomber of the people were burned quicke.[3] After whiche crueltye, followed such murder universally in the cytye and in the fieldes, that the fathers feared theyr sonnes, and the brethren theyr brethren. Whyche unquietness ceased not, untill God's severe vengeaunce was once powred forth upon suche as obstinatly refused and persecuted Chryst Jesus and hys doctryne.

Egesip. Lib. i. ca. 44.

Actes 13.

But to returne to the entreatment and preservation of Christes Church at thys tyme. It is evydent, that moste sharplye it was persecuted, and yet dayly did it increase and multiplye. It was compelled to fly from citie to citie, from realme to realme, and from one nation to another; and yet so wonderously was it preserved, that a great number of those whom the wycked pryestes, by their bloody tirannye, exiled and banished from Hierusalem, wer kept alyve til God's vengeaunce was powred forth upon that most wicked generation. The remembraunce of this, beloved in the Lord, is unto my heart such comfort and consolation, that neither can my toung nor penne expresse the same. For thys assuredly is my hope and expectation, that like as Chryste Jesus appeared to hys Disciples, when ther was nothyng in theyr hearts but anguishe and

---

[1] Hegisippus, an ecclesiastical historian of the second century. Only a few fragments of his work have been preserved by Eusebius. But Knox here refers to five books on the Jewish Wars, once attributed to Hegisippus, and now considered to be the work of a later author, which was published at Paris in 1510, and in later impressions, under this title: "Historia de bello Judaico, Sceptri sublatione, Judaeorum dispersione, et Hierosolymitano excidio, a Divo Ambrosio Latine facta."

[2] Tyrannical.

[3] Burned alive.

desperation; and like as he preserved and multiplied their nomber under the most extreme persecution: So shall he do to his afflicted flocke within the Realme of England thys daye, in spite of all his enemyes. First, I say, this is my hope, that a juste vengeaunce shalbe taken upon those bloud-thirstie tyrantis, by whom Chryste Jesus in hys members is now crucified amonges you. And after that, his veritie shal so appeare to the comfort of those that now do mourne, that they shal heare and know the voyce of their owne pastor. And thys shal our merciful God doe unto us, to let us knowe, and in practise understande that his promyses ar infallible, and that he wil not intreate us according to the wicked weakenesse of our corrupte nature; whyche alwayes is readye to fall from God, to distruste hys promyses, and to forget that ever we have receaved benefite or comfort from God's hande, when trouble lieth upon us, or when extreme daunger doeth appeare.

AS GOD DID TO HIS AFFLICTED CHURCH IN JUDEA, SO SHALL HE DOE THE SAME IN ENGLAND.

And therfore, Beloved in the Lord, albeit you fynde your heartes some tymes assaulted with dolour, with grudging, or wyth some kynde of desperacion; yet dispaire not utterlie, neither be ye troubled above measure, as that Chryste Jesus shoulde never visit you agayne. Not so, deare Brethren, not so; for such imperfections rested wyth Chrystes own Apostles of a long tyme; and yet dyd they not hynder hys gayne-commyng unto them. No more shal our weaknes and imperfections hinder or let the brightnes of his countenaunce, and the comfort of his Word, yet once againe to shine before us; provyded alwayes, that Judas, his obstinacy, his impenitencye, and traiterous heart be absent from us, as I doubt not but it is from al the members of Chrystes body, who ar permitted some tymes to fal, so that of the most fervente professors they become fearfull denyers of the most knowen trueth. But they are not permitted of any continuaunce to blaspheme, neyther to remayne in unbeliefe and desperacion to the end, as in Christes Apostles plainly maye be sene.

OUR IMPERFECTION MAY NOT HINDER GOD TO BEE MERCYFULL.

GOD'S ELECT ARE PERMITTED SOME TYMES HORRIBLY TO FAL.

And that more clearelye we maye understand our tymes and

estate wythin the Realme of Englande, thys daye, to agree with the tyme and estate of Chrystes Discyples, immediatly after his death, lette us consider what chaunced to them before and after the same.

Before Chrystes passyon, as they were instructed by Chrystes owne mouth of many thynges appertayning to that kyngdome of God, whych they neither perfectly understode, neither wor‑ thelye then regarded; so wer they advertised and oft admo‑ nished, that Christe their master should suffer a cruell death, that they should be ashamed, slaundered, and offended in hym; that they shoulde flye from hym; and finally, that persecution and trouble, from time to time, shoulde apprehende them. Wyth these most dolorous tidynges he also promysed, that he shold arise upon the third day; that he shold see them againe to their comfort and consolation; and that he shoulde myghtelye delyver them from all troubles and adversyties.

<small>THE STATE OF CHRISTIS CHURCHE BEFORE AND SHORT‑ LY AFTER HYS DEATH.</small>

But what avayled all these admonitions to Chrystes Disci‑ ples before his death, or in the extremyte of their anguishes shortelye after the same? Did they feare, and verely looke for trouble before it came? Or did they looke for any comfort when the forespoken trouble was come? It is moste evydente that no such thyng did enter into their heartes. For before Chrystes death, theyr greatest mynde was upon worldly honor, for whyche some tymes they debated and contended among themselves; yea, even when Chryste was most earnestly preach‑ yng of his crosse. And after hys death, they were so oppressed with anguishe, wyth care, wyth doloure and desperacyon, that nother could the witnessing of the women, affyrmynge that they hadde seene Christ; nother the grave, lefte emptye and voyde; nother the angels, who did appeare to certifie his resurrection; nother yet the very voice and presence of Chryst Jesus him‑ selfe, remove al doubtes from theyr afflycted heartes; but from tyme to tyme theyr myndes wavered, and fully could not be established, that their Lord and Master was verely rysen to their comfort, accordynge to hys former promyses.

<small>NOTE.</small>

<small>LUKE 22.</small>

<small>LUKE 24. JOHN 20. MATHEWE THE LAST.</small>

TO CHRIST'S AFFLICTED CHURCH. 243

In thys case consider I the true Professors of Chrystes holy Evangell to bee thys daye in the Realme of Englande. For these dayes of our present dolor and trybulation have been before spoken and blowen in our eares long before they came. Our weaknes and frayle infirmite was also painted forth before oure eyes; but who would have beleeved that the dayes of our trouble had been so nygh? Or that so short a tempeste shoulde have overthrowen so great a multitude? I thinke no man within the whole realme. For al men appeared to lyve in suche careles securitie, as that the immutable sentence of God, pronouncing that whosoever will live godly in Christ Jesus shall suffer persecution, had nothing appertayned to our age. And such a bolde confidence (or rather a vayne perswacion) had a great number, of theyr own strength, that if they had continued without any backslydyng, they myghte have been judged rather angels then men. *(margin: THE TROUBLES OF GOD'S ELECT WYTHIN ENGLANDE FORESPOKEN.)* *(margin: 2 TIM. 2.)*

But, Beloved in the Lord, the sworde of anguishe and of dolor hath nowe perced the tender heart of Chrystes Mother, (that is, of his very Churche), that the cogitacions of many heartes are suffycently revealed. The fire is come, whiche as it hath burnt awaye with a blaste the stubble, hay, and wood; so, in trying the golde, silver, and precious stones, it hath founde suche drosse and duste, that the whole masse may appeare to be consumed.

For who now calleth to mind, that the same voyce which forespake our dolours, forespake also oure everlastynge comforte wyth Chryste Jesus? Who delighteth now in hys amiable promyses? Who rejoyceth under the crosse? Yea, who rather doeth not feare, tremble, grudge, and lament, as that there were no helpe in God, or as that he regarded not the trouble which we suffer? These ar the imperfections that continually remayne in thys oure corrupte nature; the knowledge wherof ought to move us earnestlye to crye, "O Lord, increase our fayth, be mercyfull unto us, and lette us not drowne in the deepe for ever." Whyche if we doe wyth unfained heartes, then yet shal Chryste Jesus appeare to oure comforte; his power shalbe knowen to the prayse and glorye of hys owne name, in despyte of all hys conjured enemyes. And thys is the chiefe and principal cause of my comforte and consolation in these moste dolorous dayes, that neyther can our infirmities nor daylye desperacion hinder or let Christ Jesus to returne to us agayne.

<small>THE CAUSE OF COMFORT.</small>

The other cause of my comfort is, that I am assured that the judgemente of these tyrantes that now oppresse us shall not slip, but that vengeaunce shal fal upon them without provision. For sufficiently they have declared the malice of their myndes. They have violated the law and holy ordinaunces of the Lord our God. They have opened their mouthes agaynst his eternal veritie. They have exyled his trueth, and establyshed their own lyes. They dayly persecute the innocentes, and stoutly maintaine open murtherers. Their heartes ar obdurate, and their faces are become shameles like harlots; so that no hope of repentance nor amendment is to be had of them. And therfore destruction shal sodenly fall upon them. But with what kinde of plagues they shalbe stryken in thys lyfe, and whom God shal appointe to execute hys vengeaunce upon them, that remit I to his good pleasure and forther revelation. But theyr manifest iniquitie is unto me an assured assuraunce, that longe they cannot escape the vengeaunce, of them most justly deserved. But in the meane season, beloved Brethren, two things ye must avoid. The former, that ye presume not to be revengers of your own cause, but that ye resigne over vengeaunce unto Him, who only is able to requite them, according to their malicious minds. Secondly, that ye hate not with any carnal hatred these blinde, cruel, and malicyous tiraunts; but that ye learne of Chryst to pray for your persecutors, lamenting and bewayling that the Devyl shold so prevaile against them, that headlynges they sholde runne body and soule to perpetuall perdicion. And note well that I saye, we may not hate them with a carnal hatred; that is to say, only because

<small>WHY GOD SHOULDE SODENLY STRIKE THE PAPISTS IN ENGLAND.</small>

<small>WHAT WE OUGHT TO AVOYDE IN EXTREME TROUBLE.</small>

<small>MATTH. 5.</small>

they trouble our bodyes: For there is a spiritual hatred, which David calleth a perfecte hatred, whyche the Holy Ghoste en- gendereth in the hartes of Godis elect, against the rebellious contemners of his holy statutes. And it is, when we more lament that God's glorye is suppressed, and that Christes flocke is defrauded of their wholsome foode, than that oure bodies are persecuted. ^{PSAL. 119.} ^{PERFECT AND GODLYE HATRED.}

With this hatred was Jeremy inflamed, when he prayed, "Lette me se thy vengeaunce taken upon thine enemies, O Lord." With thys hatred may we hate tyrantes, and earnestly may we praye for theyr destruction, bee they Kynges or Quenes, Princes or Prelates. And further ye shall note, that the prayers, made in the fervency of this hatred, are before God so acceptable, that oft times he that praieth obtaineth the self-same thing that the externall words of hys prayer do meane; as David, Jeremye, and other of the Prophetes, sawe with their corporall eyes the hote vengeaunce of God poured forth upon the cruel tyrantes of their age; and I am assured that some, which this daye do sobbe and grone under your tyranful Bishops, shal se, upon the pestilent Papistes within the Realme of England.[1] ^{JEREMY 17, 18.}

This my affirmation proceedeth not from anye conjecture of manis fantasie, but from the ordinarie course[2] of God's judgementes against manifest contemners of his preceptes, from the beginnynge: Which is this, ^{THE ORDINARIE COURSE OF GODDES JUDGMENT.}

Fyrst, To rebuke and notifie, by his messengers, suche sinnes as before the world are not knowen to be sinne.

Secondly, To provoke to repentaunce.

Thyrdly, To suffre the reprobate to declare their owne impenitencie before the world.

And laste, To poure upon them so manifest vengeaunce, that

---

[1] "In the latter part of Queen Mary's reign, great scarcity and sickness prevailed, many persons of all ranks died, and much distress prevailed. The awful death of Gardiner is well known."—(Note by the Editor of the British Reformers.)

[2] In the orig. edit. "cause."

hys Churche may be instructed, as well of his power, as of his severe judgementes againste inobediencie. This was the ordre of his judgemente againste Pharao, againste Saul, againste Jeroboam, againste Herode, againste the Scribes and Pharisees, and againste the whole citie of Jerusalem.

EXO. 7, 8, 14.
1 REG. 15.
2 REG. 13.

Our eares have hearde, and oure eyes have sene, the fyrst thre diettes of the Lordes judgement executed against the pestilent Papistes within the Realme of England. For we have heard their sommoninge and citation duely executed by the messengers of Goddes Worde. We have hearde them accused and convicted before theyr owne faces of theft and murther, of blasphemye againste God, of idolatry, and finally, of al abominations. Whiche crimes beyng layde to their charge in their own presence, they were not able to denye; so potent, so playne and evident was Goddes Worde, whereby their secrete botches and olde festred sores were discovered and reveled.

PAPISTES HAVE BENE SOMMONED.

PAPISTES HAVE BENE ACCUSED AND CONVICTED.

We know that long processe of tyme hath bene graunted by God's lenitie to their conversion and repentaunce; and howe litle the same hath avayled, these present daies may testifye. For who now doth not espie their malice to encreace, and their obstinacy to be suche, as none can be greater? Shall we then thinke that God will give over his cause, as that he wer not able to prevaile against tyrants? Not so, deare Brethren, not so. But even so assuredly as our God lyveth, by whose Spirit was styrred up some of his elect firste to espie the greate abominations of those tyrantes in this oure age; which his messengers in despite of their tyrannye God preserved to proclayme and notifie, before their owne faces, such sinnes as the worlde knew not to be sinne: And as assuredlye as we have espied them still to continue in malice agaynste God, agaynste hys eternall veritie, and agaynste the messengers of the same, so assuredly shall we se Goddes extreme plagues poured forth upon them, even in this corporall lyfe. That some of us maye witness to the generation that shall follow, the wonderous workes that the Lorde hath wrought, and will worke in thys

TIME OF REPENTANCE HATH BENE GRANTED TO PAPISTES.

THE DUE OF EXECUTION APPROCHETH.

our age. Neither shall these plagues (more then the Worde of God which passed before) worke in them any true repentaunce, but still in a blind rage they shal rebel against the Majestie of God. For the deadlie venime of that malicious serpent, their father the Devell, can never be purged from their cankred hartes. And therefore, after these plagues, of whome some wee have hearde and sene, (for what a plague was it to the false Bishop of Doresme,[1] before his owne face to be called murtherer and thiefe, and of the same so to be convicte, that neither could him self deny it, neither any of his Proctors or divine Doctors, being present with him, durst enterprise to speake one worde in defence of hys cause). After these plagues, I saye, of whome some we have sene, and the reste we shortly loke for, resteth the last, the unquencheable fyre, which is prepared for their porcion.

[margin: PAPISTES SHAL REBELL AGAINST GOD TO THE ENDE.]
[margin: TONSTAL CONVICTED OF MURTHER AND THEFT TO HIS FACE AT BARWICKE.]
[margin: THE LAST PLAGUE OF PAPISTES.]

And therefore, yet again, dearly Beloved in oure Savioure Jesus Christ, hope you against hope, and againste all worldly apperaunce. For so assuredly as God is immutable, so assuredly shall he styr up one Jehu or other to execute hys vengeaunce uppon these bloudde-thyrsty tyrauntes and obstinate idolators. And therfore abide ye paciently the tyme that is appoynted to our correction, and to the full ripenes of their malicious myndes. Be not discouraged although the Bishops have gotten the victorie. So did the Benjamites, (natural brethren to our Bishops), defenders of whoredome and of abominable adultery, twise prevaile againste the Israelites, who foughte at God's commaundement: Ye shall consider, beloved Brethren, that the counsails of God are profound and inscrutable: The moste juste man is not innocente in hys sight.

There maye be secrete causes why God sometimes will permit the moste wicked to prevayle and triumphe in the moste un-

---

[1] Dr Cuthbert Tonstall was translated to the See of Durham in 1530, was deposed in 154 , but restored in 1553, and died in November 1559, aged 85. (See the Account of his Life in Surtees's History of Durham, vol. i. pp. 66-71.)

juste action; but yet will he not longe delaye to execute his wrath, and justly deserved vengeance, upon such as be proude murtherers, obstinate idolators, and impenitente malefactors. And therefore have they not greate cause to rejoice: For albeit thei have once prevailed agaynst flesh, yet shal God shortly bringe them to confusion and shame for ever.

Let Wynchester,[1] and his cruel counsell, devise and study till hys wits faile, howe the kyngdom of his father, the Antichrist of Rome, may prosper: And let him and them drink the bloudde of Goddes sainctes till they be droncke, and theyr bellyes burst, yet shall they never prevaile long in their attemptes. Their counsailes and determinacions shalbe like the dreame of a hungry or thyrstie man, who in his slepe dreameth that he is eatinge or drinckinge; but after he is awaked, his pain continueth, and his soule is unpacient and nothinge eased. Even so shall these tyrantes, after their profounde counsayles, long devices and assured determinations, understand and know that the hope of ypocrites shal be frustrate; that a kingdome begunne with tyranny and bloudde, can neither be stable nor permanent; but that the glorie, the riches, and mainteiners of the same, shalbe as strawe in the flame of fyre. Altogether with a blaste they shal be consumed in such sorte, that their palaces shal be a heape of stones, their congregations shal be desolate; and such as do depend upon their healpe, shal fal into destruction and ignominie with them.

<small>JOB 15.</small>

<small>ESA. 22.</small>

And therefore, beloved Brethren in our Saviour Jesus Christ, seying that neither can our imperfections nor frayle weakenes hinder Christe Jesus to retourne to us by the presence of hys Worde, neither that the tyrannye of these bloude-thyrstie wolfes may so devour Christes small flocke, but that a great numbre shal be preserved to the prayse of Goddes glory; neither that these moste cruell tyrauntes can longe escape Goddes vengeaunce; let us in comforte lift up oure heades, and constantlye loke for the Lordes deliverance, with heart and voyce say-

---

[1] Dr Gardiner, Bishop of Winchester.

inge to our God, "O Lord, albeit other lordes then thou have power over our bodyes, yet lette us onely remember thee and thy holy name." To whome be prayse before the Congregation. Amen. God the Father of our Lord Jesus Christ, by his omnipotent Spirit, guide and rule your hartes in his true feare to the enae.
Amen.

☞ Written at Depe, the laste of Maye . An . M.D.Liiij.

A FAITHFUL ADMONITION

TO THE PROFESSORS OF GOD'S

TRUTH IN ENGLAND.

M.D.LIV.

FROM the two preceding Epistles, it will be seen that, after visiting various parts of France and Switzerland, Knox had returned to Dieppe in May 1554. Dr M'Crie speaks of his having undertaken a second journey, and supposes him to have returned to Dieppe in the month of July following, to "inform himself accurately of the situation of his persecuted countrymen, and to learn if he could do any thing for their comfort."[1] In support of this statement he refers to one of the Reformer's letters, which has the date, "At Diep, the 20th of July 1554," with this note:[2] "After I had visited Geneva, and uther partis, and returned to Diep to learn the estait of Ingland and Scotland." There is no doubt that Knox left Dieppe for Geneva towards the end of July; but that previously he had accomplished two distinct journeys within the course of four months, is neither proved by the words quoted, nor at all probable.[3] We may therefore safely conclude, that he still remained at Dieppe, between the last of May and the 20th of July, for the purpose of obtaining the desired tidings from his English friends; and this obviously, in the interrupted modes of communication, would be attended with considerable delay.

It was during this interval, and under the influence of the feelings excited by learning the state of affairs in England, that Knox completed the following Admonition. In the letter already mentioned as written from Dieppe on the 20th of July, which was addressed to Mrs Bowes, and will be found in

[1] Life of Knox, vol. i. p. 135.
[2] This letter was published by Knox himself in 1572, with his Answer to Tyrie the Jesuit, when this explanatory note was probably added.
[3] It may be noticed that it required eleven days to make the direct journey between Dieppe and Geneva. See Letter of Beza, in the Zürich Letters, vol. ii. p. 131. (Parker Society.)

a subsequent part of the present volume, he refers her "to a General Letter written by me in great anguish of heart to the Congregation, of whom I hear say a great part, under pretence that they may keep faith secretly in the heart, and yet do as idolators do, begin now to fall before that idoll." In order to secure a greater circulation to this General Letter or Admonition, it was committed to the press; and if "Kalykow," the fictitious place of printing, could be identified with Dieppe, or some neighbouring town, it must have been completed on the same day with the above-mentioned letter, as it also bears in the fictitious imprint the date the 20th of July 1554.

The object of this Admonition was twofold. The one was, to animate those who had made a good profession to perseverance, and to avoid the sin of apostatizing, or appearing to conform to the "abominable idolatry" re-established in England; the other, to point out the dangers to be apprehended when the kingdom became subjected to the dominion of strangers, as would necessarily result from the projected alliance of Queen Mary with Philip of Spain. This marriage was celebrated on the 25th of July 1554. It was provided by the treaty for that alliance, and confirmed by Act of Parliament, that, on the celebration of their nuptials, Philip should, during their marriage, "have and enjoy, jointly together with the Queen his wife, the style, honour, and Kingly name of the realm and dominions unto the said Queen appertaining, and shall aid her Highness, being his wife, in the happy administration of her realms and dominions."[1]

Knox, in his Admonition, uses very strong language in reference both to the Queen and her Royal husband, and to other persons who had chiefly been instrumental in restoring the idolatrous worship of the Church of Rome. In accusing Mary of breach of public faith, it may be remarked, that immediately upon her accession, she declared that "she meaned graciously

[1] Rymer's Foedera, as quoted in Sir H. Nicolas's Chronology of History, p. 337.

not to compel or strain other men's consciences *otherwise than God should, as she trusted, put in their hearts a persuasion of the truth through the opening of His Word unto them.*" But a few days later, on the 18th of August, she issued a proclamation, in which this concession is followed by these significant words: " Until such tyme as further order, by common consent, may be taken therein."[1] Her first Parliament assembled on the 5th of October 1553. In the following month, Cranmer, Ridley, and Latimer, were committed to the Tower of London on a charge of treason, in connection with the usurpation of Lady Jane Grey, who enjoyed the honours of Sovereignty only thirteen days. On the 20th of April following, after a disputation for some days on the controverted heads of religion, at Oxford, they were tried and condemned for heresy; but for upwards of twelve months no orders were issued for their execution. The reports, however, of such proceedings, and that the sufferings of the English Protestants were daily increasing during this fearfully rapid subversion of the true religion, could not fail to fill Knox's mind with the deepest sorrow. But, both to himself and others, the publication of the following Admonition was attended with effects which he could not anticipate.

In the following year, when acting as one of the pastors of the English Congregation at Frankfurt, the unmeasured language which he uses in this work, in mentioning the Queen of England and her intended husband, served as the foundation of a charge against him, and led to his expulsion from that city, as will more particularly be detailed in the next volume of his Works; but, what was of much more serious import, it was strongly alleged to have proved most calamitous in the case of his persecuted brethren in England. Some of the leaders in the English congregation, partly in vindication of their own conduct, addressed a letter to Calvin, dated September 20th,

---

[1] Council-Book, and Wilkins's Concilia, quoted by Archdeacon Todd in his Life of Archbishop Cranmer, vol. ii. p. 383.

1555; and, after referring to the circumstances which occasioned Knox's departure from that city, they stated: "This we can assure you, that that outrageous pamphlet of Knox's added much oil to the flame of persecution in England. For before the publication of that work, *not one of our brethren had suffered death:* but as soon as it came forth, we doubt not but that you are well aware of the number of excellent men who have perished in the flames; to say nothing of how many other godly men besides have been exposed to the risk of all their property, and even life itself, *upon the sole ground of either having had this book in their possession, or having read it;* who were perhaps rescued from the sword at greater cost and danger of life than the others offered their necks to it."[1]

It would be attributing too much importance to this Admonition to imagine that the fires of Smithfield might not have been kindled if it had been suppressed, or that the Bishops of Winchester and London might have thirsted in vain for the blood of Cranmer and other martyrs; but there can be no hesitation in believing that the obnoxious terms applied to Queen Mary and to her husband, as well as to Gardiner, Bonner, and the Marquess of Winchester, may have contributed, in no small degree, in evoking that spirit of persecution which has so indelibly stamped the character of blood on her reign.

The old edition, of the title of which an exact copy is given on the next leaf, has been carefully followed. The text, as it occurs in Dr M'Crie's manuscript volume, seems to be a mere transcript of the printed edition, omitting most of the marginal notes, and changing, but not improving, the style by adopting the Scotish orthography, which in this, and probably throughout the rest of that volume, ought perhaps rather to be regarded as that of the transcriber than of the author.

[1] Original Letters, relative to the English Reformation, vol. ii. p. 762.

A FAYTH-
full admonition

*made by Iohn̄ Knox, vnto the profes-
sours of Gods truthe in England, wherby thou mayeſt learne howe God wyll
haue his Churche exerciſed with
troubles, and how he defendeth it in the ſame.*

Eſaie. ix.
*After all this ſhall not the Lordes
wrath ceaſſe, but yet ſhall
hys hande be ſtretched
out ſtyll.*

Ibidem.
Take hede that the Lorde roote
thee not out bothe heade and tayie
in one daye.

In small 8vo, black-letter, 63 leaves, not paged, sign. A to I 3, in eights, excepting A, which has only 4. On the last leaf is this Colophon:

**Imprynted at Kalykow the
20. daye of Julij.**

1554.

Cum gratia & priuilegio ad Imprimendum solum.

THE EPISTLE OF A BANYSHED MANNE OUT OF LEYCESTER SHIRE, SOMETYME ONE OF THE PREACHERS OF GODDES WORDE THERE; TO THE CHRISTEN READER WYSHETH HEALTH, DELYVERAUNCE, AND FELICITIE.[1]

THERE hath been no tyme, syth the fyrst fashionynge of man, which hath not had her manyfold myseries and great troubles, by which God chaistened and punished all men for their evel lyfe and unthanckfulnes to hym, continually refusyng his callyng and warnyng; wherof the ryghteous and juste had their partes, althoughe it was for their commoditie and profit, (but to the utter destruction of the wycked and ungodly) for judgement begynneth at the faythful, which are called the Housholde of God in the Scripture; and the punyshment wherby God chasteneth them cometh always to them for the best, either to the bringyng of pacience, or the acknowlegyng of their synnes, or for the avoidynge of the eternall condempnation. And their fashion is, when they perceave the hande of the Lorde to be upon them, or upon others, by any maner of trouble, as povertie, syckens, banishment, fallynge away of faithful frendes, encreasyng of foes, or any other lyke trouble, immediately they turne to God, are hertely sorye for their synnes and unthankfulnes, confesseth them selves giltie, and calleth earnestly for mercye, whiche God for and in Jesus Christ graunteth unto them, of his great goodnes according to his promise.

1 PET. 4.

So as in the myddest of their troubles he hath used al wayes to comforte them, yea, helpe and deliver them, as it appeareth by Noe, Abraham, Loth, and the Patriarkes; David and Ezechia, kynges; Helye, Hieremy, and Daniel, prophetes; Susanna, a woman; Peter, Paule, and the reste of the Apostles; together with all good persones, in all tymes and ages, who, in their great troubles, chaunges of estates and kyngdomes, and destruccion of their common wealthes, after they had turned to God, from whence those plagues came, found relief, helpe, comforte, and deliveraunce, in these and the lyke miserable necessities.

Thys was the only remedye and defence for all good men: thyther hath

---

[1] The writer of this Epistle has not been ascertained. It is not contained in Dr M'Crie's MS. volume, along with the transcript of Knox's Admonition.

bene their chef refuge, there fastened they their hope, and rested not continually callyng upon Hym, untyl they obteyned their requestes: or els that whiche made moste for Goddes glorie and their commoditie and profyt. But contrarie wyse it is wyth the pervers and ungodly. For, so sone as they are plagued or punyshed, they grudge against God, they hate hym, and speake dispitefully against hym; they ascribe theyr plagues to evel luck or to misfortune; they are nothyng moved by them to acknowledge their great sinnes: therfore they call not upon him; but eyther they do runne in dispaire or in contempt of God; and therfore it can not be thought that their punyshmentes are tokens of the rest and quietnes that they maye have after thys lyfe, but rather to be the begynnyng of their tormentes whiche they shall then suffre. The

GENES. 4. examples wherof are lykewyse set out to us in the Holy Scriptures, as of Cain, of the Jewes, (as wel before the commyng of Christ as after his ascention,) of wycked Jesabel, of Judas the traitor, and of the thefe whiche was hanged upon the left syde of our Lorde Jesus Christe; with divers and many mo who in all their troubles, either grudged againste God, forsoke hym, or spake wordes of despite against hym and his prophetes, or els fell into dispaire, or in contempt of hym, any of which are causes of Goddes further displeasure, and of sendyng of his greater plagues to haist their destruction.

Yet the order of the punyshmentes of God (wherin he declareth his merciful nature) is to be observed of us; which is, he plagueth not commonly al offenders with one maner of plagues and in one time, although they be all a lyke gyltie; but he stryketh some sorer then others, and begynneth in some one countrie or citie, that the residue mighte be moved by the example of their punishmentes, and have tyme and place to turne to hym, who seketh not the death of a synner,

EZECHIE 18.
3 REG. 21. but hys amendement and lyfe, as appeareth by the storye of Achab, after his wyfe Jesabel had caused Naboth to be put to death. Howbeit where he threat-
EZECHIE 14. neth to punyshe the earth wyth some one plague, as honger, noisome beastes, the sworde, or pestilence; he threateneth all four at once upon Jerusalem, which bear the name of his people, but were disobedient unto hym; whiche may worthely make us fear the more because we (the people of England) are in the lyke case; amonge whom he hath sent alreadye the devourynge sworde, and a greate sort of slowe-bellyed, hote, and cruel beastes to destroye. But let us follow the examples of all good men, in doinge as the Lord our God

PSAL. 50. commaundeth us yet in these our plagues, whyche is, to turne to hym wyth all oure hartes, and call upon him; it is he onelye that maye, can, and wyll delyver us. Let the vaine truste of man's helpe be forgotten, leave off to seke swete water in filthy puddels; what comfort can the sycke man have of one that is moche sycker then hym selfe, and loketh for nothynge els but for death? Let the noble men of England leave inconstancie, luste, and covetousnes, and turne to God aryght, and let the people do the same. Lyke as there is no man that feleth not, or feareth not, some great plague to come upon him because of his synne; even so let every man repent, turne to God, and cal for helpe betyme, for there hath bene no tyme sence the ascencion of our Lord Jesus Christ wherin there hath been greater plagues than there is now in our tyme. For besyde bloody warre, sudden death, great untruth, open perjurie, division, straunge consumyng fyres, chaunge of great estates and common wealthes, overflowyng of great cities and landes by water, honger and povertie without petie; so as it should appeare that God causeth the very elementes to fyght agaynst the world, which somtyme he caused to defend his people; EXODI. 14. he hath suffred also that trueth of his Word and the true manner of worshipping of him according to the Scriptures, to be cleane taken away as it was by Christ threatned to the Jewes, in the Gospel of S. Matthew. And in token of MATHEI. 21. his further indignation, the honger and thirst after hym and his kingdom is taken from the most parte of the whole realme, that it may be altogether voide of that good blessyng which Jesus Christ our Lorde speaketh of in the gospel of S. Matthew, sayeng, "Blessed are they which honger and thirst after ryghteousnes," &c.

He suffreth for thy unthankfulnes, O Englande, false teachers to be a burthen unto thee, whiche yf thou doest receave and allowe their doctrine, be thou wel assured his great wrath commeth shortly after to thy distruction. This is the accustomed order of God when he is mynded to destroy. First, he sendeth lyeing spirites in the mouthes of their prestes or prophetes, which delyted in lyes, then suffred he them to be disceaved by the same to their destruction,[1] as he dyd wyth Achab. Be warned yet, by this and other suche good and true bokes, Gentel Reader, so shal thou be sure to be kept in savegarde in the tyme of the plague to come, wherein you shalt also fynde moche comforte. It wil move thee to styck fast to the trueth of God's Word, and to flee from the wicked ydolatrie of the abhominable Masse, which doth no more save thee from hurt, then dyd the painting of develysh Jesabel save her REG. 2. from death when she was headlong hurled out at a wyndow, at the commaundement of Jehu.

---

[1] In the orig. edit., words ending like *destruction*, are usually printed *destruccion*, and *whole*, as *hole*, peculiarities which have not been retained.

GRACE, MERCY, AND PEACE, FROM GOD THE FATHER OF OURE LORDE JESUS CHRIST, WITH THE PERPETUAL COMFORTE OF THE HOLY GHOST, BE WITH YOU, FOR EVER AND EVER. SO BE IT.[1]

HAVYNGE no lesse desyre to comforte such as now be in trouble within the Realme of Englande, (and specially you, for many causes moste deare to me) then hath the natural father to ease the grief and payne of his dearest childe; I have considered with my selfe, what argument or parcel of Goddes Scriptures was moste convenient and mete to be entreated for your consolation, in these most dark and dolorous dayes. And so, as for the same purpose I was turnyng my boke, I chansed to see a note in the margine written thus in Latyn, "*Videat Anglia*, Let Englande beware." Which note, when I had considered, I founde that the matter written in my boke in Latin was this:[2]

"Seldome it is that God worketh any notable worke to the conforte of his Churche,[3] but that trouble, feare, and laboure commeth upon suche as God hath used for his servauntes and workmen. And also tribulation most commonlye foloweth that Churche where Christe Jesus is moste truely preached."

This note was made upon a place of Scripture written in the fourteenth chapter of S. Mathewes Gospel: which place declareth, That after Christ Jesus had used the Apostles as minis-

---

[1] In place of "So be it," MS. M. has "Amen."

[2] A NOTE MADE UPON THE SENDYNG OF CHRISTES DISCIPLES TO THE SEA, THE MIRACULOUS FEDINGE OF THE PEOPLE.—(*Marginal note.*)

[3] "Churche," in MS. M. is uniformly written "Kirk."

ters and servauntes, to fede (as it had been by their handes) fyve thousand men, beside women and children, with five barley loaves[1] and two fisshes, he sent them to the sea, commaunding them to passe over before him to the other side.[2] Whiche thing as they attempted to obey, and for the same purpose did travail and rowe forth in the sea, the night approched, the wynde was contrarie, the vehement and raging storme arose, and was like to overthrowe their poore bote and them. When I had considered (as doloure and my simplicitie would suffre) the circumstances of the text, I began to reken and aske accompt of my selfe, (and as God knoweth, not without sorowe and sobbes), whether at any tyme I had been so playne by my tunge, as God had opened his holy wil and wisedome in the matter unto me, as myne owne penne and note dyd beare witnesse to my conscience. And shortly it came to my minde, that the same place of Scripture I had entreated in youre presences, what tyme God gave oportunitie and space that you should heare, and Goddes messenger should speake the wordes of eternal lyfe. Wherfore I thought nothing more expedient, then shortly to cal to mind againe suche thinges as then I trust were touched; albeit peradventure neither of me so plainly uttered, neither of you so plainly perceaved, as these moste dolorouse daies declare the same to us.

It shall not be necessary to entreat the texte worde by worde, but of the whole summe to gather certaine notes and observations (which shal not farre disagree from the estate of these daies) it shalbe sufficient.

<small>THE FYRST NOTE. JOHN. 6. MATH. 14.</small> And First, it is to be observed, That after this great miracle that Christ[3] had wrought, he neither would retaine with him selfe the multitude of people whome he had fedde, neither yet his disciples. But the one he sent awaye, every man to returne to his place of accustomed residence; and the other he sent to

---

[1] In the original edition, here and elsewhere, "looves."

[2] WHAT CHAUNSED TO CHRISTES DISCIPLES AFTER THE FEDING OF THE PEOPLE IN THE DESERT.—(*Marg. note.*)

[3] In MS. M. "his Majestie."

the daunger of the seas; not as he that was ignoraunt what should chaunce unto them, but knowinge and forseing the tempest, yea, and appointinge the same so to trouble them.

It is not to be judged, that the onely and true Pastoure would remove and sende away from him the wandering and weake shepe;[1] nether yet that the only provident Governour and Guide woulde set out his rude warriours to so great a jeopardye, without sufficient and moste juste cause.

Why Christ removed and sent awaye from him the people, the Evangelist S. John declareth, saying, "When Jesus JOHN 6. knewe that they were come, and to take hym up, that they might make hym King, he passed secretly (or alone) to the mountaine." Wherof it is playne what chieflye moved Christ to send away the people from him;[2] because that by him they sought a carnal and worldly libertie, regarding nothing his heavenly doctrine of the kingdome of God his Father, which before he had taught and declared unto them plainly; shewing them,[3] that suche as shuld folowe him must suffre for his names MATH. 10. sake persecution, must be hated of al men, must deny them selves, must be sent forth as shepe among wolves. But no parte of this doctrine pleased them, or could entre into their hertes; but their whole minde was upon their bellies, for suffising JOHN 6. wherof they devised and imagined that they wolde appoint and chose Christe Jesus to be their worldlye King; for he had power to multiplie bread at his pleasure. Whiche vaine opinion and imagination perceaved by Christ Jesus, he withdrew him selfe from their company, to avoide al suche suspicion; and to let theym understand that no such honoures dyd agre MATH. 20. with his vocation, who came to serve, and not to be served: And when the same people sought him againe, he sharply rebuked them, because they sought him more to have their bellies IOH. 6.

---

[1] CHRIST SUFFERETH NOT HIS SHEPE AND PASTOURES TO BE DISPERSED AND TROUBLED, BUT FOR CAUSES REASONABLE.—(*Marg. note.*)

[2] WHY CHRIST SENT AWAY THE PEOPLE FROM HIM.—(*Marg. note.*)

[3] In MS. M. "schawing unto them."

fed with corruptible meat, then to have their soules nourished with the lively bread that came down from heaven. And thus in the people ther was juste causes why Christ should withdraw him selfe from them for a tyme.

Why the Disciples should suffre that great daunger, feare, and anguish, S. Marke in his Gospel plainly sheweth, saying, "That theyr hertes wer blynded, and therfore dyd nether remember nor consyder the myracle of the loaves." That is, albeit with their handes[1] they had touched that bread, by which so great a multitude was fed; and albeit also they had gathered up twelfe baskets full of that which remained of a few loaves, which, before the miracle, a boye was able to have borne; yet dyd they not rightly consider the infinite power of Christ Jesus by this his wonderful miracle.[2] And therfore of necessitie it was, that in their owne bodies they should suffre trouble for their better instruction.

When I depely consider (dearly beloved in our Saviour Christ) how aboundantly, and how miraculouslye the poore and smale flocke of Christe Jesus was fedde within the Realme of Englande under that electe and chosen vessel of God to glorye and honour, Edward the Sixte; and nowe againe beholde, not only the dispersion and scattering abrode, but also the apperinge destruction[3] of the same, under these cursed, cruel, and abhominable idolaters; methinkes I see the same causes to have moved God, not only to withdrawe his presence from the multitude, but also to have sent his welbeloved servauntes to the travels of the seas, wherin they are sore tossed and turmoylled, and appearantly moste lyke to perishe.

What were the affections of the greatest multitude that folowed the Gospel in this former reste and abundaunce, is easy to be judged, yf the lyfe and conversation of every man should have bene throughlye examined. For who lyved (in

---

[1] In MS. M. "with their awn handis."
[2] THE DISCIPLES DYD NOT RIGHTLY CONSYDER CHRISTES WORKE.—(Marg. note.)
[3] Probable or apparent destruction.

that rest) as that he had refused him selfe?¹ Who lyved in that reste, as that he hadde been crucified with Christ? Who lyved in that reste, as that he had certainly loked for trouble to come upon him: Yea, who lyved not rather in delicacye and joye, sekyng the world and pleasures therof, caryng for the fleshe and carnal appetites, as thoughe death and synne had cleane been devoured? And what was this els, then to make of Christe an earthlye Kynge? The worde that we professed, dayly cryed in our eares, That our kingdom, our joye, our reste and felicitie, neither was, is, nor should be in the earth, neither in any transitory thinge therof, but in heaven, "into which we muste entre by many tribulations." But alasse! we sleped in suche securitie,³ that the sounde of this trompet coulde of manye never be perfytly understanded, but always we perswaded our selves of a certain tranquillitie, as though the troubles, wherof mencion is made within the Scriptures of God, appertained nothing at al to this age, but unto suche as of longe tyme are passed before us. And therfore was our Heavenly Father compelled to withdrawe from us the presence of his veritie (whose voice in those dayes we could not beleve), to the ende that more earnestly we may thrist for the same, and with more obedience imbrace and receave it; yf ever it shal please his infinite goodnes in suche abundaunce to restore the same agayne.

I meane nothinge of those that folowed Christ onely for their bellies; for suche, perceiving that they could not optaine their hertes desire of Christ, have grudged and left him in bodye and herte; whiche thinge their blasphemouse voices spoken against his eternall veritie dothe witnesse and declare. For suche, Brethren,⁴ be ye not moved, for in the tyme of their profession they were not of us, but were very dissemblers and hypocrites; and therfore God justly permitteth that they blaspheme the

NOTA. 2.

IOHN 18.

ACTS 14.

1 IOHN 2.

---

¹ Denied himself.
² In MS. M. "Note. Our case at this day in Scotland, 1603."
³ In MS. M. is this marginal note:
"Allace, we sleip yit : Lord! in mercy wakin us."
⁴ In the orig. edition, "brother;" in MS. M. "brether."

truthe, whiche they never loved.¹ I meane not that ever suche dissemblinge hypocrites shal imbrace the veritie, but I meane of suche as, by infirmitie of the fleshe, and by natural blyndnesse, (which in this lyfe is never altogether expelled), they coulde not geve the very obedience which Goddes Word required, neither nowe, by weaknes of faith, dare openly and boldly confesse that which their hertes knowe to be moste true, and yet lamenteth and mourneth both for the imperfection by passed and present. From suche shal not the amiable presence of Christe Jesus for ever be withdrawen; but yet agayn shal the eyes of their sore troubled hertes beholde and se that light of Christes Gospel, wherin they moste delyte.

NOTA. 2.

The Ministers who were the distributours of this bread (the true Worde of God), wherwith the multitude within Englande was fedde, lacked³ not their offences, which also moved God to sende us to the sea. And because the offences of no man are so manifest unto me as are myne owne, only of my selfe I wyl be the accusoure.

It is not unknown unto many, that I (the moste wretched) was one of that nombre whom God appointed to receave that bread, (as it was broken by Christ Jesus,) to distribute and geve the same to suche as he had called to this banket, in that parte of his table where he appointed me to serve. It is not in my knowlege nor judgement to define, nor determine what portion or quantitie every man receaved of this breade, neither yet howe that whiche they receaved agreed with their stomackes. But of this I am assured, that the benediction of Christ Jesus⁴ so multiplied the portion that I receyved of his handes, that during that banket, (this I writte to the prayse of his name, and to the accusation of myne owne unthankfulnes,) the bread never failed when the hongry soule craved or cryed

---

¹ HYPOCRITES ARE MADE MANIFEST IN THE DAYE OF TROUBLE.—(*Marg. note.*)

² In MS. M. in the margin, "Note this was found trew;" and a few lines lower down, "He meanis himself."

³ In MS. M. "wantit not."

⁴ In MS. M. "his holie name."

for foode; and at the ende of the banket, myne owne conscience beareth wytnesse, that my handes gathered up the crummes that were lefte in suche abundaunce, that my basket was ful amonge the reste.

To be playne, myne owne conscience beareth recorde to my selfe, how smale was my learning, and howe weake I was of judgment, when Christ Jesus called me to be his stewarde; and howe mightely, daye by daye, and tyme by tyme, he multiplied his graces with me, if I should concele, I were moste wicked and unthankful.[1]

But, alasse! howe blynded was my herte, and howe little I dyd consyder the dignitie of that office, and the power of God that then multiplied and blessed the bread whiche the people receaved of my handes, this daye myne owne conscience beareth witnesse to my selfe. God I take to recorde in my conscience, that I delyvered the same bread that I receaved of Christes handes; and that I mixed no poison with the same; that is, I teached Christes Gospel without any mixture of mennes dreames, devises, or phantasies. But, alasse! I did it not with suche fervency, with suche indifferency,[2] and with suche diligence, as this day I know my dutye was to have done.

Some complained in those dayes, That the preachers were undiscrete persones, yea, and some called them raylers, and worse, because they spake against the manifest iniquitie of men, and especially of those that then were placed in authoritie, aswel in the Courte, as in other offices universally throughout the Realme, both in cities, townes, and villages. And amonge other, peradventure, my rude plainnesse displeased some, who did complaine that rashly I did speake of mennes faultes; so that al men myght knowe and perceave of whom I meant. But, alasse! this day my conscience accuseth me, that I spake not so plainly as my dutie was to have done: for I ought to have

---

[1] TO DENY OR CONCEIL THE GYFTES OF GOD WHICH WE HAVE RECEYVED IS UNTHANCKFULNES.—(*Marg. note.*)

[2] "Indifferency," impartiality.

said to the wicked man expressedlye by his name, "Thou shalt dye the death." For I fynde Jeremye the prophete to have done to Pashur the hygh priest, and to Zedechias the kinge. And not only him, but also Helias, Eliseus, Micheas, Amos, Daniel, Christe Jesus him selfe, and after him his Apostles, expressedly to have named the bloude-thristy tyrantes abhominable idolaters, and dissemblynge ypocrites of their dayes. Yf that we the preachers within the Realme of Englande were appointed by God to be the salt of the earth,[1] (as his other messengers were before us,) alasse! why helde we backe the salt, where manifest corrupcion dyd appere?[2] (I accuse none but my selfe). The blynd love that I did beare to this my wicked carcase, was the chefe cause that I was not fervent and faithful enoughe in that behalfe: for I had no wil to provoke the hatred of all men against me; and therfore so touched I the vices of men in the presence of the greatest, that they might se themselves to be offenders; (I dare not saye that I was the greatest flatterer); but yet, nevertheles, I wold not be sene to proclaime manifest warre against the manifest wicked; wherof unfainedly I aske my God mercye.

As I was not so fervent in rebuking manifest iniquitie, as it became me to have been, so was I not so indifferent a feeder as is required of Christes stewarde.[3] For, in preaching Christes Gospel, albeit myne eye (as knoweth God) was not muche upon worldly promotion, yet the love of frendes and carnal affection of some men with whom I was most familiar, allured me to make more residence in one place then in another, having more respect to the pleasure of a fewe, then to the necessitie of many. That daye I thought I had not synned, yf I had not bene idle; but this daye I knowe it was my dutie to have had consideration how longe I had remained in one place,[4] and how many

---

[1] THE PREACHERS ARE NAMED THE SALT OF THE EARTH.—(*Marg. note.*)

[2] THE CONFESSION OF THE AUTHOR.—(*Marg. note.*)

[3] PREACHERS OUGHT TO FEED CHRISTES FLOCKE.—(*Marg. note.*)

[4] This feeling may have had its influence, at a later date, in 1560, when

OF GOD'S TRUTH IN ENGLAND.

hongry soules were in other places, to whome, alasse! none toke payne to breake and distribute the breade of lyfe.

Moreover, remaining in one place I was not so diligent as myne office required; but sometyme, by counsel of carnal frendes, I spared the bodye; sometyme I spent in worldlye busynesse of particular frendes; and sometyme in takyng recreation and pastyme by exercise of the body.

And albeit men may judge these to be light and smale offences, yet I knowlege and confesse, that onles pardon should to me be granted in Christes bloude, that everye one of these three offences aforenamed, that is to saye, the lacke of fervencye in reproving synne, the lacke of indifferency in feedyng those that were hongrye, and the lacke of diligence in the execution of myne office, deserved damnation.[1]

And besyde these, I was assaulted, yea infected and corrupted with more grosse sinnes; that is, my wicked nature desyred the favours, the estimation and prayse of men; against whiche, albeit that somtime the Spirite of God dyd move me to fyght, and earnestly dyd stirre me (God knoweth I lye not) to sobbe and lament for those imperfections; yet never ceassed they to trouble me, when any occasion was offered. And so prively and craftely dyd they entre into my brest, that I could not perceave my selfe to be wounded, tyl vain-glorie had almoste gotten the upperhande.[2]

[3] O Lorde! be merciful to my great offence, and deale not with me accordyng to my great iniquitie, but accordinge to the multitude of thy mercyes; remove from me the burthen of my synne; for of purpose and mynde, to have avoyded the vayne displeasure of man, I spared lytle to offende thy Godly Majestie.

Thinke not, beloved of the Lorde, that thus I accuse my selfe

---

the class of Superintendents in Scotland was appointed to supply the lack of ordained ministers in the several parishes of their respective districts.

[1] THE LACKE OF FERVENCY OF REPROVYNG, OF INDIFFERENCIE IN FEEDING, AND DILIGENCE IN EXECUTYNGE, ARE GREAT SINNES.—(*Marg. note.*)

[2] SPIRITUALL TEMPTACIONS ARE NOT SONE ESPIED.—(*Marg. note.*)

[3] THE PRAYER OF THE AUTHOR.—(*Marg. note.*)

without juste cause, as though in so doynge I myght appere more holy, or that yet I do it of purpose and intent, by occasion therof to accuse other of my Brethren, the true preachers of Christ, of lyke or of greater offences. No, God is judge to my conscience, that I do it even from an unfayned and sore troubled herte, as I that knowe my selfe grevously to have offended the Majestie of my God, duryng the tyme that Christes Gospel had free passage in Englande. And this I do to let you understande, that the taking awaye of the heavenly breade, and this greate tempest that nowe bloweth against the poore Disciples of Christe within the Realme of Englande[1] (as touching our parte[2]), commeth from the great mercye of oure Heavenly Father, to provoke us to unfained repentance, for that neither preacher nor professoure dyd rightly consider the tyme of our merciful visitation. But altogether so we spent the tyme, as thoughe Goddes Worde had bene preached rather to satisfie our fantasies then to reforme our evel maners; which thing, yf we earnestly repente, then shal Jesus Christ appeare to oure comforte, be the storme never so great. "Haste, O Lord, for thy names sake!"

THE SE-
CONDE
NOTE.

The Seconde thyng that I fynd to be noted, is the vehemencye of the feare which the Disciples endured in that great daunger,[3] beyng of longer continuaunce then ever they had at any tyme before.

MATH. 8.

In Saint Mathewes Gospel it appereth, that an other tyme there arose a great stormy tempest, and sore tossed the bote wherin Christes disciples were labouring;[4] but that was upon[5] the daye lyght, and then they had Christe with them in the bote, whome they awaked, and cryed for helpe unto him, (for

---

[1] THE TROUBLES OF THESE DAYES COMMETH TO THE PROFYT OF GODDES ELECT.—(*Marg. note.*)

[2] As it respects us.

[3] THE GREATE FEARE OFF THE DISCIPLES.—(*Marg. note.*)

[4] THE DISCIPLES ALSO BEFORE THIS TYME WERE TROUBLED IN THE SEA.—(*Marg. note.*)

[5] Was nigh, was close upon.

at that tyme he slept in the bote), and so were shortly delyvered from their sodain feare. But nowe were they in the middest of the raging sea, and it was nyght, and Christ their comfortour absent from them, and commeth not to them, neither in the fyrst, seconde, nor third watche. What feare, trowe you, were they in then? and what thoughtes arose up out of their so troubled hertes duringe that storme? Suche as this daye be in lyke daunger within the Realme of Englande, dothe by this storme better understande, then my penne can expresse. But of one thynge I am wel assured, that Christes presence wold in that great perplexitie have been to them more comfortable then ever it was before; and that paciently they would have suffered their incredulitie to have been rebuked, so that they might have escaped the present death.

But profitable it shalbe, and somwhat to our comforte, to consyder every parcel of their daunger.[1] And First, ye shal understande, That when the disciples passed to the sea to obey Christes commaundement, it was faire wether, and no suche tempest sene:[2] But sodenly the storme arose, with a contrarious flawe of wynde, when they were in the middest of their journey. For if the tempest had bene as great in the beginninge of their entraunce to the sea, as it was after when they were about the middest of their journey, neither wolde they have aventured suche a great daunger; neither yet had it been in their power to have attayned to the middest of the sea:[3] And so it may be evydently gathered, that the sea was calme when they entred into their journey.

Secondly, it is to be marked, By what meanes and instrumentes was this great storme moved. Was the plunging of their oares and force of their smale bote, suche as myght stirre the waves of that great sea? No, doutlesse; but the Holy Ghost declareth that the seas were moved by a vehement and con-

---

[1] In MS. M. "this thair daunger."
[2] WHAT TYME THE TEMPESTE DYD ARRYSE.—(*Marg. note.*)
[3] THE SEA WAS CALME WHEN THE DISCIPLES TOKE THEIR BOTE.—(*Marg. note.*)

trary wynde,¹ whiche blewe against their bote in the tyme of darkenesse. But seyng the wynde is neither the commaunder nor mover of it self, some other cause is to be inquired, which hereafter we shal touche.

And last, it is to be noted and considered, What the disciples dyd in all this vehement tempest. Truely they turned not back to be dryven on forlande or shore by the vehemency of that contrary wynde; for so it myght be thought, that they could not have escaped shipwracke and death. But they continuallye laboured in rowyng against the wynde, abyding the ceassing of that horrible tempeste.

Consider and marke, beloved in the Lord, what we reade here to have chaunsed,² to Christes disciples, and to their poore bote;³ and you shal wel perceave, that the same thynge hath chaunsed, dothe, and shal chaunse, to the true churche⁴ and congregation of Christe (whiche is nothing els in this miserable lyfe but a poore bote) travelyng in the seas of this unstable and troublesome world, towarde the heavenly porte and haven of eternal felicitie,⁵ which Christ Jesus to his electe hath appointed.

This myght I prove by the posteritie of Jacob in Egipte; by the Israelites in their captivitie; and by the Churche duryng the tyme that Christ him selfe dyd preache, (and somtyme after his Resurrection and Ascension;) againste whome the vehement storme dyd not rage immediatly after they entred into the bote of their travail and tribulation. For the bloudy sentence of Pharao was not pronounced against the seede of Jacob, what tymo he firste dyd entre into Egipte. Neither was the cruel counsel and develish devise of proude Haman invented by and by after Israel and Juda were translated from their possessions. Neither yet, in the tyme of Christ Jesus beyng conversant with

EXOD. I.

ESDR. I.

---

¹ WHAT MOVED THE SEA.-(*Marg. note.*)
² In MS. M. "have cumin."
³ THE TOSSED BOTE IS A FYGURE OF CHRISTES CHURCH.—(*Marg. note.*)
⁴ In MS. M. "the same thingis hath cumin, doth, and sal cum to the trew kirk;" in other words, has happened, does, and shall happen to the true church.
⁵ In MS. M. "everlasting felicitie."

his apostles in the fleshe, was there used any suche tyranny against the saintes of God, as shortly after followed in the persecution of S. Steven and other disciples. But al these in the beginning of their travail, with a contrary wynde, had alwaye some calme; that is, albeit they had some trouble, yet had they not extreme persecution. [ACT. 7, & DEIN.]

Even so, moste dearly Beloved, is happened nowe to the afflicted Churche of God within the Realme of Englande. At al tymes the true Word of God suffred contradiction and repugnauncie. And so the wynde blewe against us, even from the beginning of the late upspryng of the Gospel in England; but yet it could not stoppe our course, tyl nowe of late dayes, that the ragynge wynde bloweth without briddel upon the unstable seas, in the myddest whereof we are in this houre of darknesse.

To wryt my minde plainly unto you, beloved Brethren: This wynde that alwayes hath blowen againste the Churche of God, is the malice and hatred of the Devel, which rightly in this case is compared to the wynde.[1]

For as the wynde is invisible, and yet the poore Disciples feale that it troubleth and letteth their bote; so is the pestilent envy of the Devel workynge alwayes in the hartes of the reprobate, so subtile and craftye, that it can not be espied by Goddes electe, nor by his messengers, til firste they feale the blastes thereof to blowe their bote backward. And as the vehement wynde causeth the waves of the sea to rage,[2] and yet the dead water neither knoweth what it dothe, neither yet can it ceasse nor refrayne: so that both it is troubled by the wynde, and also it selfe doth trouble Christes disciples and their poore bote. So by the envie and malice of the Devel, ar wicked and cruel as wel subjectes as princes (whose hertes are lyke the raginge sea), compelled to persecute and trouble the true [SIMILE.]

---

[1] THE MALICE OF THE DEVEL COMPARED TO THE WYNDE.—(*Marg. note.*)

[2] THE SEA CAN NOT BE QUIET WHAN THE WYNDE BLOWETH OUTRAGIOUSLY.—(*Marg. note.*)

Churche[1] of Christe; and yet so blynded are they, and so thral under the bondage of the Devel, that neither can they see their manyfest iniquitie, neither yet can they cease to runne to their owne destruction. And hereof, England, hast thou manifest experience. For in the time of Kynge Henry the Eyght,[2] howe the wolfe, that wycked Wynchester, and other, by the vehement wynde of Syxe Bloudye Articles[3] (by the Devell devised) intended to have overthrowen the poore bote and Christes disciples, is too evidently knowen alredy. But then had we Christ Jesus with us sleping in the bote, who did not despise the faythful crying of suche as then were in trouble; but by hys myghty power, gracious goodnes, and invincible force of his holy worde, he compelled those wicked wyndes to cease, and the ragyng of those seas to be stilled and calmed.[4] So that all the heartes of Goddes electe, within the Realme of Englande, dyd wondre at that soddeyn chaunge, while that under a Lambe the fearful edge of that devouring sworde was taken from the neckes of the faythful. And the tyranny of those ravenynge and bloude-thristy wolves (I mean of wyly Wynchester and of some other his brethren, the sonnes of the Dyvel,) was repressed for a tyme.

But yet ceassed not the Devell to blowe hys wynde,[5] but

---

[1] In MS. M. "the trew kirk," the word kirk being uniformly substituted in this copy for "church."

[2] THE WYNDE THAT BLEWE IN KYNGE HENRY THE EYGHT DAYES.—(*Marg. note.*)

[3] The "Bloody Articles" referred to, were enacted in the year 1539, and consisted of a determination on the following six articles: 1. That in the sacrament of the altar, after the consecration, there remained no substance of bread and wine, but under these forms the natural body and blood of Christ were present. 2. That the communion in both kinds was not necessary to salvation to all persons by the law of God. 3. That the marriage of priests was not to be allowed. 4. That vows of chastity ought to be observed by the law of God. 5. That the use of private masses ought to be continued. And, 6. That auricular confession was expedient and necessary, and ought to be retained in the Church.—(Todd's *Life of Cranmer*, vol. i. p. 281.) A legal sanction was thus given to the principal errors of Popery, excepting the Papal supremacy.

[4] A QUIET CALME WAS UNDER KYNGE EDWARD THE SEXT.—(*Marg. note.*)

[5] THE FIRST SECRETE PESTILENTE WYNDE THAT BLEWE IN THE TYME OF GOOD KYNGE EDWARDE THE SEXT.—(*Marg. note.*)

by his wicked instrumentes founde the meanes, how, against nature, the one broder¹ should assent to the death of the other: but he could not hynder the course of the travelyng bote, but forth she goeth in despyte of the Devel; who then more cruelly raged, perceyvyng his owne honour and service, that is, his detestable Masse, to be disclosed and opened before the people, to be dampnable idolatrye, and assured damnation to suche as put their trust in it.² And therfore began he more craftelye to worke, and fynding the same instrumentes apt enough, whose labours he had used before, he blewe suche mortal hatred betwene two, whiche appeared to have bene the chefe pillers under the kinge. For that wretched (alas!) and miserable Northumberlande could not be satisfied, tyl such tyme as simple Somerset³ most unjustlye was bereft of his lyfe. What the Devel, and his membres, the pestilent Papistes, meant by his awaye-takinge, God compelled my tounge to speake in mo places then one. And specially before you, and in the Newe Castle, as Syr Robert Brandlinge⁴ dyd not forget of long tyme after. God graunt that he may understande al other maters spoken before him then, as at other tymes, as rightly as he dyd that myne interpretation of the vyneyarde, whose hedges, ditches, toures, and wynepresse, God destroyed, because it would bring forth no good frute. And that he maye remember, ESA. 5. that what ever was spoken by my mouth that daye, is now

¹ Sir Thomas Seymour, Lord Admiral, was brother to the Protector, Edward Duke of Somerset. This ambitious, unprincipled man was beheaded for treasonable practices, in 1549. The warrant of his execution, says Archdeacon Todd, " was unfeelingly signed by the Protector, and uncanonically by Cranmer, the interference of bishops in a cause of blood being contrary to the ancient canon laws."— (*Life of Cranmer*, vol. ii. p. 143.) But the Protector himself, before the end of the year, was displaced from his office and imprisoned, (chiefly by the intrigues of John Earl of Warwick, afterwards Duke of Northumberland); and suffered the same fate as his brother the Admiral.

² THE DEVEL RAGED WHEN THE MASSE MISCHEFE WAS DISCLOSED.—(*Marg. note.*)

³ See notes 2 and 3, p. 278.

⁴ Sir Robert Brandling was Mayor of Newcastle in 1532, 1536, 1543, and 1547. In this last year, the Protector, Duke of Somerset, assembled his army at Newcastle for the invasion of Scotland; and after his return, he conferred the honour of knighthood on Brandling.

MARCKE WELL.

complete and come to passe; except that the final destruction and vengeance of God is not yet fallen upon the greatest offendoures, as assuredly shortly it shal, unlesse that he, and suche other of his sorte, that then were enemies to Goddes truth, wyl spedelye repent, and that earnestly, of their stubburne disobedience. God compelled my tounge, I say, openly to declare,[1] That the Devel and his ministers intended only the subvercion of Goddes true religion, by that mortal hatred amonge those which oughte to have bene moste assuredly knyt together by Christian charitie, and by benefites receyved. And especially that the wycked and envious Papistes, by that ungodlye breache of charitie, diligently minded the overthrowe of hym, that, to his owne destruction, procured the death of his innocent frende.[2] Thus, I saye, I was compelled of conscience oftener then once to affirme, that suche as sawe, and invented the meane how the one should be taken awaye, sawe and shoulde finde the meanes also to take awaye the other;[3] and that al that trouble was devised by the Devil and his instrumentes, to stoppe and let[4] Christes disciples and their poore bote; but that was not able, because she was not yet come to the myddest of the sea.

Transubstantiation,[5] the byrde that the Devel hatched by Pope Nicolas, and sythe that tyme fostered and nurryshed by al his children, prestes, freres, monkes, and other his conjured

[1] THIS WAS AFFIRMED BOTH BEFORE THE KYNGE AND ALSO BEFORE NORTHUMBERLAND AFTENER THAN ONCE.—(*Marg. note.*)

[2] "His innocent friend." The Duke of Somerset, after his imprisonment, in 1549, had been pardoned, but was afterwards condemned, and beheaded, January 22, 1552. Strype says, "His death was brought about by a faction, headed by the proud Duke of Northumberland;" and, after mentioning the persons who were most active therein, he adds, "In the end, what became of Northumberland himself, the great wheel of all, that procured the Duke of Somerset's death? He also perished, not long after, unpitied by all."—(*Ecclesiastical Memorials*, vol. ii. 306–7.)

[3] The Duke of Northumberland did not escape. For the share he had in supporting the claims of Lady Jane Grey to the Crown, he was beheaded on the 22d of August 1553. See *supra*, page 169.

[4] "Let," hinder.

[5] The doctrine of Transubstantiation was established by Pope Innocent III., at the Council of Lateran, A.D. 1215. Nicolas I. was Pope from A.D. 858 to 867.

and sworne souldiers, and in this laste dayes, chiefly by Stephen Gardiner and his blacke broode in England,—Transubstantiation (I saye) was not then clearly confuted and myghtely overthrowen, and therfore God put wysedome in the tounges of his ministers and messengers to utter[1] that vayne vanitie; and specially gave such strength to the penne of that reverend father in God, Thomas Cranmer, Archebysshop of Canterbury,[2] to cut the knottes of develyshe sophistrie, lyncked and knyt by the Devel's Gardener, and his blynd bussardes,[3] to holde the veritie of God[4] under bondage, that rather I thinke they shal condemne his workes, (whiche, notwithstanding, shal continue and remaine to their confusion,) then they shal enterprise to answere the same. And also God gave boldnesse and knowlege to the court of Parliament to take awaye the rounde clipped God,[5] wherein standeth al the holines of Papistes, and to commaunde common breade to be used at the Lordes table; and also to take awaye the moste parte of superstitions (kneling at the Lordes Supper excepted) whiche before prophaned Christes true religion.

Then, deare Brethren, was the bote in the middes of the sea,[6]

---

[1] To disclose.

[2] TRANSUBSTANTIATION OVERTHROWEN BY THOMAS CRANMER, ARCHEBYSSHOP OF CANTERBURY.—(*Marg. note.*)

[3] Buzzards, a degenerate kind of hawk, but figuratively applied to a senseless, ignorant fool.

[4] In 1550 Cranmer published "A Defence of the True and Catholick Doctrine of the Sacrament of the Body and Blood of our Saviour, Christ." Gardiner, in 1551, answered this in "An Explication and Assertion of the True Catholic Faith, touching the most blessed Sacrament of the Altar, with a Confutation of a Book written against the same." In reply to this, Cranmer published his well-known work, "An Answer, by the Reverend Father in God, Thomas Archbishop of Canterbury, Primate of all England, and Metropolitan, unto a crafty and sophistical Cavillation, devised by Stephen Gardiner, Doctor of Law, late Bishop of Winchester, against the True and Godly Doctrine of the most holy Sacrament of the Body and Blood of our Saviour, Christ." London, 1553, folio.

[5] THE ROUND GOD WAS TAKEN AWAY BY ACTE OF PARLYAMENT.—(*Marg. note.*)
—The Act of Parliament respecting the Sacrament of the Altar, and of the receiving thereof under both kinds, was passed in December 1547.

[6] WHAN ALL THE PAPISTICALL ABOMINACIONS WERE REVELED, THEN WAS THE BOTE IN MIDDEST OF THE SEA.—(*Marg. note.*)

and sodenly ariseth the horrible tempeste, moste fearful and dolorouse: Our Kyng is taken away from us; and the Devel bloweth in suche organes[1] as alwaye he had founde obedient to his preceptes, and by them he enflameth the harte of that wretched and unhappy man (whom I judge more to be lamented than hated), to covet the Imperial Crowne of England[2] to be establyshed to his posteritie; and what thereupon hath succeded, it is not now necessary to be written.

<small>TWO SPE-CIAL NOTES OF THIS DIS-COURSE.</small> Of this short discourse, beloved in the Lorde, you maye consyder and perceyve two special notes:

<small>THE FYRSTE NOTE.</small> The first, That the whole malice of the Devel hath alwayes this ende, to vexe and overthrowe Christes afflicted Churche: For what els intended the Devel, and his servauntes, the pestilent Papistes, by al these their craftie policies, durynge the tyme that Christes Gospel was preached in Englande, then the subvercion of the same Gospel, and that they myght recover power to persecute the saintes of God; as this daye, in the houre of darknes, they have obtained for a tyme, to their owne utter destruction?

Let no man wonder thoughe I saye, that the crafty policies of pestilent Papistes wrought al mischiefe; for who could better worke mischief, than suche as bore authoritie and rule? And who, I pray you, ruled the roste in the courte all this tyme, by stoute corage and proudnes of stomack, but Northumberland? But who, I pray you, under Kynge Edwarde, ruled al by counsel and wyt?[3] Shall I name the man? I wil wryte no more plainly now then my tounge spake, the laste sermon that it pleased God that I should make before that innocent and moste godly kynge, Edwarde the Syxte, and before his

---

[1] "Bloweth in such organes,"—inspires such instruments.

[2] "To covet the Imperial Crowne of England," in the person of Lady Jane Grey, who had married Lord Guilford Dudley, fourth son to the Duke of Northumberland. The Duke was "the unhappy man" who is here alluded to.

[3] WHO RULED ALL BY WYT UNDER KYNGE EDWARDE THE SEXTE.—(*Mary note.*)

counsell at Westminster, and even to the faces of suche as of whom I ment: Entreatynge this place of Scripture—"*Qui edit mecum panem, sustulit adversus me calcaneum suum;*"¹ that is, "He that eateth bread with me hath lifteth up his heele against me," I made this affirmacion, That commonlye it was sene, that the most godly princes hadde officers and chief counseilours moste ungodlye,² conjured enemies to Goddes true religion, and traitours to their princes. Not that their wickednesse and ungodlynesse was spedely perceyved and espied out, of the said princes and godly men, but that for a tyme those crafty colourers could so cloke their malice against God and his trueth, and their holowe hertes towarde their lovinge maisters, that, by worldly wysedome and pollicie, at length they attained to high promotions. And for the proofe of this myne affirmation, I recited the histories of Achitophel, Sobna, and Judas; of whom the two former had hyghe offices and promocions, with great authoritie, under the moste godly princes David and Ezechias; and Judas was purse-maister with Christ Jesus. And when I had made some discourse in that matter, I moved this question:—

JOH. 13.
PSAL. 40.

2 REG. 17.
ESA. 23.
MATH 26.
JOHN 12.

"Why permitted so godly princes so wicked men to be upon their counsell, and to beare office and authoritie under them?"

QUESTIO.

To the which I answered, That either they so abounded in worldlye wysedome, foresight, and experience, touchinge the governement of a common wealth, that their counsail appeared to be so necessarie, that the common wealth could not lacke them; and so, by the coloure to preserve the tranquilitie and quietnes in realmes, they were maintained in authoritie.³ Or els they kept their malice, which they bare towarde their maisters and Goddes true religion, so secrete in their breastes, that no man could espie it, til, by Goddes permission, they wayted for

RESPONSIO.

---

¹ The Latin words are omitted in MS. M.

² GODLY PRINCES COMMONLY HATH MOST UNGODLY COUNSAILLERS.—(*Marg. note.*)

³ THE ENNEMYES OF THE VERITYE MANYE TYMES APPEARE TO BE MOST PROFITABLE FOR A COMMON WEALTHE.—(*Marg. note.*)

suche occasion and opportunitie, that they uttered all their mischiefe so plainlye, that al the worlde myght perceave it.[1] And that was moste evident by Achitophel and Sobna;[2] for of Achitophel it is written, that he was David's most secrete counsailour; and that bycause his counsel in those dayes was lyke the oracle of God.

And Sobna was unto good Kynge Ezechias somtyme comptroller, somtyme secretary, and last of al treasurer; to the which offices he had never bene promoted under so godly a prince, yf the treason and malice which he bare against the Kinge, and against Goddes true religion, hadde been manyfestly knowen. No, quod I; Sobna was a crafty foxe, and could shewe suche a faire countenaunce to the Kinge, that neither he nor his counsail coulde espie his malicious treason; but the prophete Esias was commaunded by God to go to his presence, and to declare his traitorouse herte and miserable ende.

Was David, sayd I, and Ezechias, princes of great and godly giftes and experience, abused by crafty counsailers and dissemblyng hypocrites? What wonder is it then, that a yonge and innocent Kinge be deceived by craftye, covetouse, wycked, and ungodly counselours?[3] I am greatly afrayd, that Achitophel be counsailer, that Judas beare the purse, and that Sobna be scribe, comptroller, and treasurer.[4]

This, and somwhat more I spake that daye, not in a corner (as many yet can wytnesse), but even before those whome my conscience judged worthy of accusation: And this daye no more do I wryte (albeit I maye justly, because they have declared themselves more manifestly); but yet do I affirme, that under that innocent Kinge pestilent Papistes had greatest

---

[1] MYSCHEFE AT THE LENGTH WILL SO UTTER IT SELFE, THAT MEN MAYE ESPIE IT."—(*Marg. note.*)

[2] "Sobna," in our present version, "Shebna." The transcriber of MS. M. here adds on the margin : "1603. O Lord, help us, and be mercifull to us in Scotland this day!"

[3] IF DAVID AND EZECHIAS WERE DISCEAVED BY TRAYTOROUSE COUNSAYLERS, HOWE MOCH MORE A YONGE AND INNOCENT KYNGE.—(*Marg. note.*)

[4] THE AUTHOR MYGHT FEARE THIS INDEED.—(*Marg. note.*) In MS. M., the transcriber adds on the margin, "We may feir this day."

authoritie. Oh! who was judged to be the soule and lyfe to the counsel in every matter of weaghty importance? Who but Sobna.[1] Who could best dispatche busynesses, that the rest of the Counsel might hauke and hunt, and take their pleasure? None lyke unto Sobna. Who was moste franke and redy to destroye Somerset and set up Northumberlande? Was it not Sobna? Who was moste bolde to crye, Bastarde, bastarde, incestuous bastarde, Mary shal never raigne over us?[2] And who, I praye you, was moste busy to saye, Feare not to subscribe with my Lordes of the Kinges Majesties moste honourable Prevy Counseil? Agree to his Graces last wil and parfit testament, and let never that obstinate woman come to authoritie. She is an erraunt Papist: She wil subvert the true religion, and will bring in straungers, to the destruction of this common wealth. Which of the Counsel, I saye, had these and greater persuasions against Marye, to whom now he crouches and kneleth? Sobna the Treasurer. And what intended suche trayterous and dissembling ypocrites by al these and suche lyke craftie sleightes and conterfait conveaunce? Doutles the overthrowe of Christes true religion, which then began to florishe in England; the libertie wherof fretted the guttes of suche pestilent Papistes, who now hath gotten the dayes which they longe loked for, but yet to their owne destruction and shame; for, in the spyt of their heades, the plagues of God shall stryke them. They shalbe comprehended in the snare which they prepare for other; for their owne counsels shal

PAULETT IS PAINTED.

CAIPHAS PROPHECIED.

---

[1] Under the character of Shebna, Knox refers to Sir William Paulet, created in 1551 Marquess of Winchester, who was successively Comptroller, Secretary, and Lord Treasurer to Edward the Sixth, and was continued in that office by Queen Mary. He had declared himself to Cranmer in favour of Lady Jane Grey, and had railed against the Princess Mary, as here intimated; yet when Cranmer was committed to the Tower, in September 1553, he was not ashamed to sit among his examiners, and treat him with severity. During seven reigns of political and religious discord, he enjoyed a course of prosperity, likening himself to the pliable willow, not the stubborn oak. He died in 1572, having attained the great age of 97.

[2] THE TREASURERS WORDES AGAINST THE AUTHORITIE OF MARY.—(*Marg. note.*)

>JUDGE AT THE ENDE.

make them selves slaves to a proude, mischevous, unfaythful, and vile nation.

>THE SECOND NOTE.

But nowe to the Seconde note of our discourse, which is this: Albeit the tyrauntes of this earth have learned, by longe experience, that they are never able to prevaile against Goddes truth; yet, because they are bounde slaves to their maister the Devil, they can not ceasse to persecute the membres of Christ, when the Devel blowes his wynde in the darknesse of the night;[1] that is, when the light of Christes Gospel is taken away, and the Devel raigneth[2] by idolatry, supersticion, and tyranny.

This moste evidently may be sene, from the beginninge of this worlde to the tyme of Christ, and from thence til this daie.

>GEN. 21. GEN. 28.

Ismael myght have perceaved that he could not prevaile against Isaac, because God had made his promise unto him; as no doute Abraham their father teached to his whole household. Esau

>EXOD. 5, 6. 7, 8, &c. JOHN 5 & 12.

lykewyse understode the same of Jacob. Pharao might plainly have sene by many miracles[3] that Israel was Goddes people, whome he could not utterly destroye. And also, the Scribes and Phariseis and chiefe prestes were utterly convict[4] in their conscience that Christes whole doctrine was of God, and that, to the profite and commoditie of man, his miracles and workes were wrought by the power of God; and therefore that they could never prevaile against him. And yet, as the Devel styrred then, none of those could refraine to persecute Him, whome they knewe moste certainly to be an innocent.

This I wryt, that you shall not wonder, albeit now ye se the poysoned Papistes, wicked Wynchester, and dreaming Duresme, with the rest of theyr faction (who somtymes were so confounded, that neither they durst nor could speake nor wryte in the defence of their heresies,) nowe so to rage and triumphe against the eternal truth of God,[5] as though they had never assayed the power of God speaking by his true messengers.

---

[1] TIRAUNTES CAN NOT CEASSE TO PERSECUTE CHRISTES MEMBRES.—(*Marg.note.*)

[2] "Raigneth," in MS. M. "ringeth."

[3] "By many miracles," in MS. M. "by manifest miracles."

[4] Fully convinced.

[5] THE POWER OF GODDES WORD PUT

OF GOD'S TRUTH IN ENGLAND.

Wonder not hereat, I saye, beloved Brethren, that the tyrantes of this worlde are so obedient, and redye to folowe the cruel counsels of suche disguysed monsters;[1] for neither can the one nor the other refraine, because both sortes are as subjecte to obey the Devel, their prince and father, as the unstable sea is to lyft up the waves when the vehement wynde bloweth upon it.

It is fearfull to be heard, that the Devel hath such power over any man, but yet the Worde of God hath so instructed us. And therfore, albeit it be contrary to our phantasie, yet we must believe it; for the Devel is called the Prince and god of this Worlde, because he raigneth,[2] and is honoured by tyranny and idolatry in it. JOHN 12. 2 COR. 4.

He is called the Prince of Darknes, that hath power in the ayre. It is said, That he worketh in the children of unbelefe, because he styrreth them to trouble Goddes elect; as he invaded Saul, and compelled him to persecute David; and lykewyse he entered into the herte of Judas, and moved him to betray his Maister. He is called Prince over the sonnes of pride, and Father of al those that are lyers and enemies to Goddes truthe; over whom he hath no lesse power this day, then somtymes he had over Annas and Caiphas, whom no man denieth to have been led and moved by the Devel to persecute Christ Jesus and his moste true doctrine. And therefore, wonder not, I say, that now the Devel rageth in his obedient servaunts, wyly Wynchester,[3] dreaming Duresme, and bloudy Bonner, with the rest of their bloudy, butcherly broode: for this is their houre and power graunted to them; they can not ceasse nor asswage their furious fumes, for the Devil, their sire, stirreth, moveth, and carieth them, even at his wyl.[4] But in this that I EPHES. 2. 1 REG. 16, 18. JOHN 13. JOHN 8.

PAPISTES TO SILENCE WITHIN ENGLAND, EXCEPT IT HAD BENE TO BRAGGE IN CORNERS.—(*Marg. note.*)

[1] PRINCES ARE REDY TO PERSECUTE AS THE MALICIOUSE PAPISTES WIL COMMAUND.—(*Marg. note.*)

[2] "Raigneth," in MS. M. "ringeth."

[3] WILY WINCHESTER, DREAMYNGE DURESME, BLOUDYE BONNER.—(*Marg. note.*)

[4] THIS IS THE CAUSE BEFORE OMITTED, WHI THE WYNDE BLEW TO TROUBLE CHRYSTES DISCIPLES.—(*Marg. note.*)

declare the power of the Devell workinge in cruel tyrauntes, think you that I attribute or gyve to hym or to them power at their pleasure? No, not so, Brethren,[1] not so: for as the Devel hath no power to trouble the elementes, but as God shal suffre; so hath worldlye tyrauntes (albeit the Devel hath fully possessed their hertes) no power at al to trouble the saintes of God, but as their bridle shal be lowsed by Goddes handes.

And herein, deare Brethren, standeth my singuler comforte this day, when I hear that those bloudy tyrauntes within the Realme of Englande doth kyl, murther, destroy, and devoure man and woman, as ravynous lyons nowe loused from bondes. I lyft up, therfore, the eyes of myne herte (as my iniquitie and present doloure wil suffer), and to my Heavenly Father wil I saye:—

<small>THE PRAYER OF THE AUTHOR.</small> "O Lorde! those cruel tyrauntes are loused by thy hande, to punish our former ingratitude, whom, we trust, thou wilt not suffer to prevail for ever; but when thou haste corrected us a lytle, and hast declared unto the worlde the tyrannye that lurked in their boldened[2] breastes, then wilt thou breake their jawe-bones, and wilt shut them up in their caves againe, that the generation and posteritie folowynge may prayse thyne holy name before thy congregacion. Amen."

When I feele any taste or motion of these promyses, then thinke I myselfe most happy, and that I have received a juste compensacion, albeit I, and al that to me in earth belongeth should suffer the present death; knowynge that God shal yet shewe mercy to his afflicted Churche within Englande, and that he shall represse the pride of these present tyrauntes, lyke as he hathe done of those that were before our dayes.

<small>EXHORTA-CION.</small> And therefore, beloved Brethren[3] in our Savioure Jesus Christ, holde up to God your handes, that are fainted thorowe feare, and let your hertes, that have in these dolourouse dayes

---

[1] In the original edit. "brother;" in MS. M. "brether."

[2] "Boldened," swelled with pride.

[3] In the original edit. "brother;" in MS. M. "brether."

sleeped in sorowe, awake, and heare the voyce of your God, who sweareth by him selfe, That he wil not suffer hys Churche to be oppressed for ever; neither that he will despyse our sobbes to the ende, yf we wil rowe and stryve against this vehement wynde. I meane, yf that we wil not runne backe headlinges to idolatrie, then shall this storme be aswaged in despite of the Devel. Christe Jesus shall come with spede to your delyveraunce;[1] he shal pearce thorowe the wynde, and the raging seas shal obey, and beare his feete and body as the massie, stable, and drie land. Be not moved from the sure foundacion of your fayth. For albeit that Christe Jesus be absent from you (as he was from his disciples in that great storme) by his bodely presence, yet he is present by his myghtie power and grace. He standeth upon the mountaine[2] in securitie and rest; that is, his fleshe and whole humanitie[3] is now in heaven, and can suffer no suche trouble as somtymes he dyd; and yet he is ful of petie and compassion, and doth consider al our travail, anguish, and labours; wherfore, it is not to be douted but that he wil sodenly appeare to our great comforte. The tyrantes of this world can not kepe backe his coming, more then might the blustering wind and raging seas let Christ to come to his disciples, when they loked for nothing but for present death.

And therefore, yet agayn, I saye, beloved in the Lorde, Let youre hertes attend to the promises that God hath made unto true repentaunte sinners; and be fullye persuaded wyth a constant fayth, that God is alwayes true and just in his performance of his promises. Yow have hearde these dayes spoken of very playnly, when your hertes could feare no daunger, because yow were nyghe the lande, and the storme was not yet risen; that is, ye were yonge scholers of Christ, when no

---

[1] THE COMMYNG OF CHRIST TO HIS DISCIPLES UPON THE SEAS IS OPENED.—(*Marg. note.*)

[2] CHRIST IS SURE UPON THE MOUNTAIN.—(*Marg. note.*)

[3] "His flesche and whole humanitie," that is, his human nature, his body.

persecution was seen or felt. But now ye are come into the middest of the sea (for what parte of Englande herde not of youre profession?) and the vehement storme, wherof we than almoste in every exhortacion spake of, is now suddenly risen up. But what! hath God brought yowe so farre furth that you shal, both in soules and bodies, every one perish? Nay. My whole trust in Goddes mercy and truthe is to the contrarie. For God brought not his people into Egypte, and from thence thorowe the Red Sea, to th'entent they should therein perish,[1] but that he of them shuld shewe a most gloriouse delyverance. Neither sent Christe his Apostles into the middest of the sea, and suffred the blusteringe storme to assault them and their bote, to th'entent thei shuld there perish; but because he wold the more have his great goodnes towardes them felt and perceaved, in so mightely delivering them owt of the feare of peryshinge; giving us therby an example that he wold do the lyke to us, if we abyde constant in our profession and fayth, withdrawinge our selves from supersticion and idolatrie. We gave yow warning of these dayes long agoo. For the reverence of Christes bloud let these wordes be marked: "The same truth that spake before of these most dolorouse dayes, forspake also the everlasting joye prepared for suche as shuld continue to the ende." The trouble is come, O deare Brethren! looke for the comforte, and (after the example of the Apostles) abyd in resistinge this vehement storme a little space.

<small>MARKE THESE WORDES.</small>

The thyrd watch is not yet ended: Remember that Christe Jesus came not to his Disciples till it was the fourth watch,[2] and they were then in no lesse daunger than yow be nowe; for theyr fayth faynted, and their bodies were in daunger. But Christe Jesus came when they loked not for him: And so shal he do to yow, yf you wil continue in the profession that yow have made. This darre I be bold to promise, in the name of Hym

---

[1] GOD NEVER BROUGHT HIS PEOPLE INTO TROUBLE TO TH'ENTENT THAT THEY SHULD PERYSH THERIN.—(*Marg. note.*)

[2] CHRIST CAME NOT TO HYS DISCIPLES TIL THE FOURTH WATCH.—(*Marg. note.*)

whose eternal veritie and glorious Gospel ye have harde and receaved; who also putteth in to myn heart an earnest thrist (God knoweth I lye not) of your salvation, and some care also for youre bodies, which nowe I wil not expresse.

Thus shortly have I passed thorowe the outrageous[1] tempest, wherein the disciples of Christe were tempted, after that the great multitude were, by Christe, fedde in the deserte, omittinge many profitable notes which myght wel have bene marcked in the texte, because my purpose is, at this present, not to be tediouse, nor yet curiouse, but onlie to note such thinges as be aggreable to these most dolorouse dayes.

And so, let us nowe speake of the ende of this storme and trouble, in which I finde foure thinges cheiflye to be noted.

First, That the Disciples, at the presence of Christe, were more affrayed then they were before. 1.

Secondlye, That Christe useth no other instrument but his worde, to pacifie their hertes. 2.

Thyrdlye, That Peter, in a fervencie, firste left his bote, and yet after feared. 3.

Last, That Christe permitted neyther Peter, nor the rest of his Disciples, to perish in that feare, but gloriously delivered al, and pacified the tempeste. 4.

Theyr greate feare, and the cause therof, are expressed in the texte in these wordes: "When the Disciples sawe him walking upon the sea, they were afrayed, sayinge, that he was a spirite. And they cryed thorowe feare."

It is not my purpose in this treatise to speak of spirites, nor yet to dispute, whether spirites, good or bad,[2] maye appeare and trouble men; neither yet to inquire why mannes nature is affrayed for spirites, and so vehementlie abhorreth their presence and company. But my purpose is only to speake of thinges necessarie for this tyme.

And, firste, let us consyder that ther was three causes why

---

[1] In the orig. edit. "outrages."   [2] In MS. M. "good or evill."

the Disciples knewe not Christe,[1] but judged him to be a spirite.

1. The first cause was, The darknesse of the nyght.
2. The second cause was, The unaccustomed vision that appeared. And,
3. The thirde was, The daunger and tempest, in which they so earnestly labored for the savegard of their selves.

The darknesse (I say) of the nyght letted theyr eyes[2] to see hym; and it was above nature, that a massye, hevy, and weyghtie body of a man (suche as they understode their Master Christe to have) shuld walke, go upon, or be borne up of the water of the ragynge sea, and not sincke. And, finally, the horroure of the tempest, and great daunger that they were in, perswaded them to loke for none other but certaynly to be drouned. And so al these three things, concurrynge together, confirmed them in this imagination, That Christe Jesus, who came to theyr greate comforte and deliveraunce, was a fearfull and wicked spirite appearyng to their destruction.

What here chaunsed to Christe Jesus him self,[3] that I myght prove to have chaunsed, and dayly to chaunce, to the veritie of his blessed worde, in al ages from the begynnynge. For as Christe hym self, in this their trouble, was judged and estemed by his Disciples, at the firste syght, a spirite or phantastical[4] body; so is the truth and syncere preachinge of his gloriouse Gospel, sent by God for mannes most comforte, delyveraunce from synn, and quietnesse of conscience, whan it is firste offered, and truly preached; it is, I saye, no lesse but judged to be heresye and disceavable doctrine, sent by the Devil to mannes destruction.

The cause herof is the darke ignoraunce of God, which, in every age, from the beginning, so overwhelmed the world, that

---

[1] THREE CAUSES WHY CHRISTES DISCIPLES MYSKNEW HYM.—(*Marg. note.*)

[2] In MS. M. "lettit thair eis," hindered their eyes.

[3] WHAT CHAUNSED TO CHRIST, THAT ALSO IN ALL AGES CHAUNSETH TO HIS HOLY WORDE.—(*Marg. note.*)

[4] "Phantastical," fancied.

sometymes Goddes veray electe were in lyke blyndnes and erroure with the reprobate: as Abraham was an idolatere; Moses was instructed in al the artes of the Egyptianes; Paule, a proude Pharisey, conjured[1] agaynst Christe and his doctrine; and many in this same our age, when the truth of God was offred unto them, were sore affrayed, and cried agaynst it, only because the darke cloudes of ignoraunce had troubled them before. But this matter I omitte and let passe, til more opportunitie.

<small>JOS. 24.</small>

The chefe note that wold have yowe wel observe and marcke in this preposterous feare of the Disciples, is this:—

<small>NOTA.</small>

The more nyghe[2] deliverance and salvacyon approcheth, the more stronge and vehement is the temptacyon of the Churche of God:[3] And the more nyghe[2] that Goddes vengeaunce approcheth to the reprobate, the more proude, cruel, and arrogant are they. Whereby it commonly commeth to passe, that the veray messyngers of lyfe are judged and demed to be the authors of al mischefe. And this in many histories is evident. Whan God had appoynted to delyver the afflicted Israelites, by the hand of Moses, from the tyranny of the Egyptians, and Moses was sente to the presence of Pharao for the same purpose, such was their affliction and anguyshe by the crueltie which newly was exercysed over them, that with open mouthes they cursed Moses, (and no doute in their hertes they hated God who sent hym,) alledgyng, that Moses and Aaron was the whole cause of their last extreme trouble.

<small>EXOD. 5, 6, &c.</small>

The lyke is to be seen in the boke of Kynges, both under Eliseus[4] and Esaias the prophetes. For in the dayes of Joram, sonne of Achab, was Samaria beseged by the king of Syria. In which Samaria, no doute, (albeit the kinge and the most multitude were wicked) ther was yet som membres of Goddes electe Church, which wer brought to such extreme famin, that

<small>4 REG. 5.</small>

---

[1] Sworn.
[2] "The more nyghe," in MS. M. "the more neir."
[3] THE FEARE IS GREATEST WHAN DELIVERAUNCE IS MOST NYGH.—(*Marg. note.*)
[4] In our present version, Elisha.

not only thinges of smal price were sold beyond al measure, but also women, agaynst nature, were compelled to eat their owne children. In this same citie Eliseus the prophete most commonly was conversant and dwelt, by whose counsel and commaundement, no doute, the citie was kepte; for it appeareth the kinge, to laye that to hys charge, when he hearing the piteous complaint of the woman (who for honger had eaten her owne sonne), rent his clothes, with a solemne othe and vowe that the head of Eliseus[1] should not stand upon his body that daye. Yf Eliseus had not ben of counsel that the cytie should have bene kept, why should the kynge more have fumed against him then against other? But whether he was the author of the defendinge the citie, or not, al is one to my purpose, for before the delyveraunce was the Churche in suche extremitie, that the chiefe pastore of that tyme was sought to be killed by suche as shoulde have defended hym.

The lyke is redde of Ezechias,[2] who defending his citie Jerusalem, and resisting proude Sennacherib, (no doute obeying the counsel of Esaias,) at length was so oppressed with sorowe and shame by the blasphemouse wordes of Rabsakes,[3] that he had no other refuge but in the temple of the Lorde (as a man desperate and wythout comforte) to open the disdaynfull letters sent unto hym by that hautye and proude tyraunte.

ESA. 36, 37.

By these and many histories mo, it is moste evident that the more nigh salvation and deliveraunce approcheth, the more vehement is the temptation and trouble.

This I writ to admonishe you, that albeit yet you shal se tribulation so abounde, that nothing shal appere but extreme misery, without al hope of comforte; that yet ye declyne not from God. And that albeit somtymes ye be moved to hate the messengers of lyfe, that therfore you shal not judge that God wyl never shewe mercy after. No, deare Brethren, as he hathe entreated[4] other before you, so wil he do you.

[1] In the old edit. Elizeus.
[2] In our present version, Hezekiah.
[3] In our present version, Rabshakeh.
[4] In MS. M. "intreatit," dealt with.

OF GOD'S TRUTH IN ENGLAND. 293

God wyll suffer tribulation and dolour abounde,[1] that no maner of comforte shalbe seen in man, to th'entent, that when delyveraunce commeth the glorie maye be his,[2] whose onlye worde maye pacifie the tempestes moste vehement.

He drowned Pharao and his army.[3] He scattered the great multitud of Benedab.[4] And by his aungel killed the hoist of Sennacherib. And so delyvered his afflicted, when nothinge appeared to them but utter destruction. So shal he do to you, beloved Brethren, yf paciently ye wil abyde his consolation and counsel. God open your eyes that ryghtly ye maye understande the meaning of my wrytinge. Amen. EXO. 4.

But yet, peradventure, you wonder not a lytle why God permitteth suche bloud thristye tyrauntes to molest and greve his chosen Church: I have recited some causes before, and yet mo I could recite, but at this tyme I wyl holde me content with one. The justice of God is suche, that he wil not powre forth his extreme vengeaunce upon the reprobate, unto suche time as their iniquitie be so manifest, that their very flatterers cannot excuse it. Pharao was not destroyed, till his owne housholde servauntes and subjectes abhorred and condempned his stubburne disobedience. Jesabel and Athalia were not thrust from this lyfe into hell, tyll all Israel and Juda were wytnesses of their crueltie and abhominations. Judas was not hanged, til the princes of the prestes bare wytnesse of his traitorouse acte and iniquitie. NOTA.
EXO. 10.
JEZABEL,
ATHALIA,
AND JUDAS.

And to passe over the tyrauntes of olde tyme whom God hath plagued, let us come to the tyrauntes whiche nowe are within the Realme of Englande, whome God will not longe spare. Yf Steven Gardiner, Cuthbert Tunstal, and butcherly Bonnar, false byshoppes of Wynchester, Duresme, and of London, had for their false doctrine and traitorous actes suffered death, GARDENER,
TUNSTAL,
BUTCHERLY
BONNAR.

---

[1] WHY GOD SUFFERETH TRIBULATION TO ABOUND AND CONTINUE.—(*Marg. note.*)

[2] In MS. M. "the glorie may be to his Majestie allone."

[3] In MS. M. "his great armie."

[4] In MS. M. "Bennadab;" in our present version, Benhadad.

when they justly deserved the same, then woulde errant Papistes have alledged (as I and other have herde them do) that they were men reformable, that they wer mete instrumentes for a common wealth; that they were not so obstinate and malicious as they were judged; neither that they thristed for the bloude of any man. And of Ladye Marye,[1] who hath not herde, that she was sober, mercyful, and one that loved the common wealthe of Englande? Had she, I saye, and suche as now be of her pestilent counsel, bene sent to hell before these dayes, then should not their iniquitie and crueltie so manifestlye have appeared to the worlde. For who coulde have thought that suche crueltie could have entered into the hert of a woman, and into the hert of her that is called a virgine, that she would thirst the bloud of innocentes, and of suche as by juste lawes and faythful wytnesses, can never be proved to have offended by them selves?

4 REG. 11.
MATH. 14.

I fynde that Athalia, through appetite to raigne, murthered the seed of the kinges of Juda. And that Herodias' doughter, at the desyre of an hooryshe mother, obteyned the heade of John the Baptist. But that ever a woman, that suffred her selfe to be called the moste blessed Virgine,[2] caused so muche bloud to be spilt for establishing of an usurped authoritie, I thinke is rare to be founde in Scripture or Historie.

3 REG. 18.
2 REG. 21.

I fynde that Jesabel, that cursed idolatress, caused the bloud of the prophetes of God to be shedde, and Naboth to be murthered unjustly for his owne vineyard; but yet I thinke she never erected halfe so many gallowes[3] in al Israel as myschevous Mary hath done within London alone.

---

[1] THE PRAYSE OF WYNCHESTER, DURYSME, AND OF LADY MARY, BEFORE THESE DAYES.—(*Marg. note.*)

[2] Strype gives an account of a sermon preached before the Convocation, in October 1553, by Harpsfield, Archdeacon of London, in which he thus parodied the words written of Deborah (Judges v. 7, 8) as applicable to "our right illustrious Queen," Mary of England:—"Religion ceased in England, it was at rest, until Mary arose, a Virgin arose in England."—(*Memorials*, vol. iii. p. 40.)

[3] "Half so many gallowes." Sir Thomas Wyatt and others, when the marriage of Philip and Mary was proposed, in January 1554, had taken

But you, Papistes, wyl excuse your Mary the virgine;¹ wel, let her be your virgine, and a goddes mete to maintaine such idolatrers, yet shal I ryghtlye laye to her charge that which I thinke no Papist within Englande wyl justifie nor defende. And therfore, O ye Papistes! here I wyl a lytle turne my penne unto you. Answere unto this question, O seede of the Serpent! Would any of you have confessed two yeres ago, that Mary, your mirrour, had bene false, dissembling, unconstant, proud, and a breaker of promyses,² excepte suche promyses as she made to your god the Pope, to the great shame and dishonoure of her noble father? I am sure you would full lytle have thought it in her. And now, doth she not manifestlye shewe her selfe to be an open traitoresse to the Imperiall Crown of England, contrary to the juste lawes of the Realme, to brynge in a straunger, and make a proude Spaniarde kynge, to the shame, dishonoure, and destruction of the nobilitie; to the spoyle from them and theirs of their honoures, landes, possessions, chief offices and promotions; to the utter decaye of the treasures, commodities, navie, and fortifications of the Realme; to the abasyng of the yeomanry, to the slavery of the communaltie, to the overthrowe of Christianitie and Goddes true religion; and, finally, to the utter subversion of the whole publicke estate and common wealth of Englande?³ Let Northfolke and Suffolke, let her owne promyse and proclamation, let her fatheris testament, let the cytie of London, let the auncient lawes and actes of Parliamentes before established in Englande, be judges betwixte myne accusation and her moste traytourus iniquitie.

First, her promyse and proclamation dyd signifie and declare,

arms to prevent a union from which they anticipated many calamities to England. But their ill-concocted scheme was speedily suppressed, and seventeen gallows were erected in the most public places of London, when forty-seven persons were executed.

¹ A DIGRESSION TO THE PAPISTES QUENE MARY, CHASTES DEARLYNGES.—(*Marg. note.*)

² A LIVELYE PICTURE OF MARY, THE UTTER MYSCHEFE OF ENGLAND.—(*Marg. note.*)

³ WHAT COMMODITIES THE SPANYSSHE KYNGE SHALL BRYNG TO THE REALME OFF ENGLAND.—(*Marg. note.*)

That neither she would bring in, neither yet mary any straunger. Northfolke, and Suffolke,[1] and the cytie of London, doth testifie and wytnesse the same. The aunciunt lawes and actes of Parliament pronounceth it treason to transferre the Crowne of Englande into the handes of a forreyn nation. And the othe made to observe the sayd statutes cryeth out, That al they are perjured that consent to that her traitorous facte. Speake now, O ye Papistes! and defende your monstrous maistres; and deny, yf ye can for shame, that she hath not uttered her self to be borne (alasse therfore!) to the ruyne and destruction of noble Englande. Oh! who would ever have beleved (I wryt nowe in bytternesse of herte) that suche unnatural crueltie should have had dominion over any reasonable creature! But the saying is too true, that the usurped government of an affectionate woman is a rage without reason.

<small>A TRUE SAYINGE.</small>

Who would ever have thought that the love of that Realme, whiche hath brought forth, whiche hath nurryshed and so noblye mayntayned that wicked woman, should not somwhat have moved her herte with pitie? Who seeth not nowe, that she, in all her doynges, declareth moste manyfestlye, that under an Englyshe name she beareth a Spaniardes herte?[2] If God (I say) had not for our scourge suffred her and her cruell counsell to have come to auctoritie, than could never these their abhominations, crueltie, and treason, agaynst God, agaynste his saynctes, and agaynst the Realme, whose liberties they are sworne to defende, so manifestly have bene declared.

And who ever could have beleved that gloriouse Gardener, and trecherouse Tunstal, (whome al Papistes praysed for the love they bare to theyr countrey,) could have become so manifest traytoures, that not only agaynst theyr solemne othes, that

---

[1] According to Foxe, the Martyrologist, upon the death of Edward the Sixth, the Princess Mary pledged her word to the Protestants of Suffolk, in answer to their petition, that she would not interfere with the public profession of the Protestant religion.—(See Todd's *Life of Cranmer*, vol. ii. p. 384.)

[2] UNDER AN ENGLISHE NAME SHE BEARETH A SPANIARDES HARTE.—(*Marg. note.*)

they should never consent nor agre unto, that a foren straunger shuld raygne over England, but also that they wold adjudge the Imperial Croune of the same to appertayn to a Spaniarde by inheritaunce and lyneal dissent? O traytours, traytours, how can yow for very shame shewe youre faces?

It commeth to my mynde, upon Christemas daye, in the yere of oure Lorde 1552, preachinge in Newcastle-upon-Tyne, and speakinge agaynste the obstinacie of the Papistes, I made this affirmation, That who so ever in his herte was enemie to Christes Gospel and doctrine, which then was preached within the Realme of Englande, was enemy also to God, and secrete traytours to the Croune and common wealth of Englande. For as they thristed nothinge more than the Kinges death, which their iniquitie wolde procure; so they regarded not who shuld raign over them, so that their idolatrie myght be erected agayn. Howe these my wordes at that tyme pleased men, the crymes and action intended agaynste me dyd declare:[1] But let my veray enemies nowe saye [from] their conscience, if those my wordes are not proved true.

And what is the cause that Wynchester, and the reste of his pestilent secte, so gredely wold have a Spaniarde to raygn over England? The cause is manifest. For as that hel[2] natyon surmounteth al other in pride and whordome, so, for idolatrie and vayne papistical and devellysh ceremonies, thei may rightly be called the veray sonnes of superstition.[3] And therfore ar they founde and judged by the progeny of Antichrist, most apte instrumentes to maynteyn, establysh, and defende the kingdom of that cruel beast, whose head and wounde is lately cured within England, which (alasse, for pitie!) must nowe be brought into bondage and thraldome, that pestilent Papistes mayo raygne without punishment.[4]

---

[1] AGAYNST ME WERE WRITTEN ARTICLES, AND I COMPELLED TO ANSWERE, AS UNTO AN ACTYON OF TREASON.—(*Marg. note.*)

[2] In MS. M. "hell," evidently for "haill," or whole.

[3] SPANIARDES SONNES OF PRIDE AND SUPERSTITION.—(*Marg. note.*)

[4] WHY WYNCHESTER WOLD HAVE SPANIARDES TO RAIGN OVER ENGLAND.—(*Marg. note.*)

TO WYN-
CHESTER.

But, O thou beast! I speake to you Wynchester, more cruel than any tygre, Shal neither shame, neyther feare, neither benefytes receyved, brydel thy tyrannouse crueltie? Aschamest thou not, bloudi beast, to betraye thy natyve countray, and the liberties of the same? Fearest thou not to open such a doore to al iniquitie, that whole England shal be made a common steue to Spanyardes? Wilt thou recompence the benefittes which thou hast receyved of that noble Realme with that ingratitude? Remembrest thou not, that England hath brought thee furth? that Englande hath nurrisshed thee? that England hath promoted thee to riches, honoure, and hyghe promotion? And wilt thou nowe, O wretched caytyve! for al these manifolde benefittes receyved, be the cause that England shal not be England? Yea, verely, for so wilt thou gratifie thy father the Devel, and his lyeftenaunt the Pope, whom, with al his bagage, thou labourest nowe, with tothe and nayle, to florysh agayn in England. Albeyt lyke a dissemblyng hypocryte and double faced wretch, thou beynge therto compelled by the invincible veritie of Goddes holy Worde, wrotest long agoo thy boke, intitled, "True Obedience,"[1] agaynst that monstrouse whore of Babylon, and her falsly usurped power and authoritie: But nowe, to thy perpetual shame, thou returnest to thy vomitte, and art become an open arch-papist agayne. Furthermore, why

[1] THY BOKE OF TRUE OBEDIENCE, BOTH IN LATINE AND IN ENGLISH, SHALL REMAYNE TO THY PERPETUALL SHAME AND CONDEMPNATION OF THY CANCREDE CONSCIENCE.—(*Marg. note.*) This refers to the treatise by Bishop Gardiner, "De Vera Obedientia Oratio," written to justify the English Parliament in giving to Henry the Eighth the title of Supreme Head of the Church. He therein stated his desire "to withdraw that counterfeit vain opinion out of the common people's minds, which the false *pretended power of the Bishop of Rome* for the space of certain years had blinded them withal." This was first printed at London, by Berthelet, 1534, 8vo; and reprinted at Hamburgh in 1536, 4to, with a preface by Bishop Bonner, also inveighing against the Pope. From this edition it was "translated into English, and printed by Michal Wood, with the Preface and Conclusion of the Translator. From Roane, xxvi. of Octobre, M.D.liii," small 8vo. Nothing can exceed the terms of abuse employed by the Translator in mentioning Gardiner, Bonner, Weston, and other "Arch-Papists" in England at this time.

sekest thou the bloud of Thomas, Archbisshoppe off Caunterbury, of good father Hugh Latimere, and of that most learned and discrete man, Doctor Ridlaye, true Bisshoppe of London? Doest thou not consyder, that the lenitie, the sincere doctrine, pure lyfe, godly conversation, and discrete counsel of these three, is notablie knowen in mo realmes than England? Shamest thou not to seke the destruction of those who labored for the savegard of thy lyfe, and obteyned the same, whan thou justly deservest death?

O thou sonne of Satan! wel declarest thou, that nothyng can mollifie the cruel malice, nor purge the deadly venom of hym, in whose hert the Devel bearyth the dominion. Thou art brother to Cayn, and felowe to Judas the traitour; and therfore canst thou do nothinge but thrist the bloude of Abel, and betraye Christe Jesus and his eternall veritie.

But thus, deare Brether, must the sonnes of the Devel declare their own impietie and ungodlines, that whan Goddes vengeaunce (which shal not sleape) shal be poured furth upon them, al tounges shall confesse, acknowledge, and saye, that God is righteous in al his judgementes. And to this ende are cruel tyrauntes permitted and suffered for a space and tyme, not only to live in wealth and prosperitie, but also to prevayle and obteyn victorie, as touchinge the flesshe, over the veray saynctes of God, and over such as enterpriseth to resiste their furie at Goddes commaundemente. But nowe to the subsequente, and that that followeth.

<small>THE WICKED MUST DECLARE THEIR SELVES.</small>

<small>APOCALIP 13.</small>

The instrumente and meane wherwith Christe Jesus used to remove and put awaye the horrible feare and anguysshe of his Disciples, is his only worde. For so is it written: "But by and by Jesus spake unto them, saying, Be of good comforte: it is I; be not affrayed."

The natural man (that cannot understand the pouer of God) wold have desyred some other presente comforte in so greate a daungere; as either to have had the heavens to have opened, and to have shewed unto them such light in that darknesse, that Christe myght have been fully knowen by his own face; or els that the wyndes and ragyng waves of the seas soddenly shuld have ceassed; or some other miracle that had bene subjecte to al their senses, whereby they myght have perfitly knowen that they were delyvered from al daunger. And truly, equall it had bene to Christe Jesus to have done any of these (or any worke greatter) as to have sayd, "It is I; be not affrayed." But willyng to teach us the dignitie and effectuall power of his most holy word, he useth no other instrument to pacifie the great and horrible feare of his Disciples but the same his comfortable worde, and lively voyce. And this is not done only at one tyme, but whan so ever his Churche is in such straite perplexite, that nothing appeareth but extreame calamytie, desolation, and ruyn; then the first comforte that ever it receyved, is by the meanes of his worde and promise. As in the troubles and temptations of Abraham, Isaac, Jacob, Moses, David, and Paule, may appeare.

NOTA.

To Abraham was geven no other defence, after that he had discomfited foure kinges, (whose posteritie and lynage no doute he, beyng a straunger, greatly feared) but only this promyse of God, made to him by his holy worde : "Fear not, Abraham, I am thy buckler," that is, thy protection and defence.

ABRAHAM.

GEN. 15.

The same we find of Isaac, who flyinge from the place of his accustomed habitation, compelled therto by hunger, gat none other comforte nor conducte but this promyse only, "I shall be with thee."

ISAAC.

GEN. 16.

In al the jorneyes and temptations of Jacob, the same is to be espied : As when he fledd from his father's house for feare of his brother Esau ; when he returned from Laban ; and when he feared the inhabitauntes of the region of the Cananites and Pheresites, for the slaughter of the Sichemites committed by his sonnes; he receaveth no other defence but only Goddes worde and promyse.

IACOB.

GEN. 29, 31, 32, 35.

And this in Moses, and in the afflicted Church under hym, is most evidente. For when Moses him self was in such despera-

MOSES.

tion, that he was bolde to chyde with God, saying, " Why hast thou sent me? for syth that tyme that I have come to Pharao to speake in thy name, he hath oppressed this people: neither yet hast thow delyvered thy people." EXOD. 5.

This same expostulation of Moses declareth how sore he was tempted; yea, and what opinion he had conceaved of God; that is, That God was eyther impotente, and could not delyver his people from such a tyrauntes handes, or els, That he was mutable and unjust of his promyses. And this same, and sorer temptations assaulted the people; for in anguisshe of herte they both refused God and Moses (as we before have partely touched). And what meanes used God to comforte them in that greate extremitie? Dyd he strayght waye soddenly kil Pharao, the great tyraunte? No. Dyd he send them a legion of aungels to defend and delyver them? No such thynge. But he only recyteth and beateth in to their eares his former promises to them, which oftentymes they had before. And yet the rehersal of the same wrought so mightely in the hert of Moses, that not only was bitternes and desperation removed away, but also he was inflamed with such boldnesse, that without feare he went agayne to the presence of the Kynge, after he had bene threatened and repulsed by hym.

This I writte, beloved in the Lorde, that ye, knowynge the Worde of God[1] not onely to be that whereby were created heaven and earth, but also to be the power of God to salvation to al that beleve; the bryght lantarne to the fete of these that by nature walke in darkenesse; the lyfe to those that by synne are dead; a comforte of suche as be in tribulation; the tower of defence to suche as be moste feble; the wysedome and great felicitie of suche as delyteth in the same. And to be shorte, you knowe Goddes Worde to be of suche efficacie and strength, that therby is synne purged, death vanquyshed, tyrauntes suppressed, and, finally, the Devel, the author of all myserie, overthrowen and confounded. This (I say) I write, that ye know- ROM. 1. PSAL. 119.

[1] THE POWER AND EFFECTUAL OPERATION OF GODDES WORDE.—(*Marg. note.*)

ynge this of the holy Worde, and moste blessed Gospel and voyce of God, (whiche once you have herde, I trust to your comforte,) may nowe in this houre of darkenesse and moste ragynge tempeste, thriste and praye, that ye may heare yet once agayne this amiable voyce of your Saviour Christe, "Be of good comforte: it is I; feare not." And also, that ye maye receave some consolation by that blessed Gospel, which before you have professed, assuredly knowyng, that God shalbe no lesse mercyfull unto you then he hath bene to other afflicted for hys names sake before you. And albeit that God by and by remove not thys horrible darknesse, neither yet that he soddenly pacifieth this tempeste, yet shal he not suffer his tossed bote to be drowned.

EXOD. 14.
4 REG. 9.

Remember, Brethren, that Goddes vengeaunce plagued not Pharao the fyrst yeare of his tyranny. Neyther dyd the dogges devoure and consume bothe the fleshe and bones of wicked Jezabel, when she first erected and set up her idolatrie; and yet as none of them escaped due punishment, so dyd God preserve his afflicted Churche in despite of Sathan, and of his blynde and moste wretched servauntes; as he shal not faile to do in this great tempest and darkenesse within the Realme of Englande. And therfore yet agayne, beloved in the Lorde, let the comforte of Goddes promises somwhat quycken your dulled spirites. Exercise your selves now secretly, in revolving that which somtymes you have herde openly proclamed in your eares; and be every man nowe a faythful preacher unto his brother. Yf youre communication be of Christ, assuredly he wyll come before you be ware. His worde is lyke unto swete smellynge oyntment, or fragrant flowres, which never can be moved nor handled, but forth goeth the odoure to the comforte of those that standeth by; whiche is nothyng so delectable yf the oyntment remayne wythin the boxe, and the floures stande or lye wythout touchyng or motion.

LUCÆ 24.
SIMILE.

Marke well, deare Brethren, before that Christe spake, his Disciples judged hym to have bene some wycked spirite, which was to them no delectable savoure; but when he speaketh, the swete odoure of his voyce pearseth their heartes. For what comforte was in the heartes of the Disciples when they herde these wordes: "Be of good comforte, it is I;" that is, judge not that I am a spirite come to your destruction: No, I am come for your delyveraunce. It is I, youre Maister; yea, your Maister most familiar. It is I, whose voyce and doctrine you knowe, for ye are my sheepe. It is I, whose workes you have sene, although perfytly ye consydered not the same. It is I, who commaunded you to entre into this journey, and therfore am I come to you now in the houre of your trouble; and therfore, be not affrayed; this storme shall ceasse, and you shalbe delyvered. ^{MATH. AND JOH. SUPRA.}

What comforte, I say, deare Brethren, was in the hertes of the Disciples, hearing Christes voice, and knowynge hym by the same, can neither the tounge nor penne of man expresse; but onely suche as after longe conflicte and stryfe (whiche is betwixte the fleshe and the spirite, in the tyme of extreme troubles, when Christ appereth to be absent) feleth at laste the consolation of the Holy Ghost, can wytnesse and declare.

And Peter geveth some external signe what Christes wordes wrought inwardly in his herte. For immediately after he heard his Master's voice, he sayeth, "Lorde, yf it be thou, commaunde me to come unto thee upon the watters." Here maye be sene what Christes voyce had wrought in Peter's herte; truely not onlye a forgettynge and contempt of the great tempeste, but also suche boldenesse and love, that he coulde feare no daunger folowyng; but assuredly dyd beleve, that his Maister Christes puissaunce, power, and myghte was suche, that nothyng myght resiste his worde and commaundement: and therfore he sayeth, "Commaunde me to come," as thoughe he woulde saye, I desyre no more but the assuraunce of thy commaundement. Yf thou wilt commaunde, I am determined to obeye;[1] for assuredlye I knowe that the waters can not prevaile against me, yf

---

[1] NOTE, THAT PETER CONSIDERED NOT HIS OWN WEAKNESSE.—(*Marj* note.)

thou speake the worde: so that what so ever is possible unto thee, by thy will and word may be possible unto me.

Thus Christe, to instruct Peter further, and us by his example, condescended unto his petition, and commaunded him to come. And Peter quickly leavyng the bote, came downe from it, and walked upon the waters to come to Christe. Thus farre of Peter's facte, in whyche lyeth great aboundaunce of doctrine; but I will passe over al that especially appertaineth not to the qualitie of this time,[1] within the Realme of Englande.

Before it is sayd, welbeloved Brethren, That somtymes the messengers of lyfe are judged to be very messengers of death; and that not onely with the reprobate, but also with Goddes electe. As was Moses with the Israelites, Jeremie with the citie of Jerusalem, and Christe him selfe with his Apostles. But that is not a synne permanent, and that abydeth for ever with Goddes electe; but it vanysheth awaye in suche sorte, that not onely they knowe the voyce of their pastour,[2] but also they earnestly study to obey and folowe it, with the daunger of theyr owne lyves. For this is the special difference betwixte the children of God and the reprobate.

THE ELECTE. The one obeyeth God speaking by his messengers, whome they imbrace wyth unfayned love. And that they do, sometymes[3] not onely against al worldly appearaunce, but also against civile statutes and ordinaunces of men. And therfore in their great extremitie receyve they comforte beyonde expectation.

THE REPROBATE. The other alwayes resysteth Goddes messengers, and hateth his Worde. And therfore, in their great adversitie, God either taketh from them the presence of his Worde, or els they fal into so deadly desperation, that although Goddes messengers be sent unto them, yet neyther can they receave comforte by

---

[1] The "qualitie," &c., that is, the circumstances of this time. The other words are omitted in MS. M.

[2] THE SHEPE AT LENGTH KNOWE THE VOYCE OF THEIRE OWNE PASTOURE — (*Marg. note.*)

[3] In MS. M. "sumtymes, as Peter heir."

Goddes promyses, neyther folowe the counsel of Goddes true messengers, be it never so perfite and fruteful. Hereof have we many evident testimonies within the Scriptures of God.

Of Saul, it is plaine, that God so lefte him, that neither wolde he geve him aunswere by prophete, by dreame, nor by vision. _{1 REG. 28. SAUL.}

To Ahas kynge of Juda, in his great anguyshe and feare, whiche he had conceyved by the multitude of those that were conjured[1] against hym, was sent Esay the prophet, to assure him by Goddes promise, that his enemyes should not prevaile against him. And to confirme him in the same, the prophete requyred him to desire a signe of God, either from the heaven, or beneth in the depe; but suche was the deadly desperation of him that alwayes had despised Goddes prophetes, and had moste abhominably defiled him selfe with idolatrye, that no consolation could entre into his herte, but desperatlye, and with a dissemblyng and fained excuse, he refused all the offers of God. _{2 REG. 16. AHAS.} _{ESA. 7.}

And albeit God kept touch with[2] that hipocrite for that tyme (whiche was not done for his cause, but for the safetie of his afflicted churche),[3] yet after escaped he not the vengeaunce of God.

The lyke we reade of Zedechias, the wretched and laste kynge of Juda before the destruction of the citie of Jerusalem; who, in his great fear and extreme anguyshe, sente for Jeremie the prophet, and secretly demaunded of him howe he myght escape the great daunger that appeared when the Caldees beseged the citie. And the prophete boldly spake, and commaunded the kynge, yf he would save his lyfe and the cytie, to render and geve up him selfe into the handes of the Kinge of Babylon. But the myserable kynge had no grace to folowe the prophetes counsel, because he never delyted in the sayd prophetes doctrine, neither yet had shewed unto hym any frendly favoure. _{JERE. 37 38}

---

[1] "Conjured," combined, sworn.
[2] In MS. M. "keipit tuiche with," that is, relieved this hypocrite.

[3] GOD SOMETYME SHEWETH MERCY TO AN HYPOCRITE FOR THE CAUSE OF HIS CHURCHE.—(*Marg. note.*)

But even as the enemies of God, the chief prestes and false prophetes, required of the kynge, so was the good prophet evel intreated; somtymes caste into prison, and somtymes judged and condempned to dye. The moste evident testimonie of the wilfull blyndynge of wicked idolatrers, is written and recited in the same prophete Jeremye, as followeth:

<small>JEREM. 42.</small> "After that the cytie of Jerusalem was brente and destroyed, the kynge ledde awaye prisoner, his sonnes and chiefe nobles slayne, and the whole vengeaunce of God powred out upon the disobedient; yet ther was lefte a remnaunt in the lande to occupie and possesse the same, who called upon the Prophete Jeremye to knowe concernyng them the will and pleasure of God; whether they should remain styl in the land of Judea, as was appointed and permitted by the Caldees, or yf they shoulde departe, and flye into Egypt." To certifie them of this their doute, they desyre the Prophete to praye for them unto God. Who <small>READE THE TEXT, JERE. 42.</small> condescendynge and grauntyng their petition, promised to kepe backe nothing from them which the Lorde God should open unto hym. And they, in lyke maner, taking God to recorde and witnesse, made a solempne vowe, to obey what so ever the Lorde should aunswere by hym. But when the Prophete, by the inspiration of the Spirite of God, and assured revelation and knowledge of his wyll, commaunded them "to remain stil in the lande" that they were in, promysyng them yf they so would do, that "God would there plante them," and that he would repent of all the plagues that he had brought uppon them, and that he would be wyth them, to delyver them from the handes of the kynge of Babilon. But contrarywyse, "yf they would not obeye the voyce of the Lorde," but would, agaynst his commaundement, go to Egypte, thynkinge that there they should lyve in reste and aboundaunce, without any feare of warre and penurye of victualles, then the veray plagues whyche they feared shoulde come uppon them and take them. For (sayeth the Prophet) it shal come to passe, that all men that obstinatlye wyll go to Egypte, there to remayne, shall dye either by sworde, by

honger, or pestilence. But when the prophete of God hadde declared unto them thys playne sentence and wyl of God, I praye you, what was their aunswer? The texte declareth it, saying:

"Thou speakest a lye; neither hath the Lorde our God sente thee unto us, commaundyng that we shoulde not go into Egypte; but Baruch the sonne of Neriah provoketh thee agaynste us, that he maye gyve us into the power of Caldeys, that they myghte kyll us, and lead us prisoners unto Babylon." And thus they refused the counsail of God, and folowed their owne fantasies. JEREM. 43.

Here may be espied in this people great obstinacie and blyndnes. For nothyng which the Lord had before spoken by this godlye prophete Jeremie had fallen in vayne. Their owne eyes had sene the plagues and myseries, which he had threatened, take effecte in every point, as he had spoken before; yea, they were yet greene and freshe both in mynde and presence, (for the flamme and fyre wherewith Jerusalem was consumed and brent was then scantly quenched;) and yet could they not beleve his threateninges then spoken, neither yet could they folowe his fruteful counsail geven for their great wealth and savegarde. And why so? Bycause they never delyted in Goddes trueth, neither had they repented their former idolatrie, but stil continued and rejoyced in the same, as manifestly appereth in the xliv. chapter of the same Prophete.[1] And therfore would they and their wyves have bene in Egypte, where all kynde of idolatrie and superstition abounded, that they, wythout reproche or rebuke, myghte have their bellies full therof, in despite of Goddes holy lawes and prophetes. GREAT BLINDNES JERE. 44

In wrytinge herof it came to mynde, that after the death of that innocent and moste godlye kynge, Edwarde the Sixte, whyle that great tumulte was in Englande for the establyshyng of that moste unhappye and wycked Womanes authoritie, (I mean of her that nowe raigneth in Goddes wrath,) entreatinge the same argument in a towne in Buckinghamshyre, named

---

[1] AS PAPISTES WOLDE HAVE LEAGUE WITH THE EMPEROURE.—(*Marg. note.*)

Hammershame,[1] before a great congregation, with sorowful herte and wepynge eyes, I fel into this exclamation:[2]

"O Englande! now is Goddes wrath kyndled againste thee. Nowe hath he begonne to punyshe, as he hath threatened a longe whyle, by his true prophetes and messengers. He hath taken from thee the crowne of thy glorie, and hathe lefte thee without honoure as a bodye without a heade. And this appeareth to be onely the begynnynge of sorowes, whiche appeareth to encrease. For I perceave that the herte, the tounge, and the hande of one Englyshe man is bente agaynst another, and devision to be in the whole realme, whiche is an assured signe of desolation to come.

"O England, Englande! doest thou not consider that thy common wealth is lyke a shippe sailyng on the sea;[3] yf thy maryners and governours shall one consume another, shalte thou not suffer shipwracke in shorte processe of tyme?

"O Englande, Englande! alasse! these plagues are powred upon thee, for that thou woldest not knowe the moste happy tyme of thy gentle visitation. But wylte thou yet obey the voyce of thy God, and submitte thy selfe to his holy wordes? Truely, yf thou wilt, thou shalte fynde mercye in his syght, and the estate of thy common wealth shall be preserved.

"But, O Englande, Englande! yf thou obstinatly wilt returne into Egypt; that is, yf thou contracte mariage, confederacy, or league, with such princes as do mayntayne and advaunce ydolatrye, (suche as the Emperoure, which is no lesse enemy unto Christe then ever was Nero;)[4] yf for the pleasure and frend-

---

[1] Hammershame, or Amersham, in Buckinghamshire, a place formerly noted for the general reception of the doctrines of Wicklyffe; and during Queen Mary's reign, several of the inhabitants were subjected to persecution.

[2] WHAT WAS SAYD IN HAMMERSHAME WHEN UPROURE WAS FOR ESTABLYSHING OF MARYE IN AUTHORITY.—(*Marg. note.*)

[3] A COMMON WEALTH COMPARED TO A SHYPPE SAYLING ON THE SEA.—(*Marg. note.*)

[4] Luther, writing of the Emperor Charles the Fifth, in a letter to Bugenhagius and others of his associates, in 1540, said, "The Emperor was, is, and will continue to be, a servant of the servants of Satan. I would hope that he serves, being subject to vanity,

shippe (I saye) of suche princes, thou returne to thyne olde abhominations, before used under the Papistrie, then assuredly, O Englande! thou shalte be plagued and brought to desolation, by the meanes of those whose favoures thou sekest, and by whome thou arte procured to fall from Christ, and to serve Antichrist."

This, and muche more,[1] in the doloure of myne herte, that daye, in audience of suche as yet maye beare recorde, God wolde that I should pronounce. The thynge that I then most feared, and whiche also my tounge spake (that is, the subversion of the true religion, and bryngynge in of straungers to raigne over that realme), this daye I see come to passe in mennes counsels and determinations. Whyche yf they procede and take effecte, as by men is concluded, then so assuredlye as my God lyveth, and as those Israelites that obstinatlye retourned into Egypte agayne were plagued to the death; so shall Englande taiste what the Lorde hath threatened by his prophetes before.[2] God graunt us true and unfayned repentaunce of oure former offences.

God, for his great mercies sake, stirre up some Phinees, Helias, or Jehu, that the bloude of abhominable idolaters maye pacifie Goddes wrath, that it consume not the whole multitude. Amen.

But to retourne to oure matter: Of the premisses it is plaine, That suche as contemneth Goddes eternall veritie and grace, can neither in their troubles receave comforte by Goddes messengers;[3] neither yet can they folowe the counsel of God, be it never so profitable: but God geveth them over, and suffereth them to wander in their owne vanities to their owne perdition.

---

not willingly, or in ignorance. We pray against him and for him, and we believe that we shall be heard."— *Epist. a de Wette*, 1920. (*Note by Editor of the British Reformers.*)

[1] In MS. M. "This mekill and mair."

[2] THE ENDE SHAL DECLARE.—(*Marg. note.*)

[3] ENNEMYES TO THE TRUTH RECEAVETH NO COMFORTE OF GODDES MESSENGERS.—(*Marg. note.*)

Where as, contrary wyse, suche as beareth a reverence to Goddes moste holye worde,¹ are drawen by the power and vertue of the same (as before is said) to beleve, folowe, and obeye that whych God commaundeth, be it never so harde, so unapparent, or contrarie to their affections. And therfore, as God alwaye kepeth appointment with them, so are they wonderouslye preserved, when Goddes vengeaunces are poured forth upon the disobedient. And this is moste evident in Abraham, at Goddes commaundement, leavynge his countreye, and goynge forth he knewe not whyther; which was a thynge not so easye to be done, as it is to be spoken or redde. It appeareth also in Abraham belevyng Goddes promyses, agaynst all appearaunce; and in Abraham offeryng his chyld Isaac, agaynst al fatherly love and affection natural. The same is to be said in Moses, Samuel, Helias,² Micheas,³ and other of the prophetes, whiche, at the commaundement of Goddes worde, boldly passed to the presence of tyrauntes, and there to them dyd their message, as charge was gyven unto them.⁴

GEN. 12.
GEN. 15.
GEN. 22.
EXODI. 5, 7,
10.
1 REG. 15.
3 REG. 21.

OBJECTION. But lest that some should alledge, that these examples appertayneth nothyng to a multitude, bycause they were done in singuler men.⁵

AUNSWERE. To aunswer to this objection, We wyll consyder what the power of Goddes Word hath wrought in many at one instaunte.⁶

EXODI. 32. After that the Israelites hadde made the golden caulfe, and so fallen to idolatrie, Moses, commyng down from the mountaine, and beholding their abhominations, (the honoure that they gave to an idol,) and the people spoiled of their eare-rynges and jewels, to their great rebuke and shame, was inflamed with suche zeale, indignation, and wrath, that, firste he brake the

---

¹ THE GODLY AND CHOSEN OF GOD.— (*Marg. note.*)
² Elijah.
³ Micaiah.
⁴ In MS. M. "Geven thame be the Lord."
⁵ "In singuler men," that is, in the case of individual men.
⁶ GODDES WORDE SOMTYME MOVETH AND DRAWETH GREAT MULTITUDES.— (*Marg. note.*)

OF GOD'S TRUTH IN ENGLAND. 311

tables of the commaundementes; then he beate their caulf to powder and gave it them to drynke,[1] to cause them understande that their filthy guttes should receave that which they worshipped for God. And, finally, he commaunded that every man that was of God should approche and come nygh unto him. And al the sonnes of Levi (sayeth the text) came to him; to whom he sayd, "Thus sayeth the Lorde God of Israel, Let every man put his sworde upon his thygh, and go in and out from porte to porte[2] in the tentes; and let every man kil his brother, his neyghbour, and every man his nigh kynsman.[3] And the sonnes of Levi dyd accordynge to the worde of Moses. And there fell the same daye of the people nyghe three thousande." It is evident by this historie, that the power of Goddes Worde, pronounced by the mouthe of a man, prevailed at one tyme in a great nombre againste nature, and compelled them to be executores of Goddes vengeaunce, regardynge nothynge the affinitie nor nyghnes of bloud; and also, that their doynge so wel pleased Moses, the ambassadoure of God, that he sayde unto them, "Consecrate your handes this daye everye man in his owne sonne, and in his owne brother, that a fortunate benediction may be geven to you this daye." As though Moses shoulde saye, Your father Levi prophaned and defyled his handes, kyllyng the Sichemites in hys blind rage, which moved his father Jacob, in his laste testament, to dampne, execrate, and curse that his most vehement and ungodly zeale; but, because in this worke you have preferred Goddes commaundement before bloude, nature, and also affection, in place of that rebuke and curse, you have obtayned blessyng and prayse. EXODI. 32.   GENES. 34.   GENES. 49.

The lyke puissaunce and vertue of Goddes Worde[4] workynge JEREM. 21, 32

---

[1] WHY MOSES CAUSED THE ISRAELYTES TO DRYNCKE THE POWDER OF THEYR GOLDEN CAWLFE.—(*Marg. note.*)

[2] "Port," gate, or entrance.

[3] A SHARPE SENTENCE AGAYNST IDOLATRERS.—(*Marg. note.*)

[4] "The reader will recollect, that the sons of Levi became the executioners of God's vengeance by the especial command of the Most High: nothing else would have warranted their proceedings."—(*Note by the Editor of the British Reformers.*)

in a multitude, is to be redde in the Prophete Jeremye; who perceavynge the tyme of Goddes vengeaunce to drawe nygh, and the citie of Jerusalem to be beseged, boldly cryed oute in his open sermon, saying, "He that remayneth in this cytie shal dye, either by sworde, by honger, or by pestilence. But he that shal go forthe to the Caldeys, shall lyve, and shall fynde his soule for a praye." Thys myght have appeared a disceyvable, sedicious, and ungodly sermon, to commaunde subjectes to departe from the obedience and defence of their native prince, ryche cytizens and valiaunte souldeours from their possessions and stronge holdes, and to wyll them to render them selves, wythout al maner of resistaunce, into the handes of straungers, beyng their enemies. What carnall man would not have judged these persuasions of the prophete moste foolyshe and false? And yet in the hertes of suche as God had elected and appointed to lyfe, so effectually wrought this sermon, that a great nomber of Jerusalem lefte their kynge, their cytie, ryches, and frendes, and obeyed the Prophetes counsaile. For so maye be espied by the answere of Zedechias the kinge, when Jeremie counsayled that he should also rendre him selfe into the handes of Nabuchodonozer; he sayeth, "I feare these Jewes that are fled to the Caldees, lest perchaunce they give me into their handes." Hereoff it is plain that many wer departed from hym, whom he feared more than he dyd his enemies.

Many mo testimonies myght be brought, to declare howe myghtelye Goddes Worde, spoken by man, hath wrought in the hertes of great multitudes. As in the hertes of the Ninivites, who, at Jonas preachinge, damned their former religion, conversation, and lyfe. And in the hertes of those three thousand, who at Peter's fyrste sermon, openly made after Christes ascension, acknowledged their offences, repented, and were by and by[1] baptized. But these premisses are sufficient to prove, aswel that Goddes Worde draweth his electe after it, against worldlye appearaunce, agaynst natural affections, and agaynst cyvil

[1] "By and by," soon after.

statutes and constitutions: as also, that suche as obey Goddes speakyng by his messengers, never lacketh juste rewarde and recompensation. For onely suche as obeyed the voyce of the Prophete founde favour and grace, to the prayse and glorie of Goddes name, when his juste judgementes toke vengeaunce upon the disobedient. But nowe shortly, by notes, we wyl touche the rest of Peter's acte, and Christes mercifull delyveraunce of them; which is the ende of all troubles sustayned by Goddes electe. <small>JEREM. 39.</small>

And Fyrste, That Peter, seynge a myghty winde, was afrayed, and so, when he began to syncke, he cryed, "Lorde, save me," are three thynges principally to be noted.

The fyrste, From whence commeth the feare of Goddes electe. 1.

The seconde, What is the cause that they faint and fal in adversitie. 2.

The thirde, What resteth wyth them in the tyme of this feare and downe-synckynge. 3.

And fyrst, it is playne, that so long as Peter had his eyes fixed uppon Christe, and attended upon no other thynge but the voyce of Christe, he was bolde and without feare. But when he sawe a myghty wynde, (not that the wynde was visible, but the vehement storme and waves of the sea, that were styrred up and caried by the wynde, were sene,) then began he to feare, and to reason, no doute, in his herte, that better it had bene for him to have remained in his bote, for so myght Christ have come to hym; but nowe the storme and rage of wynde was so vehement, that he coulde never come to Christe, and so he greatly feared. Wherof it is plain, that the only cause of oure feare that have left our bote, and through the stormes of the sea wolde go to Christ with Peter, is, that we more consyder the daungers and lettes[1] that are in our journey, then we do the almyghtie power of Hym that hath commaunded us to come to him self. And this is a synne common to al the electe and chosen children of God, that when so ever they see a 1.

<small>THE CAUSE OF FEARE.</small>

[1] "Lettes," hindrances.

vehement trouble appearing to let them and dryve them backe from the obedience of God, then begynne they to feare and to doute of Goddes power and good wyll.

<small>GENE. 12.</small> With this feare was Abraham strycken when he denyed his
<small>EXOD. 3.</small> wyfe. This storme sawe Moses when he refused to be Goddes
<small>ESA. 36, 37.</small> messenger. And Ezechias sore complaint declareth, that more he beleved, consydered, and loked upon the proude voyces and great power of Sennacherib, than he dyd the promises of the Prophete.

This I note for this purpose, That albeit this late and moste ragyng storme within the Realme of England, have taken from you the presence of Christe for a tyme, so that you have douted whether it was Christ whiche you sawe before, or not. And albeit that the vehemencye of this contrarie wynde that would dryve you from Christe, have so occupied your eares, that almoste you have forgotten what He was that commaunded you
<small>MATH. 11.</small> to come to hymselfe, when that he cryed, "Come unto me, all ye that labour and are burthened, and I shall refreshe you."
<small>APOCA. 18.</small> "Passe from Babilon, O my people," &c. Albeit, I saye, that this ragyng tempest have strycken suche feare in youre herte that almoste all is forgotten; yet, dear Brethren, despaire not, suche offences have chaunsed to Goddes electe before you. Yf obstinately ye shal not continue, yet shall you finde mercy and grace. It had bene your dutie in deide, and agreable to your profession, to have loked to Christ alone, and to have contemned all impedimentes; but suche perfection is not alwaye with man, but happy is he that feleth him selfe to syncke.

2. The cause that Goddes electe begynne to faynte and to synck downe in the tyme of greate adversitie, is feare and unbeleve, as in Peter doth appeare; for so longe as he neither feared daunger, neither mystrusted Christes worde, so longe the waters (above, and contrarie to their nature) dyd obey and serve his feete as they had bene the drie, solide, and sure ground. But so soone as he beganne to despaire and feare, so soone began he to syncke. To instructe us, that lyvelye fayth maketh

OF GOD'S TRUTH IN ENGLAND.

man bold,[1] and is able to carye us thorowe suche parelles as be unscapable[2] to nature. But when fayth beginneth to faynt, then beginneth man to syncke downe in every daunger; as in the histories before rehersed it maye appeare, and in the pro- 3 REG. 18. phetes it is playne. For Helias, at Goddes commaundement, passing to the presence of King Achab, in the fervency of his faythe, obtained the fire to come from heaven, and to consume his sacrifice, by which also he was made so bolde, that in the presence of the kyng he feared nothing to kyl his false prophetes. But the same Helias, hearyng of the manacyng and 3 REG. 19. threateninges of cursed Jezabel, and consydering that the wrathe of a wycked woman could by no reasonable meanes be appeased, he saw a storme and feared the same, and so he prepareth to flye; which he dothe not without some syncking downe; for he began to reason and to dispute with God, which never can be done by the creature wythout foolyshnes and offence.[3] The same we fynde in Jeremie, and divers mo.

But the question maye be asked, "Seyng Christe knewe before QUESTION. what should happen to Peter, why dyd he not either let hym[4] from commynge from his bote? or els, Why dyd he not so confirme him in fayth, that he should not have douted?"

To the whiche maye be thus answered: Albeit that we AUSSWERE coulde render no reason of this worke of Christe, yet were the worke it selfe a sufficient reason. And it were enough to answer, that so it pleased Hym, who is not bound to render a reason of all hys workes.[5] But yet yf we shall marke with diligence to what office Peter was to be called, and what offences longe rested wyth him, we shal fynd moste juste and necessarie causes of this worke of Christe, and downe synckyng of Peter. It is playne that Peter had many notable PETER'S VERTUES. vertues, as a zeale and fervency towardes Christes glorie, and

---

[1] LYVELY FAYTH MAKYTH MAN BOLDE. —(*Marg. note.*)

[2] In MS. M. "unskapabill," not to be escaped.

[3] THE CREATURE CAN NEVER DISPUTE WITH GOD WITHOUT SYNNE.—(*Marg. note.*)

[4] "Let hym," hinder him.

[5] GODDES WORKES BY THEM SELFE ARE A SUFFICIENT REASON.—(*Marg. note.*)

a redynesse and forwardnesse to obey his commaundementes. But it is lyke playne, that of longe continuaunce there rested with Peter a desyre of honoure and worldly reste,[1] (and that moved hym to persuade Christe that he should not dye.) There rested wyth hym pryde, presumption, and a truste in hym selfe; whiche presumption and vaine truste in his owne strength, unlesse it had bene corrected and partly removed, he had never bene apte nor mete to have fedde Christes flocke. And such synnes can never be fullye corrected and reformed tyll they be felte, knowen, and confessed. And doutless, so arrogant is our nature, that neither will it knowe, neither confesse the infirmitie of the selfe, unto suche tyme as it have a tryal by experience of the selfe. And that is moste playne by Peter, longe after this tempeste; for when Christ said to his Disciples, "This nyght shall ye all be slaundered in me," Peter boldly bragged and sayd, "Albeit that all should be slaundered, and should flie from thee, yet shall I not be slaundered, but I am redye to go to prison, and to dye with thee."

This was a bolde presumption, and an arrogant promyse, spoken in contempt of all his brethren, frome whiche he could not be reduced by Christes admonition. But the more that Christ shewed hym that he should denye hym, the more bolde was he to affirme the contrarie; as thoughe his Maister, Christe, the author of all truth, yea, rather the Truth it selfe, should make a loud lye. And therfore of necessitie it was that he should prove in experience, what was the frailtie of mannes nature; and what was the imbecillitie and weaknesse of faith, even of those that were hys chiefe Apostles, which had continually hearde his heavenly doctrine, sene dayly his wonderful miracles, whiche had heard them selves so many admonitions and exhortations of hym, which also had folowed and obeyed hym in many thinges. That imbecillitie and weaknesse of fayth, yf Peter had not proved and felte it in hym selfe, neither could he ryghtlye have praysed Goddes infinite goodnes, and imbrased

[1] THE VICE THAT LONGE RESTED WITH PETER.—(*Marg. note.*)

hys free mercy; neither had he bene apte and mete to have bene a pastoure to the weake shepe and tender lambes of Christ; but he should have bene as presumptuouse a boaster of his owne strength as the Papistes are of their free wyll. And he should have bene as proude a contempner and despiser of his weake brethren as the arrogant Papistes, that contempne and dispise all godly and great learned men, though they be a thousande partes more excellent then they.

But to correct and reforme both presumptuouse arrogancy, and fraile imbecillitie and weaknes of faith, Peter was permitted once to sincke,[1] and thryse most shamefully to refuse and denye his Maister; to the intent that, by the knowledge of his owne weaknes, he myght be the more able to instructe other of the same; and also, that he myght more largely magnifie Goddes free grace and myghty delyveraunce. And that Christ taught hym before his fall, sayeng, "When thou arte converted, LUCE 22. strengthen thy brethren;" as though Christ shoulde have sayde, Peter, yet arte thou too proude to be a pastoure, thou canste not stoupe, nor bowe thy backe down to take up the weake shepe; thou dost not yet knowe thine owne infirmitie and weaknes, and therfore canst thou do nothinge but despyse the weake ones; but when thou shalt be instructed by experience of thyne owne selfe what hydde iniquitie lurketh wythin the nature of man, then shalt thou learne to be humble, and to stoupe amonge other synners. And also, thou shalt be an example to others, whyche after shall offende as thou dyddest; so that, yf they repente as thou dyddest, they nede not dispayre of mercy, but maye truste moste assuredly of Christe to obtaine grace, mercy, and forgevness of their sinnes, as thou dyddest.

This frute have we to gather, dear Brethren, of Peter's down-synckynge in the sea, (which was a secrete knowledge and privie admonition that he after should denye Christe), That we are assured by the voyce of Christ, that yf in the tyme of our trouble and extreame daunger, we crye with Peter, we shalbe

[1] WHY PETER WAS SUFFRED TO SYNCKE AND FALL.—(*Marg. note.*)

delivered as he was. And if we mourne for our denial of Christ as he dyd, we shal fynde the same grace and favour at Christes hande that he founde.

3. But nowe let us touche the Thirde note, which is this: That with Goddes electe,[1] in their greatest feare and daunger, ther resteth some smal sparcke of faith, which, by one meanes or other,[2] declareth it self, albeit the afflicted persone in fear or daunger doth not presently perceave the same. As here, in Peter, is moste clear and manifest; for perceyving him selfe to synck down, he cryed, saying, "Lorde, save me;" which wordes were a declaration of a lyvely and quick faith, which lay hyd within his afflicted and sore affrayed herte, whose nature is (I meane of faithe) to hope against hope, that is, against al appearaunce or lycklyhode to loke for helpe and delyveraunce, as the wordes of Peter wytnesseth that he dyd. He sawe nothing but the ragyng sea redy to swalow him up: He felte nothyng but hym selfe synckyng downe in body, and sore troubled in herte; and yet he cryed, "Lorde, save me."[3] Which wordes first declare, that he knewe the power of Christ able to delyver hym; for folyshnesse it had bene to have called for that helpe of hym whome he had knowen to be impotent and unable to helpe.

THE NATURE OF FAYTH.

The calling for Christes helpe by prayer, in this extreame daunger, declared also that Peter had some hope, through his gracious goodnesse, to obtayne delyveraunce. For in extreame perils, impossible it is that the herte of man can crye for Goddes helpe wythout some hope of hys mercye.

It is also to be noted, That in his great jeopardye Peter murmureth not agaynst Christe. Neither dothe he impute or laye any cryme or blame upon Christe, albeit at his commaundement he had lefte his bote. He sayeth not, Why lettest thou me synke, seying that I have obeyed thy commaundement? Moreover, Peter asked helpe at Christe alone, of whom he was

---

[1] WHAT RESTETH WITH GODDES ELECTE IN THEIR GREATEST DAUNGER.—(*Marg. note.*)
[2] In MS. M. "a meane or other."
[3] PETER KNEWE THE POWER AND GOOD WYLL OF GOD.—(*Marg. note.*)

perswaded bothe could, and would, helpe at a pynche. He cryed not upon Abraham, Jacob, Moses, Samuel, David; neither upon any other of the Patriarkes, Prophetes, or Saintes departed; neither yet upon his owne felowes in the bote, but UPON CHRIST, at whose commaundement he had left the bote.

All these thynges together consydered, declare that Peter, in this his extreame feare and daunger, had yet some sparke of fayth, (albeit in that present jeopardie he neither felte consolation nor comforte); for these premisses are undoubted tokens that he had faythe. But now to the ende, which is this:

"And immediatly Jesus stretched forth his hande, and caught hym, and sayd unto him, O thou of lytle fayth! wherfore dyddest thou doubt? And when they were come into the shyppe, the wynd ceassed. And they that were in the shyppe came and worshipped him, saying, Of a truth thou arte the Sonne of God. And immediatly the shippe was at the lande whyther they went."

Hereof first is to be noted, That God is alwaye nyghe to those that calleth upon hym faythfully; and so willyng is he to delyver them, that neither can feare nor extreame daunger hynder his godly hande. Peter was synckyng downe, and loked for no other thyng but present death, and yet the hande of Christe prevented hym. That which was[2] visibly and openly done to Peter in that his great peril, is invisibly and secretly done to Christes holye Church, and to the chosen members of Christes mystical body in al ages. PSAL. 144.

How nygh and redy was the hande of God to delyver his people Israel, when they were almost overwhelmed with desperation, in the dayes of Moses and Hester, the historie doth wytnesse! Howe nygh was God to Daniel amongest the lyons; to Jonas in the whale's bellye; to Peter in prison, is lykewyse moste evidently declared in the Holy Scriptures. Howe sod- EXOD. 14. HESTER 7, 8, 9.
DANIEL 6.
JON. 3.
ACT. 12.

---

[1] HOWE NYGH GOD IS IN EXTREME PERILL TO DELYVER HYS ELECT THAT FAYTHFULLY CALL UPON HYM.—(*Marg. note.*)

[2] In the old copies, "That that was."

denly, and beyonde all expectation, was David many tymes delyvered from Saules tyranny, his owne herte confessed, and compelled his penne to wryte, and tounge to synge, sayeng, "He hath sente from above, and hath delyvered me; he hath drawen me forth of many waters."

<small>PSALM 18.</small>

Erecte your eares, dere Brethren, and let your hertes understande, That as oure God is unchaungeable, so is not his gracious hande shortened this daye. Our feare and trouble is great, the storme that bloweth agaynst us is sore and vehement, and we appeare to be drowned in the depe. But if we unfaynedly knowe the daunger, and wil call for delyveraunce, the Lordes hande is nygher than is the sworde of our enemyes.

<small>GOD FLATTERETH NOT HIS ELECT.</small>

The sharpe rebuke that Christe Jesus gave to Peter, teacheth us that God dothe not flatter nor conceale the faultes of his electe, but maketh them manifest, to the end that the offendours may repent, and that others maye avoyde the lyke offences.

<small>PETER WAS NOT FAYTHLESSE.</small>

That Chryst called Peter "of lytle fayth," argueth and declareth (as we before have noted) that Peter was not altogether faythles, but that he faynted, or was uncertayne in hys fayth: For so soundeth the Greke terme ὀλιγίπιςῶς,[1] wherof we ought to be admonished, that in passynge to Christe throughe the stormes of this worlde, is not onely requyred a fervent fayth in the begynnyng, but also a constancie to the ende. As Christ sayeth, "He that continueth to the end shalbe saved." And Paule, "Onles a man shall stryve lawfullye, he shall not be crowned." The remembraunce of this oughte to put us in mynde, that the moste fervent man, and suche as have longe continued in profession of Christe, is not yet sure to stande at al houres, but that he is subjecte to many daungers, and that he ought to fear his owne frailtie;[2] as the Apostle teacheth us, saying, "He that standeth, let hym beware that he fal not." For yf Peter, that began so fervently, yet faynted or he cam to Christ, what

<small>MATH. 10.</small>
<small>2 TIM. 2.</small>

---

[1] This Greek term is omitted in MS. M.

[2] SUCH AS HAVE STAND LONG MAY YET FALL.—(*Marg. note.*)

ought we to feare, in whome suche fervencye was never founde? No doute we ought to tremble and fear the worst, and, by the knowledge of our owne weaknesse, wyth the Apostles incessauntly to pray, "O Lorde! increase our fayth." Christes de- LUCÆ 17. maunde and question, askyng of Peter, "Why doutest thou?" contayneth in it selfe a vehemencye, as Christe wolde saye, NOTA. Whether doutedst thou of my power, or of my presence, or of my promyses, or of my good wil? Yf my power had not bene sufficient to have saved thee, then coulde I neither have come to thee through the stormy sea, neither have made the waters obey thee when thou begannest to come to me. And yf my good wil had not bene to have delyvered thee and thy brethren, then had I not appeared unto you; neither had I called upon thee, but had permitted the tempest to devoure and swalowe you up. But consyderyng that your eyes saw me present, your eares hearde my voyce, and thou Peter especially knewest the same, and obeyedst my commaundement, why then doutedst thou? Beloved Brethren, yf this same demaunde and question ware layd to oure charge, we should have lesse pretence of excuse then had Peter;[1] for he myght have alleged, That he was not advertised that any greate storme shoulde have rysen betwixt hym and Christ, whiche justly we can not allege. For syth that tyme NOTA. that Christ Jesus hath appeared unto us by the bryghtnes of his worde, and called upon us by hys lyvely voyce, he hath continually blowen in our eares that persecution and trouble should folowe the word that we professed; which dayes are now present. Alasse! then, why doute we through this storme to go to Christ? Support, O Lorde! and let us syncke no further.

Albeit that Peter fainted in fayth, and therfore was worthy CONSOLA-
moste sharplye to be rebuked, yet doth not Christ leave hym in TION.
the sea, neither longe permitted he that feare and tempest to continue; but first they entered both into the bote, and ther-

---

[1] WE HAVE LESSE PRETENSE OF EXCUSE THEN PETER HAD.—(*Marg. note.*)

after the wynde ceassed; and laste, their bote¹ arrived without longer delay, at the place for which they longe had laboured.

O blessed and happy are those that paciently abyde this delyveraunce of the Lorde! The ragynge sea shall not devoure them. Albeit they have fainted, yet shall not Christ Jesus leave them behynde in the stormye sea, but soddenly he shal stretch forth his myghtye hande, and shall place them in the bote amonge their brethren; that is, he shall conducte them to the nombre of his electe and afflicted Churche, with whome he wil continue to the ende of the worlde.

<small>MATH. 28.</small>

The majestie of his presence shal put to silence this boisterous wynde, the malice and envye of the Devell, whiche so bloweth in the hertes of princes, prelates, kynges, and of earthly tyrauntes, that altogether they are conjured agaynst the Lorde,² and against his annointed, Christe;³ in dispite of whom, he safely shal conduct, convey, and carye his sore troubled flocke to the lyfe and reste for which they travel.

<small>PSAL. 2.</small>

Albeit, I saye, that somtymes they have faynted in their journey, albeit that weaknes in fayth permitted them to sincke, yet from the hande of Christe can they not be rent;⁴ he may not suffre them to drowne, nor the deape to devoure them. But for the glorie of his owne name he must delyver, for they are committed to hys charge, protection, and kepyng; and therfore muste he kepe and defende suche as he hath receyved from hys Father, from synne, from death, from Devell and hell.

<small>JO. 10.</small>

<small>JOAN. 7.</small>

The remembraunce of these promisses is to myne owne herte suche occasion of comforte, as neither can any tounge nor penne expresse; but yet, peradventure, some there is of Goddes electe that can not be conforted in this tempest, by any meditations of Goddes election or defence; but rather beholdyng suche as somtymes boldely have professed Christes veritie, nowe to be

---

¹ Boat, or ship.
² WORLDLY PRINCES ARE CONJURED AGAINST GOD.—(*Marg. note.*)
³ In MS. M. "Christ Jesus."
⁴ THE SCHEEPE OF CHRIST CAN NOT BE RENT FROM HIS HAND.—(*Marg. note.*)

returned to their accustomed abhominations;[1] and also, themselves to be overcommed with feare, that againste their knowlege and conscience they stoupe to an idole,[2] and with their presence mainteineth the same. And beyng at this point, they begynne to reason, whether it be possible that the membres of Christes bodye maye be permitted so horribly to fall to the denyall of their Heade, and in the same to remaine of longe continuaunce? And from this reasoning they enter in dolour, and from dolour they begynne to syncke to the gates[3] of hell and portes of desperation.

The doloure and feare of suche I graunt to be moste juste. For, oh! how fearfull is it, for the love of this transitorie lyfe, in presence of man, to denye Christe Jesus, and his knowen and undoubted veritie!

But yet to suche as be not obstinate contempners of God and of al godlynes, I woulde geve this my weake counsaile, That rather they should appeale to mercy, than by the seveire judgementes of God to pronounce agaynst themselves the fearfull sentence of condempnation; and to consider that God concludeth all under unbelefe, that he maye have mercye upon all;[4] that the Lorde kylleth and geveth lyfe; he leadeth downe to ROM. IL. hel, and yet lyfteth up agayne.

But I wyll not that any man thinke, that by this my counsaile, 1 REG. 2. I either justifie suche as horriblye are returned backe to their vomete, either yet that I flatter suche as maintaineth that abhominable idole with their dayly presence. God forbyd; for then were I but a blynde guyde leadyng the blynd headlinges to perdition. Only God knoweth the doloure and sobbes of my herte for NOTA. suche as I heare dayly to turne backe. But the cause of my counsail is, that I knowe the conscience of some to be so tender, that whensoever they fele themselves troubled with feare, wounded with anguyshe, or to have slydden backe in any point, that

---

[1] THE TEMPTATIONS OF GODDES ELECTE NOW IN ENGLAND.—(*Marg. note.*)
[2] The Romish Mass.
[3] In MS. M. "to the zettis."
[4] GOOD CONSAILL TO THE INFAYTH.— (*Marg. note.*)

then they judge their fayth to be quenched, and them selves to be unworthy of Goddes mercies for ever. To suche directe I my counsail, to those, I meane, that rather offendes by weaknes and infirmitie then of malice and set purpose.[1] And I woulde that such should understande and consider, that all Christes Apostles fled from hym, and denyed hym in their hartes. And also I wold they should consyder, that no man ever from the begynnynge stode in greater feare, greater daunger, nor greater doute, then Peter dyd when Christes presence was taken from hym. Yea, no man felt lesse comforte, nor sawe lesse appearaunce of delyveraunce; and yet neither were the Disciples rejected for ever, neither was Peter permitted to drowne in that depe.

<small>MATH. 28.</small>
<small>NOTA.</small>

<small>OBJECTION.</small>
But some shall[2] objecte, Fayth was not utterly quenched in them; and therfore they got delyveraunce, and were restored to comforte.

<small>AUNSWERE.</small>
Answer: That is it which I wold that the afflicted and troubled consciences in this age should consider, that neither feare, neither daunger, neither yet douting, nor backslyding, maye utterlye destroye and quenche the fayth of Goddes elect,[3] but that alwayes there remaineth with them some roote and sparke of faith; howbeit in their anguyshe they neither fele nor can decerne the same. Yet some shal demaunde, How shall it be knowen in whome the sparke and roote of Fayth remayneth, and in whom not; seyng that al fleeth from Christ, and boweth downe to idolatrie? Harde it is, and in a maner impossible, that one man shall wittyngly judge of an other, (for that could not Helias[4] do of the Israelites of hys dayes,) but every man maye easelye judge of hymselfe. For the roote of Fayth is of that nature, that longe it wyll not be ydel,[5] but of necessitie, by processe of tyme, it wyll sende forthe some

<small>3 REG. 19.</small>

---

[1] TO WHOME APARTEINETH THE FORMER COUNSAILL.—(*Marg. note.*)

[2] In MS. M. "sum will."

[3] THE ROOTE OF FAYTH REMAYNETH

WITH GODES ELECT IN GREATEST DAUNGER.—(*Marg. note.*)

[4] Elijah.

[5] THE ROOTE OF FAYTH IS NOT IDELL. —(*Marg. note.*)

braunches that maye be sene and felte by the outwarde man, yf it remayne lyvely in the herte; as you have herd it dyd in Peter, compellynge hym to crye upon Christ when that he was in greatest necessitie. Wilt thou have a triall, whether the roote of fayth remayneth wyth thee or not?[1] I speake to such as are weak, and not to proude contempners of God.

1. Fealest thou thy soule fayntynge in fayth, as Peter felt his body sincke downe into the waters?

2. Arte thou as sore affrayed that thy soule should drowne in hel, yf thou consentest or obeyest idolatrye, as Peter was that his bodye shoulde drowne in the waters?

3. Desyrest thou as earnestly the delyveraunce of thy soule, as Peter dyd the delyveraunce of his body?

4. Belevest thou that Christ is able to delyver thy soule, and that he wyl do the same accordynge to his promise?

5. Doest thou call upon him wythout hypocrisie, nowe in the daye of thy trouble?

6. Doest thou thrist for his presence, and for the lybertie of his worde agayne?

7. Mournest thou for the great abhominations that now over-flowes the Realme of England?

Yf these premisses,[2] I say, remaine yet in thy harte, then arte thou not altogether destitute of fayth; neyther shalt thou descende to perdition for ever. But mercifullye shal the Lorde stretche forth his myghtie hande, and shal delyver thee from the very throte and bottome of hell. But by what meanes that he shall performe that his merciful worke, it neither apperteyneth to thee to demaunde, nor to me to defyne.[3] But this is requisite, and our bounden deutie, that suche meanes as the NOTA. hande of our God shall offer (to avoyde idolatrie) we refuse not, but that willyngly we embrace the same, albeit, partly it disagree to our affections. Neither yet, thinke I, that soddenly,

---

[1] A TRYALL OF FAYTH IN TROUBLE.—(*Marg. note.*)
[2] If these things.
[3] IT APERTEYNETH NOT TO MAN TO KNOWE, NOR TO ENQUIRE, HOWE GOD WYL DELYVER.—(*Marg. note.*)

and by one meanes, shal all the faythful in Englande be delyvered from idolatrie.¹ No, it may be that God so strengthen the hertes of some of those that have fainted before, that they wyl resist idolatrie to the death; and that were a glorious and triumphant delyveraunce. Of others God maye so touche the hertes, that they wyll rather chuse to walke, and go as pilgremes frome realme to realme, sufferyng honger, colde, heate, thrist, wearines, and povertie, then that they wyl abyde (havyng al haboundaunce) in subjection of idolatrie. To some may God offer suche occasion, that in despite of idolaters (be they princes or prelates) they maye remayne within their owne dominions, and yet neyther bowe their knees to Baal, neither yet lacke the lyvely foode of Goddes moste holy Worde.

NOTA.

Yf God offer unto us any suche meanes, let us assuredlye knowe, that Christe Jesus stretched forth his hande unto us, willyng to delyver us from that daunger wherin many are lyke to perishe; and therfore let us not refuse it,² but with gladnes let us take holde of it, knowyng that God hath a thousand meanes (very unapperyng³ to mannes judgement) wherby he wyll delyver, supporte, and conforte his afflicted Churche. And therfore, moste dearly beloved in our Saviour Jesus Christ, considerynge that the remembraunce of Christes banket (whereof I doute not some of you taisted with comforte and joye) is not yet utterlye taken from your mynde; and that we have entered in thys journey at Christes commaundementes; considering that we feele the sea wyndes blowe contrary and against us, as before was prophecied unto us; and that we see the same tempest rage againste us that ever hath raged against Christes electe Churche; and consideryng also that we feele oure selves ready to fainte, and lyke to be oppressed by these stormy seas, let us prostrate oure selves before the throne of grace, in the presence of our heavenlye Father, and in the bytternes of oure hertes

REPETITION.

---

¹ DIVERS WAYES OF DELIVERAUNCE.—(*Marg. note.*)
² THE MEANES OFFERED BY GOD TO AVOID IDOLATRIE ARE NOT TO BE REFUSED.—(*Marg. note.*)
³ Unapparent, unlikely.

let us confesse oure offences; and for Christe Jesus sake, let us seek after delyveraunce and mercy, sayeng, wyth sobbes and grones from our troubled hertes:

"O God! the Heathen are entred into thyne inheritance: They have defiled thy holye Temple and have prophaned thy blessed ordinaunce. In place of thy joyfull sygnes, they have erected their abhominable ydoles. The deadly cuppe of al blasphemy is restored agayne to their harlottes hande. Thy prophetes are persecuted, and none are permitted to speake thy worde frelye: The poore shepe of thy poore pasture are commaunded to drynke the venemouse waters of mennes traditions. But, O Lorde! thou knowest howe sore they greve us: But suche is the tyranny of these most cruel beastes, that playnlye they saye, ' They shall roote us out at once,[1] so that no remembraunce shall remayne of us in earth.' COMPLAYNT. PSAL. 79. PSAL. 74. APOCAL. 17. PSAL. 74 & 83.

"O Lorde![2] thou knowest that we are but fleshe, and that we have no power of our selves to withstand their tyranny; and therfore, O Father! open the eyes of thy mercy upon us, and confirme thou in us the worke whiche thyne owne mercy hath begon. We acknowlege and confesse, O Lorde! that we are punished moste justlye, bycause we lyghtly regarded the tyme of our mercyfull visitation. Thy blessed Gospell was in oure eares lyke a lover's songe, it pleased us for the tyme; but alasse! oure lyves dyd nothynge agree with thy statutes and holy commaundementes. And thus we acknowledge that our owne iniquitie hath compelled thy justice to take the lyght of thy Worde from the whole Realme of Englande.[3] But be thou myndfull, O Lorde! that it is thy truthe which we have professed, and that thy enemys blasphemeth thy holy name, and our profession[4] with out cause. Thy holy Gospel is called heresye, and we are accused as traytours, for professyng the same. Be PRAIER AND CONFESSION. APPEALING TO MERCY. ESAY 33.

[1] In the old edit. "at ones."
[2] In MS. M. "O Lord, thy Majestie knawis."
[3] The words "of England," omitted in MS. M.
[4] In the old edit. "possession."

mercyfull therfore, O Lorde! and be salvation unto us in thys tyme of our anguishe. Albeit our synnes accuse and condempne us, yet do thou accordynge to thyne owne name. We have offended against thee: Oure synnes and iniquities are without nombre, and yet art thou in the middes of us. O Lorde! albeit that tyrauntes beare rule over oure bodies, yet thristeth our soules for the comforte of thy Worde.

JEREM. 4.

"Correct us therfore, but not in thy hote displeasure; spare thy people, and permitte not thyn enheritaunce to be in rebuke for ever. Let suche, O Lorde! as now are most afflicted, yet ones agayne prayse thy holy name before thy congregation. Represse the pride of these bloode thristye tyrauntes; consume them in thyne anger according to the reproche which they have laid against thy holy name. Powre forth thy vengeaunce upon them, and let our eyes behold the blood of thy saintes required of their handes. Delaye not thy vengeaunce, O Lorde! but let death devoure them in haist; let the earth swallowe them up; and let them go downe quick to the helles. For there is no hope of their amendement, the feare and reverence of thy holy name is quite banished from their hertes;[1] and therfore yet againe, O Lorde! consume them, consume them in thyne anger, and let them never bringe their wicked counselles to effect; but, according to the godly powers, let them be taken in the snare whiche they have prepared for thyne electe. Looke upon us, O Lorde! wyth the eyes of thy mercy, and shewe petie upon us, thy weake and sore oppressed flocke: Gather us yet ones agayne to the holsome treasures of thy moste holye Worde, that openly we may confesse thy blessed Gospell within the Realme of Englande. Graunt this, O Heavenlye Father, for Christe Jesus thy Sonnes sake. Amen."

Yf on thys maner, or otherwyse, (as God shal put in our hertes) with out hipocrisie in the presence of oure God, (respecting more his glory then our private wealth,) continuallye

[1] AGAYNST THE ENNEMYES OF GOD.—(*Marg. note.*)

we powre forth our complaint, confession, and prayers; then so assuredlye as our God lyveth, and as we feall these present troubles, shal our God hymselfe ryse to our defence, he shall confounde the counseilles of our enemyes, and trouble the wyttes of suche as moste wrongfully troubleth us. He shall sende Jehu to execute hys juste judgementes againste ydolatours, and against suche as obstinatly defendeth them. Jesabel her selfe shall not escape the vengeaunce and plagues that are prepared for her portion. The flatterers and the mainteners of her abhominations shal drink the cuppe of Goddes wrath with her. And in despite of the Devell, shall yet the glorye of Christe Jesus, and the bryghtnesse of his countenaunce so shyne in oure hertes by the presence of his grace, and before our eyes by the true preaching of his Gospel, that altogether we shall fall before him and saye:

"O Lorde! thou arte our God, we shall extol thee, and shall confesse thy name, for thou haste brought wonderous thinges to passe accordynge to thy counseilles, which albeit appear to be farre of, yet are they true and moste assured. Thou haste broughte to ruyne the palaces of tyrauntes; and therfore shal the afflicted magnifie thee, and the citie of tyranfull nations shal feare thee. Thou haste bene, O Lorde, a stronge defence to the poore, a sure place of refuge to the afflicted in the tyme of his anguisshe." Esaie 25.

This no dout, dear Brethren, shal one day be the songe of Godes electe with in the Realme of Englande, after that God hath poured forth his vengeaunce upon these inobedient and blood-thristy tyrauntes, which now triumpheth in all abominations; and therfore, yet agayne, beloved in the Lord, abyde patientlye the Lordes deliveraunce, avoiding and flyeng suche offences as may seperate and devyde you from the blessed felowship of the Lorde Jesus at his seconde comming. Watche and praye, resist the Devel, and rowe against this vehement tempest, and shortly shal the Lorde come to the comforte of Of Goddes Elect. Exhortation.

[ISAI. 25.] your hertes, which nowe are oppressed with anguyshe and care; but then shal ye so rejoyse, that through gladnes you shall saye, "Behold, this our God, we have wayted upon him, and he hath saved us: This is our Lorde, we have longe thristed for his commyng, now shal we rejoyce and be glad in his salvation." So be it. The great Bishop of our soules, Jesus our Lorde, so strengthen and assist your troubled hertes with the myghtie comforte of his Holy Ghoste, that earthlye tyrauntes nor worldly tormentes have no power to dryve you from the hope and expectation of that kingdome, which for the electe was prepared from the begynnyng by our Heavenly Father, to whome be all prayse and honour, now and ever. Amen.

Remember me, deare Brethren, in your dayly prayers. The grace of our Lorde Jesus Christ be wyth you all. Amen.[1]

Yours with sorowfull herte,

JOHN KNOX.

Imprynted at Kalykow, the 20. daye of Julij 1554.

Cum gratia et priuilegio ad Imprimendum solum.

---

[1] In MS. M. after "Amen," the date, "the 20. day of Julij 1554," is inserted, and precedes the words, "Yours with sorowfull herte, JOHN KNOX." The words, "Imprinted at Kalykow," are of course omitted in the manuscript. The imprint is here repeated, in order to show that the work was apparently printed at this date; whereas, according to MS. M., the date would apply to the Author having then finished the writing of his Admonition.

EPISTLES

TO MRS ELIZABETH BOWES, AND
HER DAUGHTER MARJORY.

M.D.LIII.—M.D.LIV.

It would appear from a passage in Knox's latest publication, his "Answer to Tyrie the Jesuit," printed in 1572, that he had in his possession the various letters which he had addressed to his mother-in-law, Mrs Bowes. One of these letters he subjoined, in order to show "what a troubled conscience craves in the day of battle;" and also to "declare to the world what was the cause of our great familiarity and long acquaintance; which (he adds) was neither flesh nor blood, but a troubled conscience upon her part, which never suffered her to rest but when she was in the company of the faithful, of whom (from the first hearing of the Word at my mouth) she judged me to be one." After referring to the conflicts in spirit which she sustained, he says, "Her company to me was comfortable, (yea, honourable and profitable, for she was to me and mine a mother,) but yet it was not without some cross; for besides trouble and fasherie of body sustained for her, my mind was seldom quiet, for doing somewhat for the comfort of her troubled conscience, whereof this rude letter is the least and of basest [feeblest] argument, *among many which lie beside me*, and so must do, by reason of my inability in more sorts than one." The letter thus selected is the one dated at Dieppe, the 20th of July 1554.[1]

During Knox's ministrations at Berwick and Newcastle, he became acquainted with the family of Bowes. Sir Ralph Bowes of Streatlam, whose will is dated in 1482, had three sons, the eldest of whom, George, was knighted on the field

[1] See it printed as No. II., page 343.

of Floddon in 1513. His third son, in 1550, is styled Richard Bowes of Aske, captain of Norham castle. He married Elizabeth, daughter and co-heir of Sir Roger Aske of Aske, in Yorkshire, by whom he had two sons and several daughters. The eldest son, Sir George Bowes, was afterwards knight-marshal to Queen Elizabeth; and Robert Bowes, the second son, was sent ambassador to the court of Scotland in 1578. Mrs Bowes appears to have experienced deep religious impressions, approaching to melancholy, and Knox's letters testify his care and anxiety in suggesting comfort to her troubled conscience. With Marjory Bowes, described in the pedigree of the family[1] as the fifth daughter, Knox formed an attachment, which, although approved and countenanced by her mother, was opposed by the other relations. Notwithstanding this opposition, they formally pledged themselves to one another "before witnesses;" and it probably was not till July 1555, when Knox visited Scotland, or it might be a few months later, that the marriage actually took place. In the following year, Mrs Bowes and her daughter embarked in a vessel for Dieppe, and Knox having joined them in the month of July, they proceeded thence to Geneva, where he resumed his ministerial labours.

From the "Livre des Anglois à Genève,"[2] we learn that, on the 13th of September, John Knox, Marjory his wife, Elizabeth her mother, his servant James, and a pupil named Patrick, were admitted members of the English congregation; and in December that year, Knox and Goodman were elected ministers.

The following letters are those to which Knox refers; and along with a few others of a later date, they have been preserved in the Manuscript collection of Knox's pieces, in the possession of the Reverend Dr M'Crie, already so frequently quoted. This

---

[1] See the pedigree of the Bowes of Streatlam in M'Crie's Life of Knox, Appendix, vol. ii., No. xix.

[2] This curious tract, excerpted from the Registers at Geneva, was edited by John Southernden Burn. London, 1831, 8vo.

quarto volume was transcribed in the year 1603, as appears from the short marginal notes. It consists of nearly 500 pages, not reckoning more recent additions on the blank leaves, such as the transcript of a letter from John Welsh, or the table of contents at the end. But no portion of the volume is in Welsh's own hand, as Dr M'Crie conjectured. The following title is prefixed:

"THE EPISTLES OF MR JOHN KNOX, worthy to be read because of the authority of the wryter, the solidity of the matter, and the comfortable Christian experience to be found therein. Ed'. [Edinburgh,] 11 February 1683, H. T. m. p." The title is followed by a note, in a smaller hand, but apparently written at the same time: " This booke belonged somtyme to Margaret Stewart, Widow to Mr Knox, afterward married to the Knight of Faudonsyde: Sister shee was to James Earle of Arran."

This volume came into the possession of Wodrow the historian, and being separated from the rest of his manuscript collections, it was thus announced for publication in April 1804, by Maurice Ogle, bookseller in Glasgow: "The Posthumous Works and last Remains of the late eminent and pious Reformer, Mr John Knox, (whose fame is in all the Churches,) &c." According to the prospectus, it was to consist of five numbers, making one handsome volume octavo, containing about 560 pages; and, it is added, "As the manuscript is wrote in language not common in the present day, the Publishers have been at considerable pains in getting it transcribed into modern language." The project does not appear to have met with sufficient encouragement; and Mr Ogle having put the volume into the hands of the late REV. DR M'CRIE, this in some measure led to his undertaking the composition of his LIFE OF KNOX, one of the most important biographical works in modern times.

Having had the most liberal use of the manuscript from the present possessor, the REV. THOMAS M'CRIE, D.D., I beg leave to express my grateful sense of this important favour, not the less esteemed, in my having had no occasion to plead a promise to the same effect, voluntarily made to me many years ago by his distinguished Father, when consulting him regarding an earlier plan than the present, of publishing a collective edition of the Reformer's Writings.

It is only necessary to add, that this series of Religious Letters, addressed to Mrs Bowes and her daughter, is now, for the first time, printed entire. Although it is very apparent that the Letters are not arranged according to strict chronology, I have thought it expedient to follow the arrangement of the manuscript, as the transcriber had evidently adhered either to that of the original Letters, or a copy prepared for publication by Knox himself. The Letters of a date posterior to 1554, chiefly addressed by Knox to other individuals, will be included in a subsequent volume of his Works.

CERTANE EPISTILLIS AND LETTERIS OF THE SERVAND OF GOD JOHNE KNOX, SEND FROME DYVERSE PLACES TO HIS FREINDIS AND FAMILIARIS IN JESUS CHRYST.

THE FIRSTE LETTER
TO HIS MOTHER-IN-LAW, MISTRES BOWIS.

RYCHT DEIRLY BELOVIT[1] MOTHER in oure Saviour Jesus Chryst. When I call to mynd and revolve with myself the trubillis and afflictionis of Godis electe frome the begynning, (in whiche I do not forget yow,) thair is within my hart tuo extreme contraries; a dolour almaist unspeakabill, and a joy and comfort whilk be mannis sences can not be comprehendit nor understand. The cheif caussis of dolour be two: the ane is the rememberance of syn, whilk I daylie feill remanyng in this corrupt nature; whilk was and is sa odius and detestabill in the presence of oure hevinlie Father, that by na uther sacrifice culd or myght the same be purgeit, except by the blude and deth of the onlie innocent Sone of God. When I deiplie do considder the caus of Chrystis deth to haif bene syn, and syn yit to duell in all flesche, with Paule I am compellit to sob and grone as ane man under ane heavie burdene; yea, sumtymes to cry, "O wreachit and miserabill man that I am! wha sall delyver me fra this bodie of syn?"

The uther caus of my dolour is, that sic as maist gladlie wald remane togidder, for mutuall comfort ane of another, can not be sufferit sa to do. Since the first day that it pleasit

[1] In MS. M. this phrase is usually written as one word, "Deirlibelovit."

the providence of God to bring yow and me in familiaritie, I have alwayis delytit in your company; and when labouris wald permit, ye knaw I have not spairit houris to talk and commune[1] with yow, the frute whairof I did not than fullie understand nor perceave. But now absent, and so absent that by corporall presence nather of us can resave comfort of uther, I call to mynd how that oftymes when, with dolorous hartis, we haif begun our talking, God hath send greit comfort unto baithe, whilk now for my awn part I commounlie want. The expositioun of your trubillis, and acknawledging of your infirmitie, war first unto me a verie mirrour and glass whairin I beheld my self sa rychtlie payntit furth, that nathing culd be mair evident to my awn eis. And than, the searching of the Scriptures for Godis sueit promissis, and for his mercies frelie givin unto miserable offenderis, (for his nature delyteth to schew mercie whair maist miserie ringeth,[2]) the collectioun and applying of Godis mercies, I say, wer unto me as the breaking and handilling with my awn handis of the maist sueit and delectabill ungementis,[3] whairof I culd not but receave sum comfort be thair naturall sueit odouris.

But now, albeit I never lack the presence and plane image of my awn wreachit infirmitie, yit seing syn sa manifestlie abound in al estaitis, I am compellit to thounder out the threattnyngis of God aganis obstinat rebellaris; in doing whairof (albeit as God knaweth I am no malicious nor obstinat synner) I sumtymes am woundit, knawing my self criminall and giltie in many, yea in all, (malicious obstinacie laid asyd,) thingis that in utheris I reprehend. Judge not, Mother, that I wrait theis thingis debassing my self uther[4] wayis than I am; na, I am wors than my pen can express. In bodie ye think I am no adulterer; let sa be, but the hart is infectit with foull lustis, and will lust, albeit I lament never sa mekill. Externallie I commit na idolatrie; but my wickit

---

[1] In MS. M. "commoun."
[2] Reigns.
[3] Ointments.
[4] In MS. M. "utheris."

hart luffeth the self, and can not be refranit fra vane imaginationis, yea, not fra sic as wer the fountane of all idolatrie. I am na man-killer with my handis; but I help not my nedie brother sa liberallie as I may and aucht. I steill not hors, money, nor claithis fra my nychtbour; but that small portioun of warldlie substance I bestow not sa rychtlie as his halie law requyreth. I beir na fals witnes aganis my nychtbour in judgement, or utherwayis befor men; but I speik not the treuth of God sa boldlie as it becumeth his trew messinger to do. And thus in conclusioun, thair is na vyce repugnyng to Godis halie will, expressit in his law, whairwith my hart is not infectit.

This mekill writtin and dytit befoir the resait of your letteris, whilk I ressavit the 21st of June. Thay war unto my hart sum comfort for dyvers caussis not necessar to be rehersit; but maist (as knaweth God) for that I find ane congruence betwix us in spreit, being sa fer distant in bodie. For when that digestlie I did avys with[1] your letter, I did considder that I myself was complenyng evin the self sam thingis at that verie instant moment that I ressavit your letter. Be my pen, frome a sorowfull hart, I culd not but burst forth and say, "O Lord, how wonderfull ar thy workis! How dois thou try and prufe thy chosin children as gold by the fyre! How canest thou in maner hyd thy face fra thy awn spous, that thy presence efter may be mair delectabill! How canest thou bring thy sainctis low, that thou may carie thame to glorie everlasting! How canest thou suffer thy strang faithful messingeris in many thingis yit to wressill with wreachit infirmitie and febill weaknes, yea, and sumtymes permittis thou thame horribillie to fall, partlie, that na flesche sall have whairof it may glorie befoir thee; and partlie that utheris of smaller estait and meaner giftis in thy Kirk myght resave sum consolatioun, albeit thay find in thame selves wickit motionis whilk thay are not abill to expell!"

My purpois was, befoir I ressavit your letter, to have exhortit you to pacience, and to fast adhering to Godis promises, albeit

[1] In other words, when I deliberately examined.

that your flesche, the Divill, and uther your enemyis, wald persuad you to the contrare; for, by the artis and subteliteis that the adversarie useth aganis me, I not onlie do conjecture, but also planelie dois sie your assaltis and trubill. And sa lykwys in the bowellis of Chrystis mercie, maist ernistlie I beseik you, by that infirmitie that ye knaw remaneth in me, (wars I am than I can wryt,) pacientlie to beir, albeit that ye haif not sic perfectioun as ye wald; and albeit also your motionis be sic as be maist vyle and abominabill, yet not to sorrow abuf measure. Gif I, to whom God hes gevin greatter giftis, (I wryt to His prais) be yit sa wrappit into miserie, that what I wald, I can not do, and what I wald not, that with Sainct Paule I say, I daylie, yea everie hour and moment, I devys to do, and in my hart, ficht I never sa fast in the contrarie, I perform and do. Gif sic wreachit wickitnes remane in Godis cheif ministeris, what wonder albeit the same remane in yow? Gif Godis strangest men of war be beattin bak in thair face, that what thay wald they can not distroy nor kill, is it any sic offence to yow to be tossit as ye compleane, that thairfoir ye suld distrust Goddis frie promissis? God forbid, deir Mother! the power of God is knawin be oure weaknes; and theis dolouris and infirmities be maist profitabill to us, for by the same is oure pryde beattin doun, whilk is not easie utherwayis to be done. By thame ar oure misereis knawin, sa that we, acknawledging oure selves misterfull,[1] seikis the Phesitioun. By thame cum we, be the operatioun of the Halie Spreit, to the hatred of syn; and be thame cum we to the hunger and thrist of justice; and to desyre to be dissolved, and sa to ring[2] with oure Christ Jesus, whilk without this battell and sorrow this flesche culd never do. And sa fra the dolouris I proceid to the comfort.

As the caussis of dolour be two, whilk ar present syn, and the laik of sic company as in whome we maist culd delyt; sa is the caussis of my comfort not ymaginit of my brane, but pronuncit first be God, and efter graftit in the hartis of Godis

---

[1] "Misterful." necessitous. [2] Reign.

children by his Halie Spreit. Thai ar lykwyse two, whilk is a justice inviolable offerit be oure flesche befoir the trone of oure heavinlie Father, and ane assureit hoip of that generall assemblie and gathering togither of Godis dispersit flok, in that day when all tearis salbe wipit fra oure eis, when death salbe vincuist,[1] and may na mair dissever sic as feiring God this day in the flesche murnis under the burdene of syn. Off oure present justice, notwithstanding syn remane in our mortall bodeis, ar we assureit by the faithfull witnes of Jesus Chryst, Johne the Apostle, saying, " Gif we confes oure synnis, faithfull and just is God to remit and forgive our synnis." Mark the wordis of the Apostill, Gif we confes oure synnis, God man[2] forgive thame, becaus he is faithfull and just. To confessioun of synnis ar theis thingis requisit: first, we man acknawledge the syn; and it is to be notit, that sumtymes Godis verie elect, albeit they have synnit maist haynouslie, dois not acknawledge syn, and thairfoir can not at all tymes confes the same; for syn is not knawin unto sic tyme as the vaile be taken fra the conscience of the offender, that he may sie and behald the filthines of syn, what punishment be Godis just jugementis is dew for the same. And then (whilk is the second thing requisit to confessioun) begynnis the haitred of syn, and of oure selves for contempnying of God and of his halie law, whairof last springis that whilk we call hoip of mercie; whilk is nathing els but a sob fra a trubillit hart, confoundit and aschamit for syn, thristing remissioun and Godis frie mercie, whairupon of necessitie man[2] follow this conclusioun, God hes remittit and frelie forgevin the syn; and why? For "He is faithfull and just," sayeth the Apostill. Comfortabill and mervelous caussis! First, God is faithfull, ergo, He man[2] forgive syn. A comfortable consequent upon a maist sure ground! for Godis fidelitie can na mair faill nor can him self.

Then lat this argument be gatherit for oure comfort; the office of the faithfull is to keip promeis; but God is faithfull, ergo, He man[2] keip promeis. That God hes promissit remissioun

---

[1] Vanquished.   [2] "Man," must.

of synis to sic as be repentant, I neid not now to recit the places. But let this collectioun of the promissis be maid; God promisses remissioun of synis to all that confessis the same, but I confes my synnis, for I sie the filthines thairof, and how justlie God may condemp me for my iniquities. I sob and I lament for that I can not be quyt and red[1] of syn; I desyre to leif a mair perfyt lyfe. Thir ar infallible signis, seillis, and takinis, that God hes remittit the syn; for God is faithfull that sa hes promissit, and can na mair deceave nor he can ceis to be God. But what reasone is this? God is just, thairfoir He man[2] forgive syn? A wonderous caus and reasone in deid! For the flesche and naturall man can understand nathing but the contrar, for thus man[2] it reasone; the justice of God is offendit be my synnis, sa God man[2] neidis have a satisfactioun, and requyre ane punissment. Gif we understand of whome God requyris satisfactioun, whether of us, or of the handis of his onlie Sone, and whais punisment is abill to recompens oure synnis, than sall we haif greit cause to rejose, remembering that God is a just God; for the office of the just man is to stand content when he hes ressavit his dewtie. But God hes ressavit alredie at the handis of his onlie Sone all that is dew for our synnis, and sa can not his justice requyre nor craif any mair of us, ather satisfactioun or recompensatioun for our synnis.

Advert, Mother, the sure pilleris and fundatioun of oure salvatioun to be Godis faithfulnes and justice. He that is faithfull, hes promissit frie remissioun to all penitent synneris, and he that is just, hes ressavit alredie a full satisfactioun for the synnis of all thais that imbrace Chryst Jesus to be the only Saviour of the warld. What restis than to us to be done? Nathing but to acknawledge oure miserie and wrechednes, whilk na flesche can do sa unfeanidlie as thai that daylie feillis the wecht of syn. And thairfoir, Mother, caus haif ye nane of disperatioun, albeit the Divill rage never sa cruellie, and albeit the flesche be never sa fraill, daylie and

---

[1] "Red," rid, free.   [2] "Man," must.

hourlie lusting aganis Godis halie commandementis, yea, stryving aganis the same. This is not the tyme of justice befoir oure awn eis; we luke for that whilk is promissit, the kingdome everlasting, preparit to us fra the begynning, whairof we ar maid airis be Godis apoyntment, reabillit[1] thairto be Chrystis death, to whome we shall be gatherit, whair efter we sall never depart; whilk to remember is my singular comfort, but thairof now I can not wryte. My commendationis to all whome effeiris.[2] I commit you to the protectioun of the Omnipotent.

At Londoun, the 23d of Juin, 1553. Your Sone unfeaned,

JOHNE KNOX.

II.[3]

Ryse, Lord! streache out thy hand: forget not the sobbis of the oppressit.—PSA. lxxix.

RYCHT DEARLY BELOVIT MOTHER in our Saviour Jesus Chryst. Now is our dolour apoyntit be God, and foirspoken be his Prophetis, cum upon us, as the dolour of a woman in the birth of hir first chyld; and sa is it cum, as with your eiris, baith opinlie and privatlie, oftentymes ye haif hard declarit. When I remember your greit infirmitie, and the strang battell that continewallie ye ficht, and callis to mynd how small comfort ye haif in erth, I am compellit to sob and grone to Him that onlie may gif strenth, comfort, and consolatioun (without help of any creature) unto yow, in theis maist dolorous dayis. And gud hoip I haif that my petitioun sall not be repellit, but for Chryst Jesus sake acceptit and grantit; albeit not in sic sort as ye and I glaid-

---

[1] A forensic term, to rehabilitate, to restore a right or privilege which had been forfeited.

[2] "Effeiris," concerns.

[3] In the margin, "The Second to his Mother."—In this letter, as published by Knox himself, (see page 333) there are some slight verbal discrepancies and omissions; but these need not be pointed out, as the letter, with Knox's marginal notes in 1572, will be given along with his Answer to Tyrie

lie wold, yit I dout not but in sic sort we sall obteane it, as his glorie and our everlasting comfort and profit requyreth.

It hath not bene without the maist speciall providence and favour of God, that, theis many dayis bypast, ye haif bene grevouslie temptit, and sair assaultit, to revolt and turne back agane to that abominabill and blasphemous ydolatrie; whilk now in Godis anger is erectit, befoir the utermaist of his plaguis be pourit furth upon the stuburne and inobedient, whilk never wald delyt in the treuth of his Word; and thairfoir of his just judgementis maist justlie hes he gevin thame over, according to thair hartis desyre, to delyt in leyis, to thair eternall dampnatioun. In the dayis, I say, belovit Mother, that na aperance thair was that ever sic abominatioun suld have taken place, sa suddenlie, within this Realme of Ingland, ye wer tempted and assaltit to turne bak agane to idolatrie; whilk tempting spirit, God our hevinlie Father permittit to trubill you, partlie for that he wald haif yow exercisit in the battell befoir the greit danger aprocheit, least perchance ye might have bene overthrawin, gif improvyditlie baith occasioun and temptatioun at anis had assaltit yow; and partlie, that by continewall repugnance ye might learne how odious is all kynd of idolatrie in the sight of God. For Sathan usis seldome to tempt, but in thai thingis whairwith he knawis God maist to be offendit with, as pryd, lust, covetousnes, adulterie, idolatrie, and sic uthir; the committers whairof, and contineweris in the same, pronouncis Paule to haif na portioun in the kingdome of God.

This is my hope, belovit Mother, That in your continewall battell sa fer ye haif profittit, that in this case almaist ye neid na Admonitioun of me. But becaus it is my bound dewtie, not onlie be a commoun Christiane cheritie, [but also for that most unfeaned familiaritie[1]] and tender love, according to godlines, that we haif keipt since our first acquentance, to do the utermaist of my power for your comfort. Be pen thairfoir will I wryt, becaus the bodeis ar now put asunder to meit agane at

[1] The words within brackets are omitted in MS. M.

Godis pleasure, that whilk by mouth and face to face ye haif heard. Gif man or angell sall labour to bring yow back fra the confessioun that anis ye haif gevin, lat thame in that behalf be accursit, and in na part (concernyng your faith and religioun) obeyit of yow. Gif ony trubill yow abufe measure, whether thai be majestratis or carnell freindis, thai sall beir thair just condempnation unles thai spedilie repent. But whasaever it be that sall solist or provok yow to that abominable ydoll, resist yow all sic baldlie unto the end; learnyng of the Halie Gaist not to defyle the tempill of God with idollis; nethir yit to gif your bodelie presence unto thame; but obeying God mair nor man, avoid all apeirance of iniquitie. The necessitie that all men hath sa to do, (that willinglie will not dissave him self,) I remit, partlie to that whilk oft ye haif hard, and partlie to a Generall Letter writtin be me in greit anguis of hart to the Congregationis,[1] of whome I heir say a greit part, under pretence that thai may keip faith secret in the hart, and yit do as idolateris do, begynnis now to fall befoir that idoll. But O, allace! blind and dissavit ar thai, as thai sall knaw in the Lordis visitatioun; whilk, sa assuredlie as our God liveth, sall schortlie aprehend thai bak-starteris amanges the middis of idolateris. With verie greif of hart I wrytt, better it had bene unto thame never to have knawin the treuth, then sa suddanlie, to Godis greit dishonour, to have returnit to thair vomit. God of his infinit mercie grant unto thame spedie repentance; for gif the syn sleip lang, I feir it sall awake to thair perpetuall confusioun!

But now, Mother, comfort yow my hart (God grant ye may!) in this my greit afflictioun, and dolorous pilgremage. Continew stoutlie to the end, and bow you never befoir that idoll, and sa will the rest of warldlie trubillis be unto me mair tollerable. With my awn hart, I oft commune, yea, and as it wer comforting myself, I appeir to triumphe, that God sall never suffer yow to fall in that rebuke. Sure I am that baith ye wald feir and aschame to commit that abominatioun in my presence,

[1] Referring to his Faithful Admonition: See page 254.

wha am but a wrechit man, subject to syn and miserie lyke to your self. But, O, Mother! thocht na erthlie creature suld be offendit with yow, yit feir ye the presence and offence of Him, who, present in all places, searcheth the verie hart and reynis; whais indignatioun anis kendillit agains the inobedient, (and na syn mair inflameth his wraith than idolatrie doith,) na creatur in heavin nor in earth, that onlie is creatur, is abill to appease[1] the same. And thairfoir, deir Mother, avoid and flie from it, evin as from the deth everlasting. Verie lufe and cairfull solicitude (whilk God knawith my hart taketh for yow) compellis me to dowbill[2] sa oftymes and rehers a thing,[3] being uncertane when God sall grant any oportunitie to visit yow agane. But the Spreit of the Lord Jesus sall, be his omnipotent and invincibill power, supplie in yow that whilk wanteth of warldlie comfort, that the glorie may be knawin to be our Godis allane, wha for a tyme useth to comfort, sustene, and feid a[4] creature be another. But in the end, he drawis us (his awn image) to him self, that be him allane, without the help of all uther, we may live, rejose, ring, and triumphe, as he hes promissit be Jesus Chryst his Sone.

Ane thing will I not conceill fra yow, Mother, that nether ar we sure, not yit in our hartis glorifie God as oure dewtie requyreth, sa lang as that we haif the carnell comfort and defence of creaturis with us. The haill man in bodie and saule sall evidentlie prove this conclusioun. For this bodie, that liveth be meit, drink, clothing, and nurischement, we sie it subject to infirmitie, yea, to mutabilitie and syn, as the finall death of all man declaireth. And the saul even of the verie elect, liveing be the lyvelie word of our heavinlie Father, having a teacher that careis flesche, is alwayis flowing and trubillit with sum feir; as in Chrystis Apostillis and many utheris, maist manifestlie we ar instructit. But when all erthlie creature ceassis, then sall the sufficiencie of Godis Spreit

---

[1] In MS. M. "apais."
[2] To repeat.
[3] One thing.
[4] Feed one.

wirk his awn work. And thairfoir, belovit Mother, feir not the battell that ye susteane, nether yit the infirmitie that ye find ether in flesche or spreit. Onlie absteane fra externall iniquitie, that ye mak not your memberis servandis to syn, and your imperfectionis sall have na power to damp you; for Chrystis perfectioun is imputit to be youris be faith whilk ye haif in his blude. Be assurit, Mother, willinglie I wald not disceave yow: gif any sic infirmitie wer dampnabill, lang ago I wald haif schewit you the treuth. But na mair nor God is displeasit, albeit that sumtymes the bodie be seik, and subject to diseassis, and sa unabill to do the calling; na mair is he offendit, albeit the saule in that case be diseassit and scik. And as the naturall father will not slay the bodie of his chyld, albeit throcht[1] sicknes it faynt, and abhoir comfortable meittis, na mair (and mekill less) will our heavinlie Father slay our saullis, albeit throucht spirituall infirmitie and weaknes of our faith sumtymes we refus the lyvelie fude of his comfortable promissis. Whair the contempt of God is, by his grace, removeit, and a love of justice, and of the lyfe to cum ingraftit in the hart, thair is the infallible seall and testimony of the Holie Ghoist, wha sall performe his awn work in dew seasone; for the power of God is knawin in our infirmitie. And thus commit I you to the protectioun of Him, wha by grace hes callit yow fra darknes to lyght; by faith hes purgeit your conscience and hart; and of his frie mercie sall glorifie you, according to his promeis maid unto thame that obedientlie receave the message of lyfe in Chryst Jesus our Lord: Whois omnipotent spreit rest with yow for ever.

At Deip, the 20th of July 1554: (Efter I had visitit Geneva and uther partis, and returnit to Deip to learn the estait of Ingland and Scotland.)[2]

[Postscript.]—My awn estait I can not well declair; but God sall gyd the futstepis of him that is wilsome,[3] and will feid

---

[1] "Throcht," through.
[2] See *supra*, page 253.
[3] Wandering, uncertain of one's course, in a state of dreariness.

him in trubill, that never greitlie solistit[1] for the warld. Gif any collectioun myght be maid amang the faithfull, it wer na schame for me to resaif that, whilk Paule refussit not in the tyme of his trubill. But all I remit to His providence, that ever caireth for his awn: Rest in Christ.

Your Sone, with trubillit hart,

JOHNE KNOX.

III.

Grace and peace frome God the Father of our Lord Jesus Chryst, rest and be multiplyit with yow. Amen.

BELOVIT SISTER, efter maist hartlie commendatioun, the rememberance of your continewall battell is dolorous unto me; yet feir I nothing less than your victorie by Him wha ever hath vincuist when Sathan apeirit to have possessit all. The art of your adversarie, deir Sister, is subtill; in that he wald cause yow abhour that, and hait it whairin standis onlie salvatioun and lyfe. Jesus, be interpretatioun, is a Saviour, be reasone that he saveth his pepill fra thair synnis; and Chryst is callit Annoyntit, (as Esay doith witnes,) the Spreit of God hath anoyntit our Savioure in sa fer as he is man; thair is gevin unto him all power in heavin and erth, that frome him, as frome a fountane, maist abounding and ever flowing well, we may receave all that we haif lost be the transgressioun of a man.

Now, Sister, our adversarie, knawing that the rest and tranquilitie of our conscience standeth in this, that we do imbrace Jesus to be the onlie Savioure of the warld; and that we learne to apply the sueitnes of his name, whilk precelleth the odouris of all fragrant smelling spyces, to the corruptioun of our woundis; he labouris to mak that name odius, and this he dois as enemy, not sa mekill to yow, as unto Jesus Chryst,

[1] That never was greatly solicitous.

wha by his awn power hes brokin doun his heid, and also sall triumphe above him in his memberis. Ye ar seik, deir Sister, and thairfoir na wounder albeit ye (not of your self, but be his continewall assaultis) abhour the succour of maist hailsum fude. I said unto yow, that I was sure that alwayis ye remanit not in that bitternes of hart, for uthir wayis perceaved I, baith be your wordis and conditionis. Gif alwayis ye haitit Jesus the Sone of God, and abhourit the redemptioun that is be his blude, ye suld never sa seik comfort nor consolatioun at God, nether be my prayeris nor familiaritie of my company; but me suld ye hait as doith the rest of the wickit warld: For sic as be reprobate can never love God, nor the memberis of Chrystis bodie, but must neidis persecut thame, and cheiflie sic as in whome the Spreit of God worketh aboundantlie. Witnes King Saule, wha to his deth persecut David; albeit David at all tymes was beneficiall unto him. The contrarie spreit, ringing in the twa, permittit never concord to stand. Farther, Sister, sic as taistis the cup of disperatioun without any motioun or thrist of grace, never taistis any sueitnes of Godis promissis. The contraire whairof I have knawin into yow, whairto I am sure your awn conscience must neidis beir witnes. And sa, Sister, ye ar seik, but sall not die. Your faith is weak and sair trubillit, but ye ar not unfaithfull, nor yit sall not your infirmitie be impute unto yow.

Remember, deir Sister, what ignorance, what feir, and what apeirance of incredulitie remained in Chrystis Discipillis efter thai had heard his maist plane doctrine, and efter thai had sene the power of his workis a langer tyme than ye haif yit continewit in Chryst. That is not sa diligentlie and sa oft rehersit by the Evangelistis without a maist speciall caus; but to be a comfort unto us, that albeit baith feir and doutis remane in our conscience, evin of lang tyme, yit is thair na danger to sic as anis hes imbracit God in his promissis; for his Majestie is sic, that he can not repent him of his giftis. To embrace Chryst, to refus idolatrie, to confes the truth, to love the memberis of Chrystis bodie, ar the giftis of God; thairfoir he can not repent that he hath maid yow pertaker thairof. But leist ye suld wax neglegent, and desyre to remane in this wickit lyfe, his godlie wisdome permitteth yow to taist a litill of that bitter cupe that his awn Sone, our Lord Jesus, did taist in greattest aboundance; and it is profitable, that sa ye do to the mortificatioun of the wickit carkas.

Efter the wrytting of theis preceiding, your brother and myne, Harie Wickleif, did adverteis me be wrytting, that your adversarie tuke occasioun to trubill yow, because that I did start bak fra yow rehersing your infirmities. I remember my self sa to have done, and that is my commoun consuetude, when any thing perceth or tuicheth my hart. Call to your mynd what I did standing at the cupburd in Anwik:[1] in verie deid I thought that na creature had bene temptit as I wes. And when that I heard proceid fra your mouth the verie same wordis that he trubillis me with, I did wonder, and fra my hart lament your sair trubill, knawing in my selfe the dolour thairof. And na uther thing, deir Sister, meant I; and thairfoir think not that I either flatter yow, or yit that I conceill any thing fra you: na, for gif I had bene sa myndit, I had not bene sa plane in uther cassis. My uther greit labouris permittis me not to wryt as I wald. I will pray for your continewance with Chryst.

At Newcastell, in greit haist, the 26th of Februar 1553.[2]

Your Brother,

JOHN KNOX.

IV.

DEIRLY BELOVIT SISTER in Jesus oure Lord, in the instant moment that your messinger delyverit me your letter was I sitting at my buke, and in contemplating Mathowis Gospell in this

---

[1] Alnwick, in Northumberland.
[2] This must have been February 1552-3, as Knox, in February 1553-4, was journeying in Switzerland.

place whairin the Parrable of gud seid is sawin, the enemy also sawing wickit cokill amung the same, I revolved sum maist godlie Expositioun, and amangis the rest Chrisostome, wha nottis upon thir wordis: "The enemy did this, that we may knaw that whasaever is belovit of God hes the Divill to his enemy; and thairfoir aucht we maist rejos when we find the Divill maist rage aganis us, for that is an evident signe that we ar not under his bondage, but ar frie servandis to Jesus Chryst; to whome becaus the Devill is enemy, he man also declair him self enemy to us." In reiding of this his halie judgement, your battell and dolour was befoir my eis; and as I prayit God that ye myght be assistit to the end, sa wissit I that ye had bene present with me; and evin at the sam instant callit your servand, whairof I praisit my God, and adressit me to wryt efter the reiding of your letter as I myght. The place of Luke's Gospell, tuiching thame that sall seik and sall not find, aucht not to discorage yow, for it doith not meane that any thristing for salvation by Jesus Chryst salbe disceavit; but of sic as seikis to enter in the kingdome of God by uther wayis than be Chryst onlie, as ye do knaw thair is a great noumber doith. And whair Chryst sayis, "Thair is few that ar chosin," that is trew in respect of the reprobat. For all Ingland this day is callit, but ye knaw how mene is the noumber that obeyis the voce of the caller. And thairfoir aught ye greatlie to rejois, knawing your self to be ane of the small and contempnit flok to whome it hes pleasit God our Father to give the kingdome.

The pane of my heid and stomock trubillis me greitlie; daylie I find my bodie decay, but the providence of my God sall not be frustrat. I am chargeit to be at Widderingtoun[1] upon Sounday, whair I think I sall also remane Monunday. The Spreit of the Lord Jesus rest with yow. Desyre sic faithfull as with whome ye communicat your mynd, to pray, that at the pleasur of our gud God, my dolour, baith of bodie and spreit, may be releved sumwhat, for presentlie it is very bitter. Never found

[1] In Northumberland, eight miles from Morpeth.

I the spreit, I prais my God, sa aboundant whair Godis glorie aught to be declairit; and thairfoir I am sure thair abydis sumthing that yit we sie not.

Frome Newcastell, 1553.[1]   Your Brother in Chryst,

[JOHN KNOX.[2]]

V.

Thair is na condempnation to sic as be in Christ Jesus, to whome be all prais.

DEIRLY BELOVIT SISTER, efter maist hartlie commendatioun. In my conscience I judge, and be the Halie Spreit of my God, am fullie certifeit that ye ar a member of Chrystis bodie, sair trubillit and vexit presentlie; that the lustis and vane pleasuris of the flesche may be mortifeit, ye may schortlie rest and rejos heirefter in honour and glorie, whairto yit never atteanit mortal creature; but first thai confessit thame selves almaist brunt in hell. Whairfoir perseveir, albeit the battell be strang, that the glorie of your delyverance may be ascrybit and hallielie gevin to God allone. I think it best ye remane till the morow, and sa sall we commoun at large, at efter none. This day ye knaw to be the day of my studie and prayer unto God; yit gif your trubill be intollerabill, or gif ye think my presence may releas your pane, do as the Spreit sall move yow, for ye knaw that I wilbe offendit with nothing that ye do in Godis name. And O how glaid wald I be to feid the hungrie and gif medicene to the seik! Your messinger faund me in bed, efter a sair trubill and maist dolorous nyght, and sa dolour may compleane to dolour when we twa meit. But the infinit gudnes of God,

---

[1] The year 1553, in several of the undated letters, has probably been supplied by Knox or the original transcriber.

[2] The signature has been cut out evidently by some ignorant person, to serve as an autograph of the Reformer, and one or two words on the other side of the leaf are lost.

wha never dispyseth the petitionis of a sair trubillit hart, sall, at his gud pleasure, [free us from these][1] panis that we presentlie suffer, and in place thairof, sall croun us with glorie and immortallitie for ever. But, deir Sister, I am evin of mynd with faithfull Job, yit maist sair tormentit,[2] that my pane sall have no end in this lyfe. The power of God may, aganis the purpois of my hart, alter sic thingis as apeiris not to be alterit, as he did unto Job; but dolour and pane, with soir anguische, cryis the contrair. And this is mair plane than ever I spak, to lat yow knaw ye have ane fellow and companyoun in trubill: and thus, rest in Chryst; for the heid of the Serpent is alredie brokin doun, and he is stinging us upon the heill.

Fra Newcastell, 1553. In greit haist,
Your Brother,
JOHNE KNOX.

VI.

DEIRLIE BELOVIT SISTER in our Saviour: Efter the sycht of your letter, ressavit fra your servand upon Saturday the 19 of this instant December, I partlie was moved in my spreit, weying with my self your continewall trubill, whilk proceideth fra the infirmitie and weaknes of your saule, whilk ever thristis[3] the presence of your Fatheris mercie, whilk na mortall man can haif at all tymes. Yea, Sister, the maist perfyt is oftymes left without all sence and feilling thairof; and that, partlie becaus syn must neidis be mortifeit day by day; and na fyre sa tryis the gold, as that kynd of croce tryis oure faith, whill it burne and consume in us; not onlie the vane glorie of the warld, but also that blind lufe we beir to our selves, sa that in verie deid we hait and abhour our selves, becaus we find nether constancie

---

[1] A small portion of the MS. is cut out: see note 2, page 351. The words, however, were previously quoted by Dr M'Crie, (vol. i. p. 97.)

[2] Still grievously tormented
[3] Ever thirsts, or longs for.

nor perfectioun in this oure coruptit nature; and thairfoir ar we compellit to sob and grone for delyverance by Him wha hath promissit and sall not disceave.

This battell knaweth not the cairles of the warld, and thairfoir thai leif as brute beastis, onlie seiking sic thingis as may pleas the flesche and appetitis thairof, seldome beholding (allace, the mair pitie!) the end whairto man is creatit; not sa mekill heir to live, as it wer, for a moment, in that whilk flesche reckonis to be pleasure, as for to inherit the kingdome preparit for sic as unfeanidlie thristing thair salvatioun to stand in Chryst, by the redemptioun whilk is by his blude, doith suffer with him; as it is apoyntit be the providence of our Father, that the memberis salbe correspondant and lyke to the Heid, wha, in anguische of extreme dolour, cryit, "My God, my God! why hes thou forsakin me?" O wordis maist dolorous, and voce maist lamentabill, to be hard proceid frome the mouth of the Sone of God! Considder, deir Sister, he was na debtour to syn nor deth; and yit, this did he suffer not onlie to mak satisfactioun to the justice of God, whilk we wer never abill to do, but also to put us in comfort that his suffering was not in vane, but evin for our exempill; that in maist extremitie, yit we sall luke for delyverance whilk we must neidis ressave, gif we thrist for the same. Sister, albeit we heir not alwayis Godis Word vocallie crying unto us, to put us in memorie, that all that is in earth is transitorie, yit have we the hand of our Father, that sufferis us not to sluggische and sleip in wantonnes, vane glorie, and fleschlie pleasuris. I knaw weill, that the purpois of Sathan is to slay and distroy; but his consallis salbe confoundit, as that thai wer in purchassing leif to trubill just Job.

Upon Monunday I was with your dochtir Bowis, wha hath hir hartlie commendit unto you, and unto our sister Marjorie. Sche forgot nane of your directionis, but did declair unto me baith your greif and hir awn, whilk I find baith to proceid fra a fountane. Prais be unto God, I left hir in gud comfort, refering thankis unto God for all his benefittis. I was not, as yit I am, in gud case to have travellit; for I had lyne Thurisday at nyght, and Fryday all day, sair trubillit in the gravell. I knaw the caus and originall, but I can not remeid; but He wha willeth me to suffer, sall at his pleasure. It wilbe efter the 12 day befoir I can be at Berwik, and almaist I am determinat not to cum at all: ye knaw the caus. God be mair mercifull unto sum then thai ar equitable to me in judgement. The testimony of my awn conscience absolves me befoir His face, wha lukis not upon the persone of man.

With trubled hart and weak bodie, at Newcastell, this Tyisday, 22 of December 1553.

Your Brother,
JOHNE KNOX.

I may not answeir the places of Scripture, nor yit wryt the Expositioun of the Sixth Psalme, for everie day of this weik must I preache, if the wickit carkas will permit.

VII.

DEIRLIE BELOVIT SISTER in our Saviour and onlie Mediatour Jesus, wha is the first begottin of the deid; the sole and soverane Prince, exaltit above all poweris and potestatis whatsoever; that be him may we, now sair afflictit and punissit in absence of our brydgrome, receave immortallitie and glorie, when he sall returne to restoir the libertie to the sonis of God; of whilk noumber ar ye and I, belovit Sister, whome the enemy doith trubill, not without permissioun of our heavinlie Father, to farther mortificatioun of this wickit flesche. Be persuadit of the mercifull presence of our Lord God and Father, for he doith not truble you in signe of his wraith, absence, or not regarding of yow: Na, deir Sister, everie sone whome the Father loveth he chastineth. But not ever will He threattin;

but fra tyme to tyme giveth, and sall gif rest, as our utilitie sall requyre. Whilk thing may be unto your hart (as it is unto myne) maist comfortable rememberance, whill that ye may espy the providence of our God to be sic, as his awn word dois witnes: that is, that sumtyme He dois turne away his face apeirandlie evin frome his elect, and than ar thai in anguische and cair; but mercifulliere turnis He unto thame, and gevis gladnes and consolatioun; whilk, albeit it remane but the twinkling of ane eie, yit is it the arlis-penny[1] of his eternall presence. Rejois, Sister, and continew. My Brother[2] hath communicat his haill hart with me, and I persave the mychtie operatioun of God: And sa, lat us be establissit in his infinit gudnes, and maist sure promissis; whais omnipotent Spreit be your comfort for ever.

Fra Newcastell, 1553.

Your Brother in Jesus Chryst,
JOHNE KNOX.

VIII.

He cumis and sall not tarie, in whome is oure comfort and finall felicitie.

DEIRLIE BELOVIT SISTER in Jesus our Soverane, rejois now and be glad frome the hart, for that whilk lang the Prophetis of God hath cryit, appeireth now schortlie to cum to pas, The elect of God to suffer, as thai haif done fra the begynning. And why sall ye rejois thairintill? Becaus it is a sure seill and testimony of that word, whilk we profes to be the verie trew and infallibill Word of God, to the whilk, wha adheiris sall not be confoundit; and also, becaus our glorie cannot be perfyt whill first we taist of that cupe, whilk albeit it be unpleasing to the

---

[1] A piece of money given in earnest of a bargain or mutual engagement.

[2] Dr M'Crie considers that Knox here refers to his brother, William Knox, who is mentioned in a subsequent letter. See page 361.

flesche, yit is it maist hailsum and profitable for us. The caus of theis my wordis, is not suddane chance that newlie is happinit, but the perpetuall and constant cours of Godis trew Word fra the first declaratioun thairof to the warld. O miserable, unthankfull, and maist mischevous warld! what salbe thy condempnatioun, when He, that hes sa oft gentillie provokit ye to obey his treuth, sall cum in his glorie, to punish thy contempt? Wha sall hyd thee frome the presence of that lyoun whome thou did persecut in everie age? What sall excuse thee, that sa tiranfullie hath sched the bluid of sic as faithfullie labourit to bring thee frome blind ignorance and idolatrie, when that stubburne contempneris sall cry, " Mountanis fall on us, and hyd us fra the presence of the Lord!" Deir Sister, we salbe placeit in maist securitie with the Lamb, in whais blud we ar purgeit.

Urgent necessitie will not suffer that I satisfie[1] my mynd unto you. My Lord of Westmureland[2] hes writtin unto me this Wednesday, at sex of the clok at nyght, immediatlie thairefter to repair unto him, as I will answeir at my perrell. I culd not obteane license to remane the tyme of the sermone upon the morrow. Blissit be God, wha dois ratifie and confirme the treuth of his Word fra tyme to tyme, as our weaknes sall requyre! Your adversarie, Sister, doith labour that ye suld dout whither this be the word of God or not. Gif thair had never bene testimonyall of the undoutit treuth thairof befoir thir oure ageis, may not sic thingis as we sie daylie cum to pas, pruif the veritie thairof? Doith it not affirme, that it salbe preachit, and yit contempnit and lychtlie regairdit be many; that the trew proffessouris thairof salbe haitit with father, mother, and uthiris of the contrarie religioun; that the maist faithfull sall cruellie be persecutit? And cumeth not all theis thingis to pas in our selves? Rejois Sister, for the same word that foirspeaketh trubill doith certifie us of the glorie subsequent. As for my self, albeit the extremitie suld now aprehend me, it is not cumin

[1] Explain, or testify.
[2] Henry Nevylle, Earl of Westmoreland, Lord-Lieutenant of the Bishopric of Durham.

unlukit for. But, allace! I feir that yit I be not rype, nor abill to glorifie Chryst be my death, but what lacketh now, God sall performe in his awn tyme.

Whair God sayith, "It repenteth me that I maid Saule king," he meanis not that Saule at any tyme was a member of Chrystis bodie; but that he was a temporall officer promovit of God, and yit maist inobedient to his commandement; and thairfoir, that He wald provyd another to occupy his rowm. And yit whair He sayis, "I repent," we must understand him to speik efter the maner of men, attemperatting him self to our understanding. For uther wayis God repenteth not; for befoir, his Majestie knew the inobedience and rebellioun of the wickit king. But, Sister, God the Father can not repent, that he hath ingraftit us memberis of Chrystis bodie; for that wer to repent the honour of his awn Sone, yea, and his awn gud work in us. Abyde pacientlie, and gif na place to the temptatiounis of the adversarie. Let him schute his dartis in his dispyte. But say ye in your hart, The Lord is my defender, and thairfoir sall I not be confoundit. Dolour salbe but for a moment, but ever and ever sall we ring with Jesus our Lord; whais Halie Spreit be your comfort to the end. Be sure I will not forget yow and your company, sa lang as mortall man may remember any erthlie creature.

Frome Newcastell, 1553.

Your Brother,

JOHNE KNOX.

IX.

MAIST DEIR SISTER, whome I reverence as it becumis in all godlines: Thinking it my bundin dewtie to visit yow alwayis trubillit, I have rather takin occasioun be reassone of this messenger, wha partlie can recyte my present impedimentis, whilk all I remit to the mercifull providence of my gud God; to whais protectioun I unfeanidlie commit yow and utheris, for whome I am mair soriefull than for my self. But as for yow, Sister, I onlie lament your corporall trubill, whilk albeit it be painfull, yit it is transitorie, and schortlie sall have end, the dolour thairof recompensed abufe all that manis hart can ask or devys. For the afflictionis of this lyfe ar not worthie of that glorie that salbe schewin furth in us, whome God our Father hath appoynted to be lyke to the ymage of his onlie Sone Jesus Chryst; whome it behuffit to suffer dolour in sic sort, that he was compellit to cry in anguische of hart, "My God, my God, why has thou forsakin me." Whilk afflictioun did God our Father lay upon his bak, not onlie for a satisfactioun to his godlie justice, but also for maist singular comfort to sic as be trubillit, as of necessitie must everie member of Chrystis bodie be at a tyme or other. For seing we haif a Bischope that by experience hes learnit in him self to have compassioun upon our dolouris and infirmities, we aucht of gud reassone to quyet our selves, undoutitlie knawing that He wha hes vincuist in him self hes vincuist for us: for na dettour was He to deth nor dolour, but all he suffirit for our caus. A portioun whairof the providence of our God will that we sum tyme also taist, not onlie to mortifie in us the pleasures and affectiouns of the flesche that ringis in utheris, but also to lat us feill in our selves how horribill is syn, and what it is to abyd the hait displesure of Godis wraith for ever, that we, assured of our redemptioun in Chrystis blude, may unfeanidlie render thankis for his fatherlie mercie, wha correcteth everie sone whome he ressaveis to his favour to the end foirsaid. And sa, gif flesche wald suffer greatlie, aucht we to rejose that it hes pleasit the gudnes of oure God to prent in our hartis the seall of his mercie.

Oure impaciencie (albeit we aucht to fecht aganis it) is not dampnabill, seing we be memberis of Chrystis bodie, thairin ingraftit be faith, whilk is the frie gift of our God, and not proceiding of our workis; out of whilk we can not be cut be na assaultis of our adversarie, whome it behuffis to rage aganis us, becaus he is a spreit confirmit in malice aganis God and his elect. But lat us not feir him, seing he is confoundit and [his head broken],[1] and dois abyd onlie that day, when he salbe committit to torment for ever. Rejois, Sister, and be constant, for the Lord cumeth and sall not tarie: and this committing yow to the protectioun of Him wha can not dissave sic as incallis his name. My commendationis to thois that effeiris.

At Carleill, the 26 of July 1553.

Your Brother,
JOHNE KNOX.

IX. 2[2]

DEIRLIE BELOVIT SISTER in Jesus oure Savioure: The adversarie can not uthirwayis do but declair him self contrair to God, and noysum to the memberis of Chrystis bodie. Your dolour, pacientlie abiddin, is unto God ane acceptabill sacrifice, for it doith mortifie unto yow that whilk ringeth in the maist part of the warld, as I haif written unto yow befoir. That ye ar of that folische sort of men that sayith in thair hart, "Thair is no God." I wonder that the Devill aschamis not to allege that contrair yow; but he is a lier, and father of the same. For gif in your hart ye said thair is no God, why then suld ye suffer angusche and cair be reassone that the enemy trubillis yow with that thought? Wha can be effrayit day and nyght for that whilk is not? In that ye lament the absence of your Fatheris amiabill presence and face, ye beir witnes thair is a God; in that ye absteane fra iniquitie at the commandement of our God, ye testifie also thair is a God. Belovit Sister, sic as denyis God in thair hart, as thai can not be sorie for na kynd of syn; sa thai fulfilling thair appetitis, regard na thing Godis

---

[1] In MS. M. "his prokin."
[2] This letter is omitted to be numbered in MS. M.

preceptis. I may not wryt sa large as I wald, corporall trubill and labour impeidis me. My brother, Williame Knox,[1] is presentlie with me. What ye wald haif frome Scotland, let me knaw this Monunday at nyght, for he must depart on Tyisday. Uthir matteris, as I may, I sall answer. Rest ye in Chryst and feir not. 1553.

Your Brother unfeanid,

JOHNE KNOX.

X.

DEIRLIE BELOVIT SISTER in our Lord Jesus, the trubillis susteanit be yow, as thai ar to the mortificatioun of the wickit flesche, sa ar thai dolorous unto me; not that I feir any deidlie dampnatioun to follow thairupon, but that I lament your corporall unquyetnes, and maist that ye ar effrayit whair thair is na caus. What wounder that the Devill provok yow to ydolatrie, seing he durst do the same to the naturall Sone of God. I am sure that your hart nether thristis nor desyris to invocat or mak prayer unto breid,[2] nor unto any uthir creature, but to the leving God onlie; and in that ye abhour idolatrie, sa lang it is na syn unto yow, albeit a thousand tymes upon a day thair with ye wer assaltit. Allace, Sister! your imbecilitie trubillis me, that I suld knaw you sa weak that ye suld be moveit for sa small a matter. But your weaknes is not rackinit, but by Jesus our Lord it is excuissit. For "he breakis not doun the bruisit reid," nor yit quenchis furth the smoking flax, whilk wordis to us ar maist comfortable. How weak that ever we be, he will not cast us away, but will feid and mak us strong. And thairfoir Paule gloreis in his infirmitie, affirmyng, that when he is

---

[1] In September 1552, the Council granted a patent to William Knox, merchant, giving him liberty for a limited time, to trade to any port of England, in a vessel of a hundred tons burden.—(Strype's *Memorials*, vol. ii. p. 295. M'Crie's *Life of Knox*, vol. i. p. 90.)

[2] The Romish host.

weak, than is he in greatest suretie. The smal and imperfyt knawledge that now we haif sall everie day incres, whill we be delyverit fra this mortall carkas, and sall sie and behold the glorie and wisdome of our God for ever. It is not necessarie to put me in rememberance to call for your delyverance. In Godis presence I wryt, as oftin as I find the Spreit to call for my self, that sa oft forget I not yow; whilk cumeth not of me, but of the Halie Spreit that sa teacheth me. And albeit I wald ceas, your self wald ceas, and all uthir creature, yit your dolour continewallie cryeth and returnis not void fra the presence of our God. And thairfoir, Sister, abyd pacientlie that finall and sure delyverance; remember that the halie Sone of God cryit thrys with teiris; and in place of sweit, blude flowit fra his bodie throuch vehemencie of his paine. And yit must he neidis drink of the cupe preparit of his Father. Gif sa sufferit the naturall Sone in whome thair was never syn nor deceat, what becumis it us to do? Stand in Godis promisses, and the end salbe joyfull. Great labouris, and partlie trubill of mynd, will suffer me to wryt na mair. The Spreit of the Lord Jesus assist you to the end. 1553.

Your Brother,

JOHNE KNOX.

XI.

DEIRLIE BELOVIT SISTER, efter hartlie commendatioun: As I can call to mynd, thair restis na thing in your wryttings whairunto I haif not ansuerit, except Godis repentance that he maid Saule king. For understanding whairof, ye sall considder, that the Spreit of God man[1] attemper and submit him self oftymes to our weaknes, and speik unto us, wha by corruption ar maid ignorant and rude, sa that we may understand what he worketh by his incomprehensibill wisdom and inscrutabill providence.

[1] "Man," must.

Whill that yit thair is na sic thing in our God, as the vocall wordis, and first sence appeireth unto us. As when David sayeth, "Rebuke me not, O Lord, in thy hait displeasure;" and in the buke of Exodus, "The Lord was angrie with Moses." And sindrie other places of Scripture dois attribute unto God not onlie sic memberis as be in man, but also sic affectionis and mutabill passionis whilk, nevertheles, ar not in God, wha alwayis in him self remanis stabill, constant, holie, and just. And of that sort is that maner of speaking, "It repenteth me that I haif maid Saule king," that is, My justice is compellit to erect and thrawe doun the rebellious king from that estait and dignitie whairunto I have placeit him; and sa sall I appeir to repent my former work. The Scripture attributis to God sic conditionis, qualiteis, and affectionis, as his Majestie appeireth to schaw in his workis upon his creatures. As when he plagues the warld, than sayis the Scripture, "God did it in his anger." When he delyveris sic as lang have sufferit trubill, then sayis the Scripture, "God streichit out his hand." "God liftit up his eis, his face, or countenance," and yit na sic thing can be in the Godheid. And thairfoir, Sister, think not that God is changeabill and doith repent, albeit sa appeir; and that sa speikis the Scripture for to instruct oure infirmitie. For befoir he apoyntit Saule to be king, his Majestie knew his inobedience, and how he was to be abjectit;[1] nether pleasit Saule him in Jesus his Sone, but always was reprobat, and never did imbrace the promeis of remissioun and reconciliatioun in the seid promissit, albeit the Lord did promote him to warldlie dignitie; whilk is na sure signe of Godis everlasting love and favour, seing thairunto is placeit as weill the ungodlie as godlie.

Then wald ye inquyre, How sall we be assured of Godis favour that changeth not? By his awn word, whilk assuris us, that sic as knawing and lamenting thair awn corruptioun and greit infirmiteis, and yit imbraces the satisfactioun whilk is be the redemptioun in Chrystis blude, ar surelie ingraftit in Chrystis

[1] Cast away.

bodie, and thairfoir, sall never be separatit nor rent fra him; as witnesseth Him self saying, "Furth of my handis can nane reif."[1]

Luke farther of this matter in the othir letter, written unto yow[2] at sic tyme as many thocht I never suld wryt efter to man. Haynous wer the delationis laid aganis me, and many ar the leis that ar maid to the Consall.[3] But God ane day sall distroy all leying toungis, and sall delyver his servandis frome calamitie. I luke but ane day or uthir to fall in thair handis; for mair and mair rageth the memberis of the Devill aganis me. This assault of Sathan hes bene to his confusioun, and to the glorie of God. And thairfoir, Sister, ceas not to prais God and to call for my comfort; for greit is the multitude of enemyis, whome everie ane the Lord sall confound.

I intend not to depart fra Newcastell befoir Easter: my daylie labouris must now incres, and thairfoir spair me sa mekkill as ye may. My ald maladie trubillis me sair, and na thing is mair contrarious to my helth than wrytting. Think not that I werie to visit yow; but unles my paine sall ceas, I will altogether becum unprofitable. Work, O Lord, evin as pleaseth thy infinit gudnes; and relax the trubillis at thy awn pleasure, of sic as seiketh thy glorie to schyne. Amen! I bid yow hartlie fairwell in Christ, our Soverane.

At Newcastell, the 23 of Marche 1553.

Your Brother,

JOHNE KNOX.

XII.

The Lord sall put end to all trubillis.

DEIRLIE BELOVIT SISTER in our Saviour Jesus Chryst: The manifald and continewall assaltis of the Devill rageing aganis yow, and trubilling your rest, whill ye thrist, and maist ernest-

---

[1] Pluck away.
[2] See *supra*, page 357.
[3] When summoned to London, chiefly at the instigation of the potent Duke of Northumberland; but he was honourably acquitted.

lie desyre to remane in Chryst, doith certifie unto me your verie electioun, whilk the Devill invyis in all the chosin of God. And albeit his artis be subtill, and tormenting painfullie, yit thairof followith greit commoditie; a haittret of your self, wha may not, nor can not, resist as ye wald his temptationis, and a continew[all] desyre of Goddis support; whilk tua ar maist acceptabill sacrifices in Goddis syght. Whair the adversarie wald persuad, that it makith na thing what ye think, becaus it sall not be impute, thair he is compellit to beir witnes to the treuth. But not of a trew intent. Trewlie nether thocht nor deid salbe imput unto yow, for thai ar remittit in Chrystis blude; but thairfoir do ye not rejois in thochtis and workis repugnyng to Goddis expres commandement; but dois lament and murne that any sic motioun suld remane in yow; and desyris to be maid frie fra that corruptioun by your campioun, Chryst: and sa ye salbe as he hes promissit. Other thingis, as tyme will permit, I will maist gladlie fulfill. I laude and prais my God, asking fra my hart, that sic as hes professit his Sone Jesus, contemp not his admonitionis to the end. Amen.

Fra Carleill, this Fryday, efter sermone, 1553.

    Your Brother in Chryst Jesus,

           JOHNE KNOX.

XIII.

Chryst hes appeirit to dissolve the workis of the Devill.

DEIRLIE BELOVIT SISTER in Jesus oure Lord: Perceaving be your letter the subtill assaultis of the Devill, I must neidis lament your greit trubill, not that I feir any danger eternall, but that I pitie the anguische of your hart, willing to rejois in Jesus and in the redemptioun that is be his blude. And not the less be art and disceat of that serpent Sathan is impeadit sa to do, whilk nether is imput for syn presentlie, nor yit sall appeir efter to your confusioun; for it is not ye that wickidlie judgeis of the Sone of God, but your enemy that wold persuad you sa to do.

Whome learne to resist in the face, not standing with him in questioun and debait, but suddanlie repelling all his disceat as unworthie to be ansuerit unto, seing it is contrarie the principallis of your faith. He wald persuad yow that Godis Word is of na effect, but that it is a vaine taill inventit be man, and sa all that is spokin of Jesus the Sone of God is but a vaine fabill. Do ye not persave that the Devill, in that his persuasioun, is the self same spreit that Jesus affirmes him to be—a man-slayer and a manifest lier? Why do ye not here lauche him to skorne, and mock him in your hart, seing he dois deny the thing whilk your eis may sie, and your earis heir, your sensis understand, and all the poweris of your saule grant and confes? He sayis the Scriptures of God ar but a taill, and na credit is to be gevin to thame. Allace, Sister! that ye suld not espy his manifald deceit.

The Word of God sayis, "That in the begynning God creatit the heavin and the erth of nathing;" making and produceing all creatures, whome his Majestie gydis and reullis to this day. And albeit that the Devill did persuad sum philosopheris to affirme that the warld never had begynning, yit the vereteis following in the same Word of God sall compell him, evin the Devill him self, to grant and acknawledge God allane to be Creatour, and the warld not to haif the begynning of it self. The voce of God said to the woman efter hir offence, " In dolour sall yow beir thy children." I pray yow, Sister, is it not a manifest and impudent lie to affirme and say that this word is vaine? Doith not your awn hart witnes that the Word of God is trew, and takis effect in everie woman befoir sche be mother? And the same voce that denunceth the pane upon the woman, pronunceth also, The seid of the woman, whilk is Jesus oure Lord, suld break doun the serpentis heid, and dissolve the workis of the Devill, whilk ar syn and deth. The voce of God affirmeth, that corporall deth entured into the warld be syn, for be ane man entirit in syn, and be the means of syn came in deth, sa that deth passeth throcht all men, becaus all men synnit.

Belovit Sister, dois not your awn hart justifie Godis Word to be trew? Feill ye not syn working into yow to your greit displesur? And knaw ye not be experience of all that ar passit befoir yow, that statute it is to all men to die? And the same voce that affirmeth syn to be the caus of deth, doith also affirme Jesus to be the autour and caus of lyfe. Seing thairfoir that ye ar compellit to grant the ane, (for wha can deny that deth devours not this mortall carkas,) why dout ye the other to be trew? But ye dout not. It is your enemy that sa wald persuad yow: contemp him in the face, and his assaltis sall not hurt yow: Stik ye onlie[1] to the treuth of Godis Word: Onlie, I say beleif and ye salbe saif. And albeit ye find not sic perfectioun as ye desyre, yit cry with the man that was sair trubillit, "Lord, I beleif, help my unbeleif." That ye are lyke to Francis Spera,[2] the Devill leyis. Allace! may ye not easelie persave ye wer never a preacher; yea, never did deny any part of Chrystis doctrine befoir the warld; yea, never did blaspheme Chryst in your hart: for gif sa ye had done, ye never suld efter have soucht for remedie; and ye seik to me the minister of Chryst, whilk is in deid to seik Chryst him self. The nature of the dampnit and reprobat is ever to flie fra Chryst.

Thair hes na temptatioun yit apprehendit yow whilk dois not commoniie assalt the elect of God. The Devill is sa subtill that he can caus his temptationis appeir to be the cogitationis of our awn hartis. But sa thai ar not, ye hait thame, lamentis and murnis for thame, whilk is the testimony of your faith; whilk albeit God suffer to be tryit as throcht the fyre, yit sall he not suffer it to be quenchit; for whome he hes geven to his Sone Jesus ar ressavit in sure custodie, and salbe lyke to his glorifeit bodie. Be not effrayit albeit the tempter trubill yow; remember how bald he was with oure Captane and Heid. Did he not call him frome Jerusalem to the Montane, and boisting him self

---

[1] Adhere only.

[2] Francis Spira, a lawyer of Padua, whose case is well known: He died under great remorse of conscience, in consequence of having, by terror of the Inquisition, abjured the Protestant faith.

to be the Lord of the Warld, did promeis the glorie thairof to Chryst gif he wald fall doun and wirschip him? whilk tentatioun was greatter and mair bold than any that he hes usit aganis yow. Say to him when he assaltis yow, Avoid, Sathan; the Lord confound thee. And albeit that ye find not sic sueitnes as ye wald, yit be ye sure that the sob of your hart persis the heavin, and doith not returne without the petitioun grantit of God, as that your utilitie dois requyre. Remember, Sister, that the tempter departit fra Chryst onlie for a tyme, and thairfoir be not discorageit, albeit he returne to yow with new and dissaitfull assaltis. Do ye not espy ye ar not within his girne;[1] for gif ye wer, to what purpois suld he trubill you? He is a roaring lyon seiking whome he may devour; whome he hes devourit alredie, he seikis na mair. Befoir[2] he trubillit yow, that thair is not a Saviour, and now he affirmis that ye salbe lyke to Francis Spera, wha denyit Chrystis doctrine; doith not the ane of theis tentationis mak the uthir a lie, sa that ye may espy thame baith to be leis? He sayis, That ye ar not yneucht sorie for your offences. Ansuer unto him, That your sufficiencie standis not within your self, nor yit in your repentance, but in the sufficiencie of Jesus Chryst. And ye haif caus to prais God that suffereth yow not to rejois in syn, nether yit to trust in your awn justice;[3] but ye desyre onlie to be found clothed with Chrystis justice, as ye ar by faith in his blude.

Think not, Sister, that I esteme it any trubill to comfort yow; be sa bold upon me, in godlines, as ye wald be upon any flesche, and na uthir labouris save onlie the blawing of my Maisteris trumpet[4] sall impeid me to do the uttermaist of my power. I will dailie pray that your dolour may be releiveit, and doutis not to obtene the same, to the glorie of oure God, and youre comfort everlasting. Fra Newcastell, 1553.

      Your Brother,
          JOHNE KNOX.

[1] Snare.
[2] Formerly.
[3] Righteousness.
[4] The preaching of the Gospel.

XIV.

RYCHT DEIRLIE BELOVIT SISTER in oure Soverane Jesus Chryst: Verie dolour and anguische of hart will not suffer me at this instant to ansuer youre letter: but to call for yow I will not ceas, and doutis not to obtene of Godis frie mercie youre continewance in Chryst. Faithfull is He that hes commandit us to pray ane for another, promising that oure petitionis ar acceptabill, yea, and that we sall give lyfe to sic as synneth not unto deth. To syn to deth is, to blaspheme the word of lyfe whilk anis we haif professit, and to fall back (not of fragilitie, but of hatred and contempt,) to sic ydolatrie and abominatioun as the wickit mantenis; whairof I am maist surelie persuadit in the Lord Jesus, that youre hart sall never do. Ye are ingraftit in the bodie, and be Him ye salbe defendit, but not without dolour; for it behuffis everie member of his bodie to suffer with the Heid. That fals and leying spreit dois according to his wickit and dissavabill craft, when he wald caus yow beleif that I know your rejectioun. Na, fals Devill! he leis: I am evin equallie certified of your electioun in Chryst, as that I am that I myself preacheth Chryst to be the onlie Saviour, etc. I have ma signis of your electioun than presentlie I can commit to wryt.

At Newcastell, in haist, 1553.

Your Brother,
JOHNE KNOX.

XV.

Frome the eyis of his Sanctis sal the Lord wype away all teiris and murnyng.

DEIR MOTHER AND SPOUS, unfeanidlie belovit in the bowells of oure Saviour Chryst Jesus, with my verie hartlie commendationis: I perusit baith your letteris, not only directit to me, but also it that sorrowfullie compleanis upon the unthankfulnes of your brother as also of myne, that ye suld not have bene equallie maid privie to my coming in the countrie with utheris, whairof the enemy wald persuad yow (ane argument maist fals and untrew) that we judge you not to be of our noumber.

Deir Mother, be not sa suddanlie moveit, he is your enemy that sa wald persuad you. God I tak to recorde in my conscience, that nane is this day within the Realme of Ingland, with whome I wald mair glaidlie speik (onlie sche whome God hath offirit unto me, and commandit me to lufe as my awn flesche exceptit,) than with you. For your caussis principallie interprysit I this journey; for hearing my servand to be stayit, and his letteris to be takin, I culd na wys be pacifeit, (for the maist part of my letteris was for your instructioun and comfort,) till[1] farther knawledge of your estait; and that ye wer na soner advertisit, only want of a faithfull messinger was the caus: for my cuming to the countrey was sa sone noysit abroad, that with greit difficultie culd I be convoyit fra a place to another. I knew na sic danger as was suspectit be my brethrene. For as for my letteris, in thame is nathing conteanid except exhortatioun to constancie in that treuth whilk God hes opinlie laid befoir our eyis, whilk I am not myndit to deny whenever sic questioun sal be demandit of me. But the cause moveing me that for a tyme I wald have bene close, was, that I purposit (gif sa had bene possible) to have spokin with my Wyfe, whilk now I persave is na thing apeirand,[2] whill God offer sum better occasioun. My brethren, partlie be admonitioun, and partlie be teiris, compellis me to obey sumwhat contrair to my awn mynd; for never can I die in a mair honest quarrell, nor to suffer as a witnes of that treuth whairof God hes maid me a messinger, whilk with hart I beleive maist assuredlie; the Halie Gaist beiring witnes to my conscience, and with mouth, I trust to God, to confes, in presence of the warld, the onlie doctrine of lyfe. Notwithstanding

[1] Until I had.   [2] Is not apparent, (not like to be,) until.

this my mind, gif God sall prepair the way, I will obey the voices of my brethrene, and will gif place to the furie and rage of Sathan for a tyme. And sa can I not espy how that either of yow baith I can speik at this tyme. But gif God pleis preserve me at this tyme, whairof I am not yit resolved, then sal thair lak in me na gud will that ye may knaw the place of my residence, and farthir of my mynd.

But now, deir Mother, haif we cause to rejois, for oure heavinlie Father, wha callit us be grace to wryt in our hartis the signis and seallis of our electioun in Chryst Jesus his Sone, begynnis now to correct our crukedness, and to mak us lyke, in suffering afflictionis, schame, and rebuke of the warld, to the greit Bischope of our saullis; wha by mekill tribulatioun did entir in his glorie, as of necessitie man everie ane to whome that kingdome is apoyntit. And thairfor, Mother, be na thing abasched of theis maist dolorous dayis, whilk schortlie sal have end to oure everlasting comfort: Thay ar not cropin upon us without knawledge and foirsycht. How oft have ye heard theis dayis foirspokin? thairfoir now grudge not, but pacientlie abyd the Lordis delyverance. He that foirspak the trubill, promissis everlasting pleasure by the same word: albeit the flesche complene, dispair na thing, for it must follow the awn nature; and it is not dampnabill in the syght of oure Father, albeit the corrupt fraill flesche draw back and refuse the croce; for that is as naturall to the flesche as in hunger and thirst to covet reasonable sustenance. Onlie follow not the affectionis of the flesche to commit iniquytie; nether for feir of deth, nor for love of lyf, commit ye idolatrie; nether yit gif your presence whair the same is committit, but hait it, avoid it, and flee frome it. But your letter makis mention that ye haif pleasure and delyt in it: na, Mother, I espy the contrarie, for ye compleane and lament that sic motionis ar within you; this is na sign that ye delyt in thame, for na man compleanis of that whairin he delytis. Ye ar in na wors case, tuiching that poynt, nor yet tuiching any uthir whairof ye desyre to be red, than was the Apostill, when with gronyng and anguische of hart he did cry, "O unhappie man that I am, wha sal delyver me fra this bodie of syn." Reid the haill chapter, and gif glorie to God that lattis you knaw your awn infirmitie, that frome Chryst allone ye may be content to resave that whilk never remanit in corruptibill flesche, that is, the justice whilk is acceptabill befoir God, the justice by faith and not by workis, that ye may glorie in Him wha frelie givis that whilk we deserve not. And thus, nether feir that nor uthir assaltis of the Divill, sa lang as in bodie ye obey not his persuasionis.

Schortnes of tyme, and multitude of cairis, will not lat me wryt at this present sa plentifullie as I wald. Ye will me to charge you in suche thingis as I mister, God grant that ye may be abill to releif the neidie. Ye may be sure that I wald be bold upon you, for of your gude hart I am persuadit, but of your power and abilitie I greitlie dout. I will not mak you privie how ryche I am, but off[1] Loundoun I departit with less money then ten grottis; but God hes since provydit, and will provyd, I dout not, heirefter aboundantlie for this lyfe. Either the Quenis Majestie, or sum Thesaurer will be XL. poundis rycher by me, for sa mekill lack I of dewtie of my patentis.[2] But that litill trubillis me. Rest in Chryst Jesus.

1553.   Your Sone,

JOHNE KNOX.

XVI.

Behald a littill and He sall cum, that sall tak away the captivitie of Israel.

DEIRLIE BELOVIT MOTHER in oure Soverane Jesus Chryst: The remembrance of that croce that daylie ye suffer is unto me

---

[1] "Off," out of, from. The allusion in this letter clearly refers it to the month of January 1553-4, when Knox was constrained to leave England.

[2] The amount due of his stipend, as one of the King's Chaplains, when he fled from England, and went to Dieppe.

a scharpe spur priking me, (when ells I wald be sleuchfull,) to call upon my God for comfort of his Holie Spreit; not onlie to my self, but unto sic as taistis of that cupe that is maist proper to[1] the sonis of God, whairof in theis partis thair be na small noumber, whome with I being partlie practisit,[2] do the better learne the art of the adversarie, wha by ane of tua meanis trubillis us the memberis of Chrystis bodie.

First, he gais about for a tyme to extenuat syn, and makes us to think nathing of it, affirmying, evin as he did to the first woman, that the transgressioun of Godis commandementis be na sic matter as we esteame thame, and sa laboureth to bring us in contempt of God. And often it is that Godis elect offendis maist haynouslie in this, (for na synfull flesche hes to glorie in the self); frome the whilk when thay are callit back be Goddis frie mercie unto repentance, then dois oure enemyie rage as a roreing lyoun, labouring to bring the weak and infirme to disperatioun; whilk boith God permittis to exercise his elect, leist thay suld rejois in this warldlie vanitie.

Beware of an assalt of that wickit spreit, (he is a liar and the father of lies,) for maist commounlie he goith about to undermynd oure faith, labouring to persuade us that we haif not the thing whilk God hath witnessit that we haif—I meane a lyvelie faith; and this is na new practise of his, but is the same that he usit aganis oure heid Jesus Chryst, when, after Chrystis baptysme, (whairin the Fatheris voce was heard, crying, "This is my weil-belovit Sone, in whome I am weill pleasit,") the Tempter durst beir Chryst in hand[3] that he was not the Sone of God, because he was in wildernes hungrie without comfort, and sa furth, as I suppose ye understand the temptatioun. Deir Mother, he that is sorie for absence of vertew is not altogider destitut of the same, for the hungrie saule can not the infinit gudnes of God send emptie away. Oure hunger cryis unto God, albeit we understand not the same.

[1] Most suited for.
[2] Frequently in conversation.
[3] Express his doubt.

Theis thingis, becaus I have writtin unto you befoir at large I now but tuiche, whilk I wald not have spokin at all, war not I feir that ye suld think me to have forget yow. Mother, be ye na thing abaschit, for God sall put end to all oure dolouris. The trubillis of this lyfe, in bodie or in spreit, declairis us to be memberis of Him wha hes passit befoir us in glorie by afflictionis of all sortis. The flesche can do nathing under the croce, but grudge and lament, and na wounder albeit it sa do, for the corruption thairof compellis it in luffing the self to murmure aganis God. But mercifull is He that will not requyre of us his weak creatures (having a will, but lacking power,) abufe that whilk flesche can give; and that is na thing at all, as witnesseth the Apostill Paule, saying, "I know that in me, that is in my flesche, remanis na gude." Yf any gude appeir, it nather is of us, nor fra us, but it is the free gift of Him wha willeth weill to his awn afflictit creaturis. The cheif sign of Goddis favur is, that we knaw and understand oure selves unfeanidlie to be na thing without his support, and that we dispair of all things within oure selves, for then must we thrist the help of oure God. And na mair can God deny his mercie and grace to sic as askith, than he can ceas to be God. And thairfoir, deir Mother, abyd patientlie the Lordis delyverance, for he sall cum when leist expectatioun is; whais Halie Spreit rest in yow for ever.

1553. Youris to his power,

JOHNE KNOX.

XVII.

DEIRLIE BELOVIT MOTHER,[1] with my verie hartlie commendatioun: Efter the wrytting of my uthir letters, whilk hes lyne besyd me of a lang tyme for want of a beirer, I ressavit your letters as I returnit fra Kent, whair I was labouring befoir the

[1] In the margin of the MS. "To his Mother and to his Spous."

resait thairof. I was assured of your trubill, and of the battell of my awn flesche, befoir God; and I suspect a greatter to ly upon yow baith than that your letters declairis to me. As for your spirituall cross, deir Mother, it behuffit Chryst to suffer and sa to enter into his glorie, and of necessitie everie member of his bodie, in his awn degree and tyme, man suffer with the Heid. But dampnation is thair nane to sic as anis hes bene ingraftit within that bodie, as that I am (sa fer as creature can be) maist surelie persuadit ye ar, as all signs and takinis maist evidentlie schawis, as I have written unto yow in dyvers letteris.

It pleassis me verie weill that the enemy assaltis yow with dyvers and new assaltis, for that is the maist sure prufe that by his ald trickis he hes not prevalit. Remember, Mother, that sa lang as he that persewes a castell or strong hold, is continewallie schutting his artailyerie or ordinance, that thair is within it sum strenth, that he wald have overcum and bet doun; otherwys fulischnes and vane it wer to spend the force of his ordinance whair na resistance wer maid. And thairfoir, deir Mother, ye remember weill, and I am rejosit of your remembrance, whair ye wryt that onlie the regenerat man fyghtis the battell. It is evin sa indeid: sa spirituall can we not be in this lyfe, but ever the flesche will mak repugnance. But sa carnell may we be, that the power of the Spreit is altogether quenchit, and thais personis, as Paule speakis of thame, after they haif ceissit to murne, giveis thame selves all halelie to filthines, to performe the same in all gredines. It is not sa with yow, Mother: Ye lament and murne that ye can not haif sic perfectioun as God and his Word requyreth. Ye fight with the weak strenth that is left, whilk albeit apeiring weak in your syght, yit befoir God it is maist valient. A sob to resist sic assaltis is maist acceptabill in presence of Him wha requyris nathing mair than that we knaw and confes oure imperfectionis, whilk is the maist triumphand victorie that we can schaw, fighting under that danger. Dispair not, Sister, ye haif brether heir, evin sic as ar judgeit to be maist perfyt.

My greit labouris, whairin I desyre youre dailie prayers, will not suffer me to satisfie my mynd tuiching all the proces betwene your Husband and yow, tuiching my matter concernyng his Dochter. I prais God hartlie, baith for your baldnes and constancie. But I beseik you, Mother, trubill not your self too muche thairwith. It becumis me now to jeopard my lyfe for the comfort and delyverance of my awn flesche, as that I will do be Godis grace; baith feir and freindschip of all erthlie creature laid asyd. I have writtin to your Husband, the contentis whairof I trust oure brother Harie will declair to yow and to my Wyfe. Yf I eschape seiknes and imprisonment, be sure to sie me soone. Yit, Mother, depend not upon me too muche, for what am I but a wreachit synner? Gif ye resave any comfort, it cumis frome above, fra God the Father, wha sall provyd for yow aboundantlie. What ever becum of me, remember, Mother, the giftis of God ar not bound to any one man, but ar commoun to everie man (in his measure) that incallis the Lord Jesus; whais Omnipotent Spreit rest with yow for ever.

The 20 of September 1553.

Your Son,

JOHNE KNOX.

XVIII.

The Lord sall put end to all dolouris at his gud pleasur.

RYCHT DEIR BELOVIT MOTHER, efter maist hartlie commendatioun: I have ressavit youre letter fra youre sone, Mr George, the piteous complayntis whairof dois perce and trubill my hart, having na comfort but that the treuth of God assureis me, that frome the handis of Jesus Chryst may nane reif: for seing that he is sent of God his Father, a triumphand victour to conques the kingdome, it suld redound to his dishonour gif any suld tak the spoilze fra him. Ye haif committit your self to his protectioun, and hes forsakin all saviouris but him allane. The knawledge of youre synis dois trubill and displeas yow. Ye knaw that his blude is a sufficient satisfactioun for all beleiveris thairinto; and albeit the Adversarie wald persuad yow that ye beleif not, trust not his disceavabill leis. Ye believe, and is also sorie, that mair constantlie ye can not beleive, and thairfoir pray, "O Lord, incres my faith." Our faith is not worthie of and for the self of remissioun of synis, and of the lyfe everlasting. But Jesus Chryst is all sufficiencie to us, whais Justice and Halines we imbrace and resave by faith; whilk never can be perfyt in us, but that his mercie will accept it, how faynt and febill that ever it be, for his awn infinit gudnes and promeis sake. And thairfoir, abyd patientlie the Lordis delyverance to the end, remembering that oure Heid is entirit into his kingdome be trubillis and dolouris without noumber; yea, it may be said, that everie hour was anguische and pane, incressing in oure Saviour Jesus fra the hour that his Majestie ressavit oure mortall nature, untill the randering up the Spreit in the handis of his Father; efter that, maist lamentablie he had complenit in theis wordis, "My God, my God, why hes thou forsakin me;" whilk wordis, deiplie considderit be us, sall releive a greit part of oure spirituall croce. For gif sic wes the onlie Sone intreatit, and gif it becumis the memberis to be lyke to the Heid, why suld we dispair under sic tribulationis? He did not onlie suffer povertie, hungir, blasphemy, and deth, but also he did taist the cupe of Godis wraith aganis syn, not onlie to mak full satisfactioun for his chosin pepill, but also that he myght learne to be pitifull to sic as ar temptit. And thairfoir dispair not, for youre trubillis be the infallible signis of youre electioun in Chrystis blude, being ingraftit in his bodie. As for the assaltis of youre enemy, sumtyme allureing yow to idolatrie, sumtyme to uthir manifest iniquitie, sa that ye obey him not altogether, thair is na danger; but rather, the feilling of his continewall assaltis is the sign that he hath not gottin victorie over yow, but that thair is in yow a spounk[1] of faith, whilk youre heavinlie Fathir sall never suffer to be quenchit nor put out, but will keip and incres the same for his promeis sake.

Deir Mother, sa may and will I call yow, not onlie for the tender affectioun I beir unto yow in Chryst, but also, for the motherlie kyndnes ye haif schawn unto me at all tymes since oure first acquaintance, albeit sic things as I have desyrit, (gif sic had pleasit God,) and ye and utheris have lang desyrit,[2] ar never lyke to cum to pas; yit sall ye be sure, that my lufe and cair toward yow sall never abait, sa lang as I can cair for any erthlie creature. Ye sall understand, that this 6 of November, I spak with Sir Robert Bowis[3] in the matter ye knaw, according to youre requeist; whois disdanefull, yea dispytfull, wordis hath sa persit my hart, that my lyfe is bitter unto me. I beir a gud countenance with a sair trublit hart, whill that he that oucht to considder matters with a deip judgement, is becumin not onlie a dispyser, but also a taunter of Godis messingeris, (God be merfull unto him!). Amangis utheris his maist unpleasing words, whill that I was about to have declarit my hart in the haill matter, he said, " Away with youre rethoricall reassonis! for I will not be persuadit with thame." God knawis, I did use no rethorick nor collourit speach; but wald haif spokin the treuth, and that in maist simpill maner. I am not a gud oratour in my awn caus; but what he wald not be content to heir of me, God sall declair to him a[4] day till his displeasure, unles he repent. It is supponit, that all the matter cumis by yow and me. I pray God that youre conscience wer quyet and at peace; and I regaird not what countrey consume this my wickit carkas; and war not that na manis unthankfulnes sall move me (God supporting my infirmitie) to ceas to do profit unto Chrystis congregatioun, that dayis suld be few that Ingland suld gif me breid. And I feir, that when all is done, I salbe drivin to that

---

[1] Spark.
[2] Meaning evidently his marriage with her daughter, Marjory Bowes.
[3] An elder brother of Mrs Elizabeth Bowes's husband.
[4] "A," one.

end; for I can not abyd the disdanfull hattred of thais of whome not onlie I thocht that I might have craveit kyndnes, but also, to whome God hath bene be me mair liberall than thay be thankfull. But so must men declair thame selves. Afflictionis dois truble me at this present; but yit I dout not to overcum, be Him wha will not leif comfortles his afflictit to the end; whais Omnipotent Spreit rest with yow. Amen.

Be youris unfeanid in Chryst,

JOHNE KNOX.

XVIII. 2.[1]

Grace and mercy.

DEIRLIE BELOVIT MOTHER, with my verie hartlie commendatioun: This last of Februar by-past I ressavit fra yow and fra my deirest Spouse letteris, whilk, when I read, partly did trubill me, knawing your continewall anguische. But, Mother, thair is na danger of everlasting death: Ye lack not faith, as divers tymes I have written unto yow; but now is weak and infirme in faith, whilk God permittis into yow of verie love, for greatter caussis than our carnell judgement can understand. But ane thing I will baldlie speik, not flattering yow, that your infirmitie has bene unto me occasioun to serche and try the Scripture mair neir than ever I culd do for my awn caus, and yit I have susteanit trubill baith in saule and bodie. Fear not, Mother, that the cair of yow passis fra my hart. Na! He to whome nothing is secreit, knawith that I never present my self be Jesus Chryst befoir the throne of my Fatheris mercie, but thair also I commend yow; and seldome it is that utheriswys ye pass fra my remembrance. The verie instant hour that youre letteris was presentit unto me, was I talking of yow, be reassone that thrie honest pure wemen wer cum to me, and was compleanying thair greit infirmitie, and wes schawing unto me the

[1] This letter is omitted to be numbered in MS. M.

greit assaltis of the enemy, and I was opinnyng the cause and commodities thereof, whereby all oure eis wypit at anis,[1] and I was praying unto God that ye and some utheris had bene thair with me for the space of twa hours, and evin at that instant came youre letteris to my handis; whairof ane part I red unto thame, and ane of thame said, "O, wald to God I mycht speik with that persone, for I persave that thair be ma tempted than I." I wryt na lie unto yow, but the verie treuth of oure communicatioun what tyme I ressavit youre letteris.

Rejois, Mother, and abyd pacientlie the day of oure finall delyverance, when all bitterness salbe removeit, and we possessit in the fruitioun whairfoir now we grone and thrist. Cum, Lord! and tarie not.

At Londoun, the 1 of Marche 1553.

Youre Sone,

JOHNE KNOX.

XIX.

The Lord leideth to hell, and lifteth up againe of his meir mercie.

RYHCT DEIRLIE BELOVIT MOTHER, with my hartlie commendatioun: I ressavit your letteris fra youre sone, Mr George, and sum frome Roger Widderringtoun, making mentioun of youre sair assaltis and spirituall trubillis, sa behuffit it the flesche to be dejectit, that without hypocrisie ye may cry, "Haif mercie upon me, O Lord, on whome thair is na gudnes; but as I am sold under sin, sa find I nathing but sin and iniquitie in this my maist wickit flesche." This confessioun, deir Mother, I think ye may gif unfeanidlie, and gif sa ye do, maist happie ar your trubillis, whairby ye haif leirnit to gif God his awn glorie; that is, that fra his gudnes by Jesus Chryst ye ressave grace and

[1] All our eyes weeped at one time.

mercie everie day and moment, offering na thing in recumpens agane to him but youre greit unworthines, whilk be his awn hand ye desyre to be diminissit. I knaw youre cupe to be maist bitter, but profitable and hailsome it is that sa the flesche be nurtirit to mortificatioun thairof, whilk unles God him self suld lay upon youre back ye culd not be content to beir it, for we can do nathing but love oure selves; and the mair that we sa do, the less comfortabill to us ar Godis promissis. Dispair not, Mother, your synnis (albeit ye had committit thousands ma) ar remissabill. What! think ye that Godis gudnes, mercie, and grace, is abill to be overcum with youre iniquitie? Will God, wha can not dissave, be a lier, and lose his awn glorie, becaus that ye ar a synner? Did he not proclame his awne name in the earis of Moses, saying, "I the Lord, mercifull, benyng, forgiving syn, transgressioun, and iniquitie?" Hes He not sworne be him self, that he delyteth not in the deth of a synner, but rather that he convert and live? Is not dolour for syn the work of God? Sall he begin to work, and sall he not bring his purposis to pas? Mother, rather sall hevin and erth perische, then the synner that lamentis for offence committit, and askis mercie for Chrystis sake, sall not be heard in maist oportunitie. I suppose ye had committit idolatrie: Is that any greatter than was Petir's denyall of Chryst? But, Mother, I espy that ye be forgetfull of the admonitionis gevin unto yow. In dyvers wryttings I have declarit, that ye must mak a divisioun betwene the suggestionis, assaltis, and temptationis of the Devill, and youre act and work. Everie cogitatioun that trubillis yow is not youre awn work; gif thay wer youre awn work, why compleane ye of thame, why dispyt ye thame and youre self baith. Remember that Paule sayis, I work it not, but syn that remanis in me; and yit he did the thing that he wald not have done, and sic things as he wald have done, that culd he not do; yit did he not ressave the sentence of dampnatioun, becaus Chryst is deid for syn, and for synneris that maliciouslie abydis not in contempt of God.

Becaus, God willing, I think to be with yow schortlie, be reasone of other labouris, now I may wryt na mair: rejois and abyd the delyverance of the Lord, wha never did confound thay that callit for his grace be Jesus oure Savioure; whais Omnipotent Spreit rest with you to the end.

London, 1553.

Yours to his power,

JOHNE KNOX.

XX.

DEIRLIE BELOVIT MOTHER, with my verie hartlie commendatioun: Your letter, ressavit on Fryday at nyght, at the first reading did trubill me not a litill, for this ye wryt: "Allace! wreachit woman that I am, my bodie is far wrang, for the self same synnis that ringit in Sodome and Gomore, whairfoir thay perissit, ringis in me, and I have small power or nane to resist." Theis wordis, at the first syght, did greatlie trubill me; but proceading in youre letter, and finding the thingis whairof ye compleane to be assaltis whairin ye delyt not, but for removeing of the same dois pray, and willis me with yow instantlie to pray, I began to tak corage, assureing my self it was but youre infirmitie, and not iniquitie confirmit in the hart, nor yit compleit in act.

Deir Mother, my dewtie compellis me to adverteis yow, that in comparing your synnis with the synnis of Sodome and Gomorhe ye do not weill, but thairintill ye offend, becaus ye imput unto Godis Halie Spreit a spot wha onlie hes preservit yow fra sic horribill iniquitie; yit ye, as ane unthankfull ressaver, dois not acknawledge the same, but rather accusis youre self of sic abominabill crymes, as God forbid that ever ye suld commit. Mother, lyke as the man offendis that excussis his offence, sa he that confessit cryme whair nane is committit, is injurious to the power and operatioun of God, for he randeris not unto God dew thankis for that whilk he hes ressavit. But, Mother, the cause of this youre unthankfulnes I tak to be ignorance in yow, that ye knaw not what wer the synnis of Sodome and Gomore, whilk ye may learne of Ezekiell the Prophet to have been pryd, whairwith I think ye be not greatlie trubillit; fulnes of meat, that is ryotus and exces in thair aboundance, and idilnes to provoke filthie lustis in thame; unmercifulnes to the pure, because thame selves did suffer na trubill; and of thir precedentis did insew schamles foirheidis to commit, and that with violence and injurie pretendit aganis strangeris, all abominatioun and unnaturall filthines, as the historie dois manifestlie schaw. In whilk of theis, Mother, ar ye giltie? of nane of all, in my conscience I affirme; and gif I understud uthir wayis, I wald not flatter yow. Do yow think that everie sturring and motioun of the flesche, or yit everie ardent and burnyng lust, is the syn of Sodome? God forbid that sa ye sall think. Dois not Paule teache unto yow, that the flesche lusteth aganist the spreit, evin in thame of maist perfectioun? Doth he not cry and bewaill him self in theis wordis: "O wrechit and unhappie man that I am, wha sall delyver me fra this bodie of deth;" and yit the same Apostill, immediatlie thairefter, as it wer rejoising aganis syn and deth, affirmis, " that thair is na condempnatioun unto sic as be in Chryst Jesus." Mark weill, the Apostill sayis not, Thair is na syn in thame that ar in Chryst Jesus, but thair is na condempnatioun unto thame, &c., as he wald say, Of necessitie it is, that syn remane in this corrupt flesche during this lyfe naturall, for sic is the corruptioun thairof, that frome a poysonit fontane must spute furth bitter watter, and frome a corrupt rute or stock must neids spring and proceid wickit frutis, whilk ar rebellioun in the flesche, lustis, concupiscence, vane wordis and cogitationis, distrust of Godis promissis, grudgeing under the croce, and sic uthiris, to the last sob of breth remaning in the maist mortifeit. Theis of thair nature, I grant, ar worthie of dampnatioun, but by faith in Chrystis blude ar they purgeit and cleane abolissit, sa that thay nether may dampn nor hurt us, (except that the knawledge of thame moveth us to lament and bewaill oure miserie, and that to us is maist profitabill, leist that be securitie and rest we suld contemp and lychtlie regard the graces and free giftis of God). And thairfoir, deir Mother, for the tender mercies of God, quyet youre hart in his infallibill promissis, for all worketh to youre singular profit. The justice of Jesus Chryst must quenche and extinguishe youre syn; the lyfe of Chryst must swallow up your deth; the power of Chryst must overcum youre weaknes and infirmitie; the victorie of Chryst must appeir in that ye ar not abill to resist by youre self aganis the fyrie and dangerous dartis of the Devill, enemye to all Godis elect. Allace! Mother, wald ye not that Chrystis glorie suld appeir? Gif in yow war nether found syn, deth, weaknes, nor imperfectioun, what neid had ye of Chrystis benefittis? Remember, Mother, that Jesus the Sone of God come not in the flesche to call the just, (not that any sic can be found, but thair is that sa esteamis thame selves,) but he come to call synneris, not to abyd and rejose in thair auld iniquitie, but to repentance; that is, to ane unfeaned dolour for the offences committit, and to a daylie sorrowing, yea, and haittred for that whilk resteth, with a hoip of mercie and forgivenes of God by the redemptioun that is in Chrystis blude.

Considder, Mother, repentance conteanis within the self a dolour for syn, a haittred of the same, and yit hoip of mercie. How can ye lament and bewaill for that ye knaw not? How can ye hait that whilk doith not trubill yow? or, How sall ye cry for mercy whair na offence is confessit? Allace! suld I have yow a scholler now in theis thingis whairin ye haif bene sa lang exercisit, and whairof ye haif heard my judgement sa oftentymes baith by word and wryt. This wryt I not to confound yow, but to certifie yow that I will flatter na part of your infirmitie. Albeit it can not move me; but I man tak a cair of yow, and will instruct yow to the uttermaist of my power; but it is a croce to me to remember how easilie the adversair, wha is the accuser of oure brethren, woundis yow. Resist him, Mother, and he sall flee fra yow; resist him, I say, in faith, and obey not the lustis of the flesche, and he salbe confoundit and his dartis quenchit. "Thair is na condempnatioun to thame that ar in Chryst Jesus, that walk not efter the flesche;" thay walk efter the flesche that, without feir or reverence to God, obeyis the wickit appetitis thairof, and studeis be all meanis to fulfill the same, as God forbid that ye do.

Ye inquyre, How can ye avoyd the sentences pronuncit aganis huirmongers, adulterers, and sic uthiris? I ansuer, That gif ye be sic ane as obstinatlie continewis in sic iniquitie, and purposeth not to avoid and absteane fra the same, than assuredlie sic sentences ar spokin aganis yow sa lang as that ye delyt in that malignitie; but gif ye confess youre syn, desyreing delyverance thairfra, God is potent to remit the same. I regard not what sumtymes ye haif bene, ("for sumtymes we wer darknes, but now lyght in the Lord,") but what unfeandlie ye desyre to be, that ye ar in Godis presence; for "blissit ar thay" pronuncit to be, be Jesus Chryst, "that hungeris and thristis for ryghteousnes;" to whome is also maid a promeis that thay salbe replenissit. Ye cannot hunger and thrist for thingis that ye haif aboundantlie, but for thay thingis that ye lack and neid. Abyd, Mother, the tyme of harvest, befoir whilk must neidis goe the cald of winter, the temperat and unstabill spring, and the fervent heit of summer: to be plane, ye must neidis saw with teiris or ye reap with gladnes; syn must in yow ga befoir justice, deth befoir lyfe, weaknes befoir strenth, unstabillnes befoir stabilitie, and bitternes befoir comfort. But in all theis sall sic as pacientlie will abyde the Lordis delyverance, wha will cum when leist is oure expectatioun, vincus and triumphe to his everlasting prais. Amen.

This Saturday, at Newcastell, when my vocatioun calleth me to other labour; but God sall frelie give what lacketh in me.

Youre Sone,

JOHNE KNOX.

XXI.

Blissit be thois that murne for ryghteousnes sake, &c.

BELOVIT MOTHER, with my hartlie commendatioun in the Lord · Let not your present dulnes discorage yow above measure: the wisdome of our God knawis what is maist expedient for our fraill nature. Gif the bodie suld always be in travell, it suld faynt and be unabill to continew in labour; the spreit hes his travell, whilk is a sobbing and murnyng for syn, fra whilk unles it sumtymes suld rest, it suddanlie suld be consumit. It doith na mair offend Godis Majestie that the spreit sumtyme lye as it were asleip, nether having sence of greit dolour nor greit comfort, mair than it doith offend him that the bodie use the naturall rest, ceassing fra all externall exercise. Ye sall consider, Mother, that the eyis of God dois perse mair deiplie than we be war of. We, according to the blind ignorance whilk lurketh within us, do judge but as we do feill for the present; but He, according to his eternall wisdome, dois judge thingis lang befoir thai cum to pas. We judge that caldnes and anguische of spreit ar hurtfull, becaus we sie not the end whairfoir God dois suffer us to be trubillit with sic temptationis; but his Majestie, wha onlie knawis the mass whairof man is maid, and causeth all thingis to work to the profit of his elect, knawis also how necessarie sic trubillis ar to dantoun the pryd of oure corrupt nature. Thair is a spirituall pryd whilk is not haistelie suppressit in Godis verie elect children, as witnessis Sanct Paule. God hath wrocht greit thingis be yow in the syght of uthir men, with whilk (unless the mell of inward anguische did beat them doun) ye myght be steirit up to sum vane glorie, whilk is a vennoume mair subtill than ony man do espy. I can wryt to yow be my awn experience. I have sumtymes bene in that securitie that I felt not dolour for syn, nether yit displeasure aganis myself for any iniquitie in whilk I did offend; but rather my vane hart did thus flatter myself, (I wryt the treuth to my awn confusioun, and to the glorie of my heavenlie Father throuch Jesus Christ,) "Thow hes sufferit great trubill for professing of Chrystis treuth, God hes done great thingis for thee, delyvering thee fra that maist cruell bondage.[1] He has placeit thee in a maist honorabill vocatioun, and thy labours ar not without frute; thairfoir thow aucht rejois and gif prais unto God." O Mother! this was a subtill serpent wha thus culd pour in vennoume, I not perceaving it; but blissit be my God wha permittit me not to sleip lang in that estait. I drank, schortlie efter this flattrie of myself, a cupe of contra poysone, the bitternes whairof doith yit sa remane in my breist, that whatever I have sufferit, or presentlie dois, I reput as dung, yea, and my self worthie of dampnatioun for my ingratitude towardis my God. The lyke, Mother, mycht have cumin to yow, gif the secreit brydill of afflictioun did not refrane vane cogitationis; but of this I have writtin to yow mair planelie in my other letteris. And thus I commit yow to the protectioun of the Omnipotent for ever.

Youris at his power,
JOHNNE KNOX.

XXII.

Greit ar the trubillis of the ryghteous, but the Lord delyvereth thame out of thame all, &c.

DEARLIE BELOVIT SISTER, whome I no less tendir than it becumis a weak member to do another, sa fer as the frailtie of this corrupt nature will permit: When I revolve the sair and continewall trubill ye suffer, sumtymes also I remember the charge thryse at a tyme[2] gevin to Petir be Chryst him self, saying, "Feid my

---

[1] On the margin of the MS. "galleis," referring to his protracted captivity on board of the French galleys after the surrender of the Castle of St Andrews, in July 1547.

[2] At one time, together.

lambis; feid my scheip; feid my scheip." Whairby the wisdome of God wold signifie unto us twa thingis maist worthie to be notit, and ever to be borne in mynd, not onlie of the scheip, but also of the pastour. First, that to the flock of Chryst sa necessarie is the lyvelie Word of God, that without the same na whyle can thay continew in the trew knawledge of God. For as by it (that is, by Godis Word) the saule begynnis to ressave life, sa be the same Word ressavis it strenth and perpetuall consolatioun, be the Spreit of oure Lord Jesus remanyng in oure hartis by trew faith, whairof Godis Word is mother, nurse, and mantener; for that meanis Chryst, when he commandis his lambis and scheip to be fed and gydit. Lambis we ar when we can not for infirmitie and weaknes degest any part of Godis Word, but as it is brokin unto us by oure pastouris; as wer the pepill of the Jewis efter Chrystis deth, resurrectioun, and ascensioun, hearing thame selves justlie condempnit, for that thay cruellie, and without cryme committit aganis thame, sched the blude of the innocent Sone of God: hearing thair dampnatioun, I say, thay cryit, "Brethren, what sall we do?" Whilk wordis declair thame to be lambis weak, yea deid, and yit desyrous to be fed. And lyke unto theis ar all this day, that, heiring the greit abominationis whairin lang thay have bene blindit, unfeanidlie thristis to knaw the treuth and obey the same.

And for sic, na dout, God dois provyde ane Petir or uther; that is, sic as unfeanidlie beleiving Jesus to be the Sone of the liveing God, ferventlie thristis the same knawledge to be dispersit abrode in the earis of many scheip. We ar to be fed efter sum knawledge, and efter oppin professioun of Chryst, for yit many thingis comfortable to oure hartis, and profitabill for oure eruditioun, remanis hid for us; as wer the self-same pepill efter baptisme continewallie abyding together in the doctrine of the Apostillis, whilk thing declarit evidentlie that everie day thay desyreit to be fed with Godis Word. And scheip we ar, to be gydit, (for sa do I understand the third kynd of feiding) by Godis Word, all the dayis of this oure transitorie and troubilsum lyfe. For lyke as scheip hes na judgement to descerne betwix the hailsum and noysum gers,[1] (but be the regement[2] of thai pastour,) sa hath not the flock of Chryst wisdome to avoid sectis and heresis, (yea, abominatioun and idolatrie,) but by Godis Word, whilk aucht purelie and sinceirlie to sound fra the pastouris mouth. The scheip hes discretioun be Godis frie gift to discerne betwene the voice of the pastour and the voice of the stranger, and to follow the pastour and flie fra the cruell murtherer and theif. But gif the pastour sleip, and altogether keip his toung close, than surelie sall the verie scheip ga astray, not that thay can perische for ever, (for that is impossible, seing that Chryst Jesus, the onlie soverane scheiphird, hes takin thame in his protectioun;) but that thay may be scatterit in the day of darknes and mist, as oftymis hath the elect bene; and yit ar gatherit agane be the voice of that pastour, wha not onlie feidis, but also maist tendirlie loveis his scheip committit to his protectioun be God his Father, by him to ressave lyfe, and that aboundantlie; and thairfoir provydis he sum Peteris to be send in everie age, to call agane the scheip to the onlie pastour of thair saullis, Jesus Chryst, whais voice the scheip heir and thristis for. Of whilk flock and number I am maist undoutedlie persuadit that ye ar ane, albeit weak and sair trubillit. Sister, remember that the power, myght, and vertew of Jesus oure Savioure is maid knawn in oure weaknes. He dispyssis not the lame and krukit scheip; na, he tackis the same upon his back and bearis it to the flock becaus it may not ga;[3] that sa the unspeakable mercie and kyndnes of the Scheiphird may be knawn and praisit of us his scheip. War we alwayis strang, than suld we not taist how sweit and mercifull the releif of oure God is fra theis daylie cairis; and sa suld we grow proude, negligent, and unmyndfull, whilk estait is maist dangerous of all uthiris.

But now almaist I had forget my self, for breiflie intendit

---

[1] To discern between wholesome and noisome grass.
[2] Rule or government.
[3] Cannot go.

I to have spokin onlie of the tua observationis whilk I thocht worthie to be notit upon the commandement of Jesus Chryst to Petir; whairof the former was, that Chrystis flock neideth, in youthheid, in strenth, and in age, to be fed and reulit be Godis Word. Whairto this will I add, that the maist evident tokin by the whilk the scheip of Chryst is discernit and knawn fra the goatis and swyne of the world, is, that the scheip thristis ever for the voice of the awn pastour, and loves unfeanidlie sic as bringeth it unto thair earis. The goatis and porkis baith hait the Word of God and the messingeris thairof. And in this thing I think, Sister, ye have greit caus to rejois, for had ye not bene ane of Chryistis scheip, na dearer had I bene unto yow than to utheris that daylie thristis my blude and distructioun. The secund note I merk on Chrystis wordis to Petir, [is] whairin apeireth the cair and diligence of a trew pastour unto Chrystis flock; for Chryst wald say, "Petir, thou confessis that thou beiris ane unfeanid love unto me, that sall thou declair in feiding of my lambes, in nurissing of my scheip, and in gyding of the same." A thing ryghtlie expoundit and weyit of Petir, commanding the same to all pastouris in the wordis, "Feid sa muche as in yow is, the flock of Jesus Chryst." O, allace! how small is the number of pastouris that obeyis this commandement; but this matter will I not deplore, except that I (not speiking of utheris) will accuse my self, that doith not, I confess, the uttermaist of my power in feiding the lambis and scheip of Chryst. I satisfie, peradventure, many men in the small labouris that I tak; but trewlie I satisfie not my awn conscience. I mycht be mair diligent in going fra place to place,[1] although I suld beg, and preache Chryst: I suld be mair cairfull to comfort the afflictit, and yow amangst many. I have done sumwhat, but not according to my dewtie. The sclander and feir of men hes impeadit me to exerceis my pen sa oft as I

---

[1] Knox before this time, or during the latter part of King Edward's reign, (and also for some months subsequently,) was engaged in preaching in different parts of England.

wold; yea, verie schame hath callit and haldin me fra youre company, when I was maist surelie persuadit that God had apoyntit me at that tyme to comfort and feid youre hungrie and afflictit saule. And this, Sister, whill I revolve with my self, I think I am criminall and giltie; for mair aucht I to regard the afflictioun ye susteane than any sclander of suche as ethir knaweth not, or will not knaw, the necessitie of thame that labour under the croce maist heavie and unpleasing. God of his infinit mercie remove not onlie fra me all feir that tendeth not to godlines, but also fra uthiris suspicioun to judge of me uthirwayis than it becumeth a member to judge of another. As for my self, I do confess, my ryght eare, my ryght thombe, and ryght toe, must be sprinkillit with the blude of the Lamb, whairwith Aarone and his sonnis war consecrat and apoyntit to that Preistheid; that is, my best work must be purgeit with Chrystis blude; and of ane thing I rejois, that I find in to my self a compassioun of youre trubill. Mervelous ar the workis of oure God!

It may be that a caus of youre trubill is a tryell of us, that profess oure selves pastouris; yea, and of uthiris that ar callit ernist professoris, to examyne and try out what cair and solicitude we will tak of the weak and infirme scheip. Gif we be, as we ar named, trew pastouris and Christiane professoris, thair can na member of Chrystis bodie suffer within the reache of oure knawledge, but thairupon we must neidis be compacient; for that is the nature of lyvelie memberis, ane to suffer with another, studeing alwayis to support what it may. Ye ar in a part the caus presentlie that I am in theis quarteris; for knawing youre sair anguischis, and the rare noumber of thame that can rychtlie lay the medicine to the wound, my conscience prickit with verie pitie, compellit me to remane, contrarie my determinat purpois. Now, Mother, rest in Chryst, and be in comfort for now and ever.

Youre Sone,
JOHNE KNOX.

XXIII.

Oure last enemy, Death, salbe devourit, and than we sall meit to oure eternall comfort.

ALBEIT I do thrist, deirlie belovit Mother, no less to sie yow than sumtymes I have thristit to sie that whilk of erthlie creaturis is maist deir unto me, yit do the daylie trubill discorage me in a part that oure temporall meitting sall not be sa suddane as we baith requyre; and yit my esperance and hoip is in God, that we sall meit, evin in this lyfe, to baith oure comfortis; and thairfoir I hartlie requyre yow, in the bowells of Chryst Jesus, to be of gud comfort, and pacientlie to beir this distance of oure bodies. I trust oure spreits call to ane God, throuch oure Lord Jesus Chryst, in whais presence we ar alwayis present notwithstanding the distance of places. And thairfoir rejois, I say, deir Mother, albeit for a tyme ye be destitute of that comfort whilk God sumtymes did minister unto yow be my mouth. His providence allane knaweth what is maist expedient and maist profitabill for us. The Discipillis culd never be persuadit the corporall departing of thair Maister suld be to thame schortlie efter matter of joy and occasioun of baldnes; and yit the same thai felt trew in experience. God hes gevin unto yow many probationis of his fatherlie love and cair whilk he beiris toward yow; for what love was that whilk God did schaw unto yow when he callit yow fra the doungoun of darknes and frome the bondage of idolatrie, efter that sa lang ye had bene plongeit in the same, to the bryghtnes of his mercie, and to the libertie of his chosin children to serve him in spreit and veritie. How mercifullie did God luke upon yow, when he gave yow baldnes rather to forsaik freindis, contrey, possessioun, children, and husband, then to forsaik God, Chryst Jesus his Sone, and his religioun, knawin and professit. Was it not ane assureit sign of Godis favour towardis yow, that in the tyme of blasphemous idolatrie he brought yow in the bosome of his Kirk, and thair fed yow with the sweit promeissis of his mercie; and now in the end, hath he brocht yow hame agane to youre native contrey, in whilk I trust ye salbe compellit to do nathing aganis youre conscience, whilk aucht and must be reulit be Godis Word onlie. Theis ye aucht, deir Mother, to esteme signis and tokinis of Godis great love towards yow, whilk dois not change as doith the love of mortall men, as oftin ye have hard declared and affirmed. Your unthankfulnes and impacience doith perchance trubill yow, but turne youre eyis fra youre self and fra youre awn worthines; and when ye ar stingit with these fyrie and venemous serpentis, direct youre eyis to Jesus Chryst crucifeit, wha onlie is oure redemptioun, sanctificatioun, and justice. Thay that be haill neid na phisitioun; and sic as wer not stingit had na pleasure upon the brasin serpent; but the seik and woundit finding na remedie els whair, can not dispyse the salvatioun prepareit, whilk onlie consistis in Chryst Jesus. And thairfoir let not the remorse of youre conscience trubill yow above measure, but knaw weill that ye ar brocht to a sensibill feilling in youre imperfectionis, to the end that ye may glorie in Chryst Jesus allane. The pryd of this corrupt flesche is sic, that sa lang as we feill not oure selves utterlie destitute of all gudnes, we can not but defraud God of his glorie, usurping to oure selves that whilk is not ouris. And thairfoir dois God beat doun this dampnabill pryd in his chosin children be the verie knawledge of thair awn synis, to the whilk thay cum not at thair first entres with God, but do atteane unto it be dyvers experiences of thair awn unthankfull and corrupt nature. David at his first familiaritie with God wald never haif thocht that he suld haif committit adulterie and murther; nether yit wald Petir have confessit that in him did lurk the abnegatioun and denyall of his Maister. But experience did teache the ane and the uthir, that in manis nature, evin efter regeneration, thair is na stabilitie but sa lang as God assistis with his Halie Spreit.

Blissit ar thay that, utterlie refussing thame selves, do haillie depend upon Chryst Jesus allane; whais Omnipotent Spreit rest with yow now and ever. Amen.

1554. Your Sone,

JOHNE KNOX.

XXIV.[1]

DEIRLIE BELOVIT SISTER,[2] in the commoun faith of Jesus our Saviour: The place of Johne, forbidding us to salut sic as bringeth not the hailsome doctrine, admonisseth us what danger cumeth be fals teacheris, evin the destructioun of bodie and soule. Whairfor the Spreit of God willeth us to be sa cairfull to avoyd the company of all that teachis doctrine contrarie to the treuth of Chryst, that we communicat with them in nathing that may appeir to manteane or defend thame in thair corrupt opinioun. For he that biddis thame Godspeid, communicatis with thair syn; that is, he that apeiris, be keiping thame company, or assisting unto thame in thair proceidings, to favour thair doctrine, is giltie befoir God of thair iniquitie, baith becaus he doith confirme thame in thair error be his silence, and also confirmes utheris to credit thair doctrine, becaus he opponis not himself thairto. And sa to bid thame Godspeid is not to speik unto thame commounlie, as we, for civill honestie, to men unknawin, but it is, efter we have hard of thair fals doctrine, to be conversant with thame, and sa intreat thame as thai had not offendit in thair doctrine. The place of James teachis us, belovit Sister, that in Jesus Chryst all that unfeanidlie profes him are equall befoir him, and that ryches nor warldlie honouris ar nothing regairdit in his syght; and thairfoir wald the Spreit of God, speiking in the Apostill, that sic as ar trew Christianis suld have mair

---

[1] The old numbering of the letters, in MS. M., stops with No. 23. The next letter is that to his Afflicted Brethren, already printed at page 231.

[2] In the margin of the MS., "To Marjorie Bowis, wha was his first wyfe."

respect to the spirituall giftis whairwith God had dotith his messingeris, nor to externall ryches, whilk oftymes the wickit possessis, the having whairof makis man nether nobill nor godlie, albeit sa judge the blind affectionis of men. The Apostill dampneth sic as preferis a man with a goldin chayne to the pure; but heirof will I speik no more. The Spreit of God sall instruct your hart what is maist comfortable to the trubillit conscience of your Mother, and pray ernistlie that sa may be. Whair the adversarie objectis, Sche aucht not think wickit thoughts; answer thairto, That is trew, but seing this oure nature is corruptit with syn, whilk entirrit be his suggestioun, it must think and wirk wickitlie be his assaltis; but he sal beir the condigne punisment thairof, becaus be him syn first entirit, and also be him it doith continew whillis this karkais be resolved. And whair he inquyris, What Chryst is; answer, He is the seid of the woman promissit be God to break down the serpentis heid, whilk he hath done alreadie, in him self appeiring in this oure flesche, subject to all passionis that may fall in this oure nature, onlie syn exceptit; and efter the death suffirit, he hath, be power of his Godheid, rissen againe triumphant victour over deth, hell, and syn, not to him self, for thairto was he na dettour, but for sic as thristis salvatioun be him onlie, whom he may na mair lose, nor he may ceas to be the Sone of God and the saviour of the warld. And whair he wald perswade that sche is contrarie the word thairinto, he leis according to his nature, whairin thair is na treuth; for gif sche wer contrarie the word, or denyit it, to what effect sa ernistlie suld she desyre the company of sic as teacheth and professeth it? Thair is na doubt but he, as he is the accusatour of all Godis elect, studieth to trubill hir conscience, that according to hir desyre sche may not rest in Jesus oure Lord. Be vigilant in prayer.

I think this be the first Letter that ever I wrait to you.
In great haist, your Brother,
JOHNE KNOX.

XXV.[1]

The Spreit of God the Father, be Jesus Christ, comfort and assist you to the end. Amen.

TOUCHING the sonis of Jacob, who cruellie, contrar to thair solempned promeis and othe, did murther and slay the citizens of Sichem; whasa ryghtlie marketh the Scriptures of God sall easelie espy thame maist grevouslie to have offendit. For albeit the transgressioun of the young man was haynous befoir God, yit wer thai na civill majestratis, and thairfoir had no autoritie to punish. And farther, thai committit treasone, and, in sa fer as in thame was, blasphemit God and his halie name, making it odious to the nationis round about, seing thai, under the pretence of religioun, and of ressaving them in league with God and with the pepill, did disceatfullie as also cruellie distroy, the haill citie suspecting na danger. Albeit some laboureth to excus thair syn be the zeall thai had, that thai myght not suffer thair sister to be abusit lyke ane harlot, yit the Spreit of God, speiking in their awn father, efter lang advysement, in the extreamitie of his deth, utterlie dampneth thair wickit act, saying, " Semioun and Levi, brethren, &c., Lat not my saule entir in their consall, nor yit my glorie into thair company; for in thair furie thai killit a man, and for thair lust distroyit the citie. Cursit is thair heit or rage, for it is vehement; and thair indignatioun, for it is intractable. I sall dispers thame in Jacob, and scatter them abrod in Israel." Heir may ye espy, Sister, that God dampneth thair het displeasure and cruell act, as maist wickit and worthie of punishment. But perchance it may be inquyrit, Why did God suffer the men that had professit his name, be ressaving the sign of circumcisioun, sa unmercifullie to be intreatit? I myght answer, God sufferis

---

[1] There is no name affixed in MS. M. to this, or the next letter, but they were evidently addressed to his mother-in-law, Mrs Bowes.

his awn, in all ageis, be the ungodlie to be cruellie tormentit. But sic was not the case of thir men, whom, na doubt, the justice of God found cryminall, and worthie the deth. For thai did abuse his sacramentall signe, receaving it nether at Godis commandement, nor having any respect to his honour, nor to the advancement of his name, nor yit trusting in his promissis, nor desyreing the incres or multiplicatioun of Godis pepill; but onlie for a warldlie purpois, thinking thairby to have attaynit ryches and ease, be joyning thamselves to Godis pepill. And sa the justice of God faund thaim worthie of punisment and sa permittit thaime, justlie on his part, to be afflictit and distroyit be the ungodlie; whilk is a terribill exempill to sic as, in caus of religioun, mair seikis the profit of the warld nor eternall salvatioun. But heirof na mair.

Thus brieflie and rudlie have I writtin unto yow, becaus I remember myself anis to have maid yow a promeis sa to do, and everie word of the mouth of the faithfull (yf sa impeid not God) aught to be keipit. And now rest in Chryst. After this I think ye sall resave na mair of my handis. In haist, with sair trubillit hart, youris as ever in godlines,

JOHNE KNOX.

XXVI.

BELOVIT SISTER, efter my hartlie commendatioun: Tuiching the Angell of God send to warsill with Jacob, the matter salbe maid easie to understand gif ye sall merk in what estait standeth Jacob, departit fra Laban. He was to enter into his native landis, but not without great danger of his lyfe, seing befoir him was Esau, wha befoir had conspyrit his deth. And albeit Jacob had a promeis of God to be keipit, and also a commandement to entir into the land, and not to feir; yit when he cumis to the verie poynt whair danger apeireth, was sair affrayit, feiring the tiranny of his brother Esau; as be giftis and rewardis, be directioun of his messingeris, be devyding of his companyis to avoyd the uttermaist of his brotheris hatred, evidentlie may be espyit. This weaknes and imbecilitie resting in all men, (yit not imputit for syn in Godis elect,) the mercifull providence of oure God supportis as that his wisdome thinketh and judgeth to be expedient. And albeit he useth not a[1] medicine to everie pacient, yit to everie ane of his chosin pepill giveth he at a tyme or other sum sure and undoutit significationis, that he knaweth thair infirmitie, takith cair for the same, and that he will not suffer them to perische for ever; albeit the warld and the Divill rage maist violentlie to oppres and confound us that be maist feable and fraill. And heirof have we ane image maist lyvelie payntit furth, in the wersilling[2] of Jacob with the Angell. Jacob feirit that his brother Esau suld vincus and overcum him, God wald witnes the contrarie, by that he maid him abill to resist and prevaile during the haill nyght against ane angell, a spirituall creature, wha allone, be Godis power, is of greatter puissance and myght then all erthlie creatures.

And this wald God speak to the hart of Jacob, "O, Jacob, why feiris thou man, whilk is but flesche, bonis, and blude, seing I have maid thee[3] abill to ganestand a spirituall creature? This nyght that thou hes indurit in wersilling, signifeith unto thee, and unto Godis elect efter thee, all tyme of transitorie trubill, whairunto I have supported thee, not onlie to confirme thee in my promisseis, but also for comfort of sic as sall heirefter suffer adversitie, that my verie Angell hath not prevalit against thee. And thairfor will I now change thy name frome Jacob, whilk signifeith a supplanter, deceaver, or ane that is weak, whilk name was gevin to thee, by that thou in thy nativitie aprehendit the heill of thi brother; and did also, be consalie of thy mother Rebecca, receave fra thi father the benedictioun, without his knawlegde, whilk he provydit for thy bro-

---

[1] "A." one or the same.
[2] Wrestling.
[3] "Thee" and "thy," frequently written in MS. M. "the" and "thi."

ther Esau, whilk albeit apeirit to proceid fra the consall of the woman, meanyng deceit. Yit becaus I was autour thairof, and moveit hir hart and mynd thairto, now will I change that name, and thow salbe callit Israell, whilk signifeis strong be God; for be me thou hes ever bene defendit, and sall also be to the end of this transitorie battell; and sa art thou victour not onlie of men, but also of Godis, that is of angellis, spirituall creatures."

Be this paraphrase upon the last part of the text, ye may espy what is ment be the warselling of Jacob with the Angell all nyght, and what be the changeing of Jacobis name. The Angell touchit the marie or principall synow of Jacobis thigh, whairby he become crukit, and did halt, to witness unto him, that it was not be his awn power that sa lang he had resistit. The thigh, ye knaw, is the principall part that susteanis man to stand; and thairfoir being maymit or crukit in that part, he is unabill to wersell: And yit (a matter greatlie to be wonderit,) Jacob wald not suffer the Angell to depart whill he gave unto him the benedictioun, (a response befoir writtin,) and this was done at the spring of the morning. Heirby is signifeit, that oure victorie proceideth not frome oure awne strenth, but from the gudnes of Him, wha, by his Spreit, poureth into us understanding, will, sufficiencie, and strenth; for without Him can we do na thing. And leist we suld glorie, as that some power resteth with us, (for ever wald the flesche rest in the self,) it is necessaire that our thighis be touchit and we maid crukit; that is, that all hoip and comfort of the flesche be tackin fra us, that we may learne to depend upon the promissis of our maist faithfull God.

Let us not despair, albeit all the strenth, not onlie within us, but also apeiring in uthiris, vanische and forsake us. Remember, Sister, that God never brocht any excellent work to pas whill first mannis judgement was dispairit thairof; and this his Majestie doith to notifie his power to the sonis of men. Abell cryit not vengeance upon Cayen the murtherer, whill first his blude was cruellie sched. Joseph obteanit not dominioun and power, whill first he sufferit great trubill and imprisonment, and in opinioun of his father was deid. Moses was not ressavit in protectioun of Pharois dauchter whill first he was exponit to the danger of the flude. And finallie, Jesus Chryst, oure champioun and heid, did not obteane victorie above all his enemyis, sa that efter thay might not trubill nor molest him any more, whill first he sufferit the vyle deth of the cross.

And sa, Sister, albeit we be dejectit evin to the ground, yit with Jacob lat us hald fast the Angell; that is, the promissis of oure God; and na dout benedictioun sall follow in the spring of the mornyng; that is, efter the cludie stormes of theis dolorous nyghts whairinto we fight, (not onlie aganis flesche and blud,) and yit that wer a battell too strong for oure puissance, but also aganis spirituall wickitnes in heavinlie thingis; that is, sumtyme aganis despair, whilk wald call all Godis promissis in dout, and sumtyme aganis confidence in oure self, whairwith almaist everie living man is infectit, albeit, allace! everie man doith not espy it. It is a syn, dangerous and odious in Godis syght; and happie ar thois that sa be intreatit in the mercie of God, that they find na cause to rejois in thame selves. After lang debait, Paule came to this knawledge, that when he found greatest weaknes in him self, than did he glorie that the vertew and power of Jesus Chryst myght abyd in him. Wha ernistlie can cair for meit, that feilleth not the pane of hunger? Wha unfeanedlie thristis for drink, that sustenis not the dolour of drought? And wha with fervent hart can desyre to be rid and delyverit fra the cairis and doloris of this wickit flesche, that taistis not the bitternes and anguischis thairof. And sa, Sister, ar trubillis verie profitable for Godis chosin pepill, as weill to humill the proudnes borne with us, as to ingender in us a thrist and desyre of the lyfe everlasting.

Jacob thocht he had sene God face to face when he saw

the Angell, and be him atteanit to sa great knawledge; for he understude be commonyng with him, what everie poynt of his conflict ment, and whairfoir he was maid impotent of his thigh. And heirunto was not Jacob altogether disceavit; for albeit he saw not the pure and verie substance of God as he is in his awn essence, whilk, as God affirmeth to Moses, na man can sie and live; that is, na living man (in this mortall lyfe) is abill to sie, perse, and behald the nakit substance of God, as his Majestie is, in his awn bewtie and glorie, for that sicht is reservit to the lyfe everlasting, whair and when we sall sie as we ar sene; and thairinto sall stand oure great comfort and felicitie: Albeit, I say, Jacob saw not God sa, yit saw he the gudnes of his God, the power of his God, and the mercifull providence of his God, tacking cair for him, to delyver him frome pursuit of his enemyis whome sa greatlie he feirit, and instructing him in sic caisis as aperteanit to his present comfort. And sa he saw God face to face; that is, he had a trew and undoutit knawledge of Godis will and present favour towards him; for that is to sie God. As Jesus Chryst answereth unto Philip desyreing to sie the Father, "He that seith me," sayis Chryst, "seith the Father;" that is, He that understandeth the caus why I am cumin in the warld, and sa beliveis in me, (whilk is to sie me be faith,) the same man sieth the Father; that is, understandis and knawis, that God the Father beireth ane unfeaned favour toward him. Chryst heir meaneth not of any corporall syght, but of the eyis and syght of faith, whilk perseth throcht the cloudis of darknes; that is, throcht the wraith of God whilk oure synis doith deserve, to the bryghtnes of the glorie of oure Fatheris face, whairin we behald mercie and grace, in that he hes gevin to us salvatioun and lyfe in his onlie Sone Jesus Chryst. That oure Savioure ment not here of any corporall syght, it is plane; for Judas and many uther reprobat sawe the same face and visage of Jesus Chryst, yea, also his workis and wonderous signis that either Petir, or any uther of the Apostillis saw in the mortall flesche.

And yit, na reprobat saw and considderit God the Father mercifull to thair offences in Jesus Chryst. And sa, the textis ar not repugnant, for the text of Moses meanis, that na mortall creature in this lyfe, for the dulnes and infirmitie of this corrupt nature, is abill to behald the nakit presence of God as he is in his awn substance and essence. And all other textis making mentioun that men hes sene God, or spokin to God face to face, meanis that God reveallis and notifeis him self to sic as he will, and in sic forme and similitude as his wisdome knawis to be expedient for thair infirmitie. And thairby doith he instruct thame of his consall and Godlie will, as ye may persave, be his visionis schawin to Esay and Ezekiell, and other ma Propheitis of God, whairof to wryt, my uthir greit labouris permitteth not.

The contentis of your uther letter, ressavit lang ago, I beir not now in mynd; but I knaw your letter to be in custodie, and sa, at sum convenient lasure, efter advysment with your doutis, I will do diligence to resolutioun thair of; or yf ye sall wryt the same doutis agane, yf possibill be I will answer thame befoir I go. Be fervent in reiding, fervent in prayer, and mercifull to the pure, according to your power, and God sall put end to all dolouris, when leist is thocht to the judgement of man.

Your Brother unfeaned,
JOHNE KNOX.

APPENDIX:

CONTAINING

THE TREATISE BY BALNAVES
ON JUSTIFICATION BY FAITH,
AS REVISED BY KNOX.

M.D.XLVIII.

THE following Treatise is reprinted entire from the original edition, which was published at Edinburgh in the year 1584. The reason for its appearance as an Appendix to this volume has already been assigned;[1] the work itself having been revised, and transmitted for publication to Scotland, by Knox while detained a prisoner in France. After an interval of thirty years, as related in the Epistle Dedicatory to the Lady of Ormiston, which follows the facsimile of the old title-page, it was accidentally discovered, and committed to the press, long subsequently to the death of Knox as well as the Author. In the following biographical notice of Balnaves, the minuteness of some of the details may be excused, as tending to vindicate his character; while his Letters which are appended, serve to illustrate some portions of Knox's history.

HENRY BALNAVES of HALHILL, the author of this Treatise, was a lawyer of distinction, and was eminently serviceable in promoting the great cause of the Reformation in Scotland. We are informed by Calderwood, that he was a native of Kirkcaldy, and we assume the year 1502 as the probable date of his birth. "When he was a childe, (meaning in his youth,) he travelled through Flanders to Culen [Cologne], understanding that poor children were putt to the schooles, and interteaned by the commoun purse of the town. There he profited both in the lawes and in religioun. After his returne to the countrie, he was interteaned by Sir Johne Melvill, laird of Raith,[2] who had alreadie some taste of the true knowledge of God. Thereafter, he went to Sanct Andrewes, and became procurator before the Commissar, but resorted often to the Raith. He was after made Treasurer-Clerk by Sir James Kirkaldie, laird of Grange, who had to wife Jonet Melvill, daughter to the laird of Raith. Thus was Mr Henrie advanced for his wisdome and learning; and after employed in ambassadge to King Henrie the Eight.

---

[1] See *supra*, page 3.
[2] Sir John Melville of Raith was executed on a charge of treasonably corresponding with England, in 1548-9. See note in vol. i. p. 224.

He was in honour and estimatioun under the reigne of King James the Fyft, not without invy and malice of the cleargie for his religioun."[1] It is probably a mistake to suppose that Balnaves was a person of humble origin;[2] but this account serves to show, that he not only raised himself to distinction by his own talents and learning, but that his residence abroad must have extended over several years. As the patronage of Melville of Raith, whose property lay in the parish of Kirkcaldy, was the means of first bringing him into notice, this benefit was ultimately repaid by his constituting one of that family heir to his property of Halhill.

The name of the university at which Balnaves took his degree of Master of Arts has not been ascertained. We find, however, that, on the 7th of December 1526, "Magister Henricus Balnavis, Alb.," or Albanus, (implying his being a native of that district of Scotland, north of the Firth of Forth,) was incorporated a member of St Salvator's College, St Andrews.[3] In the Consistory Court of the metropolitan See, many important causes were then decided; and his practice in that Court may have qualified him for the higher employments which he obtained within a few years after the institution of the Court of Session, in 1532. The precise time of his admission as an Advocate is uncertain. In a series of extracts from the Acts of the Lords of Council and Session, under the date 16th of November 1537, there is a "Memorandum.—At this tyme, the cheiff Advocates in Sessioun wer, Mr Hendrie Lauder, Mr Thomas Marjoribanks, *Mr Henrie Balnavis*," with five others, who are named.[4] On the 3d of December that year, "In an action moved be James Kirkaldy of the Grange, on the one part, aganis David Erle of Crawfurd, on the other part, tuiching the mater advocat before the Lordis, anentis the landis of Ruthulot, Murdocairny, and Star," "Maister Henry Bannayis" appeared as Prolocutor for James Kirkaldy of the Grange.[5]

On the 31st of July 1538, Balnaves was raised to the Bench

---

[1] History of the Church of Scotland, Wodrow Society edition, vol. i. p. 158.

[2] A family of that name had been settled in Fife at an earlier period.— Laurencius de Balnavis is mentioned in the notorial instrument of Perambulation of certain lands in Fife, in 1395. (*Registrum Prioratus Sancti Andreæ*, p. 3.)

[3] Acta Rectoris Univ. S. Andreæ.

[4] MS. Collections from Acts of Parliament to the year 1621, and of Council and Session to 1592, written apparently before 1630, and probably for Sir Thomas Hope, but called erroneously Lord Fountainhall's Collections, from the volume, now in the Editor's possession, having subsequently belonged to him.

[5] Acta Dom. Conc. et Sess., vol. ix. fol. 47^b, and fol. 52^b.

as an Ordinary Lord of Session, and took his seat under the designation of Halhill. This property in Fife he had acquired by purchase, as we learn from a Charter to himself and Christian Scheves, his spouse,[1] in the following year, of the lands "of Easter Collessy, now called Halhill." Balnaves was one of the Commissioners appointed to Parliament, in November 1538, and his name is occasionally found in the Parliamentary proceedings until November 1544.[2]

After the death of James the Fifth, leaving his infant daughter Mary heir to the crown, Sir James Melville[3] states, that it was through the influence of Sir James Kirkaldy of Grange, Balnaves, and others of the reformed religion, that Hamilton, Earl of Arran, afterwards Duke of Chatelherault, was chosen Governor, "wher as he appearit to be a trew Gospeller." The return from France of his natural brother, the Abbot of Paisley, who was afterwards Archbishop of St Andrews, had the effect of changing the Governor's line of policy; but Balnaves was previously advanced to the important office of Secretary of State. The precept of his appointment, as recorded in the Register of the Privy Seal,[4] is in the following terms:—

"*Balnavis.*—Preceptum littere Magistri Henrici Balnavis de
" Halhill facien. eum Secretarium Domine Regine et Custodem
" omnium Signetorum ejusdem pro omnibus diebus vite sue, etc.
" Apud Edr. vltimo Februarij, Anno Domini I^m.v^c.xlij."

In the first Parliament of Queen Mary, 12th March 1542-3, Balnaves is accordingly described as Secretary. He was one of the speakers for the secular party, in favour of the act introduced by Lord Maxwell, to allow the use of the Sacred Scriptures in the vulgar tongue.[5] In the same Parliament, he was one of three Commissioners sent to England to treat with Henry VIII. for the projected alliance between Prince Edward and the infant Queen of Scots; having, in Knox's words, "so travailled, that all things concerning the marriage were agreed upon except the time of her deliverance to the custody of Englishmen."[6] The Act and Instructions are dated the 13th March 1542-3.[7] The Commissioners met at

[1] See No. I., page 419.
[2] Acta Parl. Scot., vol. ii. pp. 352, 355, 368, 383, 384, 403, 446.
[3] Melville's Memoirs, (Bannatyne Club edit.) p. 71.
[4] Regist. Secreti Sigilli, lib. xvii. fol. 30.
[5] Vol. i. p. 99.
[6] Vol. i. p. 102.
[7] See letter from the Council of Scotland, to Henry VIII., dated the 20th of March 1542-3. (State Papers, vol. v. p. 270.)

Greenwich in the month of June, and concluded their deliberations on the 1st of July, returning to Scotland in the course of that month. According to the treaties of pacification and marriage, settled on the 1st of July, there can be no doubt that this projected alliance would have permanently conduced to the prosperity of both kingdoms. In regard to Balnaves, one effect of this employment seems to have been the occasion of his afterwards becoming a pensioner of the English monarch, and attaching himself to the English interest or faction.

In consequence of the change alluded to in the Governor's policy, and the increasing influence of Cardinal Beaton, Balnaves was superseded in his office of Secretary, and was subjected to a temporary imprisonment in Blackness Castle. This happened in November 1543, when the Governor and Cardinal made a progress through Fife and Angus, and caused the Earl of Rothes, Lord Gray, and Balnaves to be apprehended.[1] On the 24th of March 1544, "ane boy was sent with ane writting of my Lord Governouris to Mr Henry Balnavijs, *in the Blaknes.*" He had been liberated before the 4th of June, as on that day, and again on the 14th, "ane boy was send furth of Linlithgow *to Halhill* with writtingis of my Lord Governouris to Maister Henry Balnavis." On the 26th of April 1545, the Treasurer, "be my Lord Governouris precept and speciall command deliverit to Mathew Hamiltoun, Capitane of the Blakness, for the expensis of Maister Henry Balnaves, in the tyme of his being in ward within the said Castle of Blakness, in lxviij. crownis of the Soun,[2] £74 : 16 : 0." But this temporary imprisonment did not prevent him resuming his judicial duties, as his name occurs in the Rolls of Parliament, 7th November 1544, and in the Records of the Lords of Council and Session, 11th July 1545.[3]

On the 29th of May 1546, Cardinal Beaton was murdered in his Castle of St Andrews. That Balnaves was cognizant of the previous scheme, undertaken at the instance of Henry the Eighth, to apprehend or slay this able and resolute opponent to the designs of the English monarch, can scarcely be doubted; yet, although he subsequently coöperated with the chief perpetrators of that most daring act, he cannot be accused as "one of the assassins," as George Chalmers more than once terms him;[4] nor is it the fact, as Spottiswood asserts,

---

[1] Vol. i. p. 116.
[2] A crown of the Sun, the name of a gold coin, valued at £1 : 2 : 0.
[3] MS. Collections, *ut supra.*
[4] Chalmers's Life of Queen Mary, vol. iii. pp. 184, 185, 340.

that he entered the Castle of St Andrews "the day after the slaughter."¹ By entering the Castle of St Andrews, which formed a place of resort to such persons as had rendered themselves obnoxious to the Popish rulers, it is no doubt true that Balnaves, in similar circumstances with Sir David Lyndsay and Knox, fully identified himself with the conspirators; but in the act itself, as he had no concern, we may conclude that he was instigated to this measure, either on the ground of personal attachment to the parties who were the actual perpetrators, or from religious motives, as it involved the sacrifice of his worldly honours and emoluments. It is important, therefore, to prove that he had no direct concern in this tragical event.

Upon examining the subsequent records of the Lords of Council and Session, it appears that he was present on the 4th of June, again on the 28th, (there being a blank in the Registers after the 9th of that month); also on the 1st, 3d, 5th, 19th, 23d, 26th, 27th, 28th, 30th, and 31st of July. Now, on the 10th of June, a summons of treason, under the Great Seal, had been issued by Parliament against the conspirators, who are specially named. They are again specially denounced by an Act of Privy Council on the penult of July, the Queen Regent, the Governor, Chancellor, and other noblemen being present. On the previous and following days, Balnaves's name occurs in the sederunt of the Privy Council. As his name does not occur on the 13th of August, or any subsequent meeting of Council and Session, we may safely assert that he entered the Castle not earlier than the middle of August. On the 3d of August, when the same persons were present, including Balnaves, " It being inquirit be my Lord Chancellar at the haill Prelatis, Erlis, Lordis, and Barronis above written, Quhether it be tresoun to slay ane Chancellar of the Realm or nocht?—Quha all declarit, That conforme to the Commoun Law, it wes tresone to sla the Chancellar."² This of itself should be sufficient to vindicate him from the charge of being an associate in the murder of the Cardinal and Chancellor of Scotland, upwards of nine weeks previously. His former intercourse with England was sufficiently well known; and it had no effect, even while the power of the Cardinal was uncontrolled, in tending to disqualify him from acting as a Judge and Privy Councillor. We may therefore conclude, that Balnaves having resigned, or

¹ History, vol. i. p. 167.—The passage is already quoted in the footnote, vol. i. p. 182.

² Regist. Secreti Concilii: Acta, vol. i., fol. 35, and 35ᵇ.

been deprived of his office as a Lord of Session, entered the Castle of St Andrews some time between the middle of August and the month of October.

During their abode in the Castle of St Andrews, Knox himself relates that Balnaves, John Rough, and Sir David Lyndsay, were the persons " who travailled" with him to undertake the office of the ministry.[1] On the 20th of November 1546, Balnaves and the Master of Rothes proceeded as agents to solicit aid from Henry the Eighth, engaging to deliver the Castle.[2] They returned with an assurance of his assistance, upon condition they would promote the marriage between the young Queen and Prince Edward. In February following, the King granted a subsidy of £1180, with a supply of provisions for support of the garrison; and among other pensions, Balnaves was to receive £125, payable from the 25th of March. He is also said to have received the sum of £300 from Edward the Sixth, who continued the same line of policy, found so advantageous by other English monarchs, " of establishing the English policy by corruption;" and we learn that a further sum of £60 was paid " to Henry Balnaves, remaining in France."[3] On his return from England in February, Balnaves was enjoined to use his utmost endeavours to induce the nobility to withdraw themselves from their allegiance to the Governor; but the death of the English monarch, in the early part of 1547, frustrated their expectations.

These negotiations were renewed; and in a contract, which is dated at the Castle of St Andrews, 9th of March 1546-7, the subscribers being " ever dedicate to the service of our late Maister the Kynges Majestie that dead ys, King Henry the Eight;" in their own name, and that of their friends, "partakers with thame, being also true and faithfull men," engage to carry into effect the proposed alliance between Edward and Mary, to deliver up the son and heir of the Governor, and to promote the unity of both realms. It is signed,

    NORMAND LESLYE, Master of Rothes.
    MASTER HENRY BALNAVES of Halhill.
    JAMES KYRKCALDY of the Grange.
    DAVID MONYPENNY of Pitmuly.
    WILLIAM KYRKCALDY.[4]

---

[1] This was probably in May 1547: See note in vol. i. p. 185.

[2] Diurnal of Occurrents, p. 43.

[3] Chalmers's Life of Queen Mary, vol. iii. p. 342.

[4] Rymer's Foedera, vol. xv. p. 133.

Two days later, or on the 11th of March, Patrick Lord Gray signed articles of a similar tenor; Norman Lesley, James Kirkcaldy, Henry Balnaves, and Alexander Quhytlaw of New Grange, being witnesses.[1] In connection with this agreement, Balnaves had undertaken another journey to England; and he addressed a letter to the Protector, Duke of Somerset, upon his reaching Berwick, on the 18th of April, which is now printed, probably for the first time, from the original in the State Paper Office.[2]

In August 1547, the Castle of St Andrews having surrendered to the Governor, Balnaves, with the chief persons within the Castle, to the number of six score, were carried as prisoners to France.[3] It was during his captivity at Rouen that he wrote the following Treatise on Justification, which, as already stated, was revised by Knox, who divided it into chapters, with a Summary of the contents; and having prefixed to it his Epistle, (which forms the commencement of the present volume,) sent the manuscript to Scotland; but during the lifetime of both Knox and the Author, the work was considered as lost. "How it was suppressed," the former says in 1566, "we know not;" and allusion is made, in the Dedication, to his earnest desire, *as almost nothing more so*, that it should be diligently sought out and preserved from perishing. It has been mentioned as having been actually printed in 1550, and described as two distinct works;[4] but the publication of such a Treatise in Scotland at that time would not have been tolerated; and the title given to it, in 1584, might easily mislead any one who had not an opportunity of examining the original, which is of considerable rarity.

Of the actual resignation or deprivation of Balnaves as a Lord of Session, as already noticed, no mention occurs in the public records, but these are not fully preserved. When Robert Carnegie of Kinnaird was nominated by the Governor to the place of a Temporal Judge, 4th July 1547, it is specially assigned, in the letter to the Lords of Session, as a reason for his appointment, "that thair is diverse of their College deceist,

---

[1] Rymer's Foedera, vol. xv. p. 144.

[2] See No. II., page 418.

[3] Upon the 24th of July 1547, the King of France send in Scotland sixteen galleons to siege the Castle of St Andrews, and upon its surrender, the Lairds of Grange, elder and younger, Norman Lesley, the Laird of Pitmilly, Balnaves, Knox, and others who had taken refuge there, to the number of six score persons, were carried as prisoners to France; the galleons having set sail on the 7th of August.—(*Diurnal of Occurrents*, p. 44.)

[4] Mackenzie's Lives, vol. iii. p. 147; Herbert's Typographical Antiquities, vol. iii. p. 1482.

and utheris absent, wherthrough they ar not an sufficient number to decyd caussis."¹ A notice in the Treasurer's accounts, however, shows that his forfeiture took place during his captivity in France. On the 5th of December 1548, the messenger who was sent to Fife to summon an assize on the Laird of Raith, at the same time was directed to "execute summondis of treason upon the Laird of Petmillie (Monypenny) and Maister Henry Balnaves."

In the Parliament held at Edinburgh in March 1556, the forfeiture of the Lairds of Grange, Ormiston, Brunstone, and of Balnaves, was rescinded by direction of the Queen Regent.² Having soon after returned to Scotland, we find him taking an active part in managing the affairs of the Congregation. After the accession of Queen Elizabeth, who favoured the Protestant party in Scotland, Balnaves was again called upon to engage in the stirring events of that period. For the purpose of negotiating with, and supporting, the Lords of the Congregation, Sir Ralph Sadler and Sir James Croft were, in August 1559, sent with secret instructions to reside at Berwick. On the 3d of that month, the Queen issued a warrant for £3000 to be paid to Sadler, "to be by him employed accordinge to suche instructions as we shall give hym;" and he was duly authorized "to rewarde any maner of persone of Scotlande, with such sommez of money as ye shall think meete," out of the said sum. Two similar letters of credit, each for £3000, were dispatched to Sadler, on the 5th of October and in November following.³ It has already been noticed,⁴ that on the 20th of August, they addressed a letter to Knox by the return of his messenger, expressive of the desire, "that Mr Henry Balnaves, or some other discrete and trustie man, might repayre, in suche secret maner, and to such a place, as I have appoynted here, to the intent we might conferre with him touching their affayres." For so Sir James Croft wrote on the same day to Secretary Cecil.⁵ Balnaves, whom Knox there styles "A MAN OF GOOD CREDITE IN BOTH THE REALMES," was accordingly despatched, and arrived at Berwick on Wednesday, the 6th of September, at midnight. His mission was so far successful, that he obtained from Sir Ralph Sadler, in the Queen's name, a promise of £2000 sterling, which was to be shipped at Holy Island

---

[1] MS. Collections, *ut supra*.
[2] Sir James Balfour's Annals, vol. i. p. 305.
[3] Ellis's Original Letters, the Third Series, vol. iii. p. 332.
[4] Vol. ii. p. 38.
[5] Sadler's State Papers, v. l. i. p. 399.

with "as much secrecie as possible." On the 8th of September, Sir Ralph Sadler, in a letter to Secretary Cecil, recites at great length the "long talke" he had with Balnaves on the state of parties in Scotland. A letter addressed by himself to Sadler and Crofts, from Stirling, on the 23d of that month, also contains some important information on the same subject: both letters are published in Sadler's State Papers.[1] On the 21st of October, after sermon, Balnaves came to Randolph, and requested him to inform Sadler and Croft of various proceedings of the Lords of the Congregation. On the last of that month, Cecil writes from Court, and says, " If Balnaves shuld come, it wold prove dangerous; and therefore it is thought better that he be forborne until the matter be better on foot."[2]

In a subsequent letter addressed to Croft, from Edinburgh, on the 4th of November, Balnaves refers to some accusations of his want of diligence in writing intelligence, and in not having bestowed the money he had received upon the common affairs, but upon particular individuals. He states in reply how the money had been expended for the support of the troops that were enlisted; the payment to each of the six companies of foot soldiers, extended monthly to £290 sterling, that of 100 horsemen to £230; and that 500 crowns were given to the Earl of Glencairne and Lord Boyd, which, he says, "was the best bestowed money that ever I bestowed, either of that or any other." " But in tymes to cum, (he adds,) I shall save myself from such blame, with the grace of God. I think I deservit more thanks. It was presumit that I had receyvit twenty thousand crownis, and would not bestow it as every man wold. This is the commoditie that I had for my travell; but I serve God principallie in this matter, and consequentlie that thing which may tender the common-weale of baith thir Realmes, as God beareth witnes to my conscience, and I am hable to justifie when tyme and occasion suit: so I take the less care of tales."[3] Sadler and Croft, in a joint letter to Randolph, on the 5th of November, thus refer to his vindication: " And whereas we perceyve by Balnaves lettres, that he laboureth to excuse himself of such things as he supposeth us to charge him withall, which, as we take it, he gathereth of such communication and talke as we had with [Cockburn of] Ormeston, you shall declare unto him, on our be-

---

[1] Sadler's State Papers, vol. i. p. 461. Balnaves's letter is subjoined as No. III. page 420.

[2] Ib., vol. i. p. 532.

[3] Keith's History, vol. i. p. 403; and reprinted as No. V. at page 423.

half, that the care which we have of their commen accyon, moved us to say our mynds frankly to the saide Ormeston, wherein we mynded nothing lesse then to offende Balnaves; and therefore pray him to thinke of us whatsoever we say, that we be no less carefull of their well doing then he is; and that we do not only take all his doings in goode parte, but also rest his assured frends to our power."[1]

For the purpose of communicating speedy and accurate intelligence between the chiefs of the Congregation, Knox was appointed to attend those of Fife, and Balnaves was sent to act as Secretary to the noblemen in the West. This was in the month of November. On the 15th of that month, Croft informs Cecil of a rumour that young Lethington and Balnaves had come to England. A letter, however, from Balnaves was brought by Thomas Randolph, (sometimes called Randall, and who also assumed the name of Barnaby,) who accompanied Secretary Maitland in this journey. They came by water to Holy Island, and were secretly admitted by Croft into the Castle of Berwick.

In February 1559-60, it was resolved to send Lord James Stewart, Lord Ruthven, the Master of Maxwell, Secretary Maitland, Wishart of Pitarrow, and Balnaves, to a conference with the Duke of Norfolk, on the 25th of that month, at Berwick. On this occasion, they came by sea from Pittenweem, "as the way by lande is both daungerous and longe;"[2] and the result was the settling the treaty of Berwick, by which the aid of the English government was openly afforded, and the Reformation in Scotland before long fully established.[3]

Of the subsequent history of Balnaves, after the establishment of the Reformation, there is not much to relate. According to Knox,[4] at the Parliament held in May 1563, Kirkcaldy of Grange, Balnaves, and two others, "were restored." The records of that Parliament are not preserved, but any act rescinding their forfeiture must be assigned to an earlier date; and took place, as we have seen, in March 1556. But this later act might refer to compensation for the losses, or restoration of their heritable property, and not of their personal privileges; as in fact, on the 11th of February 1563, Balnaves had been reappointed to a seat on the Bench, upon

---

[1] Sadler's State Papers, vol. i. p. 548.
[2] Ib., vol. i. p. 705.
[3] See *supra*, vol. ii. p. 45-52, where a copy of the Treaty is inserted; and note 1, p. 52.
[4] See vol. ii. p. 381.

the occasion of a vacancy. This we learn from the following entry in the *Acta Dominorum Concilii et Sessionis:*

"*Vndecimo Februarij Anno Domini, etc.* lxij°.

"Sederunt, &c.

"*Hic intravit M. Henricus Balnavis, Ordinarius.*

"Compeirit Maister Henrie Balnavis of Halhill, and pre"sentit ane writting of the Quenis Grace, subscrivit with hir "Gracis hand, desyring the Lords to admitt him an Ordinar in "place of umquhill Sir Jhone Campbell of Lundy knycht, as "at mair length is contenit in the said writing, of the dait at "Edinburgh, the xvij. day of Januar, &c. According to the "quhilk writing, the saidis Lordis ressavit, and ressavis the "said Maister Henry in ane of thair Ordinar, and quha maid "faith," &c.

On the 29th of December 1563, Balnaves was named one of the Commissioners appointed to revise the Book of Discipline. It is also stated, but upon no sufficient evidence, that he acted as one of the Assessors to the Earl of Argyle, in the mock trial of Bothwell, for Darnley's murder.[1]

In the proceedings that took place in England, after the Earl of Murray was chosen Regent, accusing Queen Mary as accessory to her husband's murder, Balnaves was one of the Regent's attendants or assessors. The inquiry was commenced at York on the 4th of October 1568, adjourned to Hampton Court on the 30th, and continued there and at Westminster in the month of December.[2] It does not appear that Balnaves took any active part in the pleadings; but the persons referred to, George Buchanan, and John Wood the Regent's Secretary, had each a suit of black velvet, Secretary Maitland an allowance of £200, and Balnaves various articles of dress, amounting to £231 : 4 : 3. The chief items of articles furnished for his use may be quoted from the Treasurer's accounts : "Item, the xvj. day of September, be my Lord Regent grace precept to Maister Henrie Balnavis of Halhill, ix. elnes ij. quarteris of fyne blak weluote, the elne vij. lib. Summa lxvj. lib. x. s. Item, iij. elnis of fyne tripe weluote, the elne xx. s. Summa iiij. lib. x. s. Item, iiij. elnis ij. quarteris of blak Inglis freis, the elne xx. s. Summa iiij. lib. x. s.; with various other furnishings, amounting to £18. 19. 11. Item, v. elnis j. quarter of fyne blak claith, the elne vj. lib. xs. Summa xxxiv. lib. ij. s. vj. d. Item, xij. elnis of blak

[1] Keith's History, and Brunton's and Haig's Senators of the College of Justice, p. 62.

[2] Goodall's Queen Mary, vol. ii. pp. 108, 307.

damas, the elne iij.lib. x.s. Summa xlij.lib. Item, viiij.elnis iij. quarteris, half quarter of satene, the elne iij.lib. v.s. Summa xxviij.lib. xvj.s. x.d. Item, viij. elnis ij. quarters of cowgraine taffeteis, the elne iij.lib. x.s. Summa xxix.lib. xv.s. Item, ane hat, as the said precept with the acquittance of resait schawin upon compt beiris, xl.s."

In the Convention held at Stirling on the 12th of February 1568-9, " The haill Lords of the Previe Counselle, and utheris of the Nobilitie and Estaittis above writtin, allowit the proceedingis of my Lord Regentis Grace and Lordis Commissionaris that wer with him in the realme of England: The same proceedings being declarit and red to them."[1] It may further be noticed, that after Balnaves's return from England, he appears to have received the sum of £300.[2] His name also occurs in the Records of Privy Council, although there is no evidence of his having been formally readmitted. He still continued however in the performance of his judicial functions till within a short period of his death. On the 20th of June 1569, he being personally present, there was presented before the Lords of Session a deed, which was ordered to be registered, dated at Balmuto and Edinburgh on the 11th and 12th day of that month, being a contract of marriage entered into betwixt David Boiswell of Balmuto for himself and Christian Boiswell his lawful daughter on the one part, and Mr Henry Balnaves, liferenter of the lands of Halhill, and one of the Senators of our Sovereign Lordis College of Justice, and James Melvile, his son adoptive, and fear of the saids lands of Halhill, on the other part; that "the said James Melvile sal, God willing, marie and tak to his spousit wyf the said Christiane Boiswall, and sall solempnizat and compleit the band of matrimonie with hir in face of the haly kirk and congregatioun, conforme to the law of God now establischit within this realme of Scotland, betuix the day and dait heirof and the feist of Lambes next," &c.[3]

Balnaves died at Leith in the month of February 1569-70.

---

[1] Reg. Secr. Concilii, p. 103.

[2] In the Treasurer's accounts, opposite August 1571, but evidently inserted in the wrong place, is a slip: "Item, be my Lord Regentis grace speciale command, to Maister Henrie Balnavis of Halhill, knycht, iij.ᶜlib." In the margin of the slip is written, probably by Balnaves himself. "*To mend the dytement of me in this buke.*"

[3] Register of Deeds, &c., vol. ix. 1566-1569.—The following is a facsimile of his signature in 1539, as one of the Auditors of some public accounts.

A copy of his Confirmed Testament is annexed at page 427; and it proves his gratitude to the family of his early patron, in making James Melville, his adopted son, heir of the estate of Halhill.

During the whole course of his active life, the political and religious conduct of Balnaves exhibits a rare degree of consistency under adverse circumstances. Melville, who, in his younger days, had been sent to France as one of Queen Mary's pages of honour, visited Scotland in June 1559, to ascertain for his Royal Mistress the state of public affairs, and the intentions of her natural brother, Lord James, Prior of St Andrews, better known as the Regent Earl of Murray. He was introduced to Lord James by Balnaves, and from his account of their interview, contained in his Memoirs, the following passage may appropriately conclude the present biographical notice:

"Master Hendre Belnaves (says Melville) was then in great credit with hym (Lord James, Prior of St Andrews) *and loved me as his awen sone, be some acquaintance I had with him in France, and plesoures I had done to him during his banishment.* He first shew unto me, sa far as he knew of my Lord James intention; and encouragit me to be plane with the said Lord James, and assured me of secrecie, and of honest and plain dealing; FOR HE WAS A GODLY, LEARNIT, LANG EXPERIMENTED, WYSE COUNSELLOR; and past with me to the said Lord Pryour."[1] Knox also, who had enjoyed such long and confidential intercourse with Balnaves, mentions him as "an old professor;"[2] and elsewhere[3] speaks of him as highly esteemed as a man of learning as well as piety.

In regard to the following Treatise, it is valuable as exhibiting Knox's sentiments on an important point of Christian doctrine, while his notes and summary entitle it in some respects to a place amongst his own writings. On this subject, the biographer of Knox remarks, "In reading the writings of the first Reformers, there are two things which must strike our minds. The first is, the exact conformity between the doctrine maintained by them respecting the Justification of sinners, and that of the Apostles. The second is, the surprising harmony which subsisted among them on this important doctrine. On some

---

[1] Memoirs of Sir James Melville of Halhill, (Bannatyne Club edit.) p. 81. Edinb. 1827, 4to.
[2] Vol. i. p. 99.
[3] Ib. p. 226.

questions respecting the Sacraments, and the external government and discipline of the Church, they differed; but upon the Article of FREE JUSTIFICATION, Luther and Zuinglius, Melancthon and Calvin, Cranmer and Knox, spoke the very same language. This was not owing to their having read each other's writings, but because they copied from the same Divine original. The clearness with which they understood and explained this great truth is also very observable. More learned and able defences of it have since appeared; but I question if it has ever been stated in more scriptural, unequivocal, and decided language, than in the writings of the early Reformers. Some of their successors, by giving way to speculation, gradually lost sight of this distinguishing badge of the Reformation, and landed at last in Arminianism, which is nothing else but the Popish doctrine in a Protestant dress. Knox has informed us, that his design, in preparing for the press the Treatise written by [Mr] HENRY BALNAVES,[1] was to give along with the Author, his 'Confession of the Article of Justification therein contained.' I cannot, therefore, (Dr M'Crie adds) lay before the reader a more correct view of our Reformer's sentiments on this fundamental Article of Faith, than by quoting from a book which was revised and approved by him."[2]

In quoting the above passage, the intelligent Editor of the British Reformers, in 1831, subjoins,—" May we not say, that more *learned* defences of the doctrine of Justification by Faith perhaps have since appeared, but it would be difficult to point out any of equal *ability*, in all essential respects?"

APPENDIX.

I.

ABSTRACT OF A CHARTER OF CONFIRMATION TO BALNAVES OF THE LANDS OF HALHILL. 1539.

Carta confirmationis Mro. Henrico Balnavis et Christinæ Scheves suæ sponsæ in conjuncta infeodatione et heredibus inter

---

[1] Dr M'Crie, by mistake, here styles him *Sir* Henry Balnaves.

[2] M'Crie's Life of Knox, vol. i. p. 390.

ipsos legitime procreatis seu procreandis; quibus deficientibus, legitimis et propinquioribus heredibus seu assignatis dicti Magistri Henrici quibuscunque super cartam illis factam per Alexandrum Cummyng de Inneralochy,[1] de data 8 die Augusti 1539: DE OMNIBUS et singulis terris suis de Estir Cullessy nunc vocatis *lie Halhill,* cum molendinis earundem et suis pertinentibus jacentibus infra Dominium et Vicecomitum de Fiffe, Tenend. de Rege, &c. REDDENDO summam viginti octo marcarum monetæ Scotiæ, unacum decem bollis avenarum et duobus duodenis pulturarum, secundum tenorem cartæ feodifirmæ per Regem et suos prædecessores dicto Alexandro Cummyng et prædecessoribus suis desuper confectæ ad terminos in eadem contentos INSUPER de novo dando concedendo et confirmando dicto Mro. Henrico ejus Sponsæ eorumque prædictis totum jus titulum, &c. Testibus, &c., dat. apud Petlethy, 10 die Augusti 1539.[2]

II.

LETTER FROM BALNAVES TO THE LORD PROTECTOR, DUKE OF SOMERSET. 1547.

Pleaseth your most nobill Lordschip, be aduerteseth my dewite remembred, this day, aboute sevyn of the clok, I arryved at Bervik, and sall, with Goddis grace, mak deligence towarde your Lordship. The wyndes hes bene some parte contrarius sens Setterday that I come from the Castell of Sanct Andrewes, wharthrou I ame some parte euill disposeth; so except I happyn to gett the better horses for my selfe, it wilbe ane greit hender to my passage. If it be your most nobill Lordship's pleasour, I think best that Jhone Lesly be conveyed abrode in the contre with some gentilman in halking or huntyn whill I haue spokkyn some thingis at lenth to your Lordship; And then that he be send fore, and that this be not knowin to hym, but always that he be weill treated, and know no thing of my cuming, whill your Lordship aduertess hym efterwartis.

---

[1] A charter of the lands of Eister Cullessy was granted to Sir William Cumming of Innerlochy, knight, *alias* Marchmont Herald, and Christian Prestoun, his spouse, 18th September 1507. These lands are included in the subsequent charter to William Cumming, their son and heir, and Margaret Hay, 14th July 1513.— (Registrum Magni Sigilli, lib. xiv. No. 187.)

[2] Ib. lib. xxvi No. 310.

Schir Jhone Borthwik[1] come frome the Castell with me. All other thinges I refferr to forther declaratione at my returnyng toward your good Lordship, whome Almyghty Gode have in his eternall tuitione. Frome the Kingis Majestes towne of Berwyk, the xviij. of Aprill, Anno &c. xlvij°.

Your Lordship's most hummill seruitour at command,

M. H. BALNAVES.

To the Ryght Noball Lord Duke of
Somyrseit, Lord Protectour and
Governour of the Kingis Majestes
Most Nobill Personne, &c.
Be deliuered with deligence.

III.

LETTER FROM BALNAVES TO SIR RALPH SADLER AND SIR JAMES CROFT. Sept. 23, 1559.

RICHT WORSHIPFULL,

After most heartie commendacion: Having occasion by oportunitie of this bringar Mr Whitlaw, I thought it good to advertise you of the proceedings here since myn arriving and departing from you. The 16 of this instant I cam to Striviling, where I founde the Lords, together with my Lorde of Arrane. The matiers I had in hand, as secretlie as it was possible, I communicate to a fewe nombre, and purpose was taken with suche diligent spede as might to gett our men togither; no daye prefixit, but that all countreis shulde be warned to be in readines upon the space of 4 dayes warning, and then to have the certaintie of my Lorde Dukes mynde in this cause. We past to Hamilton the 19 of this instant, and there, after all our purpose was opened up to him, he gladlie subscribed all the bonds we had made, bothe towards religion and other affaires of the commenweale. And he, togither with the rest of the Lords, wrote to Therle of Huntley, that he shulde joyne him to them, and com forwards with all his freends. It is beleved he shall be upon this side. Nowe we beyng in Hamilton, woorde cam to us, the Frenchmen ware entred to the fortefyeng of Leitht, whiche thing displeaseth not a littell the Lords, who

---

[1] An account of Borthwick is given in vol. i. p. 533, Appendix, No. viii.

incontinent wrote to the Quene Regent,[1] to cause them desist from the saide entreprise, or ells the hole nobilitie and commonalltie of the realme woolde provide remedie. There was no aunswer brought again of their lettre at this tyme. Notwithstanding finall conclusion is taken by the Lords, to convene with all the force and strenght they maye, the 15 of this next moneth, and not to depaurte a sounder, till they accomplishe the change of this authoritie, and have their intent of the Frenshe men, ether by one meanes or other. And bicause we feare the fortefyeng of Leitht in this meane tyme, if it be possible, with suche nombre as maye be gathered of our men, we make to take Edinburgh, to the effect the Frenchmen maye be impeded of their intreprise; and bicause we woolde be sure of the Castell of Edinburgh to freende, there is lettres sent to my Lorde Erskyn with secret credit. I trust he shall mete my Lorde Prior this next Soundaye, to common upon this matier. As suche matier takith effect, I shall advertise you tyme by tyme; but the passage is verie difficill. My Lorde of Arrane is verie desireous to have Mr Randolph to common with; and to that effect, has sent this bringar with his owne direction, who can open all these maters at lenght to your M. as he shall be requyered. Moreover, if we shall not have the lyke thing I brought with me, sped here with diligence, about the latter end of this next moneth, it is not possible to kepe our men any long tyme togither. Therefore I praye your M. have respect hereto, and advertise with this bringar me, what tyme the same maye be lippened to be received, that I maye appoint summe secret man to that effect. For it is not possible to my selfe til-be absent from the Lords of Counsaile, while these maters take summe staye. This entreprise of Leitht hathe inflamed the harts of our people to a woonderfull hatred and despite of Fraunce, wherthrough I thinke there shall folowe a playne defection from Fraunce for ever. Thus, not molesting your M. with longer lettre, I committ you to the tuicion of Almightie God. From Striveling in hast, the 23 of Sept. 1559.

By your M. assured freend at power,
HENRY BALNAVES of Halhill.

There has chancit laitly slauchter between the Grames of Eske and the Maister of Maxwell, who is our frend; and if the sam shall not be stayit by sum meanes of your Warden

---

[1] Their letter, or rather manifesto, may be found in Knox's History. See vol. i. p. 413. It bears date at Hamilton, 19th of September 1559.

of the West Marches, it shall make the said Maister Maxwell to be so impedit, that he may not bring furth his men to us in our necessite. Good it were, if he may, that sum remedy was providit herein, by the means whereof we may have without lett, the force and strength the said Maister Maxwell may make to us.

IV.

Extract of a Letter from Thomas Randolph to Sadler and Croft. Oct. 22, 1559.

This daye beyng the 21, after the sermone Mr Balnaves cam and requeyered me to write unto your honours as here foloweth. The 18 of Oct. we cam to Edinburgh withoute impedement, and the 19 wrote a lettre to the Regent, who went the daye before to Lythe: the substance of the lettre was, that she shoulde cause incontinent the Frenche depart from Lythe. And because she woolde presently give no answer by the bearer, but sought to protract tyme, the xx. of this instant wee sent a trumpett to requyer answer withoute further delaye. And forasmuche as in all her dooyngs she seketh nothing but to protract tyme, we intend shortlie to proclayme her enemye to the commen wealthe for suche causes as shall be alledged; and that the governement shall be used by the counsell alreadie chosen, whereof the Duke and Therle of Arrain are principall. Item, To mayntayne this matter, we cannot kepe our companyes together, howbeit the nobles remayne. Therfore we thinke no fewer than 3000 footemen, and 300 horsemen, necessarie to be kept for 3 monethes, to recover Lythe again; wherfore it woolde please our freends, with all possible diligence, to hast hither money for the payment of these souldiers for the saide tyme, or at the least for two monethes; and if this be not spedilie aunswered, it shall repent us and our freends bothe, for good will is in us, but our power is not to furnisshe accordingly. And assure their honors in my name, the lytell money I brought with me hathe servid more to these effects then if they had bestowed themselfes five thousand pounds, as the dede hathe shewed from the begynnyng. Item, It is concluded the xxj. of this present, with the consent of the Lords of the Congregacion, nobles and barons assembled, that the Regent shall be deposed, and this to be proclaymed upon Mondaye, which is the 23.

The hope of all concord this daye is taken awaye, by reason that blood is drawen largely on every side. Thus muche have I charge of Mr Balnaves to write.

This daye it was concluded in counsell that there should be levied three thousand men more, and every nobleman to contribute to his abilitie, and to give any adventure they can to expell the Frenche, whereunto I see them so inclyned, that I think it not possible for them long to remayne.

Kircaldie in hast cam unto me, to requyer me, from the Lords of the Congregacion, to dispatche this berer with suche credit as he hathe to saye, desiering you to lend them summe power oute of hand. The rest I referre for lack of tyme, most humblie taking my leave. 22 Oct. an°. 59. *Hora tercia.*

V.

LETTER FROM BALNAVES TO SIR JAMES CROFT. Nov. 4, 1559.

After most hearty commendations, Rycht Worschipfull, this is to certifie, that the mater has evill chancit the Lord of of Ormestoun,[1] who by the Erle Bothwell was this last Tusday at nycht besyde Haddyngtoun takin, hurt, and spolzeit of that he hadde. How sone this word came to the Lords, they upon Weddinsday raid to Crechtoun, four hundrecht horsmen, thre hundrecht futemen, and certan peces of ordinance, trusting to have found there the Erle Bothwell; but he was departit suddanly upon ane hors without sadill, bout, or spoures. And then the Lords tuke the house, and put in the sam fifty hagbutars to keip it, and send the capitan of the said hous to the Erle Bothwell, desiring hym to restore the money, and redress the wrong done to the Lord of Ormestoun, or ellis they wold spolze the said house, and destroy it. As zit thay have resavit no answer of hym, bot this day ar ryddyn agane to that end, if he satisfie thame not, to performe the thing they promist him. Upoun Weddinsday last, the Frenchmen being advertest in Leyth of the small number left in this town, ischit furt and cam suddanly upoun certan pecis of ordinances lyand upoun the hill between Leyth and Edinburgh, schoting at Leyth, and put the futemen, whiche was but ane few or small number, fra the said ordinance, and tuke two of the sam, one whiche was brokyn, and ane other, and chasit the futemen in with small

---

[1] John Cockburn of Ormiston: See vol. i. p. 455, note 2.

hurt; and so maid suche a frey to the town, that all was out of order the space of two hours. Thar was slane of our syde pure men, wemen, and bairns in the sowborbs of the Cannogait, ten or twelve persones, and of the Frenchmen as many or mo, as thamselfs hes grantit; amangs the whiche they want two capitans, whiche thay understand to be takyn, but thay ar dead indeid. All this mischance happinnit through the takyn of the Lord of Ormestoun. As for his hurt, he will not be any thing the worse; but the lose of the money greves us sore, more for the discovering of the mater, nor the want of the money. Howbeit the sam is ane great dammage to us; for it shall not be possible to us till keip our men togydder without money, and that was the caus of the last written I send, our necessite being so great. And yit if heasty remead be not providit for oure support, it will be too true that I wrot; for we sall suffer the present dammage, and peraventure when you wald support us it shal be too lait, without the heastier expedition be maid now presentlie, considering that whiche was sent is lost.

It now behuffit me to answer to some points whiche are laid to my charge, as doing my duety in the thing committit to my credit. The first, That I was too slaw in advertesement geving. I answerit that in my last letter, that I gave sufficient advertesement to provide money in the letter I sent with Alexander Whitlaw, advertesing how every thing was appointit to be done as it is succedit indeid; and therfore desirit the money to be in reddyness about the last day of October, or soner: and this advertesement was geven be me sax weicks before the tyme. As for ony other materis of wecht or importance, I had none, till the tyme we cam to Edinburgh; and so thar is na suche great caus of sleuthfulnes toward my part. And as for my importunete in writtein, if you did know how I was urget therto by the Lords, and also the necessite which cravet the sam, that mycht be easily borne with; but if I had writtyn to the Counsale, I wold have writtyn no less, hearing of thame by mouth-speaking, as I did heir of you, assuring ayd, as necessite requirit. And as for keiping of closurs, that standit not in my hand you know; thay whiche sent me for that money must needis be upon counsale of disponing therof, whiche was not possible to keip close, by reasone of the listing of the men of warre. It is knowing that we are not hable, without support of others, to susteyn suche charges, and therfore our adversaries presumes we have support of you; yea veraly our awin selves cannot keip the sam close, because thar is so many being upon counsale whiche cannot be brought to ane few number, as the materis now standis with us.

Last, where it is reportit to you, that the money I receyved was not bestowed upoun the commoun affaires, but upoun particular persones, &c. That is most ontrue, who evir reportit it, as I schall clerly schew; for there was ane thousand futemen incontinent listit, whiche are payit ane monethes wages with the said money. And because thay thought more necessarie to have futemen then horsmen, ther was listit agane 500 futemen, whiche ar likewyse payit ane monethes wages. And ane hundreth horsmen at the leading of the Lord of Gray and Alexander Whitlaw, whom I payit at the command of Mr Randolph, as having commission from you. And I deliverit to the Erle of Glencarn and Lord Boyd 500 crowns, which was the best bestowed money that ever I bestowed, ather of that or any other; the which if I had not done, our hoyll interprise it hatht bene stayd, both in joyning with the Duke, and cuming to Edinburgh, for certan particular causes that war betwix the saids Lords and the Duke, which war sett down by that meanes be me so secrete, that it is not knowen to many. Here is the hoyll mater oppynnit upoun bestowing of the said money. Now judge you my ple. But in tymes to cum I shall save myself from such blame with the grace of God. I think I desservit more thanks. It was presumit that I had receyvit twentie thousand crowns, and wold not bestow it as every man wold. This is the commoditie that I had for my travell, bot I serve God principallie in this mater, and consequentlie that thing whiche may tender the common weale of baith thir realmes, as God bearetht witnes to my conscience, and I am hable to justifie when tyme and occasion suit; so I take the less care of tales. Had I suit sum mennis appetites, thar hatht been no word of the money bestowing; but hatht I done that, I culd not have answerit to you upoun my honour, as I dar now baldly write and speake.

The man whom you desyre will be sent to you freely instruckit, how soone lasser may be had, and sum stay of thir present besyness. The payment of our futemen extendis monethlie everie ansenye[1] (whiche ar now sex in number) to £290 sterling. The hundretht horsmen extends to monethlie, in ordinarie payment, £230 sterling. By this you may calkill what twa thousand futemen and thre hundreth horsemen will

[1] Ansenye, or enseinyie, a company of soldiers.

tak monethlie, whiche is the least number the Lords desyris to have furnesat at this tyme. And as for the money lost by the Lord Ormestoun, the Lords will send you thar writtyn upoun the sam as the mater hatht chancit. If Mr Randolphe hatht not bene her present, I wold have writyn oftiner to you; notwithstanding as materis occurris, and as I may have lesar, (whiche is rare) you shall be advertest. Thus not molesting you longar, I committ you to the tuition of Almychty God. From Edinburgh the 4th day of November, anno Dom. 1559.

    Your much assured frend at power,
      HENRY BALNAVIS of Halhill.

VI.

LETTER FROM BALNAVES TO SADLER AND CROFT. Nov. 19, 1559.

Ryght Worshipfull, after my most harty commendations, having no other maters to write at this tyme to you nor they whiche ar knowing manifestlie by common report; and also the bringer hereof can at more lentht declare nor is neidfull to me till write; yet thought I it nedefull to show you that, notwithstanding theis lait alterations and changes, there is no purpois alterit which ever was begun here by the Lordes and Nobilite of this realm, ether concerning the menteyning of true religion, or keping of this realme in the ould liberte thereof from the tyranny of Frenchemen. And to declare thare myndes to the Quenes Majestie, they have send Mr Secretarie Ledington fully instructed with thar myndes, to whois returning the Counsales of our syde makes residence in Glasguow and Sanctandros for the keping of the contries in order, and making of mo frendes, as we doubt not but thay will incresse daly; and the rather that it be knowing we have your frendship, as at more lentht the bringer hereof, Mr Randolphe, will shew you, whom I committe to the tuition of Almy^{t}y God. From Sanctandros, the 19 of November 1559.

    Your loving frend at power,
      HENRY BALNAVES of Halhill.

To the Ryght Worschipfull
 Kny^{t}es, Sir Rauff Sadler
 and James Crofte, be
 these deliverit.

VII.

MAISTER HENRY BALNAVES.
Apud Leith,
xvij⁰. *Martij* 1571.

THE TESTAMENT TESTAMENTAR AND INVENTAR of the gudis, geir, and dettis pertening to umquhile MAISTER HENRY BALNAVES OF HALHILL, ane of the Senatouris of our Soverane Lordis College of Justice the tyme of his deceis, quhilk wes in the moneth of Februar, the yeir of God I^m.v^c.lxix. yeris, faithfullie maid and gevin up partlie be him self upon the thrid day of Januar, the yeir foirsaid, and partlie be JAMES MELVILL, his sone adoptive, quhome the said umquhile Mr Henry, the tyme foirsaid, be his latterwill underwritten, nominat, constitut, and maid his Executour testamentar, as the same at lenth beiris.

In the first, The said James Melville, executour foirsaid, grantis that the said umquhile Maister Henry had, the tyme of his deceis foirsaid, the gudis and geir following pertening to him, as his awne proper gudis and geir, viz., Upoun his manis of Halhill, sextene drawand oxin, price of the pece v.lib. vj.s. viij.d. Summa lxxxv.lib. vj.s. viij.d. Item, foure ky, thairof tua with thair followaris, price of the pece ourheid iiij. lib. Summa xvj.lib. Item, twa stottis, price of the pece xl.s. Summa iiij. lib. Item, xxiij zewis, price of the pece xv. s. Summa xvij.lib. v.s. Item, xxxiiij. hoggis, price of the pece x.s. Summa xvij.lib. Item, in the barne and barneyard of Halhill, lxx. bollis of aittis, price of the boll ourheid, xiij.s. iiij.d. Summa xlvj.lib. xiij.s. iiij.d. Item, in ten bollis of peis, price of the boll xx.s. Summa ten lib. Item, xxvij. bollis of beir, price of the boll xxvj.s. viij.d. Summa in money xxxvj. lib. Item, threttene bollis of quhete, price of the boll thretty shillings. Summa xix.lib. x.s. Item, in utensilis and domicilis, by the airschip, estimat to xxvj.lib. xiij.s. viij.d.

Summa of the Inventar ij^c.lxxviij.lib. viij.s. iiij.d.

Followis the Dettis awing to the Deid.
Item, Thair was awing to the said umquhile Mr Henry be his tennentis of Petconty, of the fermes thairof, for the crop and

yeir of God I^m.v^c.lxix. yeiris, thre chalderis, nyne bollis victuall, price of the boll xx.s. Summa lix.lib. Item, be Johne Brad, for the males of the bowhous of the Mertymes terme preceding his deceis, nyne lib. Item, be the tennentis of Lethame, of thair teindis of the said yeir x.lib. x.s. Item, be Duncane Levingston, collectour of the Quotis of the Testamentis of Contributioun appertening to him as ane of the Lordis of the Sessioun, conforme to Robert Scottis clerk thairof ticket maid thairupon, thrie skoir nyne pundis viij.s. And becaus it mycht happin that the said umquhile Mr Henry had intromettit with mair of the Lordis contributioun nor he aucht to haif done, Thairfoir he willit that the same be recompansit and satisfeit be the said sowme of lxix.lib. viij.s., and payit thairwith.

Summa of the Dettis awing to the deid, j^c.xlvij.lib. xviij.s.
Summa of the Inventar with the Dettis, iiij^c.xxvj.lib. vj.s. viij.d.

Item, The said umquhile Maister Henry grantit him to be awand to the Laird of Sanct Monanis ane hundreth pundis, to be payit howsone the airis of Culluthie redemis the fyve merk land of Sanct Monanis, quhilk I wodset to the Laird upon twa hundreth and fyftie merkis, becaus I gaif thame the reversioun upoun ane hundreth merkis alanerlie: als, becaus in the contract maid betuix me and the said Laird, registrat in the bukis of Counsale, I wes obleist to gif him ane hundreth pundis money; and he being desirous to haif that hundreth pundis put in the reversioun, to the effect the saidis landis suld be the langer unredemit: Thairfoir, he consentand to the discharge of ane hundreth merkis contenit in the said contract, he aucht to haif but onlie the said hundreth pundis, uthirwayis na thing but as law will, for I am na forder obleist.—Item, I am awand for the few males of Halhill, of the Mertymes terme preceding my deceis, nyne pundis xviij.s. iiij.d. Item, for the few males of Petcontie and Muirfeild, of the Witsunday and Mertymes preceding his said deceis, xxij.lib. ij.s. Item, to Helene Boiswell, for hir fe, as his Wifes testament beiris, tuelf pund. Item, to the said James Melvill, executour, gevin up to be awing to Johne Rutherfurd, for his half yeiris fe, liij.s. iiij.d. Item, to Alexander Duncane, for his fe, xx.s. Item, to Alexander Johnstoun, for his fe, xx.s. Item, to Isobell Robertsoun, for hir fe, lix.s. Item, for the Witsonday males of his chalmer, xij.lib. Item, to Thomas Davidsoun, ypothecar, for medecine gevin to the defunct, and as his acquittance gevin thairupoun sen his deceis beiris, nyne pundis, tua schillingis, vj.d.

Summa of the dettis awing to the deid, I^c.lxxij.lib. xv.s. ij.d.
Restis of fre geir, the dettis deducit, iij^c.xxxiij.lib. xj.s. ij.d.
Na division.

Followis the Deidis Latterwill, and Legacie maid be him upoun the thrid day of Januar 1569 yeiris, befoir Johne Robertsoun and Johne Rind, witnesses.

In the first, The said MAISTER HENRY constitut his sone adoptive, JAMES MELVILL, his only Executour and intromettour with his haill movable gudis. And becaus the gudis that he had ar only the plenising of his landis and manis, he himself could mak na speciall inventour thairof, bot committit the same to Thomas Myldis, his greve, to be maid be him, with aviss of his said sone, quhilk he appeirit to be als sufficient in all pointis as gif he had maid and subscrivit the same with his awin hand. Item, he ordinit quhatevir be contenit in Alexander Clerkis compt buke, the same to be payit with uther small triffles and soumes. Item, he left to Thomas Fyllane, ane boy at the scule with Maister William Riñd, in Sanct Johnestoun, to put him to ane craft, fourtie pundis : Of the quhilk he willit to haif na diminutioun, notwithstanding, peradventure, he left mair nor his fre gudis extendit to. Item, to Johne Robertsoun, twentie pundis. Item, to Alexander Clerkis wyf, his awne horse that he raid on, becaus he is not ane horse to pas in testament as airschip; nor yit willit he that the horse he gaif to the said Johne Robertsoun be put in testament, becaus I disponit the same to him twa yeiris syne. Item, in ane taken to Alexander Clerk, he left the lang burd, the lang sadill, and furme thairwith. Item, the bed that he lay in he left to the hospital, tymmer, and all utheris thingis pertaining thairto, except the cover thairof. Item, he left to his said Sonis wyf his damuss gown lynit with velvet, and the rest of his claithis of silk he left to be disponit be his said Sone. Item, he left to him the haill airschip, and utheris quhatsumevir being in the Halhill to his awne use, except ane fute of silver to ane cup with ane vice, quhilk pertenis to the said Helene Boiswell, and is hir awne. Item, he left his ryding coit and cloik to the said Thomas Myldis. Item, to Williame Patersoun, wrytar, my goun of serge, lynit with blak furring, and pewit in the breist with his Bibill. Item, to Christiane Scheves, sister to Patrik Scheves, xx.lib , gif it may spair; and the rest, gif ony be, I commit to the discretioun of my said Sone to gif to the purest and maist neidfu l of my freindis. And ordanis the Witsundayis chalmer maill and servandis feis to be payit of the reddiest of my gudis. Item, levis to the puir of Edinburgh, ten pundis. Item, to the boy of my chalmer, Johne Thomsoun, xl. s.

Sic subscribitur,
Maister Henry Balnaves of Halhill, with my hand.

Item, upoun the xx. day of Januar, the yeir abovewritten, he left to Patrik Scheves of Kenback foure scoir merkis, nochtwithstanding that he wes curatour to him, and that the said Patrik wes in his danger, and he not in his, and for helping him to pleneis his grund. Providing that gif it salhappin him to call or persew his executouris or intromettouris with his gudis, for ony caus preceding of the said Maister Henry, in that caise he willit be thir presentis, that his legacie expire, and be null of the self. And that the comptis be haid of his tyme of his curatorie, as salbe gevin up.

Sic subscribitur,
Mr Henry Balnaves of Halhill, with my hand.

Ita est. Willielmus Patersoun <i>Notarius in premissis requisitus.</i>

Compositio Quotte xx. merkis.   Summa quotte tuentie merkis.

We, Mrs. Robt. Maitland, etc., Commissaris of Edinburgh, speciallie constitute for confirmatioun of testamentis, be the tennour hereof, ratefeis, apprevis, and confermis this present Testament or Inventour, insafar as the samin is dewlie and lauchfullie maid of the gudis and geir above specifiit, and gevis and committis the intromissioun with the samin to the said James Melvill, sone adoptive to the said umquhile Mr Henry Balnaves, his onlie executour and intromettour with his haill movabill gudis, conforme to the lattir-will abovewrittin; reservand compt to be maid be the said James thairof, as accordis of the law. And he being sworne, hes maid fayth trewlie to exerce the said office; and hes fundin cautioun that the gudis and geir above specifiit salbe furthcumand to all parteis havand interes as law will; **as ane Act maid therupoun beris.**

THE CONFESSION
of Faith, conteining how the troubled
man should seeke refuge at his God,
*Thereto led by faith: with the declaratiõ of the
article of iustification at length. The order of
good workes, which are the fruites of faith: And
how the faithful, and iustified man, should walke
and liue, in the perfite, and true Christian
religion, according to his vocation.*
Compiled by M. *Henry Balnaues of Halhiil,* &
one of the Lords of session, and Counsell of SCOTLAND,
being as prisoner within the old pallaice of *Roane:*
In the yeare of our Lord. 1548.
*Direct to his faithfull brethren, being in like trouble or more.
And to all true professours and fauourers of the
syncere worde of God.*
Act. 1. Hab. 2. Rom. 10.
*He shall come, and shall not tary, in whome who beleeue,
shall not be confounded.*

¶ Imprinted at Edinburgh, by
Thomas Vautrollier. 1584.

In small 8vo, printed in Roman letter,
Sign. A to Vij., in eights.

To the Right Honourable and Vertuous Ladie, Alison Sandilands, Lady of Hormistoun,[1] Thomas Vautroilier,[2] her humble Servitour, wisheth Grace and Peace in Christ Jesus.

WHILE I consider, Noble Lady, how that after the miserable saccage of Jerusalem, utter wrake and overthrow of the cietie and temple thereof, lamentable leading till, and being in captivitie of the Jewes; and to the eyes of man the unrecoverable desolation of that whole common-weale, having nowe, as it were, lying so many years deadly buried; yet at the last, besides their deliverance which was most wonderful; how, I say, that wherin their greatest beautie and highest felicitie ever did stand; yea, the onely glorie wherein any people could excell, that is, the Lawe of God given by Moyses, was found out amongst the old and desperate ruines, undestroyed, unviolated, and safely preserved, as is to bee seene by the holy historie (2 Chro. xxxiv; 2 Kings xxii.) I can not but acknowledge the wonderful providence and exceeding great mercy of our God, in preserving from tyme to tyme his blessed law and word, (wherein onely consisteth the glorie and felicitie of his Church upon the face of this earth,) from depravation, corruption, and destruction, in whatsoever extreame dangers; howsoever the blinde Papistes cannot see this, without a visible and glistering succession of a

---

[1] Dame Alison Sandilands, daughter of Sir James Sandilands of Calder, is mentioned by Knox, in his History. (See vol. i. p. 237.) She became the wife of John Cockburn of Ormiston, in East Lothian. As their son, Alexander (*ib.* note 3, p. 185), who died in 1564, was Knox's pupil, it is most probable that this Treatise, from being discovered at Ormiston, had originally been transmitted to some of that family. This lady survived the publication only a very short period. According to the confirmation of her Testament, "Ane rycht honorabill lady, Dame Alesoun Sandelandis, auld Lady Ormestoun, relict of umquhil Johne Cockburne, laird of Ormestoun, deceissit upon the 21st day of October 1584." Richard Bannatyne, who is styled one of her servitors, signs as witness.

[2] Thomas Vautroullier, the Printer, was a French refugee, settled in Loudon, but who came to Scotland in the year 1584. (See Introductory Notice in vol. i. p. xxxii.; and Herbert's Typographical Antiquities.)

church to do the same. The like perswasion whereof, now in the whole body of the Scripture, now in some parts or portions of the same, the histories of tymes and memories of men do recorde; so that God's carefull providence and mercyful preservation, hath alwayes beene bent hereaway.

And if it be lesome[1] to compare small, base, and litle thinges unto such as are great, highe, and mightie; surely there was a certein prettie, learned, and godly Treatise, compyled by a divine Lawier, and honourable Sessioner of the King's Majestie his Session and publicke Counsell, which through the injuries of time, negligence of keepers, great and carefull distractions of the Author, was so lost, and, to the opinion of all, perished, that being earnestly coveted, greatly desired, and carefully sought for and searched out by some good, godly, and learned, as having some intelligence of the Author's travels in that part; yet it could never bee had, as desperate at any tyme to have beene able to bee recovered, untill to manis appearance of mere chance, but most assuredly by the mercyfull providence of our God, a certeine godly and zealous Gentleman, privy to the desires of some that so earnestly coveted it, being in the towne of Hormistoun in Lothiane, findeth the same in the handes of a child, as it were serving to the childe to playe him with, and so receaved and recovered the same. And as this Treatise was a prettie and gentill strand[2] of the aboundant fountaine of the Scriptures; Why might it not in this point savour of the own source, spring, and beginning? Why might not the birth, in such a case, follow the nature and condition of the womb; and, Why might not the daughter this farre even resemble the mother, or be of the same fortune, and, as it were, subject to the same fatalitie with her?

Wherefore, this Treatise comming to my handes as a singular token of the finder's loving-kindnes, and liberall will, and affection towards mee; considering the worthiness, utilitie, compendious learning, and singular godlines thereof, I could not either bee so inique[3] to the honourable fame of the godly Author; either so ingrate to the loving propiner and offerer unto me, either envious to the common-wealth of Christianitie, or sacrilegious towards God in suppressing his glorie in this point, as not to commit the same, by my travell, to a longer and more lastie[4] memorie: that so, in this raritie of trustie and

M. HENRY BALNAVES.

RICHARD BANNANTINE.

[1] Lawful.
[2] "Strand," or "strynd," a small stream, a rivulet.
[3] Unjust.
[4] Enduring, lasting.

faithfull handmaides, and great store of treasonable dealing of vile hyrelings, this lawful and loving daughter might, after a maner, and some what ancillat or famulat[1] (so to speake it after the Latines) to the owne mother, that is, to the Scriptures, whereof shee floweth and proceedeth.

And surely not a few nor small reasons moved mee to utter the same, Worshipful Lady, under the shadow of your name, and as it were dedicat it, at least my paines and travels in setting it out, unto your Honour. For, it being found and recovered in your ground and holding, and after a maner being the birth thereof; who can so justly as yee nowe and yours challenge the right of the same, after God's calling to his mercies the Author? It is also a work bredd and broght forth in that affliction and banishment for Christ's sake, in the which yee did breede and bring forth your dearest children. It is the worke of a faithfull Brother and most trustie Consellour, participant of all the afflictions, and continuing constant to the end, and in the end. It is such, that when as it was (I wot not howe) negligently letten bee[2] amongest the handes of babes to play them with, it was through God's providence recovered by that godly gentleman, your Ladyship's Secretarie.[3] It was RICHARD BANNANTINE. by that notable servant of God, whome the Larde, your husband of godly memorie,[4] and yee did ever so duetifully reverence, and JOHN KNOX. he so fatherly and Christianely love you, so earnestly cared for, and so diligently sought out and inquired of, that it might be preserved from perishing, as almost nothing more. And as the Booke of the Law, found in the Temple by God's providence, was presented to Josias, to renew again the covenant betwixt God and his people, and to bring them againe under his right obedience, and found them in his true knowledge and worshipping, which all now a long time had beene put in oblivion: Who wot[5] but the like is resembled and shadowed to you, and given you to understande and learne in finding this pendicle[6] of Godis lawe and word in your dwelling, that yee and yours may be put in mind of your duety towardes God, constantly to abyde by his trueth, and to see that hee bee truely served in your dominion: that yee and yours, thus first seeking the kingdome of

---

[1] Be an handmaid and servant.
[2] Allowed to be.
[3] Of Richard Bannatyne, Knox's faithful servitor, or amanuensis, who survived till the year 1605, some notices will be given in the concluding volume.
[4] John Cockburne of Ormiston died at Edinburgh, 2d November 1583, appointing by his will 'Alys Sandilands,' his spouse, executrix.
[5] Who knows.
[6] Compendium, or summary.

God and righteousnes thereof, then all other things may bee cast unto you. In case yee or they faile in so doing, it may be a testimonie against you or them, that God hath offered him self, even to be found by you, and in your ground, and yet ye have not rightly regarded him.

Surely these, with other reasons besides my duetie towards your Honour, moved me to set out this small Worke chiefly under your name. The utilitie whereof (I doubt not) shall be found so profitable, the delite so pleasant, the dignitie so excellent, that whosoever readeth it shall find them[1] greatly commodate[2] by the goodnes of God, the fountain thereof, joyfully delited by the Author or writer, and honorablie decored[3] throgh your meane, whereby they injoye the use of it.

Now, as to that that rests,[4] God ever preserve your Ladyship and yours, in his true feare; graunt you good dayes and long life, to the furtherance and advancement of his glory, and helping to the building up of the worke of his Church, and your eternall confort.

[1] Find themselves.
[2] Benefited.
[3] Adorned.
[4] That which remains.

JOHN KNOX, THE BOUND SERVANT OF JESUS CHRIST, UNTO HIS BEST BELOVED BRETHREN OF THE CONGREGATION OF THE CASTLE OF ST ANDREWES: &c.

[*See this printed at pages 5 to 11.*]

THIS Worke following, conteineth three principall parts. The First parte, How man, being in trouble, should seek refuge at God alone. And that naturally all men is subject to trouble, and howe profitable the same is to the godly. Last, of the cruell persecution of Sathan and his members against the chosen of God.

The Second part conteineth, How man is released of his trouble by faith and hope in the promisses of God, and therefore declareth the Article of Justification, proving that Faith onely justifieth before God, without all deserving or merite of our workes, either preceding or following faith. With a solution to certaine contrarie arguments, made by the adversaries of Faith and this Article; with the true understanding of such Scriptures as they alledge for them.

The Third and last part conteineth, The fruites of Faith, whiche are Good Workes, which every man should worke, according to their owne vocation, in every estate.

All this plainely may be perceaved in the life of our first parent Adam, which by transgression of God's commandement, fell in great trouble and affliction: from which hee should never have beene released, without the goodnesse of God had first called him. And secondly, made unto him the promisse of his salvation; the which Adam beleeving, before ever hee wrought good workes, was reputed just. After, during all his life, hee continued in good workes, striving contrarie Sathan, the worlde, and his owne flesh.

The Author,
unto the Faithfull Readers.

The love, favour, mercy, grace, and peace of God the Father, God the Sonne, with the illumination of God the Holy Ghost, bee with you all, my welbeloved Brethren, which thirste after the knowledge of the Word of God; and most fervently desire the same, to the augmentation and increasing of the Church of Christ, dayly to flourish in godly wisedome and understanding, through faith unfained, ever working by love. Amen.

THE I. CHAPTER.

1. *What should be the study of man: And what man should do in time of tribulation.*

As desirous as the wild hart is (in the most burning heat and vehement drouth) to seeke the could fontaine, or river of water, to refresh his thirst: So desirous should we be, O Lord God, to seeke unto thee, our Creator and Maker, in all our troubles and afflictions; and say with the Prophet David, " Wherefore art thou sad or sorowfull, O thou my soule or sprit, and why troubles thou me? Beleeve and hope surely in God;" that is, confide in his mercy, and call to remembrance the tyme by-past, how mercyfull, helply, and propiciant he hath bene to the fathers, and delivered them of their troubles: Even so shall hee do to thee if thou beleevest unfainedly in him, and seek hym in his worde; not inquiring his name,[1] what they call him, nor what similitude, forme, or shape, he is of, for that is forbidden thee in his lawe. Hee is that he is; the God of Abraham, Isaac, and Jacob; and the God of the fathers, to whome he made the promis of our redemption. He would show his name no other waye to Moyses (Exo. iii.), but commanded him to passe to the people of Israel, and say unto them, " He which is[2] hath send me to you, that is my name from the beginning, and that is my memorial from one generation to another."

PSAL. 41 & 42.
PSAL. 76.
PSAL. 21 & 104.

THE II. CHAPTER.

1. *How man comes to the knowledge of God.*
2. *Where shold man seeke God; and how he should receave him.*
3. *And by whome we should offer our petitions.*

By faith are wee taught to knowe God the Father, Maker and Creator of al, heaven, earth, and all creatures; whom we should

---

[1] That is, The maner how he will deliver.—(*Marginal note.*)

[2] That is, He, which of him self hath power and being, by whome all had their beginning, life, and moving.—(*Marg. note.*)

beleeve to be Almightie, of infinite power, mercy, justice, and goodnes; and that he created, in the beginning, all thing of nought, as the Scripture teacheth us, (Gen. ch. i.) And that by the Word (which is the Sone of God) he made all thing which is made: who is equall to the Father in devine nature and substance, without beginning, in the bosome of the Father, which was with God in the beginning, and was also God. And at the prefined and preordinate time, by God the Father was send into the world, and made man, taking our manly nature and cloathing him with the same, and dwelled among us. And after long time conversing amongst us, teaching and preaching the realm of heaven, being exercised in al trobles and calamities, in the which this our mortall body is subject (except sin only); finaly, for our sakes, suffered the most vile death for our redemption; and rose from the same the third day for our justification. And after forty daies ascended to the heavens, and sittes at the right hand of the Father, our advocat, as testifies the Holy Scriptures of him. And thereafter send the Holie Spirit to instruct his Disciples of all veritie, as hee had promised of before, who proceeding from the Father and the Sonne, the third person of the Trinitie, descended upon the Disciples in a visibile signe of fyrie tounges; by whome all creatures is vivificat and hath life; is governed, ruled, sustained, and comforted, without the which all creatures would turne to nought.

2. Of this maner knowe thy God, three Persons distinct in one substance of Godhead: confound not the Personnes, nor devide not the Godhead. But beleeve fearmly and indoubtedly as thou art teached in the Symbole of the Apostles, and of the holy man Athanasius, confessed in the holy church of Christ. Ascend no higher in the speculation of the Trinitie, than thou art teached in the Scriptures of God. If thou wilt have knowledge of the Father, seek him at the Sonne.[1] If thou wilt know the Sonne, seek him at the Father: For none knoweth the Sonne but the Father, and none may come to the knowledge of the Father but by the Sonne. And also Christ being desired of Phillip, one of his Apostles, to show them the Father (answeared), "This long time I am with you, and ye have not knowen mee, Phillip! He who hath seene me hath seene the Father;[2]

---

[1] That is, Give credit to the doctrine which Jesus the Sonne of God hath teached.—(*Marg. note.*)

[2] That is, Though my Father wer present, no other workes should he work then I have wroght in your presence; nor yet other doctrine should he teach to you nor I have done.—(*Marg. note.*)

beleevest thou not that I am in the Father, and the Father in me?"

Therefore, what ever thou desirest which good is, seeke the same at the Son; for the Father hath given all thing in his power. For that cause Christ commanded us all to come unto him, and seeing he hath al things given to him, and also commandeth us all to come to him, great fooles we are which seeke any other way, of the which we are incertaine, either in heaven or in earth. As concerning our salvation, wee are sure he loveth us, and will heare us according to his promise; "Greater love than this can no man showe, but that he put his life for his frendes:" Yea, verily, we being his enemies, he willingly gave him selfe to the death to get us life, and to reconcile us to the Father. Therefore, if we will have our thirst and drouth quenched and refreshed, seeke unto Christ, who is the fontain of lively water, "of the which, whosoever drinketh shall never thirst, but it shalbe to him a fontaine of running water to everlasting life."

^{3.}
^{MATH. II.}
^{JO. 4.}

THE III. CHAPTER.

1. *The fruit of tribulation unto the faithfull.*
2. *God is a peculiar Father unto the faithfull; what care he takes of them, and wherfore.*
3. *Tribulation the signe of God's love.*
4. *The judgement of the wicked concerning tribulation; what they do, and why they despaire therein.*

THIS vehement drouth and thirst had David, the holy Prophet, when he said, "O God, thou art my God,[1] of most might and power: therefore I seeke thee early in the morning; with most ardent desire my soule thristeth after thee, and my flesh desires thee." Great and fervent was this desire of the holy man, as ye may read the 62d Psalm, which teacheth us howe profitable, holesom, and commodious the trobles, afflictions, and incommodities of the world are to the faithfull and godly men. In so much, that the flesh, which ever of the own nature is adversarie and enemy to the spirit, drawing and entising the same from the true worshipping of God; with frequent troubles and calamities is so brokin and debilitat, that it takes peace with the spirit, and altogether most fervently seeks God, saying, "Bet-

¹
^{PSAL. 62.}
^{RO. 8.}

---

[1] That is, Thou alone art sufficient to save thogh all men be enemyes.—(*Marg. note.*)

ter is thy goodnes, mercy, and benignitie, the which thou showest to thy faithfull flock, then this corporall life; therefore my lippes shall never cease to praise thee." O happy is that trouble and affliction, which teacheth us thys way to know our good God, and moves this thirst in our soule, that we may learn to cry unto our God as the fathers did, "O thou my God!" (as David and S. Paul say in divers places.)

"I give thanks (sayth Paule) to my God for you, my bretheren." Howbeit hee be God to all creatures by creation; yet to the faithfull he is one speciall and peculiar God, whose troubles and afflictions he seeth and shal deliver them thereof, even as he did his people of Israell forth of the handes of Pharao, without all our deservings or merites. Therfore, let us not looke upon our merites, worthines or unworthines, but only to his mercy and goodnes, putting all our trust, hope, and beliefe into him, and into no other thing either in heaven or earth; and say with the Prophete David, "O Lord, my strength, I shall love thee." "The Lord is my surenes, my refuge, and my deliverance." And after, "Be unto me a God, defender, and a house of refuge, that thou mayest save me, for thou art my strength; and for thy names sake thou shalt lead me and nourish me." That is, I put no confidence in my owne strength, wit, nor manly power, but only into thy mercy and goodnes, by the which I am defended and preserved from al evils, and led and keeped in all goodnes; for thou takest care upon me, and art my only refuge, and strength unwinneable, in all my troubles and adversities.

Therefore, my welbeloved Bretheren, let us rejoice greatly of this our litle trouble and afflictions, and consider them to be good and not evil; the signs and tokens of the goodwill of God toward us, and not of ire nor wrath; and receave them forth of his hands, nether of chaunce, accident, nor fortune, but of his permission and certaine purpose, to our weale, as the tryall and exercysion of our faith. And that hee punisheth us, not that wee bee lost thereby, but to drawe and provoke us to repentance, according to that saying, "I will not the death of a sinner," &c.[1] In the which he requireth of us obedience, faith, and calling upon his name, as the Prophet David teacheth us, saying, "Call upon me in the day of thy trouble, and I shal deliver thee, and thou shalt honor me." That is, Beleeve me ever present with them which unfainedly call upon me, and I shall not abstract my favor, helpe, and supply from them; but shall so deliver them, that they may therfore give me

---

[1] Quhat God requires of us in time of tribulation.—(*Marg. note.*)

great thankes and praise: for I desire no other thing of man. This maner of trouble brings patience, and patience proufe, and proufe hope, which frustrates not, but greatly conforts the faithfull. ROME. 5.

The world hath another judgement of this trouble, and the wicked man, when the same happeneth to him, hee grudges and murmurs contrarie God, saying, " Why hath God punisht me? What have I done to be punisht of this maner?" Then gathers he in his heart, Had I done this thing, or that thing, soght this remeady or that remedy, these thinges had not happened to me. And so thinkes, that they are come to him either by chaunce or fortune, or neglecting of manly wisdome. Thus he fled from God, and turneth to the help of man, which is vaine. In the which finding no remeadie, finally in his wickednesse despaires, for hee can do no other thing, because al things wherin he put his trust and beliefe hath left him, and so rests no consolation. 4.

PSAL. 59, 61. 106.

THE IV. CHAPTER.

1. *What do the faithfull in time of tribulation.*
2. *What we have of our owne nature, and what of Jesus Christ.*
3. *What Adam did after his transgression.*
4. *The goodnes of God showen unto Adam.*
5. *What Adam wrought in his justification.*
6. *To Abraham, being an idolater, was made the promise that he should be the Father of many Nations; and the conclusion thereupon.*

But the godly say, O my good God, thankes and prayse be to thee, who hast visited thy froward child and unprofitable servant, and hast not suffered me to runne on in my wickednes, but hast called me to repentance. I know my offenses; justly have I deserved thys punishment, yea, and ten thousand times more for my sins, the which sore repenteth me. 1.

Our wicked nature teacheth us to fly from thee, to diffide or doubt of thy mercy and goodnes; and to excuse in our selfes our sinne and vice, and object the same in another, as our forefather Adam did; having no respect to person, or love of any creature more then he had; for contrarie his owne fellow, which was of his owne flesh, he objected the crime, to excuse himselfe! Yea, and also against God, thinking that the good 2.

work of God, making the woman, and geving her to hym in fellowship, was the cause of his sin and fall, as the Scriptures saye (Gen. ch. iii.) But faith in the bloud of thy onely begotten Sonne Christ Jesu, leadeth us to thy mercy-stoole, and hope conforteth us, that wee are not overcome in this battell; knowing perfectly that the flesche is subject to these bodyly afflictions, that the dregges of sin may be mortified in us, the which we have of our forefather Adam.

3. Thys corruption of nature teacheth us what we have of our first parentes, and what we are of our selfes; which being considered, shal lead us to the knowledge of God, in whome we shall find goodnes, mercy, and justice, as we may clearly perceave in our first parent. For, after he had transgressed the law and commandement of God, he fled from him, whom God followed, moved of love toward his handie work, and called him again; in the which he did shew his goodnes. And when he accused Adam of his sin, he was not penitent, nor trusted not in the mercy of God, or asked forgevenesse, but excused hys transgression and fault. Neverthelesse, God of his infinite mercy made the promes of salvation or ever he would prononce the sentence contrarie the man or woman; saying to the serpent, "I shall put enymity betweene thee and the woman, and betweene thy seed and the woman's seede. The Seed of the woman shal tread downe thy head, and thou shal sting the same on the heele." Adam was conforted with these words, and through faith in thys promis was of wicked made just, that is, receaved again in favour, and through faith in the bloud of Christ to be shed, was accepted as just.

4. And thereafter God manifested his ire and wrath contrarie sinne, which of his righteous judgement he can not suffer unpunished, and pronunced the sentence, first against the woman, and then against the man; and ejected them forth of Paradise, cloathing them with skinne coates;[1] saying, "Behold, Adam is made as it were one of us, knowing good and evil;" that is as much to say, O miserable man! now thou mayest perceave thy state, and the fruites thou hast gotten for the transgression of my commandement. What is thy knowledge that thou hast learned nothing but to fly from thy Maker, to passe from life to death, from great pleasure to all miserie? And so Adam is spoyled of all the noble gifts he was indued with in his creation, as here after [in] time and place at more length shalbe

NAHU. 1.
NU. 14.
GENE. 3.

---

[1] Skinne coates were the signe and remembrance of their mortalitie.—(*Marg. note.*)

showen. Read with order the third chapter of Genesis, and thou shalt understand this matter clearly.

Nowe, yee may see what was our first parentes part in the obteining of this promisse of God. Verylie, no more then he had of his creation, but rather lesse; for beyng but dust and clay, hee made no evill cause; but being made man, he disobeyed his Maker, trangressed his law, usurping glorie to hym selfe, and knowledge which became him not to seeke; for the which he deserved nothing but eternall dampnation. 5.

Abraham, in his father's house, an idolater as he was, and the rest of his house, made no good cause to God, nor merite to obteyne the promisse, that he should bee the father of all faithfull; but only beleeved in the promis of God, as hereafter shalbe discussed. But even as thei were accepted as just through faith, without all their merites or deservinges; so shall wee bee which are the sonnes of Abraham, and heires of the promisse. 6. GENE. 11 & 22 JOSU. 24.

No other way shold we seeke but the order taught us in the Scriptures of God, that is, if wee wilbe sure of our salvation, and have passage to the Father, passe unto Christ, who sayeth, " I am the waye, the trueth, and the life; no man commeth to the Father but by me." If yee had knowledge of me, ye should also have knowledge of the Father. Therefore, if we will walke right in the way, go with Christ, and walk in him. If wee will not bee deceaved, passe unto him; for he is the veritie who can nether deceave, nor be deceaved; and if we wil not die the eternal death, he is the life. These gifts may we have of no other but of him, and by him only through faith in the mercy of God, by the operation of the Holie Spirit. JO. 14.

THE V. CHAPTER.

1. *The consolation of Adam expelled from Paradise.*
2. *The consolation of Adam, whiche hee tooke of his two sons, turned in dolor.*
3. *What Adam did when hee receaved Seth for Abell, whome Cain slew.*
4. *The confort of Adam in all afflictions, and example left to us therinto.*

GREAT was the trouble and affliction both of body and spirite, which was in Adam, standing trimbling before God, whome hee had so highlye offended, perceaving him self deceaved of the 1.

false promise made by the Serpent, which was, that he shuld not die, howbeit hee eat of the aple, but should bee like unto God, knowe good and evill; being therefore ejected forth of that pleasant garden of all delite and pleasure, into the miserable earth, to eat his bread with the sweat of his face. Trust well, he was sore penitent now, and would have suffered great torment upon his body, to have satisfied for his offences; but that could not be, nor might not stand with the justice of God. What was his confort then? Nothing but this promise, which he apprehended by faith, and beleeved him to be in the favour of God; for that promiseth Seedes sake. This conforted his spirite, or els of despair he had perished in this sorrow and trouble; for he found no remeady in himself.

2. For his bodily consolation, God sent him two sonnes by naturall propagation to his owne image and similitude. This was no litle consolation and confort to Adam; but this bodilie confort[1] turned shortly into great displeasure, when the one brother slewe the other, of malice, by which Adam was destitute of all succession. Thus dolorously lead he his life a long time, desiring ever at God succession in place of Abell.

GENE. 3.

3. Of whome God had pitie and compassion, and sende him a sonne named Seth, of whome descended the promissed Seed, that God might be found true in his sayings; for rather would he have raysed Abel from death to life, then his promise shuld not have beene fulfilled. By this was the dolor and trouble of Adam converted into joy and gladness; for the which hee gave thankes unto God, saying, "God hath sent me another seed for Abell, whome Cain hath slain." Here he saith not that he hath gotten a sonne in place of Abell, howbeit by naturall generation he begat him, and Eve bare him of her bosom; but saith, God hath sent me another seede for Abell, ascriving the same to the gift of God, and not to the work of man. This is a notable example to al the faithful, to receave all thinges forth of the handes of God, giving him ever thankes therfore, as the holy fathers did; not contemning the work nor helpe of man, whom God maketh the instrument to do that thing which is his godly will to performe.

GENE. 4.

MARKE WELL.

4 Let us herefor tak example of our forefather, That like as he was subject to trobles and afflictions all the daies of his life in this miserable world; evin so are we, and let us take therefore all thing in patience, thinking us to have deserved the same justly, how just that ever we be, or appear to the world. Trust

---

[1] All pleasure of earthly thinges turnes and ends in sorrow.—(*Marg. note.*)

well there is, nor was never man which descended of Adam by naturall propagation, juster nor he was after his fall; for there is no mention in the Scripture of any offense done by Adam, contrarie the lawe of his God, after his expulsion forth of Paradise. And as for his first rebellion and corrupting of hys nature, we are all gilty of that as he was, and then also gilty of our sinnes proceeding of that rebellion; wherefore we may well be worse then he, but no better. Thinke well, he confessed him justly punished, and thought he deserved more punishment than ever was put upon him. Taking ever consolation of the sweet promises of God, in the which he beleeved; and in all his troubles conforted him with hope to be delivered of them, as all faithfull doe; and to be restored to the glorie hee was ejected from for his owin foolishnes; without al merits or deservings of himself, which ware nothing in him, and much les in us.

There hath beene no difference betweene the expulsion of Adam forth of Paradise, and Lucifer out of the Heavin, if the promisse had not beene made to Adam. Through faith in the which promise he ever hoped victory against the Devill,[1] who had deceaved him; and that by power and strength of the promissed Seed, and not through any power or might of him self. Even so should we do, confiding in the promisses of God, and the merites of the promised Seed, Christ Jesu, to be delivered of the tyrannie of the Devill, the calamities and trubles of thys miserable world.

THE VI. CHAPTER.

1. *Wherfore we should rejoyce in tribulation.*
2. *Under what pretext the wicked pursues the just.*
3. *Whereby ryseth the dishonoring of God.*
4. *The diversitie of opinions, touching the Article of Justification, and who are just before God.*
5. *What is the substance of Justification; and why the Article therof should be holden in memorie.*

To the faithful, these bodily afflictions and troubles are marveilous necessarie, for by them the faith is tryed, and made more pretious then gold, which is purified by the fire; for by

1. 1 Pet. 1.

---

[1] This victorie sall we obtein in the generall resurrection, for then both body and soule shalbe glorified.—(*Marg. note.*)

many troubles it is needefull to us to enter in the realme of heaven, by firme and constant persevering in faith, as sayth S. Paul. And also, it behoved Christ to suffer, and so to enter into his glory; that is, not for him self, but for us. Therfore the godly men, in theyre troubles and afflictions, take great consolation and confort, and anchors them upon God alone by faith; to whome they can come no other way, and thinke them no better nor greater then their Maister, Christ, but should take both confort and consolation of his word, saying, "Seeing the world hath persecuted mee, they shal persecute you also." This persecution is a communion with the passions of Christ, in the which wee have great matter to rejoyce, so we suffer not as homicides, theefes, or evill doers, but for Christ's sake and his word, as S. Peter sayth in his First Epistle, the fourth chapter.

<small>ACT. 14.</small>
<small>LUC. 24.</small>
<small>JO. 15.</small>

2. But in this matter take no care what the world judge of thee, but to thy owne conscience and the Scriptures of God: for the judgemente of the world pronunces contrarie to the Word of God, calling them, which professes the same, heretikes, seditious men, and perturbers of common weales. Therfore they thinke they punish justly, in birning, slaying, banishing, and confisking of landes and goodes. And howbeit the faithfull suffer all patiently and undeserved, yet they say they suffer justly as traitors, heretickes, homicides, perturbers of common weales, and evill doers. Let these sayinges not move thee, faithfull Brother, but confort thee with thy Maister Christ, who was called by the adversaires of veritie, a seducer of the people, a drunkard, a devourer or glutton, an open sinner, conversant amongest them, and an authorizare of their sins. His Apostles were called heretikes, and their doctrine heresie. The Prophets were called perturbers of common weales, and traitors to their countrie; prophesying contrary the common weale and libertie of the realme, as ye may reade of Elias and Jeremie in divers places of his Prophesie. Which Scriptures I praye you reade, and ye shall perceave no difference betwene the blasphemations of the Prophetes of Christ himselfe, and his Apostles, and the faithfull in these dayes; for all was and is done by the wicked under colour of holynes.

<small>JO. 7.</small>
<small>MATH. 27.</small>
<small>MAR. 2.</small>
<small>LUC. 5.</small>
<small>3 REG. 18.</small>
<small>JER. 20, 21, 25, 26, & 27.</small>

3. Herefore, let us seek refuge at our God, and sticke fast to his Word, who can nether deceave, nor be deceaved; for the world is full of deceit, and judgeth ever the wrong part; of the which unjust judgement commeth all the diversity of opinions, and sectes ruling this day in the church of Christ, to the dis-

<small>PSAL. 90.</small>

honoring of the name of God, deminishing of his glory, and no little perturbation of common weales. The cause hereof is the neglecting of faith, and taking from the same her due office, which is, to justifie only by her selfe, without the deeds or workes of the law.[1] That is, man of wicked is made just by the mercy of God, through faith in the bloud of Jesu Christ, without the deeds or workes of the law. This I dare affirme, because the Scriptures of God testified the same to be true, as herafter shalbe declared at length.

Here ryseth the contention; for some brags and boastes them to have faith, and have no works; and others rejoysing them to have faith, attribute and give the justification to works: others have workes, and looke nothing to faith, as hipocrites: and others again there are, the which have nether faith nor workes, as the plaine wicked and ungodly. My welbeloved Brethren, let us auctorise neither of these persons; for all they impung this Article of Justification. Against the first speakes S. James, in his Epistle. Against the next, Saint Paule speakes in his Epistles to the Romans, and Galathians, and divers other places. And against the other two kindes of men, the whole Scriptures speakes. 4.

By these considerations moved, I thought necessarie for my owne erudition and your confort, my welbeloved Brethren, to declare and forth show my beliefe concerning THE ARTICLE OF JUSTIFICATION, as the Scriptures teaches mee, having no respect to man's opinion, that thereby we may have consolation through our mutuall faith, and be more ready to give coumpt and reak- oning to all which aske of us any question of our faith. Al- wayes in this and all other thinges, submitting my selfe to the Scriptures of God, and aucthoritie of the faithful church of Christ, which is governed, ruled, keeped, and defended from all spot of heresie by the Holie Spirit; who moves this ardent thirst in our soule to seeke Christ, the fontaine of living watter; love and charity in our harts to Christ, our brother's salvation as our owne. The fondation and groundstone hereto is faith, and the shielde or buckler to defende us with against the fiery dartes of Sathan, at the which he ever shoots, becaus it is our victorie against him, and gets dominion of the world; but if he finde us destitute or disarmed of our shield, he shal wound us so, that hee may safely or lightly take us captive to his realme. Ther- fore, this our faith shold never be idle, but ever working by love; that is, to bee ever cled with our shield, being vigilant and

ROMA. 1.
1 PET. 3.

JO. 4.

1 JO. 5.
EPH. 6.

---

[1] Whereby man is made just.—(*Marg. note.*)

walkfull, because our said adversarie Sathan is ever going about us, as it were a roaring lion, seeking for the prey to devour or swalow; against whom we shold resist stoutly into faith, taking in our hand the sword of the Spirit, which is the Word of God, with the rest of the armour perteyninge to a Christian knight, specified by S. Paule, Ephesians the sixth chapter.

1 PET. 5.

5. The substance of the Article of Justification, is to cleave and stick fast by our God, knowing him our Maker and Creator, and to beleeve firmly and undoubtedly that wee are not righteous nor just of our selfs; nor yet by our workes, which are lesse nor wee; but by the helpe of another, the onely begotten Sonne of God, Christ Jesu, who hath delivered and redeemed us from death, the devill, and sinne; and hath given to us eternall life, as hereafter at length shalbe declared.

Above all thing the saide Article is to be holden in memorie, recent among the faithfull. And at every tyme and houre, driven and inculcat in their eares as it were a trumpet. Without the which faith (which is the fondation of the Christian religion and church of Christ) is made so darke and mistie, that no place shalbe founde where upon to build the perfite workes of faith.

THE VII. CHAPTER.

1. *What obtained Adam and Eve, seeking wisdome contrarie God's commandement; and what they which seekes justification other wayes then teacheth the Scriptures.*
2. *Whereby is the wicked man made just.*
3. *Where may Sathan enter, and where not.*
4. *What wrought the lawe into Adam, and the office thereof unto us.*

1. THE ground-stone and sure firme rock, whereupon all godly workes and vertues are builded, our said adversarie Sathan vexed in the Paradise;[1] when in the beginning he persuaded and entised our forefather Adam, and Eve, to leave their faith into God, their Maker and Creator, and consent to his false perswasion, which was, that through their owne wisdome, strength, and power, they might be made equall and like unto God, who gave them life, and promised the same ever to endure, with all pleasures and commodities in Paradise.

[1] The persecution of Sathan.—(*Marg. note.*)

The Devill perceaving the woman voide and without faith,[1] love, and feare of God, said, "Howbeit ye eat of the fruicts of this trie, ye shall not die the death; ye know not wherefore God hath forbidden you to eate of the same, but I shall show you the cause. God knoweth, that in what soever daye yee shall eate of the fruict of this trie, your eyes shall be opened, and ye shall be like Gods, knowing good and evill." This same persuasion hath all the wicked, which perswades man to trust to his owne workes, merites, power, and strength, therby to be made just, and to get greate rewarde of God, for doing of workes not commanded by God, but invented by man's vaine conceat, thinking that God shallbe pleased therewith. But surely, even as our forefather was deceaved, so shall we be if we consent thairto. Heerefore give trust to no thing in this case or matter, but to God and his word; keeping ever faith pure and clean, without all mixtion of works in the making of a wicked man just; and then our adversarie shall get no place to enter to deceave us. GEN. 2.

Ye shall understande that Adam knew good and evill before the eating of the aple, for that teached him the law of nature, and the other great wisedome hee was cloathed with, as yee may reade in Ecclesiasticus, the seventeenth chapter, saying, "God created them with the spirit of knowledge, and with wisedome and understanding. Hee fulfilled the harts of them, and shew unto them good and evill. His judgementes and justice also he shew to them." What then was the knowledge Adam got of the eating of the aple? Onely, that he had offended his good God, transgressed his law, the which shew to him his offences and sin. By this knowledge he understood that hee was fallen from the good state in which he was created, and shuld have remained (if he had obeyed the law of his God), into the miserable estate of sin; for he had never knowen what the trangression of the lawe had bene if he had not sinned. The law before taught him what he should doe and leave undone, what was good and what was evill;[2] and after he sinned, the lawe uttered the same to him, and broght him in knowledge thereof; for it can do no other thing to the sinner but trouble his minde, and bring upon him great feare and dread. This 3. ROM. 3.

---

[1] That is, Sathan, after he perceaved the woman doubt of the faith and verity of Godis word, durst affirme the contrarie, saying, "Though ye eate of the tree ye shall not die;" whereto the woman giving credit, transgressed Godis command; and so to doubt of Godis promis is rute of all wickidnesse.—(*Marg. note.*)

[2] The office of the law.—(*Marg. note.*)

<small>GEN. 3.</small> proves the sayings of God to Adam, inquiring, Who hath showen unto thee that thou was naked; but that thou hast eaten of the tree, of the which I commanded thou shouldest not eat?

4. This hatred and enimity is old, which Sathan hath moved contrary mankind, and had the beginning at the first creation of man, of malice conceaved, to bring man in the same rebellion he was in. This persecution of Sathan shal endure to the latter judgement: Therefore let us bee walkefull and diligent, ever <small>1 PET. 29.</small> armed with our shield [of] faith, the Word of God ever printed in our hartes, taking no care of worldly troubles, hoping hastely to be delivered therefrom; considering we have no permanent citie here, but as pilgrimes, travailing to and fro, beholding <small>1 PET. 2. HEB. 13.</small> and looking for that heavinly citie and place, prepared to us from the beginning of the world.

THE VIII. CHAPTER.

1. *Wherefore Cain slew Abell: Howe long God suffered the Article of Justification to be pursued by the seede of Cain.*
2. *What paine hee tooke at last, and howe Sathan reserved his seede.*
3. *Whereof sprang the Idolatrie, whiche abounded betweene the dayes of Noe and Abraham; and under what pretext it was defended.*

1. SHORTLY hereafter, the said adversarie (a mankiller and lyer) <small>1 JO. 3.</small> perswaded and entised the one brother to slaye the other, of malice, without any cause but that the one brother, Abell, being just and godly, offered into faith a more pleasant and acceptable sacrifice unto God, then the other,¹ Cain, who was wicked, and an hipocrit, whose sacrifice pleased not God, becaus the person was not acceptable to him. Therefore God looked to Abell, and to his workes; unto Cain and his workes he looked not.

2. There followed against the saide Article, the perpetuall perse- <small>GENE. 4.</small> cution of Sathan, intolerable by the sonnes of Cain, while God was compelled (provoked of his ryghteous judgement) to drowne the whole worlde, and once to purge the same from sin; reserv-

---

¹ Cain gloried hee was the first begotten, and thought therefore he was acceptable. But Abel knew him self a sinner, seeking for Godis favor by that promised Seed alone.—(*Marg. note.*)

ing and defending (through his mercy onely) the perauthor of faith and righteousnesse, Noe. Neverthelesse, Sathan keped his seed in the third sonne of Noe, Cham, as testifies the historie. GENE. 2.

After this, the whole world, rysing in a madnes and fury, impugning this Article of Justification, finding and inventing innumerable idols and religions, with the which they pretended to please God; with their owne works and inventions, everie one making to him selfe a particular or peculiare god or gods. The which is no other thing but to think, that without the help of Christ, of their owne power, workes, and inventions, they may redeeme them selves from sin and all evils, and please God with their free will and naturall reason.

From Noe unto Abraham, our saide adversarie Sathan, so covered this article, that no outward testimony is found therof in Scripture. And, trust well, the Fathers, all this time had many pleasant workes, invented of their own conceat, good intention, and naturall reason, having some footsteppes of the examples of the holie fathers, by which they beleeved to please God; but it was not so indeed, because they followed the examples of the fathers in the outward workes and ceremonies, but not in faith, and so all became idolaters.[1] And the same ceremonies, and most shining workes, appeare to be most excellent in the offspring and posteritie of Cham; because his nephew Nimrode began first to be myghtie in the earth, and usurped to him the kingdome of Babilon. It is not to presume that the preaching of Noe, and the Word of God taught to him and his sonnes by the mouth of God, and his maner of sacrifice, was past from their memory; but man is lyghtly drawn from faith and the word, to his owne conceat, and vain intention, to the exercising of the outward deed, in the which man wil never be sene to do evil, so there appeare any maner of outward holines in his works; the which he defends to be holy and good, because the holy fathers did so; and have no respect to faith, which maketh the work acceptable and pleasant in the sight of God, without the which al is but idolatrie, how holy that ever the worke appeare. And so enters Sathan, and rules mightiely, as he did amongst the fathers to the time of Abraham. 3.

GENE. 4.
GENE. 3.

MARK DILI-
GENTLIE.

[1] The wicked florish in earth.—(*Marg. note.*)

THE IX. CHAPTER.

1. *God renewed to Abraham the promise made to Adam of the blessed Seed, wherto Abraham beleving is pronounced just.*
2. *Though the just be ever persecuted, at last they prevaile.*
3. *Wherfore are we brethren to Jesus Christ.*
4. *The wrong judgement of the fleshly man touching the chosen of God.*

1. GOD of his infinit mercy and goodnes, moved of love, which he bears to mankind, (seeing our adversary ruling so mightely,) would steir up this Article of Justification in Abraham, that his Church should not perish, commanding him in these words: "Passe furth of thy father's house, and from thy freends, and furth of thy own countrie, and cum into the land which I shall showe thee." That is asmuch to say, As thy father, his household, and the whole countrie in the which now thou makst thy dwelling, thy whole nation and kindred ar all idolaters; therefore of my mercie and grace, without thy merites or deservings, I will call thee to the faith, and raise up in thee the ground-stone of my Church, and make thee the father of all the faithfull. This exposition ye shall finde in the book of Josua, the twenty-fourth chapter, for the Scripture is the best interpreter of it selfe.

GENE. 12.

2. And [God] so stirred up this article in the person of Abraham, in these words, saying, "I shall make thee in a great nation, and shall blesse thee, and shall magnifie thy name. And thou shalt be blessed; I shal bless them that bless thee, and curse them that curse thee, and in thee shall all nations of the earth be blessed." This is the renewing of the promes maid to Adam in the Paradise, "That the Seed of the woman should tread down the serpent's head." Heir shall ye finde the beginning of the faith of Abraham; who past forward as God commanded him, to whome he gave credence, and surelie beleved in his promisse; and left all worldlie affections, committing him wholy into the hands of God, depending only upon his word, beleeving the same trew; hoping to obtein all things which were promised him by the Word of God, of the which he had deserved no thing; for the Scriptures testified him to be no other but an idolater as his father was. After this, God drave and inculcat this Article of Justification in the eares of Abraham, saying, "Dreid not, Abraham, I am thy defender, and rewarde above measure, &c. Thou shalt have him to be thy heire that shall passe forth of thy bosom. Thy seede shalbe

GENE. 21.

as the starres of the heaven. Abraham beleeved God, and it was reputed to him for ryghteousnesse," &c. Here ye see the proceeding of this article from faith to faith, ever continuing in more perfection day by day. ^{JO. 4.} ^{GEN. 15.}

Then began Sathan, our adversary, newly to impung this article, ever to annul the promise of God; and as he perswaded Cain to pursue Abel, even so perswaded he Ismael to pursue Isaac; Esau, Jacob; and the rest of the brethren, young Joseph, whom they sold, as testifies the historie. Thus still continued the old hatred and enmitie betwen the seed of the serpent and the seed of the woman.[1] That is, the wicked pursue ever the chosen and godlie, which ar the woman's seed that treadeth down the serpentes head. For even as Christ, the blessed Seed, hath obteined victory of our adversary; so shall we by faith in him, of whose flesh and bones we are, and he of ours: That is, we are members of his body, and brethren to him, by two reasons; the one is, that he is made man and of our flesh, the naturall begotten sonne of the glorious Virgin Marie, and so of Adam, is said our brother. The other reason is, that by him, and through him by faith in the mercy of God, we are the sons adoptive of God, and so his brethren, and fellow-heires of the heritage with him. [3.] [JO. 5.] [EPH. 6.] [JO. 7.] [MATH. 27.] [MAR. 2.] [LUC. 5.]

The fleshlie man and worldly judgement is deceaved in the knowledge of this seed, as our mother Eve was; for she said, after she had conceaved and borne Cain, "I have gotten or possessed a man by God;" that is, according to the promis made by God, I have gotten the seed that shal tread down the serpentes head. Here she looked not into faith, but tooke the fleshlie reason of the first begotten sonne. But when she saw hee slew his brother, then she understoode him to be the seede of the serpent. Therfore, when she bare Seth she held her peace, because she knewe her selfe deceaved before in the opinion of Cain: And then cleaved to faith as Adam did, saying, "God hath given to mee an other seede, for Abell whome Cain hath slaine." [3 REG. 18.] [JERE. 20, 21, 25, 26, & 27.] [PSAL. 90.]

Abraham beleved of his fleshly judgment, that Ismaell was the promised seed; as appeareth by the answear he made to God, when he said to him, "Sarai shall bare unto thee a sonne, whome I am to bless," &c. Abraham smiled in his harte, and said, "Wold to God Ismael might live before thee."[2] But here- [GEN. 17.]

---

[1] The seede of the serpent, and the seede of the woman.—(*Marg. note.*)

[2] As he would say, Sufficient have I receaved of thy mercy, in that thou hast given to me a sonne of whom I am content.—(*Marg. note.*)

after admonished by the mouth of God to obey Sarai, and expell Agar and hir sonne, for he should have no parte of heritage with Isaac, he understood spirituallie, and obeyed the voice of his wyfe.

GEN. 21.

4. The seed of the serpent contended with the seed promised in the bosome of that noble and godlie woman Rebecca, being both of one conception. This contention moved the mother to say, "Better I had remained still barren, then to have this displeasure." To whome God gave consolation, saying, "There is in thy bosom conceaved two sundry nations, and two people shalbe devided of thy belly." That is, thou knowes not which of them is the seede of the promesse, the youngest have I chosen, to whome the eldest shall serve. This is conforme to the sayinges of S. Paule (Rom. ix.) But, trust well, she understood spiritually by faith that Jacob was the promised seede, when shee procured and laboured so diligently that he should get the blessing of his father, and defrauded the eldest, Esaw. This was not known to Isaac, for he wold not only that Esawe should succeede to the heritage, but to have gotten the blessing also, which Jacob obtained by perswasion of his mother. Nevertheless, Esaw remained with the heritage in his father's house, and ceased not still to pursue Jacob, who at last was compelled to fly for feare of his life. And so ever the seede of the serpent pursues the chosen, conforme to this beginning: Let Abell dye and Cain live. But finally, the seede of Jacob succeeded to the land of promission, and injoyed the heritage; howbeit they were long troubled and afflicted in Egipt.

GEN. 25.

GEN. 27.

THE X. CHAPTER.

1. *The wrong opinion of the Jewes of the promised Seede.*
2. *Wherin the ungodly place justification.*
3. *Sathan moves his members against the true professours of faith.*
4. *Jeremie, the prophet of God, resisted the whole ecclesiasticall power of the Jewes.*
5. *The head of the serpent troden downe by the death of Jesus Christ.*
6. *The article of justification preached after the death of Christ.*

1. YE shall understand that the Jewes had a fleshly opinion of this promised Seede: for they understood that the Messias which

was promised to them, should rule temporaly as David did; and establish his realme in great quietnes and rest, with all pleasure and voluptuousness, as yee may understand by the desire of the mother of the sons of Zebedee. Her sons, being with Christ and his Apostles, were of the same opinion, as testified the aunsweare of Christ, saying to them, "Yee knowe not what ye aske." But the spirituall knowledge which the fathers had, was farre different therefrom, who understoode in the spirit that the realme of Christ was spirituall and not temporall, to the which they were led by faith. MATH. 20.
MAR. 10.

By this yee shall understande, not only that the fleshely judgement is deceaved in knowledge of this Seede. but also of the persecution of Sathan; ever perswading the wicked and ungodly, which are his seede, to persecute the woman's seede of the promisse; that is, the chosen, who, according to the promisse of God, obtaine victorie by faith in the bloud of Christ. For Sathan, intending to destroye this Article of Justification, may not suffer the preaching thereof; that is, that by grace, through faith, and not of our owne righteousnesse and workes, we ar made safe, please God, are receaved into favour with him, and accepted as righteous and just, not of our merites or deservinges; but through the merits of Christ Jesu our Saviour.

2. By the contrary, the wicked trusts in their owne strength and merites, and will have their good works, invented by them selfe, without the commandement of God, a part of their salvation. And who will not authorise the same, they persecute of deadly hatred, and must needes dye as Abell did. So, Let Abell dye and Cain live; that is our law, sayeth the ungodly.

3. In the church of the Jewes, our saide adversarie ceased not to impung this Article, and perswade the wicked to persecute the godly, and kill the prophets for preaching the same. For 4. defence of the which, Jeremie the Prophet resisted the whole ecclesiastical power and authoritie of the church of the Jewes, that is, the multitude of the wicked, being a few number of the chosen that assisted to him, as yee may reade Jeremie, the twenty-sixth chapter. Not the less, afterward, hee was stoned to death for the same cause, which is the reward of man, that is, which man giveth for the true preaching of this article. So, Let Abell dye and Cain live.

5. Finally, the persecution of Sathan, our adversary, perswaded the death of Christ, his Apostles, and Martyres, and their true successours, all for this article. But ever Christ got victorie, and triumphed by his Word only. In so much as he got vic-

torie of the Devill, hell, and death; of the lawe, sinne, the world, and the fleshe, through his death and resurrection.

6. So, by faith in his bloud, al the Prophets, Apostles, Martyres, and Confessors, with their bloud have watered the Church, and have left a sure testimonie to us, for confirmation of this Article, that in the bloud of Christ, and not in their owne bloud, workes, or deedes, they are made safe, and have gotten the realme of heaven, conquest and purchased to them by Christ, and not by them selfes, nor their merites. The which confession is the cause that the godly ar ever persecuted by the wicked. So, Let Abell dye and Cain live; that is our lawe.

THE XI. CHAPTER.

1. *How Sathan hath deceaved the worlde after Christ, and wherewith he hath cled him.*
2. *An evident argument, showing them which this daye are called Bishoppes, to be the Church malignant.*
3. *An exhortation to them which enter in the church by the Popes authoritie; and of his power to make bishops.*
4. *Wherein the wicked Jeues gloried, and wherein the Pope and his kingdome.*

1. Now our adversary, perceaving by the death of Christ that the promise made in Paradise was fulfilled, and his head troaden down, that is, his power and strength by the sheding of the bloud of Christ; this Article of justification laid so abroad, and the Church of Christ is so strongly edged with the same, that all his imaginations, with the which he deceaved mankind, had no place to pervert the perfite faith. Then invented he a new maner of habite, which hee founde in the same church amongst the slouthfull ministers, whome (by processe of time seeing them idle and not occupied in the reading, teaching, and preaching of the Scriptures) hee provoked to invent workes of their own conceite. And also to abuse the holy sacramentes, and good workes of God, with vaine superstitions, the which they call good workes. And by this meanes he hath so drawen them from faith, that they knowe not what the same is; nor what Christ is, but as it were, a theefe hanged upon a gallous or gibbit innocently; or like another maner of prophane history of Hector, or of the great Alexander: And therefore hath provoked them to pursue this article more cruelly then ever it was

pursued from the beginning of the worlde. Them selfes by worde confessinge the same with their mouth, reading, singing, and, of their maner, dayly teaching and preaching the same. And yet, nevertheleste, dayly burning, killing, and banishing the true faithful preachers of the said article and confessours therof. And so ever shall Abell dye and Cain live; that is our lawe, say they.

Our said adversarie, that he should not be perceaved, hath transformed him selfe in to an angell of light. That is, in forme of holynes, he hath entred in the church in wonderfull subteltie;[1] for hee hath cled him with the most honest and shining works, invented this day by mennis wit or reason, (yea, with the same works commanded also by God,) and by them maintaineth and defendeth him self wholy. Yet verilie, he hath cled him with the blessed sacrament of the body and bloud of Christ; for hee can well disguise him in workes, with pride, vaine glorie, hipocrisie, diffidence, dispaire, idle faith, as to beleeve the historie onely, presumption of the owne merites, &c. But in perfite faith, which is the ground-stone of this article of justification, he can never enter. Therefore, under colour of holines he hath caused, and dayly causeth, the Prelates of the Church (as they call them), who should of their vocation have (to the shedding of their bloud) defended this article, pursue the same most cruelly with all tormentes invented by man's wit, under the false pretence of good workes, having no respect to faith. And so shall Abell dye and Cain live.

Ye shall understand, that the oft repeating of the death of Abell, and the life of Cain, is no vaine storie nor purpose, but the true similitude of the Church of Christ, which, first watered with the bloud of Abel, remaineth example to this houre, and shal to the seconde comming of Christ to the latter judgement. In the which two persons is set forth to us the perfite knowledge of the church, which consistes in the godly and ungodly.[2] And ever the perfite and just churche is pursued with the wicked, and never pursueth, by which the Disciples and servauntes of Christ are knowen, as testifie the Holy Scriptures.

I exhort you which are adversaries to this article of justification, consider with your selfe if ever ye read the history in canonical Scriptures, or prophane histories, that ever the true and perfite Church, from the beginning of the world to this

---

[1] Where may Sathan enter and rule.—(*Marg. note.*)

[2] Which shalbe separate when the Lord shal send forth his angels in his harvest.—(*Marg. note.*)

houre, persecuted any, but ever was persecuted, and the godly glad thereof. Herefore, the forme and order of this tyrannicall persecution used this day by them having the ecclesiasticall power in their handes, against the faithfull professours of this Article, I judge to be of the Devill, and may say truely to them, as Christ saide to the Scribes and Pharisies, "All the bloud which is shed, from the bloud of Zachariah, whome they slew betwene the altare and the temple, shall come upon these cruell tirantes," which impunge this article, and slaye the faithfull professours thereof. Against these sayings, the adversaries of faith and veritie crye,[1] "The Canon lawe, the aucthoritie of the Church, the long consuetude, the expmples of the Fathers, the Bishop of Rome's aucthoritie, the generall counsels; Heresie, heresie!" So there is no remeady, but, Let Abel dye and Cain live; that is our lawe.

<small>LUC. 11.</small>

3. My hartes! yee which have entered in the Church of Christ, by the Bishoppe of Romes law and aucthoritie, with his faire bulles, your shaven crounes, smearing you with oyle or chreame, and cloathing you with all ceremonies commanded in your law. If yee thinke you therethrough the successours of the Apostles and fathers of the church, ye are greatly deceaved, for that is but a politike succession or ceremonial. The succession of the church is farre otherwyse, the which requireth you to have knowledge in the Scriptures of God, to preache and teache the same, with the other qualities and conditions conteined in the Scriptures, as hereafter shalbe shown in the speciall vocationis: Of the which, if ye be expert, and your vocation lawfull, according to the Worde of God, doubtles ye are the successours of the Apostles, and have the same auctority they had committed to them by Christ. And, if ye want the saide conditions and qualities, yee are but reaving wolfes, clede with shepe skinnes, what authoritie that ever the Bishop of Rome give you. For it is no more in his power to make a bishop of him which can not preache, nor hath the knowledge to rule the flocke committed to his care, according to the Word of God, then it is in his power to make an asse to speake or bee man, or yet cause a blinde man to see. Therefore, I pray you, learne the Scriptures, that ye may walke in youre vocation right: For of your succession yee have no more matter to glorie, then the Jewes had to glorie against Christ, calling them the sonnes of Abraham, whom he called the sonnes of the Devill. They gloried in the carnall succession, and ye glory in the politike or cere-

<small>1 TIM. 3.</small>
<small>TIT. 1.</small>

<small>NOTE WEL.</small>

<small>JO. 8.</small>

---

[1] The voyces of the wicked.—(*Marg. note.*)

moniall succession; and all is one thing. God sende you knowledge and understanding of his Worde, that yee may cease from your tyrannie, and the true faithfull may live in rest and quietnes.

THE XII. CHAPTER.

1. *The division of justice in generall, with the definition of every part thereof.*
2. *The cause that no man is just by the law.*
3. *Scriptures and examples proving all men (except Jesus Christ) to be sinners.*

LET us passe forewarde in the discussing of this Article of JUSTIFICATION;[1] for knowledge of the which, necessarie it is to showe what justice is of man, what of the lawe, either of God or man; which being shortly discussed, wee shall the more easily come to the knowledge of our Christian Justification; which is a thing farre above all law, either of God or man; for it is the justice by the which a wicked man is made just, through faith in the bloud of Jesus Christ, without the works of the lawe; because of the deedes of the law no flesh shalbe made just before God,[2] as the Apostle saith. This is asmuch to say as, because no man fulfilleth the law, nor doth the deedes and workes of the same, in the pure and cleane estate, as the lawe required them to bee done, according to the puritie of the same, therfore the law can pronunce none just before God. ROM. 3. GALATII. 2.

This worde justice, or righteousnesse generally,[3] by the philosophers is taken commonly for the obedience and outwarde honesty, according to all vertues of morall maners, the which a man may doe and performe of his owne power and strength. This is called an universall or general justice, after the philosophicall definition. The same, S. Paule called the righteousnesse of the law or workes, because the transgressours of this justice are punished as wicked and unrighteous: for whome the lawe is made and ordinate, as Saint Paule sayeth (1 Tim. ch. i.), for the just needeth no law. These morall maners and discipline, is the most excellent rayment or habite wherewith man may bee cled. Nevertheles, they cannot make a man just before

---

[1] The entres to the Article of Justification.—(*Marg. note.*)

[2] The cause that no man is just by the law.—(*Marg. note.*)

[3] Justice in general.—(*Marg. note.*)

God, nor is not the justice which we speak of here in this Treatise.

The Politike or Civill Justice is, the obedience which every subject and inferiour estate of man giveth to their prince and superiour, in all the worlde. The which proceedeth of the lawe of nature, and is a good worke; without the which obedience (to the punishment of the wicked and defence of the just) no common-weale might bee conserved and kept in rule and order, but all would run to confusion. Therefore are princes and higher powers commanded of God to be obeyed, as his good worke, for they ar the ministers of God unto good. Neverthelesse, yee shall never finde man so just in fulfilling this justice; but the lawe of nature shall accuse him that hee hath not done his whole duetie, whiche the same requireth. Neither the prince to the subject, nor the subject to the prince, nor equall to equall, that is, neighbour to neighbour. The knowledge of this lawe of nature is borne with man, prented in his harte with the finger of God. And therefore, let every man consider his owne estate, and hee shall perceave, that if God wil accuse him with this law, he shall not be found just, "because of the deedes of the law no flesh shalbe found just before God." Notwithstanding, hee which doth the deeds of this law and is obedient thereto in doing and leaving undone, according to the external works, is so reakoned just before man,[1] and liveth in the same; and therefore hath the name of justice.

The Ceremoniall Justice is, the obedience and fulfilling of the statutes, ordinances, and traditions of man, made by the Bishop of Rome, and other bishops, counsels, schoolemaisters, and householders, for good rule, and order, and maners, to bee kept in the church, schooles, and families. This is a good work, and necessarie to be had with these conditions;[2] that is, that they be made not repugnant to the law of God; and that through keping of them, no man thinke him the holyer before God; nor yet therefore to obteine remission of sinnes, or to bee found rightuous before God. Nor yet that the same may bind or oblish any man to the observing of them, under the paine of deadly sinne. Neverthelesse, how well that ever ye observe or keep them, that is, this Law Ceremoniall, ye shall not bee found just therethrough before God, becaus of the deeds of the lawe no flesh shalbe found just before him.

---

[1] What is to be just before man.—(*Marg. note.*)

[2] The thinges which should be eschewed in keeping ceremonies.—(*Marg. note.*)

The Justice of the Law Morall, or Moyses Law, which is the law of God, exceedeth and is far above the other two justices. It is the perfite obedience required of man, according to all the works and deeds of the same. Not only in externall and outward deed, but also with the inward affections and motions of the hart, conforme to the commandement of the same, saying, "Thou shalt love thy Lord God with all thy hart, with all thy mind, with all thy power and strength: and thy neighbour as thy selfe." This is no other thing but the law of nature, prented in the hart of man in the beginning; now made patent by the mouth of God, to man, to utter his sin, and make his corrupted nature more patent to him selfe. And so is the lawe of nature and the lawe of Moyses joined together in a knot, which is a doctrine teaching all men a perfite rule, to know what he should do, and what he should leave undone, both to God and his neighbour. ^{DEUT. 10. MATH 22. MAR. 12.}

The Justice of the Lawe is, to fulfill the law, that is, to doe the perfite workes of the lawe as they are required from the bottome of the hart; and as they are declared and expounded by Christ: And whosoever transgresseth the same, shall never be pronounced just of the law. But there was never man that fulfilled this lawe to the uttermost perfection thereof (except onely Jesus Christ). Therefore, in the lawe can we not finde our justice, because of the deedes of the lawe no fleshe shalbe made just before God. 2. ^{MATH, 5, 6, & 7.}

For the probation hereof, wee will showe the aucthorities of the Scripture from the beginning; how the most holy fathers were transgressours of the law, and therefore could never be made righteous by the same. And if they which were most holy could not be found just by the deeds of the law, much lesse may the wicked be pronounced just by the same! Therefore, wee must take this conclusion, with the Apostle S. Paule, "All have sinned, and have neede, or are destitute, of the glory of God;"[1] and are made just, freely by grace, through faith in the bloud of Jesus Christ. ^{ROM. 3.}

Adam, first, in the Paradise, transgressed the law, and therefore the same accused him, and condempned him and all his posteritie, as rebels and transgressours of the same to the death. Neverthetes, the law remaineth still holy, just, and ^{GEN. 3.}

---

[1] That is, By original sinne all man is become blind, and is fallen from that image of God (which was, integritie of nature, justice, and righteousnes) in which man was first created, and now is cled with the contrarie.—(*Marg. note.*)

good, requiring the same holynesse, justice, and goodnesse of us, as testified S. Paule (Rom. vii.); And because wee doe not the same, the lawe ever accused us, and pronounced us rebelles and transgressours as our forefather Adam was; who might never be pronounced just by the law, because of the deeds of the law, no flesh shalbe made just before God.

3. And seeing all men gotten by naturall propagation hath descended of Adam, he is corrupted and rebel to the law as Adam was; for he might get no better sonnes nor his nature was. This corruption is so infixt in the nature of man, that hee is never cleane purged thereof, so long as this mortall body of sin and the spirit remaineth together. And that is the cause why wee fulfill not the lawe, in the pure and cleane forme as the same requireth the deedes thereof to be done. For this cause S. Paule sayeth, "Now I worke not this evill, but the sinne which dwelleth in me; for I know there dwelleth in me (that is, in my flesh) no good; for the good which I would, that doe I not, but the evill which I would not, that doe I." As Paule wold say, so rebellous is my wicked nature to the affections of my spirit, that the very things which I know good and would doe, for weakenes may I not complete. I would love, feare, honor, and thanke God, with all my hart, and all my strength, and adheere to his promise, in every houre, and all tribulation; but by the wicked fleshe I am impedite to doe the same. For howbeit, I have feare and love begun into me, yet are naturall securite and concupiscence impediments, that they be not pure and perfite as the law requireth. And albeit I have faith begun in me, which teacheth that God is true in all his promisses, yet natural dubitation and imbecillity causeth me frequently to doubt if God shall deliver.[1] And so murmurs sometime the fleshe, and loves not God with all the hart. Here, my hartes, ye may learne at the Apostle to know this corruption of nature: for he gives the example in himselfe, and in no other, teaching every one of us to judge our selfe and not our neighbour.

ROM. 7.

ORIGINAL SINNE.

This corruption of nature is called Originall Sinne, which is the wanting of originall justice, that should have beene in man according to his first creation. This corruption of nature followed the fall of Adam, in all men, that the nature of man may not truely obey the lawe of God, nor fulfill the same, for the inherent faultes and concupiscence in the hart of man, engendred of this corrupted nature, and so can not be pronounced just by

---

[1] Let every man judge, if in time of tribulation hee finde not this battel within him self.—(*Marg. note.*)

the lawe, because, of the deedes of the law no fleshe shal bee made just before God.

From Adam to Noe, from Noe to Abraham, and from Abraham to Moyses, induring the which space and time we can finde none of the holy fathers (which lived under the law of nature) pronounced just by the deeds of the law; but all were sinners and transgressours of the lawe, as Adam was, as testifieth the whole history of Genesis. Therefore, the justice of a Christian man shall we not finde in the law, because, of the deedes of the law no flesh shal bee found just before God.

Moyses, who was mediatour betwene God and his people of Israell, in giving of the law of the two tables, (which is but a declaration of the lawe of nature right understand.) fulfilled not the lawe, as yee may reade in the booke of Numbers, the twentieth chapter,[1] where Moyses and Aaron ar both reprehended of God for their diffidence and incredulitie, the which is the breaking of the first commandement of God; and a great and weightie sin, howbeit the reason of man cannot consider it; yea, veriely greater and weightier before God then either slaughter or adulterie. In the sight of man the crime appeares but small;[2] for God gave commandement to speake to the stone, or rock, in presence of the people, and charged the same to give water; but they spak to the people with a doubt, saying, "May not God give you water out of this rocke?" and then stroke upon the stone twise, which gave water aboundantly. But God would not pretermit the punishment of their unfaithfulnes, saying, "They should never enter in the land promised to the people of Israell." And Moyses also testified no man to be innocent before God, but by favour and imputation of grace through faith. And howbeit Moyses repented sore the said offence, and prayed fervently that he might enter into the land of promise, he was not heard; for God would not alter his sentence, as yee may collect of the saying of Moyses (Deut. ch. iii.), where God saith to him, "Speak no more to me of that matter; thou shalt not passe over the water of Jordane." Here ye may see that man can finde no justice in the lawe which is of value before God. [EXOD. 34.] [EXOD. 35.]

Job, who was commended by the mouth of God the most just in earth, could finde no justice in the law. For howbeit he was innocent in the sight of man, hee might not enter in judgement with God; because the justice of man is nothing before

---

[1] The breaking of the first commandement.—(*Marg. note.*)
[2] The sin of Moyses, and punishment therof.—(*Marg. note.*)

God, as ye may reade in his booke, and alledges the starres of heaven not to bee pure in the sight of God, much lesse are men to stande in judgement with his law to bee pronounced just. Therefore the holy man Job concluded his booke with confession and repentance, granting him to be a foolish sinner. And so by faith in the promised Seed was receaved in the favour of God, and accepted as righteous, the which is the justice that is of value before God.

<small>JO. 6, & 15.</small>

<small>JOB ULTIMO.</small>

David, the figure of Christ, of whome God speaketh, saying, "I have found a man according to my hartes desire," sayth, "Enter not in judgement with thy servant, O Lorde; for in thy sight no man living shal bee made just or righteous;" that is asmuch to say, after the mind of the Prophete, If ye wilbe justified by the law, ye must enter in judgement with God. Who is he that liveth so godly and holy in the earth, which may or can defend his cause, being called to the justice seate of God to give accompt and reakoninge of all thinges which hee aught to God, and by his lawe justly hee may require? There is not one, as the Prophete saith. Therefore, O Lord, if thou shalt call us to judgement, and aske question of oure life and maners, according to the rigour of thy lawe, there shalbee to us no hope of salvation. S. Augustine, expounding the said verse, saith, "There is no man living upon earth excepted in this cause, no, not the Apostles;"[1] and concluded with these words, "Let the Apostles say and praye, O Father of heaven, forgive us our debtes as wee forgive our debtours. And if any would say unto them, Why saye yee so? What is your debt? They would aunsweare, saying, Because no living creature shal bee founde just in thy sight." And in another place, expounding the said wordes, "Enter not in judgement with thy servant, O Lorde;" that is, stande not in judgement with mee, asking from mee all thinges which thou hast commanded, and given me charge to doe, and [to] leave undone; for thou shalt finde me guiltie if thou enter in judgement with me. Therefore saith hee, "I have neede of thy mercy, rather then to enter with thee in judgement."

<small>1 REG. 18 & 16.</small>

<small>PSAL. 124.</small>

And S. Bernard, in the sermon which he maketh and writes in the day of All Saintes speaketh after this maner,[2] "But what may all our justice be before God? Shal it not be reputed or esteemed like unto the menstruous cloth of a woman, according to the saying of the Prophete? And if it be sharply accused,

---

[1] Augustine concluded all men to have sinned.—(*Marg. note.*)

[2] Marke the wordes of S. Bernard. —(*Marg. note.*)

all our justice shalbe found unrighteousnes. What then shalbe our sins, when our justice may not answer for the selfe? Therefore, let us cry with the Prophete, 'Enter not in judgement with thy servant, O Lord;' and with all humility run to the mercy of God, which onely may save our soules." Here ye may clearly understand, by the holy Fathers saying, that they understoode the Scriptures, and Article of Justification, as we do, finding no righteousnes in the law, but only through faith in the mercy of God.

The saide Prophete saith, "If thou, O Lord, shall keepe our iniquities, and laye up our sins in store, O Lord, who shall sustaine or abide?" S. Augustine, expounding these words, saith, "The Prophete said not, I shall not susteine; but, Who may susteine or abyde thy judgement, if thou wilt accuse? He saw the whole life of man circumvolved with sinnes, all consciences to be accused with their owne thoughts; and no cleane, pure, and chast hart to be found, presuming in his own righteousnes. Therefore, if a cleane or chaste heart cannot bee found, presuming in his owne justice, let all men with the hart in faith unfainedly presume in the mercy of God, and say unto him, If thou, O Lord, shall keepe or laye up in store our iniquities, O Lord, who shall or may abyde it?" Where then is the hope of our salvation? With thee, O Lord; for the helpe and satisfaction or sacrifice for our sinnes is with thee;[1] as it followeth in the next verse of the same Psalm. What is this sacrifice, but the innocent bloud of Christ shedd, which hath deleted and put away our sinnes, the onely price given to redeeme all prisoners and captives forth of the enemies handes. Herefore, help and satisfaction is with thee, O Lorde; for if it were not with thee, but that thou woldst bee a just judge, and not merciefull, and wouldest observe and keepe all our iniquities, and seeke them of us, who might abyde it? Who should stand in thy judgement, and say, I am innocent? Therefore our onely hope is, that helpe, mercy, and favour is with thee!

O ye which are adversaries to faith, prent these wordes in your hartes which yee reade with your mouthes, but take no care of them, and then yee shall not impung this Article of JUSTIFICATION, but saye with us the wordes of the Prophete, "Enter not into judgement with thy servant, O Lorde, for in thy sight no living creature shal bee found just."

[1] Sacrifice for our sinnes.—(*Marg. note.*)

THE XIII. CHAPTER.

1. *The justice of a Christian.*
2. *The questions of the wicked against the manifest will of God, taught in the Scriptures.*
3. *Tokens declaring the serpentes seede.*

1. Now, sithens our forefathers, which lived most just, could not be made just in the deedes of the lawe, or in no law could finde this justice by the which a wicked man is made just; of necessitie we are compelled to seeke the justice of a Christian man without all lawe, or workes of the lawe; and of another then our self, which is just and innocent, that no law may or can accuse; and through his justice we must be made just, for of our selfes we are not just, nor no man, as the Prophet saith, (the 13th Psalme), and the Apostle (Rom. iii.) "All men have left God, and altogether are become unprofitable; none of them is found good, except one, which is the man Christ Jesu, the only begotten Sonne of God; by whom, and by his merits, through faith in his bloud, we are all receaved into the favour, grace, and mercy of God the Father; accepted as righteous and just, without all our merites or deservinges, to the everlasting life." This is the justice of a Christian, which at length shal bee declared (with God's grace) hereafter.

2. Here the adversaries will move three questions, to see if they may impugn the trueth.[1] The first is, Wherfore gave God the law to man, or what availed the giving of the same, if man of his owne power and strength may not fulfill the lawe? The second question is, If man may not be made just through the deedes and works of the law, wherefore should man do any good works? The third is, How were the fathers made just, and by what meanes? To the first question concerning the giving of the lawe, the cause wherefore it was given, and why we fulfill not the same, I will answere unto it presently. And the other two questions shal bee discussed with the Article of Justification; that is, with the discussing of the justice pertaining to a Christian man; and in the forthsetting of good workes, which followed faith as the true fruites thereof.

But first, yee shall note and keepe well in memorie, that the wicked ever objects questions and causes unto God,[2] on this

---

[1] The objections of the wicked.—(*Marg. note.*)

[2] The nature of the wicked.—(*Marg. note.*)

maner; when any thing occurres which transcendeth their fleshely wit and reason, then say they, Wherefore did God this or that thing? the which sayinges declareth them to be the serpentes seed, of whom they learned that lesson. For it was his first proposition, made unto our mother Eve in Paradise, saying, "Wherefore hath God commanded you that ye should not eat of all the trees in the Paradise?" Thus he perswaded the woman to give him answere of the cause not perteining her to know, and so brought her to confusion. Even so doth the ungodly and sonns of the Devil, inquiring at God the causes of his secret judgements; as, Wherefore hath God chosen one and rejected another? with other such unprofitable questions of the predestination and forescience of God. But in all such matters which are above our capacitie and reason, let us saye with the Apostle, "O highnes! O deepenes! O profoundnes! of the riches, of the knowledge, and of the wisedome of God! How incomprehensible are the judgements of him, and unsearchable are the wayes of him! For who hath knowen the minde of the Lord, or who hath beene his counsellour? or who hath first given to him, that hee should give againe to them? For of him, and by him, and in him, are all thinges; to whome be honour, praise, and glorie for ever."

<small>3.</small>

<small>ROM. 2.</small>

Herefore, my well beloved Bretheren, inquire ye nothing of the workes of God, and of his secret judgementes, but as his Worde teacheth you; and seeke no cause of his workes more then of his divinitie, but be content to knowe those thinges which are in your capacitie, and under judgement of the reason of man. For, as Job sayth in his booke, "If God hastely inquire us, who shall answeare unto him, or who may say unto him, Wherefore doest thou so? He is God, whose ire no man may resist." Read the whole tenth chapter for confirmation of this matter. And I exhort you, by the mercy of God, to reade the Scriptures, not as they were a prophane historie of Hector, Alexander, or other gentill histories, nor yet as the manly science of Plato, Aristotle, the Bishop of Rome's lawe, or others, which are but the science of men, and may be judged by the reason of man; but with an humble hart, submit you to God and his Holy Spirit, who is Schoolemaister of his Scriptures, and will teache you all veritie necessarie for your salvation, according to the promisse of Jesus Christ. For the understanding of the Scriptures is not of manly wisedome or knowledge, but the godly men, moved by the Holy Spirite, have spoken and forth showen the perfite knowledge of the

<small>NOTE WEL.</small>

<small>JOB 9.</small>

<small>JO. 14, 16.</small>

Scripture, as Saint Peter saith in his Second Epistle, the first chapter, "Therefore think the Scriptures not difficil, but to the fleshly man which shal get no understanding thereof."[1] They deceave you which say, The Scriptures ar difficil, no man can understand them but great clearkes. Verily, whome they call their clearkes knowe not what the Scriptures meane: Feare nor dread not to reade the Scriptures as yee are taught here before; and seeke nothing in them but your own salvation, and that which is necessarie for you to knowe. And so the Holy Spirit, your teacher, shall not suffer you to erre, nor go beside the right waye, but lead you in all veritie. And so will we passe forward to the question before rehearsed, Wherefore God gave the Law? as we are taught by his Scriptures.

THE XIV. CHAPTER.

1. *An introduction to answere the first question of the wicked.*
2. *To what creatures God gave law, and why he gave the law to man.*
3. *Of Adam's gifts before his fall hath no man experience.*
4. *The law given to Moyses, and why man may not fulfill the law.*

1. THERE can nothing be perfitly understand without the ground and foundation be sought and knowen. So, for the true knowledge of this question, ye must begin at God, and know him, as he hath commanded in his Scriptures, and seeke him no other wayes; and by him yee shall get knowledge of your selfe.

God, being without beginning, as he is without ending, in the beginning made all creatures perfite, right, and good; and, last of all, man,[2] to his owne image and similitude; male and female hee made them; whom hee indued and cled with most excellent gifts of nature and godly vertues, with originall justice, full integritie, the law of nature imprented in his hart, with power to do the same of his own freewil; and put him in the paradise of pleasure, that he should labour and keepe the same, with commandement to eate of the fruites of al the trees of Paradise, and forbad him to eate of the fruites of the trie of knowledge of good and evill, standing in the middes of the Paradise; adjoyning the paine if he transgressed this commandement, saying, GENE. 1 & 2. "Whatsoever day thou eatest of the same thou shalt dye the death."

[1] Whome to the Scriptures are difficil.—(*Marg. note.*) [2] In edit. 1584, "men."

2. Not only gave God a lawe to man, but also to beast, sunne, moone, elementes, and all his creatures in their kindes, the which they should not transgresse nor overpasse. That in his creatures hee might be glorified and have obedience of them, to that effect hee made them, and gave them the lawe. This exposition yee shall finde in the 148 Psalme, where the Prophet exhortes all creatures, animate and inanimate, to preach and forthshow the glorie of God, because he said the word and they were made, and gave commandement and they were created. So the law was given to man, to the effect he should knowe his Maker, glorifie him, and obeye him; for obedience is the fulfilling of the law.[1] To obeye God, is to love God, with all thy hart, with all thy mind, power, and strength;[2] and thy neighbour as thy selfe. This lawe was prented pure and cleane in the hart of Adam, who had free will and power of himself to do the same. For God made man in the beginning, and left him in the power of his owne counsell; hee gave to him his preceptes and commandements, saying, "If thou wilt keepe the commandementes, they will keepe thee," &c. Hee put before him fire and water, that hee might put his hand to which of them hee liked. He layd before him life and death, good and evill, saying, What ever shall please him shal bee given to him, &c. ECCLE. 15.

3. The perfection of Adam, and knowledge of the law, the righteousnesse and integritie of him in his creation, with the excellent gifts and godly vertues he was indued with, are unspeakeable, as saith Ecclesiasticus, the 17th chapter, "God created man of the earth, and made him after his owne image and similitude, turned and converted him againe in the same, and cled him with vertues according to himself," &c. Read the whole chapter, which will instruct you of these noble vertues and qualities of Adam. What might hee want, being perticipant in vertues to the godly nature? Nothing at all. And so all the workes of God were made perfite;[3] the which he never altered nor changed. No more did he his lawe; but after the fall of man, by his Prophetes and holy Preachers, hee set forth and uttered his lawe in the same forme and pure estate as it was created; that man thereby might the more perfitely knowe his weakenes and imperfection. Therefore the Apostle saith,

[1] The cause why God gave the law to man.—(*Marg. note.*)
[2] What it is to obey God.—(*Ibid.*)
[3] All creatures of God were perfite in their first creation.—(*Marg. note.*)

<small>RO. 3. & 7.</small>
<small>ROM. 4.</small>
"By the law is the knowledge of sinne." The lawe is not sinne, but sinne is not knowen but by the law. That is the cause why the law workes anger and hatred.

4. The law of Moyses of the two tables, was but a uttering and declaration of the law of nature; and that proves the sayinges of Christ. For when he had made a long sermon, teaching his Disciples and the people the perfection of the lawe of Moyses, as ye may read the 5th, 6th, and 7th chapter of S. Mathew, concludes on this maner: "All things whatsoever ye wil men do to you, doe ye the same to them: For this is the law and Prophetes." Here ye see the law and all the preaching of the Prophetes joyned in a knot to the lawe of nature, which teacheth us what we should doe, and what we should leave undone. This lawe was perfitly prented in the heart of Adam, who wanted no perfection to fulfill, observe, and keepe the same, to the uttermost perfection thereof.

For transgression of the commandement of God, our forefather Adam was exiled and banished forth of Paradise, and spoiled of the integritie, perfection, and all the excellent qualities, dignities, and godlie vertues with the which he was indued by his creation, made rebell, and disobedient to God in his owne default:[1] And therefore hee might not fulfill the law to the perfection as the same required. For the lawe, remaining in the owne perfection, just, holye, and good, requireth and asketh the same of man to be in deed fulfilled. But all men proceeding from Adam, by naturall propagation, have the same imperfection that hee had. The which corruption of nature resisteth the will and goodnes of the law, which is the cause that wee fulfill not the same, nor may not of our power and strength, through the infirmitie and weakenes of our flesh, which is enemie to the spirit, as the Apostle saith.

<small>ROM. 7 & 8.</small>

O miserable man! accuse not God but thy selfe, because thou fulfillest not the lawe. For howbeit thou, in thy default, fell from thy goodnes and perfection of nature (by the which of thy own friewill and power thou might have fulfilled the law) into evilnes and imperfection, and hath corrupted thy nature: Nevertheles, God remained just, good, true, and unchangeable, and his lawe also, which requireth of thee her duty, not according to the fragilitie of thy nature, but to the puritie of her nature, according to the good will of God. Therefore impute no fault to God, nor yet to his lawe, that thou fulfillest not the

---

[1] Why man may not fulfill the lawe.—(*Marg. note.*)

same; but to thy selfe, and thy corrupted nature, which obeyed the will of the Devill, and resisted the good will of God.

THE XV. CHAPTER.

1. *What remained in man after his fall, and what may man do thereby.*
2. *The opinion of the Philosophers, touching the wickednes of man.*
3. *The office of the lawe, and what shall man, accused thereby, doe.*
4. *The conclusion of Paule, and evasion of Sophistes therefrom; with arguments convincing them as lyers.*

NOTWITHSTANDING, after the fall of man, remained with our first parents some rest and footsteppes of this lawe, knowledge, and vertues in the which hee was created, and of him descended in us;[1] by the which, of our free will and power we may do the outward deedes of the law, as is before written. 1.

This knowledge deceaved and beguiled the Philosophers; for they looke but to the reason and judgement of man, and could not perceave the inward corruption of nature, but ever supposed man to bee cleane and pure of nature,[2] and might of his own free wil and naturall reason, fulfill all perfection. And when they perceaved the wickednes of man from his birth, they judged that to be by reason of the planete under whome he was borne, or through evill nourishing, upbringing, or other accidents; and could never consider the corrupted nature of man, which is the cause of all our wickednes. And therefore they erred, and were deceaved in their opinions and judgements. 2.

But the perfite Christian man should looke first in his corruption of nature, and consider what the law requireth of him; in the which he finding his imperfection and sinnes accused; for that is the office of the law, to utter sinne to man, and giveth him no remedy; then of necessitie is he compelled either to dispaire, or seeke Christ, by whome hee shall get the justice that is of value before God, which can not be gotten by any law or works, because by the deedes of the lawe no fleshe shalbe justified before God. 3.

[1] Men may work outwarde workes of the law.—(*Marg. note.*)   [2] The opinion of Philosophers.—(*Marg. note.*)

4. Yee shall not mervell of the oft rehearsinge of these wordes, that OF THE DEEDES OF THE LAW NO FLESHE SHALBE MADE JUST, that is, declared, reputed, found, or pronounced just before God; for they are rehearsed before the forthsetting of the Article of Justification, that it may seeme the more cleare; and to that effect the same wordes were spoken by the Apostle, Romans the third chapter, of this maner, "We know what ever the lawe speaketh, to them it speaketh whiche are in the lawe, that all mouthes may bee stopped, and all the worlde made subject unto God, because by the deedes of the law no fleshe shal bee made just before him." And therefore I have repeated them so oft, because they lead all men to the perfite knowledge of their Justification which is in Christ.

This proposition of the Holy Spirite is so perfite, that it excludeth (if ye will understande the same right) all the vaine, foolish arguments of sophistrie, made by the justifiers of them selfes, which perverte the wordes of S. Paule (as they doe the other Scriptures of God) to their perversed sence and mind, saying, That the Apostle excludeth by these wordes the workes of the law ceremonial, and not the deeds of the law of nature and morall law of Moyses. The which shameles sayings are expresly evacuat by the wordes of the Apostle; insomuch that no man of righteous judgement can denye, but shall feele the same, as it were in their hands. By this probation the law speaketh to all, that is, accuseth all men that are under the law. All men are under the law of nature or the law of Moyses: Therefore the Apostle speaketh of the law of nature and Moyses, and of all men, which he comprehendeth under Jewe and Gentill, as he proveth by his argumentes in the first and second chapters to the Romans; and concludeth in the third chapter, "All men are sinners." If all men bee sinners, none is just: If none bee just, none fulfill the lawe: If none fulfill the lawe, the lawe can pronounce none just. Therefore concludeth he, "that of the deedes of the law no flesh shalbe founde just before God." The same is proved by David in the 13th Psalme.

ARGUMENTE AGAINST SOPHISTES.

Here ye see by the words of the Apostle, he intendes to prove and declare all men sinners; that is, to stoppe all men's mouthes, and to dryve them to Christ by the accusation of the law. No law may make or declare all men sinners, and subdue the whole world to God, but the law of nature and Moyses. Therefore, under that word LAW the Apostle comprehended the law morall, and not the law ceremonial only; becaus it fol-

2. ARGUMENT.

loweth in the text, "The knowledge of sinne is by the lawe:" And also, "I knewe not sinne, (sayth S. Paule,) but by the lawe. ROM. 3. Nor I had not knowen that lust or concupiscence had bene sinne, were it not the law said, Thou shal not lust." Therefore ye cannot eschew, but confesse that the Apostle speaketh of the law morall; yea, of all lawes, and all men, because hee excepts none. Therefore let us conclude with the Apostle and the Holy Spirite, that the justice of God is without the law ROM. 3. made patent and forthshowen by the lawe and prophetes; and then shall we come to our justice, which is Christ, as S. Paule saith, the First Epistle, the first chapter, to the Corinthians.

If yee will saye of your vaine conceate (as ye which are adversaries to faith ever objects vanities), that the Apostle, in his conclusion, comprehendeth not all men proceeding from Adam by naturall propagation, but that some just men are excepted; ye shall not finde that exception in Scripture of any man except Christ, who beeing both God and man, is expresly except- ESA. 53. ed, because hee never contracted sinne; fraude nor deceat 1 JO. 3. was never found in his mouth. By this exception, all other are excluded, because there is no other who can be found just but he. For that cause he only fulfilled the law, and satisfied the same. By whome all which beleeve are accepted as just, without the deedes of the lawe, through faith in the bloude of Jesu Christ. Let us passe forward, therefore, in the Scriptures for to finde the justice of a Christian man which can not be founde in the lawe, nor deedes thereof.

THE XVI. CHAPTER.

1. *The diversitie of names of that justice which is acceptable before God.*
2. *Justice is plainly reveled in the Evangell.*
3. *What is to live in faith, or by faith.*

THE justice whereof we have made mention in the beginning, 1. and that is so cruelly and tyranously persecuted by our adversarie Sathan, is called the justice of God; the justice of faith; and the justice of a Christian man:[1] the whiche is all one thing glued and joyned together, that by the same wee are in Christ, and hee in us, by the mercy of God, purchased by Christ

[1] The justice of a Christian man hath divers names.—(*Marg. note.*)

through faith in his bloude, without all our deservings, either preceeding or following the same. And it is so farre different from the other justice of the law, as darkenesse from light, and heaven from earth; becaus it wilbe alone, and not participant with any other thing, that Christ may have his due honour, who obtained this justice from the Father, and is the price thereof.

And, first, it is called the justice of God, because it proceedeth only of the mercy of God. Secondly, the justice of faith, because faith is the instrument, whereby in Christ we obteine the mercy of God, freely given to us for Christes sake. And, thirdly, it is called ours, because by faith in Christ, without all our deservinges, wee receave the same, and are made, reputed, and compted just and accepted in to the favour of God. And all three are one justice, devided by sundrie names, as is before saide, which is this ARTICLE OF JUSTIFICATION. As, by example, almes-deede is but one name, and yet after the common maner of speaking it is appropriat truely to three; that is, to the Giver, to God, and to the Receaver. In almes, the poore and indigent have no part but only to receave and give thankes. The giver freely giveth of his liberalitie and substance; and for God's sake. So it is properly called the almes of the giver, and justly attribute unto God, becaus for his sake it is given; and also to the receaver, becaus he is made rich therewith. In the like maner, this justice of God proceedeth of his aboundant mercy and grace, favour, and goodnes, which hee beareth toward mankind that is poore; yea, above all povertie, laden with sinne, having neede of the grace and mercy of God, destitute of all confort and consolation; and therefore is called his justice by reason of the giving. And it is called the justice of faith, or the justice of Christ, because faith is the instrument, and Christ the purchaser of the same. And it is called ours, by reason of participation of all Christes merits, which we have through faith in his blud, without our merites or deservinges.

Therefore, even as the sick man receaveth his health,[1] the poore his almes, and the drye earth the raine, without all their merites or deservings; so receavest thou of God this justice, which is of value before him, by such instruments as God provideth mediately thereto, He being the immediate cause. The phisition giveth thee his counsel in thy sickenes, exerciseth his labours upon thee, by the creatures of God, according to his vocation; thou doest nothing but suffer to worke in thee til

---

[1] An apt similitude.—(*Marg. note.*)

thou be healed. And then, at commandement of the good phisition, thou keepest good dyet, not to get thy health, but that thou fall not againe in sicknesse. The poore man, receaving his almes, hath no parte thereunto onely but to receave; the man that giveth beeing the instrument, whome God hath made the stewarde of that his gift. The earth receaved the raine, and hath no part thereinto but to receave; the labourer or plowman beeing the instrument to open the pores of the earth, hat the raine may descend into it, and then it bringeth forth fruite in due time. Even so it is with man.

It is called the justice of God, and not of man or of free wil, but of God. Not that justice by which God is just, but the justice with the which man is cledd, and, by the mercy of God, of wicked made just; as Saint Augustine saith, in his booke of the Spirite and the Letter, the 20 chapter, in obteining of the which, we neither worke nor give any thing to God, but receaveth and suffers God to worke in us. Therefore, it is farre above all justice of the law which man doth and worketh, the which are also the works of God; both becaus they are of the law, and man may do them of his own free will and power, as to the externall work. And also they are the gift of God; but alwayes they may have no place in this Article of Justification before God, except yee will exclude the merites of Christ, (whiche God forbid!)

This justice was covered in the Olde Testament under ceremonies and sacrifices, but is make knowen and patent unto us now, by the Evangell of Jesu Christ, from faith to faith; that is, not from one faith to another faith, but from that faith by the which wee receave the evangell of God, through hearing of his word, and with gladnesse accepte the same, in continuall perseverance growing dayly in perfiter knowledge of God, through faith in Christ, til we give up the spirit into the handes of the Father of heaven; never doubting for whatsoever tentation or trouble in adversitie but receaving all thinges from God, and of his handes. as our forefather Abraham did, and judge all for the best. Then followeth the formall conclusion, THE JUST SHAL LIVE IN FAITH, that is, ever continue in sure trust, hoping to obtain the thing he looketh for, which is remission of sinnes, the gift of the Holy Spirite, and everlasting life, all purchaste by Christ, without our merites or deservinges.

2.

ROM. I.

3.

This is the faith of the which the Prophete Habakkuk speaketh, "The just shall live by his faith." The just man and faithfull hath never respect to any thing, but only to faith in

Christ. And what ever he work or do, referreth all to Christ; and so remaineth he in Christ, and Christ in him, conforme to the saying of S. Paule, "I live now, no not I, but Christ liveth in me; for so much as I live in the fleshe, I live in the faith of the Sonne of God, who hath loved mee, and given himselfe for mee." Here ye may see to live in the faith,[1] is to beleeve in Christ, joyned unto him continually by faith; then live wee in Christ, and Christ in us, from faith to faith, having no respect to workes or merites, but onely to the merites of Christ. And so the just liveth by his faith.

GALATH. 2.

THE XVII. CHAPTER.

1. *The definition of Faith.*
2. *What faith the Fathers had before Christes incarnation, and whereby they were safe.*
3. *Good workes are a testimonie to faith.*
4. *Wherefore workes please God.*
5. *The methode of S. Paule in writing and teaching, and the necessitie of good workes.*
6. *Wherefore justice is ascribed unto man.*
7. *Who spoyleth God of his glorie.*

1. THE Apostle defineth and declareth what faith is, saying, "Faith is the substance of thinges hoped or looked for: the argument or matter of thinges not seene, without the which it is impossible to please God." That is, faith is the true and perfite thought of the hart;[2] truelie thinking and beleeving God, the which a man doth when he beleeveth his Word, and putteth his sure trust in the mercy of God, which is to beleeve that his sinnes are forgiven him for Christes sake only, the wrath of the Father pacified, and he receaved in favour, and accepted as just; and firmely and undoubtedly beleeveth the Father of heaven to bee ever merciefull, gentle, helpfull, and favourable unto him for Christes sake, without all deservinges of his deedes or merites, either preceeding faith, or following the same. This is the justice of God, which is made patent and revealed by the Sonne of God, Christ Jesu, in his evangell, as said is before.

HEB. 2.

2. In this faith only in Christ were all the fathers, to the comming of Christ in the fleshe, made just without the deeds of the

JER. 23 & 23.
ESA. 4 & 45.
EZECH. 34.

[1] What is to live in faith.—(*Marg. note.*) [2] The definition of faith.—(*Marg. note.*)

lawe.[1] And therefore, all the promisses of the comming of Christ, are to bee referred to that promise made in Genesis, the third chapter, "That the seede of the woman shall treade downe the serpent's head," &c. And so the faith of the fathers in the Old Testament, and our faith in the Newe Testament, was and is one thing; howbeit they had other externall rites, objectes, ceremonies, and signes, then we have. And they beleeved in the comming of Christ to fulfill all promisses and prophesies spoken of him. And we beleeve he is come already, and hath fulfilled al which was spoken of him in the Law and Prophets; and hath ascended to the heavens, and sitteth at the right hande of the Father, our Advocate. And as the fathers beleeved the first comming of Christ, ever desiring and looking for the same by faith; even so now wee beleeve and looke for his second comming, and most fervently desire the same, to bee delivered of this mortall bodye of sinne, that wee may rule eternally with him in glory. That the fathers were safe by faith without the deeds of the law, S. Peter testifieth,[2] saying, "Wherfore now tempt ye God to put a yoke upon the neckes of the disciples, the which neither wee nor our fathers might beare; but by the mercy of Jesus Christ, we beleeve to be made safe as they were." And S. Augustine, in the 157 Epistle, saith, "Therefore, if the fathers (being unable to beare the yoke of the old lawe) beleeved them to be made safe by the mercy of our Lord Jesu Christ; it is manifest that the same mercy, or grace, made the old fathers to live just by faith." Now ye may see clearely that the old fathers were all made safe through the mercy of God, without all the deedes of the law. Then, how will you make your selfe safe with workes, which never did so good workes as the fathers? So there can bee no better conclusion to exclude your workes in the Article of Justification, then S. Paule maketh, saying, "That a man is made just by faith without the deedes of the law." Therefore faith onely justifieth before God. Ye shall understand that it is all one thing to say, Faith onely justifieth, and to saye, Faith without workes justifieth. As by example, if one saye, The goodman is in the house alone, or he is in the house without any body with him. This is all one maner of speaking. The Scripture saith, " Man is made just by faith without the workes of the law;" therefore we may well say, that faith onely justifieth.

 For confirmation hereof, yee shall reade the second chapter to

ACT. 15.

ROM. 3.

[1] The faith of the Fathers before the incarnation of Christ.—(*Marg. note.*)

[2] Marke the wordes of S. Peter.— (*Marg. note.*)

the Hebrews, before rehearsed, in the which yee shall finde the histories briefly repeated by the Apostle, testifieng the fathers to bee made safe by faith, referring nothing to workes; except onely that the workes beare a outwarde testimonie of the faith. Abell, by faith, or in faith, offered to God a more acceptable sacrifice then Cain did, by the which hee obteined witnesse that hee was just; God bearing witnesse of the offerings; and by the same hitherto speaketh, being dead. God looketh first to the hart of man, before hee looke to his workes; as testifieth the voyce of God, saying, "I judge not after the sight of man: for hee seeth the thing whiche appeareth outwardly, but I beholde the hart;"[1] that is, the man is first made just by faith, and accepted in the favour of God (as Abell was) and then his workes are acceptable and please God, because they are wrought in faith. That it is the mind of the Apostle S. Paule to exclude all workes, (either going before or following faith,) to bee of the substance of the Article of Justification, proved clearely the arguments and matters of his Epistle, specially to the Romans, Galatians, Hebrews; in the which he laboureth so diligently, that all the sophistes and workers, that are justifiers of them selfes, may not get a corner to hyde them into, from his conclusions, without they deny Christ and his office; at the least in effect (as they doe after their maner.) But the wisedome of God and his Holy Spirite deceaveth them; for when they wrest and throwe the Scriptures to their minde in one place, they are compelled in another place of the same Scripture to confesse them selfes lyers. In the Epistle to the Romans, from the beginning to the twelfth chapter, and in the Epistle to the Galatians, to the fifth chapter,[2] with all laboure and diligence he setteth forth the justice of God to bee through faith in Jesu Christ, without all workes of the lawe. And when he hath established the same Article of Justification, then setteth he forth the workes of righteousnes, in the which a Christian man shal live becaus the just shal live in faith. This order ye may see in the saide Epistles; and in the Epistle to the Hebrews, hee declareth the office of Christ, his priesthood and sacrifice, and giveth faith her place, (the eleventh chapter.) All his laboure was to exclude the mixtion which now these fained workers would have joyned in with faith, and the benefite of Christ; which is no other thing but the worke of the Devil our

---

[1] The man is first just before the workes be good.—(*Marg. note.*)

[2] The purpose of Paule in his Epistles to Romans and Galatians.—(*Marg. note.*)

adversary to make the death of Christ in vaine, as the Apostle sayeth, "Therefore if justice be of the law, or by the law, Christ's death is in vaine." GALATH. 2.

But thinke not that I intende through these assertions to exclude Good Workes. No, God forbid! for good workes are the gift of God, and his good creatures; and ought and should be done of a Christian, as shalbe showen hereafter at length in their place. But in this Article of Justification, yee must either exclude all workes, or else exclude Christ from you, and make your selfes just; the which is impossible to do, because we are wicked and can do no good at all which can be of value before God, or pacifie his wrath; except Christ first make our peace. For that is his office,[1] for the which he came in the world, and suffered death. So, if yee will not exclude Christ, exclude your workes; for in this case there is no concurrence, more then there is betweene darknes and light: For what participation hath righteousnesse with iniquitie? or what fellowship hath light with darknesse? The definition of this justice is made plaine by S. Paule, Romans, the third chapter, which I exhort you to reade. Consider worde by worde, conceave and prent them well in your harts; then shall ye be able to contend and fight valiantly against Sathan and his Sophistes, of whom yee shall have victorie by faith, which is our victorie that overcommeth the world. 2 COR. 6. 1 JO. 5.

"The Justice of God is, by the Faith of Jesu Christ, in all and upon all which beleeve in him. There is no distinction or exception: All have sinned, and have need (or are destitute) of the glorie of God; but they are made just by his mercy, freely without the workes, by the redemption which is in Christ Jesu; whome God hath proponed or layd before a sacrifice or satisfaction by faith in his bloud, to the forthshowing of his justice for remission of the sinnes bypast; the which God hath suffered to the forthshowing of his righteousnes at this time; that Hee may be just, and justifie him which is of the faith of Jesu Christ. Where then is thy glorie or vanting? It is excluded. By what law? Of workes? No, but by the law of faith. Therefore we beleeve surely a man to be made just by Faith, without the deedes of the Law."

Now, I pray you tell me what plainer words may be spoken, or termes invented, to exclude ALL our works, merites, or power, to be participant with God in this Article of Justification?

---

[1] The office of Jesu Christ is to pacifie the wrath of God, which our workes may not doe.—(*Marg. note.*)

They are as plaine and cleare as the sonne in mid-day. Neverthelesse, because the wordes are so pretious, and necessarie above all things to be imprented and continually keeped in the hart of man, I will make some declaration of every part and particle of this definition; and prove by authoritie of Scripture, this justice of God (by the which a man is made just) to be without all works or power of man, only by faith in the mercy of God.

PSAL. 5.   Of this justice, David speaketh, saying, "Lead me in thy justice, O Lord, because of my enemies: direct my way in thy sight." That is, O Lorde, my God, for thy greate goodnes, singuler kindnes, and naturall love thou wast ever wont to show unto sinners and mankind, bee to me a governour, guider, and convoyer in all perilles and daungers; suffer never my minde to decline from the right waye, for any maner of strength or
PSAL. 10.   feare of my enemies. And also, "In thy justice, O Lorde, deliver me;" that is, for thy goodnesse and mercy. And after, "Judge
PSAL. 43.   thou me, O Lorde, and discusse my cause;" that is, take my defence upon thee, for I am not able of my self to resist. Therfore, in thy justice deliver me, and be unto me a strength in-
PSAL. 70.   vincible. So shall ye finde in divers and sundrye Psalms, and other places of Scripture; as Daniell, ninth chapter, "Justice and righteousnes unto thee, O Lord, but unto us confusion and shame of face." In the which chapter, ye may read what justice or holynesse that holy Prophete ascriveth unto him, or to the most holy of the people, amongest whome assuredly there was many good punished with the wicked, but none which might ascribe righteousnes to themself[es].

6. Sometime yee shall finde in Scripture this worde, Justice,
PSAL. 4.   ascribed unto man; as David saith, "Heare me, who called on thee, O Lorde, of my justice," &c. That is, God, the author, giver, and keeper of my innocencie, hath looked upon me: and, "Judge me, Lord, after my justice, and according to my inno-
PSAL. 7.   cency which is in me." Here he forthshoweth not his vertues or his righteousnes which are in him, with these words; because
PSAL. 142. he saith in another place, "Enter not in judgement with thy servant, O Lorde, for in thy sight no living thing shalbe found just." And the Holy Ghost is never contrarie to himself.[1] But here he called the justice of God his, by imputation. And also, hee was innocent of the thinge which was layde to his charge by King Saule, who ever accused him of treason, and usurping of the crowne of Israell. In the 16th Psalm, hee saith, "Heare

---

[1] The Holy Ghost is never contrarie to himselfe.—(*Marg. note.*)

my justice, O Lorde, and give attendance to my desire and prayers." Here hee calleth his justice, his petition. And in innumerable places of Scripture, yee shall finde this word, Justice, sometime ascribed to God, and sometime to man;[1] because of the receaving of the same from God. But ever the Scripture makes the selfe plaine, by the sentence that goeth before, or els followeth, or in some other place. Therefore, take good heede upon the reading of the Scriptures, that ye deceave not your selfes, ascribing any deede or power of yours to the Article of Justification; for it may suffer none but only Christ's merits, because the merites of man are impure and imperfite, and may not abyde the justice of God, nor stand in his sight.

It followeth in the definition of this Justice: "By the faith of Jesu Christ in all, and upon all, which beleeveth in him." Here ye may see our faith, that we beleve in Jesu Christ, called His faith, as it is in deede. And the faith also of God, and by the same reason as the justice is called before, because it is the gift of God, as S. Paule saith, Ephesians, the second chapter, and is the instrument by the which we obteine the mercy of God, remission of our sinnes,[2] the gift of the Holy Spirite, and everlasting life, all for Christes sake, without our deservings; by the which wee are joyned in Christ, and Christ in us, as the pretious stone is joyned in the gold ring. So let all our delite and pleasure bee to imbrace Christ in our hart, by faith in his bloude; for faith is the thing which Christ desireth of a sinner. "Beleeve, sonne, thy sinnes are forgiven thee." And also, "All which beleeve in mee (saith Christ) shall not dye eternally." And to the woman, in the seventh chapter of S. Luc, "Thy faith hath made thee safe." *MATH. 9. JO. 11. ROM. 10.*

It followeth in the definition: "There is no distinction nor exception: All hath sinned, and hath neede of the glorie of God." That is, all wanteth that justice which God approved or judged to be glorie. And so all men are sinners and rejected from God, and can not be made just by the lawe, because the same accused sinne,[3] and is like a mirrour in thy hand to consider the forme of thy face, which can do no other thing but show thee thy deformitie. God hath concluded all under sin, that he may have mercy upon all. The Scripture hath concluded all under sin, that the promise may be given, through the faith of Jesus Christ, to all which beleeve. *3 REG. 8. 2 PAR. 6. 1 JO. 6. ECCLE. 7. ROM. 2 GALATH. 3*

[1] Why justice is ascribed to man.—(*Marg. note.*)
[2] The faith of Jesus Christ, and what wee receave thereby.—(*Marg. note.*)
[3] The law is a mirrour.—(*Marg. note.*)

It followeth in the definition: "But they are made just, Freely, by the grace of God, through the redemption which is in Jesu Christ." Here ye see the Apostle purposeth to exclude all your merites in deserving of this justice; to the effect he may (as in all his Epistles and labours he intended) set foorth the glorie of God, and the benefite of Christ; the which can nowise be highlier set forth, then in the making of a wicked man just and freely; that is, for nothing and without deserving. For that cause, Christ is made to us from God, wisdome, justice, holynes, and redemption; that he which rejoyseth may rejoyse in the Lord. And that meaneth the Apostle Paule, and the Prophet Jeremie, which will have all our vertues given unto God, as wisedome, strength, and riches, which are in our power to use and exercise, as the gifts of God; much more justice, which is not in our power. For we are made, and make not our selves; the which we do, if we deserve it, either for workes preceding or following the justification, to have any part of the substance thereof. And so would ye drawe the glorie of God to you in one part, the which God will not suffer, as the Prophete Esay saith, "My glorie will I give to no other." Either must yee make your selves just, or els bee made just by God: if yee make your selves just, ye are not allowed of God; so the glorie redoundeth to your selfe of your owne worke. This the Holy Spirite will never approve nor consent unto, as ye read, the Second Epistle to the Corinthians, the 10th chapter, Colossians third, Philippians third, Galatians sixth.

1 COR. 3.
JERE. 9.

NOTE.

ESA. 42 & 48.

That wee are made just Freely by the mercy of God, declareth S. Paule, for confirmation of this his assertion, "By grace (saith he) ye are made safe through faith, and that not of your selfes, it is the gift of God: Not of workes, that none have matter to glorie or rejoyse." This same he affirmeth in his Epistle to Titus, the third chapter, and Romans, the eleventh chapter, where hee saith, "If it bee of grace, then it is not of workes: Otherwise grace were no grace."[1] Here ye may see this justice is of mercy, freely, without all oure merites or deservinges.

EPHE. 2.

Yee are made just by the redemption which is in Christ Jesu, and not in your selves; for Christ hath redeemed us from the curse of the lawe, and is made for us accursed: That is, hee suffered the paine which the curse of the lawe injoyned to us by sinne: In whome wee have redemption by his bloude, remission

GALATH. 3.

---

[1] That is, Remission of sinnes were not freely given.—(*Marg. note.*)

of our sinnes, according to the riches of his mercy and grace." What wordes may bee more plaine to prove this justice onely by faith in Christ, excluding our merites. Yee have the same assertion in the Epistle to Titus, the second chapter; Galatians, the fourth, and Apocalypsis, the fifth chapter, where it is written, "Thou art worthie, O Lord, to take the booke, and open the seales of it; for thou art slaine and hast redeemed us to God in thy bloud;" hee saith not in our workes, but in thy bloud. Here ye may see and consider our sinnes were no light thinges; considering there was no other thing whiche might pacifie the wrath of the Father,[1] but the bloud and death of his onely begotten Sonne Christ Jesu, to bee made man for that cause. And now for vaine invented imaginations of ignorant sophistes, (which will not onely be their owne redeemers, but also redeeme others,) this pretious bloud is repute in vaine, or a light thing!

It followeth, "Whome God hath layde before a sacrifice or satisfaction through faith in his bloud, to the forthshowing of his justice, for remission of the sinnes by-past, the which God hath suffered, (or in the suffering of God,) to the forthshowing of his justice at this time; that he may be just, and justifie him which is of the faith of Jesu Christ." Here the Apostle aboundeth in wordes, to exclude all sophistrie and vaine conceate of workes, which men intende, and would intende to make satisfaction for sinne. For hee setteth forth Christ here the full sacrifice and satisfaction for sinne; and therefore he called him the Mediatour of the New Testament, by intercession of his death. And also, "Christ offered a sacrifice for sinnes, and for ever sitteth at the right hand of God, beholding till his enemies bee made his foote-stoole." And S. John saith, "If any shall sinne, we have an Advocate before the Father, Jesus Christ, who is just, and he is satisfaction for our sinnes; not only for ours, but for the whole world's, and that through faith in his bloude." For there is nothing may bring us thereto but faith only; and no satisfaction may be but Christes death, "Who hath once dyed therefore, and shall not dye againe; death shall have no more dominion of him." In the which hee hath declared him just, in fulfilling the promise made of him in the Lawe and Prophetes; that is, that He was to make us just, which could not make our selves just.

And where hee saith, "For remission of sinnes bypast, the which God hath suffered," &c., understand not that of the

[1] The wrath of God against sinne.—(*Marg. note.*)

sinnes by-past, before the comming of Christ onely, but also of all sinnes committed to the worldes end. For these wordes are spoken foorth of the mouth of God, with whome all things is present, as yee may consider by the wordes of Christ, speaking to the Jewes on this maner: "Before Abraham was, I am." Howbeit Abraham was dead a thousand yeares before his incarnation. So to the penitent all sinnes are bypast; therefore the remission of sinnes by-past, in Christes bloude, indured to the end of the worlde.

<small>JO. 8.</small>

This is necessary to know for two causes principally. The one is, for confounding of the heresie of the Novatians,[1] which pervert the sayings of the Apostle, whereupon they would inferre that man once beeing justified, and thereafter falling in sinne, may have no place of repentance; whiche were the perverting of all the Scriptures of God, and his promisse in the bloud of Christ, who is the Lambe of God that taketh away the sinnes of the world; and our Advocate, Sacrifice, and Satisfaction. Howbeit the Apostle speaketh plainly, that it is impossible to be renewed to repentance through renewing of baptisme; for that were to crucifie Christ againe, not in his fleshe, but in thy fleshe, which would be new baptised.

<small>HEB. 6.</small>
<small>JO. 1.</small>
<small>1 JO. 2.</small>

The other cause is, to exclude their opinion, which think that Christ satisfied but for Originall sinne onely,[2] and that baptisme giveth, or hath purchaste grace to man, after the baptisme, that he may satisfie for his owne sinnes by recompensation, as God were a marchant to chop and change with man: That if Christ was the first marchant, they shalbe the next! And this is as great a heresie as the other, by the which they would make the death of Christ but a vaine trifle, and chaunge faith into workes of man's making, the which is the work of the Devill, that ever intended to impung this Article of Justification by the mixtion of workes. This opinion S. John confoundeth in his First Epistle, the first and second chapters, where he declareth, first, "If a man say he hath no sinne, hee deceaveth himselfe." And then, "If man sinne (as doubtlesse all men doeth), he sayeth, Wee have an Advocate, Christ Jesu, who is just, and is a satisfaction for our sinnes." Moreover, all men, howe just that ever they bee, neede dayly to praye, "Forgive us our debts, as we do our debtours;" the which prayer were not necessarie, nor Christ had never taught the same, if we might have satisfied for our owne sinnes at any

<small>NOTE.</small>

---

[1] The heresie of the Novatians.— (*Marg. note.*)

[2] The false opinion of Sophistes.— (*Marg. note.*)

time. So, Christ is ever our satisfaction, and we dayly sinners; therefore we ought ever to pray, " Forgive us our debts, as we forgive our debtours."

It followeth in the definition, "Where is thy glorie? By what lawe is it excluded? Of works? No, but by the law of faith: and concludeth man to be made just by faith without the deeds of the lawe." Ye shall understand, that glorie[1] in this place, is taken for the sure trust and beleefe which men putte in their owne workes and merites; the which the Apostle will have cleanly excluded forth of this article, and given wholly to Christ, who deserveth the same, becaus he is obteiner thereof to us, through faith in his bloud. The which faith will have no thinge participant with it in this case, more then the sight of the eye will have or suffer the finger in it to help the sight. No, it can not suffer a mote, but ever waters, being hurt till the mote be taken foorth. Even so faith foorthshoweth all thing to the glorie of God, and merites of Christ, without all workes or merites of man.

If Abraham had beene made just of works, then had he wherein to rejoyse, but not before God. And also, hee had not obteined that name to be called the Father of the faithfull, but the father of workers. Therefore the Scripture saith, "Abraham beleeved God, and it was reakoned to him for righteousnesse." In the which Scriptures, yee shall not onely finde this justice whiche is of value before God, attribute and given whole to faith in the mercy of God; but also the workes expresly excluded. For either wee must be made just by faith only, or by workes only; because they may not bee mixt, without Christes death be in vain: For to him that worketh, saith Paule, the rewarde is not impute according to grace or mercy, but according to debt. But to him which worketh not; that is, confideth not in his own merites, but beleeveth in Him which justifieth the wicked, his faith is compted to him for righteousnesse, according to the purpose of the mercy of God; and that without workes. For the probation and sure understanding of this assertion, yee shall reade the whole fourth chapter of Romans, the fifteenth of Genesis, the second, third, and fourth Galatians, and second to the Ephesians, which wordes shalbe showen in this subsequent chapter.

ROM. 4.

GEN. 15.
ROM. 4.
GALATH. 1.
HEB. 2.

[1] What is glorie.—(*Marg. note.*)

THE XVIII. CHAPTER.

1. *The cause wherefore God loveth us.*
2. *Whereby commeth the heritage.*
3. *The constance of Abraham in faith, and his obedience.*
4. *Jesus Christ payeth for us that which the Law requireth.*
5. *Who spoileth Christ of his office.*

1. "By grace yee are made safe by faith, and not of your selves: It is the gift of God; not of workes, that no man rejoyse." "We are his handywork, created in Christ Jesu unto good workes, the which God hath prepared that we should walke in them."

Verily, these wordes are worthy to be written in letters of golde, and ever imprented in the hart of man, because they conteine the whole somme of the Evangell of Christ; and also exclude all the vaine sophisticall arguments made contrarie this Article of Justification; because in this Epistle there is no question of the law (as in the Epistles to the Romans and Galatians): But it is written to the Gentiles, being confirmed in the faith, and also persevering thereunto; whome the Apostle certifieth of their justification in the first three chapters; and then setteth forth to the end of the Epistle, the workes of righteousnes, in the which true Christians should live, according to their vocation; upon the which wordes I will make some short declaration according to the Scriptures.

2. "By grace ye are made safe;" that is, by the grace and mercy of God, and aboundant love he hath to mankinde; because hee hath made us, hee would not wee should perishe: For hee loveth his owne worke.[1] Hee saith, "I will not the death of a sinner, but that hee convert and live." Hee made us, that hee should love us, for no man hateth or invyeth his own worke. "This grace we get by faith in Jesus Christ, the which is not our worke, but the gift of God." "For wee are not of our selves able or sufficient (as of our selves) to thinke a good thought; but all our abilitie is of God," as the Apostle saith, the Seconde Epistle to the Corinthians, the thirde chapter, and Galathians, the third chapter, "If the heritage bee of the lawe, then it is not of the promisse;" but by the promisse God gave it to Abraham, Ismaell, and Esau, which were the eldest sonnes, who succeeded not to the heritage; but Isaac and Jacob, whiche were heires of the promisse, succeeded.

EZECH. 18 & 33.

EPH. 2.

[1] Wherfore God loveth us.—(*Marg. note.*)

Wee are not made safe through workes, that none should glorie, because God will not have us rejoysing in our selves in any parte of his giftes, as the Apostle saith, " What hast thou that thou hast not receaved? And if thou hast receaved it, why rejoysest thou, more then thou haddest not receaved it?" Ye see workes excluded forth of this Article, that man hath no matter to glorie, but to referre all the glorie unto God, as is before rehearsed. And that man hath nothing to glorie into, but in the crosse of Jesu Christ, by whome wee should crucifie the worlde to us;[1] that is, wee should esteeme all that is in the worlde wicked, as the Apostle sayth to the Galathians, the sixt chapter. 1 COR. 4.

Yee shall not mervell that our salvatioun is ascribed and attribute to the mercy of God through faith, excluding all workes, because the reasoun is here shewen by the Apostle, in these wordes: " For we are the handyworke of God, created in Jesus Christ unto good workes." That is, forsomuch as we live, have life and understanding, and beleeve, it is of God, and not of our selves, because hee is our Maker and Creator. Why should the earthen or clay-pot extoll the self against the potter, of whom it hath all which it hath? Or the branche against the tree, of which it hath all the substance to bring forth the fruite? As Christ giveth the parable in the Evangell of Saint John, the 15. chapter, the which yee shall reade that yee may understande the wordes of Christ, and similitude in the whiche the Father is declared to bee the husbandman, or the labourer; and Christ the wine tree; and us Christians to be the branches or the bearers. For the branche hath two offices,[2] the one is, if it remaine with the tree, fresh and greene, it bringeth forth good fruite of the substance of the tree, and not of the self; the other is, if it wither, and bring forth no fruite, it must be cut off and brint. Therfore, if thou wilbe a Christian, and remain in Christ, by faith ever joyned to him, thou shalt bring forth good fruite of his substance, and not of thyne; of the which the glory perteineth to him, and not to thee. And if thou will be the withered branche, that is, wicked, and bring furth no fruite, thou art prepared for the fire, there to serve with the Devill and his angels. And this is sure, if thou wilt either glorie in thy workes, or yet that thou art thy own Saviour, or any part thereof, as concerning this Article of Justification. But to re- ACT. 17. PSAL. 99. ESA. 45. JERE. 18. ROM. 9.

---

[1] To bee crucified with Christ.—(*Marg. note.*)

[2] The office of the branche.—(*Marg. note.*)

maine in Christ by faith,[1] and suffer him to worke in thee, which thou doest when thou workest the workes commanded in the Scriptures of God, and attributs them to Christ, to be his workes working in thee: then shall he make thy imperfection perfite,[2] that nether the Devil nor the Law dare accuse them, because they are the workes of Christ, and for his sake receaved of the Father by faith. So there is heir no thing to thee to glory of, but to say with the Apostle, "He that wil glorie, let him glorie in the Lord," &c.

<small>1 COR. 1.
2 COR. 10.
JERE. 9.</small>

This glory of workes is excluded by the law of faith; of the which law the Apostle maketh mention, saying, "The law of the Spirite of life in Christ Jesu, hath delyvered me from the law of sinne and death." That is, the mercy of God, the gift of the Holy Spirit, remission of sinnes, and everlasting life, purchased to us through faith in Christ; by the which we live in ryghteousnes, free from sinne and death. And so it is called the law of faith, which excludeth all glory of works, because we receave, and give no thing but glory and honour unto God, which is the sacrifice of praise and thanksgiving. In this we should live in righteousnes, and worke the workes of God; and not become thrall again to sin and death, from the which we ar freed freely, without our merits or deservings, through faith in the bloud of Christ, our Saviour and Advocate.

<small>ROM. 8.</small>

<small>ROM. 4.</small>

Therefore let us conclude with the Apostle,[3] and establish for an infallible conclusion, man to be made just by faith, without the deeds of the law, as prove the Scriptures before rehearsed, and by the example of Abraham, who had no mixtion of works in his justification. The which we must affirme to be trew, because the Scriptures affirme the same, and testifie him to be justified by imputation through faith, because hee beleeved God, and gave sure trust to his promise; howbeit the same appeared not possible, as indeed it was [not] to the judgment of man. Nevertheles, hee doubted not in his faith, but beleeved hope against hope;[4] and therefore it was compted to him for righteousnes; not onely to him, but of the same maner to us which beleeve, and are sonnes to Abraham by faith. And trust well, Abraham did many noble and heroicall works of the law of nature; but none of these works were participant of his justifica-

<small>GENE. 15.
ROM. 4.</small>

---

[1] Who remaineth in Christ.—(*Marg. note.*)

[2] Wherfore the law nor Sathan may not condemne the works of the faithfull.—(*Marg. note.*)

[3] The conclusion of Paule.—(*Marg. note.*)

[4] That is, He beleeved the promise of God, albeit the same appeared impossible to nature or manlie power.—(*Marg. note.*)

tion before God, but only beare witnes to his faith, and obedience to God in his righteousnes, as shalbe showen hereafter.

The most excellent work amongst the Jewes was circumcision,[1] which was given to Abraham, and commanded to be used in all his posteritie for the signe and token of the band and covenant betwene God and him.[1] The which was long after the justification of Abraham, as ye may read Genesis, the 17. chapter. And the Apostle sayeth, "Abraham receaved the signe of circumcision, the seale of the justice of faith," &c. Therfore this work made him not just, nor yet had any parte of his justification. Neverthelesse, God reahearsed to him at that time the promise, saying, "Abraham, walke before me, and be perfite; and I shall put my covenant between me and thee; and shall multiplie thy seede exceedinglie; and thou shalbe the father of many nations." And after this, God tempted Abraham; that is, searched or espyed out his faith; commanding him to take his sonne Isaac, whome he loved, and offer him in a sacrifice, &c. Consider this commaund, and ye shall perceave it a great temptation of the faith of Abraham; and conferre the same with the Scriptures going before, where God gave commaund to him that he should put away his sonne Ismael; for the seed of the promise should be fulfilled in Isaac. Neverthelesse, the faith of Abraham was so firme and constant,[2] that he rather hoped and surely beleved, that God was to raise Isaac from death to life, then that his word should be fals, or of none effecte. And therefore God said unto him, and confirmed the same with an othe, saying, "Because thou hast done this thing, and hast not spared thy onely begotten sonne, I shall bliss thee, and multiply thy seede as the starres of the heaven, and sand of the sea shore; because thou hast obeyed my voice and charge." Heir yee see and find the promisse repeated again, which was made to him long before. But it is not saide here, that because Abraham did this worke, it was compted to him for righteousnes; but that hee was commended by the mouth of God, for his obedience and perseverance in faith. For the faithful shuld live by faith, daylie persevering, and increasing day by day more and more perfite, which is from faith to faith; giving ever thanks and praise unto God, and obeying his command.

Yee shall take this conclusion,[3] That no man can be called

---

[1] Circumcision after justification.—(*Marg. note.*)

[2] The obedience and constancie of Abraham.—(*Marg. note.*)

[3] No man living wickedly is called just.—(*Marg. note.*)

just which liveth wickedly; but hee which is godly, and liveth well, is called just. Nevertheless, his good life or workes have no participation of this Article, because they are excluded by the Apostle, in the wordes before rehearsed for a conclusion, "That man is made just before God by faith, without the deedes of the lawe." Upon the whiche wordes, S. Augustine saith, "These wordes are not to bee understande so, that a man receaving the faith, if he live afterwarde wickedly, shalbe called just; but hee is made just without all his workes, that he may live in righteousnes[ness] and work well."

Christ is the end of the law (unto righteousnes) to all that beleeve; that is, Christ is the consummation and fulfilling of the lawe, and that justice whiche the lawe requireth; and all they which beleeve in him, are just by imputation through faith, and for his sake are repute and accepted as just. This is the justice of faith, of the which the Apostle speaketh, Romans the 10. chapter: Therefore, if yee wilbee just, seeke CHRIST and not the Law, nor your invented workes, whiche are lesse then the lawe. Let HIM bee the mark whereat ye shoote, and let him never passe foorth of your harte: whereto seeke yee that thing which already hath taken an end. Is it not written in the Evangell of S. Luc. the 16. chapter, "The Law and Prophetes are unto the time of Johne, from the which time the kingdome of God is preached and foorthshowen," &c. And S. Johne, in the 1. chapter of his Evangell, saith, "The Law is given by Moyses; but Grace and Veritie ar given by Jesus Christ." These two words are expounded by S. Paule: Grace, that is the mercy of God whereby we ar made safe through faith in Christ, and not of works. Verity is the fulfilling of the promises of God, for the which Christ was made servant to circumcision, for the veritie of God, to confirme the promises of the fathers. Here ye see Christ will have no mixtion with the law, nor works therof, in this Article of Justification, because the law is as contrarie to the office of Christ as darknes to light, and is as farre different as heaven and earth.¹ For the office of the law is to accuse the wicked, feare them, and condemne them, as transgressours of the same. The office of Christ is to preache mercy, remission of sinnes, freely in his bloude, through faith, give consolation, and to save sinners. "For hee came not in to this world to call them which are just, or think them selves just, but to call sinners to repentance."

The office of Christ, John the Baptist declareth, saying,

---

¹ The office of the lawe.—(*Marg. note.*)

"Behold the Lambe of God! Behold him which taketh away the sinnes of the world!" It is not I, sayeth John, nor the law, repentance, or workes of repentance, which I preache, that taketh away your sinnes; but it is Christ, that innocent Lambe of God, to whome I send you. And also Christ sayeth, "God send not his Sonne into the world that he shold accuse, condemne, or judge the world; but that the world should be made safe by him." And after, "It is not I (sayeth Christ to the Jewes) that judgeth you, it is Moyses which accuseth you." And so the Scriptures testifie that the Law accuseth, and Christ saveth. He sendeth none to the law;[1] but rather the law driveth and compelleth man to seeke Christ, if yee will understande it aright. The woman accused of adulterie, he sent her not to the law; but said to her, "Passe thy waye, and sinne no more." And to the man which had bene diseased thirtie-eight yeres, &c., "Behold! thou art made whole, now sinne no more, that some worse thinge happen thee not." Christ called all to himself, saying, "Come unto me all yee which labour, and are laden with sinne, and I shall refresh you." And Peter saith, "There is no salvation but in Jesu Christ: nor no other name given under heaven by the which man may obteine salvation."

Therefore, sithens no other may save but He, we should put all our trust and hope in him, and in his mercy only, and neither in the law nor works; for to all them which thinke they may bee safe by workes, or made just, Christes death is in vaine. Or, if there had beene given a lawe which might have given life, then righteousnes surely had beene of the law; but it is manifest, "That by the law no man is made just before God, because the just shall live by faith."

What wordes may bee more plaine then those are, to exclude workes foorth of this article?[2] Now, sithens the Scripture teacheth us so plainely that Christ is our Justice, our Saviour, and Redeamer, satisfaction for our sinnes, the ende and consommation of the lawe; and hath freed us from the lawe, sinne, and death, and from the kingdome of Sathan our adversarie, and bought us to the kingdome of righteousnesse without our merites or deservings; why will wee usurpe his office to our selves, and spoile Christ of his glorie,[3] or become thrall againe to that thing from the which Christ hath freed us? The which

---

[1] The law rightly considered compelleth us to seek Christ.—(*Marg. note.*)

[2] The fruites which we have of Christ.—(*Marg. note.*)

[3] Who spoyleth Christ of his glorie.—(*Marg. note.*)

we do, if we wilbe participant with Christ in the making of our selves just, or mixt any workes with the Article of Justification.

THE XIX. CHAPTER.

1. *As the good tree beareth good fruite, so the good man worketh good workes.*
2. *But as the fruit maketh not the tree good, so workes make not the man just.*
3. *For, as the tree is before the fruite, so the man is just before the work be good.*
4. *The cause why wee should worke good workes.*
5. *The Captaines in the kingdome of Christ, his subjects, and reward; and of his adversarie Sathan.*

1. THIS faith, which only justifieth and giveth life, is not idle, nor remaineth alone; nevertheles, it alone justifieth; and then it workes by charitie. For unfained faith may no more abyde
2. idle from working in love, then the good tree may from bringing foorth her fruite in due time. And yet the fruite is not the cause of the tree, nor maketh the tree good; but the tree is the cause of the fruite; and the good tree bringeth foorth good
3. fruite, by the which it is known goode. Even so it is of the faithfull man: the workes make him not faithfull, nor just, nor yet are the cause thereof. But the faithfull and just man bringeth forth and maketh good workes, to the honour and glorie of God, and profit of his neighbour, which beare witnesse of his inward faith, and testifie him to be just before man.
4. Therefore, yee must be just and good, or ever yee worke good workes, for Christ sayeth, "May yee gather grapes of thornes, or figges of thristles?" No, no, it is contrary their nature. Even so it is with man; till hee be made just by faith, as it is before writtin, hee may never doe a good worke; but what ever hee doeth is sinne; for al which is not of faith is sinne. And Christ sayeth to the Pharisies, "How can yee speake good, while yee ar yet evill?" Therefore, or ever we speak good, or do good, we must be made good, and that by the mercy of God, through faith in Christ, without al our deservings. Then shal we worke al good works in the kingdome of Christ as his faithfull subjects.

MAT. 7.

ROM. 14.
MAT. 11.

There is two kingdomes,[1] and two kinde of subjects, which

---
[1] Diverse kingdoms.—(*Marg. note.*)

are direct contrary to other, because there princes ar as contrary as ar light and darkenes; that is to say, the kingdome of Christ, and the kingdom of the Devil. To the kingdom of the Devil,[1] man is of his owne nature a perfite subject, and the sonne of ire and wrath. To the kingdome of Christ, man is made subject through his second birth or regeneration, which is by baptisme in the bloud of Christ. To this kingdome, man is bought, neither with gold nor silver, but with the precious bloud of the Sonne of God, Christ Jesus, and so is made servaunt to righteousnes to serve unto life. Therefore, who is made just by faith, through the mercy of God, and merites of Christ Jesus, must (in faith which is not idle, but ever working in love) serve Christ, and embrace him in his hart. Then shall he remaine in Christ and Christ in him, by the which joyning, through faith, sinne shall have no dominion, nor shall not rule as a prince, howbeit the dregges remaine in us; they shall not be imputed to us, if we persevere in faith, as our forefather Abraham did, ever working by love and charitie. And this is the cause why we shuld work good workes, because wee are bought to the kingdome of Christ,[2] in the which rule, as valiant captaines, Faith, Hope, and Charity, working ever righteousnes unto life.

E II. 2.

I PET.I.

The kingdome of the Devill[3] hath thre valiant captaines, which governe the same, that is, Incredulitie, Dispaire, and Envye, ever working sinne and unrighteousnes unto death; because the reward of sinne is death. In this kingdome, Sinne ruleth as a prince, having dominion; therefore, " If ye will serve sinne, and obey the same, ye are servants to that thing which ye obey, whither it be of sin unto death, or righteousnes unto life." But Christ hath redeamed us, and bought us from this realme; that even as Christ hath risen from death to the glorie of the Father, right so we should live in a new life, and let not sin have more dominion over us. There is no man so foolish, who wil thinke, he being delivered of a vile prison, by the grace and mercy of a great prince, and brought to serve in his hall, and so made tender to the prince that he is made participant of his sonnes heritage, will say, I will passe againe to prison, because he is not a part of his owne deliverance. Verily, it is even so of their sayings, which say, I wil do no good becaus Christ hath delivered me; and being delivered, I will sin and follow

ROM. 6.

---

[1] What we have of our owne nature.—(*Marg. note.*)

[2] The captaines of the kingdome of Christ.—(*Marg. note.*)

[3] The captaines of the kingdome of Sathan.—(*Marg. note.*)

all libertie of flesh: Wherfore should I do any good workes, sithens Christ hath redeamed me without my deservings?

My hartes, ye which object these sayings, reade the Scriptures, and yee shall finde another lesson taught you. And attend upon your Schoolemaister, which is the Holy Spirite, who shall teach you the right waye, that yee passe neither to the right hand nor to the wrong, but the right kingly way; that is,[1] to confesse, and ever have prented in your hartes, that by faith onely, of the mercy and grace of God, yee are made safe. And then followe the example of our Lorde Jesus Christ, giving your whole studie and cure to love, charitie, and all maner of righteous living, to the glorie of God and profit of your neighbour. Not that there through ye are made safe, but that ye may be found thankefull unto God, whome we knowe to be favorable, gentle, kinde, and mercyfull to the godly; and to the wicked, wrathfull and angrie. This is the solution to the argument made in the beginning, which proveth,[2] wherefore should we doe good if we be free from the law, and freely justified by the mercy of God, through faith, without our deservinges. Therefore, choose you now, if ye wilbe servants to sinne, or servantes to righteousnesse; subjects of the kingdome of Christ, or of the kingdome of the Devill. For wee are made free and just by grace through faith, that we shuld live in righteousnes to Christ, who hath dyed for all; "that they which live, live not now to them selves, but to Him which hath suffered death for them, and hath risen again from the same." Keeping this order, yee shall never cease to doe good works as occasion requireth.

COR. 5.

THE XX. CHAPTER.

1. *An answere to all Scriptures which our adversaries alledge for them[selves], against the Justification of Faith.*
2. *Wherfore workes are commended in Scriptures.*
3. *An argument proving that no workes justifie.*

Now, because there is some Scripturs which our adversaries wold cause to bee seene, either contrarie to the Scriptures before rehearsed for probation of this Article of Justification; or els, with them they would mixt this Article; so that faith not

---

[1] The right kingly way.—(*Marg. note.*)

[2] The answere to the question, why we shuld worke good workes.—(*Marg. note.*)

only justifieth without works. Therefore, I will rehears some of the most principal of them, and cause you understand by the same Scriptures, they are neither contrarie to this Article, nor yet have any entresse[1] with faith, in the making of a wicked man just; but followe faith as the due fruites thereof; in the which the Christian man should live, as said is before.

In the Epistle of S. James, the second chapter, it is said, "Bretheren, what profite is it, if a man say hee hath faith, but hath no works? may his faith save him?" And again, "Ye see," saith hee, "that a man is justified of workes, and not of faith only."

Here the adversaries of faith make a great feast, but they understande this saying of the holy Apostle, as they doo the other Scriptures, ever working with the Devill to make the Holy Spirite contrarie to himselfe, which is impossible.[2] But will yee understand, take heede, and read the text, ye shal see clearely that the Apostle speaketh of the historicall or idle faith; that is dead without workes, to the confusion of the wicked Christians, which have no faith but in the mouth; and not of the faith which maketh a man just before God, and obteineth remission of sinnes; by the same examples and wordes that he rehearseth. For he saith[3] the Devill troweth,[4] beleeveth, and dreadeth; but the Devill can never beleeve that Christ hath redeamed him, and purcheste to him the mercy of God, remission of sinnes, and eternall life, whiche is the faith to whome S. Paul ascriveth justification only. And also he reproved the evill Christian, which sayeth hee hath faith, and neglecteth the deeds of charitie, in cloathing of the naked, and feeding of the hungrie, whiche deeds are the fruits of faith, of the which S. Paul speaketh. Therefore, there is no contrarietie in the Scriptures before rehearsed, but concurrence.

And also the offering of Isaac, as mention is made before, was done above thirtie yeares after the justification of Abraham, to the forthshowing of his obedience, as the text proveth, Genesis the 15. chapter and 22. chapter. In the which offering, the Scripture was fulfilled, as saith S. James, "Abraham beleeved God, and it was compted to him for righteousnes." Here ye may see clearely S. James speaketh nothing of the justification before God, but of the justification before thy neighbour, becaus of the examples and authorities of the Scrip-

[1] Interest, concern.
[2] Note the minde of S. James in his Epistle.—(*Marg. note.*)
[3] Marke diligently.—(*Marg. note.*)
[4] Knoweth.

tures alledged by him, which are of works done in faith by the faithful, long after their justification. For faith onely justifieth before God, as S. Paul saieth, without works; and workes justifie before man outwardly,[1] and declare a man just before his neighbour, in exercising the deedes of charitie, which are approved before God, and acceptable to him, in them whiche are reconciliate by faith in the mercy of God, and beareth witnesse that a man is just. Therefore, yee who would alledge this authoritie of S. James to impung the Article of Justification which we confesse, understand not the Scriptures, nor have no foundation for you but ignorance and babling of words.

They alledge another text, the 10. of Actes, of Cornelius, whose prayers and almes deedes past up in the sight and memory of God. By the which words they would inferre, his works made him just, or at the least provoked God to call him to the faith, which is all one thing. For if we, by our deeds, may provoke God to love us, or to have mercy upon us; through our merits, by the same reason we may make our selves just; and so we need no other Saviour, but let Christ's death be in vaine. But, my welbeloved Bretheren, yee shall understand that God first loved us, and provoked us to love him, (wee being sinners unworthie of love, yea, enemies also,) as the Scriptures of God teach you, John, First Epistle and 4. chapter, and in his Evangell the 3. chapter, and Romans the 5. chapter. And therefore, God first preveened[2] us with love and all goodnes, and we not him; and so shal ye understand this text following of Cornelius.

The text saith, "There was a man named Cornelius, a captaine," &c., "a devout man, and one that feared God with all his houshold; which gave great almes to the people, and prayed God continually," &c. To whome the angell sent from God said, "Thy almes and prayers are past up in the sight of God," &c. Here yee see this man was faithfull and just, by the first two proprieties by the which hee is commended, which can not stand without faith; that is, devout and fearing God. Devout, is to say, a true worshipper of God. No man truely can worship God or please him but in faith, becaus it is impossible to please God without faith. Cornelius[3] worshipped God truelie, and so pleased him, therefore he was faithfull, he feared and dreaded[4] God by love, for that is the feare whereof the text speaketh.

---

[1] Workes justifie before men onely.—(*Marg. note.*)

[2] Went before, anticipated.

[3] Cornelius had faith, and thereby wroght good workes.—(*Marg. note.*)

[4] In the edit. 1584, "dread."

Therefore Cornelius was faithfull, because that love can not be without faith. The works which Cornelius wroght wer the fruites of faith, and pleased God, because God approved the same, which hee had never allowed except they had bene done in faith; for all which is not of faith is sinne. Therefore, yee must confesse that Cornelius was faithfull and just before God, or els ye must deny the Scriptures, (which God forbid!).

And then will yee say, To what effect was Peter sent for? to instruct him in the faith, and teach him what he should do? If he was faithfull, what faith was it he had? To that I shall answer, Cornelius[1] had the same faith that Adam, Noe, and the fathers had; for he beleeved the promised seede, which was Christ, and knew not that he was come; but beleeved in one God, and that the same God had promised a Saviour to redeame the world. So, God looking upon the faithfull, humble, and simple hart of Cornelius, and the fervent desire of his prayers, (which desire doubtles was conforme to the sayinges of the Prophet Esay, "O, if thou wouldest break asunder the heavens, that thou might come doune!") would not have him deceaved, to looke for Him which was already come. Therefore, he caused him send for Peter to instruct him in the present faith; and to certifie him that Christ was come, whome he looked for so ardentlie. Yee may read the text, then shall yee perceave the sermon Peter made unto him, which was only of the opening of the Scriptures, testifieing the comming of Christ in the fleshe; and fulfilling of all the promises and Prophets sayings, spoken of him before; and that he was risen from deathe, and had given Peter and the rest of his Disciples and Apostles, command to preache repentance and remission of sinnes to all which would beleeve in his name, &c. *ESA. 65.* *MATH. ULT.* *MAR. 16.* *LUC. 24.*

To the which words and preaching of S. Peter, Cornelius and his whole housholde gave firme faith, and receaved by a visible signe the Holy Spirit. The which is no other thing but this Article of Justification. For hee beleeved the Word of God, and by faith in Christ, through the mercy of God, receaved the Holy Spirit, without all working of any deede of the lawe of Moyses, but onely being under the law of nature; and so was baptised, &c. Therefore, yee can not prove, by this authority of Scripture, that either the works preceeding or following the gift of the Holie Spirite, was the cause of his justification, or yet any parte thereof. But, first, being just through the faith

---

[1] What faith Cornelius had, and wherefore was Peter sent unto him. —(*Marg. note.*)

which the fathers had, (who had also the Holy Spirit,) truely worshipped God, and feared him of love, and so he was just; and in that righteousnes wrought the fruites of faith in prayers and almes deeds. And secondly, being taught by Peter, beleeved that Christ was come, the sure Saviour of the world, and had fulfilled all which was spoken of Him by the Prophetes. By this faith was hee, by the mercy of God, made just, and receaved the Holy Spirite visiblie, without all works or deservings; and then, in the kingdome of Christ and righteousnesse, wrought the fruites of faith unto life, as all perfite Christians should doo.

They alledge another text, Galathians the 5. chapter, "Faith which worketh by love," &c. By these wordes they would inferre, of their corrupted maner, that faith onely justifieth not before God, but faith which worketh by love. By this maner of understanding,[1] they not only make the Apostle false, but also cast all downe, and destroye the same thing which hee hath builded. For in the 4. chapter of the same Epistle preceeding, with great laboures and invincible arguments hee setteth forth the Article of Justification, proving faith only to justifie, without all deedes or workes of the law. And then in the 5. chapter he beginneth to set foorth the fruites of faith, saying, "Ye are abolished from Christ which would be made just by the lawe; ye have left grace; for we, by the spirite of faith, beholde or looke for the hope of righteousnes, for into Christ Jesus neither is circumcision nor uncircumcision any thing worth, but faith which worketh by love."

In these words shortly, and in briefe termes, the Apostle excludeth all workes and lawes, sacrifices and worshippings, both of Jew and Gentill, to have any mixtion with Christ in the justification of a Christian. For if there had bene any more excellent work, or greater in estimation among the Jewes (which were the chosen people of God) then circumcision, no doubt but the Apostle would have excluded the same. And so the principall work, commanded by God, and given by him as the seale of his promise and covenant made to Abraham, being excluded forth of this Article, how can any ather worke of lesse or equall estimation have parte thereinto? Therefore the Apostle concluding shortly, and comprehending the whole estate of a Christian man, saith, "Neither is circumcision nor

---

[1] Sophistes would make the Holy Spirit, speaking in S. P. [St Paul], contrarie to him selfe.—(*Marg. note.*)

It may be noticed, that in the edit. 1584, St Paul is occasionally printed in this contracted form "S. P."

ON JUSTIFICATION BY FAITH. 501

uncircumcision any thing worth in Christ, but faith which worketh by love." He saith not, love which worketh by faith, but faith whiche worketh by love; that is, faith inwardly maketh a man just before God, who hath no neede of our workes; for the whole worlde, and all that is therein is his. And love outwardly testifieth of thy inwarde faith towarde thy neighbour, who hath need of thy works; for whose utilitie and profite thou art commanded to do good workes; to whome thy faith availeth nothing. And so this text impugneth not the Article of Justification, but fortifieth the same. PSAL. 49.
NOTE.

Ye read, love greatly extolled by S. Paule, the 1. to the Corinthians, the 13. chapter, (as it is worthy), but ye find never justification before God attribute to love, for that is not the office therof. But love followeth faith in the third degree, whose office the Apostle setteth forth in the said chapter; specially, how that love suffereth all thinges, beleeveth all thinges, hopeth all thinges, and endureth all thinges.[1] Yea, verily, some thinges which faith may not suffer, nor wil on no wayes suffer; as a light[2] superstition repugning to the Word of God, Love will, or may suffer the same to be in it, for the weakenes of the infirme brother. But faith may in no manner suffer the same, because it may be prejudiciall to the Article of Justification, and induce the mixtion[3] of works.

Also Faith, Hope, and Charitie being reakoned, the Apostle exalteth Charity to be the most excellent of the three, but giveth her none of their offices. But, if ye wil understand the text well, ye shall know the Apostle's mind by the conclusion, saying, " Now we see through a glas darkly, but then we shall see face to face: Now I know in part, but then shall I knowe, even as I am knowen: And nowe abydeth Faith, Hope, and Charitie, but the chiefest of these is Charitie."[4] As he would say, Now we ar imperfite, but then we shalbe perfite: Faith and Hope shall both perish, and vanishe awaye, but Charitie shall remaine in her perfection; for then she is in her perfection when the other two have taken effect, and are vanished away: for in the heaven there is neither Faith nor Hope, but Charitie is in her most excellent degree there, which never hath an ende.

The cause wherefore the Apostle extolleth Charitie, yee shall consider in the First to the Corinthians, the 12. chapter, the which 1 pray you read. For in that whole Epistle there is

[1] The nature of love.—(*Marg. note.*)
[2] Trifling.
[3] Mixture.
[4] Why charity is called the chiefest. —(*Marg. note.*)

no question of the Article of Justification, nor of the office of Faith, but an instruction how the Christian man should live; reproving hatred, envy, dissentions, and opinions amongst the Corinthians, which became not to be amongst Christians; therefore, he exhorted them above all thinges to Charitie, which is the band of peace, and the most excellent vertue to be had, and ever kept among the Christians; "for by that men shall know you, saith Christ, to bee my Disciples." Therefore, howbeit Charitie be the most excellent vertue, and that the whole life of a perfite Christian is faith and charitie, or faith working by Charitie. Nevertheles Charitie justifieth not before God, nor yet hath any mixtion with Faith in the making of the wicked just; but followeth Faith as the due fruites thereof, conforme to the order of Scriptures before rehearsed, and as also hereafter shalbe showen.

To impugn this article, they alledge this text, "If thou wilt enter into life, keepe the commands." By the which they would inferre, that the keeping of the commands is in our owne power of free wil; and that we, fulfilling the same according to our power and strength, may thereby obteine the kingdom of heaven by our works; the which is as agreable to the saying of Christ, as blacke and white is; as yee shall clearely understande by the Scriptures.

Christ, being asked and inquired of by the young man, what he should doe or worke that he might have eternall life, answeared on this maner, saying, "If thou will enter into life, keepe the commands." "Which ar they?" sayeth the young man. Jesus answered, "Thou shalt not kill; Thou shalt not commit adultery; Thou shalt not steale; Thou shalt speak no fals witnes; Thou shalt honour thy father and thy mother; and, Thou shalt love thy neighbour as thy selfe." Here yee see Christ teacheth the young man the workes of the second table, which concerne our neighbour onely; and speaketh no thing of the first table, which perteineth properly to God, and consisteth into faith. Therefore, by these wordes of Christ it may not be inferred that he sendeth any to the law, to obtein perfection therin, that is to say, justification or salvation; but onely to let them know what the law requireth of them, and what they wer oblished to doe; that they, seing no remeady thereinto, might seeke Christ, who came in the world to call all unto him, and not to sende them to the law, for that was the office of Moyses. What availed Christ's comming in the fleshe, if hee would have sent man to the law to get salvation? But Christ declareth plainely hereafter in the same texte, that there was no perfection to be had in the deedes of the law of mannes doing, as appeareth by the answere made to the young man, and precept given to him.

When the young man said, He had observed all the said deedes of the law from his youth, &c. howbeit hee made a lye, Christ accused him not, because it was not his office; but said unto him, "If thou wilt be perfite, go thy waye, and sell all that thou hast, and give it to the poore, and come and follow me." But when the young man harde that saying, he went away sorrowfull, and left Christ, because he had great possessions.[1] These wordes of Christ are no other thinge but the declaration of the fained man, to let his hart be knowen, which beleeved that through fulfilling of the outward deeds of the law, he might be found just before God; and also to teache us the duetie which we are bound to do to our neighbour. For, howbeit Christ hath freed us from the thraldome and malediction of the law, he will that we worke the workes of charitie, to the utility of our neighbour, and nothing draweth us so much therefrom as avarice and covetousnes. Therefore, Christ opened the young man's covetous hart, (which hee would have hidden, as all hypocrites do,) and taught him, if he would bee perfite, to followe him in whome is all perfection. And so this text maketh nothing for them which impugne this Article of Justification, but rather against them, becaus the matter of which Christ speaketh doth concerne the neighbour only, and works to be wrought to his weale and utility, which of necessitie followe the Article of Justification, as the fruits of faith done by the justified man, who may or can finde no better workes to doo nor they which are commanded in the law of God.

The adversaries of faith reading the Scriptures, where ever they finde mention made of works,[2] that part they collect not to the effect as it is spoken by the Holy Spirite, but to the intent they may impugn thereby the Holy Spirit as contrarie to him selfe. This proceedeth of the Devill, to empoyson the Article of Justification; that is, to mixt the same with workes, that hee may enter and obteine his place, by the which hee may abolishe faith, or at the least the perfite office thereof, and diminishe the glorie of God. But for eschewing of this, yee who will knowe the perfite estate of a Christian man, where ever

---

[1] The wordes of Christ uttered the hipocrisie of the young man.—(*Marg. note.*)

[2] How the wicked doo read the Scriptures.—(*Marg. note.*)

yee finde mention made of faith in the Scripture, without any adjection[1] thereto, ye shall understand it of perfite faith unfained, which, without al workes, either preceeding or following the same, justifieth. And upon this faith S. Paule groundeth all his arguments, to prove that faith onely justifieth before God, without the law or works, which he ever excludeth, as is proved by the Scriptures before rehersed.

2. And where ever ye find mention made of works in the Scriptures without any adjection, ye shall understand them of perfite workes wrought into faith. Of these workes S. Paule maketh mention in all his Epistles, after he hath set forth the Article of Justification. Therefore, the workes are but the witnessing of faith, and the obedience which is required of the just and faithfull man, to the glorie of God and profite of his neighbour, by the which the just obteineth witnessing of his faith, as is proved clearly by S. Paule to the Hebrews, the 11. chapter, where hee reakoned from the just and faithfull Abell, and their works in speciall, till he come to Gedeon, Barac, Sampson, Jepthe, David, Samuel, and the Prophetes in general, declaring them all to have done many great and excellent workes into faith. And yet ascribeth nothing to works, but to faith onely, showing the workes to be the testimonie and witnessing of their faith outwardly, and no part of their justification; concluding in this maner, "The which by faith have subdued and overcome realmes, have wrought righteousnesse, obteyned and gotten the promisse, have stopped the mouthes of lyons, quenched the violence of fire, and escaped the edge of the sworde," &c.

3. Here is a cleare solution to all the objections of workes, made by the adversaries of faith: for, seing the Apostle saith, "It is impossible to please God without faith;" where then are the works which preceede faith, and move God to give grace and favour, (which ye call *De Congruo*[2]). And then ye worke of your own strength and power, as yee say, the workes which deserve remission of sinnes and everlasting life; yea, not only sufficient to your selfe, but also superaboundant to save others, (which yee call *De condigno, et opera supererogationis*[3]).

ROM. 4. The Scriptures are plaine against your false superstitions and sophisticall argumentes; concluding that neither workes preceeding nor following faith have entres in making of a wicked man just, nor yet may save you. It is written, "All which

---

[1] Addition.
[2] Grace of congruity: See History of the Church of Christ, vol. iv. ch. v.
—(Note in British Reformers.)
[3] Of your deserving, and works of supererogation.—(Ib.)

is not of faith is sinne." How then can ye do any worke preceeding faith, that it may please God, or provoke him to love you, considering all that ye doo out of faith is sinne?[1] Will ye say that he deliteth in sin? No, no; it is a thinge most abominable in his sight; therfore, all that ever ye do, how excellent the work be in your sight, it is sin before God; and yee heape sinne upon sinne, which is abomination in his sight, as sayeth the Prophete Esay. The workes which follow faith make you not just, because or ever yee worke good works yee must be made first just, and thereafter (in faith) yee worke the workes of justice. Neverthelesse the saide workes may not save you, nor merite the kingdome of heaven to you, much lesse may they merite to others. But yee are made safe by the mercy of God, and not of workes, as S. Paule sayeth, " Not of workes of righteousnesse, which we have done, shall we be saved, but according to his mercy, God hath saved us."

<small>TIT. 3.</small>

Here yee see not onely workes excluded in generall forth of this article,[2] but also the workes of justice, which can not be done but by the justified man; Where are then your workes which deserve the kingdome of heaven of their worthinesse, not onely to your selves, but superaboundant to others? They are excluded by the Scriptures of God. Therefore I exhort you to exclude them also, and cleave to faith.

THE XXI. CHAPTER.

1. *The opinion of the wicked, seeking their owne glorie.*
2. *The workes commanded by God, and done without faith, ar abomination before him.*
3. *Whereby commeth the new birth.*
4. *Paule refuseth his workes, seeking no justification thereby.*
5. *The conclusion of all the Scriptures.*
6. *What is given to man which hath true faith.*

I MERVELL greatlie of your blindnesse which are adversaries to this article, and would ever mixt it with works, (specially of your owne making,) that yee may bee a parte of your owne salvation. But I ought not mervell thereat, because yee seek your own glory, and not the glory of God; for ever ye cry, The law, the law; Good works, good works;[3] the which yee never doe,

1.

---

[1] Marke diligently.—(*Marg. note.*)
[2] The workes of justice is excluded in the cause of justification.—(*Marg. note.*)
[3] The wicked advance them of works which they never doe.—(*Marg. note.*)

nor yet it is in your power, of your selfe, to complete according to the perfection, that yee may set them before the judgement seat of God. And this same thing did your forefathers, the Scribes and Pharisies, against Christ; and now yee, against his faithfull litle flocke, of the same blindnesse and ignorance. For, to establish your owne justice, yee neglecte the justice of God, and will not be subject thereto, as the Apostle sayeth. And Christ sayeth, "Yee are they which justifie your selves before men; but God knoweth your harts;" because that which is of great estimation in men's eyes, is abhominable before God. Even so it is of your workes not commanded by God; how honest or shining that ever they be in the sight of man;[1] for verily God wilbe pleased with no workes of man's inventioun, but with the workes commanded by him selfe. And the same should be done in faith, according to his will and not ours; for the which we are commanded, and should daylie praye, "Thy will, O heavenly Father! be fulfilled, and not ours." What better works can man doe, then the workes commanded by God, as praiers, almes-deedes, fastings, and keeping of holy dayes, and others,[2] as ye may reade, Esay the first chapter, the which God, by the mouth of the Prophet, calleth abomination. And Christ called prophecying, preaching, casting forth of devils, miracles, wonders, and signes, and many other great and excellent vertues done in his name, the workes of iniquitie; and the doers of them the workers of iniquitie, saying, "Passe away from me all yee which are workers of iniquitie; for not all which say unto mee, Lord, Lord, shall enter in the kingdome of heaven; but they which doo the will of my Father whiche is in heaven." These workes are contemned by God for no other cause, but that they ar wrought by the wicked without faith, or mixt with the Article of Justification; thinking therethrough to be made just, or to be a part of their owne justification; and therefore cannot please God, but greatly displease him, because the good worke is converted into sinne, through the iniquitie of man. Nevertheless, they appeare in the sight of man to be most excellent good, and should have a great reward, after the judgement of man; but yee see here what rewarde God giveth them.

And seing the workes commaunded by God to be done are so displeasant in his sight, wrought by the wicked without faith,

---

[1] God never was, nor wilbe, pleased with works of man's invention.—(*Marg. note.*)

[2] Workes which of them self are good, done without faith, are abomination before God.—(*Marg. note.*)

what shalbe of your workes which are not commanded by God, nor have no authoritie in his Scriptures, but invented by your selves, of your good zeale, and intention to make your selves just by them, having no respect to faith; but to the working of them of the selfe deed, yea, verily, expresse contrarie the Scripture, and plaine idolatrie! Neverthelesse, he that doth them yee make just; and he that doth them not yee condemne. Is this any other thing but to make the death of Christ in vaine, and to be justifiers of your selves? For, seeing the justice which is of value before God is not of the deedes of the law, how can it be of your deeds? Therefore Christ wil say unto you, "Passe from me, all ye workers of iniquitie; I know you not." Notwithstanding, in other places of the Scripture yee shall finde the same workes greatly commended by God, where they are done by the just man, as the fruites of faith; and reward promised to the workers of them. So they confesse them unprofitable servantes when they have done all that they can ; for Christ saide to his disciples, "When yee have done all whiche is commanded you to doe, then say, wee are unprofitable servantes; wee have done that which wee were bounde to doe." LUC. 17

And if they which fulfill all the commandements of God, are compted or repute by him unprofitable servants, what have wee to glorie in, which fulfill not one of his commandements? Now, I pray you, lay this text to your assertion, "If thou wilt enter into life, keep the commandements," and ye shal thinke shame of your sayings, insomuch as yee would impugn the Article of Justification therewith, and mixt workes with faith, to the making of a wicked man just.

Now I trust it be sufficiently proven by authority of the Scripture, as is before rehearsed at length, to the satisfaction of a Christian and godly man, that works are excluded forth of this Article of Justification, and have no participation therewith, but follow faith as the due fruites thereof, that all glorie may redound to God: howbeit, the wicked hypocrits and justifiers of themselves will never be satisfied by any authoritie of the Scripture; for they cannot nor will not be content with God, nor his Word, but ever impugn the same, to establish their owne authoritie and glorie;[1] and therefore, are never at rest nor quietnes in their conscience with God, because they reject the mercy, grace, and peace of God, the which ar the substance of the estate of a Christian, wherein the just liveth by faith, and ESAY 48.

---

[1] Hypocrites are never at rest in their conscience.—(*Marg. note.*)

ar so necessary that they should ever be blowen in at the eares of the faithful by the ministers of the Word.

Therefore, where ever the Apostle S. Paul wrote[1] or preached, (howbeit there was no question of the law, nor workes thereof), hee never pretermitted in the beginning of his Epistle, as the other Apostles in like maner used, to certifie the Christian congregation of the substance of this Article,[2] saluting them with grace, and peace;[3] which is asmuch to say, as the mercy of God, by the which ye are made just, and accepted as righteous in the favour of God the Father, through faith in Jesus Christ, our only Lord and Saviour: Rest and quietnesse in your conscience I desire to be with you, and remaine with you continually, that thereby ye may worke the fruites of faith, by charitie or love, in righteousnes, to the glory of God, and profite of your neighbour, through Jesus Christ, by whome we have this mercy and grace, and entres to the Father, and the same grace; the which grace is given to us by God in Jesus Christ, that no fleshe should rejoyce in his sight, who hath given himselfe for our sinnes, that he might deliver us out of this present wicked worlde, according to the will of God the Father, and according to the riches of his mercy, the which hee hath aboundantly shed forth upon us, by whose mercy we are made safe. He hath called us by his holy vocation, not according to oure workes, but according to his purpose and mercy, the which hee hath given to us by Jesus Christ.

ROM. 1.
ROM 5.
1 COR. 1.

GALATH. 1.
EPHE. 1 & 2.

2 TIM. 1.

And S. Peter saith, "Blessed bee God the Father of our Lord Jesus Christ, who, according to his great mercy, hath begotten us of newe into a lively hope, by the rysing of our Lorde Jesus Christ from the death." Therefore, if wee bee borne and gotten of new by mercy, it is not of workes nor of our deservinges, but freely given us by the grace and mercy of God, through faith in Jesu Christ. Nor we have no righteousnesse of the law nor workes, as is before clearly proved by the Scriptures at length. And the same S. Paule testifieth in his owne body to bee true,[4] who wrought many excellent works of the law. Nevertheless he reputeth all but filthines, that he may winne Christ and be found in him, not having his owne justice or righteousnes which is of the law, but that justice which is of the faith of Jesu Christ.

1 PET. 1.

PHILIP. 3.

[1] In edit. 1584, "writed."
[2] A repetition of the Article of Justification and substance thereof.—(*Marg. note.*)
[3] The salutation of the Apostle.—(*Marg. note.*)
[4] Paule wrought many excellent good workes, but reputeth them nothing.—(*Marg. note.*)

And, seing the holy Apostle, the chosen vessell of God, might not obteine righteousnes in the law nor works, but in the mercy of God, through faith in the precious bloud of Jesu Christ; alace! what blindnes is in us wicked and miserable sinners, which will ever glory and cry, Good works, which we never do, and will have them mixt with this Article of Justification: In so much that Christ, after our judgement, is not sufficient to save us and make us just; howbeit, it be the cause wherfore he was made man for us only.

Therefore, let us conclude with the Apostle and the holy Scriptures, that by Faith only in Christ we ar made just, without the law and workes thereof. And after man be made just by faith, and possesseth Christ in his hart, knowing perfitely him to be his justice and his life, then shall he not be idle; but even as the good tree shal bring forth good fruite;[1] because a man truly beleeving, hath the Holy Spirite, and where he is, hee suffereth not man to bee idle, but doth move and provoke him to all godly exercises of good workes; as the love of God, patience in troubles and afflictions, calling upon the name of God, and thankesgiving, and to the forthshowing of charity and love unto all. This is the order of a Christian's life, and the substance of good workes, as hereafter followeth, and as we have also touched some thing in the beginning concerning the trouble and patience thereof.

THE XXII. CHAPTER.

1. *What workes should Christians doe.*
2. *The life of man is a perpetuall battell.*
3. *What is the law of the members, and what the law of the spirite.*
4. *What sacrifice we should offer to God, and what is required that our sacrifice be acceptable.*
5. *Who followeth Christ, who goeth before him, and who is equall with him.*

BECAUSE good workes are the fruites of faith, and necessarilie must follow the same, and proceede of the justified man as the good fruits of the good tree, without the whiche no Christian man may gette witnessing of his faith; therefore, after the forthsetting of the Article of Justification, should ever men-

[1] The entresse to good workes.—(*Marg. note.*)

RO. 5.
2 TIM. 3.
PROV. 3.
HEB. 12.
APO. 3.

tion be made of good workes, and all faithfull taught to do the same. The which methode S. Paul useth in all his Epistles,¹ but specially in the Epistle to the Romans and Galathians. "For being justified by faith, we are at peace with God, by our Lord Jesus Christ." But then hastely riseth the battel and strife with the world and persecution, because all which will live godly in Christ Jesus shall suffer persecution. Then shalt thou begin to rejoyce of thy trouble, knowing surely that thou art the sonne of God, because he chasteneth all sonnes whom he loveth. This affliction, whether it be in spirit or body, bringeth patience to thee, which is the proofe of thy faith. Then conceave thou hope, whose office is to confort thee, that thou bee not overcomme in thy affliction; and so then faith and

ROM. 5.

hope being joyned together, the love, favour, and grace of God are by his Holy Spirite shed abroade in our hartes; by the which we, as valiant knightes, passe to a new battell, against the

1 JO. 5.

Devill, the World, and the Fleshe, of whome wee obteine victorie by faith, and suffer not sinne to rule over us. This methode to good workes teacheth the Apostle, Romans the 5. and 6. chapter, exhorting us, that as wee of before gave our members to bee weapons of unrighteousnes unto sinne to the death; that now wee, being justified by faith, give to God our members,

RO 6.

weapons and armour of righteousnesse unto life. For the rewarde of sinne is death,² but the grace of God is eternall life by our Lord Jesu Christ. Then let us surely beleeve, hee who

PHILIP. 1.

hath begunne the good worke in us, which is God, shall performe the same to the daye of our Lord Jesus Christ. And so, to begin good workes³ is not to suffer sinne to rule in this mortall body, that we obeye not the lustes and concupiscence of the same.

2. The whole life of man is but a battell upon the earth; and

JOB 7.

whosoever will pas fordward in the service of God, hee must

ROM. 7.

prepare him for tentation and trouble.⁴ This battell S. Paul had, and, as a knight of great experience, taught us the same; how he fand a law in his members, repugning to the law of his

3. mind; which is no other thinge but the tyrannie of the Devill, drawing and provoking man to followe the lustes and concupiscence of the flesh;⁵ not onelie in external workes, but also in

---

¹ The method of S. Paule in wreting.—(*Marg. note.*)
² The reward of sinne is death.—(*Marg. note.*)
³ The beginning of good workes.—(*Marg. note.*)
⁴ Whosoever serveth the Lord, must prepare him self for trouble—(*Marg. note.*)
⁵ The repugning of the flesh.—(*Marg. note.*)

the inwarde affections of the minde, as to doubt or diffide of the goodnesse and mercy of God; or to bee slouthfull, voyde, and emptie, of the love and fear of God. The lawe of the minde is the lawe of God provoking and calling man to doe all justice and righteousnesse, whiche the faithfull man consenteth to in his minde, to bee good and just; and yet findeth no power in him selfe to performe the same. For the whiche the holy Apostle, with an exclamation, saith, "O unhappy man that I am, who shall deliver mee of this mortall body, which is no other thing but a masse of sinne!" These wordes he saith, not as of a doubt in his faith, but of a fervent desire to be dissolved and separated from this vile life, to bee with Christ; because hee giveth thankes unto God, by Jesus Christ, by whome hee is delivered of the said battell. Read the 7. chapter of the Epistle to the Romans, where yee shall clearely perceave this matter at length. Therefore, the saintes and holy men vehemently lamente these motiones and affections of the fleshe, whiche they feele in their inward wit; reason, and manly wisdome, repugning against the spirite and will not bee subject thereto, nor may not of their own power or strength, but by the Spirite of God, which beareth witnes with our spirite that we are the sonnes of God. There are none which perceave this battell, or valiant fighting, but the just men, which confide not in their own workes, merits, or deservings, but only in the mercy of God through faith in Jesu Christ, by whom they obtein victory, and thank God. ROM. 8.

But because this mortall body of sinne is ever repugning unto the spirite, and our greatest ennemie, daylie borne about with us, the Apostle exhorteth us most fervently, by the mercy of God, to give and offer the same a quicke, lively, holy, and pleasant sacrifice unto God. And that our service and worshipping of God be reasonable; not conforming our selves to this world, but to be renewed and reformed into a new witte, knowledge, and understanding; that we may have proufe how the will of God is, how good, how acceptable, and how perfit; the which is, that we mortifie our bodies and members which are upon earth; not only to abstein from externall, outward, and grosse sinnes, as from fornication, incest, uncleannesse, avarice, indignation, wicked lustes, and concupiscence, ire, filthie communications, and like unto these, reakoned by S. Paule; but also to conceave in our harts the true and perfite feare of God, which moveth and causeth us to abhorre sinne, and detest our wicked corrupte nature, which ever resisteth the will of God, ROM. 8. ROM. 12. COLLOSS. 3.

¹ The will of God.—(*Marg. note.*)

and entiseth us to follow our owne will, wit, reason, and honest appearance of good zeale, and intention; the whiche wee should not obeye, but the will of God,[1] which is, to beleeve in him, and in Jesus Christ whome hee hath sent. And also, it is the worke of God, for the which wee should ever pray to God, "Thy will be fulfilled, and not ours."

<small>JO. 6.</small>

This doing, the kingdome of heaven is within us, as Christ saith, Luc. the 17. chapter, and the olde man mortified in our bodies, and crucified with Christ; the body of sinne abolished and destroyed, that wee serve no more to sinne, the which is no other thing, but to cast off all our affections of the fleshly man, and submit us wholely to Christ;[1] and as hee hath risen from death, that we likewise rise with him from sinne; and live a new life in the kingdome of righteousnes; no more being under the lawe nor sinne, but under grace; that is, Christ and his worde, the whiche will never teache us to sinne, but to all vertue in faith. The order hereof S. Paule teacheth, Romanes the 12. chapter, and so forth to the ende of the epistle. And S. Peter, in his First Epistle, the 2. chapter, teacheth the same.

<small>RO. 6.</small>

This quicke and lively sacrifice which God desireth of us, and is so pleasant and acceptable in his sight,[2] is a contrite and broken harte, a troubled spirit, humiliate and subject unto God. These the Prophete calleth the affections of the minde, or thoghts of the harte, which are broken, afflicted, and cast downe, by the knowledge of sinne, and place their whole hope and confidence onely in the mercy of God. The same affections of the hart hee calleth the sacrifice most acceptable unto God; and commaunded the same to be offered unto him, as it is written, "Give unto the Lord the sacrifice of righteousnesse, and put your whole hope into him." And in the 49. Psalm, he calleth the same the sacrifice of praise and thankesgeving. For we should ever praise God, that is, preache and foorthshowe in all thinges his infinite goodnes; and what ever we think, speake, or doe, direct the same to his glorie. This is a worthy sacrifice to be done by a Christian. On this maner we are taught by S. Paule to the Hebrews, and diverse other places of the Scripture.

<small>PSAL. 50.</small>

<small>PSAL. 4.</small>

To the fulfilling of this sacrifice is required that we spoyle our selves of the old man,[3] that is, our first conversation in

---

[1] To bee crucified with Christ.—(*Marg. note.*)

[2] The sacrifice pleasant to God.—(*Marg. note.*)

[3] The old man.—(*Marg. note.*)

sinne, which wee have of naturall propagation of old Adam, and is cledde, and beareth the same so long as we live after the example of Adam, ever rebels to God and his law; and clothe us with new Adam, that is Christ, with whom wee are cledde when we reforme our life to the similitude of him which restoreth again to us the image and similitude of God, to the which we were created. This is the right and true holinesse, integritie, and justice, to the which, in Christ, we are renewed by the Holie Spirit; that we should live in all justice and holines of life. In that we were created by God in the beginning, that we should walke before him;¹ therefore the Apostle commandeth us to be renewed with the spirit of the minde, and cloth us with the new man. The minde is the fountaine and beginning of all thinges; so it must be renewed, if any good works should follow. And that teacheth the Prophete Esay in these wordes: "Put away the evill of your thoughts from my eyes," &c. And so to doe good workes according to the pleasure of God and order of the Scripture, is to beginne to mortifie this sinfull body, as is before rehearsed. Then are we the good tree, whose fruite is sweete and pleasant in the sight of God, and acceptable to him. COLLOS. 3.
EPHE. 4.
ESA. 1.
MAT. 16.
MARC. 8.
LUC. 14.
1 PET. 2.

Therefore, lette us deny our selves, take our owne crosse upon our backes and followe Christ, as he hath commanded us in his Evangell. For the which he suffered death for us, leaving to us an example that we shuld follow his footstepps, and neither go before Christ, nor yet aside with him; but let us follow him;² the which we doe when we cast from us all our wisedome, righteousnesse, holines, and redemption, and receave them from Christ, who is made to us, by God, our wisdome, justice, holynesse, and redemption; and confesse us to have nothing of our selves but evill, and all our goodnes to be from God; as S. James saith in his Epistle, the 1. chapter. This our crosse³ is no other thing but the troubles and afflictions, both spirituall and corporall, that we have in this present life; the which are the probations and exercises of our faith, whereby the same is tryed and searched by our heavenly Father, to our weale; and testifie us to be the sonnes of God, and not bastardes. And therefore we should gladly accept the same, with thanksgiving from the bottome of our hart, thinking them to come to us for the best, and that we are the beloved of God, so accepting them. 1 COR. 1.
HEB. 12.
ROM. 8.

---

¹ That is, love and extoll his magnificence in all kinde of godlie life.—(*Marg. note.*)

² Who followeth Christ.—(*Marg. note.*)

³ The crosse of the faithfull.—(*Ib.*)

And then, in the greatest troubles and afflictions, raise up our hartes with faith and hope, beleeving surely our good God to be so faithfull and true, that he wil not suffer us to be overcome or confounded, and tempted above that we be able,[1] but will even give the issue with the tentation, that we may bee able to beare it; because our weak and fragill nature is known to him. He will have compassion upon us for Christ's sake, by whome wee are reconciliate to his favour. So let us not go astray, but follow Christ's footesteppes; that is, to suffer all thinges patiently, and thinke that we have deserved more for our sinnes. Also remembring that Christ our Saviour hath suffered ten thousand times more for us. On this maner we followe Christ's footesteppes, who hath borne our sinnes in his body upon the crosse; that, being dead from sinne we shuld live in righteousnes. My harts, ye which are adversaries to the Article of Justification, learn to read the Scriptures with effect, to the perfite understanding thereof; and then ye shal obteine knowledge to begin to do good workes in faith, pleasant and acceptable to God.

Since we have made mention of three kinde of personnes, that is, of them which goe before Christ, of them which goe astray from Christ, and of them which follow Christ's footesteppes, it is necessarie to let them bee knowen by them selves, that the true and faithfull may be knowen by their deedes.[2] They which confide in their owne workes, merites, and deservings, thinking therethrough to obteine the kingdome of heaven, and satisfie for their owne sinnes, not onely for them selves, but also of the superaboundance of their merits for others; of the which they make marchandise: These are they which goe before Christ; and are called Antichristes, or contrarie to Christ, because they usurpe his office, and wilbe justifiers of themselves and others.[3] They which thinke faith not sufficient to justifie without workes, but will have their own good deeds joyned, to helpe Christ in their justification; these are they which go astray from Christ, and wilbe equall with him in their owne justification. For none of these hath Christ suffered death.

Therefore, hee shall abstract from these two kindes his wisedome, righteousnes, holines, and redemption; and shall suffer

---

[1] God will not suffer us to bee tempted above that we may susteine. —(*Marg. note.*)

[2] Who goeth before Christ.—(*Marg. note.*)

[3] Who goeth astray from Christ.—(*Ib.*)

them to contend with the law in the latter judgement, whose workes being accused, and the puritie and cleannes required, according to the perfection of the lawe; all their noble workes and deedes of good zeale and intention shalbee found abomination in the sight of God, how excellent or shining that ever they be before men; to whome it shalbe said, " Passe your waye LUC. 16. from mee, ye workers of iniquitie." Lucifer was throwen downe MATH. 7. out of the heaven, because hee would have made him equall with God.¹ Adam forth of Paradise, becaus he pretended to know more then was given him in commandement to know, &c. The Pharisie, of whom Christ maketh mention, pretended no LUC. 18. other thing but a great rewarde for his good workes. The same thing pretende all they which impugn this Article of Justification; for will ye compare their sayings and doinges, it is the same selfe thing, but of another arrayement. Nevertheles they are as like as a [one] egge is like another; and so they are not of Christes little flocke, which hee hath chosen, and follow him.

The thrid kind of personnes are they which putte all their trust, hope, and confidence in Christe, take his crosse upon their backes, and dayly followe Christ in his footsteppes,² neither declining to the right hande nor to the left; that is, grounded in faith, ever working by charitie, absteining from evill, and doing good works, in the which they put no confidence; but thinke when they have done all whiche is commanded them to doo, nevertheles they think them selves but unprofitable servants. They lay their sinns upon Christes backe, and follow him by faith, ascribing all their wisedome, justice, holynesse, and redemption to Christ, and nothing to them selves nor their merites; because they are sinners, and through the dregges of sinne left in them, of the old corrupted man, their workes are not perfite according to the perfection which the law requireth. Therefore, they may not stande in judgement with them, of their owne power and strength, but beleeve the same workes, through faith in Christ, to bee accepted as obedience to the lawe, and through Christes merites made perfite. These are they to whome it shalbee saide: " Come unto MATH. 27. mee, yee blessed of my Father, and possesse the kingdome of heaven, prepared unto you from the beginning of the worlde." Against the which the Lawe hath no place to accuse, nor condemne their workes of any imperfection, because

---

¹ The punishment of pride.—(*Marg. note.*)   ² To follow Christ.—(*Marg. note.*)

they are Christes workes, made by him perfite, through faith in his bloud.

THE XXIII. CHAPTER.

1. *What the reason of man perswadeth to be done in the matter of religion.*
2. *Argumentes against good zeale and good intention.*
3. *The Papisticall church this day, is worse then the external church of the Jewes, in the dayes of the Prophets and Christ.*
4. *What fruite bringeth the good zeale of man.*

THE blinde reason, witte, and understanding of man (which is but the desires and appetites of the fleshly man) is the cause why wee misknowe the good and perfite order to doe good workes taught us in the Scriptures,[1] neglecting the Worde of God, and following our own will, which teacheth us good zeale and good intention. This our reason affirmeth good, and thinketh that God shall approve the same according to our desire, whiche is but flesh (I meane of the whole man, and all that is in him). But the Spirit and Word of God teacheth us to walke in the spirite, and not to performe the desires and lustes of the fleshe. For the flesh ever contendeth against the spirite, and the spirite against the flesh. Therefore, we are commanded to fight valiantly against the desires of the fleshe, and to absteine from the lustes and appetites thereof; and to followe the will of God, which is to walke in the Spirite, and clothe us with Christe Jesus.

This order the Apostle teacheth, Galathians the 5. chapter; Romanes the 8. chapter and 13.; and S. Peter in his First Epistle, the 2. chapter.

O miserable, blinde, and ignorant man! why doest thou neglect the good worke of God, to invent good worke of thy owne making? thinking therethrough to please God, saying, Thou doest it of a good zeale and intention; which is asmuch to say as, that thy minde and intentione are good in the selfe. And, because thou thinketh the same good, God after thy judgement should approve the same as good. Thou are deceaved, because thou understandest not the Scriptures, or will not understande the same. It is written, That the whole thoght of man, and all

[1] All men depending upon his own reason is deceaved.—(*Mary. note.*)

ON JUSTIFCATION BY FAITH. 517

the cogitations of his hart, is ready, given, and bent upon evill at all time. And also the witte, understanding, and conceat of man, and the thought of his harte, are prone, ready, and inclined to evill, from his youthhead and young age.¹ And David sayeth, "The Lord knoweth the cogitations of man's hart that they are vaine." Nowe, my hartes, where will yee finde your "good zeale and good intention?" either is it evill of the self, or else God is false, the whiche can not bee. Yee may call it "good," but God, who hath better knowledge thereof then ye have, by his Word testifieth all that is in you to bee but evill, as he hath declareth by the mouth of Moyses, commanding that we do not that thing which wee think good; but that thing which hee hath commanded us to do, that should we do;² and neither adde to his Word, nor take therfrom, but walk in the way the which the Lord hath commanded. This showeth thee that thou should not followe thy "good zeale and intention," thinking therethrough to please God, or fulfill his will, the which thou can not fulfill but by his Worde. For all man of them selves are but lyers, and full of vanitie. GEN. 6. GEN. 8. PSAL. 43. DEUT. 12. JERE. 11. PSAL. 115.

Great is the difference betwixt the will of God, and the will of man; the thought of God and the thoughtes of man; the wayes of God and the wayes of man. As saith the Prophete, in the person of God, "My thoughts and cogitations ar not yours, nor your ways mine; but as the heavens ar exalted above the earth, even so ar my wayes and cogitations from yours." This is no other thing but to teach us to follow the will and commande of God, and not ours,³ who hath declared in His Scriptures, plainly, what we should doe and leave undone, that we neede to seeke no further. So doing, we shal procure the blessing of God, if wee take his erudition and teaching: as David sayeth, "Blessed is the man whom thou, O Lord, instructeth, and of thy law teacheth him." And if we will followe our own teaching, doing workes of our owne intention (the which wee think good), we shal procure the plagues and punishments threatened by the Prophet Jeremie, the 19 chapter, because we doe the thing which he hath not commanded⁴ nor spoken to us, nor yet hath ascended in his hart. Trust well, the people thoght they did a great excellent worke to God, and ESA. 53. MICH. 6. PSAL. 93. JERE. 15 & 19.

---

¹ The confutation of good zeale and good intention.—(*Marg. note.*)
² The commandement of God contrarie our good zeale.—(*Ib.*)
³ All which man shold doe is conteined in the Scriptures.—(*Marg. note.*)
⁴ Who doth workes not commanded by God in his Scriptures, incurris his malediction.—(*Ib.*)

sacrifice to please him, when they spared not their owne children, to kill and offer sacrifice unto God of their innocent bloud! This was their "good zeale and good intention."[1] But they had no command of God for them; and verily yee have lesse for you to make such sacrifice as yee doe dayly, to deceave the poore people, and to purchase to your selves great riches, goods, and possessions. Therefore, I exhort you, by the mercy of God, to cast away that "good zeale and intention;" and follow the Word of God as he hath commanded you in the Scriptures, for they beare witnes of him, and show to man what is his will. Seeke no further, nor confound not the works of God with thy vain thoghts.

3. Through the vaine conceate of man, used in these words "good zeale and intention," have all the abuses now ruling in the church of God risen, [so] that the sayings of the Prophet, spoken to the people of Israell, are complete this day in the church of Christ, and may be said to us as they were said to the Jewes.[2] "Even as the theef is ashamed when he is taken, even so is the house of Israel ashamed, they and their kinges, their princes, priests, and prophets, saying unto the tree or stocke, Thou art my father, and to the stone, Thou hast begotten me. They have turned their backe to mee, sayeth the Lord God, and not their face. And in the time of their trouble and affliction they shall say, Rise and deliver us." Then shall the Lord say unto them, "Where are thy gods which thou hast made thee? Let them arise and deliver thee in the time of thy trouble. Thy gods were verily in nomber according to the nomber of thy cities, O Juda! What! wilt thou contend with me in judgement? Ye have all left me, sayeth the Lord."

Now, I pray you, conferre these words of God, here plainly spoken, with the doings of these dayes now ruling in the church, and then yee shall perceave the abuse of God's Word. We praye commonly the Pater Noster (that is, Our Father), to the image of this or that saint made of tree or stone. And specially to this or that altar wee kneele, which is by our selves or our predicessours founded upon such a saintes name, whose picture is well graved in a stocke or stone, and with costly colours painted. And the blessed Sacrament of the body and bloud of Christ, after their maner, offered dayly to this or that Saint, and called "his messe;" for doing of the which there

---

[1] The fruites of good zeale.—(*Marg. note.*)
[2] The wordes of Jeremie ar true this day.—(*Marg. note.*)

is not a syllable in God's Word for you, but the contrarie expressly commanded; both that yee should have no graven images nor worshippe them; nor yet invent any maner of worshipping of God, but as God hath commanded by his Word. And for your defence ye have onely these wordes, "good zeale and intention," the which is expresly contrarie the first commandement of God. For even as we are forbidden and inhibite to have strange gods, so are wee inhibite to have strange worshippings of God.[1]

<small>EXOD. 20. LEVIT. 26. DEU. 5. PSAL. 81. 96, & 113.</small>

Blessed be God, the matter is so patent and plainely set forth in these dayes, concerning the said vaine workes invented by man, to the confusion thereof, by the godly men which laboure day and night in his Scriptures, to the edification of Christ's chosen litle flocke, that it is not needful to abide long upon the discussing of these matters; but onely to remit you to the Scriptures, and the saide godly declarations made thereupon; against the superstitious worshipping of Saintes; going in pilgrimage; purgeing in purgatorie; hallowing of water, or other elements; foundatioun of masses to publike or private idolatrie; offering or sacrifices making, not commanded in the Word of God; choice of meats; forbidding of marriage in the church of God; and abominable abuses of the whole Christian religion, by the shaven, oincted, or smeared priests, bishops, monkes, and friers; having onely there vocation of man, and by man. Therefore, we let the specialities of them passe, and referre the same to thy judgement, good reader. Thankes be to God, these abuses and groundes are not unknowen; and we will passe forward to the knowledge of the workes commanded us to doe, and work, by the Scriptures of God, as the fruites of faith.

THE XXIV. CHAPTER.

1. *What workes Pastors should teach unto their flocke.*
2. *Wherefore the yoke of Christ is sweete, and his burden light to Christians.*
3. *Vocation mediate and immediate.*
4. *Vocation in generall, by the which all true Christians are equall, made Kinges and Priests in Christ's bloude.*

IF any will ask or inquyre, What workes should the faithfull doe? I can finde no perfiter answear to make thereto, then the

---

[1] Strange worshipping of God is not conteined in the Scriptures.—(*Mary. note.*)

Evangell teacheth us. As S. Luke sayeth, the 3. chapter, John the Baptist preaching repentance in remission of sinnes; the people inquired at him what they should doe. To whom he answeared, saying, " He that hath two coates give to him that hath not one; and he that hath meate, let him doe in like maner." This is no other thing but to exercise the deedes of mercy and charitie toward thy neighbour, as the prophet Esay sayeth, " Breake thy breade to the hungry [and] needie; and the poore who are cast out bring into thy house; when thou seest the naked, clothe him: contemne or despise not thy owne flesh." This is the forthshowing of thy faith, which S. James desireth of thee in his Epistle. Thou art taught the same, with the other works of charity to thy neighbour, Ezechiel the 15.

The publicans and open sinners inquired in like maner, what they should doe. To whom he answeared, saying, " Yee shall doe no further then that which is commaunded you to doe," as he would say, Decline and cease to doe evill, and learne to doe good, as yee ar teached by the prophete Esay, the 1. chapter. And David teacheth you the perfection of religione, saying, " Come to me, my sonnes, and heare me, and I shall teach you the feare of the Lord. Who is he who liveth and loveth to see good dayes, let him refraine his toung from evill, and his lippes that they speake no fraude. Decline from evill, and doe good; seeke peace, and followe the same." Therefore, passe your waye, and sinne no more; for I will not send you to the lawe to get remeady of your sinnes. But looke in the law, and behold what is ordeined you to do; the which will declare you to be sinners and transgressours; and then ye shall seeke Christ for remeady, whose forerunner I am. It is he in whome ye shall finde remeady. Therefore, I say unto you, " Beholde the Lambe of God, which taketh awaye the sinnes of the world."

And being inquired of the souldiers, what they should doe, he answered, saying, " Yee shall strike nor hurt no man; nor yet do wrong or injurie to any personne, but bee content of your wages. Which is as much to say, as oppresse none;"[1] take no person's geare violently; yee are publicke officers, depute by princes and magistrats for keeping of good rule and order amongst the people, for rest and quietnes of the common weale; for the which cause ye have your wages. Your office is

---

[1] The vocation and office of men of warre.—(*Marg. note.*)

honest, and the good worke of God; therefore looke on your own vocation, and do that justly which is commanded you, and exceede not your bounds.

Here is a good order taught you, which are Ministers of the Worde, to learne the auditour in generall or speciall to doe good works; that is, to show them the works commanded by God, the right fruits of repentance and faith; to the which ye should send them, and not to vaine workes invented by man, which is no other thing but to heape sinne upon sinne.

And Christ, being asked by the Jewes, "What shall we doe," say they, "that we might work the workes of God?" answered, saying, "This is the worke of God, that yee beleeve in him whome hee hath sent."[1] Here hee sent them not to the law (howbeit the law be the worke of God), but to faith, which is not the work of man but the work of God, which hee worketh in man. Therefore Christ saith to us, "Beleeve, and yee shall bee safe;" and so let us say with S. Peter, "Lord, to whome shall we passe? Thou hast the words of life; wee will seeke no other, but beleeve in thee." Yee shall consider, that Christ, after hee had refreshed the people with their corporall foode, then he taught them the perfection of a Christian man, and fed them with the spirituall foode; and they which receaved the same did follow him. The rest left him, which had no faith, but tooke his doctrine carnally, and of externall and outwarde workes; as did the young man, to whome Christ made the answer, as is before rehearsed, Mathew the 19 chapter. By the which Scriptures, we are taught to follow Christ, becaus there is no perfection but in the following of him.[2]

Therefore, as wee have receaved our Lorde Jesus Christ, let us walke in him, being rooted and builded in him, and confirmed in the faith as we have learned, abounding in the same with giving thanks, as the Apostle saith, Colossians the 2. chapter. For hee is the fountaine of all goodness, and the head of our felicitie, and let us have respect to no other thing, nor laye no other foundation: For as the Apostle saith, "No man may lay another foundation nor that which is already layde, the which is Jesus Christ.[3] Let us build upon this foundation, gold, silver, and precious stones, which are the workes of God, commanded in the Holy Scripture, to bee wrought into faith; every

---

[1] Faith is the worke of God.—(*Marg. note.*)

[2] There is no perfection but in Christ.—(*Ib.*)

[3] Christ is the head and foundation of our felicitie, upon whom we should build good workes.—(*Marg. note.*)

one according to his vocation, in the which we should walke worthely, as wee are called, with all humilitie, and meeknesse, and patience, supporting one another in love and charitie; carefull to keepe the unitie of the Spirite in the band of peace, as we are taught by the Apostle, Ephesians the 4. chapter.

<small>MATH. 11.</small> And Christ saith, "Take my yoke on you, and learne of me, that I am meeke and lowly in hearte: and yee shall finde rest unto your soules. For my yoke is easie, and my burden light." The which wordes Christ would never have spoken, if hee had laden us with the law; for that burden is so weightie that neither we nor our fathers might beare it; as S. Peter saith in the Actes of the Apostles, the 15. chapter.

But verily the yoke of Christe is easie, and his burden is light, to the faithfull and chosen;[1] for they lay all upon Christ's back, and follow him through faith, confiding nothing in their owne workes nor merites; but ever working all good according to their vocation, giving all glorie and honor unto God. Not exceeding the boundes of their vocation, which is the best rule that the faithfull can have to doe good workes; to the knowledge thereof we will make some short declaration, and then make an ende.

Yee shall understande that there is two kindes of godly vocations.[2] The one is immediate[3] by God, as the prophetes were called in the Old Testament; yea, and as David to be a king, and Moyses a governour, to the people; and as the Apostles in the New Testament. The other is mediate[4] by man, (and immediate by God), as Josue in the Old Testament was called by Moyses to be governour to the people, at the commandement of God. And as Timothy and Titus were called by S. Paule to bee bishops; and as all they which nowe are called to be bishops, which are lawfully made, according to the Word of God, and authoritie of the magistrates. Therefore, to the knowledge of every man's vocation, I remit him to the Word of God and his own conscience, which are his inward and most sure judges.

4. There is a generall vocation,[5] by the which we ar called by Christ and his Word to a Christian religion, through the which wee are made one body and one spirite; even as we are called in one hope of our vocation. For, that charitie is required of

---

[1] Wherefore Christes yoke is asie and his burden light.—(*Marg. note.*)

[2] Of generall and speciall vocations.—(*Ib.*)

[3] Immediate vocation.–(*Marg. note.*)

[4] Mediate vocation.—(*Ib.*)

[5] Vocation generall.—(*Ib.*)

us by the Word of God which maketh and bringeth us together in one body, through mutuall conjunction of faith working by charity; therefore charity is called the band of peace.¹ There is but one fellowship of all the faithfull, and one body; that is, one church, whose only head is Christ. In this church is, nor should bee, no division; for there is in this vocation and Christian religion but one body, one faith, one baptisme, which is the seale of our religion, marked by God with the bloud of his only begotten sonne Christ Jesus our Lord, in whose bloud we are baptised; one God, and one Father of all, which is upon all, and by all, and in us all. And therefore the Apostle testifieth us all to be but one body, that is, one church in Christ.² For into one Spirit, and by one Spirite, the whole universall congregation of the faithful is governed, ruled, strengthened, and kept. There is but one marke or ende, to the which all the faithfull contend or shoote at: that is, eternal life. Wee are all the Sonnes of one Father, and participant of one heritage, as we are called in one hope of our vocation.

1 COR. 12.
EPHE. 4 & 5.

And seing we have but one Lord, which is Jesus Christ; it is convenient that his servantes bee of one minde, and not devided through discord and envie. There is but one profession of faith in all this Christian religion and vocation; for howbeit wee see in these our dayes many sundry professions and opinions of faith, there is but one true faith; which is that faith which the Apostle of our Lorde Jesus Christ, together with the patriarches and prophets, have professed, and given to all nations through their teaching and preaching, as testifie the Holy Scriptures. Upon the which foundation, the whole church of Christ is builded. Therefore, by one baptisme, we are al made clean and purified, and by the which we ar ingrafted in Christ, and made the people of God, purified from our sinnes, and altogether buried with Christ. There is amongst us all but one power or strength of baptisme; and in one name of the Father, Sonne, and the Holy Spirite, we are baptised: And so are we made one body into Christ, being many members, compacted and joyned together into him. For the more perfite understanding of this body, yee shal reade the whole 12. chapter of the 1. Epistle to the Corinthians, the 4. and 5. to the Ephesians, in the which yee shal finde this mater declared by the Apostle at length.

1 COR. 3.
EPHE. 2.
ACT. 9, 14, & 20.
ROM. 5.
1 COR. 12.

MATH. 38.

¹ Charitie is the band of peace.—(*Marg. note.*)
² Why the faithfull are called one body.—(*Marg. note.*)

In this generall vocatione there is no distinction of persones, for all men are equall before God, of one estate. By one generall promise al are called to the faith, under one Lord and King, Jesus Christ, who hath shedd his bloud for all which beleeve in him. Therefore, all Scriptures which make mention that there is no exception of persons before God are referred to this generall vocation in the Christian religion, as Romans the 2. chapter, where the Apostle intending (under Jewe and Gentill comprehending all men) to prove them sinners, sayeth, "Before God there is no acception of persons." And Peter sayeth, "In veritie I have found that God is not an accepter of persones, but in all nations and people hee is accepted unto him which feareth Him and worketh righteousnesse." And S. James sayeth, "My brethren, have not the faith of our glorious Lord Jesus Christ in respect of persons." And S. Paul saith, to the confounding of the false Apostles which seduced the Galathians through great authoritie, and also to show him selfe equal in power with James, Peter, and John, that "God is not a respecter of the person of man;" but in this vocation of Christian religion, by baptism, through faith in the bloude of Christ, all men are equall, both Jewe and Gentill, servand, free man and woman, all are one in Christ Jesus, the sonnes of Abraham by faith, and according to the promise, heirs; that is to say, all which beleeve are the sonnes of God, therfore are they free, and heirs of eternal life.

<small>MAR. 16.
JOB 33.</small>

<small>ACT. 10.</small>

<small>JA. 2.</small>

<small>GAL 2.</small>

<small>GALATH. 3.</small>

To this generall vocation perteineth the sayings of S. Peter in these words: "Yee are a chosen generation, a royall priesthoode, a holy nation, and a people set at liberty; that ye should forthshowe the vertues of Him that hath called you forth of darknesse into a mervelous light," &c. The same is said by Moyses, Exodus the 19. chapter. Here yee see in this vocation there is no acception of persons. We are all the holy people of God which beleeve unfainedly;[1] yea, kinges oincted[2] in baptisme by the Holie Spirit; and priests, making sacrifice to God dayly of this our sinful body mortified, from sinne, and offer a holie and acceptable sacrifice, after the maner above written, conforme to the teaching of the Apostle, Romans the 12. chapter. But beware ye call not your selves kings in office and dignitie, nor priests in administration of the word and holy sacramentes, for that perteineth to a speciall vocation, or office by the selfe. Therefore, I exhort you which reade the Scriptures, take heede

<small>1 PET. 2.</small>

<small>NOTE WELL.</small>

---

[1] Al faithful are kinges and priests.   [2] Yea, kings anointed.
—(*Marg. note.*)

that yee confound not the works of God, for if yee doe yee shal not escape error. These speciall vocations shall follow in their owne places.

If we will looke dayly to this Christian vocation, we shal have perfite knowledge what works we shuld doe, and what works we should leave undone. The neglecting hereof, is the cause of al the enormities and abuses now ruling in the church of Christ through the whole world. For, considering wee are all members of one body, and all members have not one office, but every one serveth other in their owne place; as when the eares heare any thing, the eyes casteth the sight what it should be, then the feete and hands prepare them to pursue or defend, to stand or flee. And al these members, and whole body obey the head, and awaite upon the direction of the same.[1] Even so, we being all members of one body (which is the Church) whose heade is Christe, should, in our estate and office, according to the gift of God, and grace given to us, differing one from another, serve, in our speciall vocation, every one another in our owne estate, not invying the gift of God in our neighbour, but as the Apostle saith, "Let us love brotherly fellowshippe, in going before another in honour and reverence." In doing hereof, there would be no strife in the body; but if a member were troubled, hurt, or had any disease, all the other members would have compassion of it. And if one member were glad or joyfull, all the other members would rejoyce with the same, as the Apostle saith, the 1. to the Corinthians, the 12. chapter. If wee knew this perfitly, none would usurpe another's office or dignitie (to the whiche he were not called), but would be content of his own vocation, and give to every man his duetie; "Tribute to whom tribute is due, custome to whome custome perteineth, feare to whome feare belongeth, and honour to whome it perteineth." The which are all compleit by this saying, "Love thy neighbour as thy self;" for the love of thy neighbour worketh no evill. Therefore the Apostle saith, "Owe nothing to any man, but that ye love together." These wordes being observed, ye fulfil the whole law. Therefore this love, one to another, is ever debt, and should ever bee payde.[2] For, will the prince and superiour do his duetie to the subject, and the subject his duetie to the superiour, there would bee no disobedience. The minister of the Word to the auditour[3] and flocke committed to his care; the auditour to the minister of

EPHE. 5.

ROM. 12.

ROM. 13.

---

[1] Every member should serve in his owne vocation.—(*Marg. note.*)
[2] Love is ever debt.—(*Marg. note.*)
[3] Auditory.

the Worde, there would be no division in the church. The
father and mother to the children, and the children to the parents, there would bee no dishonouring. The lord to the servant, and the servant to the lord, there would bee no contempt
nor trouble in the Common weale. And so would we all looke
upon Christ our head, and be ruled with his Word, and seek
no other way beside it; nor mixt the civill or politicke estate
with the Word of God, but every one to serve in the owne
rowme and place; then should there be no question of politick
works, nor no other works of any law to be mixt with faith,
which justifieth onely before God, as it is before written; but
every faithful person should, by the Word of God, know their
own vocation, and diligently exercise them therintill; and
seeke no further knowledge nor wisedome, but that that is needfull to them to know;[1] and that with meeknesse and sobernes
ever working the works of God, which ar the fruits of faith, to
the honour of God, and profite of our neighbour.

THE XXV. CHAPTER.

1. *All estate of man is conteined within one of these four speciall vocations.*
2. *The offices of princes, magistrats, and judges.*
3. *Wherefore judges are called the sonnes of God; wherefore and in what case they should be obeyed.*

To the more perfite knowledge and understanding of our speciall vocations in the which we should walk, according to the
Word of God, and gift of the Holy Spirite, we will devide all
the estate of man in four offices, dignities, or speciall vocations:[2] that is to say, In the office of a prince, under whom
we comprehend all kind of man, having generall administration
in the common weale or jurisdiction of others: In the office of
the administration of the Word of God, under whom we comprehend all power ecclesiasticall: In the father and mother,
under whom wee wil comprehend al householders having special families: And in the subject or servand, under whom we
wil comprehend al estate of men subject to other.

If thou be called to the office, estate, or dignitie of a King,

---

[1] Men shuld seeke no knowledge but it which is profitable.—(*Marg. note.*)

[2] The division of the estaits of men. —(*Marg. note.*)

Prince, or any supreme power, having jurisdiction of people in the civil ordinance,[1] consider thy estate, and know thee perfitely to be the creature of God, equal to the poorest of thy kingdom or dominion ; his brother by creation and naturall succession of Adam, and of nature a rebell to God ; the sonne of wrath and ire, as hee was, as the Apostle saith, Ephesians the 2. chapter ; and the innocent bloud of Christ, shed for thy redemption as for him ; and thou, called by faith, and borne of newe by baptisme in his bloud ; the sonne of God by adoption, and made fellow heire with Christ of the kingdome of Heaven, without respect of persons, the sonne of favour and grace. Therefore, the poorest and most vile within thy jurisdiction is thy brother, whom thou shouldst not despise nor contemne, but love him as thy self.[2] This is thy debt and duetie, because it is the commandement of God, whome thou should love and feare, for that is the beginning of wisdome, as Solomon saith: "The right way to rule in thy office is to knowe God,[3] of whom thou can have no knowledge, but by his Word and lawe, whiche teacheth thee what thou shouldest doe, and leave undone, according to thy vocation." PROV. 1. PSAL. 110.

And as to thy princely estate, and dignitie, and office, thou art father to all thy kingdome ; their heade in place of God, to rule, governe, and keepe them ; upon whome thou shouldest take no lesse care then the carnall father taketh upon the best beloved sonne gotten of his body ; for they are given by God to thee in government. Therefore thou shouldest begin to knowe the will of thy God, and take the booke of his law in thy hand,[4] read upon it, which teacheth thee the will of God. It should never passe forth of thy harte, nor depart from thy mouth, day and night having thy meditation thereinto, that thou mayest keepe all which is written therein; then shalt thou direct thy way, and have knowledge and understanding of the same. This being done, thou shalt get the blessing, of the which speaketh David, saying, "Blessed is the man which deliteth in the lawe of the Lord, and hath his meditation thereinto day and night." Then aske at God wisedome and understandinge, which is the knowledge of his godly will, and a harte that may receave teaching, that thou mayest judge thy people, and decerne betwixt good and evil, as thou are taught by the DEU. 17. JOSU. 1. PSAL 1.

---

[1] The office of kinges and magistrates.—(*Marg. note.*)
[2] The king should love his subjects.—(*Ib.*)
[3] No man may know God but by his Word.—(*Marg. note.*)
[4] The king should have knowledge of God's law.—(*Ib.*)

3 REG. 3.
example of Solomon. For if thou lacke wisedome, aske the same at God, who giveth abundantly: and doubt not, for he that doubteth in his faith shall obteine nothing from God. Confide JACO. 1. not in thy own wisdome, for God maketh wise men blind, which are wise in their owne conceate. His witnessing is faithful PSAL. 19. which giveth wisedome to young babes; that is, to simple hartes, bearing them selves lowly and humbly before God, not presum SAP. 1. ing in their owne wittes. For "there is no place to wisedome in 1 PET. 5. the proude brest," as saith Solomon; "for God resisteth the proude, but to the meeke and humble hee giveth grace." "The mightie and proude hee casteth downe of their seate, and exalteth the humble and lowlie in harte," as testifieth the Song LUC. 1. of the glorious Virgine Marie.

Therefore, humblie and lowly submit thy selfe in the handes of thy God, and take thought of him, being governed by his Word. Beginne at him, and set forth the true and perfite worshipping of God in thy kingdome.¹ Restore the true, pure, and syncere Christian religion; abolish, destroye, and put downe all false worshippinges and superstitions, contrarie to the Worde of God, and not commanded therein; according to the example of the noble kinges of Juda, Ezechias and Josias, as thou mayest reade the Fourth Booke of the Kinges, the 18. and 23. chapter. This is thy vocation, in the which thou shouldest walke, and orderly proceed in guiding of thy people, DEUT. 17. as thou art taught by the Worde of God; and decline not therefrom, neither to the right hand nor the left, but [walk in] the kingly way teached thee in the Holie Scriptures.

To you which are Princes, Judges, and superiour powers upon earth, perteine wisedome, knowledge, understanding, and learning, that ye may justly and truely exercise the office and charge committed to your care by God. Therefore David exhorteth PSAL. 2. you, saying, "Understand and know, O ye kings; and be learned, O yee which judge the earth. And serve the Lord in feare and reverence, and rejoyce in him with trimbling." This is your wisedome and understanding taught you in the law of DE T. 4. God. For the godly man needeth not to seeke wisedome, but in the Scriptures of God, where he shall finde how he shall behave him both to God and man, in prosperitie and adversitie, in peace and warre. Therefore, to seeke wisdome any other waye, it is nothing but foolishnes before God.² Sithens yee are

---

¹ The king should set forth the true, and destroy the false religion of God in his kingdome.—(*Marg. note.*)

² To seeke wisedome other wayes but in God's Scriptures is foolishnes. —(*Marg. note.*)

the ministers of God unto good, created and ordained by him, 1 COR. 1. as the Apostle saith, Romans the 13. chapter, it becommeth you of your office to guide and rule your subjects in all goodnesse and sweetnes, not seeking from them their landes or goodes; but seeke righteous judgement; help the oppressed; judge ZACH. 7. righteously the people and widowes cause; justifie the needfull, ESAY 1. PSAL. 81. humble, and poore, as teacheth you the Scriptures of God. Defend them from the injuries and oppressions of the wicked; and being unjustly pursued in judgement absolve them. Take EXOD. 23. from them your duety, and no more; have no respect of persons, nor take no bribes or rewardes, the which blinde the eyes LEVIT. 19. of the wise, and perverte the wordes of the just. These two DEUT. 16. thinges, that is to say, respecte of persons and rewards, perverte all righteous judgements. The first comprehendeth in it the feare and reverence of great, mighty, and rich men, love of frends, favour of kinne or affinitie, contempt of the poore, humble, and sober persons, mercy of the wicked and guilty, perill of thy own life, tinsell, or losse of fame, and losse of goodes or worldly honours. The second, that is, rewards, comprehendeth in it lucre, profite, hope, and all that infinite and insatiable goulfe of avarice. Therefore Jethro counselled EXOD. 18. Moyses to provide, for administration of justice and good order in the civill policie, wise men which feared God and were true, hated and detested avarice, the which is the roote and beginning of all evill. And so learne, yea, above all thinges, to detest avarice, vaine glorie, and particular affection of persons, if yee will walke right in the Christian religion, according to your vocation.

Your estate and office is great, and not to bee contemned, 3. but of all men to bee praised and commended; of your subjects feared, reverenced, and also loved,[1] because yee are as it were JO. 10. gods, and so called in the Scripture, by reason of participation of the power of God, committed unto you whose judgements ye exercised; and called the sonnes of God; as David saith, "I DEUT. 1. have saide, Yee are gods, and sonnes of the Most Highest;" that PSAL. 11. is, for the excellent dignity of your office I have called you my sonnes. Nevertheles, know your selves to be but men, and for to suffer death as other men doth, and in like maner as princes of earthly kingdomes, or tyrants, which have the ruling of common weales, as ye have. Therefore be just and righteous, exercising your selfe in all godlynes, according to your vocation;

---

[1] Judges should be honoured because they are participant in power with God.—(*Marg. note.*)

being sure yee shall shortly die, and give accompt and reakoning of your administration. "For ye are but flesh, and all flesh is but grasse, and all the glory of the same as it were the floure of the field; the grasse is withered, and the floure falleth, but the Word of God remaineth for ever." Therefore know Christ to be your king, ruler, guider, and governour, who shall rule you with an iron rod, and breake you asunder as it were a clay pot, or vessell of fragill earth. If ye wil not understand the will and commandement of God, his ire and wrath shall rule above your heade at all times. These sharpe threatninges are showen you in the Scriptures; Esaye, the 1.; Jeremie, the 5. chapter; David in the 2. and 81. Psalm; and Zacharie, the 7. chapter, where yee are taught the chiefe pointes of your office, and workes which yee are bound to do;[1] for neglecting of the which undoone, yee shall bee accused before God. But never for neglecting of pilgrimages, offering to images, praying to saintes, founding of masses, and abbayes of monkes and friers; making of images, belles, copes, and other such vaine superstitions; because the same are not commanded you to do, but rather the contrarie. This dare I affirme, because God's Word affirmeth the same.

Yee should be pure and cleane of life, without crime, because ye are depute by God, and ordeined to the punishment of crimes.[2] Howe can yee judge justly, being corrupted? A theef shall never punish theft; an oppressour, manslayer, adulterer, a false lyer, a dishonourer of father and mother, a disobeyer of his superiour, a covetous or avaritious man, a blasphemer of the name of God, shall never punish these crimes in others. Therefore, the Scriptures of God teache you to absteine from all such vices and crimes. For in you which ar great men, and have the care of others,[3] your crimes and sinnes are not so much to be lamented in you, as the evill example your subjects take thereof; and therethrough follow you in the same and other crimes, heaping sin upon sinne, ever, till God of his righteous judgement take vengeance, yea, and cause another as wicked as yee are punish you; as yee may reade of the punishment of the people of Israell by the open ennemies of God[4] and manifest idolaters, because they neglected the lawe of

---

[1] Whereof shall judges be accused, and whereof not.—(*Marg. note.*)

[2] A judge of corrupted life can never minister justice equallie.—(*Ib.*)

[3] Subjects follow the vices of their superiour magistrates.—(*Marg. note.*)

[4] God commonly punished the wicked by them which are more wicked.—(*Ib.*)

God, as testifie the whole histories of the kings and judges of Israell and Juda. JER. 7.

And the greatest punishment is sent by God, for doing of the most excellent work, after the judgement of man, becaus it was not commanded by God;[1] for no thing from the beginning of the world hath ever bene so displeasant in the sight of God, as to invent any maner of worshipping of him which he hath not commanded. For this cause king Saull was ejected, and all his posteritie lost and fell from the kingdome. In the which example, yee shall consider that the workes wrought by King Saull were right excellent in the sight of man, and also done by him of a good intent, and for a good cause. Hee offered sacrifice for feare that the people should not passe from him, hee being then prepared for battell against the enemies of God. He did show the deede of mercy in saving of the life of an aged and impotent king. And for the love hee had to the worshipping of God, assented to the people, and kept the fattest bestiall, most pretious cloathing, and jewels of gold and silver, to offer the same to God in a sacrifice. Was this not a good zeale and intention? But ye may read the great punishment which God laide upon him, which shal remaine for an example in all ages to come.

1 REG. 15. 2.

1 REG. 15.

THE XXVI. CHAPTER.

1. *The office of a Bishop.*
2. *Bishoppes should not mixt them with worldly matters.*
3. *If the flocke perish, their bloud shalbe required of the Bishop.*
4. *Bishops should exhort their flock to frequent the reading of the Scripture.*
5. *Bishoppes can doe no good workes, without they preach the Word of God.*
6. *The punishment of Bishops which leave that undone which God commandeth, and attende upon their owne superstitions.*

IF thou bee called to the office of a Bishop or Minister of the Worde of God, preach the pure and syncere worde to the flocke committed to thy charge; counsell and confort the weake and feeble; minister the sacramentes in their due forme, according to the Word of God. Exceede not the boundes of thy vocation, but walke thereinto, conforme to the ordinance of the Holy

1.

[1] Marke diligently.— (*Marg. note.*) [2] See page 535, note 1.

Spirite, taught thee in the two Epistles of Saint Paull, written to the first bishop that he made, called Timotheus, and to another called Titus. There thou shalt finde the workes which thou art bound to doe, and what is thy office; specially in the First to Timothy, the 3. chapter, and to Titus, the 1. chapter. There is nothing left unexpressed, that is necessary to thee to work, in the Scriptures of God. Thou art commanded to be a mirrour, or example to thy flocke, in teaching of the word, in good life, and honest conversation; in love and charitie, in faith and chastitie; ever exercising thy selfe in reading, exhorting, and teaching; the which if thou doe, thou shall save thy selfe and others. 1 TIM. 4.

2. Thou should not meddle thee with secular affaires or busines, for that is not thy vocation. Follow the example of the Apostles in all ryghteousnesse and godly living; in faith, love, pacience, meeknes, and sweetnes, as thou art taught. If yee wil remember dayly upon the office yee are called to which are bishops, yee shal find you to have a great charge and worke to doe, and not a great dignitie or lordeshippe. But alace! now yee take thought of the lordshippe, dignitie, rent, and profite, and looke never to the worke yee should doe; the cause thereof is, the neglecting of your vocation; the which, if yee will understand perfitely, yee would not omit the charge and commandement given to you by God, and invent vaine superstitious workes, not commanded. The principall work yee should doe is to preach and teach; which yee never doe, because ye can not; and to excuse you, ye have, as yee say, others to whom yee commit the cause and charge. Yee are blinde and know no thing; they to whom yee commit the charge know as litle or lesse. So perish the poore people in ignorance; for yee are blinde, and leaders of the blinde, and therefore both fall in the myre. 2 TIM. 2.
3 TIM. 6.

3. Neverthelesse, the bloud of them shalbe required at your hands,[1] as the Prophete Jeremie sayeth, the 23. chapter, and Ezechiah, the 34. chapter, the which I pray you reade; for there yee shall see clearely your deeds laid before you, with sore threatnings. EZI CH. 34.

4. Yee should not onely your selves continuallie reade and teache the Scriptures, but also yee should command the flocke in your charge to seeke their spiritual food in the same. This was the order in the church of Christ in the beginning: The

---

[1] The bloud of the flocke perished for fault of spiritual food, shalbe required at the bishope.—(*Marg. note.*)

minister of the worde to teache and preache, and the auditors to reade, that therby they might take the teaching the better; as the Thessalonians did at the preaching of the Apostle, as ye may reade and consider in the Acts of the Apostles, the 17. chapter: And Christ teacheth us to search the Scriptures, for they beare witnesse of him. And S. Paul sayeth, "All thinges which are written, they are written to our learning, that through patience and consolation of Scriptures, we may have hope, that is, of eternall life." The which is the marke whereat shoote all the faithfull; for in the Scriptures of God all things are contained necessarie for our salvation. Alace! thinke yee not shame (which are bound and oblished, under the paine of eternall damnation, to teache your flocke this maner of doctrine,) to inhibit and forbid them to looke upon the Scripture, either to heare or reade them? This is farre different from the order of the Apostles, yea, and of the holy Fathers of the Church long time after, as appeareth clearly by the teaching of Chrisostom, writting upon the 1. chapter of S. Mathew, (the 2. and 5. Homilie,) where he, with a great lamentation, reproveth the secular men and householders,[1] which alledged the reading and teaching of Scriptures perteined not to them; exhorting them to give attendance to the Scriptures, that they might instruct there families and household how they should live, according to the order of the Scripture, and as becommeth Christians. But by the contrarie, yee would that none of your flocke or auditors should know them, lest your misdeeds wer espyed.

The feeding of your flocke, the attendance and care yee should take thereupon, is so necessary,[2] that without the doing thereof yee can doe no good works at all according to your vocation, which can please God; because in neglecting of this, yee neglect faith, out of the which all good workes should spring. So should all your good workes follow faith. And this principal point of your vocation is the cause that S. Paul, departing from Ephesus to Jerusalem, called before him the ministers of the word in the congregation, certifieing them, he would not returne againe in bodily presence; and therefore hee left to them this legacie, saying, "Attend, and take heede unto your selves, and to the whole flock, in the which the Holy Spirit hath put you bishoppes to guide and rule the church of God, the which he hath redeamed with his bloud. For I knowe,

---

[1] The complaint of Chrisostom.—(*Marg. note.*)

[2] Without a bishope preache truelie, he can do no good worke before God.—(*Marg. note.*)

after my departing, there shall enter in amongst you ravening wolves, which shall not spare the flocke. And of your selves, there shall rise men, speaking wickednes, that they may leade disciples to follow them.[1] Therefore, bee diligent and vigilant, keeping in memorie, that by the space of three years, I ceased not, day and night, with teares and weeping, warning and admonishing every one of you," &c.

If the Apostle had knowen any better work or more excellent, to have beene left in memorie or legacie to the ministers of the word, he would, no doubt, have expressed the same. And even so S. Peter, in his First Epistle, the 5. chapter, exhorteth you to feed the flocke of Christ committed to your charge; even as Christ said to him thrise, " Feede my sheep;" so sayeth he to you, Feede the flocke committed to you, every one within his boundes, according to your vocation. This food is the Word of God, and wo be to you which doe not the same, because it is your vocation.[2] For the Apostle saith, " Wo be to me if I preach not the Evangel," &c. For the neglecting of this good work undone, yee shalbe accused before God, but not for the neglecting of the other vaine superstitious workes invented by man; but rather yee wilbe accused for the doing of them. And it wilbe said unto you, Wherefore have yee left the command of God undone for your statutes and traditions?

Yee should teache everie estate of man, how they should behave them in their conversation; the poor to the rich, and the riche to the poore; the servaunt to the maister, and the maister to his servaund. And give your selves forth for an example in deed, to be followed, as yee are teached by the Apostle; and play not the tyrant or the lord upon the inferiour ministers and estates of the church; but, from the bottome of your harte, bee as it were a forme, or rule to the flocke, as S. Peter teached you in the First Epistle, the 5. chapter. Labour continually in your vocation, as the good knights of Christ, being ready, if neede require, to suffer death for the flocke; resisting the unfaithfull, and eshewing prophane and worldly triffles, as yee are taught by the Apostle. If ye will attend upon these workes, which are good, taught and commanded you to doe, as the fruits of faith, ye should finde your selves so wel occupyed in the Scripture, that there shalbe no place found to your vaine superstitions above written, which are not commanded by God

---

[1] The legacie of Paull unto bishops.—(*Marg. note.*)

[2] That is, sorrow and eterne damnation abideth you.—(*Marg. note.*)

nor his word. For in the using of them, ye do that which is not commanded you, and leave that undone which is commaunded.

For this cause God suffereth you to be contemned and cast off. Because ye have left him, he hath left you, and will punish you after the same manner as ye have sinned. For the contempt of God and neglecting of his worde, Hely the chiefe priest was deposed, and all his posteritie, of the priesthood; his sonnes killed in battell; the ark of God put in the handes of his enemies; and the people also heavely tormented, as testifieth the historie. MALACH. 2.
SAP. II.
1 REG. 2.
3 REG. 2.
1 REG. 2.

The holy king David, for the slaughter of Urias, and adultery of Bathsheba, the sonne of his owne body defiled his daughter; the one sonne slew the other; and also defiled his wives and concubines, in publike presence of the people; and usurped the crowne of his realme, as yee may read the Second booke of the Kings,[1] the 13, 15, 16, and 18 chapter. This example of David perteineth as well to you as to princes,[2] and to all estates of the world, that they may learne not to sinne. And if they fall in sinne, that they dispaire not, but turne to repentance, and come unto God, whose will is that all bee safe, and come to the knowledge of the veritie.

THE XXVII. CHAPTER.

1 *The office of the fathers to the sonnes; householders to their families; and of husbandes to their wifes.*
2. *What kinde of men were chosen to bee bishops in the primative Church.*

IF thou bee an householder, rule and guide thy familie and houshold; bring up thy children in all godlynesse and honestie, exercising thy selfe in thy occupation faithfully and truely, without deceate or fraude to thy neighbour, either in word or deede. "Love thy wife, even as Christ hath loved the church;" for thou art debtbounde to love thy wife, even as thy owne body. "There is no man which hated or detested his own body, but nourisheth and feedeth the same as Christ the church: For we are members of his body, of his flesh, and his bones; for that 1.

EPHE. 5.

COLLOS. 3.

---

[1] So according to the Septuagint and Vulgate, but in our present version, the Second Book of Samuel.

[2] The punishment of David perteineth to bishops aswell as to princes. —(*Marg. note.*)

cause man shall leave father and mother, and cleave unto his wife, and they shalbe two in one flesh." And in like maner, "Thou woman be subject to thy husband, as if it were to the Lord; for the man is thy head, even as Christ is the head of the congregation." And, as the church is subject to Christ, even so be thou subject to thy husband in all lawfull things. This is your vocation in the which ye should walke, according to the commandement given to you by the Apostle, Ephesians the 5. chapter, and Colossians, the third, in these wordes, "Let every man love his wife as himself, and let the woman feare and dread the husband:" This is the commandement of God.

<small>1 PET. 3.</small>

If ye, men and women, wold take care upon your vocation, how honourable the estate of the same is, and what yee ought every one unto another, there were none of you who would commit adulterie, or defile your owne bodies, nor defraude one another of their duety and right. For thou man hast not power of thy owne body but the woman: Nor thou woman hast not power of thy owne bodie, but the man. Therefore, there is neither of you that should give your bodies to other men or women, nor abstract one from another that mutuall love which yee are commanded to have together. This doing, ye exercise the good work of God. Be not outrageous nor thraward upon the woman, but teach her with meekenes and sweetnesse, forbearing her somewhat, as the weakest vessell. And thou, woman, pretend no dominion upon thy husbande, but obey him as thy lord, taking example of the obedience of that noble woman Sarai. If ye wold keep this order and rule in your own vocation, there would be no strife betwixt you, but all godlines and love. No man would contemne or disdaine his wife, nor no woman her husband; but every one love other, as their own body, and take care one for another in all things.

<small>1 COR. 7.</small>

<small>COLLOS. 3.
1 PET. 3.
1 TIM.</small>

Thou, man, should dayly and hourely exercise thee, according to thy vocation; and labour diligently for sustentation of thy wife, children, and familie, that thou mayst minister unto them their necessaries; for if a man take no thought of his owne, and specially of his houshold and familie, hee hath denyed the faith, and is worse then an infidele. Suffer not thy children nor servants to be idle, but see ever that they bee occupied in some good and vertueous occupation. For that is the right way to keep them from vice and sinne, because idlenes is the beginning of all evill. Teach them the law of God; use all things with discretion; and provoke not your children to anger,

<small>1 TIM. 5.</small>

<small>PSAL. 77.
DEUT. 6.</small>

but bring them up in good teaching, discipline, and correction, and in the erudition of the Lord. Give unto your servants that thing which is just and right; what yee promisse, paye them, knowing well that ye have a Lord in heaven.

COLOSS. 3. 4.
EPHE. 6.

And thou, woman, exercise thee in nourishing and up-bringing of thy children; in ruling all thinges within thy house, as thou hast commandement of thy husband; take care upon his direction, as thy head, and transgresse not his commandement, for that is the will of God. I meane not of evill, but of all goodnesse; because I speake of the fruites of faith, and workes of righteousnesse. Yee are all bound to doo the workes whiche God hath commanded you to do, in his holy Scripture, of mercy, love, and charitie, by reason of your vocation in the Christian religion; and these other workes in your speciall vocation. In doing of the which, thinke that ye do the good work of God, and please him, if yee worke them in faith, (albeit hypocrites commend not the same). Beeing occupied on this maner daylie, there shall bee no place to vice, for your minde is occupied upon other busines.

It is but idlenes to you, to passe in pilgrimage to this or that sainte, to sit the halfe of the daye in the church, babling upon a paire of beades, speaking to stocks or stones, the thing which neither thou nor they knowe; and neglecteth the good worke of God, the which thou art bound to doe.[1] If thou wilt praye right, learne the Lordes Prayer in the toung thou understandeth; thy Creede, that is the Articles of thy beleeve;[2] the Ten Commandements of God. And dayly at thy rysing, and downlying at night, have some space to thy contemplation thereinto, and teache thy housholde the same maner. And occupie the rest, as is before saide, according to thy vocation, not exceeding the bounds thereof, nor seeking no other workes but them which are commanded in the holy Scriptures, and are necessarie to be done, as is written to Titus, the 3. chapter. Let the faithfull which are of our number bee ever ready, and learne to doe good workes to all necessary uses, that they bee not unfruitefull. For the faithfull can never bee idle, because unfained faith worketh ever by charitie.[3] But they which knowe not their owne vocation, can never bee faithfull therefore they can never worke good workes, but all is evill, whatsoever thing they do or worke without faith; becaus all which is not of faith is sinne. Therefore, if thou wilt worke well, be faith-

ROM. 4.

---

[1] Right prayer.—(*Marg. note.*)
[2] Belief.
[3] The unfaithles worke no good workes.—(*Marg. note.*)

full, and looke ever to thy vocation; and thou shalt finde thy conscience teaching thee both to do good, and eschew evill, at all times.

Ye should be pure and cleane in your conversation, for good example giving to your children and familie. For as they see you doe so shall they learne; and are ever rather inclined to do evill then good, by reason of this corrupted nature of man.[1] Therefore, teach them to love and feare God, to know his lawe, being ever your selves an example to them, and as it were, a mirrour to looke into, in all godly life and conversation. For if they behold you living together, (in great love and charitie, chastitie and temperance; being mercifull to the poore; supporting the indigent after the quantitie of your riches; at love and charitie with your neighbour; ever speaking good of all creaturs, detracting none,) they shall followe the same doings; by the which ye shalbe called the faithfull fellowship of Jesus Christ, and true subjects of his realme.

2. Your vocation is good and holy, and it becommeth you to know the Scriptures; for in the primitive church, the bishops were chosen commonly forth of your number. A godly and honest householder, who lived in chast matrimonie, ruled and guided his household well, brought up his children in subjection and reverence, in all maner of godly teachings. Hee, having this outward witnessing, is commanded by the Apostle to be chosen to the office of a bishop. When this order was kept in the Church of Christ, the Worde of God flourished.

1 TIM. 3.

Therefore, woe be to you which saye, that laickes, or secular men and householders, should not know the Scriptures, read them, or teach their houshold the same. Yee impugn the Holy Spirite, and dishonour the olde fathers of the church, which taught the contrarie; as by example of Chrisostome, before rehearsed.[2] It is even alike to you to say, temporall or secular men should not heare the Worde of God, read and teach their families the same, as to say they have not a soule; for the Word of God is the foode of the soule, and if yee will abstract the foode, without the which the soule must perish, yee shall make man as a brutishe beaste. And if yee will admit them to heare the Word, yee should admit them to read the same, and talke thereupon; for what availeth the hearing, if a man should not conceave, and keepe in memorie that thing which he heareth, and live thereafter. For Christ sayeth, "Blessed

DEUT. 8.
MATH. 4.

---

[1] The life of the fathers should be cleane, because it is a mirrour to the sonnes.—(*Marg. note.*)

[2] Marke diligently.—(*Ib.*)

are they which heare the Word of God, and keepe the same. The oft reading of the Word, and communication thereof, keepeth the same ever recent in memorie; and digesteth in thy hart, by continuall meditation, some confort and consolation; and abstracteth thee from vice and sinne, leadeth and convoyeth thee to all godlie living. Therefore David calleth that man blessed, which deliteth in the lawe of God, and hath his meditation therein day and night.

Wo, wo, be unto you, therefore, which would abstract this blessing from any man or woman, the which God pronounceth with his mouth. These doings of yours beare witnesse of you, that ye ar not the ministers of the Word of God, or true successors of the Apostles; but false teachers, subverters of the word, and very antichrists. Wherfore, I exhort you whiche are the faithfull, whatsoever estate or vocation yee be called to, that yee both gladly heare the Word of God, reade it, teache your children, family, and subjects the same; and conforme your life thereto, ever working the deedes of charitie and mercy in all godlinesse, according to your vocation; and give no credit to them which teacheth you the contrarie, for they are false teachers and members of the Devil, which withdraw you from that thing which is your salvation.

THE XXVIII. CHAPTER.

1. *The duetie of the maister unto the servant, and contrary.*
2. *Of the subject to the prince.*
3. *Of the sonne to the father.*
4. *The honour which the sonnes ought to the parents.*
5. *The divelish doctrine of pestilent Papisticall preists, in the cortrarie thereof.*

If thou be a subject, servaunt, sonne, or daughter, be obedient to thy superiour. First, unto thy prince, as the supreame power, and to every one having power from him, for they are the ministers of God, whom thou shouldest obey and not resist, ordeined by God to the revenge of evill doers, and loving of the good doers; which is the will of God, as yee ar taught, Romanes, the 13. chapter, and the First of Peter, the 2. chapter. Your duetie is, to honour al men, love brotherly fellowship, feare God, and honour the king; be obedient to him, not onely for feare and dreadour of his ire, but also for hurting of your

conscience, because it is the will of God, in all thinges not re-
2. pugning to his command. Give to thy prince and superiour
his duetie; or what ever he chargeth thee with concerning temporall riches; inquire not the cause, for that perteineth not to
thy vocation. Hee is thy head, whom thou shouldst obey:
trangresse not his lawes; be not a revenger of thy owne
cause, for that is asmuch as to usurpe his office: so thou walk-
est not aright in thy vocation. Looke not to his faultes or
vices, but to thy owne. Disobey him not; howbeit he bee evill
and doe the wrong (which becommeth him not of his office);
grudge not thereat, but pray for him, and commit thy cause to
God. Be not a perturber of the common weale, but live with
thy neighbour at rest and quietnesse, every one supporting
others as members of one body; forgiving gladly and freely
one another, if there be any complaint amongest you, even as
the Lorde hath forgiven you. Be sweete, meeke, bening, humble, and patient, one with another, as it becommeth the saintes
and welbeloved of God, having compassion one of another.
Above all these have love and charitie, which is the bond of
perfection; for charitie coupleth together many members in
one body. This are yee taught by the Apostle, Colossians, the
3. chapter, and in other places before rehearsed.

Here yee finde aboundance of works commanded you to doe
by God, and neede to seeke no others. There is none which
can work these good workes but the faithfull; from doing of the
which, the faithfull and justified man can not cease; but ever
worketh as he findeth occasion, according to his vocation: hee
looketh ever to his owne faultes and sinns, and not to his neigh-
bours.[1] But if he perceave any fault or vice in his neighbour,
hee lamenteth the same, and considered greater vices to be in
him selfe; and therefore hath compassion of his neighbour,
and neither blasphemeth, bakbiteth, or dishonoreth him; but
counselleth and conforteth him, as his owne body, of brotherly
love and affection.

3. Yee children, obey your parents with great humilitie; love,
feare, and honour them; for that is the command of God, and
the first which hath promise (as concerning thy neighbour) that
it may be well to thee, and that thou live long upon earth.
4. This obedience and honour consisteth not in wordes onely, nor
in salutations, but also in ministring all thinges necessarie unto
them. Remembring, as they ministred unto you in your tender,
feeble, and poore youthheade, even so do yee to them in their

[1] The faithfull lament the faults of others.—(*Marg. note.*)

feeble, impotent, and poore age. Neglecting this good work undone, yee can doe no good worke that can please God. There is no colour of godlines may excuse you from this good worke: howbeit your wicked and ungodly pastors have taught you to found a soule masse with your substance, and suffer father and mother to begge their breade. This is a devilish 5. doctrine, to convert the good worke of God into idolatry. The Scribes and Pharisies, their forefathers, taught the same, as testifie the wordes of Christ.

Yee servauntes, obey your carnall lords and maisters, with feare and trembling, with simplenesse of hart, as it were unto Christ; not in eyes service, as it wer to please men, but as servants of Christ; doing the will of God, not onely to them which are good, and well instructed in maners, but also to the wicked and evill. What ever yee doe, worke the same with your harte, as it were to the Lord, and not to man, knowing surely ye shall receave from the Lord the reward of the heritage: Therefore serve the Lord Jesus Christ. Be not flatterers nor lyers, backbiters, nor detracters; serve not your maisters onely in their presence, but also in their absence, without deceat or dissimulation. Take thought of the thinges given you in charge, and obey their will, even as to God, who looketh upon your inward mindes. Pretend not to be equall with your lord or maister, because yee are both of one Christian religion, but serve him the better. Have love and charitie with your equall fellowe servantes, as all members of one body, exercising you in all good workes, according to your vocation in the Christian religion.

Now yee see that we which professe the true faith of Jesus Christ, and ascribeth the Justification of man before God onely to Faith, without all workes, merits, or deservinges on our parte; that we are not the destroyers of good workes, but the mainteiners, defenders, and foorthsetters of the same, as the fruites of faith; as I have before at length showed.

Therefore, I exhort you which blaspheme us, saying, we would destroy all good workes, because we affirme with the Scriptures of God, Faith onely to justifie before God, to remord[1] your conscience; and reade the Scriptures with an humble hart and spirit, which shall teach you the right way, by the grace of the Holy Spirit, who will lead you in all veritie. And then I doubt not but yee shall aggrie with us, and contemne and despise the vaine superstitious workes, not commaunded in the

[1] To excite to remorse.

Scripture, but invented of man's vaine conceate, as we doe. And altogether, as it becommeth the faithfull members of Jesus Christ, worke the workes of God, which are commanded us in his holy Scriptures; every one according to his vocation, proceeding of love, furth of a cleane and pure hart, of a good conscience, and of faith unfained, which worketh by charitie, to the profite of thy neighbour, and glorie of God. To whom be all praise, honour, and glory, for ever and ever. AMEN.[1]

[1] In the work as first published in 1584, there here follows the address To THE READER, and A BRIEFE SOMMARIE OF THIS BOOKE, already printed at the commencement of the present volume, as having been added by Knox to the original Treatise in 1548.

www.ingramcontent.com/pod-product-compliance
Lightning Source LLC
Chambersburg PA
CBHW071430300426
44114CB00013B/1382